SOCIAL WORK
RESEARCH METHODS

SOCIAL WORK RESEARCH METHODS

FROM CONCEPTUALIZATION TO DISSEMINATION

BRETT DRAKE

George Warren Brown School of Social Work
Washington University

MELISSA JONSON-REID

George Warren Brown School of Social Work
Washington University

PEARSON

BOSTON   NEW YORK   SAN FRANCISCO
MEXICO CITY   MONTREAL   TORONTO   LONDON   MADRID   MUNICH   PARIS
HONG KONG   SINGAPORE   TOKYO   CAPE TOWN   SYDNEY

Senior Series Editor: *Patricia Quinlin*
Series Editorial Assistant: *Carly Czech*
Marketing Manager: *Laura Lee Manley*
Production Supervisor: *Liz Napolitano*
Editorial Production Service: *Black Dot/NK Graphics*
Composition Buyer: *Linda Cox*
Manufacturing Buyer: *Debbie Rossi*
Electronic Composition: *Black Dot/NK Graphics*
Interior Design: *Black Dot/NK Graphics*
Cover Designer: *Kristina Mose-Libon*

For related titles and support materials, visit our online catalog at www.ablongman.com

Between the time website information is gathered and then published, it is not unusual for some sites to
have closed. Also, the transcription of URLs can result in typographical errors. The publisher would appreciate
notification where these errors occur so that they may be corrected in subsequent editions.

ISBN-13: 978-0-205-46097-7

Library of Congress Cataloging-in-Publication Data

Drake, Brett.
  Social work research methods : from conceptualization to dissemination
/ Brett Drake, Melissa Jonson-Reid. — 1st ed.
    p. cm.
  Includes bibliographical references and index.
  ISBN 0-205-46097-6 (alk. paper)
  1. Social service—Research—Methodology. I. Jonson-Reid, Melissa.
II. Title.
  HV11.D17 2007
  361.0072--dc22
                              2007030857

Printed in the United States of America

10 9 8 7 6 5   V092 15

Microsoft product screen shots reprinted with permission of Microsoft Corporation.

*We would like to dedicate
this book to our children,
Harrison and Thomas.*

BRIEF CONTENTS

CONTENTS

CHAPTER 3   SPECIFICATION 37

CHAPTER 4   DESIGN 69

CHAPTER 11   IMPLEMENTATION 209

CHAPTER 16   INTERPRETATION AND DISSEMINATION 387

PREFACE

oth of the authors teach social science research at the PhD and MSW levels. We also do a lot of research, most of it federally funded. Unfortunately, when it came time to pass along our skills to our students through teaching, we found that we were unable to settle on a single text. The main problem we faced was that we couldn't find a *practical* book that covered the *whole* research process. This book started out as a series of different booklets written to supplement the other texts we were using. One day we figured that we might as well go the distance and complete a book on the subject. In doing so we were guided by a number of specific goals:

We Wanted to Write a Completely Stand-Alone, "Soup-to-Nuts" Book

We wanted this book to be a guide to the basic research process, including all necessary core skills. Sometimes people use the expression "soup-to-nuts" to mean "absolutely everything, starting at the beginning and ending at the end." We wanted this book to be soup to nuts.

This book is meant to include everything you need to *actually do* a research project, from deciding to do the work to mailing it to a publisher. This is why we included so much statistical material. Methods and statistics influence each other, and you can't really do either without doing both. Even if your class or your project does not require you to do statistical analyses, you will have to read journal articles that do use advanced statistics. We hope our book can help you both perform analyses and better understand those analyses you read about in the literature.

Of course, this does not mean it includes all you will ever need to know. Many other researchers, statisticians, and philosophers of science have written more detailed or more advanced work that applies to the various stages of the research process. Each chapter includes references for further reading. These sources were not selected through a comprehensive critical review. Lack of inclusion is in no way reflective of the quality or worth of an article or text, but merely the limits of space and the applied nature of this book.

We Wanted to Write a "How-To" Book

Our goal was to help students *do* a research project. We think students are more likely to remember some-thing they have *done* than something they have *read about.*

- The book follows a *step-by-step format*, like instructions for assembling a child's toy. You start at the beginning and work your way forward; and at the end, you have a product.

- The book includes *five very detailed examples,* so students can "follow along" with the process. The examples were chosen to cover the broadest range of methods and statistics possible. In our experience, students learn better if they have something to refer back to. *These examples are complete.* Discussions of conceptualization, human subjects issues, literature searches, forms, data dictionaries, electronic databases, and quantitative or qualitative analysis programs are given for each. Each example culminates in a finished product such as a publishable paper, a PowerPoint presentation, or a poster of the type that might be displayed at an academic conference.

- The book includes *coverage of four common computer programs* that you may use in the research process: Excel (a spreadsheet), SAS and SPSS (statistical analysis packages), and NVivo (a qualitative research tool). We understand that your school may use different packages, but these four are fairly representative, and we hope that the many examples and screenshots we provide will help you to painlessly move forward with your projects.

We Wanted to Demystify Science and Show That It Is Something Anyone Can Do

It is too easy for researchers (like us) to slip into jargon or to teach students things just because we were taught them. We have tried to avoid these problems.

- *The language we use is intentionally simple.* We see no useful reason to perpetuate the use of clumsy jargon that serves only to make science unreadable to almost everybody. It is actually much harder to write simply than to use jargon.

- *We tried to limit content to those things that are necessary to doing beginning science.* Relevant philosophical and historical issues are covered, but only when they are likely to matter in the real world. Many other texts include a lot of content that we just didn't think was critical to completing a research project.

WE WANTED TO COVER BOTH BASIC AND APPLIED SCIENCE

This is not just a book on ivory-tower research. This is also not a book on how to evaluate just your own or your agency's practice. It is both. These types of research are more similar than different, and we hope that you will be equally well served whether you are doing basic or applied science. We have two chapters directly applying the principles in the book to practice settings, and one of our five examples is an internal evaluation by a social service agency.

WE WANTED TO COVER MORE THAN EXPERIMENTAL DESIGNS AND SURVEY DATA

True experimental designs can do things other designs can't do (like assessing causality), but they are not the right tool for every job. Surveys can be a great way to get information but also aren't always the best way to go. Most textbooks focus heavily on these two areas. While we cover both these areas, we also cover descriptive, exploratory, and correlational methods in equal detail. We place substantial emphasis on preexisting data, such as secondary or administrative data. This brings our book more in line with the type of research that is done by students and professors in the field and reported in journals.

WE WANTED OUR BOOK TO BE A PLACE WHERE STUDENTS COULD GET "THE STRAIGHT INFO"

Both of us have experience teaching, publishing, and running large federal grants. We tried to include a good many pointers we have picked up along the way, particularly around contentious or otherwise problematic issues. Is it OK to be a positivist? What do grant reviewers look for? Do scientists value qualitative research? We tried to give simple and (relatively) unbiased answers to these and similar questions.

WE WANTED TO SHOW STUDENTS HOW RESEARCH IS A WHOLE PROCESS, NOT JUST SEPARATE PARTS

Good research happens when all the components of research (specification, design, implementation, analysis, dissemination) flow logically and complement each other. Doing this is hard. The main thing you learn as an old researcher is how to anticipate what will happen next and make sure that what you're doing makes sense as a whole. Real research is not pretty. We tried very hard to make sure that students understood the "two steps forward, one step back" reality of doing research. The process of doing research is a process full of dead ends and false starts. Our examples and our discussion of the research process reflect this. Most textbooks tend to portray research as a thing that can be done in a certain "correct" way. This just isn't the case, and we hope that our approach helps students to anticipate and accept the multiple problems they will encounter as they begin to learn to be researchers.

WE WANTED TO SUPPORT STUDENTS IN USING EVIDENCE-BASED PRACTICE

We think Evidence-Based Practice (EBP) is the most exciting new idea in the helping professions to come along in a long time. However, in order to do EBP, you must have a set of specific skills, including the ability to ask empirically answerable questions, the ability to find the best available evidence, the ability to critically evaluate that evidence (hard to do!) and the ability to apply that evidence in combination with your professional judgment and client factors. Many of the core skills for EBP are taught in this book, and we wanted to make it very clear how you could use those skills in your future work with people. We therefore included a set of EBP modules, which are sprinkled throughout the book, so that you could see how you can use what you are learning in a practice setting.

As a final note, we'd like to say that this book is meant for students at both the PhD level and the master's level. We've taught both levels of research, and the basic content is pretty much the same. The how-to nature of the book lends itself to such flexibility, as the process of research is a constant, no matter what level you're at. This book is a beginning, not an end. There is much more to learn. We hope students will use this as a launching pad and continue to explore well beyond this guide.

ACKNOWLEDGMENTS

The authors wish to thank Ed Spitznagel, PhD, for his review of and feedback on the analysis chapters; Vernon Loke for his assistance with the SPSS commands and output for the analysis chapters; and TAs Charlotte Bright, Sun Ha Choi, Marcia Ollie, Hiie Silmere, and Lisa Tracey for the help with fine-tuning questions and exercises, many of which were incorporated into the analysis chapters. We would like to thank our PhD students from the foundations of data analysis and research methods courses and our MSW students from our research methods courses for the past 4 years who have been our helpful and patient consumers of various versions of many of the chapters in this text. Finally, we would like to thank Associate Dean Shanti Khinduka, Associate Dean David Cronin, and Dean Edward Lawlor, and our family for their support and assistance.

BRETT DRAKE AND
MELISSA JONSON-REID
St. Louis, Missouri

INTRODUCTION

In this text, we give you a step-by-step practical guide to social science research. We have structured the text to follow the research process from specification (thinking about what your question is) through dissemination (telling people what you found). Because people often learn best from examples, we give you examples to follow. We present five fictitious researchers and their projects throughout the text, following the researchers from their first thoughts about their research to their final research products. As applicable, chapters close with a module devoted to evidence-based practice. This applies content from each chapter to the photos of the evidence-based practice. As an applied text, our goal is to provide an understandable and practical foundation to the entire research process.

Welcome to the world of social science research. If you ask a number of different professors what social science is, you will probably get a number of vague, unsatisfying, and contradictory answers. One of the reasons for this is that different professors may place emphasis on different aspects of social science. One professor may emphasize social science as an extension of the methods of "hard sciences." In other words, social science is about applying the techniques of areas like chemistry to the "softer sciences" like psychology or social work. Other people see social science from the perspective of how the information generated is useful or not in improving people's lives. Such a perspective tends to view social science research as a field needing to use the best method to answer a question related to some sort of applied intervention or policy. Still other scientists are focused on complicated philosophical debates about scientific approaches and see this as key to the development of social science. This latter group will contend that the way you view the conduct of science is the key to understanding what results from the study.

Why the confusion? Social science is what Thomas Kuhn (1962) called a "preparadigmatic science," meaning people don't agree on how exactly to do it. For example, physics is currently a paradigmatic science. People basically agree on what "heat" is and how to measure it. The social sciences are still in search of broadly accepted unifying principles and so are best described as preparadigmatic. This is especially true with regard to research. One example is how social scientists view the principle of objectivity. Put simply, objectivity is the idea that researchers can and should stand apart from what they are studying, so as not to bias and contaminate their subjects. Some researchers accept only objectivist methods, but some others reject the whole idea of objective science. These researchers may share very little in common and can have difficulty respecting or even understanding each other's work.

We have chosen a pragmatic path for this text. We are part of the second group of scientists in the introductory paragraph—the applied social scientists. From our perspective, social science research is about adding to our understanding of individuals, groups, communities, and psychological or social issues so as to support the interventions, programs, and policies that enable people to live more satisfying lives. Of course, issues related to people can be much more difficult to study because human behavior can be affected by neurobiological factors, psychological factors, social factors, the societal context, and interactions between these levels of influence. Some readers might already recognize this idea as the ecological framework posited in the late 1970s (Bronfenbrenner, 1979). We believe this makes social science inherently messier. Answers to complex questions may come from some of the same methods used in the hard sciences but may also include methods specific to social science inquiry. Such a focus on the use of data generated also allows for variation in philosophical approach. It is true, however, that the basic quantitative and qualitative research methods and analytic techniques in this book are based on the notion that there are constructs that can be sufficiently described and understood to be examined. This information is then communicated publicly and open to critique and further study.

SECTION 1.1
DEFINITIONS

We'll start the book by introducing you to some basic, important, and sometimes misunderstood definitions and terms used in social science. We will define these terms as we have observed them used in the field by researchers, and we will indicate when there are multiple or contradictory definitions. Because the social sciences are a preparadigmatic field, we have to try hard to avoid confusion and be very careful in how we define things. We think that the following terms are absolutely essential to your understanding of social science:

- Science
- Pseudoscience
- Approaches to science
- Empirical
- Objectivity
- Theory
- Induction/deduction
- Evidence-based practice/policy

SECTION 1.1.1: DEFINING *SCIENCE*

Science involves looking at "facts" in a way that makes sense and then telling people what is found. We place quotes around the word "facts" because scientific information is always open to change and development. At one time we believed the world was flat, but then our ability to observe objects in the sky and explore the oceans changed that. The shape of the world did not change, but our ability to observe it did. Eventually this led to a general acceptance of a new fact—the world is round.

SCIENCE IN MODERN SOCIETY IS EMPIRICAL, LOGICALLY STRUCTURED, AND PUBLIC

- For a review of what is and isn't "empirical," see below.

- By "logically structured," we mean that science is done according to a clear and explicit plan that makes sense. For example, scientific polling is done using precise methods that are written down and adhered to, that make sense and seem to work. Following a formal structure is necessary for assuring the quality of your work. You need to be able to tell people exactly how you did what you did, so they can judge your work or even *replicate* it (do it themselves to see if they get the same results). What are some ways you can evaluate whether your work is logically structured? Think about someone who asks you for your recipe for a favorite dessert. That recipe needs to be constructed in such a way that a person who has never made that dessert can follow the steps and come up with a similar outcome. As a general rule, we like to imagine that someone is criticizing our work or our approach to a project. Can we clearly and reasonably defend why we did what we did in a way that makes sense?

- Science is not a thing one person does. It is an endeavor of the human race. Your little part of science is made public and becomes the culmination of the work of others and the basis of future work (we call this knowledge building). If your work isn't public, nobody else can check it or try to replicate it.

No one study or effort ever proves anything on any theory, but if continued study appears to find similar results we place more confidence in the theory behind it (Sokal & Bricmont, 1998).

APPLICATION OF SOCIAL SCIENCE

Some people define *science* by what it tries to do. The example in the nearby box discusses this from the perspective of what some people call "basic science" versus "applied science." Put simply, basic science is about

generating knowledge. Applied science is about using science to help people.

BASIC AND APPLIED SCIENCE COMPARED

Dr. Basicscience: What I want to do is find out about important underlying "laws" of human and social behavior (for example, people are more likely to recall or be influenced by things that happened recently). I want to conduct scientific studies with the goal of creating basic knowledge. Once we discover these laws, others can use them to help people through direct services or policy. I understand this may take a long time. I am successful to the degree that I discover and rigorously test these principles across individuals or societies. In my view, the social sciences should closely model themselves after the more established sciences like physics. Strict adherence to the scientific process is important to me. Issues regarding the philosophy of science are likely also important to me.

Dr. Appliedscience: I am not quite as interested in advancing science for its own sake. I am more interested in using scientific tools to help people. I do social science in a way that gives me answers that can be used to improve policy and practice. I am successful to the degree that my work reaches "the trenches" and improves policy or practice. I am very interested in using scientific approaches that are technically valid, but they must also be practical. I am still interested in the quality of methods, but I also want to be able to translate findings to the real world. I may be less interested in debates about the philosophy of what I do.■

Social science can also be about understanding meaning, building theory, and discovering constructs. Sometimes quantitative approaches do not lend themselves well to this type of inquiry. So, in social science we also use qualitative methods such as case study interviews or content analysis or focus groups. In our view, it is not the method that makes something good science but the way in which it is executed.

QUALITATIVE RESEARCH IN SOCIAL SCIENCE

Let's say that a student decides to do some qualitative research on how hospitalized people feel about being in a hospital. That student picks some people (without any clear reasoning for whom he picks), asks whatever questions seem appropriate at the time, and writes a report filled with his opinions about what was said. This would be an example of very bad qualitative research, and few people would say it is scientific. It is not scientific mainly because it follows no clear logical structure. For example, nobody can really tell what the researcher was trying to do or what he did or how he came to his conclusions. Nobody can go out and replicate what was done.

This research could have been much improved if the researcher had paid more attention to his question, his sample, and how he asked questions. He needed an organized way to record data and tell people how he analyzed his data. If these things are done in a logical and structured manner, and if he reports his process, then this would be an example of qualitative research that is clearly scientific. Students often ask us if qualitative work is really scientific. In our view, good-quality qualitative research is scientific.

If what you do is clearly and logically structured; if it is based on observation of people, or things, or measurable constructs; and if you clearly tell people what you did, then you have a fairly good claim to be doing science. Of course, science can be of varying degrees of quality. We agree with Pawson (2005) who writes,

The acid test of research quality is whether a study provides good explanation and this involves examination of how it jockeys for position amongst competing explanations. Inquiries are judged to be competent only when they secure a place in a developing network of explanations. Research quality is confirmed only when synthesis is achieved.

Another way to better understand science is to go into a little more detail about the opposite of science: pseudoscience. Pseudoscience is often described as something that is not science but pretends to be. How can we determine if an area of "inquiry" is scientific? A series of main principles you can use is shown in Table 1.1.

TABLE 1.1. Identifying Pseudoscience: Questions You Can Ask.

WHAT IS THE RESEARCHER'S FOCUS?

Science: The main focus is on following an approach that will provide the best understanding of what is being observed. The validity of the approach is important, and the conclusions must follow the data.

Pseudoscience: Pseudoscientists attempt to support a predetermined conclusion or belief. Supporting preexisting conclusions is more important than the validity of the approach. This is called "arguing from a conclusion."

WHAT IS MOST IMPORTANT?

Science: Evidence

Pseudoscience: Conclusions

WHO ARE THE PROPONENTS OF THE FIELD? WHERE DO THEY WORK AND PUBLISH?

Science: Scientists tend to have formal training in their area and to be employed by reputable organizations. Their work is published in peer-reviewed scientific journals and occasionally the popular press.

Pseudoscience: Pseudoscientists tend not to be formally trained in the area and not employed by reputable organizations, and their work tends to be published in the popular press but *not* in peer-reviewed journals.

WHAT IS THE HISTORY OF THIS FIELD? DOES IT CHANGE AS NEW EVIDENCE ARISES?

Science: Scientific theories are constantly changing, either radically (like quantum physics) or incrementally (like evolution). Relatively unchanging principles or claims persist only in the continuing presence of strong affirmative evidence.

Pseudoscience: Claims made by pseudoscientists rarely change. Assertions that do not change and are not supported by evidence are almost certainly pseudoscience. *Example:* Astrology

CAN THE RESEARCHER'S ASSERTIONS BE DISPROVEN?

Science: Truly scientific inquiry must be designed so that one can *fail* to show the hypothesized result. The better the chance for failure, the stronger the test.

Pseudoscience: Tests are often not done and, when done, are not fair tests of the theory or idea.

WHAT HAPPENS WHEN A TEST FAILS TO SHOW THE ANTICIPATED RESULT?

Science: Unexpected findings invite replication and, once established, provide the basis for changing theory. Anomalous (weird) findings are very exciting to scientists.

Pseudoscience: Anomalous findings are rationalized away or ignored. Anomalous findings threaten pseudoscientists, who tend to attack the findings or the researchers who produced them.

WHAT DATA ARE FOCUSED ON?

Science: Any data that bear on the issue being studied are fair game. Data that appear to disagree with existing theoretical positions are especially important and require study.

Pseudoscience: Data that support the conclusion are sought after, and data that do not are ignored.

Sometimes pseudoscience can be very hard to distinguish from real science. Like most things in life, there can be gray areas. For example, reputable scientists have studied psychic phenomena (although they have thus far failed to find clear evidence), but most people would regard paranormal psychology as a pseudoscience. The current debate about intelligent design is another example. Whereas we would consider religiously derived and unfalsifiable positions to be unscientific, others disagree.

SECTION 1.1.2: DEFINING APPROACHES TO SCIENCE

There tends to be very strong camps regarding how we should think about science. This is such a confused and sometimes contentious topic that we considered ducking the issue by leaving it out of the book. However, you'll probably run into it as you begin to consume social science research, so it's helpful to understand some of the terms. One term that is frequently used and misused is *positivism*. A basic understanding of what positivism is (and how people react to the term) is essential.

Positivism, often credited to Auguste Comte, is the orientation that the basis for science should be observation of the world, and that this observation leads to the uncovering of natural laws (we look at real things and figure out laws). It was a reaction against knowledge being based on authority on metaphysical principles (such as religious doctrine). Positivism suggests that:

- *The first way you can know about the world is by observing reality.* Observations of reality are valid scientific evidence. Objective reality exists.

- *The second way you can know about the world is through constructing and testing logical principles based on observations.* Science therefore consists not only of documenting evidence but of constructing ideas from this evidence. You must then rigorously test these ideas.

- *There are natural laws that can be discovered.* This is pretty much a restatement of the prior point, said differently.

- *We are building knowledge, refining and adding to our knowledge base.*

TO BE A POSITIVIST OR NOT A POSITIVIST?

Perhaps Bruce Thyer said it best when he said, "Few contemporary philosophers of science defend logical positivism, yet positivism itself remains the dominant philosophy, both in social work and in all other scientific fields" (Thyer, 2002, p. 471). People engaged in thinking about the philosophy behind science have lots of reasons to disparage or abandon positivism. These include problems with verifiability (how can you ever prove that something is *always* true *all the time?*) and the inability of

a positivist approach to answer many important philosophical questions (such as understanding value). On the other hand, some of the basic ideas of positivism when used in a practical sense (reliance on empirical data and reason) do appear to be dominant in virtually all scientific research, including social science research. If this confuses you, you aren't alone. By the way, you should know that there is a long history to positivism, and many subtypes (including logical positivism). For an excellent and massively detailed online review, see www.iep.utm.edu/l/logpos.htm, hosted by the University of Tennessee.

EXAMPLES OF POSITIVIST SCIENCE

Modern Bridges

We build suspension or box girder or other kinds of bridges because we found a bunch of rocks (iron ore) and played around with them (metallurgy), developed a mathematical science of how natural forces work based on observation and experimentation (physics), and *applied* these basic principles to practical matters (engineering). We did not guess how to do it nor did we assume that we should deconstruct the narrative of iron because maybe tin was just as strong in somebody else's reality. It was a cumulative scientific accomplishment built on discovered natural laws and centuries of knowledge building.

Systematic Desensitization

Behaviorist psychology is a particular form of psychology stressing objectively measurable behaviors. Through experimentation, researchers discovered that two key principles in behavioral psychology are habituation (the reduction of a natural response over repeated exposures) and extinction (the reduction of a learned response following cessation of reinforcement or punishment). The process up to this point has been an example of basic science. These principles were then *applied* in a method called "systematic desensitization" in which clients with phobias (such as a fear of cats) are exposed to imagined stimuli (imaginal desensitization) or to real cats (in vivo desensitization). Research shows that, over time, these types of phobias decrease with this kind of treatment.■

BEYOND POSITIVISM

Some social scientists do not like positivist approaches, and you often hear such statements as, "We've moved beyond positivism." This means that positivism is too narrow an approach to make room for consideration of subtle but important subjective factors, the changing nature of human society, or what is often termed the "socially constructed" nature of human reality. In a theoretical way, these points are very valid. From a philosophical point of view, a simplistic adherence to the concept of objective reality can be troubling. For example, many would suggest that positivism cannot allow for the different ways different people view or respond to the same objective situation. There has been a concern that the subjective flavors of human experience can be lost through strict adherence to a philosophically positivist position. Because of these concerns, many people resist the label "positivist" and try to do science in different ways. A few of the more commonly used labels associated with these approaches are described here.

Feminist research is actually quite varied, with many leading theorists and authors, but most feminist researchers share the following:

- An assertion that women are oppressed in our society
- A commitment to reducing the oppression of women
- Respect for the subjective points of view of women

As such, feminist research is innately political, both in assumptions (the ideas it is based on) and in goals (the things it is used to achieve). We do not mean this as a criticism of feminist research. We find it difficult to criticize political aspects of social science when those political aspects are made clearly explicit, as they are for many feminists. There is a consistent grassroots feel to feminist perspectives, which often gain data directly from the subjective experiences of women. While feminist research can be quantitative, such as documenting pay imbalances, it is more commonly qualitative.

Feminist research often seeks to involve research subjects in attempts to organize politically or otherwise engage in political action. Some call this "participatory" research. Using this model, the execution of the research can therefore in itself be seen as a practical, political attempt to reduce the oppression of women. Feminist research approaches may be a good fit for researchers interested in research as a form of social action. However, because feminist research supports a particular political agenda, feminist researchers are particularly vulnerable to being placed in an awkward position should their results not be consistent with their assumptions or goals. This can result in serious ethical conflicts, as we will discuss in Chapter 2.

Participant action research (PAR) is a political orientation, a paradigm, and a set of research methods. Many people trace its origins through the work of Kurt Lewin and Paulo Freire. It is political in that it starts with the assumption that combating social injustice should be a core function of social research and that the people being studied must have a role in this process. Participation of subjects and other stakeholders is seen as necessary for several reasons:

- Inclusion allows for research that more truly reflects the perspectives of all involved. This supports both the validity and utility of the research.
- The long-term goal is that after the researcher leaves, other study participants can keep the research structure going to meet their own needs. Inclusion of the people in the process allows them to develop ownership and the skills necessary to keep the program going.

Paradigmatically (at the broadest level), PAR is all about getting the researcher and the subjects to participate *together* in the research process. Ideally, a wide variety of individuals should be included, including users of services, providers of services, other members of the community, and researchers. This inclusion is collaborative, not simply researcher driven. All participants have a role in shaping questions, approaches, analysis, and interpretation. PAR is not simply standard research with some side consultation of clients or other stakeholders; rather, it is research in which all participants are critical players at each stage of the process.

Apart from these differences, PAR is similar to more traditional forms of research. Standard techniques (surveys, administrative data, qualitative methods) can be used. The emphasis is not on what methodological tools are used but on who uses them and for what political purpose. As such, PAR is more a commitment to mobilization or capacity building than a specific set of techniques. PAR can be very much like feminist research, is often unambiguously political, and may cause some discomfort among researchers who consider themselves more objectively oriented. Like feminism, PAR is best seen as a blend of political/social action and research, bringing with it strengths and weaknesses of both.

Postmodernism is essentially a European philosophical movement, rooted in the works of Nietzsche, Heidegger, Foucault, Derrida, and others. More recently, it has spread to a wide variety of disciplines, including history, literature, and the social sciences. Postmodernism is best understood as including the following principles:

- All products of the enlightenment (including reason, objectivity, mathematics, modern democratic liberalism, political and social paradigms, and theories) are characterized as "modernism."
- Modernism is an interlocking set of constructs created by one group (White European males in positions of power) to maintain and assert its power.
- This is done through controlling the world views of others.

- The assertion that modernism must be viewed with great critical suspicion. This includes the specifics of modernism (such as customs, institutions, and the like) as well as the overarching "objectivist" paradigm of modernism (the idea that reality or truth can exist).

- A perspective, point of view, definition, or argument is often termed a *narrative*. Sometimes an overarching paradigm (such as a belief in the value of objectivity) is referred to as a *metanarrative*. Metanarratives are viewed as serving the power interests of those who created them and should be deconstructed and destroyed.

- Deconstruction could be termed the methodology of postmodernism. Deconstruction begins with the assumption that any thought, narrative, custom, or institution was previously "constructed" by power-holders to meet their own needs.

- The process of deconstruction is the process of attempting to understand the reasons why concepts exist as they do, especially how the constructs meet the needs of those in power. The postmodernist seeks to criticize and understand the nature of these constructs from his or her own perspective and therefore tries to free him- or herself from the covert, embedded meanings that formerly composed the construct and controlled reality.

- A primary venue for postmodernist exploration involves conversation and interaction between individuals, such that individual voices can be heard and understood. Such "authentic" communication is the basis of greater understanding.

- Beyond deconstruction, postmodernists offer no new structure or framework for doing science or building knowledge, as such new frameworks would obviously serve the interests of those creating them and be no more valid than prior modernist constructs.

Postmodernism is valued by many for its critical stance toward dominant and/or harmful paradigms. Unfortunately, if there isn't a real world out there (or something like it), it is hard to see what science is supposed to be for or how a social problem can be systematically addressed, or how a practitioner can demonstrate accountability.

SECTION 1.1.3: DEFINING *EMPIRICAL*

In ancient times, truth was based more on the authority of the source or on religious belief than on evidence. This wasn't very practical and didn't advance human knowledge much. Nowadays, we want knowledge to be grounded in "facts." In the strictest sense, empirical things are real things that you can observe and (often) count. By "observe," we mean both direct observation (such as the number of times a child correctly identifies a shape) and also observation by other means, such as psychological testing or responses to survey or interview questions.

Empiricism is the philosophy of basing your scientific conclusions only on empirical facts. An empiricist is someone who accepts only observable or measurable things as evidence. The empiricist wants "just the facts, ma'am." The word *facts* is a bit misleading, as science is a building process. For the scientist, facts are rarely absolute, and our understanding of them can change in the face of new information.

It should be noted that different researchers will consider different things to be empirical. Strict behaviorists, for example, will not accept descriptions of internal feeling states as empirical, while many other researchers would. The use of the term *empirical* can also vary by context. Sometimes this can be confusing, so more examples are in order.

WHAT'S EMPIRICAL? SOME EXAMPLES

Example 1: The Feeling State of "Depression"

If we are talking, and you say, "I'm depressed" or "That person is depressed," you are probably just telling me your subjective judgment. This casual statement is not based on any careful observation. Most scientists who wanted to know if you were depressed would use a formal method, such as giving you the Beck Depression Inventory (a test designed to yield a score showing how depressed someone is). This is because the BDI is a well-known structured and standardized scale (in other words, people have studied it and mostly agree that it really measures depression).

Now here is where the notion of what is empirical gets messy. So long as we are interested in assessing the presence of depression as a construct operationalized in an agreed-upon manner across studies (see Chapter 5), someone saying "I'm depressed" has little empirical value. However, if we are interested in gathering data about how people describe their mental state or how clients define their needs, their statement "I'm depressed" may have great empirical value.

Example 2: Astrology versus Astronomy

Astrology uses empirical data (observations of the stars and planets), but the assertions it makes (for example, "People born under the sign of the fish are sensitive and artistic") are not systematically connected to these observations and are not subjected to change based on data. The relationships between stars and people that form the heart of astrology are not subject to empirical challenge by those who believe in it. Astrology itself is therefore not empirical. On the other hand, one could study the history of astrology, the level of belief in astrology in a given population, or the perceived impact of astrology on a person's life.

Astronomy uses some of the same data astrology does (the locations of stars, etc.), but bases conclusions on these data. Any factual or theoretical assertion is open to revision based on new evidence. Astronomy lives and dies by what the evidence says and is therefore an empirical science.■

SECTION 1.1.4: DEFINING *OBJECTIVITY*

Objectivity in science is the notion that real things exist and that they should be studied as they are, with the investigator being as neutral (unbiased) as possible. Most scientific designs seek to put the researcher in an objective stance toward the subjects of the study. Absolute objectivity is really a goal more than a reality, with the investigator's biases (some unknown to him or her) normally moving science away from the best case of "pure" objectivity. There are approaches to doing science that attempt to remove such biases, such as double-blind designs (see the following).

ENHANCING OBJECTIVITY: DOUBLE-BLIND DESIGNS

Let's say I want to see if people put a puzzle together faster after taking 100 mg of caffeine. I don't want the people to know if they got the caffeine or not, so I give half of them caffeine pills and half sugar pills. In this way, the subjects are "blind" to the intervention. But this might not be good enough for me, because I know who got what pills and therefore might treat them differently and introduce bias by how I handle the subjects. I could make it a "double-blind" study by having my assistant administer numbered pills without knowing who gets caffeine and who gets sugar. In this way, we can't compromise the objectivity of the situation.

As noted in the section on "Defining Approaches to Science," research is sometimes purposively conducted from a more subjective viewpoint. Further, many subjects in the social sciences do not lend themselves to the scrutiny of randomly assigning individuals or double-blind investigations. For example, one does not randomly assign a child to be abused so that the effects of that abuse can be studied in a more objective manner. To do so would be unethical and inhumane.

SECTION 1.1.5: DEFINING *THEORY* (SIMPLY AND PRACTICALLY)

A **theory** is an idea. Usually, theories will describe how one thing relates to something else, what we will later call "the relationship between two constructs." "Stress causes parents to be more likely to physically abuse their children" is a theory. "Most metals get softer as temperature increases" is a theory. Remember that:

■ Theories are never perfect or finished. They are always under revision. This is why they are called "theories" and not "truths."

■ Theories are tested when they give birth to testable statements, called hypotheses. Once you have a hypothesis, you can make up a test to check it. Based on what you find, you can accept, drop, or revise the theory. This is what most people mean when they talk about the **scientific method.**

Under the scientific method, you: (1) describe your theory, (2) create a testable prediction (hypothesis) from your theory, and (3) test the hypothesis. Later, you (4) revise your theory, if necessary.

EXAMPLES OF THEORY

Evolution

We believe natural selection causes more fit animals to survive and pass their genes forward, thus making the next generation more capable of survival. It is interesting to note that recently, we have modified the theory of evolution to suggest that this change is probably not gradual but occurs more in "steps." This shows how theories can change over time in the face of new evidence.

Catharsis

Believe it or not, when violent TV first became an issue, some scientists believed that watching violence on television would make people *less* violent because it would allow them to "let out" their violent emotions in a safe way (Siegel, 1956). This is based on Freudian theory and the notion of "catharsis." Unfortunately, the data we have seen suggest, if anything, a very mild positive association between viewing violence and participating in violence, so the theory of catharsis is pretty much discredited, at least as it applies to TV viewing.■

EXAMPLE OF THE SCIENTIFIC METHOD

One researcher had a *theory* that group pressure could make people change their minds about things they knew to be true. He developed a *general hypothesis* that "if people are around other people who state something is true, they will be more likely to agree, even if the statement is clearly wrong." He *tested this theory* by having a bunch of people pretend to be study participants (actually they were actors). These actors made obviously wrong statements about the lengths of lines that the whole group (including one real subject) was looking at. The real experimental subject was then asked for his judgment. Amazingly, the real subject often agreed with the obviously wrong statements previously made by the fake subjects (Asch, 1955).■

Not everyone agrees with everything we've said above. There has been a considerable debate about what theory is and how to describe it. This problem is complicated by the fact that most people don't agree on the differences between a theory, a model, and a paradigm. We'd like to try to define some of these terms, but acknowledge that people are not in agreement about these terms.

Paradigms are the most general kind of ideas about how the world is. They are so general and all-encompassing that most people may not even be able to say what they are (Can a fish describe water?). Examples of paradigms include "The world is basically a good place" or "Truth is judged by observation and testing." According to Kuhn (1962), science proceeds from one paradigm to another. For example, in the Middle Ages, people believed truth could be determined by religious or other authorities. In the Enlightenment, people started believing that individuals could determine the truth for themselves through observing, testing, and thinking about what they saw and did in a rational way. Paradigms do not generate hypotheses easily and are not really very testable. Paradigms are sometimes called "frameworks," but we use the term *conceptual framework* later to mean something else entirely, so we won't use "framework" to mean paradigm in this book.

Grand theories are attempts to describe large areas of human or social behavior with single, overarching theories. A few of the many grand theories are Marxism, behaviorism, the theory of reasoned action, and humanism. They generally make assumptions about what is important to look at and set up rules for how to look at the world. For example, psychodynamics has a set of core assumptions or constructs, which includes the existence and importance of the unconscious mind, the id/ego/superego structure, the importance of psychic energy (libido), and so on. It also specifies a methodology for finding out about those constructs, which includes dream analysis and other forms of psychological sleuthing. This contrasts markedly with behaviorism, which starts with the assumption that the scientific understanding of human beings must rest on observable behaviors. While some aspects of grand theories can sometimes be turned into hypotheses and tested, the main function of grand theories is to organize a field of study and to provide a context for more specific lower-level theories that can be tested empirically.

Midlevel theories (or **midrange theories**) are more specific than grand theories. They are sometimes directly drawn from grand theories. One example of this is the midrange theory of learned helplessness, which is drawn directly from behaviorism (grand theory). Sometimes, midrange theories are not clearly drawn from any single grand theory. For example, crisis

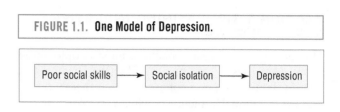

FIGURE 1.1. **One Model of Depression.**

theory (which posits that help is more effective after a crisis when given quickly and massively) is not clearly a subset of any particular grand theory. Midlevel theories are usually pretty easy to translate into testable hypotheses.

Models are very specific theories that often take the form of testable statements. Often, a model is an attempt to apply a midlevel or grand theory to a specific situation. We define a model as a specific statement about how specific constructs or variables relate to each other. Models are often drawn with lines and boxes. Models can be very complex, with dozens of constructs or variables, or they can be very simple, linking a few variables or constructs (see Figure 1.1).

More simply, the diagram in Figure 1.1 means that people with poor social skills tend to become socially isolated, and that makes them depressed. Notice that each box is a construct that is specific enough that you can reasonably hope to turn it into a measurable variable with a little work.

Practitioners and researchers often talk about "practice models" in a very general way, but these can range from paradigms to grand theories to very exact and "manualized" (written-down) statements of what to do in particular situations. That isn't what we mean by a model. For us, a model is a clearly specified theoretical idea with specific constructs. For example, the "harm/evidence model of substantiation" (Drake, 1996b) specifies that child abuse cases are substantiated only if *both* enough harm is observed and high enough levels of evidence are available. Another example of a model is the "information, motivation, and behavioral skills model" for AIDS treatment, which states that people are more likely to stick to a medical treatment if they know more, are motivated, and have the skills they need to do it (Amico, Toro-Alfonso, & Fisher, 2004).

Warning! The definitions above are those that we have found to be the most generally accepted, but these terms are not used the same way by everyone. For example, "systems theory" is clearly a paradigm, and Freud's "hydraulic model" is a midrange theory. The "medical model" isn't even a midlevel or grand theory; it's probably more like a paradigm. We believe that most researchers would not agree on where to put a particular theory in the above hierarchy. These terms just aren't that agreed-upon.

SECTION 1.1.6: DEFINING *INDUCTIVE* AND *DEDUCTIVE*

This one is a little easier, because most people agree about what these terms mean. Induction is when you look at data (facts) and come up with a theory (idea) that fits the data. Deduction is when you take a theory and try to figure out what specific facts that theory would predict. Let's look at each in more detail.

DEDUCTION IS USING A THEORY TO PREDICT A FACT

I might believe that home ownership is a good thing and makes communities stronger and safer. I could use my theory to predict specific facts and then look to see if those facts do, indeed, happen as predicted. I could, for example, predict that census tracts with higher rates of owner occupancy also have lower rates of reported crime. I could then check this against the 2000 decennial census data. Note that hypotheses are deductively derived predictions (predictions about what facts will show up based on theory). Hypotheses allow theory to be tested (Figure 1.2).

EXAMPLE OF DEDUCTION: AGE AND MORAL JUDGMENT

Kohlberg (a famous theorist in morality; see Kohlberg, 1986) says that preschoolers make moral decisions based on rules. They are not flexible and do not allow context to contaminate their simple rules of behavior. Older kids, however, do allow other considerations (like the greater good) to enter in to their conclusions. I might therefore predict the following: Given the scenario where a boy steals medicine to save someone's life, more preschoolers will say it is the wrong thing to do (rigid adherence to simple rules) while more older elementary school students will say it was the right thing to do (consideration of importance of saving life). We have moved from a theory (Kolhlberg's) to a prediction about how people will answer a question depending on their age (facts). This allows us to test the theory.■

INDUCTION IS MOVING FROM FACTS TO THEORIES

Induction happens when you make a general statement (theory) based on specific facts or observations (Figure 1.3). This is what most people do on a

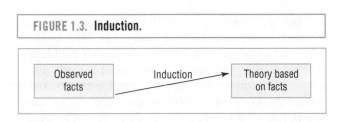

FIGURE 1.3. **Induction.**

day-to-day basis. If you notice that your dog always gets excited when he meets a new person or gets a new toy, then you might develop a theory that your dog enjoys new things. If you notice that your cat hides under the table whenever there is thunder, or on the Fourth of July, then you might create a theory that your cat hides from loud noises.

EXAMPLE OF INDUCTION: ASKING FOR DIRECTIONS WHILE DRIVING

If you keep noticing that most men won't ask for directions while driving but most women will, then you might create a theory that says, "Men are less likely to ask directions while driving than are women." This is moving from the specific observations you made of people to a general theory that you think might apply to all people (induction).

Of course, to test this theory, you will want to do the opposite, to use deductive logic (moving from theory to facts). As an example, you might take 10 men and 10 women, put them in identical driving situations, and predict that more women than men will ask for directions. If you find that eight women ask for directions and only one man does, you will claim deductive empirical support for your inductively created theory.■

Science is a circular process, moving from facts to theory (inductively), then testing that theory (deductively) against facts (Figure 1.4). Theories are very powerful but can be verified only by testing them against facts. In this way, deduction and hypothesis testing can be seen as ways to demonstrate the validity of abstract ideas (theory) through generating hypotheses and measuring observations (facts).

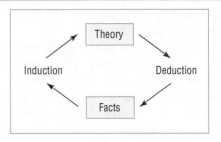

FIGURE 1.4. **The Nature of Science.**

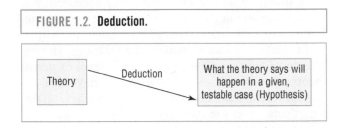

FIGURE 1.2. **Deduction.**

SECTION 1.1.7: DEFINING *EVIDENCE-BASED PRACTICE/POLICY*

The last 15 years have seen the birth of the evidence-based practice movement. Traced to origins in medicine, this movement is about the conduct, consumption, and application of research in a context where the practitioner's clinical judgment and the client's values and circumstances are also centrally important. To consume and apply the empirical research, the evidence-based practitioner must have the ability to: (1) frame a problem in term of an operationalized question that can be answered by data; (2) identify what information is needed to address the problem, search the literature, and extract the relevant information; (3) critically evaluate that information; and (4) apply the information to practice in conjunction with professional judgment, and client values and circumstances.

As stated above, this process involves the practitioner's judgment and attention to the context of a given case (patient characteristics, desires, and the like) that may alter the applicability of research (Center for Health Evidence, 2005; Sackett, Strauss, Richardson, Rosenberg, & Haynes, 2000). Evidence-based practice is absolutely not the robotic application of the research literature or so-called "best practices"; your judgment and the client's desires are critically important. Thus far, most of this discussion has occurred in the area of clinical or direct practice (Marston & Watts, 2003; Rosen & Proctor, 2003). However, the notion of basing efforts to serve people on the best empirical evidence can be extended across levels (clinical, program, community, policy)—though the effort is not without barriers (Marston & Watts, 2003; Pawson, 2005; Proctor, 2004; Zayas, Gonzalez, & Hanson, 2003).

For the beginning researcher or graduate student taking a social science research course, we believe that this paradigm offers promise as a way to understand the value of science. In other words, the principles behind the idea of evidence-based practice lead one to the conclusion that whether or not you become an "academic," you will remain a researcher as long as you seek to provide the best possible services or construct the best possible policy based on available information. As pointed out in the EBP debate, social issues are rarely neatly defined or adequately researched (Marston & Watts, 2003; Zayas et al., 2003). This requires even more careful thought and consideration on the part of the social science student. In simple terms, messy social science questions often result in messy social science research, and it may take some skill on your part to sift out what makes sense and what doesn't. This is described in more detail at the end of this chapter.

SECTION 1.2

THE ETHICS OF SOCIAL SCIENCE

Ethical issues will be addressed throughout the text as we proceed through the research process. Broadly, in social science, research is typically conducted regarding the existence, scope, and causes of an issue or problem or the evaluation of an intervention or policy. As such it is uniquely tied to practice and thus, we believe, bound by the same ethics of competence and best practice endorsed in various applied social science codes of ethics (that is, American Psychological Association *Code of Ethics,* 2003; National Association of Social Workers *Code of Ethics,* 1999; and the like). Specifically, ethics are manifested in:

- Appropriate design of a study to answer a research question, including sampling
- The ethical treatment of animal and human subjects, including informed consent and avoidance of harm
- The careful implementation of the study and accurate data collection
- The appropriate selection, use, and interpretation of statistical tests
- The honest and responsible dissemination of the results

Attention to these issues throughout the research process is critical to building knowledge in the social sciences.

SECTION 1.3

THE PROCESS OF DOING SCIENCE

We have broken the process of doing science down into six steps (Figure 1.5). Each is the subject of at least one chapter in this book, but we will take some time now to overview them. The six steps are specification, design, implementation, analysis, interpretation, and dissemination. We'd like to say that these steps follow smoothly in this order, but in real life this never happens, so don't feel bad when you find yourself having to back up a step or two.

The way we look at it, each of these six areas should result in a tangible (real) product that you must have before moving forward to the next step. Each of the steps is recursive (circular) in that it has to be done many times, checked carefully, and refined, before moving to the next step. Like writers, researchers are subject to Ernest Hemingway's observation that "The first draft of anything is #$@&." This means that each time you get

FIGURE 1.5. **The Scientific Process.**

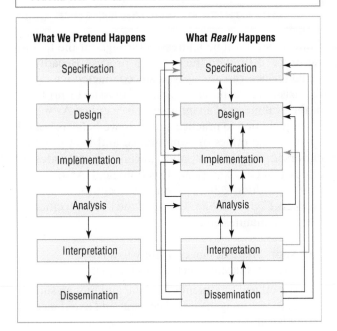

to a new step, you will have start with an idea of what to do, but when you try to work that step out, there will be serious problems. This will cause you to alter your plan. You will then repeat this process of working out your idea, encountering problems, and revising your plan, until you get it to a place where you feel comfortable with it. We've have taught master's and PhD research courses for many years, and virtually all of our students get demoralized by the many false starts in this process. When things break down, and you have to start the step over, you must realize that this is normal. It is not because you are stupid. This is how research works. You may be wondering how this possibly can be so. A simple example might clear this up. Just recently, we submitted an article for publication. The editor requested a revision that included a respecification of the problem, some changes in the design, and new analyses. In short, we had to redo the whole process after we thought we had completed all the steps. This sort of thing is surprisingly common and happens to *everyone*.

Each of the six steps is presented in Table 1.2 along with the product that each step generates.

TABLE 1.2. **Six Steps of the Research Process (How You Actually Do It).**

DESCRIPTION OF STEP	WHEN YOU'RE DONE YOU WILL HAVE:
Step 1: Specification	
Pick / refine your area of interest ↑ ↓ Find out more about your area of interest	. . . a collection (library) of information that will allow you to discuss and write about the status of knowledge and practice in your area. This can often be published as a literature review or theoretical journal article. You will be able to describe: 1. What your area of interest is 2. What is going on in the field (real world) in your area 3. Theory that is important to your area 4. Main empirical findings in your area 5. Methods used to study your area 6. Key issues needing study in your area 7. The aim of your research, including a clear conceptual framework
Step 2: Design	
Pick / refine your question and design ↑ ↓ Work through the details of the design	. . . a final written plan for how you will do the research. This can often be submitted as a grant proposal. You will be able to operationally describe: 1. Your question 2. Hypotheses (if any) 3. Theory relating to your question 4. The type of design you will use 5. Your sample and how you will get it 6. Your variables and how they will be measured 7. An implementation plan, including time line

DESCRIPTION OF STEP	WHEN YOU'RE DONE YOU WILL HAVE:
	8. The relevance of your design to the field 9. The strengths and limitations of your design 10. The degree to which your design meets ethical standards 11. An IRB application

Step 3: Implementation

Pilot / execute design ↑ ↓ Revise the design depending on problems encountered	1. Raw data in an electronic database from the number of subjects consenting or available (secondary data) 2. A second electronic database that includes variables recoded into more useful formats. This may include the merging of several databases and the creation of new variables. 3. A codebook that explains what each variable means at both of the above levels 4. A record of exactly how you did what in the process of implementing your research design

Step 4: Analysis

Analyze data ↑ ↓ Refine analyses	1. Verification of reliability validity of variables and measures used 2. Univariate statistics that describe your data 3. Bivariate statistics that show simple relationships between variables 4. Multivariate statistics that show more complex relationships, including interactions *Note:* Qualitative data analysis can proceed somewhat differently, often involving coding and categorizing responses.

Step 5: Interpretation

Interpret data and develop conclusions ↑ ↓ Refine and check conclusions against other research findings, policies, and field experience	. . . a series of graphs, tables, and summary statements. The product of this step is an ideal basis for presentation at a conference in either presented paper or poster format. 1. An assessment of answers to research question and hypotheses as originally stated, including statistical and *practical* significance 2. An assessment of strengths and weaknesses of design and data 3. An evaluation of how results correspond with prior studies 4. An evaluation of how results relate to theory 5. An evaluation of how results relate to policies and practice in the field 6. A description of key questions requiring further research

Step 6: Dissemination

Write / revise ↑ ↓ Submit for publication or release findings	Articles, book chapters, agency reports, final grant reports, master's theses, doctoral dissertations, your final assignment in a class like this one, and so on

There are several things that should be remembered about each of these steps.

- *Each step requires doing, redoing, and redoing some more.* You will note that on the left side of the table there are arrows going both ways. None of these steps are simply planned and executed without a hitch. Researchers always encounter problems that require revising what they initially planned. You should see each step as a circular process of trying, finding weaknesses, revising, and trying again. As an (extremely common) example, you may begin step 3 (implementation) with a plan for recruiting subjects. That plan may yield an unacceptably low response rate, requiring you to revise your plan and try again "on the fly."

- *Each step results in a tangible, physical product.* As each step is completed, there will be something physical (or electronic) that you can look at, evaluate, and use to figure out if you're happy with your work or not. This allows you to know when you have successfully completed each phase.

- *The product created in each step is something you must have to move to the next step.* If you are doing a full research project, you cannot bypass steps. Some more limited projects, however, will not require that you move through all the steps. For example, if your goal is to write a literature review for publication, then you will not have to go through steps 2, 3, or 4. The remainder of this book will provide far greater detail for each of these steps.

SECTION 1.4

THE ROLE OF THEORY

The most difficult and important thing for students to understand is how theories (ideas) can be linked to questions, hypotheses, and empirical observations (facts). Theory is used somewhat differently in induction and deduction, as can be seen below.

SECTION 1.4.1: THE ROLE OF THEORY IN DEDUCTION

In deduction, the whole game is about testing theory. Your role is to set up and execute a fair test of your theory. It may sound obvious, but the most important thing is to start with a theory that the data might disprove. This is called "falsifiability" or having a "falsifiable theory." The principle of falsifiability is that a test is only a real test if it can disprove your theory and that theories that are not based on real tests are not scientific. A guy named Karl Popper spent lots of his time writing about how important this is (Popper,

1959). He was upset by such theories as Freudian theory or Marxist theory because there was no test he could do that would disprove them. Because of this, Popper felt that these were not scientific theories at all but actually articles of faith. In deductive work, data are of interest mainly in that they allow you to test your theory. You begin with a theory, you set up a testable hypothesis from your theory, go find facts to test your theory, and then you tell the world if you think the facts supported your hypothesis (and therefore the theory) or failed to do so.

You are probably getting irritated by our saying things like "supported your hypothesis" and "failed to support your hypothesis." This is because scientists are innately conservative and don't like to say things like "I proved it" or "I disproved it." This is because, as we said, science is a process involving your work, other people's work, replication, and so on . . . Real conclusions in science are drawn by the human race, not by you, and even when pretty much everyone accepts a theory (such as gravity or evolution), we still call it a "theory" and not a "fact" or a "truth." This is because we know that sooner or later, some smart person will add on to the theory, or revise it, or replace it entirely. In summary, the role of theory in deduction can be illustrated as follows:

Theory → Question → Fair test → Data → Support/nonsupport
                    of question   of theory

AN ACTUAL REAL-LIFE EXAMPLE

In English

Our dog barks at night. We had the idea that our dog, being a perfect angel, only barked when the neighbor dog (clearly a bad influence) barked first. We set up a radio in the room where the dog sleeps that plays static at a low volume and masks the sound of the other dog. Our dog stopped barking, and we congratulated ourselves on our cleverness.

In Scientific Terms

Theory: Our dog barks in response to the neighbor's dog.

Question: Does our dog bark if he cannot hear the neighbor dog?

Hypothesis: If we play a radio (presumably masking the sound), our dog will bark less than if we do not play a radio.

Design: We set up a radio so our dog won't hear the neighbor dog.

Data: Our dog barked less when the radio was on.

Conclusion: Data support hypothesis. The theory is supported. We should keep the radio on (it still is on to this day).

Of course, if we were really into doing this right, we would need to repeat the process several times, sometimes with the radio off (we would expect barking), and sometimes with it on (we would expect less barking), just to be more sure. As it is, though, our dog no longer barks, and we're happy.■

SECTION 1.4.2: THE ROLE OF THEORY IN INDUCTION

When we do inductive science, we are not testing a theory, we are observing the world to get the facts we need to better describe it and to create new theories. This does not mean we are "theoryless," because everything we do in research (selecting data, specifying variables) exists in a context of ideas, whether we can clearly describe them or not. Still, the main goal of inductive research is to find out what is going on and to try to fit it to a theory accounting for it:

Question about the world	→	Observation of data	→	Description of data	→	Explanation of why the data is so (theory)

ANOTHER ACTUAL REAL-LIFE EXAMPLE

I remember taking tests as a student and noticing that some people finished fast, while some people took forever. Did finishing fast mean that you knew your stuff or that you were unprepared and just faked it? Did taking forever mean you were careful or that you were desperately trying to make up for your lack of preparation? Frankly, I didn't really know what to think. When I got to be a professor, the first time I gave a test, I kept track of the order the papers were turned in, and I recorded the grades, earliest to last. They looked something like this:

(Fastest) **AAABAABAAABBBACBCBBAABBCACBCAB** (Slowest)

My interpretation is that the fastest third of the class or so appears, in fact, to be doing better than the others, on the average. The first 10 students had 8 *A*'s and 2 *B*'s, while the remaining 20 had only 6 *A*'s. On the other hand, the last 10 students did about the same as the middle 10 students. I then created a theory: "Students finishing fast do better than other students, but there is not much difference between middle-of-the-pack and later students." This is a very basic theory that just describes what seems to happen and does not specify why it happens. Clearly more research is needed to refine my theory.■

This initial chapter has been written in an attempt to help you understand the general nature of social science research. You should have a clearer understanding of a series of important terms (such as science) and have been given an exposure to the process of how research is done and the importance of theory in research. The remaining chapters will provide more detail on the ethics, process, and nature of social science and will feature a series of examples that can serve as guides in doing your own projects. To help the reader further apply research in the field, chapters on evaluation research and clinical research are included. Also included are two chapters on quantitative analyses. These chapters are used in conjunction with computer software applications and emphasize use rather than underlying mathematics. The qualitative analysis chapter is also designed to be used in conjunction with one of the most popular qualitative analysis programs.

Like all research methods texts, we cover some things in more detail and other things less thoroughly. At a minimum, we hope that this text will help students to be better able to consume and apply existing research, as the evidence-based practice and evidence-based policy models require. We would also hope, however, that some students will decide to engage in research activities of their own, and we hope that this text can serve as a practical foundation for that endeavor. Either way, students will likely complete the text feeling that it has taught them how much they still need to know. This is normal, and we have tried to provide further recommendations for reading to assist this ongoing effort of learning to do social science research.

★ ★ ★

EBP MODULE

This section is meant to expand upon the description of evidence-based practice provided earlier in this chapter. It is meant especially for those students who plan to approach clinical practice from an EBP perspective. Evidence-based practice is a truly revolutionary approach to working with people that is getting increasing attention in social services. We believe it is also key to thinking about the role of research in social services practice at the individual, group, community, and policy level. Further, our goal is to present a research methods text in a very applied way. The use of evidence in informing all levels of practice is upheld by professional ethical guidelines, increasingly demanded by funders, and is, in our view, the best means of ensuring we are actually helping people.

We believe that your clients will do better if you understand cutting-edge research. We believe that the best way to teach you how to understand research is by helping you do some research on your own. There is an old Chinese proverb that states, "Show me, and I forget. Teach me, and I remember. Involve me, and I understand." That is why this book is designed to help you to move through the research process yourself. We don't expect that you will all do research for the rest of your lives. We do hope that you can give your clients the gift of truly informed practice.

IF YOU'RE NOT INTERESTED IN RESEARCH, BUT "JUST WANT TO HELP PEOPLE," WHY SHOULD YOU READ THIS BOOK?

You should read this book because you can't do EBP unless you understand the research process well enough to critically evaluate leading-edge research in your area. If you don't understand research issues like sampling, validity, and statistics, you won't be able to tell how well new research relates to your practice and the people you are trying to help. To really practice EBP, you must be able to critically evaluate studies of the type found in academic journals. You probably can't do that now. We hope that after reading this book you will be better at it.

We have, throughout the text, provided modules to assist you in thinking about how EBP is linked to understanding research methods and applying them whether or not you are actively doing original research. For this Chapter 1 module, we draw heavily on an unpublished manuscript on which we are coauthors (see Jonson-Reid, Drake, Hovmand, & Zayas, 2006) and wish to acknowledge the contributions of Dr. Peter Hovmand and Dr. Luis Zayas.

WHAT IS EVIDENCE-BASED PRACTICE?

It has several defining characteristics. It includes a set of implicit and explicit philosophical and values assumptions:

- *Empiricism:* Scientific data (qualitative and quantitative) provide essential information for helping professionals.
- *Accountability:* When you try to help someone, you are morally responsible to use the best available scientific data.

- *Lack of reliance on authority or precedent:* Medical and human service professionals should not act simply on the basis of what other professionals say or do or on the basis of what has been done before. They find, evaluate, and use the best available evidence in conjunction with their own best professional judgment and their best understanding of their client.

EBP includes a specific framework for practice, in which three things are prized:

1. The best available empirical evidence
2. The practitioner's own judgment
3. The client's characteristics, situation, and wants

EBP includes a set of steps for doing practice. At a minimum, these include:

- The practitioner frames a question that is empirically answerable.
- The practitioner searches for the best available evidence.
- The practitioner critically evaluates the best available evidence.
- The practitioner applies the best available evidence in conjunction with professional judgment and client factors.

When you think about it, all of the points above are really reflections of the same very simple idea: The heart of evidence-based practice is that our clients deserve treatment from professionals who use the best available human knowledge in conjunction with their own best judgment and conscious sensitivity to the client.

WHERE DID EBP COME FROM?

Central tenets of the enlightenment involved a reaction against dogmatic or arbitrary sources of authority (such as the church or monarchies), the reliance on empirical sources of data in evaluating and formulating knowledge, and the (perhaps overly optimistic) assumption that the world is entirely or largely knowable through the application of reason and evaluation of evidence. These themes pervade EBP, where the practitioner is expected to be able to autonomously apply evidence rather than simply extend traditions of practice or follow precedent.

Originally called "evidence-based medicine," EBP was first described by the Evidence Based Medicine Working Group (EBMWG), which was largely comprised of faculty of the Medical School at McMaster University in Hamilton, Ontario. The best historical introduction to EBP (then called EBM, of course) is a 1992 publication in the *Journal of the American Medical Association* (a full text version is available online at http://jama.ama-assn.org/cgi/reprint/268/17/2420). This early version has held up remarkably well over the years and still gives one of the best explanations of why EBP is important and what the underlying philosophy of EBP is. Those wishing a more recent and detailed description should see Straus, Richardson, Glaslou, & Haynes (2000).

Evidence-based practice has been described by its creators as a paradigm shift in the Khunian sense (EBMWG, 1992; see also Thyer, 2004). We agree and further assert that the philosophical conceptualization of the practitioner as independently capable of making his or her own decisions is the most important aspect of EBP. For EBM, "the underlying belief is that physicians can gain the skills to make independent assessments of evidence and thus evaluate the credibility of opinions being offered by experts" (EBMWG, 1992, p. 2421). In concrete terms, this means having the skills to "critically appraise the Methods and Results sections" (EBMWG, 1992, p. 2421) of articles, rather than just reading the introduction and discussion sections.

Over the last 15 years, many national and professional organizations have expressed support for EBP. In the United States, these include medicine (Institute of Medicine, 2001) and psychology (APA Policy Statement on Evidence Based Practice, 2005, Available online at www.apa.org/practice/ebp.html) among others. Internationally, EBP has also taken root, with some nations (such as Great Britain) being considerably in advance of the United States in their application of the model (see www.herts.ac.uk/lis/subjects/health/ebm.htm). In social work, a recent conference focused on the teaching of EBP, with a very interesting set of articles being available online at www.utexas.edu/ssw/ceu/practice/articles.html. EBP has also become a controversial area, as we will see below.

THE THREE FACES OF EBP: PRACTITIONER JUDGMENT, CLIENT FACTORS, AND BEST AVAILABLE EVIDENCE

EBP as originally set forth by EBM has three main components (Figure 1.6). These components include the practitioner's clinical judgment and experience; the client's situation, needs, and preferences; and critical application of the best

FIGURE 1.6. The Three Components of Evidence-Based Practice.

available data (EBMWG, 1992; Sackett et al., 2000). Philosophically, the inclusion of evidence, practitioner judgment, and client values causes EBP to be a method under tension. The tension exists between an essentially empiricist approach to evidence and the more elusive human judgments, preferences, and values of the practitioner and client. EBP places this tension squarely with the practitioner, forcing the practitioner to live in both rationalist and subjectivist domains while making decisions. Given that practitioners bear moral, ethical, and legal responsibility for their acts as autonomous professionals, this tension could hardly reside anywhere else.

Two parts of EBP are practitioner judgment and client factors. The assertions that clinical judgment and client factors should be part of clinical decision making were not revolutionary. By practitioner (or clinical) judgment, we mean the formal decisions that a professional makes about a course of action based on "practice wisdom" experience or mental models that practitioners have developed to help them understand and approach different situations. These mental models might reflect management experience or the knowledge of service availability in a given setting or a policy advocate's understanding of the political process in a specific area. The mental models might also include knowledge of the particular practice constraints due to eligibility requirements, funding, or other contextual factors. This aspect of EBP fits nicely with the requirements of graduate social work education to address use of *self* (CSWE, 2001), a term that has been notoriously difficult to specify in the past.

While certainly less longstanding, the last several decades have seen an enhanced focus on clients as participatory in their own care, in both medicine (McGuire, McCullough, Weller, & Whitney, 2005) and social work (Rothman, Smith, Nakashima, & Paterson, 1996), in the United States and abroad (for example, AASW, 1999). EBM posits that the practitioner must consider the uniqueness of the client situation, including preferences for interventions. This idea is very helpful to social workers when considering the application of EBP, as it provides an express framework for consideration of diversity and client self-determination as parts of the planning and implementation of services.

The emphasis on including the client perspective should not be misconstrued as EBP being restricted to individual people—quite the opposite. In organizational or community practice, where the "client" may be an agency struggling with an upcoming merger or a neighborhood seeking to reduce crime, the "client perspective" refers to the way that the organization or community sees the issues collectively, including the cultural norms and political context. Emerging models of evidence-based policy recognize this explicitly and require involvement and ownership of the policy development process by community members (Pawson, 2005).

What about research? Practitioner judgment and client situation are still informed by evidence, but by evidence outside the realm of intervention efficacy. It seems obvious that well-conceptualized theory and research that inform our understanding of the workings of policies, service systems, organizational dynamics, client culture and needs, preferences, and values are all vital aspects of EBP.

The final part of EBP is the use of the best available evidence. With regard to the use of evidence in EBM, several specific steps are generally recognized (EBPWG, 1992):

■ Formulate a clear clinical question from a patient's problem.

■ Search the literature for the best relevant evidence.

■ Evaluate the evidence for its validity and usefulness (*Note:* Evaluation is based on fairly traditional empiricist criteria).

■ Combine evidence with clinical judgment and client factors and apply (EBMWG, 1992; Rosenberg & Donald, 1995; Sacket et al., 2000; Straus & McAlister, 2000).

The above steps are almost always present in any description of EBM or EBP. Sometimes a fifth step is included wherein the practitioner evaluates the efficacy of the intervention chosen. Other steps that sometimes appear include a preliminary step where the practitioner becomes oriented to EBP and a final step in which the practitioner teaches others the EBP process.

HOW BROADLY CAN EBP BE APPLIED? SOME EXAMPLES

The process of EBP can be applied to every aspect of the helping professions. Some examples of different practice contexts may help show that EBP is not just the application of "proven" therapies by a medical doctor or psychotherapist, as follows.

At the Clinical Practice Level. Imagine yourself as a therapist in a mental health community agency. A client comes in presenting a mental health disorder that is well researched. There might be validated evidence-based practices that have been found to work well with this type of person having this type of disorder. On the other hand, perhaps the client is from a cultural background that has had little research attention. Now you must draw upon research about the culture (quantitative or qualitative) to critically assess the applicability of current knowledge. Diversity issues are not the only complicating issues. Physical and psychological comorbidity, age, living situation, and an almost limitless list of other factors will require that practitioners gain access to a broad spectrum of different kinds of evidence (including epidemiological, prognostic, and human development).

At the Program Administration Level. Imagine yourself as an administrator of a large state child welfare agency. Your goal is to improve the delivery and efficacy of services. This may spawn a number of questions regarding the nature of the people you serve or the policies you use. You may draw on evidence about populations and needs, evidence regarding how current policies enable or inhibit access to services, current outcomes for different populations served, as well as intervention literature for use within specific programs. Data needed in answering such questions may be found in the mainstream scientific literature, in internal agency reports, or even on Web sites featuring census data describing your area. Data may emerge from program evaluations in other jurisdictions similar to yours but whose methods of intervention are quite different. This evidence may help you in improving your state's services.

At the Social Development/Policy Level. Imagine yourself as someone hired by the government of a developing nation to assist with community development. You will need information about the culture and preferences of the population, the policies of a given country or region, and comparative studies about socioeconomic strategies that worked for other populations that seem to share similar circumstances. It is difficult to imagine how one could randomly assign developing nations to poverty conditions to test incredibly complex interventions that are heavily influenced by the social context. This does not mean you cannot use the best available evidence to help construct a plan that has the highest likelihood of success.

WHAT EBP IS NOT

EBP Is Not a Static Noun. EBP is best understood as an operationalized approach to decision-making (EBMWG, 1992; Sackett et al., 2000). EBM as originally conceptualized was a decision-making process, not the assertion of the scientific validity of a particular manualized practice.

EBP Is Not Simply Applying Evidence or Referring to Practice Guidelines. As Gambrill (2001) correctly points out, EBP is about the critical assessment and autonomous application of evidence not only by the practitioner but also in conjunction with the client. In reading some of the narrower definitions of EBP, it becomes difficult to differentiate EBP from a simple exhortation to use practice guidelines. The practice guideline movement predates EBP (Howard, Bricout, Edmond, Elze, & Jensen, 2003). A practice guideline can only be one of many tools for an autonomous EBP professional. For a description of this process, including a description of how clinicians might critically evaluate clinical practice guidelines, you might want to look at the excellent Center For Health Evidence Web site (www.cche.net).

EBP Is Not Expressly Micropractice in Application. Because of the origins in EBM, the language and steps involved developed around the idea of medical doctor–patient roles. It is therefore natural that they are so readily applied to the more clinical and mental health–oriented aspects of the helping professions. The ideas of EBP, however, are not limited to such application. In the United Kingdom, for example, the use of evidence-based policy is a readily accepted idea with a well-developed debate about its execution (Pawson, 2005).

IS EBP ENTIRELY MODERNIST?

It is precisely the complexity and diversity of social practice that generates strong reactions to perceptions of EBP as a strict "modernist" approach to practice. We believe that those who assert that EBP has a "modernist agenda" ignoring consideration of client (Faulkner & Thomas, 2002) or practitioner (Pope, 2003) are reacting to a narrow conceptualization of EBP. The original view of EBP values professional judgment and the subjective views and beliefs of clients. We find it better to say that EBP, as originally conceived, is partly modernist and partly not.

EBP is modernist in two ways: (1) The philosophical focus on the practitioner as capable of assessing and applying knowledge free from authority; and (2) the evidentiary component (and the specific elements of the critical appraisal process) of EBP is directly traceable to the modernist position on best possible reasoning and empirical observation.

EBP moves beyond modernism in three ways: (1) EBP's clinical judgment component relies on essentially unobservable and idiosyncratic professional experience and preferences; (2) EBP's patient factors component (that is, needs, preferences, values) is similarly free from strict evidentiary or rationalist criteria; and (3) while traditional research approaches will obviously undergird a portion of the evidence used, it is not clear that *evidence* need be defined as stemming only from research done within a tightly positivist framework. For example, the qualitative meaning of mental health within a given cultural group is clearly important "evidence" when considering how to intervene as a clinician. A feminist approach to research on the trafficking of women may provide important insight into client values and situations.

WHAT DEBATES ARE GOING ON RIGHT NOW ABOUT EBP?

There may be nearly as many different views on EBP as there are researchers or practitioners. First, we have the debate between the "original" and "narrow" conceptualizations of EBP, as discussed above. Originalists tend to use EBP as a broadly applicable process. The narrow perspective focused more on specific evidence based interventions. These two positions include very different assumptions about EBP and how to support its use. In the present text, we take the originalist position to understanding how to conduct and use research.

EBP MODULES IN UPCOMING CHAPTERS

The rest of this book includes a series of modules (in Chapters 1 through 8 and 14) discussing how the content learned in those particular chapters is relevant to evidence-based practice from the originalist perspective. Research skills are critical tools for the evidence-based practitioner, and we will highlight how these skills can be useful to anyone working under the EBP model. ■

REVIEW

1. What is meant by the statement that the social sciences are "preparadigmatic"? *Hint:* Start by describing a paradigm.

2. The text defines science as having three main characteristics. What are they? Describe each.

3. Define: replication, knowledge building, applied science, and basic science.

4. Give an area of inquiry you believe to be genuine science and one that you believe to be pseudo-science. Explain why you classified them that way.

5. What is positivism?

6. Why do some people dislike positivism?

7. What is feminist research?

8. What is PAR?

9. What is postmodernism (as applied to research)?

10. What is a theory?

11. Define: grand theory, midlevel theory, and model.

12. Give an example of deduction in science.

13. Give an example of induction in science.

14. Evidence is one of the three main parts of the evidence-based practice model. What are the other two?

15. What are the six steps of doing social science that form the framework for this text?

16. How is theory used deductively in research?

17. How is theory used inductively in research?

SUPPLEMENTAL READINGS

■ Hines, T. (2003). *Pseudoscience and the Paranormal.* New York: Prometheus Books. This enjoyable little book does a good job of framing what is and what isn't science.

■ Kuhn, T. (1962). *The Structure of Scientific Revolutions.* Chicago: University of Chicago Press. This book is possibly the most commonly cited work on the philosophy of science. Kuhn argues that science proceeds in stages of "normal" science, a "paradigmatic" state in which most people agree how science is done. Between these stages come periods of change, where the nature of science changes, and new agreements are formed about how scientists think about and do their work.

■ The *Stanford Encyclopedia of Philosophy* (http://plato.stanford.edu) is not as complete as we might like, but it does include very complete sections, such as biographies of key people in the philosophy of science.

■ *Wikipedia:* If you don't know about this, you need to. This online encyclopedia, found at www.wikipedia.org, has amazingly detailed entries on pretty darn near everything. Quality is superb as far as we have seen. If you have general questions about anything from specific books to issues and individuals, this is a great place to start. Even very specific things such as arcane statistical terms are likely to be present. As with any general resource, you may want to double-check whatever you find against another source.

VALUES AND ETHICS

When we think about values and ethics, the first and possibly only thing that comes to mind is not hurting the people we study. Most of us are familiar with at least a few well-known experiments that have hurt people badly, such as the Tuskegee syphilis study. Similarly, most of us accept that oversight by human subjects committees is a necessary, if sometimes troublesome, part of doing research on people. Unfortunately, you probably don't go much further in your consideration of values, which is a shame, because it is likely that the reason you got into this profession to begin with is to help people and make the world a better place. Values and ethics flow through the entire research process and will be addressed throughout this book, but we'd like to introduce the issue by going over some of the core issues about why we do social research and how we can make sure that the work we do is ethical, supporting both professional and personal values. Specific attention will be focused on the following issues:

- The history and core principles of research values and ethics (following)
- Values and ethics in specifying a research question (Chapter 3)
- Values and ethics in research design (Chapter 4)

- Obtaining human subjects clearance (Chapter 11)
- Values and ethics in dissemination (Chapter 16)

SECTION 2.1

DEFINITIONS

In order to discuss values and ethics in an understandable way, we would like to begin with a set of definitions of commonly used terms. We would like to caution the reader that these definitions are not necessarily agreed on by all researchers.

SECTION 2.1.1: DEFINING *VALUES*

Values can be defined as those moral principles that we subscribe to and that (hopefully) influence our actions. Individuals hold values, and professions are also frequently described as having values (Reamer, 1995). Values cannot be verified scientifically. Science is useless as a tool for determining which values are best, although data gained scientifically can be helpful in making value judgments. Put simply, you can't prove right and wrong, but the more you know, the easier it is to make choices in accordance with what you think is right.

Individual values include many things on which virtually everyone agrees (e.g., that murder is bad, that children should be loved), as well as many things on which people disagree (e.g., the rightness of gun control or abortion laws).

Professional values can be informal and general but also are expressed more formally in ethical codes. For example, the NASW (National Association of Social Workers) Code of Ethics (www.socialworkers.org/pubs/code/co-de.asp) specifies professional core values as including service (you should help people), social justice (we'll get to that later), the dignity and worth of the person (people are valuable and deserve your respect), the importance of human relationships (you should value how people relate to each other and not just focus on individuals as isolated entities), and professional integrity and competence (don't be dishonest, take advantage of people, or try to do things you aren't qualified to do).

Different values can conflict even within a profession or an individual. For example, the NASW code of ethics acknowledges that there exists a "possibility of conflicts among the *Code*'s values, principles, and standards" (National Association of Social Workers, 1999, "Purpose of the NASW Code of Ethics"). In applied professions like social work, one potential area of conflict involves tension between the profession's strong commitment to research (Code Section 5.02) and the profession's commitment to social and political action (Code Section 6.04). What is the correct course of action if disseminating research results may have temporary or long-term negative social or political consequences? The resolution of value conflicts is notoriously difficult and tends to be largely subjective. Formally established ethics codes are intended to help us with this difficult task and make values more operational in practical terms.

SECTION 2.1.2: DEFINING *ETHICS*

Ethics in research includes "codes or guidelines that help resolve value conflicts" (Gillespie, 1995, p. 4). As we will see, detailed ethical standards exist with regard to the treatment of human subjects. In addition, a range of ethical standards and issues exist at the professional level (e.g., honest dissemination of results) and at the broader level of the researcher's commitment to society (e.g., specification of research questions that might reasonably be expected to improve people's lives).

SECTION 2.1.3: DEFINING *CULTURAL COMPETENCE*

Culture has been defined in various ways (Miraglia, Law, & Collins, 1999). One author talks about culture as a set of behavior patterns and group life experiences (Lum, 2003). These factors influence all phases of social science research. Cultural competence in research is defined by Rubin and Babbie (2005) as

> . . . being aware of and appropriately responding to the ways in which cultural factors and cultural differences should influence what we investigate, how we investigate, and how we interpret our findings. (p. 497)

SECTION 2.1.4: DEFINING *SOCIAL JUSTICE*

Social justice is not an easy topic to pin down and is used rather indiscriminately. We have directly asked many students, professors, administrators, and even representatives of accrediting bodies for definitions of social justice and have not received a coherent set of responses. Certainly, views of justice vary radically between individuals. Is the death sentence socially just? Is the libertarian's view of economic justice (I made it, it's mine) better than the Marxist view of economic justice?

The most commonly quoted modern philosopher in the area of social justice is John Rawls (Nussbaum, 2001). His 1971 work, *A Theory of Justice* (Rawls, 1971) argues that the key to justice is fairness, and that everyone should have an equal chance in the world (e.g., there should be no barriers due to race, gender, or other factors). In current academic terms, it might be said that justice is partly the absence of oppression. In sports terms, it means a level playing field. Another question Rawls deals with in some depth is the distribution of resources (often termed "economic justice" or "distributive justice"). He asserts that we should tolerate the uneven distribution of resources and wealth, but only when it carries some benefit for those with the least. This is sometimes termed "the difference principle." Using this principle, it would be virtually impossible to justify the accumulation of wealth by Louis XVI or Imelda Marcos. However, it might be easier to justify the wealth held by Bill Gates. You might argue that the Microsoft corporation has added materially to the productivity of society in general and increased the tax base. You might also argue that Bill and Melinda Gates's massive charitable contributions have helped those most in need. Other people might see the wealth accumulated by Gates as problematic, no matter how much he and his wife give away. We chose this rather controversial example intentionally, hoping that you might see how questions of justice lend themselves to potentially endless debate from multiple points of view. Less ambiguous examples also exist. It is perhaps easier for people to recognize the absence of social justice as in cases of children dying of starvation in Ethiopia, international trafficking of young girls, or children growing up in extreme poverty in the U.S.

The most important values, of course, are yours—which are also hopefully in line with those of your chosen discipline.

SECTION 2.2.1: DOING NO HARM

Although the reader may associate these words with the medical profession, the value of "doing no harm" is a part of virtually all social science codes of conduct in one form or another. For example, psychologists strive to benefit those with whom they work and take care to do no harm (Principle A, American Psychological Association, 2003). How should this play out in research? One way is through becoming educated in how to do high-quality research. Bad research can hurt people. Another way is through the mechanisms protecting human subjects, which deal specifically with this issue.

SECTION 2.2.2: HELPING PEOPLE AND SOCIAL JUSTICE

But what about your personal desire to help people? Virtually all social researchers get into the field because of who they are and because of a desire to help others or society in general. We know few professors or other researchers who began with a purely academic interest in people. Indeed, the social sciences' professional codes of ethics all have some reference to making the world a better place. Here are a few examples from the introductions to professional codes of ethics:

- They [sociologists] apply and make public their knowledge in order to contribute to the public good (Principle E, American Sociological Association, 1999).
- Psychologists strive to benefit those with whom they work and take care to do no harm (Principle A, American Psychological Association, 2003).
- Social workers draw on their knowledge, values, and skills to help people in need and to address social problems (Principle A, National Association of Social Workers, 1999).
- Social workers pursue social change, particularly with and on behalf of vulnerable and oppressed individuals and groups of people (Principle B, National Association of Social Workers, 1999).

Frankly, if this isn't true for you, you might consider returning this textbook and joining a more financially rewarding profession. This brings us to a very complicated question, namely, "How should this value be reflected in research?" Because your personal values almost certainly include making the world a better place, you should try to do research that you believe in and that helps people. This is, after all, why you are learning this subject. Not all questions have equal pay-offs, and you should always try to direct your energies toward doing the best work that you feel can help the most people.

Not all research helps people right away (in fact, most doesn't), but there should be some reasonable chance that your work will move us toward the day when people can live better lives. This can be trickier than it sounds. There will be many demands on your work. Can it be funded? Is it publishable? Is it practical to do? Will the people involved let you do it? Accommodating these concerns can deform and twist your original good intentions to do beneficial work. It is surprisingly easy to end up with irrelevant academic questions, which nobody in the real world will care about.

A VERY SAD STORY

One day, one of the authors went to a conference. The speaker was discussing results from an expensive publicly funded research project. As the talk went on, the author realized three things. First, that there were probably no more than five or six people in the world who really cared about the question or the results. Second, that the author was one of those five or six people; and yet, third, the research was so academic, uninteresting, and unrelated to anything real that the author was finding it hard to stay awake and wasn't going to remember anything ten minutes after the session ended. The moral of this story is that all research isn't equally useful, and if you're not careful, it is quite possible to create work that nobody (maybe not even you) will care about.■

We would suggest that you make sure that at least *you* believe in your work. Research can be an important way of advancing social causes and advocating for better policies (Joyner & McCaughan, 2003). Of course one must be careful not to let one's desire to help influence the accurate reporting of results. For example, the need to alleviate racism is a dearly held tenet by most (if not all) social scientists and members of the helping professions. Imagine doing descriptive research documenting income inequalities based on race and gender. Some theories suggest that minority women are at very high risk for various problems due to their "double" minority status as both ethnic and gender minorities (see Barnes, 2005; United Nations, 2001). This may be true in many instances. But what happens if you have data that show that female Black college-educated professionals actually make more than White female college-educated professionals? What should you do?

The challenge is to both be accurate and fair. For example, you would not use the above findings to conclude definitively that racism no longer exists.

Meaningful work should not be about doing just what is easy or meets a course requirement. This is sure to sap your energy and enthusiasm. This is probably one of the most common issues our doctoral (PhD) students bring to us. Should they do what they want, or should they do what is easy (i.e., fundable, trendy, easily measurable, etc.)? You basically have two paths you can follow. The first choice is to be true to yourself, within reason, and try to help others. We say "within reason" because sometimes one must choose to pursue smaller steps in order to ultimately answer the larger question. You may have a more difficult path, but you will find sources of strength and energy, and you will be happier in the end. The second choice is "quicker, easier, more seductive" (Yoda, date uncertain) and involves doing what seems most expedient or popular with funders at the time. The end of that path may include your turning into a mindless automaton who is merely doing a job for the money or professional accolades. Don't do it.

SECTION 2.2.3: CULTURAL COMPETENCE IN RESEARCH

Most social science professions also have specific references in their ethical codes that uphold the value of cultural competence, though it may be called something else:

- Psychologists are aware of and respect cultural, individual, and role differences, including those based on age, gender, gender identity, race, ethnicity, culture, national origin, religion, sexual orientation, disability, language, and socioeconomic status and consider these factors when working with members of such groups (Principle E, American Psychological Association, 2003).

- They [sociologists] are sensitive to cultural, individual, and role differences in serving, teaching, and studying groups of people with distinctive characteristics (Principle D, American Sociological Association, 1999).

- Social workers treat each person in a caring and respectful fashion, mindful of individual differences and cultural and ethnic diversity (Principle C, National Association of Social Workers, 1999).

How should this value be reflected in research? Well, researchers in this area generally recommend that one be aware of the subject or subject population's cultural and experiential characteristics and how that may differ from one's own. Different sources recommend different actual means of carrying this out.

In one article, a model for culturally competent researchers included four concepts: cultural awareness, cultural knowledge, cultural sensitivity, and cultural competence. The authors defined a culturally competent researcher as someone who can apply the first three principles across all phases of the research process (Papadopoulos & Lee, 2002).

One can acquire the needed knowledge and skills in various ways. This begins with the researcher examining and challenging his or her own personal cultural value base (Lum, 2003; Papadopoulos & Lee, 2002). Developing cultural knowledge may stem from taking courses or reading books in diversity or cross-cultural psychology or related areas (see Berry, Poortinga, Segal, & Dasen, 2002, for a nice example of cross-cultural psychology); from formal (e.g., practica, internships, employment) or informal (personal) contact with persons of diverse backgrounds; and from research specific to a population that may be included in a study. For example, prior to conducting research you might go to a leader from the community of interest and ask that person to help you understand how this particular group may view the issue you are considering (Boynton & Wood, 2004).

Sensitivity to cultural differences may play out in a variety of ways in research, including the appropriate selection of measures and language use (Morales, 2001; Pan, 2003); the use of racially and/or culturally similar interviewers (Gubrium & Holstein, 2001; Twine & Warren, 2000); choosing to use specific types of research design (Israel, Eng, Schulz, Parker, & Satcher, 2005; Van de Vijver & Leung, 1997); and insuring sensitive (but always honest) portrayal of results (Rubin & Babbie, 2005).

SECTION 2.2.4: WHEN VALUES CONFLICT

We have discussed how personal values can animate you and provide energy for your work. They can also create issues and problems for some researchers. One problem that our students frequently encounter relates to research results that are unexpected and the researcher finds distasteful to his or her values or politically dangerous if disseminated. Should the data be explained away as an anomaly? Is that ethical? Other problems can occur when one researcher disagrees with another about whether or not a member of one cultural group can study another. Still other conflicts can occur in areas such as evaluation research (see Chapter 7) when an agency may put pressure on a researcher to alter or at least not disseminate negative program results. Further, sometimes researchers can (either implicitly or explicitly) inflate the relevance of statistical findings. For example, not all things that are statistically significant should be considered practically significant (this issue is discussed more in later chapters).

Although institutional review boards, coursework, mentors, and research ethics materials can help you think about these issues, ultimately it will be up to you to wrestle with your values, those of the profession, and those of stakeholders in research projects. We will see how these issues (and others) are dealt with through professional ethical codes, but first, let's review some of the history of how we got to formal codes of conduct for research.

SECTION 2.3

EXAMPLES FROM HISTORY: HARM TO HUMAN SUBJECTS

There is, unfortunately, a long history of researchers hurting people, particularly in the name of medicine. Some very well-known and respected medical researchers have been involved in some very unethical research. We now know that Pasteur's famous 19th-century vaccination experiments resulted in the death of one experimental subject, which was kept quiet until fairly recently (Geison, 1995).

On September 23, 1919, the *Journal of the American Medical Association (JAMA)* uncritically ran an article by one Dr. Udo Wile of the University of Michigan. Part of Dr. Wile's work involved using a dental drill to make holes in living people's skulls for the purpose of extracting small chunks of brain matter, which was then checked for syphilis. The work was done on mental patients at an asylum. Dr. Wile remains a respected figure at the University of Michigan to this day. For an interesting set of letters to an editor around this issue, with some people requesting that the University of Michigan cease honoring Dr. Wile's memory, see *Medicine at Michigan*, 4(2), 2002, available online at www.medicineatmichigan.org/magazine/2002/summer/letters/default.asp.

These examples give some idea how long this issue has existed, but most of us are more familiar with recent examples. We would like to review several specific and well-known events that were critical in highlighting the need for ethical standards protecting research subjects.

SECTION 2.3.1: THE HOLOCAUST

Between the late 1930s and the liberation of Europe in May 1945, the Nazi government of Germany ordered the wholesale murder of entire segments of their population, including Jews, homosexuals, Gypsies, the mentally ill, and many other groups. While the existence of the death camps is well known, some people may not be aware of the medical experimentation carried out at some camps. Perhaps most infamous was the camp at Aushwitz/Birkenau, with medical experimentation under the supervision of Dr. Joseph Mengele. Some of these experiments were supposed to have a practical purpose, such as inflicting wounds so that treatments could be compared or experimenting (completely unsuccessfully) with limb transplantation. Experimentation was also done for more general ideological purposes. People were killed and autopsied to support the Nazi pseudoscience of racial superiority.

These activities shocked the world when they were discovered and exposed, notably at the "Doctors' Trials" at Nuremberg. The Holocaust is particularly important to discussions of research ethics due to the resulting **Nuremburg Code,** which codified many modern concepts relating to the protection of human subjects. In the code, we see the main elements of modern human subjects protection already clearly spelled out: informed consent, avoidance of harm, and the weighing of risks and benefits. It is perhaps worth noting in passing that the famous "Nuremberg defense," the argument that one is not responsible if one is "only following orders," is clearly never a valid excuse for engaging in unethical behavior. If you are told to do something, that doesn't make it right, no matter who tells you to do it, and it doesn't protect you from professional sanctions or even criminal or civil prosecution.

THE NUREMBERG CODE

Nuremberg Code: **Directives for Human Experimentation**

1. The voluntary consent of the human subject is absolutely essential. This means that the person involved should have legal capacity to give consent; should be so situated as to be able to exercise free power of choice, without the intervention of any element of force, fraud, deceit, duress, over-reaching, or other ulterior form of constraint or coercion; and should have sufficient knowledge and comprehension of the elements of the subject matter involved as to enable him to make an understanding and enlightened decision. This latter element requires that before the acceptance of an affirmative decision by the experimental subject there should be made known to him the nature, duration, and purpose of the experiment; the method and means by which it is to be conducted; all inconveniences and hazards reasonable to be expected; and the effects upon his health or person that may possibly come from his participation in the experiment.

   The duty and responsibility for ascertaining the quality of the consent rests upon each individual who initiates, directs or engages in the experiment. It is a personal duty and responsibility that may not be delegated to another with impunity.

2. The experiment should be such as to yield fruitful results for the good of society, unprocurable by other

methods or means of study, and not random and unnecessary in nature.

3. The experiment should be so designed and based on the results of animal experimentation and a knowledge of the natural history of the disease or other problem under study that the anticipated results will justify the performance of the experiment.

4. The experiment should be so conducted as to avoid all unnecessary physical and mental suffering and injury.

5. No experiment should be conducted where there is an a priori reason to believe that death or disabling injury will occur; except, perhaps, in those experiments where the experimental physicians also serve as subjects.

6. The degree of risk to be taken should never exceed that determined by the humanitarian importance of the problem to be solved by the experiment.

7. Proper preparations should be made and adequate facilities provided to protect the experimental subject against even remote possibilities of injury, disability, or death.

8. The experiment should be conducted only by scientifically qualified persons. The highest degree of skill and care should be required through all stages of the experiment of those who conduct or engage in the experiment.

9. During the course of the experiment the human subject should be at liberty to bring the experiment to an end if he has reached the physical or mental state where continuation of the experiment seems to him to be impossible.

10. During the course of the experiment the scientist in charge must be prepared to terminate the experiment at any stage, if he has probable cause to believe, in the exercise of the good faith, superior skill, and careful judgment required of him that a continuation of the experiment is likely to result in injury, disability, or death to the experimental subject.

SOURCE: *Trials of War Criminals before the Nuremberg Military Tribunals under Control Council Law* No. 10, Vol. 2, pp. 181–182. Washington, DC: U.S. Government Printing Office, 1949.■

Recently, there have been several interesting debates about data related to some atrocities that occurred during the Holocaust. Experimentation on hypothermia was conducted at Dachau that involved keeping people in cold water until their body temperature dropped almost 20 degrees Fahrenheit. Many participants died very painfully. Thankfully, such experimentation cannot be done today. The modern study of hypothermia is a humanitarian endeavor with the goal of finding ways to save the lives of people who have suffered exposure. The question therefore becomes, "If the Nazi data are at all scientifically useful, should they be used in helping us to treat hypothermia?" Does the evil nature of the research render use of the data unethical, or is it unethical to ignore already existing

data (regardless of the source) that may save lives? Like many questions of this type, there is no clear answer. We would strongly recommend that students interested in this issue use the excellent NOVA (Public Broadcasting System) interactive website at www.pbs.org/wgbh/nova/holocaust/experiments.html. Be warned that the site contains disturbing images and material.

As a side note, it may be of value to note that the Holocaust was not the only example of massive state-sponsored human experimentation in World War II. Very similar experiments were carried out by Imperial Japan's Unit 731 during the 1940s. At least several thousand and possibly many thousands of Chinese, Korean, and Allied civilians and prisoners were subjected to death by freezing, G-forces (centrifuges), removal of organs, living dissection, and many other means. Fatalities in Northern China are still occurring due to the testing and dispersal of biological warfare weaponry done over 50 years ago (Williams & Wallace, 1989).

SECTION 2.3.2: THE TUSKEGEE SYPHILIS STUDY

Any sane person can identify the German or Japanese experimentation described above as unethical. There is an unfortunate tendency for us to discount what happened under the Nazis or in Imperial Japan as currently irrelevant, because these regimes were manifestly evil and totalitarian. We might believe that such things could never happen in any democratic society. Between 1932 and 1972, the United States government subsidized an utterly pointless ongoing study of syphilis that resulted in unnecessary suffering and the death of many African-American citizens. The activities carried out under the study involved denying needed medical treatment for a fatal disease (syphilis) that could have been easily and cheaply cured by the researchers after the first decade of the study. Incredibly, the work was entirely public, with results being routinely published in top medical journals. The subjects were all poor Black men with little education who were therefore easy to victimize. Some details on what happened can help us highlight a number of key issues. We will also see how the study developed and how it gradually shifted from an initially humanitarian enterprise to something utterly infamous.

In 1929 there was no cure for syphilis. Treatment, however, was believed to reduce the symptoms and to make it harder to pass on the disease. The Rosenwald Fund approved $50,000 to be spent during 1930 for demonstration treatment projects intended to control the spread of venereal disease among a rural Black population. This study, funded privately, ceased during the Depression and ended up changing into something else. That something else was the "Tuskegee Study of Untreated Syphilis in the Negro Male" funded by the Public Health Service. In a time of scarcity, it had to be cheap, and its reduced objective was the discovery of the severity of the syphilis problem and the monitoring of those infected. Such a study could produce information on the need in these communities and could help support programs to help resolve the problem.

Under an agreement with the state of Alabama, minimal treatment for syphilis would be provided as part of the study. As time progressed, however, there was little emphasis on providing effective treatment. Instead, there were active efforts made to prevent treatment, so that the course of the disease could be followed more naturally. In the 1940s, penicillin became available. It was a cheap, effective cure for syphilis. The study participants were not offered the drug, and study personnel actually prevented patients from receiving treatment to protect the "worth" of the study. Amazingly, the availability of a cure was used as a reason to continue the study because so many infected men were not likely to be available in the future, now that a cure was available (Jones, 1993). In the early 1960s, some ethical concerns were raised, even published, but there was not widespread public awareness. It was not until the existence of the program was publicized in the popular press in 1972 that congressional hearings and public outrage quickly killed the project. By this time, the effects of syphilis had disabled or killed a number of study participants. The National Research Act was enacted in 1974 as a direct result of the Tuskegee study. In 1997, President Clinton provided an overdue public apology. There are a range of important things we can learn from this study:

- The study evolved over time, from a service project designed to help people, to a research project designed to study an incurable disease, to a study designed to document the progress of a completely curable disease. This last purpose makes no real sense. We believe it is likely that the "slide" of the work's objectives made it easier for the project designers and directors to rationalize their support for the study.

- The study developed a certain momentum, and there was pressure to "keep the study going." This is commonplace but does not excuse inflicting harm. For another classic example of this kind of pressure, see Haney, Banks, and Zimbardo, 1973.

- Researchers felt the (questionable) scientific merit of their work justified hurting, even killing, people. This was a clear violation of existing medical ethics, but that didn't stop anyone.

- The people carrying out the work on the ground and in the communities were influenced by the

prestige of the involved institutions (e.g., the federal government) and may have seen themselves as simply carrying out the directives of a larger institution that they felt was beyond reproach.

- The research was carried out on a group of very poor people who were also racial minorities. It seems impossible that this study could have been carried out with a population of rich, well-educated people who knew their rights.

- The research continued to be pursued after World War II, despite the similarities to medical experimentation in the Holocaust, the example of the Nuremberg Doctors' Trials, and the existence of the Nuremberg Code. Participants were simply unable to draw similarities, as can easily be seen in both the written (Jones, 1993) and the rather chilling videotaped comments made by involved individuals (WGBH, 1993).

- There was no widespread public awareness of the project, despite many journal articles being published. The project was not secret, but it was also not really public. Mainstream media exposure, when it finally occurred, caused an instant and overwhelming public response. There's the academic press and the public press, and they are often completely out of touch with each other.

SECTION 2.3.3: THE BELMONT REPORT AND THE "COMMON RULE"

Following the unmitigated ethical disaster that was the Tuskegee Syphilis Study, the Belmont Report was produced by DHEW (the precursor to the United States Department of Health and Human Services) in an effort to more directly address the issue of human subjects protection. This report stressed three main principles:

1. *Respect for people and their autonomy.* This is largely achieved through the process of informed consent.
2. *Beneficence.* Research can only be done when harm is minimized and the gains outweigh the risks or costs.
3. *Justice.* Subjects cannot be recruited in manifestly unjust ways. For example, prisoners, poor people, children, etc. should not carry a disproportionate burden of participation as subjects.

The report can be found at www.hhs.gov/ohrp/humansubjects/guidance/belmont.htm. The Belmont Report was institutionalized in government as what is referred to as "the common rule." The "common rule" exists in many federal departments. In the United States Department of Health and Human Services, it is found in 45 CFR 46 (Title 45, HHS Code of Federal

Regulations, part 46). The common rule includes the current overarching federal human subjects requirements that, through local internal review boards (IRBs), control ongoing research. These regulations are far too extensive to print here but they do follow the above principles and can be reviewed at www .hhs.gov/ohrp/humansubjects/guidance/45cfr46.htm.

SECTION 2.3.4: MILGRAM'S OBEDIENCE EXPERIMENTS

We now will switch to a very different kind of study, one that has no biomedical component but which is purely psychological. We are going to discuss this study because it is a helpful way to get into how the concept of harm is operationalized in the social and psychological sciences.

Milgram (1963) wanted to see how obedient people would be when ordered to punish (perhaps *torture* is a better word) someone with electric shocks. To do his work, he used deception (he misled people while they were in the study). Nobody actually got shocked, but the point of the study was to see how far you can get people to go when they *think* they are shocking someone. To make this work, Milgram brought in people (real subjects), told them that they were going to help him with an experiment, and that they should shock the (fake) subject when the (fake) subject failed to perform a task the right way. Basically it looked like this:

1. Fake subject makes a mistake.
2. Milgram tells real subject to shock fake subject.
3. Real subject sends a (fake) shock to the fake subject.
4. Fake subject responds to (fake) shock by pretending to show pain.
5. Real subject believes that he or she is hurting the fake subject.
6. Above repeats, with higher shocks each time until real subject refuses to continue or until the highest shock level is reached.

The study's findings continue to amaze people to this day. About two-thirds of subjects went all the way to 450 volts, rather menacingly, if cryptically, marked "XXX" on the dial. At this point, the fake subject had shouted, pounded on the walls, demanded to be let out, and even complained of heart trouble. Even among the subjects who stopped giving shocks, no subject discontinued the procedure before the 300-volt "intense shock" level.

Concerns about the ethics of this study involve the possible psychological harm done to participants. How do people react to the knowledge that they can easily be made to severely torture another human being?

There is absolutely no chance at all that any similar study could be approved today. It is clearly unethical to do any research that has the possibility of creating such a severe psychological reaction among participants, especially when deception is involved. Interestingly, subsequent surveys of participants showed that 84% felt they had benefited from the experience and only 1% claimed to have regretted their participation (Hock, 2004). This surprisingly positive response from the subjects does not make the study ethical. Key implications of this study include:

- Avoiding psychological harm is as important as avoiding physical harm. Stress and other reactions to research must always be considered.
- Even if the majority of the subjects claim benefit from the study, this does not outweigh harming some participants.
- Psychological reactions can be difficult to predict, so researchers must err on the side of caution when evaluating risks.
- Deception is generally not acceptable when there is potential for harm to the clients. Deception was a necessary part of Milgram's work.
- Some research cannot be ethically pursued. Milgram's work simply cannot be done today. To be ethically acceptable, the work would have to be radically changed. Subjects could not be exposed to a situation where they would be asked to torture another human being under any circumstances.

SECTION 2.3.5: HOW DECEPTIVE IS TOO DECEPTIVE? REVIEWING FAKE ARTICLES

Mahoney (1977) sent out a set of mostly identical articles to 75 peer reviewers. All good scientific journals use peer review to find out if an article is worth publishing. Basically, the editor sends the article out and gets back comments from experts in the field, then uses these comments to decide if the paper should be published and to suggest changes to the authors. Mahoney had taken the time to figure out theoretical orientations of the reviewers in advance by looking at their prior work. The kicker was that he changed the findings in some of the articles to either agree or disagree with the theoretical positions of the reviewers. In short, he sent out identical articles except that they either supported or cast doubt on the opinions of the people reviewing them. Unsurprisingly, people were less likely to approve articles with findings they disagreed with. Surprisingly, however, the criticisms made (of the results people disagreed with) were largely on methodological grounds, even though all the methods were the same. The upshot is that apparently reviewers are biased against ideas they disagree with but that they express this bias by picking on the methods used, not by directly confronting theories or conclusions.

Is this research ethical? The subjects did not know they were in a study, very possibly would not have consented to be in the study had they known of it, and each paid a price in time (a precious commodity for a professor) to participate. On the other hand, there are clear benefits to the profession at large for uncovering and empirically demonstrating the presence of reviewer bias, and the study clearly could not have been done without deception. We will see below how ethical standards from different disciplines attempt to draw the line in this area, but we believe that people would be split on whether or not this work was ethical.

SECTION 2.4

EXAMPLES FROM HISTORY: OTHER VIOLATIONS OF RESEARCH ETHICS

There are many other values held by researchers and ethical codes that apply to research that have nothing to do with harm to subjects. Honesty, fairness, and social responsibility are commonly held values that are applied to researchers.

SECTION 2.4.1: MAKING THINGS UP— FABRICATION AND FALSIFICATION

The National Institute of Health (NIH GUIDE, Volume 22, Number 23, June 25, 1993) reported that T. Lee, a postdoctoral fellow at Harvard, lied about results from his research on diabetes and the human eye. According to this source, Dr. Lee both reported data from tests that were never done (fabrication) and changed results from tests that were done (falsification) so that they showed the conclusions he wanted. Both Harvard and NIH investigated the case and found that fraud occurred. Dr. Lee was prevented from receiving federal grants or serving on federal boards for a five-year period, and retractions were issued regarding the four articles that were published based on the false data. This case represents a clear example of a researcher who simply conducted his work in bad faith and can easily be seen as a clear violation of research ethics.

SECTION 2.4.2: PUBLISHING NONSENSE (ON PURPOSE)

Hundreds, possibly thousands, of professors have published papers that make no sense, but one physics professor at New York University published such a paper on purpose. You see, Dr. Sokal had become irritated with the degree to which ideas from physics were

hijacked and distorted by people pushing political or ideological causes. He wrote what he later described as "a mélange of truths, half-truths, quarter-truths, falsehoods, non sequiturs, and syntactically correct sentences that have no meaning whatsoever" (Sokal, 1996, p. 93). He then submitted his work to *Social Text,* a journal. The editors published it.

When it became clear that the article was a hoax, there was a bit of a flap. At *Social Text* they appeared to feel that Sokal's conduct had been unethical. It could be argued that the work violated the trust that academic products are presented honestly and in good will. Although not a formal research study, we suppose that Sokal's efforts could be considered a case study or a simple experiment. It ended up demonstrating the disturbingly loose criteria used to judge submissions to some journals. The ethical question boils down to this: Can you use deception in publishing an article to achieve some higher purpose, or is this simply a case of fraud or unethically bad faith?

SECTION 2.4.3: A PLAGUE OF PLAGIARISM?

In recent years some very respected historians, including Doris Kearns Goodwin and Stephen Ambrose, have been accused of plagiarism. They had included in their own works several sections of work written by others, either verbatim or nearly verbatim, without clearly crediting the sources. Some people believe that plagiarism is plagiarism, period. Others were more accepting of the authors' explanations of what happened, that their working notes inadvertently mixed quotations and impressions of what was read, and that citations were simply erroneously excluded. Were these people guilty of plagiarism or just sloppiness?

We believe that it is difficult, perhaps impossible, for anyone to be completely certain that they have avoided plagiarism. Researchers do a great deal of reading and can be subject to time pressures or other things that tempt them to be less careful than they need to be. This does not, however, mitigate the wrongness of the act or remove responsibility. Your best defense is constant care and awareness of the risk for unintentional plagiarism in your work. When in doubt, err on the side of overcitation of references, even those you only pull general ideas from. In particular, you must make absolutely certain that you do not ever make verbatim (or near-verbatim) transcriptions without citations. We hope that most plagiarism is unintentional and due to carelessness, but it is your responsibility to make sure that you do everything you can to avoid such unprofessional behavior.

The next section will build on these examples and provide you with fairly well-operationalized (and hopefully well-cited!) examples of ethical codes as found in psychology, sociology, and social work. We hope that you can use the specific ethical guidelines below as a starting point in understanding how the values and ethical principles covered in this chapter may apply to your work.

SECTION 2.5
PROFESSIONAL CODES OF ETHICS: HUMAN SUBJECTS

In this section and the next, we will see how values are operationalized into ethics. The following specific statements about what you can and can't do are taken from the American Psychological Association (APA) code of ethics, the National Association of Social Workers (NASW) code of ethics, and the American Sociological Association (ASA) code of ethics. Of these sources, the ASA code is probably the most thoroughly operationalized. The NASW code is the least specific and carries more emphasis on very general levels of social responsibility. The references below are not exhaustive but should point the reader to the sections where ethical conduct is detailed in each of the documents referenced. These ethical principles are clearly reflected in institutional review board (IRB) guidelines and codes of conduct at major universities, think tanks, and service agencies. We will begin with a summary of key ethical provisions regarding the treatment of human subjects. In addition to these codes, students may be interested in the Belmont Report, which was published in 1979 and serves as the basis for human subjects' protection by many institutional review boards. For a copy, see http://ohsr.od.nih.gov/ guidelines/belmont.html.

SECTION 2.5.1: INSTITUTIONAL REVIEW BOARDS

- IRBs should be consulted and their guidelines followed (NASW, 1999, 5.02d). You may not mislead IRBs and must follow protocols approved by IRBs (APA, 2003, 8.01; ASA, 1999, 12.01e). These protocols invariably contain subject protections in core areas, specifically informed consent, reduction of harm, and confidentiality.

SECTION 2.5.2: INFORMED CONSENT

- Informed consent must include providing information about "(1) the purpose of the research, expected duration, and procedures; (2) their right to decline to participate and to withdraw from the research once participation has begun; (3) the foreseeable consequences of declining or withdrawing; (4) reasonably foreseeable factors that may be expected to influence their willingness to participate such as potential risks, discomfort, or adverse effects; (5) any prospective research benefits; (6) limits of confidentiality; (7) incentives for participation; and (8) whom to contact for questions about the research and research participants' rights. They provide opportunity for the prospective participants to ask questions and receive answers" (quoted from APA, 2003, 8.02. Also see NASW, 1999, 5.02e, j; ASA, 1999, 12.01-02).

- Informed consent may not be required in some very specific situations, including evaluation of courses you teach, some specific kinds of naturalistic observation, and archival research, as well as some other situations (see APA, 2003, 8.05; NASW, 1999, 502g; ASA, 1999, 11.02c, 12.01). Interested researchers should read these sections carefully, as many restrictions apply. Key principles include that informed consent is often not required for data publicly available or displayed, nor is confidentiality necessarily required in these cases (ASA, 1999, 11.02c).

- Refusal to participate must not cause the subject "deprivation or penalty" (NASW, 1999, 5.02e).

- When participants are incapable of giving informed consent, an appropriate explanation must be given to participants, their assent (agreement to participate) should be sought, and written consent should be obtained from an appropriate proxy (NASW, 1999, 5.02f, ASA, 1999, 12.01d). These principles apply to children (ASA, 1999, 12.04), in which case a parent or legal guardian is generally the proxy.

SECTION 2.5.3: CONFIDENTIALITY

- Steps must be taken to protect the confidentiality of subject's data (NASW, 1999, 5.02k,l,m.; ASA 10.11, 11).

- Researchers may sometimes violate confidentiality if failure to disclose confidential information may result in threats to health or life (ASA, 1999, 11.02b).

- Limitations of confidentiality must be spelled out in advance in the consent process (APA, 2003, 8.02; NASW, 1999, 5.02l; ASA, 1999, 11.03a).

- Electronic transfers of data may imply risks to confidentiality that must be considered (ASA, 1999, 11.05).

- Evaluative data should be shared only with professionals concerned with the data and for professional purposes (NASW, 1999, 5.02i; ASA, 1999, 11.07b).

SECTION 2.5.4: SECRET TAPING OF CLIENTS

■ Video or audiotaping may occur only if the subject consents in advance, or if it is done in a public place and is not used in a way that can identify or harm participants, or if it is done in a study using deception and the subject consents during debriefing (APA, 2003, 8.03; ASA, 1999, 12.06).

SECTION 2.5.5: POWER DIFFERENTIALS, CONFLICTS OF INTEREST, AND DUAL RELATIONSHIPS

■ Power differentials may exist between researcher and subjects (e.g., professors may use their own students) but only if there are no adverse consequences for participation or non-participation. If academic credit is involved, other options must be available (APA, 2003, 8.04; ASA, 1999, 12.03).

■ "Social workers should be alert to and avoid conflicts of interest and dual relationships with participants" (NASW, 1999, 5.02o).

SECTION 2.5.6: INDUCEMENTS

■ Inducements (money, credit, etc.) may not be so large that they can coerce people to participate (APA, 2003, 8.06; NASW, 1999, 502e; ASA, 1999, 13.03). This means that you can't offer people so much money (or whatever) for participating that they end up doing things they don't really want to do.

SECTION 2.5.7: DECEPTION

■ Deception is permissible only for work that will yield valuable results and would not be possible without deception. Deception can never be used in a study involving physical harm or severe emotional distress. If deception is used, you must debrief (explain the deception to the subject) as soon as possible. Subjects then have the right to have any data associated with their participation destroyed (APA, 2003, 8.08; ASA, 1999, 12.05).

■ You may "never deceive research participants about significant aspects of the research that would affect their willingness to participate, such as physical risks, discomfort, or unpleasant emotional experiences" (ASA, 1999, 12.05b).

■ Concealing your identity may (rarely) be necessary but is permitted only if necessary, if only minimal risk to subjects is involved, and if approved by an IRB or similar body (ASA, 1999, 12.05d).

SECTION 2.5.8: DEBRIEFING

■ Subjects must be given the opportunity to "obtain appropriate information about the nature, results, and conclusions of the research, and they take reasonable steps to correct any misconceptions" (quoted from APA, 2003, 8.08; also ASA, 1999, 12.05c). If information must be withheld for scientific or humane reasons, steps must be taken to reduce possible attendant harm. If harm to clients is discovered, steps must be taken to reduce that harm.

> **NOTE:** In our experience, most studies include a discussion of how they will anticipate the possibility of emotional reactions from participants, particularly if they are asked to recall traumatic events. This usually takes the form of having a counselor available, either in person or by telephone referral. This is one of the most common ethical safeguards.

SECTION 2.5.9: MINIMIZING HARM

■ Steps should be taken to "protect participants from unwarranted physical or mental distress, harm, danger or deprivation" (quoted from NASW, 1999, 5.02j; see also ASA, 1999, 13.01b).

■ Appropriate supportive services should be provided to participants involved in evaluation and research (NASW, 1999, 5.02i).

SECTION 2.6
PROFESSIONAL CODES OF ETHICS: OTHER ISSUES

There are a number of ethical standards that do not deal directly with human subjects concerns but that are important for the researcher to know. Again, we have selected ethical standards representing the main points from psychology and social work.

SECTION 2.6.1: SOCIAL RESPONSIBILITY

■ "Social workers should monitor and evaluate policies, the implementation of programs, and practice interventions" (NASW, 1999, 5.02a).

■ "Social workers should promote and facilitate evaluation and research to contribute to the development of knowledge" (NASW, 1999, 502b).

■ Social workers should educate themselves and others about responsible research practices (NASW, 1999, 5.02p).

SECTION 2.6.2: SPECIAL POPULATIONS

- You should have knowledge of any special populations you are researching and should employ consultation from the community or experts when necessary to supplement your knowledge (ASA, 1999, 13.01d; NASW, 1999, 1.05; APA, 2003, 2.01).

SECTION 2.6.3: REPORTING AND PUBLISHING

- You never make data up, and if you find that you have published significantly incorrect data, you must tell people, usually through a published note or correction (APA, 2003, 8.10; NASW, 1999, 5.02n; ASA, 1999, 13.04b,f). You may not selectively omit relevant data (ASA, 1999, 13.04c).

- Research must be designed to minimize the chances that results will be misleading (ASA, 1999, 13.01a).

- "Sociologists disseminate their research findings except where unanticipated circumstances (e.g., the health of the researcher) or proprietary agreements with employers, contractors, or clients preclude such dissemination" (ASA, 1999, 13.04a). We take this to mean that you may not ethically choose to withhold findings that you may find disagreeable on political, personal, or similar grounds.

- "Sociologists do not make public statements that are false, deceptive, misleading, or fraudulent, either because of what they state, convey, or suggest or because of what they omit, concerning their research"(ASA, 1999, 10.01b).

- You must disclose sources of research support or funding (ASA, 1999, 13.04g).

- You must take care not to misrepresent the work of others in your writings (ASA, 1999, 13.04h).

SECTION 2.6.4: PLAGIARISM

- "Psychologists do not present portions of another's work or data as their own, even if the other work or data source is cited occasionally." We take this to mean that if your writing contains restatements of someone else's work, you must cite that person frequently, at least once per point presented, to make sure the reader knows the source of the work (APA, 2003, 8.11).

- Verbatim quotations must be indicated as such (ASA, 1999, 14a). Other presentations or descriptions of the work of others, even if not quoted or even paraphrased, must be clearly indicated as such (ASA, 1999, 14b).

SECTION 2.6.5: PUBLICATION CREDIT

- You can give authorship only to someone who worked on or substantially contributed to a project (APA, 2003, 8.12a; ASA, 1999, 15a). Individuals providing minor contributions should be acknowledged in footnotes, introductions, or similar (APA, 2003, 8.12b).

- First authorship must be given to the person who contributed the most (APA, 2003, 8.12b,c; ASA, 1999, 15b,c).

- The principal author should get the consent of coauthors prior to submitting for publication (ASA, 1999, 16.01a).

- Articles should not be submitted to multiple journals simultaneously. Book manuscripts may be submitted for review to multiple publishers simultaneously, but only if no contract has yet been signed (ASA, 1999, 16.01c)

SECTION 2.6.6: PREVIOUSLY PUBLISHED DATA

- If you use secondary data or data that have been published before, you must say so (APA, 2003, 8.13; ASA, 1999, 16.02).

SECTION 2.6.7: DATA SHARING

- Other researchers have a right to request your data to verify your results, so long as they are competent, respect confidentiality, pay for incurred costs, and do analyses only to check your findings. If they want the data for other reasons, they must get your signed written consent (APA, 2003, 8.14; ASA, 1999, 13.04e, 13.05).

SECTION 2.6.8: CONFLICTS OF INTEREST

- You must not have a financial or similar stake in the outcomes of your research. Any potential relationships implying a conflict of interest should be disclosed to IRB and appropriately noted in publications (APA, 1999, 3.06; NASW, 1999, 5.02o; ASA, 1999, 13.04).

SECTION 2.6.9: REVIEWING OTHER PEOPLE'S WORK

- Reviewers for grants, publications, and the like must "respect the confidentiality and proprietary rights" of the material they read. We take this to mean that they may not disclose or steal the ideas from materials they review (quoted from APA, 2003, 8.15; see also ASA, 1999, 17).

As you can see, there is a lot to consider when thinking about values and ethics in research. Throughout this text we will attempt to integrate these concepts as they relate to specific chapters. It is simply not possible, however, to do full justice to the topic of ethics in research in a general text like this one. Students are encouraged to take courses on ethics, pursue further reading in this area, and familiarize themselves with the particular ethical codes and institutional review requirements related to their discipline.

★ ★ ★

EBP MODULE

Concerns regarding values and ethics are important when considering evidence-based practice. We would like to return to the framework shown in Chapter 1, which highlighted three key parts of EBP: best available evidence, practitioner judgment, and client factors. We believe that ethical practice with human beings demands attention to all three of these areas, and we believe that a good understanding of current research in your area can help you to be a better practitioner across all three of these domains.

ETHICAL DUTY TO KNOW AND CONSIDER THE BEST AVAILABLE EVIDENCE

Imagine you are taking your child to the pediatrician for an ear infection. You have certain unspoken expectations. One of these is that the medical doctor you see will know what the best current research shows about ear infections and how they are treated. It would be malpractice for the doctor to take action based on an incomplete knowledge of the problem or available treatments. We fear that many social service providers do not feel that they have this same level of responsibility to their clients. There are many reasons this may be so, all of which provide fertile grounds for the practitioner to rationalize away his or her responsibility to keep up on current research:

- Social science research, as found in journals, is usually written in a needlessly academic and confusing style. Such articles are not generally written so that the average practitioner can understand them easily, if at all.
- Many areas lack sufficient good-quality research.

- Even if research exists, it may be done on a population unlike those to whom you wish to generalize the results.
- Much social science research does not find effects that are large enough to be practically meaningful.
- Many social science research findings contradict each other. Whom do you trust?
- Practitioners "just don't have the time" to keep up on publications in their field.

There are probably a lot more reasons you could think of for not keeping up to date with cutting-edge research. However, under evidence-based practice, you must do so. We would suggest that there are several compelling reasons why you should continually keep abreast of what is going on in your area. First and foremost, you have a moral responsibility to bring your clients the benefits of the best available knowledge. People come to you because they hurt, and as a human being, you have a responsibility to do the best you can for them. Part of this is being able to apply what we know. Once again, think of it in terms of medical practice. How would you feel if you found out that your child suffered more than she had to simply because your pediatrician wasn't aware of the latest facts or treatments?

Many people say social science is not sufficiently advanced in many areas, limiting how useful it can be in the real world. We believe that it is too easy to say "the research isn't there" without looking around. Sometimes the research is there and is conclusive. For example, good research shows pretty clearly that systematic desensitization is a simple and effective way to treat phobias. We feel that any practitioner who decides on a course of treatment for a phobia without considering behavioral approaches such as systematic desensitization is engaging in conduct that borders on the unethical. Of course, if you are working with other types of issues, you may well find yourself without the benefit of strong evidence in your area. What is the ethical course of action then? Do you simply say, "Sorry, chump, we don't know squat about your problem, and I'm going to fake it" and start making things up at random? We would suggest that no matter how bad the evidence is in your area, you are obligated to find and consider the *best available* evidence when treating your client. What information is available for similar kinds of problems or issues? If you can't find exactly what you need, then the best available evidence may be something closely related to what you want to find. Of course, you don't have to use poor-quality research as a basis for your practice. You need to weigh the quality of what's out there in deciding what to do. You are responsible, however, to at least know what is known and to make reasoned decisions about what information to use when you try to help people.

ETHICAL DUTY TO CONSIDER CLIENT FACTORS

We would like to report that in medicine and in the human services there is a long tradition of valuing the uniqueness and the diversity of each client. We would like to say that we have high confidence that clients are treated as human beings by all the helping professionals they run into and are not dehumanized as simply members of a given race, or as people who are poor, or as a walking mental health diagnosis. We'd like a lot of things to be true that aren't really true in all cases.

What does the above cynical whining have to do with EBP and research? First of all, under EBP, you have a responsibility to find out about the particular client you are working with. We do not restrict our use of the word *client* to individuals. By client, we may mean the person with whom you are doing psychotherapy, or the family you may be counseling, a community you may be working to improve, or even a larger entity. To begin with, you can't work client characteristics into your practice if you don't bother to find out about whom you are working with. What does this client want? How does your client see the problem? Is there information you can provide the client with that will help him in participating in his own treatment?

Next, understanding people who are not like you can be tricky, and you really should have some idea how to approach different populations. We often call this "cultural sensitivity." Of course, you do not want to stereotype all members of a given race, class, sexual orientation, or whatever as being a certain way. On the other hand, you do want to know that there may be things about some groups that are often true, that may influence how you work with them. For example, if you commonly work with certain Asian populations, you may need to understand that there may be cultural views about family relationships (e.g., how elders are viewed, responsibilities of sons to parents) that differ from Western populations. If you are working with young gays or lesbians, you probably should do some homework on what we know about the coming-out process. These things may seem obvious, but we wonder how many practitioners really bother to look at the research that exists in their area about the people they serve. Do they just refer to a summary in a dusty old textbook, or do they pull down some new

research that provides rich details about something like the coming-out process? Understanding current knowledge in these areas is not a one-time thing. The available evidence around the process of acculturation, for example, has grown rapidly in the past decade. It is important that you never stop reading and never stop learning.

ETHICAL DUTY TO REFLECT ON YOUR OWN CLINICAL JUDGMENT

Why did you do what you did with the last client? What are you going to do with the next one? Do you know if you are really helping people or not? How have other clinicians (or policy makers, or whatever) handled similar cases? All these are questions that relate both to your own clinical judgment and to research.

Evidence-based practice includes thoughtful consideration of your own practice, hopefully on the basis of data about your clients that you collect. Judgment is based on experience. Keeping simple records can help you to improve your professional judgment. Following up on clients after they leave your practice can also give you more information that can improve your learning about your own practice. Many questions, such as, "Are my clients doing better after they leave?" or "What do my clients feel was the most helpful part of the work we did?" can be answered by internal evaluations of your own practice. Chapters 7 and 8 will help you learn about ways you can answer these questions. We hope that you will not be comfortable just doing your job and not finding out if what you are doing is working or not.

Your professional judgment will also benefit from a broader understanding of the kind of work you do, the kind of people you serve, and the experiences of others in your area. Read what others have to say, in the form of either research reports, or case studies, or more general theoretical or clinical writings. This cannot help but improve your ability to make decisions in the future. Whole journals are devoted to publishing case studies where other professionals have tried to show exactly what situations they faced, explain what they did, and evaluate what happened and why. Do you face similar issues? Do you think about the problem the way they did? Are they looking at things you ignore?

We hope this section has been at least a little bit helpful. For us, the strong ethical grounding of EBP is one of its most attractive features. We hope that you find that using the process of EBP will help you to feel more assured that you are providing your clients with the best quality service possible.■

<table>
<tr><td>

1. How are individual and professional values different?

2. What are ethics? How do they differ from values?

3. Briefly outline Rawl's version of social justice.

4. What are the core ideas contained in the Nuremberg Code?

5. List three things terribly wrong with the Tuskegee syphilis study.

6. Give two core ethical principles violated by Milgram's studies.

7. When is deception permissible?

8. Define *fabrication* and *falsification*.

9. Give two strategies you can use to avoid unintentional plagiarism.

10. Define informed consent.

11. What are some special populations that require more careful attention with regard to their use as subjects?

12. What kinds of special precautions must be taken with special populations?

13. How can power differentials (e.g., teacher–student) become a concern regarding research subjects?

14. What limitations are there on inducements to get people to participate in a study?

15. What is debriefing, and why is it done?

OTHER QUESTIONS THAT CAN'T REALLY BE EVALUATED BY ANYONE BUT YOU

16. What are your own personal values with regard to the subject matter you plan to research?

17. Could your personal values conflict with any findings you might come across?

18. What would you do in such a case?

</td><td>

■ Berry, J., Poortinga, Y., Segal, M., & Dasen, P. (2002). *Cross-Cultural Psychology: Research and Applications*. Cambridge, UK: Cambridge University Press. Although this book is not specific to ethics, its overviews of culture and relevant research issues are very helpful.

■ Institute for the Study of Applied and Professional Ethics (1997). *Research Ethics: A Reader*. D. Elliot & J. Stern (Eds.) Lebanon, NH: University Press of New England. This study covers a comprehensive range of topics related to research ethics. We particularly like the case examples and the discussion of how funding and publication pressures can influence research.

■ Jones, J. (1993). *Bad Blood: The Tuskegee Syphilis Experiment*. New York: The Free Press. We can't resist but to again suggest you look at this truly frightening account.

■ Kimmel, A. (1988). *Ethics and Values in Applied Social Research*. Newbury Park, CA: Sage Publications. This readable supplement has nice case examples.

■ Oliver, P. (2003). *The Students' Guide to Research Ethics.* Berkshire, UK: Open University Press. This readable book focuses on ethical concerns in the types of projects that students are likely to carry out while in graduate school.

■ Reamer, F. (2004). *Social Work Values and Ethics*. New York: Columbia University Press. This nice overview focuses on practice but has some content relevant to research.

■ Sales, B., & Folkman, S. (2000). *Ethics in Research with Human Participants*. Washington, D.C.: American Psychological Association. This edited book covers most of the important issues in far more detail than was possible in this chapter.

</td></tr>
</table>

CHAPTER 3

SPECIFICATION

SECTION 3.1

INTRODUCTION

This chapter will show you how to pick an area, find out about it, and refine that area of interest so that you can move to the design stage. We could have divided this into two chapters, with the first being "picking a topic" and the second being "reviewing the literature." The problem with that, though, is that in our experience people almost always do these things at the same time. Napoleon is quoted as saying that "no battle plan survives contact with the enemy." It is equally true that "no research question survives contact with the literature." We will therefore look at question specification as a circular process, with your original ideas being modified by what you find in the literature, being rethought, being further refined by more literature, and so on. At the end of this chapter, you will have the tools you need to describe:

1. What your area of interest is

2. Theory that is important to your area

3. Main empirical findings in your area

4. What is going on in the field (real world) in your area

5. Methods used to study your area

6. Key issues needing study in your area, taking into consideration the ethical and practical requirements to study these issues

7. The aim and conceptual framework for your research

You may be pleased to hear that you will no longer be alone in your journey through this book. From this point forward, the research process will be illustrated with five examples, four using hypothetical data and one (Maria's project) using real data. These examples will include the entire research process from start to finish. Between them, these five examples will give you practical examples of most of the skills included in this book. Of course, five projects need five researchers, and here they are:

■ *Abigail* is a PhD student who is interested in completing a project for an advanced research methods course. If all goes well, she plans to present it at a local conference.

■ *John* is a new PhD student who is interested in the local Bosnian refugee community, with whom he has a little experience. He is short of money and desperately wants to get a grant to help subsidize his education. He is hoping to do some qualitative pilot research to help him write a stronger multimethod (meaning both qualitative and quantitative) grant.

■ *Professor Kathy* is a criminologist. Her work requires that her research assistants read through large numbers of handwritten and electronic police files to determine how many times each person in the files has been arrested and convicted, and of what offenses. Each of her research assistant coders fills out a summary form on each person's file. The problem is that her research assistants are accurate only about 80% of the time. She knows this because she has had other people check their work. Professor Kathy is desperate to do just about whatever she can to reduce errors. One afternoon, she heard a radio program on National Public Radio (all professors listen to NPR, it is written into our contracts) talking about an organization that uses classical music, which they claimed decreased clerical errors. Professor Kathy decided she would try this to see how well it might work. The more she thought about it, the more she thought it might be a good thing to really try it out scientifically. Maybe she could get a publication out of it too.

- *Maria* is a master's-level student specializing in research. She is interested in homicide rates. What kinds of people kill each other? Where do all these killings occur? She is hoping to use this question for her master's research specialization project, and she thinks it would be fun to do something at a conference, maybe to present a poster.

- *Yuan* is a master's student who has a field placement at a domestic violence facility that treats batterers. The agency is thinking of changing the treatment model they use and has asked Yuan to help them figure out if the new model will work better than the old model. Yuan is taking this opportunity to use the research for his treatment evaluation course project.

SECTION 3.2
YOUR AREA OF INTEREST

The good news is that you probably have an area of interest. For most people, there is an area that they want to understand better. Often it has to do with prior personal or professional experience. Sometimes it is something you enjoy thinking about. The challenge is taking a broad area of interest and turning it into something that can generate useful research questions. Areas of interest can be narrow or broad. One senior professor at our school is fond of telling students that "not all questions are created equal." We agree. A good area of interest will meet the following requirements:

- *Your area should interest you.* People often choose to study something because it is easy to study or because there are other people around them studying it, or because their school has very strong resources in that area. This is generally a mistake. Most people can do their best work only if they care about the thing being studied. Choose something that does not interest you, and you may find yourself "running out of gas," getting easily irritated, and being unhappy. These are bad things that can be avoided by finding a way to do what you want to do.

- *You must be able to say what your area of interest is in one sentence in simple language.* The mother of one of the authors used to say, "If you can't say

it simply then you don't understand it." If you can't spit it out in simple English, then you need to think some more.

- *Your area of interest must be small enough to guide you to specific questions.* "Children," "Behavior," and "Diversity" are too broad to be very helpful. Areas that are more focused, such as "Barriers to academic performance in young children," or "Differences in altruistic behavior between men and women," or "Child-rearing practices among the Hmong in America" are more targeted and will allow you to move more easily to specific questions.

- *Your area should have some relevance to practice.* Unless you are doing purely basic science, your area of interest will need to be one that can inform what is going on in the field. As you recall, **basic science** means "science that is meant to find out about things but has no goal of immediate practical application." This is different from **applied science,** which is science that is intended to have an impact on the real world right now. Physics is a basic science, while engineering is the corresponding applied science. In the social sciences, sociology is commonly basic science, psychology has large basic and applied branches, while social work and counseling are usually applied.

- *Your area should be important.* We suppose that all events are important to the people they happen to, but some things are far more important or are more in need of research than others. Does your area really matter? What practical benefits to humankind would come about if we knew more about your area? Issues that affect many other areas of life, such as increasing literacy or decreasing poverty, are clearly very important. This is both a practical issue and one that concerns values and ethics. Is it reasonable to waste resources on something irrelevant? Are you making the world a better place? Is there a reasonable chance that some real moral good will come from the proposed work?

- *Your area must lead to questions you can study both ethically and practically.* This means that in your area you must be able to:

1. *Specify measurable variables:* For example, "unease" is not a commonly measured construct, but there are scads of ways to study "depression." Even depression might be hard to measure for some people, for example people with serious illnesses for which standardized scales cannot be used.

2. *Collect the information for the variables ethically:* For example, let's say an individual is interested in stress levels among hostages during bank robberies. Because of the stress, retrospective recall is particularly bad among hostages, so

asking them afterward has limitations. The simplest thing would be to stage a robbery yourself and observe people as it went down. Of course, this would almost certainly hurt people (e.g., heart attacks, PTSD, etc.) and is totally unethical. Likewise, it would be extremely dangerous if the researcher tried to use "participant observation" and pose as a criminal to be included in a planned robbery. It would also be unethical not to warn the authorities to try to prevent the crime. In short, you will have very limited ways that you can ethically study stress among hostages, and you will need to think creatively. Maybe you can use voice-stress analyses?

3. *Justify access to the study population:* If you are going to interact with human subjects, then the question should be important enough to justify the intrusion—even if the questions to be asked are "harmless" and not time-consuming. Part of this includes consideration of the perspective of the group to be studied. For example, part of being culturally competent is understanding if the group to be studied also values this particular line of research (Rubin & Babbie, 2005). Further, if possible, you want to avoid sampling from a vulnerable population. For example, minors, prisoners, and individuals with developmental or mental health disabilities are considered "vulnerable populations." These individuals are considered to have limited abilities to consent to participate in research for various reasons. You must have a very important reason to include such individuals in your sample. There must be a clear benefit to the subject group (either immediately or in the future) that far outweighs consideration of their vulnerability. Even with such a rationale, human subjects clearance will be difficult, and you will have to do lots of extra work to show others (and to be sure yourself) that you aren't taking advantage of these vulnerable people.

4. *Obtain human subjects clearance from your institutional review board (IRB) and perhaps IRBs of participating agencies:* This is done by demonstrating that the study is important and can be conducted with consent and without harm to the subjects. This process is covered in detail later in the book.

5. *Locate sufficient numbers of subjects:* Some subjects are just plain hard to find. For example, you might be interested in finding out what kinds of people are more likely to commit suicide. You decide to give people personality tests and then follow them to see if they end up killing themselves. Fortunately, very few people kill themselves, so you would have to start with literally thousands of people to end up with enough completed suicides to be meaningful.

6. *Execute the research with the resources available to you:* Do you have the money and time to do it? Do the tools you need exist?

One further (if slightly repetitive) note: Determinations of moral rightness cannot be made scientifically and are not appropriate areas of interest. You can study the act of moral judgment, moral processes, or similar things, but you cannot use science to answer a moral question such as "Is eating meat wrong?" Now that we have a sense of what makes for a good area of interest, let's look at our five friends again and see where they're starting from.

- *Abigail,* who is interested in organizations and used to be a child welfare worker, has realized that "organizations" or "child welfare organizations" are probably too big an area to study. She thinks she might look at organizational climate as it affects workers. She is very uncertain as to what specific areas to look at. She thinks she might have a look at burnout, worker retention, and ways workers cope with stress. She might then see which area makes the most sense to look at.

Interesting to her?	Can she say it clearly?	Is it narrow enough?	Relevant to practice?	Important?	Practical to study?
Yes	No, but she has several ideas.	No; she needs to pick a more specific issue.	Probably	Maybe; that's not clear yet.	Unknown

- *John* is a new PhD student who isn't sure what he wants to do. He is sure he wants to do work that can lead to a dissertation grant. Dissertation grants are nice because they provide both evidence to future employers of your skills and money to do research. John has always been interested in refugees and resettlement, because he thinks that the time that a person or family is in transition may be critical in getting them a good or a poor start in their new home. It seems like an important area. Locally, the largest population of recent immigrants consists of about 30,000 Bosnian refugees. John understands that this group of refugees has a high likelihood of having had traumatic experiences prior to coming to the United States and wonders how they are dealing with those experiences. John needs to find out more about refugees and their adjustment (especially Bosnians), and he also needs to go out to the community to see what's going on firsthand.

Interesting to him?	Can he say it clearly?	Is it narrow enough?	Relevant to practice?	Important?	Practical to study?
Yes	Not quite yet	Not yet	Yes	Yes	Probably

■ *Professor Kathy* has a relatively easy time formulating a question: "Does background music change the number of mistakes made when coding files?" She is not sure yet what kind of music she will try out, or how many different types. She'll look at the literature first.

Interesting to her?	Can she say it clearly?	Is it narrow enough?	Relevant to practice?	Important?	Practical to study?
Fairly	Yes	Yes	It is relevant to researchers.	Yes, from a methodological point of view	Certainly

■ *Maria* is interested in homicide rates. She needs to produce a "master's research specialization project" by the end of the semester. She is interested in murder rates in different types of communities. Maria recently went to the dentist, where she noticed that the dentist had a computer screen that showed exactly where her fillings were. The more she thought about it, the more it amazed her that even her cavities were in a database. If cavities exist in a database, then surely many other important things must exist, somewhere, electronically. Maria decided to track down a database that would tell her about murders and then try to see what she could find about the kinds of places in which murders occur. She fired up her search engine and was on her way.

Interesting to her?	Can she say her question clearly?	Is it narrow enough?	Relevant to practice?	Important?	Practical to study?
Yes	Maria is allowing the details of her question to be firmed up after she gets a better sense of what electronic databases are available in her area. The question "Can it be practically studied?" is the first serious hurdle she must cross. If the data do not exist, she can't study it this way.				

■ *Yuan* is having his question more or less thrust upon him. Yuan is interested in domestic violence and how it is treated. Because of this interest, he is working in a domestic violence shelter during his master's practicum (internship). As part of his education, Yuan is required to do research on the practicum site. For the past several months, Yuan's agency has been wondering if it should switch to a different model of treatment that features cognitive behavioral treatment (CBT) methods. Yuan suggests to the agency that they might want to try it out in a scientific way and see if it works better. The agency, pleased to have someone who brings some research interest and skill, has decided to have Yuan work on the evaluation process as part of his practicum. Yuan's question, therefore, is, "At our agency, will subjects treated by CBT do differently than clients treated under our old system?" Yuan is one lucky dude, having found both a question and a site.

Interesting to him?	Can he say it clearly?	Is it narrow enough?	Relevant to practice?	Important?	Can it be studied?
Yes	Yes	Yes	Yes	Yes	Yes

Our buddies seem to be on their way, some with a clear idea of what they're going to do (Kathy) and some with just a vague plan (Maria). Remember, you will probably end up revising your area as you move forward, and that this doesn't mean that you're doing anything wrong. As you will recall from our illustration in the first chapter, each step of the research process is iterative, which means that you end up doing it over and over again until you get comfortable with where you are. We've done about all we can do without looking at what other people have done, so now we will tell you how to go about reviewing the literature.

SECTION 3.3

THE INITIAL LITERATURE REVIEW

The process of learning more about your area of interest is usually called the *literature review*. We find this term misleading, because there are many resources available to you that are neither journal articles nor books nor book chapters. Among the other places you can go to find out more about your area are the Internet, conferences, professional organizations, colleagues, and experts in the area. In fact, if you are at a university, your first step should probably be to have an informal chat with someone who already knows about the literature in your area, so that he or she can give you pointers as to how to proceed with your search. Don't be afraid to use the professors at your school. It is their job to help you learn. You will note that this section is titled "The *Initial* Literature Review." This is because you will keep finding more relevant sources throughout your work, and the purpose of this first section is to help you get enough stuff so that you can make some sense of the literature, not so that you are "finished." "Finishing" never happens in an absolute sense; there is always more to learn.

Section 3.3.1: Types of Literature

Most sources can be described in the following ways:

- *Empirical:* These are mainly focused on presenting new data. Most articles and many book chapters are empirical. *Example:* An article reporting findings from an experimental treatment for autism, or a study describing relationships between neighborhood poverty and rates of domestic violence.

- *Review or overview:* These sources tell you what we know about something. These are commonly found in book chapters and also in journals. *Example:* An article describing what we know about what works and what fails in welfare-to-work programs.

- *Theoretical or conceptual:* These sources present ideas, tie together prior findings in new ways, or seek in some other manner to make sense out of what we know. *Example:* An article suggesting that the current findings in a given area can be best explained through the application of a new theoretical model.

- *Other:* Other articles can be found that focus on subjects such as research methodology or the application of research findings to specific policies.

The above terms are commonly used, *but most sources are mixtures of these categories.* For example, many empirical articles have literature review sections that are longer than their methods and results sections.

Where to Find Literature

There are many places where literature lurks. The main ones include the following:

- *Journal articles:* Journal articles are the lifeblood of science. If you pursue research as a career, you will consume more of these than anything else, and you will be judged on how often and how well you write them. There will be "core" journals in your area. For a child abuse researcher, examples might include *Child Maltreatment, Child Abuse and Neglect, Child Welfare,* and *Children and Youth Services Review.* However, such a researcher would also use many journals not in his or her core, such as *Journal of Interpersonal Violence* and *Child Development.*

- *Books and book chapters:* More books exist than you might think.

- *Governmental (or similar) publications:* Again, government publications are far more common than you might expect and are often overlooked. Many are also free and can be ordered online from the government. Many are viewable online.

There are several basic approaches that we have found helpful in locating literature. You may develop others based on your area and personal style. We have listed them in the order we would pursue them in.

Surf the Web

Google Scholar is our favorite. We assume you know how to use this.

- *Ask the experts:* Go to a professor or other student in your area. Ask for quick suggestions regarding the key journals, texts, and government publications in your area. Take no more than five minutes doing this. The idea is to get pointed in the right direction. Say "Hi. I'm interested in diabetes among Latinos. What journals or books would you suggest? Are there a few studies or a few researchers I should definitely look up?"

- *Online database searches:* At our university, we have access to PsycINFO, which is a good database with many journal articles and book titles listed. Other excellent database search engines exist, such as Medline and Sociofile.

Using Search Engines

Students come to us all the time saying, quite authoritatively, "There is no literature in my area." These students are always wrong. Why? Because they are just learning how to do searches and aren't really doing a very effective job yet. Using the following technique to isolate areas of interest and find overlaps will probably help you to do a better job.

- *The goal of searching—Finding areas of overlap:* You might want to know about cocaine-exposed infants. This requires you to find two issues simultaneously—cocaine exposure and infants. When you get only the articles that have both, you will have your stuff.

- *The technique of searching:* Effectively searching a database is a bit of an art and requires practice. The main skills you need to learn for advanced searching involve embedded "and" and "or" commands and learning where to put your parentheses. We will assume you are using a search engine such as PsycINFO, which provides windows for entering search terms. Do this:

1. *Think about how to specify each area in a very inclusive way,* for example, drug or substance or cocaine, and infant or prenatal or perinatal or newborn or child. You need not be perfect the first time; as you find articles, you will learn the key buzzwords and can redo your search, but you've got to start somewhere. In many engines, you have multiple windows to use. Each of these windows will function like a set of closed parentheses.

2. *In the search window, type in a request for the intersection of these areas:* (drug or substance or cocaine) and (infant or prenatal or perinatal or newborn or child). If multiple windows are available, just type "drug" or "substance" or "cocaine" in the first window, check the "and" connector between the windows, and then type the rest of the text in the second window.

3. *See how your search goes and revise 1 and 2 above.* For example, "drug" may give you too many false hits, and you may need to exclude it.

Remember:

- "Or" *broadens* the search: "A *or* B" gives everything with *either A or B in it.*
- "And" *narrows* the search: "A *and* B" gives only those things with *both A and B in them* (see Figure 3.1).

You can also search for articles by specific authors, using their names and specifying that you are looking for the author's name. In many search engines you can write this as "au=Smith." You can also specify years of publication, language, and type of subject (human versus animal). There is no substitute for just messing around with the search engines. You may well be frustrated for the first hour or two, but you will soon

gain skill and speed in your searching. Most people find it kind of fun after they get used to it.

Neat Trick 1 (Quotes). If you are looking for a phrase in which two words almost always occur together, such as *domestic violence,* you might want to enter those words between quotes. This will register only those articles containing the words next to each other and in that order. This can really streamline your search process.

Neat Trick 2 (Wild Cards). The asterisk (*) is a "wild card" in many search systems. If you enter "abus*," you will get all words starting with "abus," such as "abused," "abusing," "abusive," "abuse," "abuser," and so on. This can be a big help with a lot of words, such as *violen*, neglect*, argument*, recover*,* and the like.

HAND REVIEW OF CORE JOURNALS

After a bit of online searching, you will say to yourself something like, "Geez, the *Journal of Imperialist Oppression* is coming up everywhere!" Why not go right to the mother lode? Hit the library, get the last 5–10 years of *JOIO,* pile them up on an empty table, and look through every issue's table of contents. This takes less time than you think, and when you find an article it is already in your hands! Focus on recent journals (see next paragraph for why). If you have online access to the journal in question, you can do this on your computer, and then download or print the articles you want.

BIBLIOGRAPHY SEARCHES

Now you're getting hot. You have lots of articles already. What is the next step? Look at the articles that are closest to what you are interested in. Read the bibliographies. Obviously, if you see good articles you don't have, you need to go get them, especially if they are cited over and over again in different articles. There are other clever things you can do too. Do some journals keep coming up time after time? If so, and you haven't already reviewed that journal, go do it. Do some author names keep coming up time after time? If so, go do an online search for that person's name.

LIBRARY CATALOGS

Your library probably has an electronic database with books and book chapters. Use it.

LIBRARY SHELVES

Hey, you've found the Library of Congress numbers for your subject, so get your bad self up to the stacks and look at all the books near the ones you found. Chances are you'll find more.

FIGURE 3.1. **Searching.**

Use a search engine and cruise the 'Net. Everyone knows how to do this already. Make sure you keep track of where you go and make sure that the sources you use are high-quality (nationally recognized institutions are good). DHHS (www.hhs.gov) is the Waiamea Bay of human services research Web surfing. Go there. You can find out about what's funded, and you can pull boatloads of documents. Once you find key people or institutions relevant to your work, go and track them down online. Many professors have their CVs or cool home pages online, which is a good way to get a listing of their work.

SECTION 3.3.2: HOW TO PHYSICALLY OBTAIN LITERATURE

There are two things you need to know: (1) The best sources are always unavailable, and (2) journal articles can sense desperation and are good at hiding. For these reasons, you should look for sources at least a month in advance of needing them. We procrastinate as much as anyone else, but this is the one place where you will get roadkilled if you procrastinate too much. With these warnings in mind, you will want to find your sources in the following locations:

- *Off the shelves*: Most journals and books are allegedly on the shelves. Go grab the journals and photocopy them. At the start of a project you will seem to spend more time photocopying than sleeping. Do not check out books unless you want the whole book. Photocopy the pertinent chapter(s) instead.

- *Online copies (Internet)*: Increasingly, full-text versions of articles are available online. This is great. Download them to a special directory you create for that purpose. You may want to print them out on paper anyway, both for ease of use and security.

- *Through your library system:* Your library may have special features that allow access to things that you can't get to online. Find out about what you have available. Your library almost certainly has an interlibrary loan system. This may be paper or electronic. In either case, you need to allow "several weeks for delivery" in our experience, even if your library claims to be able to deliver things much faster. Somehow that key reference always has something funny going on with it, and you have to wait.

- *Photocopying:* To repeat: Photocopy everything. We sometimes even photocopy chapters of books that we own (makes it possible to file them or put them in relevant binders). The first thing you must

do is make *absolutely sure* that the date, publisher, journal title, book title, page numbers, author, book editor, and whatever else you need for the citation is on the thing you are photocopying. If it isn't, write it in *immediately*. The first time you fail to do this and spend three hours trying to track something down, you will understand why.

- *Spending money:* There are some things you just plain need. Don't buy too little. Don't buy too much. Buy things that are otherwise unobtainable (like dissertations or little-known books) that you will refer to on a daily or weekly basis.

SECTION 3.3.3: HOW TO PHYSICALLY STORE LITERATURE

Stuff gets away from you. This is bad. Prevent it in the following manner:

- *Create directories on your computer for .pdf or similar downloaded articles.* In the last year or two (as of this writing in 2007) it has finally become possible to do useful lit searches almost fully online. Increasingly large numbers of articles can be downloaded, commonly in .pdf format. If you can, do it! Make sure you keep these articles somewhere safe, preferably on a backed-up network drive or periodically copied to disks.

- *Use a computer reference manager such as Endnotes.* This allows you to quickly find stuff, and you can put bibliographies together automatically. The earlier you start doing this, the easier your life will be.

- *Keep a list of whom you loan what to.* When people want to borrow your material, give them a specific date you need it back. Keep a little notebook indicating whom you loaned what to. Write your name on everything you own in thick permanent felt marker on the outside. That way, even if they don't return it, they'll feel guilty each time they use it.

SECTION 3.3.4: FIVE EXAMPLES OF PRELIMINARY LITERATURE SEARCHES

JOHN'S LITERATURE ON BOSNIAN REFUGEES

John needs to find out about refugees in general, Bosnian refugees in particular, and what we know about what makes them adjust better to our society. Unfortunately, there is nobody else in his school studying this population. He goes to a professor during office hours who teaches a human diversity course who is able to point him to some basic theoretical articles on refugee resettlement. One of these articles (Drachman, 1992) seems to provide a useful conceptual guide for how to think about the entire immigration experience. He then does a PsycINFO search using (Bosnian or Bosnia) and (immigrant or immigration or refugee), which provides 49 hits (a nice, reviewable number). This gets him a number of sources. In selecting which resources he would focus on, John favored those articles that were empirical, that helped him understand the theory and the literature, and that were published in better journals. John avoided a number of articles that were specific to things he had no special interest in (such as marital relationships, young children, and the like). The following examples all came from this first PsycINFO search:

Nesdale, D., Mak, A. (2003). Ethnic identification, self-esteem and immigrant psychological health. *International Journal of Intercultural Relations* 27(1), 23–40. This article looked at immigrants from many countries in Australia and found that ethnic self-esteem had little to do with psychological health; personal self-esteem was a better predictor. For John, it provides useful empirical data regarding the role of ethnic self-esteem and identification in promoting psychological health.

Bemak, F., Chung, R., Pederson, P. (2003). *Counseling refugees: A psychosocial approach to innovative multicultural interventions.* Greenwood Press, Westport, CT. This book describes how a Multilevel Model of therapy can be applied to refugees. It includes a number of case studies including two Bosnians. There is also a nice literature overview. For John, it provides a chance for him to see someone else's background and lit review on the subject, summary of main ideas, and it gives him a chance to "get into" two case studies of Bosnians. This is a great source for John.

Miller, K., Worthington, G., Muzurovic, J., Tipping, S., Goldman, A. (2002). Bosnian refugees and the stressors of exile: A narrative study. *American Journal of Orthopsychiatry* 72(3), 2002, 341–354. This article, from an excellent journal, does basically what John was thinking of doing. It is a superb qualitative piece that includes narrative data on 28 Bosnian refugees describing them pre-departure, during transition, and currently in Chicago. John is initially crushed. They did his idea already! No fair! Upon more reflection, though, he realizes that this just gives him more information upon which to craft a better question. He notices the average age of the person in the study is about 50. That's pretty old. How about younger people?

Cusak, K. (2002). *Refugee experiences of trauma and PTSD; Effects on psychological, physical, and financial well-being.* Dissertation Abstracts International: Section B: The Sciences & Engineering Vol 62(10), 47–78. Western Michigan University. This doctoral dissertation looks at newly arrived refugees, including some

Bosnians, and employs standardized tests to determine predictors of PTSD, quality of life, and self-sufficiency. This is an absolute gold-mine for John, because dissertations include lengthy literature reviews, which can aid the search, and this dissertation is only a year old, so most recent literature should be present. Well worth the money to order it (www.umi.com).

Witmer, T., Culver, S. (2001). Trauma and resilience among Bosnian refugee families: A critical review of the literature. *Journal of Social Work Research & Evaluation* 2(2), 173–187. This overview article looks at the literature, but, unfortunately, focuses on Bosnian Muslims only. Still, a wonderful review, which confirms John's observation that PTSD seems to be the most heavily studied issue with this population. This is a critical reading for John, who can now get a more general view of the literature.

Mollica, R., Saraljic, N., Chemoff, M., Lavelle, J., Sarajilic-Vukovic, I. Massagli, M. (2001). Longitudinal study of psychiatric symptoms, disability, mortality, and emigration among Bosnian refugees. *JAMA: Journal of the American Medical Association* 286(5), 546–554. This article focuses rather strongly on the period of early departure/camp life, looking at mainly medical and mental health symptomatology. John finds this reading useful to get a better understanding of the early transitional experiences of this population.

Weine, S., Kuc, G., Dzudra, E., Razzano, L., Pavkovic, I. (2001). PTSD among Bosnian refugees: A survey of providers' knowledge, attitudes and service patterns. *Community Mental Health Journal* 37(3), 261–271. This article looks at service providers, not refugees, and finds they are having real problems even recognizing PTSD among clients, let alone working with them. John needs this article to get a sense for service delivery issues and practical concerns regarding this population. ■

John's next step was to obtain these articles physically and to obtain the key and commonly cited references in the sources, particularly from the dissertation (Cusak, 2002) and the review article (Witmer & Culver, 2001). This provided him with a nice collection of about 40 articles. A number of trends in the literature are becoming apparent to John. First, there has been some fairly advanced empirical research, but almost exclusively in the area of PTSD, as John suspected. Second, almost all the empirical work has been done in the last few years, with few useful items being more than five years old. Third, there seems to be substantial current interest in this area, with publications in top journals. This all seems to bode well for John's choice for a dissertation topic, because it is a hot issue which has apparently only been studied along the single axis of PTSD. John never did find a journal that seemed to come up repeatedly in the search, but he did find a sufficient literature base to support his further work. His challenge now is finding an interesting and understudied part of this area which will provide the best fit for his dissertation work.

MARIA'S LITERATURE ON HOMICIDE RATES

Maria, who is interested in community homicide rates, took a backward approach to exploring her area. She started by looking for data she could find online that measured homicide rates. She did a number of Web searches and found that while it was fairly easy to get data at the county level on homicides, it was tough finding anything at a lower level. She eventually found that the San Diego Coroner's office publishes homicide and suicide counts by zip code and has been doing so for two years at www.sdcounty.ca.gov/cnty/cntydepts/safety/medical/stat/2000mestats.pdf and www.sdcounty.ca.gov/cnty/cntydepts/safety/medical/stat/2001mestats.pdf. Although Maria had not initially thought about looking at suicide rates, the data were available, and it did seem interesting. Would it follow the same patterns as homicides? She found the question interesting and exciting. Maria talked to the professor teaching her social development class about where she could get community data on zip codes to match to the San Diego data. She was told that the U.S. Census (www.census.gov/Press-Release/www/2002/sumfile3.html) was the best source. A look at the census data dictionary ("Technical Documentation," same Web page) showed her that she could easily find out a large number of interesting things about the residents of each zip code, including income, educational status, racial composition, median age, and so on. Maria now had a source for counts by zip code of suicide and homicide and a source for lots of other information about those zip codes that she could look at. She now had to find out what we know about community homicide and suicide rates. She found the following:

Centerwall, B. (1995). Race, socioeconomic status, and domestic homicide. *JAMA: Journal of the American Medical Association* 273(22), 1755–1758. This article looked at 349 killings in New Orleans and found that although Blacks appeared far more likely to commit murder than Whites, this difference vanished when neighborhood characteristics (low census tract SES measured as percentage of households with more than one resident per room) was taken into account. (Maria found this interesting. It was going to be critical for her to control for race and poverty in her study.)

Harries, K. (1995). The ecology of homicide and assault: Baltimore city and county, 1989–91. *Studies on Crime & Crime Prevention*. Vol 4(1), 1995, 44–60. This article found that three community (tract) dimensions

(poverty–violence, unemployment, stable neighborhood) explained about 50% of the variance in homicide rates, which is a lot. (This was encouraging. It looked as if she might well find that communities do have big effects. Her work would be more interesting, though, because she was looking at both suicide and homicide.)

Harries, K. (1990). *Serious violence: Patterns of homicide and assault in America*. Springfield, IL: Charles C. Thomas. This somewhat dated book contains useful information about neighborhood types and homicide rates, including theory and findings. (It's a nice general background work. Maria thought is was too bad it wasn't more recent, containing more recent references.)■

Maria couldn't find much else. She noticed that Keith Harries came up a lot, so she "Googled" him. This led her to www.ojp.usdoj.gov/ovc/publications/infores/geoinfosys2003/welcome.html, which is a Department of Justice site about how to do community mapping. It includes a wealth of citations, including:

Boggs, S. (1965). Urban crime patterns. *American Sociological Review* 30: 899–908.

Brantingham, P. J., & Brantingham, P. (1981). *Environmental Criminology*. Prospect Heights, IL: Waveland Press.

Brantingham, P. J., & Brantingham, P. (1984). *Patterns in Crime*. New York: Macmillan.

Harries, K. 1974. *Geography of Crime and Justice*. New York: McGraw-Hill.■

It seems as if Maria's literature is fairly narrow and confined to a few particular researchers. This surprised her because she was worried that this area might have been studied to death. The downside, of course, is that there will be relatively little to look at in terms of models of how she should proceed. The good news is that she gets to do some pretty interesting and cutting-edge work. She realized she needed to do a little more review of the suicide literature. She used (kw: suicide and kw: ecology). She also did (kw:suicide) and (kw: tract or kw:zipcode or kw:county). These and other searches resulted in the following:

Wenz, F. (1977). Ecological variation in self-injury behavior. *Suicide and Life-Threatening Behavior*. 7(2), 92–99. This article looked at census tracts and found that economic status at the tract level did predict suicide rates, with poorer areas having higher rates. (Maria is excited that the data on suicide seem to be converging with the data on homicide, at least as far as SES goes.)

Connoly, J., & Lester, D. (2001). Suicide rates in Irish counties: 10 years later. *Irish Journal of Psychological Medicine,* 18(3), 87–89. This article found that different factors (age distribution, urbanization) predicted suicide rates in Irish counties at different times. This is another very useful article that looks at a range of factors beyond SES.

Durkheim, E. (1897). *Le Suicide.* Paris: Felix Alcan. This author is cited by just about everyone. He outlines four possible ecological or sociological causes of suicide. "Egoistic suicides" are socially isolated people who may be depressed or subject to stressors (poverty, divorce). "Anomic suicides" result from social disruption and have to do with individual feelings of anger and unhappiness. The other two kinds of suicides ("altruistic" and "fatalistic") are rare in our society and do not seem terribly relevant. It is interesting to note that both egoistic and anomic suicides seem as though they might be more common in impoverished areas, which have lower levels of community integration and more stressors. (Talk about ancient history! Maria thought it would be nice to include some historical background about how this area came to be studied, though.)

Cutchin, M., & Churchill, R. (1999). Scale, context and causes of suicide in the United States. *Social Science Quarterly,* 80(1), 97–114. This very interesting article has a key methodological point: Scale matters. You will get different results when looking at different geographical units, and explanatory power increases at lower levels, so tracts would be better than zip codes, which would be better than counties, which are better than states, and so on. (Maria is now very pleased that she is looking at zip code rather than county figures. She is a little worried that she doesn't have tract-level data, but she just can't find any.)

Lester, D. (1999). Suicidality and risk-taking behaviors: An ecological study of youth behaviors in 29 states. *Perceptual and Motor Skills*, 88(3), 1299–1300. This study is interesting mostly because it was able to find that one factor that individual studies have found to be predictive of suicide at the individual level (drug abuse) is also predictive of suicide at the statewide level. (However, this was not a terribly exciting article for Maria.)

Jarvis, G., Ferrence, R., Whitehead, P., & Hohnson, F. (1982). The ecology of self-injury: A multivariate approach. *Suicide and Life-Threatening Behavior,* 12(2), 90–102. This source is mainly of interest for the advanced statistical methods used and the fact that low-SES, high-density housing and single-person households predicted suicidality, but family status and mobility did not. (Maria notices that housing density and living alone seem important. This tends to remind her of the Durkheim book. It seems to be worth checking out census variables that have to do with this.)

McCullough, J., Philip, A., & Carstairs, G. (1967). The ecology of suicidal behavior. *British Journal of Psychiatry,* 113(496), 313–319. This study found that old, lonely tenement dwellers and younger people from troubled families are at high risk for suicide. This is of interest because both types of person are more likely to reside in low-SES areas—more confirmation that Maria has to look at living arrangements and density.■

It looks as if there are both theoretical and empirical reasons to suspect associations between some environmental factors, such as SES, and suicide rates.

YUAN'S LITERATURE ON DOMESTIC VIOLENCE

Yuan first went to his agency to find what empirical literature they were aware of. He found several articles suggesting how treatment should be done but not much with evidence behind it. He then decided to look in the textbooks he had, but again, there were few empirical citations. He decided to do a PsycINFO search. Initially, he got few hits, but he eventually stumbled on the terms ("domestic violence," or batterer) and ("cognitive behavioral," or CBT). This worked well and yielded the following:

Dowd, L. (2002) Female perpetrators of partner aggression: Relevant issues and treatment. *Journal of Aggression, Maltreatment and Trauma.* 5(2) 73–104. This one is not really on topic, as it deals with female perpetrators, but this article is interesting and provides almost 100 citations with generally useful information about the area of battering. (Yuan is mainly interested in this work for the superb reference list. The fact that it is a fairly recent publication helps here.)

Hamsley, J. (2001). *The efficacy of domestic violence treatment: Implications for batterer intervention programs.* Unpublished doctoral dissertation. Memphis State University, Memphis, Tennessee. This study seeks to measure conflict resolutions skills, marital adjustment, and emotional functioning as outcome variables (preliminary diagnostic questionnaire, Moriarity, 1981). (Bingo! This dissertation is not too different from what Yuan plans to do, and it seems to be a "must-get." He coughed up the bucks and ordered the document (www.umi.com). This instrument sounded interesting, so Yuan Googled it. He found http://buros.unl.edu/buros/jsp/search.jsp, a Web site from the Mental Measurements Yearbook with people offering online summaries of instruments and reviews of instruments. While the actual reviews cost $15 each, and Yuan didn't buy any, he did use it to search for titles and found a number of instruments he could check out later.)

Buttell, F. (2001). Moral development among court-ordered batterers: Evaluating the impact of treatment. *Research on Social Work Practice,* 11(1), 93–107. This interesting article suggests that batterers, who have very poor moral reasoning, did not have their moral reasoning improved by a CBT program. (Yuan finds this troubling. It seems that CBT will work for some people but not for others. How will he deal with this in his research?)

Morrel, T. (2000). *Changes in self-efficacy, self-esteem and aggression in male batterers: A comparison of cognitive-behavioral and supportive group therapies.* Unpublished doctoral dissertation, University of Maryland at Baltimore. This study found that treated subjects did better, but CBT and supportive therapy had the same levels of benefit. Self-esteem and self-efficacy gains did not predict decreased spousal violence as reported by the victims. (This definitely could be an important resource.)

Stof, D., Breiling, J., & Maser, J. (1997). *Handbook of Antisocial Behavior.* New York: Wiley. (Another goldmine, this seems to be one of the major reference works in the field. It will allow Yuan to look up findings, theory, and methods in the area of violence.)

Gerlock, A. (1997). New directions in the treatment of men who batter women. *Health Care for Women International,* 18(5), 481–493. Although a bit out of date, this reference has a good review of the literature and applies feminist theory to both treatment and methodological issues. (The application of theory was particularly interesting to Yuan.)

Hanusa, D. (1994). *A comparison of two group treatment conditions in reducing domestic violence.* Unpublished doctoral dissertation, University of Wisconsin, Madison. (This is yet another doctoral dissertation with yet more dependent variables, including social skills, sex role rigidity, hostility, anger, and depression.)■

Yuan has been fortunate, finding authoritative sources (Stof, et al.) and three dissertations on the subject in the last 10 years. The dissertations should be particularly useful, because critiquing methodology as it exists in the field is often a primary focus of doctoral dissertations, and he should be able to build on their work and benefit from their experience.

PROFESSOR KATHY'S LITERATURE ON THE EFFECTS OF MUSIC

Professor Kathy did a search using (kw: music or kw:musical) and (kw: task or kw: performance or kw: completion). This resulted in 2,310 hits—too many. She narrowed her search to citations with these terms in the titles and switched "ti" for "kw," which dropped the results down to 379. This is still a lot, but she decided to go through them, quickly skimming the titles. She found the following citations:

Stephensen, V. (2002). *The Effect of Classical Background Music on Spatial Reasoning Skills as Measured by Completion of a Spatial Task: A Study of Selected College Undergraduates.* Unpublished doctoral dissertation, Universidad de Guadalajara, Mexico. Classical music and jazz were tried on people doing mazes. It turns out that Handel speeded people up, but no kind of music made people more accurate. (This was discouraging.)

Halam, S., Price, J., & Katsarou, G. (2002). The effects of background music on primary school pupil's test performance. *Educational Studies,* 28(2), 111–122. This study found that calming music increased 10- to 12-year-olds' ability to do memory and arithmetic tasks, but students did not do well with music perceived as arousing or aggressive or unpleasant. (While not looking at adults, this study does seem close to Professor Kathy's area of interest, and there did seem to be some effect from the classical music. It seems as if the kind of music is important. Maybe different types of music will need to be studied.)

Furnham, A., & Strbac, L. (2002). Music is as distracting as noise: The differential distraction of background music and noise on the cognitive test performance of introverts and extraverts. *Ergonomics,* 45(3), 203–217. This article finds that introverted people are more affected by distractions than are extraverts. (Who knew? This could be something Kathy should attend to. This study is getting more complicated by the minute.)

Johnson, M. (2000). *The effects of background classical music on junior high school student's academic performance.* Unpublished doctoral dissertation. The Fielding Institute. This article found that classical background music was more poorly associated with lower student performance than the silent control condition. This is good—more evidence that this is a worthwhile area to study.

Otto, D., Cochran, V., Johnson, G., & Clair, A. (1999). The influence of background music on task engagement in frail, older persons in residential care. *Journal of Music Therapy,* 36(3), 182–195. For older people, time spent on-task did not vary by the presence of background music. (Kathy finds it interesting that music has been studied across so many populations. It is also interesting that there seems to be a trend of some articles having positive findings, while others don't.)

Rauscher, F., & Shaw, G. (1998). Key components of the Mozart effect. *Perceptual and Motor Skills,* 86(3), 835–841. This study reviews the literature on the degree to which some classical music might or might not influence task performance. The authors conclude that there may be a slight effect, but that how it is studied makes a difference. (This one is similar to the last article. It looks as if the differences may be small or elusive. This may require a larger sample size to find small effects.)■

Professor Kathy also did some Googling, and the following citations were found on a very useful Web site at Valparaiso University. Each came with a summary of the article's findings:

Furnham, A., & Bradley, A. (1997). Music while you work: The differential distraction of background music on the cognitive test performance of introverts and extraverts. *Applied Cognitive Psychology, 11,* 445–455. For complicated tasks, music does not seem to help. (This seems OK, because Kathy plans to test the effect on a fairly simple task.)

Fox, J. G., & Embrey, E. D. (1972). Music—an aid to productivity. *Applied Ergonomics, 3*(4), 202–205. This article, based on experiments with factory workers, suggests that music does improve repetitive tasks. (This is good news; Kathy's coding work is fairly repetitive, so maybe she might find something.)

Smith, W. A. S. (1961). Effects of industrial music in a work situation requiring complex mental activity. *Psychological Reports, 8,* 159–162. Card-punchers (it has to do with old computers) did about the same with music or no music, but reported that they were happier with music. (Should she study the happiness of her student coders? Will anyone care? Probably not.)■

In summary, there seem to be several threads of research. First of all, there is research finding perhaps a slight benefit to music in terms of people doing repetitive tasks. Second, there is interest in the degree to which the introversion/extraversion of the subject may make a difference. Third, there seems to be the issue of different types of music having different effects. There is an idea that sometimes music may hurt performance if it is too annoying or intrusive. This seems like a good start.

Abigail's Literature on Child Welfare
Abigail has decided to look at child welfare supervisors and see if their particular supervisory skills predict client outcomes. She looks at the supervision literature, as supervisors seem to be an important link between workers and their organizations.

Bibus, A. (1993). In pursuit of a missing link: The influence of supervision on social worker's practice with involuntary clients. *Clinical Supervisor, 11*(2), 7–22. This article provides useful context and background for CPS supervision. (It's not really directly relevant, but it can help Abigail flesh out her introduction.)

Flynn, R. (2001). External influences on workplace competence: Improving services to children and families. In Foley, P., Roche, J., et al. (Eds.). *Children in*

society: Contemporary theory, policy and practice. (pp. 177–184). Buckingham, England: Sage Publications. This one provides a nice overview of how external sources can affect children through the workers' services. (It will be more helpful background.)

Glisson, C., & Durick, M. (1988). Predictors of job satisfaction and organizational commitment in human service organizations. *Administrative Quarterly, 33,* 61–81. These authors help us understand how workers' happiness and attitude toward the workplace can vary based on other factors. (Although it's an interesting article, it doesn't seem to bear directly on client outcomes.)

Glisson, C., & Hemmelgarn, A. (1998). The effects of organizational climate and interorganizational coordination on the quality and outcomes of children's service systems. *Child Abuse & Neglect, 22*(5), 401–421. These findings suggest that managing conflict, fostering cooperation, and helping workers assume clear roles might have a positive impact on client outcomes. (This appears more useful, more related to Abigail's specific area of interest.)

Himle, D., Jayaratne, S., & Thyness, P. (1991). Buffering effects of four social support types on burnout among social workers. *Social Work Research and Abstracts, 29,* 22–27. This article looks at supervisory social support and impacts on burnout. (Abigail hadn't thought directly about burnout. Maybe supervision affects clients mainly through lessening worker burnout? Should she study this?)

Holloway, E., & Neufeldt, S. (1995). Supervision, its contributions to treatment efficacy. *Journal of Consulting and Clinical Psychology, 63*(2), 207–213. This article asserts that there is very little research that looks at the relationship between clinical supervision and client outcomes. (Abigail had noticed this. It is nice to have someone she can cite as saying that the area isn't too strongly studied, though.)

Perry, E., Kulik, C., & Zhou, J. (1999). A closer look at the effects of subordinate–supervisor age differences. *Journal of Organizational Behavior, 20*(3), 351–57. This one provides reason to suspect that the age difference between supervisor and supervisee may be an important factor in their relationship. (It seems not to be too relevant, but maybe age is something Abigail should track in her work to see if it matters. She hadn't thought of that.)

McFadden, E. (1975). Helping the inexperienced worker in the public child welfare agency: A case study. *Child Welfare, 54*(5), 319–329. This qualitative work, although aged, provides some useful background "feel" to the issue. (It's nice to read something that makes sense on a human level, even if it is horribly out of date.)■

These sources have shown Abigail a number of things. First of all, her area has been looked at, and there seems to be a person (Glisson) who is cited a lot and seems to be the main researcher in this area. There has been work done on how organizational and supervisory factors affect workers, especially with regard to stress and burnout; and also a small amount has been done on how supervisory factors affect clients. Abigail now has to think about how she will narrow her question. The more she thinks about what she has found, the less interested she becomes. She finds herself wanting to look at something more tangible. As she is looking through the sources, one article in particular catches her eye:

Gustavson, N., & MacEachron, A. (2002). Death and the child welfare worker. *Children and Youth Services Review,* 24(12), 903–915.■

This article interests her for a number of reasons: The field of client death seems to have some linkage to theory but appears understudied with regard to child welfare workers. It is in an area that Abigail understands, and there seem to be practical implications surrounding how child welfare workers handle the death of a child on their caseload. Does it lead to them quitting? Do they become less effective if they don't deal with it well? Although most of the literature seems to look at helping professionals in general, it seems that child welfare might be a special case because child welfare workers are specifically charged with the safety of their child clients as their primary focus and make critical decisions regarding their safety on a daily basis. Furthermore, fatalities on child welfare worker caseloads are likely to be homicides, whereas many psychotherapeutic caseload deaths are suicides. Finally, the agency that Abigail worked for was interested in this issue. She seems to recall them having some kind of training on it. Perhaps they would be interested in hosting the research?

The literature that Abigail finds is scant, and she gets a good deal of it from the references in the Gustavson & MacEachron article:

Bendiksen, R., Bodin, G., & Jambois, K. (2000). The bereaved crisis worker: Sociological practice perspective on critical incident death, grief, and loss. In Lund, D. A. (Ed.). *Men coping with grief* (pp. 253–272). Amityville, NY: Baywood Publishing. Again, we get medical and police/rescue workers, but it does provide interesting ideas, including the importance of venting the pent-up emotions following a death. (This could be helpful in terms of thinking about what factors might be important.)

Burrrell, L. (1996). *The impact of experience, exposure and support on emergency worker health.* Dissertation Abstracts International, Section B: The Sciences and Engineering. Vol. 57(6-B). 4067. This very helpful dissertation includes information on the manner in which social support seems to mitigate the negative effects of client death. The sample is of medical crisis response workers (EMTs). (Social support makes a lot of sense to Abigail as a key factor; this seems worth looking at.)

Defey, D. (1995). Helping health care staff deal with perinatal loss. *Infant Mental Health Journal,* 16(2), 102–111. This article is useful because it looks at reactions to the deaths of young children, and most child abuse fatalities are quite young. (Although Abigail isn't finding lots of material directly in her area, she is finding that parts of her area have been studied in isolation. On one hand, this is frustrating, but it also suggests that there is plenty of room for her to do what she wants.)

Moore, K., & Cooper, C. (1996). Stress in mental health professionals: A theoretical overview. *International Journal of Social Psychiatry,* 42(2), 82–89. Theoretical overview articles are always useful in the early stages of a project, even if they are not exactly on topic. (This can at least give Abigail a citation for talking about stress among helping professionals in general, even if it isn't exactly the right profession.)

Rowe, M. (1997). Hardiness, stress, temperament, coping, and burnout in health professionals. *American Journal of Health Behavior,* 21(3), 163–171. Burnout may be an area of interest. (This article helps Abigail get focused on that issue and think about if it is something she wants to look at in particular.)■

As a result of her literature review, Abigail has now decided to radically switch her focus to child fatalities and how workplace and other factors are associated with better or worse worker outcomes. She thinks that she will have to look at work environment and the worker's home environment and see how these correlate with either better or worse functioning following the death of the child client. Admittedly, this is still somewhat fuzzy, but Abigail hopes it will come together a little bit better in the design phase.

SECTION 3.4
REVIEWING THE FIELD

We have looked at the academic literature, but if our work is going to be practically relevant, we need to know more about what is actually going on in the community. If you are doing basic science (science meant to find things out without concern for practical application), then you may skip this part altogether. Many times, people come to an area of interest because they have some field experience and so are already familiar with how their issues play out in practice. Sometimes, however, people decide they want to look at an issue that is new to them and about which they know basically nothing. In the world of social science, there are few things as frightening as a researcher using standardized instruments and sophisticated statistics to study an area he or she knows nothing about in a practical sense.

How do you learn more about your area? Conferences are good. General handbooks can also help, such as the *Handbook for Child Protection Practice* (Dubowitz & Depanfilis, 2000). In the end, though, there is really no substitute for experience. Is it possible for you to contact someone who does the work you are interested in? Can you buy that person lunch and get feedback about your ideas? Is there anything like a "ride-along" available in your area of interest? Once you settle on an area of career interest, the best alternative is for you to work or volunteer in the area, even if it is for only a few hours per week. There is really no substitute for having experience working with the population you study. If you don't have such experience, we strongly recommend you get some.

Among our examples, John has had experience working with Bosnians at a refugee service center, but he doesn't know much about the community otherwise. As a next step, John decides to find out about local agencies serving Bosnian refugees. His school's practicum office knows of several supervisors who work in these agencies, and the Assistant Director of Field knows one personally. John uses this contact to get in touch with this person, invites her to lunch, and is able to quickly pick up an introduction to the Bosnian social service scene in his town. It mostly revolves around the Resettlement House, a local service center for refugees that serves several hundred Bosnians. John now has at least a general idea of what science is being done and what agencies are working with the population in his area. He also decides to broaden his knowledge of the population by reading what he can find about them, attending cultural events hosted by the community, and starting to do some volunteer work at the Resettlement House. He still has not specified his question, and isn't sure what theories will guide him. This is his next task.

Abigail talks to her old supervisor and finds that there may be a great deal of receptiveness at the county, or maybe even the state, level to doing a study of workers who have had clients die. She is excited about the opportunity to do research within a system she knows so well.

Maria decides that she can make better sense of communities and violence by talking to police officers. She decides to do a number of ride-alongs in poor and

in wealthy areas. This enables her to both get a better sense for the people and events in these neighborhoods and to get feedback from police about their perspectives on what goes on and why.

Yuan, while not as experienced as Abigail, does understand how work is done at his agency. His biggest need is to understand the specific intervention being tested, CBT, and how it may be used in other agencies. It might be useful for him to contact people at other agencies who use the model and find out more about the issues that have arisen in their experience.

Professor Kathy is doing work that has practical application only to professors and research assistants. She already knows all about that, so she does nothing special to learn more.

SECTION 3.5
UNDERSTANDING YOUR LITERATURE

After your initial literature review, you need to check to see that you can answer the following questions:

1. What questions have been asked by others in my area?
2. What populations have been studied and at what level (i.e., individual, community, and so on)?
3. What constructs or variables have been looked at?
4. What instruments (tests) or other measures have been used in my area?
5. What theories exist to tell me how to think about my area or what relationships are likely to exist there?
6. What kinds of designs (experimental, correlational, and the like) are used in my area?
7. What are the main empirical findings in my area?
8. What needs to be studied next in my area?

Your next task is to look at the literature you have and try to see if you can answer the above questions. If you can't, then you need to go back and fill in the gaps with more literature. We will describe each of the above points in detail.

SECTION 3.5.1: WHAT QUESTIONS HAVE BEEN ASKED BY OTHERS IN MY AREA?

Perhaps the easiest question to answer is what research questions others have asked. Any competently written research article will tell you precisely what questions are being asked and how these questions build on prior work. Unless your area is brand new, you may notice that there will be clusters of studies that look at particular issues and reference one another. Try to see what the big issues are in your area. Note carefully exactly how the questions in your literature are phrased and try to see if these questions make sense to you. A good question should be clear, testable, and meaningful. One problem that stops many of our students dead is that they can't find many articles relating to their precise question. If you can't find literature in your area, find literature about the closest thing possible. For example, let's say you want to do a study where you try to raise the self-confidence and improve the self-image of very young amputees (4 to 6 years old). Let's say you can't find much on it. What you would do is go to the literature on adolescent or adult amputees and their adjustment and see what you could find there. You would also go to the developmental literature on young children and see what that would contribute to your work. Possibly there is a parallel literature (say, on working on psychological issues with children with cancer) that you could tap. Nobody is going to blame you for broadening your sources if there is no alternative. In short, if you can't find it, find the next closest thing.

Understanding what the questions in your area are allows you some room for creativity and critical thought. Do the questions make sense to you? Are they studied in a way that fits with what you know from your experiences in the field? Are there questions that are not asked but that strike you as critical? Time spent thinking about these things is time well spent.

SECTION 3.5.2: WHAT POPULATIONS HAVE BEEN STUDIED, AND AT WHAT LEVEL?

Researchers often focus on particular groups of people for no scientifically valid reason. For example, college freshmen are not typical Americans, but vast amounts of research have been done only on them, just because they're available. Some fields (psychology) have been criticized for focusing almost exclusively on middle-class Whites. Other kinds of work, such as poverty studies, have spent quite a lot of effort on some populations (poor inner-city residents) while largely ignoring other groups (the rural poor). You should use your common sense and see if the questions being asked match well with the populations studied. Are racial, class, sexual orientation, gender, and other critical forms of diversity within our population being well covered?

What are the units of analysis in the studies you reviewed? We'll discuss units of analysis later, but basically, the unit of analysis is the level at which you sample, score, and analyze. If I were to do a study on which city has the best quality of life, my unit of analysis would be the city. If I were to do a study on

surviving cancer after taking a given drug, my unit of analysis would be the person (cancer patient). Most studies use individuals as the unit of analysis, but other levels, including families, groups, organizations, census tracts, zip codes, cities, counties, or states are used. Sometimes the unit of analysis is a measure of time, such as a day. We recently submitted a grant in which we counted the number of violent events each day in a four-year period in an attempt to try to understand the degree to which violent sporting events might be associated with rises in violent acts. Ask yourself what level your question has been explored on, and see if you can think of other ways to look at your issue at different levels of analysis.

SECTION 3.5.3: WHAT CONSTRUCTS OR VARIABLES HAVE BEEN LOOKED AT?

Constructs (things, concepts, events, and the like) are the things we study. When we look at them in a highly operationalized form, we call them variables. In this sense, depression might be the construct you want to study, but you may operationalize depression as the subject's score on the Beck Depression Inventory. The score from that scale is now your variable representing depression. Sometimes researchers get clumsy or lazy or just plain do bad work, and you may find yourself easily confused. For example, many studies will list "mental health" as an outcome, but will measure only subject depression. This is not a global measure of "mental health" at all, just of a single part of it. Other times, a researcher may operationalize "job exit" as the person's stated intention to leave the job, while another researcher may operationalize the same construct as the actual exit. These are very different.

You should be familiar with the constructs and variables in your area. Do they include the things you want to study? Do you agree with how constructs are turned into variables? Is some key construct or variable missing? Do the constructs apply well to the people you want to study?

There may also be considerable debate in a given area regarding the appropriate construct or variable to use. For example, Papadopoulos and Lee (2002) point out that there are yet to be agreed-upon means of measuring or controlling for culture across studies and disciplines. Berry and colleagues (2002) detail several aspects of culture that one might consider in research. Further, one should always check out constructs with members of the population to be studied. Different cultures may have very different ways of defining and discussing various concepts of interest (Boynton et al., 2004; Pan, 2003).

SECTION 3.5.4: WHAT INSTRUMENTS (TESTS) OR OTHER MEASURES ARE USED?

Most studies have very specific ways of measuring variables of interest. This will commonly take the form of a score on a test (we call these tests "instruments" so that we can impress people at cocktail parties and charge more for our services). Sometimes there will be broad agreement about how to measure something. For example, the Beck Depression Inventory we mentioned above is very commonly used for measuring depression, while the CBCL (Child Behavior Checklist) is commonly used to measure children's emotional and behavioral problems. Instruments have different strengths and weaknesses. To stay with the example of the Beck Depression Inventory: This instrument gives you a continuous score, which is very useful for most statistical analyses, but it does not tell you other things. If, for example, you want to know if someone meets the current diagnostic criteria for depression, then you can't use the Beck, because it does not conform to diagnostic criteria for depression as found in the *Diagnostic and Statistical Manual of Mental Disorders (DSM-IV-TR)*. You want something such as the depression section from the *DIS-IV (Diagnostic Interview Schedule – IV)*, an instrument designed to test whether or not someone meets *DSM* diagnostic criteria.

You need to have a pretty clear understanding of what instruments exist to study the constructs you are interested in. The best way to do this is simply to see what others have used. We would also recommend the Mental Measurements Yearbook site (http://buros.unl.edu/buros/jsp/search.jsp). Another good resource specific to children and youth is *Conducting School-Based Assessments of Child and Adolescent Behavior* (Shapiro & Kratochwill, 2000). Finally one must consider whether or not a given measure has been used with your population. There may be cultural biases in instruments due to conceptual differences, linguistic issues, or other problems. *The New Handbook of Multicultural Assessment: Clinical, Psychological, and Educational Applications* (Suzuki et al., 2000) is a great resource for helping you to understand if a measure is culturally appropriate.

SECTION 3.5.5: WHAT THEORIES EXIST TO TELL ME HOW TO LOOK AT MY DATA OR WHAT RELATIONSHIPS ARE LIKELY TO EXIST IN MY DATA?

Understanding what theories to use and how to use them is very important. It is also probably the most difficult part of the entire research process. The role of theory in your work will depend entirely on the issue you are interested in studying. Just like understanding variables or instruments, a good place to start with theory is to see what other people are using. It is not plagiarism or copying to base your work on the work of others. It is how science works. We call this "knowledge building." What you can't do is take credit for the work of others.

Right now your task is to find out about the theories that are important in your area. Good articles will overview the theories on which their design is based. It shouldn't be too difficult to see what theories are commonly used or even dominant in your area. For example, in the treatment of phobias, you will quickly find that many studies test behavioral or cognitive behavioral treatments. You will find relatively few studies on phobias examining the efficacy of treatments based in humanistic theory. As in the other areas, you need to think for yourself here. Do the theories match up with the research populations, questions, and designs in a clear way? It will almost certainly be necessary to go back to the literature and find more sources on the theories that are most commonly used or most appropriate to you.

SECTION 3.5.6: WHAT KINDS OF DESIGNS ARE USED IN MY AREA?

This will make more sense to you later, but try to figure out how people are doing research on your subject. Do they all use experimental designs (see next chapter)? Do any of the articles you have found say they are "longitudinal"? Are qualitative methods used? Try to get a sense for what ways that researchers are approaching the area, so you can approach your own design with some background and the benefit of the prior work of others. You probably aren't at a place where you can really critically figure all this out yet, but don't worry, we'll get there.

SECTION 3.5.7: WHAT ARE THE MAIN EMPIRICAL FINDINGS IN MY AREA?

It can be confusing just listing out the findings from each article you read. Try to figure out what the big and consistent findings are. Which findings come up over and over again? Which hypotheses are consistently supported or are consistently not supported? Are there strong trends that generalize over time and across populations? Try to get a sense for the larger and more important empirical findings in your area. Try to determine if the findings in your area represent large and meaningful differences, or if they simply report small effects that barely manage to reach statistical significance. For example, many studies find that boys are five or ten times as likely to become delinquent as girls. This is a big difference that matters. Other studies have found that birth order may influence IQ by a point or two. This is a small difference that has no practical importance.

You ought to be able to describe the findings in your area in simple terms. You should be able to say things like, "The literature consistently reports a strong relationship between *X* and *Y*," or "We have reports only of weak or nonsignificant associations between *X* and *Y*." Don't panic, we'll teach you all about things like association and significance as we go forward. For now, just try to get a sense of what your literature says.

SECTION 3.5.8: WHAT NEEDS TO BE STUDIED NEXT IN MY AREA?

This is an easy one. Most articles end with a paragraph or so that tells the reader what kinds of research need to be done in the future. Simply go to the articles you have found and read what the authors have to say. Dissertations can be particularly good for this. This is another place to use your creativity. Start with these questions:

- What key questions are unanswered?
- What issues have been raised recently that need answering?
- What policies, events, or changes in the world suggest a new slant on the research?
- Have all important populations been studied with regard to your question?
- What strikes you as missing or important to look at?

SECTION 3.5.9: EXAMPLE PROJECTS— UNDERSTANDING THE LITERATURE

We will now look at our five friends and see how they are doing with regard to these issues.

John. John has found a decently sized literature on Bosnians. In order to find out what form his research should take, he'd like to find some important gaps in the current work that he can exploit. Two themes have emerged. First, it is obvious to John that PTSD was getting all the attention. Second, there seems to be a real lack of any focus on strengths (Witmer & Culver, 2001) in the literature. As far as researchers are concerned, the issue is mental health (meaning PTSD), and that seems to be that. Although John was originally planning to focus his work on PTSD, the lack of research in other key areas is too tempting to miss. So John searches for strengths or resiliency among Bosnian refugees and finds almost nothing except some qualitative descriptions of services that had been provided from a strengths perspective. John is starting to think that finding out more about the strengths of the Bosnians and

how these strengths help in supporting mental health and economic success might be interesting, important, understudied, and fundable. More in-depth review of his sources brought up some interesting findings in this regard. Nesdale and Mak (2003) found that psychological health was higher among refugees with higher levels of personal achievement in their new cultures. Miller and colleagues (2002) found that lack of mastery in a range of areas was among the primary issues faced by Bosnian refugees in Chicago. A very common finding is represented by Baker (1988) who claims that mastery of language is one of the most important things in adapting to life in America. How should John look at this strength stuff? He has no idea and needs some theory. One of his identified sources is a large book that seems as though it might have a nice theory review section (Bemak, Chung, & Pederson, 2003). From this source, he identified two possible theoretical models to use and found that Berry and Kim's model (Berry & Kim, 1988) seemed like a good fit. That model discussed four different types of acculturation and related them to mental health outcomes. John is beginning to believe that he would like to use this model, in conjunction with a focus on strengths, to look at different kinds of mental health and economic outcomes among Bosnian refugees.

Abigail. Abigail has chosen to look at how client death affects child welfare workers. She is beginning to think she is interested mainly in how client death may or may not lead to more or less trauma for different workers. From her readings, she has found that both a positive work environment and social support from family and friends should be helpful factors. As far as she can tell, there has been no empirical work to date looking at child welfare workers and their response to client fatality, but she does have models she can draw from that have been developed with populations of medical professionals.

Maria. Maria has found theoretical reasons why she would expect homicide and suicide rates to be higher in some zip codes as well as a modest number of studies, mainly at the county or higher levels, showing how this is done empirically. Maria is in a good position at this point because the census variables available to her will allow her to track most of the things that interest her (poverty, housing, age, race, and the like), and her level of analysis (zip code) will provide her with better (finer level) data than have been previously found at the county level.

Yuan. Yuan has found both theoretical and empirical sources that pertain to CBT and domestic violence. If anything, he has too many possible paths open to him, especially in the area of constructs and variables of interest. He has a range of outcome variables he can choose from, including a number of scales measuring various kinds of conflict or violence. He also has the option of studying events, ranging from perpetrator or spousal accounts of violence to a review of police records (if he can get them). The particular form of CBT to be used by Yuan's agency has a heavy emphasis on blocking violent behavior through teaching alternate means of conflict resolution, so some measure that looks at how the family handles conflict, and how it changes over time, would seem logical.

Professor Kathy. Professor Kathy just wants to know if playing music cuts down on errors. She is going to minimize the role of theory in her work and test just the expected relationship. This is because she doesn't care at all why music might reduce errors, she just wants to see if it does. Based on her review of the literature, it looks as though she will want to use some kind of easy-listening or classical music, because music that is more modern might be intrusive or distracting. Her key concepts are listening to nonintrusive music and performance in research coding tasks. Her population is going to be her research assistants. Her overall goal is to see if she (and other researchers) should use background music for her coders.

SECTION 3.5.10: ETHICAL ISSUES FOR OUR SAMPLE PROJECTS

There are no ethical issues at this stage that prevent the researchers from going forward with their questions of interest. In other words, none of them are proposing something so dangerous to himself or herself or so potentially harmful to subjects or so unimportant as to be a waste of resources. There will be, however, ethical considerations for our researchers as they move forward into the design of their study. These will be dealt with in detail in subsequent chapters but are overviewed here.

Maria will be using data at the zip code level from the census, assuming that similar aggregate data can be found for suicide and homicide. Her study involves little human subjects consideration, low resources, and is important. If she uses only publicly available data, then she will have no concerns about confidentiality.

John will have to carefully consider potential vulnerability due to immigration status, the sensitivity of the questions he will ask, how to address issues if a subject seems to need services, and confidentiality. It will be important for John to get to know more about the culture and the local population. Finding a local leader and discussing the issue will be an important next step.

Abigail's sample will be dealing with a traumatic issue, so care will be required to have a counselor or other resources available to support subjects who may have negative reactions. It will need to be made clear to subjects that their employment will in no way be affected by their decision to participate and that their employers will not be given access to confidential data.

Yuan's topic is important, and the agency is likely to support access to a sample. One concern is that he may be studying mandated clients, and they may potentially feel coerced into participating. Because recidivism is a harmful occurrence for the partner of the subjects as well as the clients, it is especially important that the study must not include withholding treatment that would otherwise have been provided.

Kathy has already selected a nonintrusive form of music, is sampling adults, and is not asking potentially harmful questions. She will just have to insure that students are not feeling pressured to participate due to grades or fearful of termination of a job as a research assistant. She might also have to consider possible stress reactions to the task.

SECTION 3.6
YOUR CONCEPTUAL FRAMEWORK

This is where you move from simply reporting what others have said to more carefully defining your personal area of interest. We use the term **conceptual framework** to mean what constructs and relationships you are interested in, how they might fit together, whom you are interested in (your sample), and what theories underlie your work. The issues of how, where, and when you do your study are all part of your design and will come in the next chapter. Students (and most professors) typically jump to the "how" of design before they understand the constructs they are studying (what), their population of interest (who), and the practical issues and theories underlying their work (why). This leads, almost without exception, to people who don't really understand what they're doing. This results in people having bad experiences and needing to go back to the proverbial drawing board.

TRUE STORY

Many years ago, one of the authors sat in on a session in which a senior professor's initial draft of a grant was being critiqued. Two of us (including the author) thought the grant looked fine. The final reviewer, however, pointed out that when you really looked closely, the theory being used as a basis for the work had absolutely nothing to do with the constructs that were being measured. As the reviewer went on, it quickly became apparent that the single-spaced 20-page draft we had in our hands was built on a bad foundation and needed almost total revision. The problem was that the professor had done the design first and added supporting theory only later. Because the design was not built on the theory, theory and design did not really fit together. There was no amount of revision or creative writing that could cover up the fact.

As a side note, it might be worthwhile focusing on the researcher's response. She was taking rapid notes. She did not get defensive and did not argue, she understood that the person was right, and that the person was doing her a real service. Instead of getting annoyed, she asked questions such as, "How can I approach this in a different way?" or "Do you know of any other theoretical approaches which might be a better fit?" Not only did her response show tremendous strength of character, but it was exactly the best way for her to get the feedback she needed to move forward. The grant was later funded by the federal government.■

So don't go backward. Don't start with a design; start with a clearly defined framework that describes what you are interested in. Key parts of a conceptual framework are shown in Table 3.1.

SECTION 3.6.1: CONSTRUCTS

Constructs are the things we study. They can be almost anything, from traits to opinions to events to treatment interventions to virtually anything you can think of. They all share several things in common, though. Usable constructs are easy to understand and specific and can be transformed into variables that are clearly operationalized and measured. Constructs can be concrete things, like weight (that's already a variable), or they can be more conceptual, like "depression." The less clear and specific your constructs are, the more work you will have to do in transforming them into measurable variables. Ideally, constructs should also have practical importance. Just as all questions are not equally important, all constructs are not equally important. For example, hunger was a serious social problem in the United States

50 years ago. It is a less critical issue today. Even among the very poor, obesity is probably a far greater threat to health than hunger. Concepts relating to poor nutrition (lack of the right foods, surplus of empty calories) would be a far more important thing to measure than low caloric intake, at least in the United States.

SECTION 3.6.2: RELATIONSHIPS BETWEEN CONSTRUCTS

Relationships between constructs are the things we test in our models. Many of the relationships between constructs are so obvious that you might not even notice them. For example, anyone studying delinquency is likely to understand that the construct of gender is strongly related to delinquency (there are more delinquent boys than girls). Relationships between constructs are a big part of what social science is all about. You are probably not very interested in just measuring your constructs in isolation but instead want to know how they relate to something. For example, if people using my new cancer-fighting drug have a recovery rate of 30%, I have no idea if that is good or not. I need to compare that rate to a recovery rate among similar people who don't get my drug but instead get treatment as usual. I have two constructs, treatment recovery rate with my drug (0 to 100%) and recovery rate without my drug (0 to 100%). If people who take my drug have higher recovery rates, I say that giving my drug is associated with higher rates of recovery.

The big issue is this: How do you know what relationships to look for? This is where theory comes in. There may be any number of theories relating to your constructs. These theories may describe how your construct develops or is caused (etiology), how it is spread across society (epidemiology), and what other constructs are related to it. You must know these theories. The relationships you will be looking for will come from them. If you cannot show how the relationships you are exploring or testing are derived from or related to theory, your work may not be taken seriously.

Sometimes your area is so new that there is little theory present. In these cases, your work will probably be mainly descriptive (describing what's out there) or exploratory (finding out what's there) and inductive (gathering facts on which to build new theory). However, you still need some kind of theoretical framework to specify what you want to describe. You never just go charging out with nothing in your head. It just isn't possible. Your reasons for choosing to look at what you look at in a descriptive study are probably based on some general perspective, such as a systems approach (the idea that we have to understand not only the individual, but the social systems he or she is a part of) or a developmental approach (the idea that people think, act, feel, and require different things at different ages). In such a

---

TABLE 3.1. **Key Elements of a Conceptual Framework.**

Constructs
- A description of the constructs you are interested in
- A description of the practical relevance and importance of these constructs
- A description of what theories relate to these constructs

Relationships between constructs
- A description of the relationships between constructs you expect to find
- A description of how the theories you use lead you to expect these relationships

Populations to be studied
- A description of whom you are interested in studying
- A description of how the constructs and theories you use are appropriate to this particular population

case, go ahead and state that your work is being done under the general theoretical orientation you choose and discuss how this orientation shapes your work.

This last point deserves some emphasis. If you can't find a specific theory that relates to your question, you may have to move out to broader theories or paradigmatic approaches. This is undesirable but may be necessary. You should try to find the smallest-level, best-fitting theory you can. At the broadest level, a surprisingly large number of scholarly works claim to be based on an "ecological" or "systems" theory, framework, or paradigm. This often happens when a researcher can't find a theory to tightly fit the question. What to do? Because a good deal of social research attends to factors in the environment of the subject, one can often fall back and call one's work "ecological." Of course, this is having a theory only in the vaguest possible sense and is really more of having a "paradigm" or "approach."

SECTION 3.6.3: POPULATIONS TO BE STUDIED—SPECIFICATION AND ETHICAL CONCERNS

Your conceptual framework must reference whom or what you are studying. This includes a description of the people, organizations, or whatever that you will be including in your research. You need to explain clearly how the populations you include in your conceptual framework are appropriate to the constructs you have chosen and the theory you are using. For example, many studies have been criticized for using only easily available populations. College students are common subjects, but this might not help you find out about the population as a whole.

A serious ethical concern is the underrepresentation of women and minorities in the literature, which was especially serious in decades past. People applying for grants to many federal agencies (e.g., NIMH) are required to write special sections that explain how the proposed research will sample and apply to a broad range of people. This is so that the benefits of the work can be shared by all kinds of people. There are exceptions to this, obviously. If you are studying something that mainly affects one type of person (e.g., male pattern balding, Tay-Sachs, or sickle-cell anemia), then it is reasonable to include only the people to whom that issue pertains. Furthermore, you may have theoretical reasons for sampling only one segment of the population. For example, you may want to look at African American male homosexuals exclusively, because you believe the issues facing this population may be quite different from those faced by Whites or other ethnicities. In our own work, we have often limited our research on child abuse and neglect to poorer, urban populations. We justify this on the grounds that this is a population of particular practical importance, comprising a large part of child welfare caseloads. In short, you do not have to study everyone all the time to be ethical, but you also should try not to contribute to the tendency of research in some areas to hurt a group of people by chronically ignoring them.

SECTION 3.6.4: PARSIMONY

Parsimony is a ten-buck word for "simplicity." We are all familiar with the advice, "Keep It Simple, Stupid," often abbreviated as KISS. This applies to conceptual models just as it does to most things in life. You can achieve parsimony in your model by doing the following:

HOW TO BE PARSIMONIOUS

Limit the Number of Constructs. Just include those constructs that you expect will have meaningfully large effects on the model (Figure 3.2). If income was previously shown to account for < 1% of the variance in

---

FIGURE 3.2. **Limit the Number of Constructs.**

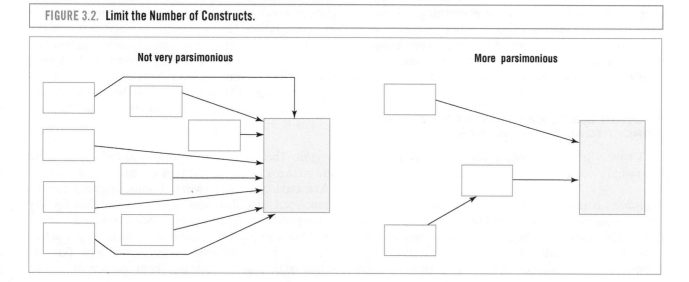

FIGURE 3.3. **Limit Relationships between Constructs.**

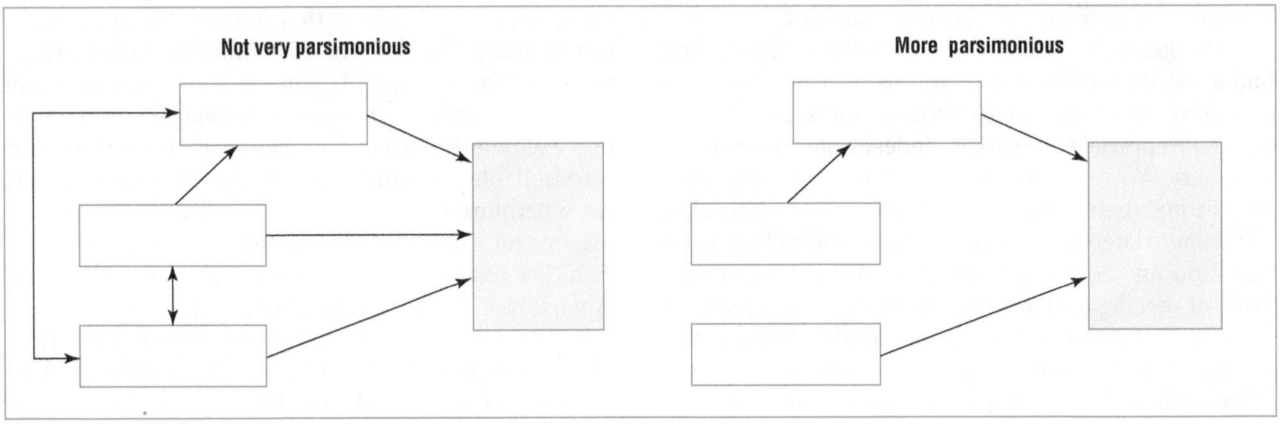

what you're studying you probably should leave it out of the model.

Include Only Relationships That You Have Good Theoretical Reason For or That Other Studies Have Found in the Past. It is tempting to say, "Gee, maybe everything relates to everything! Let's see!" This is bad. A model that specifies (draws lines for) all possible relationships between constructs is "saturated" and can cause some statistical analysis programs to refuse to run. Your model must reflect your best judgment about the most important relationships you hope to find (Figure 3.3). *Warning:* Later we will again use the word *saturated* in the qualitative analysis chapter. *Saturated* has two totally different meanings in research. A saturated theoretical model is bad, but reaching saturation in a qualitative analysis is good. Sorry about that.

Does this mean you must always use the simplest possible model? Absolutely not. In the above example, the diagram on the left is very heavily specified (almost everything is related to almost everything): If that's what theory or evidence suggests is best, however, you may have to sacrifice some parsimony. Your models don't have to be parsimonious, but you should have a darn good explanation for why they aren't.

SECTION 3.6.5: EXAMPLE PROJECTS— CONCEPTUAL FRAMEWORKS

Let's have a look at the conceptual frameworks for our five sample cases.

John. John is interested in the constructs of strengths and acculturation. He has found relatively little on this, however, and feels that he should start his research by consulting the Bosnians themselves and getting their perspective. He believes that he may therefore be

pursuing a more qualitative approach. Because John is planning to go into the community and get the perspectives of the people he is studying, he feels he should allow them considerable scope in defining strengths. As for acculturation outcomes, he is planning on seeing how well Berry and Kim's (1988) model will serve as a framework for understanding what the Bosnians have to say about their own experience. This model specifies four different acculturation outcomes. These are assimilation, in which an immigrant abandons his or her prior culture and becomes Americanized; integration, in which the immigrant maintains parts of his or her culture but also joins with the American culture; separation, in which the immigrant retains his or her culture entirely and rejects American culture; and marginalization, an early stage in the process in which the conflict and crisis of immigration cause the person to be isolated from both his or her culture and American culture. John expects that he will find that the Bosnians he talks to will be able to give him information on what strengths lead to more positive acculturation outcomes (integration) and relatively rapid transition through marginalization. He expects his subjects will report a lack of strengths to be associated with separation and extended marginalization. John expects to find local Bosnian immigrants and interview them, either individually or in groups. He intends to give them wide latitude in how they respond, but he also wants to get his core questions answered.

Abigail. The more Abigail thinks about it, the more she realizes that her question might best be phrased "Are environmental (work, family, friends) factors associated with different responses to child fatality among child welfare workers?" She consulted a reference book of psychological tests (Corcoran & Fischer, 2000) and has found some measures that look like they might be helpful in capturing her constructs of interest and answering her theoretical questions. These include the following:

- *The Impact of Events Scale (IES),* by M. Horowitz, produces two subscales measuring bad psychological outcomes of a traumatic event. These include intrusive experiences (can't stop thinking about the event, bad dreams, and the like) and avoidance (trying not to think about the event, avoiding places that make you remember it, and so on).

- *The Social Support Behaviors Scale (SSB),* by A. Vaux, S. Reidel, and D. Stewart, measures five different kinds of social support. Abigail is especially interested in the subscales on emotional support and advice/guidance.

- *The Organizational Climate Scale (OCS)* by A. Thompson and H. McCubbin measures various aspects of organizational climate as perceived by the respondent.

It seems to Abigail that these scales will let her capture many of the key constructs that her literature review cited as important. There will be a number of other constructs she may also want to measure, but the IES appears to be a good dependent measure, and the SSB and the OCS seem to provide a range of key environmental predictor factors.

Maria. Maria's constructs are homicide and suicide (in San Diego zip codes) and community characteristics (mainly race, housing, and income in those zip codes). She expects crowded housing and low income to be associated with both suicide and homicide. Her population will be the population of San Diego County but aggregated at zip code level.

Yuan. Yuan is interested in the concept of different treatment types (CBT versus treatment as usual) and how they are associated with conflict strategies and violence. He will test to see if either type of treatment has clearly better outcomes. His population is determined for him and will be people using his agency's services.

Professor Kathy. Kathy will look at nonintrusive music (classical, easy listening) and see if it improves the percentage of correct coding by her researchers.

SECTION 3.7
FORMALIZING AND PRESENTING YOUR CONCEPTUAL FRAMEWORK

In communicating your conceptual framework to others, you will have to be able to present your ideas in a clear manner using terms that others will understand. To do this, you will have to know the terms we use to describe variables, and you will need to know how to graphically represent your conceptual framework so that others can see and understand it. We will start out by becoming a little more technical in how we discuss variables. *Variables are operationalized constructs.*

But what does **operationalized** mean? Something is operationalized if it is clear how it is measured. For example, "suicide attempt history" is not operationalized, but "number of prior suicide attempts reported by the subject during the interview" is operationalized. There are lots of ways to operationalize constructs. For example, another researcher might operationalize suicide attempt history as "number of hospital admissions for attempted suicide." The goal here is simply to be clear about what concrete measure your construct is represented by.

Let's get back to variables. Variables are therefore measurable in some way, often through counting (e.g., number of arrests) or through scores from instruments (e.g., your SAT score).

SECTION 3.7.1: FOUR TYPES OF SCALES FOR VARIABLES

There are four different ways in which variables may be scaled to represent their constructs: nominal, ordinal, interval, and ratio. If you know French, you can remember this by the fact that the first letter of each scale (in the above order) spells *Noir,* the French word for "black" (as in "film noir").

Nominal scales (categorical) are just names or types that have no numerical significance. "Blond," "Republican," "Joan," and "Female" are nominal.

Ordinal scales (categorical) are not common in social research and relate to the rank order something has. For example, a ranking of the worst earthquakes in terms of fatalities (most killed, second most killed, and so on) and Olympic medals (first, second, third) are ordinal variables. Notice that these are numeric only in the sense that you know who came first and second; you do not know how much difference there was between them. For example, the winner of the 500-meter freestyle may have beaten the second place person by only .01 second, while the second place person beat the third place person by a whopping 9 seconds, but they're still listed as "first, second, third."

Interval scales (continuous) are different from ordinal variables in that the differences between numbers are the same. If we record the temperature each day on the Fahrenheit scale, then we are recording numbers where the difference between each number on our scale is the same (one degree). Interval scales lack "true zeros" (see the following).

Ratio scales (continuous) are similar to interval scales but have "true zeros." A true zero is when a value of zero means that the amount being measured is

TABLE 3.2. **Examples of Research Questions: Independent, Dependent, and Control Variables.**

RESEARCH QUESTION	INDEPENDENT VARIABLE	DEPENDENT VARIABLE	CONTROL VARIABLES
Which detergent will make my sheets their whitest?	Type of detergent	Amount of stain removed (from identically stained sheets)	
Are there more fire department calls on hot days?	Daily high temperature	Number of fire department calls	Humidity, precipitation, day of week, holiday, and the like
Does lower classroom size help learning?	Number of people in classroom	Average class score on standardized test	Teacher experience, spending per pupil, and the like

nothing. For example, the number of apples I have involves a true zero (no apples). Similarly, the Kelvin scale has a true zero (zero Kelvin is "absolute zero," a theoretical condition where there is absolutely no heat of any type present). On the other hand, many scales lack a zero altogether (you can't get a zero on the ACT, for example) or have zeroes with no real meaning (on the Fahrenheit scale, zero is just a number; it doesn't mean "no heat present"). Similarly, degrees Celsius is also not a ratio scale; even though "0 degrees" means something (the freezing point of water), it does not mean "no heat."

SECTION 3.7.2: CATEGORICAL AND CONTINUOUS VARIABLES

Variables measured with nominal or ordinal scales are generally called "categorical variables." Variables measured with ratio or interval scales are called "continuous variables" because the difference between each point on the scale is the same. Many statistics require that your variables be continuous. One confusing point is that most researchers treat scores from psychological or similar tests as continuous (usually interval), even when there is no reason to really believe that they are, if you use a strict definition.

SECTION 3.7.3: INDEPENDENT, DEPENDENT, AND CONTROL VARIABLES

Independent variables can be thought of as "predictor" or "causal" variables. Independent variables are those things you believe will predict or cause a change in the dependent variable. When drawing models, independent variables are to the left.

Dependent variables can be thought of as "outcome" variables. They are those things you believe are affected by other things in your model. When drawing models, the independent variable is the item furthest to the right. There are also "mediating" and "moderating" variables, which we will discuss below.

Control variables are other possible influences on your dependent variable that you decide to keep track of. They are included in your model to make sure that the relationship between independent and dependent variables is not due to other factors (see Table 3.2).

SECTION 3.7.4: DRAWING MODELS

Next, we need to talk about how to draw ideas out on paper. There are specific conventions that are used in social science in presenting models. If you do not use these conventions, then people will not know what you are trying to say. These graphic models are most commonly used with nonexperimental designs, which generally include more variables and more complex possibilities for relationships between variables.

CONVENTION 1

Use boxes for constructs and move from left to right, with causes or earlier factors being to the left and outcomes or later events being to the right. If things happen at the same time, stack them, one above the other (Figure 3.4). Earlier stuff or causes should be to the left. Later stuff and final outcomes should be all the way to the right. In the example in Figure 3.4, we want to look at social contact, how that relates to later depression, and how that relates to later suicide. If we were interested in looking at depression and social contact at the same point in time, and how that relates to future suicide, we'd set up the boxes like those shown in Figure 3.5.

Notice that these diagrams already tell different stories. The first says, "Social contact comes before depression, which comes before suicide," while the second says, "Social contact and depression both happen before suicide."

FIGURE 3.4. **Three Constructs In Time Order.**

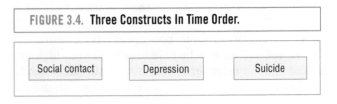

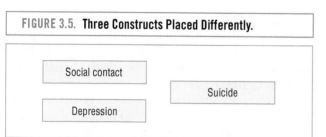

FIGURE 3.5. **Three Constructs Placed Differently.**

CONVENTION 2

Use arrows to indicate direction of expected relationships. Obviously, because time goes from left to right, arrows shouldn't go backward, except in recursive models, when you are trying to show that two variables have effects on each other. Arrows can be marked with a plus to indicate a positive relationship (they both go up or down together) or a minus to indicate an inverse (or negative) relationship (one goes up while the other goes down). In the example in Figure 3.6, depression and social contact are (inversely) associated with each other, and they are (differently) related to later suicide. This shows that people with high social contact are less likely to be depressed (and vice versa), and that people with high social contact are less likely ("−") to commit suicide and that people with depression are more likely ("+") to commit suicide.

CONVENTION 3

Mediating variables are another issue. Sometimes *A* causes *B* and *B* causes *C*. In this case, *B* is termed a "mediating" or "mediator" variable. This can easily be portrayed. In the example in Figure 3.7, we are asserting a model where lack of social contact leads to depression which leads to suicide. Depression is therefore *mediating* the relationship between social contact and suicide (less social contact leads to more depression, which leads to more suicide).

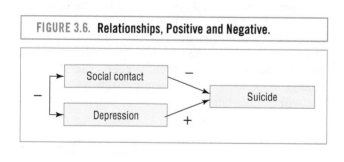

FIGURE 3.6. **Relationships, Positive and Negative.**

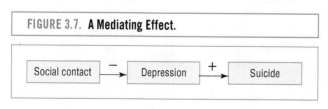

FIGURE 3.7. **A Mediating Effect.**

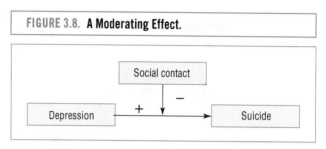

FIGURE 3.8. **A Moderating Effect.**

CONVENTION 4

Variables can also moderate. Sometimes *A* is related to *C*, but some other factor changes the relationship. We might believe that depression leads to suicide but that social contact can alter or reduce this effect. We would therefore say that depression's impact on suicide is moderated (changed) by social contact. This is drawn by putting a line from the moderating variable to the relationship (not the construct) it changes. In the example in Figure 3.8, more depression leads to more suicide, but social contact weakens ("−") that relationship (e.g., if two people are equally depressed, the one with more friends will be less likely to commit suicide). This is the same as "interaction."

CONVENTION 5

Direct and indirect effects also occur. *A* may cause *C* directly but may also do so through a third variable. *A* causing *C* is called a direct effect, but *A* causing *C* because it first effects the mediating variable *B* (which then causes *C*) is called an indirect effect. Both can exist at the same time. In the example in Figure 3.9, depression causes less social contact, which, in turn, is associated with more suicide; this is the indirect effect of depression on suicide through a mediating variable (social contact). Depression also has a direct effect on suicide.

CONVENTION 6

The strength and statistical significance of relationships can be specified. Numbers that represent the percentage of variance explained (usually these are interpreted like regression coefficients, see Chapter 14) and asterisks showing the statistical significance of the

FIGURE 3.9. **A Direct Effect (Depression to Suicide) and an Indirect Effect (through Social Contact).**

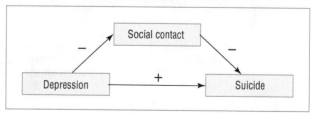

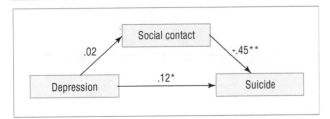

relationship are often included in models after the data have been analyzed. In the example in Figure 3.10, there is a nonsignificant (no asterisks) relationship between depression and social contact; a small, significant relationship between depression and suicide; and a moderate, also significant relationship (which is an inverse, or negative relationship; see the "−") between social contact and suicide. In plain English, we can't find any association between depression and social contact; depression is associated with a slight increase in suicide; and high social contact is associated with a substantial reduction in suicide (these are fictional data for example only). We'll get into statistical issues more later.

These basic conventions should not only help you to present your models more clearly but will also help you in understanding the literature, where such models are often employed.

SECTION 3.7.5: PUTTING IT ALL TOGETHER—PRESENTING YOUR CONCEPTUAL FRAMEWORK

It is always good practice for researchers to put their conceptual framework down on paper. This framework should include the key concepts in the framework and the expected relationships between the constructs. A diagram such as this is a necessary component in most projects and is good practice even in journal articles, although the limitations on space in journal articles often cause such diagrams not to be included. The relationships among the constructs should conform to the theory underlying your conceptual framework.

As an example, let's assume that we are interested in designing a program to reduce adolescent drug use. We think that changing whom the subjects associate with will reduce likelihood of drug use. We base this on a simplified version of peer cluster theory (Oetting & Beauvais, 1986), which looks something like Figure 3.11.

This theory suggests a number of points where we might intervene. We might try to help families before adolescents develop problems; we might try to intervene early with children at school before they fall out into deviant peer clusters; or we might intervene with the deviant peer clusters directly. Let's say that we want to intervene as the children reach school, in kindergarten and first grade. Based on the model in Figure 3.11, we would be trying to make it so that children with poor socialization do not become isolated and thus are less at risk of falling out into deviant peer clusters later and presumably therefore being at higher risk for drug use. We therefore are most interested in the first two constructs (poor socialization and academic/social failure in early grades). We might try to fix this by providing a special school/peer socialization curriculum ("NewPals") to all kindergarteners and first graders, with the goal of reducing the number of children who become socially isolated. Our model would therefore look like Figure 3.12.

Dotted boxes and arrows can be used to represent parts of the model not tested in the proposed research. You don't have to study the entire theoretical model; in fact, most studies are not complete explorations of a theory or model, but only part of it. Why even include the parts of the theory that we are not actually testing? Because it is important to show the reader how the work fits in with the theory as a whole.

This model makes a number of things clear in a visual manner: We are testing the NewPals curriculum. We are interested in how the presence of that curriculum modifies the relationship between poor socialization among incoming students and subsequent poor outcomes. We are also showing that the outcomes we will study are limited to academic and social outcomes in early grades. Even though we never deal with drugs directly, our theoretical model (which we can show has been empirically supported by reference to prior research) suggests that if we can change early social and academic pathways, then drug use will decline later.

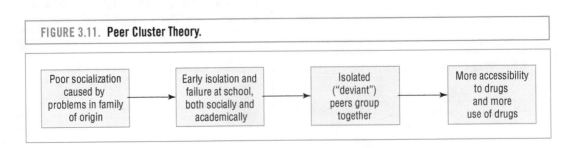

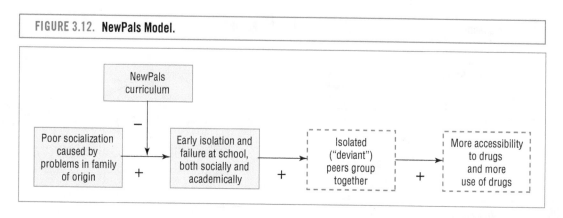

FIGURE 3.12. **NewPals Model.**

SPECIAL CASE 1

How do you draw a model for a simple experiment? Often, models of the type discussed in the preceding section are not drawn for simple experiments because such a model would not be very informative and would look like Figure 3.13. Instead, people may include a table showing each experimental condition, the number in each group, and what treatments they get over time. That might look like Figure 3.14.

Figure 3.14 is not really a picture showing a conceptual framework at all. It is a picture showing who gets what and when measurement occurs. The simple truth is that basic experimental designs are so simple conceptually (give some people X, don't give X to others, see what happens) that conceptual frameworks are generally not drawn out.

SPECIAL CASE 2

How do you draw a model for an exploratory design when you don't even know what the constructs are? Exploratory designs also do not usually include illustrations of their conceptual framework. We feel this is a mistake, because even the simplest research involves basic ideas about what is being looked at. We'd suggest something like Figure 3.15. This gives the reader some idea of what you plan to look at. In this case, the

researcher is pointing out that he or she will use an ecological model and will attempt to look at not only the woman who is battered but also at her partner and the broader community.

FIGURE 3.15. **A Model for an Exploratory Design.**

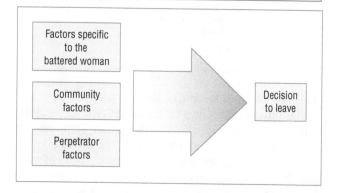

SECTION 3.7.6: EXAMPLE PROJECTS— FORMALIZING CONCEPTUAL FRAMEWORKS

Let's look at our five example cases to see how they are presenting their conceptual frameworks.

John. John is using Berry's (1988) model, which takes time into account and looks something like Figure 3.16.

FIGURE 3.13. **How Not to Draw an Experimental Design.**

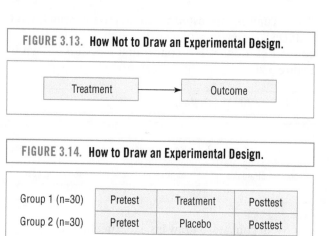

FIGURE 3.14. **How to Draw an Experimental Design.**

| Group 1 (n=30) | Pretest | Treatment | Posttest |
| Group 2 (n=30) | Pretest | Placebo | Posttest |

FIGURE 3.16. **Berry's (1988) Model.**

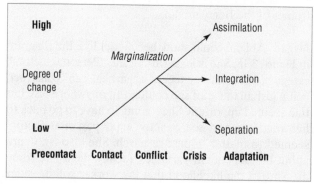

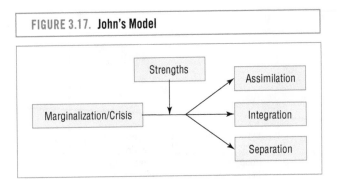

FIGURE 3.17. **John's Model**

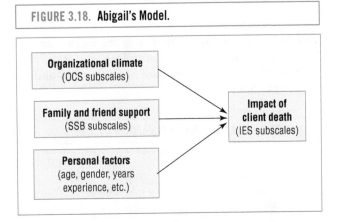

FIGURE 3.18. **Abigail's Model.**

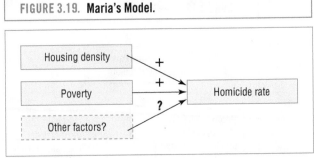

FIGURE 3.19. **Maria's Model.**

(a)

(b)

This model is interesting, because it takes a number of things into account (degree of change, type of acculturation, time) and specifies a particular sequence of events (precontact, contact, conflict, crisis, and adaptation). It also specifies that there will be a period of marginalization during crisis that either one can get stuck in or that can lead to eventual states of assimilation, integration, and separation. This model suggests to John that if he wants to understand how strengths lead to different acculturation outcomes, he will have to look at people either over a long time (contact or conflict through adaptation) or after the crisis stage and ask them to recall what it was like. John only has time for the latter, so that's what he will do. His overall model might look like Figure 3.17.

His job, of course, will be to identify what the key strengths are relative to acculturation outcomes, and how they affect the acculturation process. Notice that John is really only using the last two or three timeframes of the Berry model.

Abigail. Abigail could show her model like the diagram in Figure 3.18. She is least sure of the "Personal factors" category, which has the feel of a "garbage can" construct, being just all the stuff she couldn't fit anywhere else but that seemed important. She's going to have to go back to her readings and see exactly what personal factors seemed to matter in past research. She also isn't sure about the dependent variables. Ideally she'd like some measure of the likelihood that the worker will consider

quitting based on the fatality, but she isn't sure how to do that—maybe just a direct question on the survey?

Abigail is feeling pretty good but then realizes that she needs a theory to support her model. What theory to use? Stress and coping? Is she measuring how different kinds of social support help people cope with a stressor? Is she mainly going to use an organizational theory? That doesn't seem to fit too well.

Maria. Maria is interested in looking at how community factors influence rates of homicide and suicide. She really has two questions and two models. She already knows that poverty and housing density look like they might be important, and she wants to test this. She is also interested in exploring what other factors might be important. Her models might look like Figure 3.19a and 3.19b.

Yuan. Yuan is interested in the degree to which CBT reduces domestic violence through first improving conflict strategies. His conceptual model is shown in Figure 3.20.

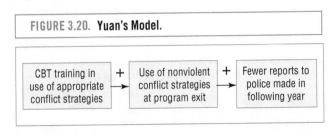

FIGURE 3.20. **Yuan's Model.**

Yuan could also draw his experimental design (not his conceptual framework) like this:

CBT Group	Pretest (conflict strategies)	CBT treatment	Posttest (conflict strategies)	Check # of police reports over 1 year
Treatment as Usual Group	Pretest (conflict strategies)	Treatment as usual	Posttest (conflict strategies)	Check # of police reports over 1 year

He will be able to place people either in the CBT or "as usual" therapy groups, then track the degree to which group membership brings about changes in conflict strategies at program exit; finally, he will be able to track the police reports made on families over the following year.

Professor Kathy. Kathy has found that music could be calming (good) distracting (bad) and that tempo could affect coding speed (Figure 3.21a). She is also interested in seeing if these factors can affect coding accuracy (Figure 3.21b).

FIGURE 3.21. Possible Effects of Music on (a) Coding Speed and (b) Coding Accuracy.

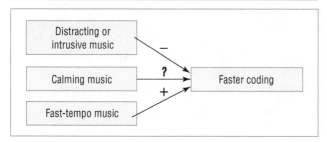

(a)

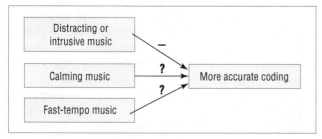

(b)

Professor Kathy could draw her experimental design (not her conceptual framework) like this:

No Music (Control condition)	Subjects code files with no background music	Check number of files coned (speed measure)	Check number of errors per file (accuracy measure)
Easy-listening Music Group	Subjects code files with no background music	Check number of files coded (speed measure)	Check number of errors per file (accuracy measure)
Classical Music Group	Subjects code files with no background music	Check Number of files coded (speed measure)	Check number of errors per file (accuracy measure)

In the above example professor Kathy has included a "no music" control condition so that she can not only compare easy listening to classical, but can also tell how each performs relative to no music.

Professor Kathy has therefore decided to pick only easy-listening and classical music. She sees no point in studying distracting or intrusive music, which seems only to hurt. She has also decided to use only medium-tempo music because she does not want to confound her research design with the issue of tempo, which she does not think will increase accuracy. She will also include a control (no music) group.

CONCLUSION

If it seems as if this must be a time-consuming aspect of the research process, you are absolutely correct! There are many critical issues involved in selecting a topic and constructs and specifying a conceptual framework that are too often given scant attention in research texts. We provide some further readings related to literature review and doing research across cultures to assist in this process. In the next chapter, we will discuss how to plan out the details of research projects, and we will see how these conceptual models play out in the design phase.

★ ★ ★

EBP MODULE

As you recall, there are several steps in doing EBP. The first two steps are formulating an empirically answerable question and finding relevant literature. Chapter 3 has already dealt with these two issues as they relate to forming a research question and searching literature to support research. This section will provide three examples to suggest how you can use these same skills as part of EBP.

FORMULATING AN EMPIRICALLY ANSWERABLE QUESTION

You know what *empirical* means, and you know what questions are empirically answerable and what aren't. What kinds of questions might you encounter in practice? Depending on the kind of work you do, these questions could be almost anything. The following examples demonstrate the range of questions that might be asked.

Example 1. Let's say you have a teenage female client who was anorexic but has been asymptomatic for a year. She and her family want information on relapse. How often does anorexia recur? The question facing you is, "What is the recurrence rate for anorexia nervosa among teenage girls like my client?" That's certainly answerable.

Example 2. You are a state midlevel social service manager who is reviewing how services are provided to abused and neglected children. The agency director has asked for a comprehensive review of service provision gateways within your agency to make sure that the right people are being served. You notice that in the past your state has offered services only to cases that are labeled by the investigative worker as "substantiated." You are aware that most other states do not restrict services in this manner. Should your state continue to restrict services to only substantiated cases, or should unsubstantiated cases also be eligible for services? This would seem to depend on the nature and degree of difference between substantiated and unsubstantiated cases. You frame the following question: "Are substantiated and unsubstantiated cases similar or different with regard to need for services?"

Example 3. You are a mental health care provider for children. You have a client presenting with obsessive-compulsive disorder (OCD). You have heard that cognitive behavioral therapy is an effective treatment for that disorder. You want to find out if that is true. Your question is, "Is CBT effective for children with OCD?"

Basically, if you need to know something to help people better, then you should be able to phrase it as an empirically answerable question using the skills you learned in this chapter.

FINDING RELEVANT RESEARCH

The way you find relevant research will depend on the kind of question you are asking. For most questions, you will follow the procedures described earlier in this chapter. However, if you are trying to answer a question of the form, "What treatment works best for X?" then there are some nice resources you should know about that we did not cover above.

Reviews and Practice Guidelines. In the EBP module in Chapter 1 we discussed the difference between evidence-based practice and evidence-based practices. If you happen to be looking for EBPs or practice guidelines in a particular area, you're in luck. There are some nifty tools available. Among these are the Cochrane Collaboration www.cochrane.org and the Campbell Collaboration (www.campbellcollaboration.org). These sites publish reviews of the best available evidence of treatment efficacy and effectiveness. The National Guideline Clearinghouse (www.guideline.gov) is a very useful source for practice guidelines. In addition, a number of specific agencies host sites listing information about empirically supported practices or programs in their area of focus. For example, the Office of Juvenile Justice and Delinquency Prevention's Model Programs Guide (www.dsonline.com) would be of interest to practitioners and administrators in the area of delinquency. Area-specific collections such as this can generally be found through the Web sites for the appropriate government or professional agency responsible for that area (e.g., the National Institute of Drug Abuse or the American Psychological Association).

Once I Find a Review or Practice Guideline, Can I Stop Searching? Summaries of research and lists of practice guidelines are generally not sufficient for the true EBP practitioner. You want not only to read someone else's summary of what's going on, you want to see the original articles for yourself. They're referenced in the reviews and are easy to locate. There may also be other, possibly more recent articles you should find. Why bother to look at the original work? There are lots of reasons. For example, you need to have some idea of what kinds of people have been used in the studies so that you can understand how well the findings will generalize (see Chapter 4) to your clients. There may be many other things about the research that limit or support its value to you not mentioned in all reviews, such as how long the follow-up periods were. We agree with Sackett and coauthors (2000), who suggest that when you are dealing with issues that you run into frequently or that are particularly important, you must always go to the primary sources. They also suggest that when dealing with less important or less commonly encountered problems, it may be possible to rely more on summaries or guidelines. This represents something of a trade-off between quality and practicality.

APPLYING BEST EVIDENCE TO PRACTICE

We will now return to our three examples above. We will see what is found, and we will see how the best available evidence might be applied to practice.

Example 1. You want to know about recurrence rates for anorexia in teenage girls. You go to PsycINFO and enter "anorexia" and "recurrence" as key words (kw). Not finding anything immediately useful, and finding a lot of articles you don't want, you tighten your search, looking for the above terms in the title only. This produces "Remission, Recovery, Relapse and Recurrence in Eating Disorders: Conceptualization and Validation of A Validation Strategy" (Kordy, H., Kramer, B., Palmer, L., Papezoya, H., Pellet, J., Richard, M., & Treasure, J. (2002). *Journal of Clinical Psychology,* 58(7), 833–846). This very interesting article looks at various ways to think about recurrence and overviews what is known about rates of recurrence in a fairly understandable way. You decide to track down some of the primary sources listed in the article and look them over too. If you think the information in the article is both useful and accessible to your client, you might even print out a copy of one or two of them and share a copy with the girl and her parents, carefully explaining the kinds of things that have been found and how the research might or might not be applicable to your client.

Example 2. Your question is: "Are substantiated and unsubstantiated cases similar or different with regard to need for services?" You happen to feel like using Google this time and put in "unsubstantiated child maltreatment." Right on the first screen, you find a couple of papers that look interesting. The first is Drake, B., Jonson-Reid, M., Way, I., & Chung, S. (2003). Substantiation and recidivism. *Child Maltreatment,* 8(4), 248–260. This very nicely written article is an empirical examination of recidivism rates among substantiated and unsubstantiated cases. Bottom line is that unsubstantiated cases come back to the system almost as often as substantiated cases do. This suggests that the substantiation label isn't all that useful as a proxy for service need. Another, older article (Drake, B. [1996b]. Unraveling unsubstantiated. *Child Maltreatment,* 1[3], 261–271) provides a coherent theoretical framework for why this might be so. Since you don't want to rely on the work of a single author, no matter how well respected, you look for more recent publications. You find one (Hussey, J., Marshall, J., English, D., Knight, E.,

Lau, A., Dubowitz, H., Kotch, J. [2005], Defining maltreatment according to substantiation: A distinction without a difference? *Child Abuse and Neglect: The International Journal,* 29[5], 479–492) that uses a different (nationally representative) data set to look at similarities between substantiated and unsubstantiated cases. This article also concludes that substantiated and unsubstantiated cases aren't very different. You backtrack the references in the Hussey and colleagues article (it's more recent) and find that there seems to be consensus in the empirical literature. On the basis of this review, you decide that it looks as though unsubstantiated cases are at fairly high risk of recidivism and are probably not all that different from substantiated cases in terms of their service needs. You report to the boss that the policy probably should be changed to allow services to unsubstantiated cases.

Example 3. Is CBT useful for children with OCD? You go straight to the Cochrane Collaboration and enter "OCD CBT" under its search panel. You find the following review: O'Kearny, R., Anstey, K., Von Sanden, C. (2006) Behavioural and cognitive behavioural therapy for obsessive compulsive disorder in children and adolescents. The conclusion given in the review is that CBT is effective for OCD in children, equally as effective as medication. The review lists find four relevant studies, which you obtain and read. To backstop yourself, you do an independent search on PsycINFO and find a few more interesting articles that were not included in the review. You satisfy yourself that CBT does appear to be an effective intervention for children with OCD. You decide to present this to the child's parents as one treatment option.

We hope this information and these examples have been helpful supplements to the broader search information given in this chapter, and we hope that you have occasion to use such approaches to obtaining the best available evidence so that the people you help can get the best possible care.■

REVIEW

1. Think of a topic in social science that interests you currently. Do you think it meets the six requirements for selecting an area of interest? Why or why not?

2. How does reviewing the literature relate to the selection of a specific research question?

3. What are the ethical considerations that are key to deciding whether or not to move forward with a question to the research design phase?

4. Explain what independent, dependent, and control variables are. Find a journal article about a study either from this chapter or in your own area. Identify the independent, dependent, and control variables.

5. What are the different scales of measurement for a variable?

6. How might culture influence the way in which a construct is measured?

7. Identify three theories from the literature that can be applied to your area of interest.

8. With regard to the question above, are these three theories best described as models, midlevel theories, grand theories, or paradigms? Justify.

9. Imagine you are interested in violent behavior among youth. Is this a practically important construct? Why or why not? Identify at least two variables that might be used to measure the construct of "violent behavior."

10. Juanita is interested in asset development in developing countries. She thinks that government support of new farming technology, proximity to water supply, strength of social networks in the community, and health are associated with accumulation of assets among households. Draw a possible conceptual framework for her study.

11. Go out there and find a research study with a really large and complicated set of variables and relationships between variables. Do you think that this article is OK with regard to the principle of parsimony? Why or why not?

SUPPLEMENTAL READINGS

■ Berry, J., Poortinga, Y., Segal, M., & Dasen, P. (2002). *Cross-Cultural Psychology: Research and Applications.* Cambridge, UK: Cambridge University Press. The review of various concepts related to culture and connections between culture and behavior is very helpful to students in specifying their conceptual framework when doing research that includes persons of diverse backgrounds.

■ Bolker, J. (1998). *Writing Your Dissertation in Fifteen Minutes a Day: A Guide to Starting, Revising, and Finishing Your Doctoral Thesis.* New York: Henry Holt and Company. This quirky and irreverent little book gives loads and loads of practical advice on how to handle a big project.

■ Cooper, M. (1998). *Synthesizing Research: A Guide for Literature Reviews.* Thousand Oaks, CA: Sage. This amazing little book is designed rather like the book you are holding now. It works you through the process of understanding literature in a logical, step-by-step way, with lots of practical applications.

■ Girden, E. (1996). *Evaluating Research Articles from Start to Finish.* Thousand Oaks, CA: Sage. This is a nice handbook-style guide to evaluating articles, which walks the reader through case studies including some specific advanced analyses (e.g., discriminant analysis) not covered in this book.

4

DESIGN

Your research design is simply your plan for answering a question. It should follow naturally from a well-specified conceptual framework (see Chapter 3). This chapter will focus on quantitative research design. Chapter 5 will go over measurement and instruments. Then Chapter 6 will review qualitative design. Sometimes people talk about "field" or "practice" or "clinical" research that is done by social service providers or agencies. The science they use is the same as the science that more formal researchers use, but there are sometimes different considerations when doing research in an agency or field setting. For this reason, we have two other chapters that specifically look at field research. Chapter 7 discusses multisubject field research or evaluation research, and Chapter 8 focuses on clinical single-subject designs ("$N = 1$" designs). To conclude our content on design, we have a review of how our five research example people did their designs in Chapter 9.

In the last chapter, you identified your question(s), operationalized your constructs, and developed a conceptual framework based on theory. This chapter will give you the basic knowledge you need to decide exactly how to design a quantitative research project that will fit with your conceptual framework and answer your question.

SECTION 4.1
SPECIFYING YOUR AIMS, QUESTIONS, AND HYPOTHESES

In this section we will introduce you more formally to aims, questions, and hypotheses and will describe what steps you can take to be sure you've done good work in specifying yours. Operationalizing may be one of the most important skills that a social scientist can have. Without clearly operationalized concepts, variables, questions, procedures, and the like, nobody (including you) really knows what you are doing, and nobody can check or replicate your work.

SECTION 4.1.1: DEFINITIONS AND EXAMPLES

If you have clearly specified your conceptual framework (as discussed in Chapter 3), it should be easy to move to a well-specified and operationalized question. In framing or posing an area of interest or question, there are a number of terms you might encounter.

Research aims are very broad statements (not questions) that include the entire intent of the work being done. They are often not so well operationalized as questions or hypotheses. An example of research aim is "to determine the association between respite care worker burnout and service provision."

Notice that we are still at a very general level. In the previous example, the two concepts "burnout" and "service provision" are not tightly operationalized yet.

Research questions are in a question (not statement) format and are often split up into more general (less operationalized) questions and more specific (well-operationalized) subquestions. This will often take the form of a hierarchy of questions. We suggest that you number and/or letter your questions so that the structure of your questions is clear (e.g., general questions 1 and 2; specific questions 1A, 1B, 1C, and 2A, 2B, 2C). Such numbering is helpful because it is easy to follow, allows clear linkage to hypotheses (use the same numbers), and provides a logical structure.

EXAMPLE RESEARCH QUESTION

Do respite care workers reporting high levels of burnout, using Maslach's model, provide the same quantity and quality of services as workers with lower levels of burnout?

This particular question is really two questions: "Is burnout associated with *quantity* of services provided by respite care workers?" and "Is burnout associated with *quality* of services provided by respite care workers?" Maslach's model of burnout includes three separate constructs (emotional exhaustion, EE; depersonalization, DP; and personal accomplishment, PA, which is inversely related to EE and DP). Basically, EE and DP are bad, and PA is good. This three-part model suggests that we need even more detailed questions, looking at each part of the construct of burnout separately. We might formally write our aim and questions as follows:

> **Research Aim:** To determine the association between respite care worker burnout and service provision.
>
>> **Question 1:** Is burnout associated with the *number of service units* provided by respite care workers?
>>
>>> **Question 1A:** Is emotional exhaustion associated with units of service provided?
>>>
>>> **Question 1B:** Is depersonalization associated with units of service provided?
>>>
>>> **Question 1C:** Is personal accomplishment associated with units of service provided?
>>
>> **Question 2:** Is burnout associated with the *quality of service* provided by respite care workers?
>>
>>> **Question 2A:** Is emotional exhaustion associated with quality of services provided?
>>>
>>> **Question 2B:** Is depersonalization associated with quality of services provided?
>>>
>>> **Question 2C:** Is personal accomplishment associated with quality of services provided?

Why go through all this hassle? We can assure you that we are not obsessive people doing this without a practical reason. Here's the thing: When you move to a design, you need to assign variables and develop procedures, and you absolutely must know exactly what questions and subquestions your design is trying to answer. You will save hours and hours (possibly even days or weeks) of time by specifying exactly what your design is supposed to do *before* you try to create a design.

Research hypotheses are statements (never questions) about the relationships you expect to find between constructs. They should be matched to your most specific level of research question. We suggest that you number your hypotheses using the same system you use to number your research questions, as shown in the prior example. This allows the reader (and you!) to easily follow what's going on. Hypotheses must be fully operationalized at the most specific level.

How do you come up with hypotheses? Hypotheses are created based on your question, which is based on theory and prior research. What does your theory say you will find? What has been found before? Look at your conceptual framework and research question to figure out what your hypotheses are. That's why you created them.

We are interested in measuring burnout with the EE, DP, and PA subscales of the Maslach Burnout Inventory (www.cpp.com). We will categorize amount of services rendered in terms of units (hours) of direct services (not including travel time, training, or consultation) as recorded on each worker's log. We will measure quality of service with the Home Service Quality Survey for Home and Community Care Home Support and Respite Services, which is used by the government of Australia and is available online at www.health.gov.au/acc/hacc/download/surveys/genquest.pdf. We will use only subscale 3, which attempts to capture quality of services from the client's perspective, and we will alter the scale slightly, using the term *caregiver* instead of *agency*.

> **Hypotheses relating to question 1 (burnout and units of service provided)**
>
>> **Hypothesis 1A:** Higher EE will be associated with fewer hours of service provided (log).
>>
>> **Hypothesis 1B:** Higher DP will be associated with fewer hours of service provided (log).
>>
>> **Hypothesis 1C:** Lower PA will be associated with fewer hours of service provided (log).
>
> **Hypotheses relating to question 2 (burnout and quality of service)**
>
>> **Hypothesis 2A:** Higher EE will be associated with lower service quality (CCHSRS, scale 3).
>>
>> **Hypothesis 2B:** Higher DP will be associated with lower service quality (CCHSRS, scale 3).
>>
>> **Hypothesis 2C:** Lower PA will be associated with lower service quality (CCHSRS, scale 3).

Notice how the numbers on the hypotheses and questions match. Notice how independent and dependent variables are now tightly operationalized.

Directional and Nondirectional Hypotheses. You will notice that the hypotheses in the example say "more burnout will be associated with *fewer* hours of service." This is called a **directional** ("one-way" or "one-tailed")

hypothesis. If we didn't know what kind of effect burnout would have, we would instead have said "burnout will be associated with differences in hours of service." This is a **nondirectional** ("two-way" or "two-tailed") **hypothesis.** Most researchers use directional hypotheses when they are confident they can predict the direction of the expected relationship, based on theory or prior work. If your research is truly a guess, not guided by as much theory as you would like, you may want to use nondirectional hypotheses.

Should You Always Have a Hypothesis?

You don't always need a hypothesis. Some researchers believe you always need a hypothesis when you are doing science. These people are wrong. Deductive approaches always look at theory and specify a fact that that theory predicts will happen. Thus, all deductive research *must* have at least one hypothesis. On the other hand, inductive research looks at facts and creates theory. Thus, purely inductive research will *never* have any hypotheses. People often try to shoehorn hypotheses into inductive research. This is simply confusion and misunderstanding about how science works. We guess that this confusion arises because many or most people who write textbooks are used to doing mainly deductive work, like true experimental designs.

Section 4.1.2: How to Create Good Aims, Questions, and Hypotheses

Aims are intended to be general, so they need not be highly operationalized. On the other hand, your aims should be simple, should make sense, and should reflect theory and prior research. Many studies have only a single aim, but others may have several. If you are exploring, describing, or testing what are clearly separate ideas, then you should have clearly separate aims.

Questions are extremely difficult to create, or at least good ones are. Every good researcher we have ever met normally goes through several revisions in crafting his or her questions. At a minimum, a good question:

- Must be clearly and simply stated
- Should be clearly related to theory
- Should be relevant to the field
- Should build upon prior work
- Must include well-operationalized constructs
- Should state the constructs in correct sequence (cause before effect)
- Must be something you can practically, empirically, and ethically answer

- Should be broken down into subquestions if it includes multiple dimensions
- Must say which relationships between constructs you are interested in
- Should refer to the population being tested
- Should specify the time frame involved (if appropriate)

Examples of poor questions include:

- Do word processors enhance literary specificity? (This is not clear.)
- Do proportions of populations that are incarcerated vary as a function of the individual's membership in major racial groups? (This is not simply stated; a better wording might be, "Do different races have different rates of incarceration?")
- What is the nature of depression? (The question does not say what we want to find out about depression.)
- Does true love make people happy? (The question does not include operationalized constructs.)
- Is the death penalty a fair punishment? ("Fairness" is not empirically testable.)
- Are arthritis symptoms reduced by exercise? (The cause is given after the effect; this should be, "Does exercise reduce arthritis symptoms?")
- Will people randomly assigned to a smoking group have higher rates of lung cancer than people randomly assigned to a nonsmoking group? (Such an experiment is not ethical.)

Hypotheses flow logically from questions and are more highly operationalized restatements of questions in the form of statements, which you will test. If you cannot easily write your hypotheses, then your questions are almost certainly not clear enough or are poorly operationalized. In this case, go back and redo the questions. A good hypothesis must meet the same criteria as a good question. In addition, it absolutely must be operationalized at a very specific level. It must clearly state the relationship between constructs, which is to be tested.

Some examples of poor and improved hypotheses are as follows:

- *Poor:* Depression affects pregnancy in girls. *Improved:* Higher levels of depression (as measured by the Beck Depression Inventory) will, over a 6-month period, increase the likelihood that 16-year-old middle-class girls in our sample will become pregnant.
- *Poor:* Men play video games more. *Improved:* After controlling for age, job type, and educa-

tional level, college freshman males will report more time spent per week playing video games than will college freshman females.

- *Poor:* Gun laws work. *Improved:* In the state of New Colobama, those 35 counties establishing handgun permit requirements in 1999 will have reductions in yearly rates of handgun crime (1998 versus 2001) when compared to the 69 counties that did not establish handgun control laws.

In the poor version of the last example, we apparently have two constructs, one stated, but unclear ("gun laws" could mean any of a range of laws). The other construct, that the laws "work," might mean almost anything (handgun crime?). We also probably have a directional assertion. To fix this awful hypothesis, we have chosen to do a large number of things:

- We narrowed "gun laws" to "handgun laws" because the vast majority of crimes are not committed with rifles or shotguns; therefore, handgun laws should theoretically make more difference.

- We put in a time frame, so we established clearly that we would be using a longitudinal design, and we knew what period of time to cover.

- We specified our second construct in a measurable way (rates of handgun crime).

- We specified a unit of analysis, the county.

- We specified a comparison group: counties without handgun control laws.

There are endlessly different ways you could improve this hypothesis; for example, you might want to break out different types of handgun crime into separate hypotheses, or you might want to include control variables to account for other factors. The remainder of the chapter will discuss many of these issues, such as choosing a time frame, specifying the population you will study, deciding on one group versus two or many groups, and so on.

SECTION 4.2

SEVEN KEY DIMENSIONS OF RESEARCH DESIGN

This section overviews seven key dimensions of research design, including ethical issues associated with these dimensions. We will look at seven dimensions of research (purpose, type of control, subjects, groups, investigator manipulation, time frame, and data type). These dimensions are combined in two broad types of design (experimental and nonexperimental) and five subtypes (true experimental, quasi-experimental, correlational, descriptive, and exploratory). First we

illustrate how the seven dimensions are related to different types of designs (see Table 4.1).

The first row in Table 4.1, "When do I use this approach?", is in many ways the most important. You need to be able to identify constructs before you can describe them, you should to be able to describe constructs before you can look for relationships between them, and you should use experimental designs if you are looking for causal relationships. You can therefore easily identify the type of design you need to use by assessing your knowledge of the constructs under study:

- If you don't know what the important constructs are, you should do an **exploratory design** and find out. This is a necessary step before theory can be built. You will be doing inductive work. It is critically important that you understand how to go about asking questions with the given population of interest (Harkness, Van Dijver, & Mohler, 2002; Pan, 2003).

- If you can identify constructs, but wish to understand them better in terms of their nature, distribution, relationship to other constructs, or other properties, you should use a **descriptive design.** Developing a greater understanding of constructs and their interrelatedness is a key step toward developing theory. Again, the focus is on induction.

- If you want to test relationships between constructs as suggested by theory, you should do a **correlational design,** unless the relationships you want to test are **causal,** in which case you want to use a **quasi-** or **true experimental design.** These approaches are deductive.

SECTION 4.2.1: PURPOSE

Experimental Designs Test for Causal Relationships. Sometimes these designs are called "randomized clinical trials" or RCTs. These causal relationships are based in theory. Because we are testing to see if the causal predictions made by a theory are reflected in fact, we are clearly doing **deductive research.** Experimental designs always start with a theory about what causes what (*example:* I think aspirin causes headaches to go away). It then moves to a design that will generate facts that will test the theory (Get 50 people with headaches; give half aspirin and half sugar pills. Wait 30 minutes, then ask everyone if he or she still has a headache). Finally, it evaluates the degree to which the facts support or refute the theory (if more people who got the aspirin say their headaches went away, then we say that we have evidence that aspirin makes headaches go away). Experimental designs test hypotheses derived from

TABLE 4.1. **Key Characteristics of Research Designs.**				
NONEXPERIMENTAL DESIGNS			**EXPERIMENTAL DESIGNS**	
Exploratory	Descriptive	Correlational	Quasi-Experimental	True Experimental
Choosing a Design: When Do I Use This Approach?				
When you cannot **identify constructs or relationships** to be studied	When you can identify constructs but cannot **describe constructs or relationships between them** well	When you can describe constructs, and wish to **test if relationships suggested by theory occur**	When you can describe constructs, and wish to **test cause and effect** relationships as predicted by theory between them.	
Dimension 1: Purpose of Research and Role of Theory				
Discover constructs and relationships, build theory. (What things exist? How do things relate to each other?)	**Describe** constructs and relationships. (When, where, how often? What is it associated with or related to?)	**Test associations** between constructs as suggested by theory. (Is X associated with Y as the theory predicts?)	**Test causal relationships** between constructs as predicted by theory. (Does X cause Y as the theory says it will?)	
These designs do not test theory, and are mainly inductive (theory-building) methods.		These designs do test theory and are therefore deductive methods.		
Dimension 2: Causality and Control—How Are They Accounted For?				
Control is normally a less important issue.		Statistical controls are usually used.	Matching or statistical	Random assignment
Dimension 3: Subjects and Sampling				
Fewer subjects sometimes allow more detailed work.	Varies greatly; many subjects are often used.	Many subjects provide statistical power. Some quasi-experimental case study designs use single subjects in time-series designs (Ch. 8).		
Dimension 4: Assignment of Subjects to Different Groups or Conditions				
Subjects are not assigned to different groups or conditions.			Multiple groups or conditions are usual.	Multiple groups are always used.
Dimension 5: Investigator Manipulation				
Investigator manipulation is not common in these designs.			Present, except in naturalistic experiments	Always present
Dimension 6: Time Frame				
May be cross-sectional (point-in-time) or longitudinal (data collected over time).				Must administer experimental and control conditions; may follow up.
Dimension 7: Data Type				
All types of data frequently used.		More objective measures (structured observations, instruments, archival records) most common.		Objective measures most common.

theory. All good experimental designs start with a hypothesis that is explicitly based on a theory. All experimental designs have hypotheses.

This is the only type of design that can be used to test causality. On the other hand, sometimes findings from these studies are difficult to translate to the field. Why? Well, the conditions under which behaviors occur and interventions are delivered are inherently not well-controlled environments. So, one cannot assume that because an idea has been tested in a controlled study the constructs will operate in similar ways across persons and settings.

Correlational Designs Test to See if Expected Relationships between Constructs Occur.

Correlational designs test for relationships between constructs, not causation. Correlational designs must have hypotheses that take the form of "*X* will be associated with *Y*" (nondirectional) or "increases in *X* will be associated with (de/in)creases in *Y*" (directional). As a simple example, you may have a theory that says that people who are burned out are more likely to quit. You can measure how burned-out people are and then see if the more burned-out ones are more likely to leave over the next year. The hypothesized relationships that you are testing for must be grounded in theory. This means that you don't just go off and look for any relationship; you have a clearly explained theoretical reason to look for the relationship you are seeking. If you just go out and see what is out there, that is not correlational; that's either descriptive or exploratory. All correlational designs have hypotheses.

Descriptive Studies Seek to Better Understand Constructs and the Relationships between Them.

A large number of studies have description as their goal. Description (obviously) involves describing the characteristics of people, things, or events within a certain category (e.g., describing the age, gender, and income characteristics of those with anorexia nervosa). Often, however, descriptive studies are intended to help us learn more about the relationships between variables (e.g., "Are there relationships between age of onset of anorexia nervosa and the person's demographic characteristics?"). The difference between descriptive and correlational studies is that the main goal of a correlational study is to test theoretically derived relationships, while descriptive studies seek to describe new relationships as they are found.

Descriptive Studies Are Never "Theoryless."

Theory is used to frame descriptive studies. Often, this theory is at the level of a paradigm or approach. Theory guides what population you are looking at, what characteristics you are describing, and how you go about your analysis. For example, if you are looking at children, you may use ideas about how kids grow up (developmental approach) or ideas about the child's home context (family systems theory) to decide exactly which things you should look at and how. Theory used in descriptive studies is typically general (paradigmatic or grand theory levels) compared to theories tested in experimental or correlational studies, which generally test specific theoretical models. Purely descriptive studies lack hypotheses.

Exploratory Designs Are Meant to Discover Constructs and Sometimes to Gain Preliminary Data about Relationships

between Constructs. They are used to gather data for inductive theory construction. These studies are done when little is known about an area or when an area is being viewed using a new method or perspective. For example, there may be no prior work about how national traumas like the terrorist attacks of September 11 affect people with preexisting anxiety disorders.

On the other hand, exploratory work sometimes involves something that has been heavily studied but takes a new slant. For example, one might look at the successes and failures of foster care from the perspective of the very young child. The constructs of interest from a child's point of view are probably totally different from those that have been studied in the literature. While many exploratory studies are qualitative, exploratory studies can be purely **quantitative.** For example, you may want to know about what makes for a successful parole experience, and you may root around in a computer database using purely statistical methods to try to figure out what factors seem to show up in people who complete their parole successfully. You would then use this data (inductively) to build theory. Exploratory research, like descriptive research, can include focus on relationships between constructs as well as on the constructs themselves. The main difference between an exploratory and a descriptive design is that the descriptive design starts with an already defined set of constructs to be studied, while exploratory designs allow constructs to develop as the research progresses. Theory is used much the same way as it is used in descriptive studies. You must know what ideas other people have about the things you are studying, and you must use (or at least acknowledge) these ideas as you decide how to frame your exploration. Exploratory designs lack hypotheses.

Ethical Considerations.

It is important not to overreach. Surely experimental designs are always better, right? We should jump to them as fast as possible, right? Wrong. When you choose a correlational or experimental design, you are asserting that reasonable theory exists that predicts associations you can test. You are basically saying you know what is going on, and you just want to test your well-considered ideas.

It is often tempting to slam together experiments in cases where the theory is weak and exploratory or descriptive designs may be more useful. Cynical people might say that this is, in fact, what is often done. There may also be ethical constraints related to the ability to randomly assign subjects. For example, it is difficult to imagine randomly assigning an abused child to "intervention" or "no intervention." Further, there are some instances, such as international social development research, where it is impossible to assign a country to a given political affiliation or economic status.

Testing a theory (deduction) before it is well developed (induction) can be a waste of time and can yield confusing results. Premature movement to experimental research has a number of risks:

1. Your design may ignore important variables, causing your test to be badly designed and your results to be confusing or even misleading.

2. You are very likely to have limited power (ability to find what you are looking for) because you don't really know what you are looking at, looking for, or how to measure it. This can cause false negatives.

3. Interpretations of your findings are likely to be wrong and may steer future research in unhelpful directions.

4. Resources are drawn away from a more correct research path, with theory testing being based on a thorough understanding of the nature of the things being studied.

Risks of Basing a Design Solely on Explanatory Power or Desire for Statistical Rigor Can Be Especially Problematic when Studying Racial Minorities or Other Diverse Subpopulations (Van de Vijver & Leung, 1997). Is there enough descriptive or exploratory data available for this population for you to feel comfortable in applying and testing your theory? Do you know enough about the community so that your research can apply the theory correctly? What key things might you be missing? Maybe you better get "on the ground" and make darn sure you know what's going on before you start testing theories. In simple language, don't go out and start studying people you know nothing about (Papadopoulos & Lee, 2002). Find out about who they are and what they think of your ideas *before* you start testing your pet theories on them.

SECTION 4.2.2: CAUSALITY AND CONTROL

CAUSALITY

If the purpose of the study is to assess causality, there are three things you must have: (1) association, (2) time order, and (3) lack of spurious causality. This is a critical principle of science, and your instructor is likely to test you on it. You had best remember it.

Association and time order are fairly simple ideas, but spurious causality is more difficult. Association merely means that the two things you are trying to link must be related. For example, if you believe that mosquito eradication programs reduce malaria, then areas with these programs should have less malaria than similar areas without such programs. The second requirement, time order, is also fairly obvious, in that the cause must happen before the effect. If mosquito prevention

programs are effective, then the malaria rates should drop *after* the program goes into effect, not before. The third issue has to do with **spurious causality** and control. Because they are so intertwined, we will discuss them together. Let's get into this by using three simple examples and one simple definition:

> **Example 1:** Homicide rates go up on the same days that ice cream sales go up. (*Note:* We don't know if this is really true, but it is a fun example).

> **Example 2:** African Americans are reported for child maltreatment more often than Whites in some states.

> **Example 3:** Among people randomly given either sugar pills or aspirin, those given aspirin report fewer headaches 30 minutes later.

Definition. Spurious causality occurs when the relationship between two factors (*A* and *B*) is, in reality, caused by a third factor (*X*) (see Figure 4.1).

In the first (hypothetical) example, we have a case that looks fishy right off the bat. We suppose that some people might believe that all that sugar in ice cream makes people go crazy, and then they go out and kill people. Most people, however, would probably believe that something else is going on. Perhaps it is possible that murder rates and ice cream sales are both driven by temperature. In this case, the relationship between ice cream sales and murder is a spurious relationship caused by the fact that temperature influences both. Because there is not a real causal link between eating ice cream and murder, we say it is a case of spurious causality (Figure 4.2).

Our next example is a bit more subtle. It is well known that African Americans have higher rates of child abuse reports than Whites. Why? Is there a bias in

---

FIGURE 4.1. Spurious Causality: The Dotted Line Indicates the Spurious (Wrong) Relationship.

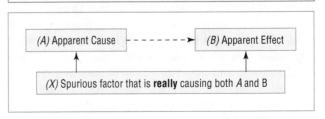

FIGURE 4.2. Ice Cream Sales and Homicide (Hypothetical).

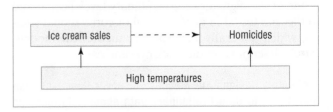

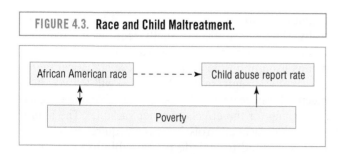

FIGURE 4.3. **Race and Child Maltreatment.**

reporting? Are there cultural differences? Our research suggests this maybe also largely a case of spurious causality (Drake, Jonson-Reid, Way, & Chung, 2003). There is a third factor driving the apparent overreporting of Black children, and this is that they tend to live in poorer areas. Once the variation in maltreatment rates based on poverty is statistically removed (we'll show you how to do that later), Blacks and Whites look pretty similar. Notice the bidirectional arrow between Black race and poverty in Figure 4.3. It would be silly to say that one causes the other, so a directional arrow is out. But they are statistically associated, so we draw the relationship as a bidirectional association, not as a causal pathway. On the other hand, we have good theory to suggest that poverty increases rates of reports (stress, resources, and so on), so we draw that directionally.

In our third example, the intervention (aspirin versus placebo) is given randomly. Assuming that the sample is correctly selected and the design is well implemented, this design should control for the problem of spurious causality. In other words, one can conclude that *A* does cause *B* in that particular study (Figure 4.4).

Now that we have a more solid grasp of the concept of spurious causality, we will move to ways in which researchers try to limit it. This is the concept of **control.**

CONTROL

Arthur Conan Doyle put it best when he had Sherlock Holmes say, "Eliminate all other factors, and the one which remains must be the truth" (*The Sign of the Four*). Control is nothing more than that. There are three main kinds of control used in research designs.

Control in Experimental Designs. Experimental designs are designs with groups that experience different conditions. If you find that the groups turn out differently, then you say that the thing done to the "experimental" or "treatment" group made a difference. Control in true experimental designs is done with random assignment.

FIGURE 4.4. **Aspirin and Headaches.**

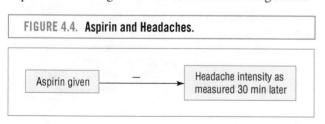

Random assignment to groups is the best method of control, but it is not without difficulty. In this method, you select your sample, then you randomly assign them to two or more groups, one of which is the control group. The word *random* means that each person has an equal chance of being placed in any group. Randomization is often done with random number lists (see Appendix A) or computer programs, although there is no theoretical reason why you couldn't just flip a coin. Randomly assigning subjects to treatment and control groups is the only sure way to control for spurious causality. Why? Given a large enough sample, spurious factors associated with individuals (for example, intelligence, attitude, whatever) will be randomly (evenly) distributed between experimental and control groups. If differences are equally divided between experimental and control groups, then any effects you find in the experimental group cannot be due to these differences. This will be true even for differences that you don't even know about. Random assignment will take care of *all* differences and is the only way to control for those "invisible" differences.

If your design has two or more randomly assigned groups, one of which is a control group (experimental condition not present), then we call your design a "true experimental design." This type of design provides the best control and is therefore the best design for eliminating the risk of spurious causality.

Is random assignment (e.g., true experimental design) the only way to eliminate spurious causality? Yes and no: In a single study, it is the only way. For the methodological purist, it may also be the only way. But if you look at entire bodies of research, it is often possible to build a completely convincing case for causality without true experimental designs, at least at the practical level.

The most obvious example may well be smoking and lung cancer in humans. Every reasonable person accepts that smoking causes lung cancer, but no true experimental design on smoking and lung cancer in humans has ever been done. It is obviously totally unethical to randomly assign people to smoking (experimental) and nonsmoking (control) conditions and check back in 50 years to see who has died of lung cancer. To our knowledge, this has never been done. Despite this, every person we know believes that science has conclusively proven that smoking causes lung cancer. Why? Because there is such an overwhelming flood of different kinds of research that all point to such a causal link. Correlational and quasi-experimental designs have shown over and over again that smokers get lung cancer more than nonsmokers. True experimental designs on animals have shown that a causal link does exist in animals. We have theoretical models explaining how smoking causes lung cancer. These models fit the data well. The bottom line is that while random assignment is the best way to eliminate spurious causality, and the only ironclad way, there are many areas in which the totality of evidence has "proven" causality, at least for practical purposes, through putting together so many strong studies using other approaches that the causal conclusion is inescapable, at least for practical purposes. If you want more examples, think about astronomy. We have never done an experiment on a star, yet we are confident that we understand certain causal relationships pertaining to them.

Control by **matching** is often used in quasi-experimental designs. As you recall, experimental designs lacking random assignment are called *quasi-experimental*. By matching subjects between groups on all the factors that you think are important (age, gender, test scores, whichever factors are most appropriate based on theory and prior research), you attempt to lessen the risk that the differences in groups are due to factors other than the experimental condition. Of course, you may fail to match on some important factor you don't yet know is important (or even exists), so this method is regarded as weaker than a true experimental design. It is important to remember that the group that does not receive the treatment condition is called the **control group** only in a true experimental design. In quasi-experimental designs, we call that group the **comparison group,** because we are not certain that we are really controlling for all important factors.

Matching can also be accomplished by using propensity score methods. For example, let's say you wish to examine the outcome of dropping out of school according to whether or not a student participated in a dropout prevention program. You have data on all the students, but there was no random assignment. It would simply be too difficult, however, to attempt to match students on enough characteristics to make the program and nonprogram groups similar. You can, however, potentially predict who entered the program based on a variety of student characteristics using a statistical model of program entry. Simply put, a propensity score is the predicted probability that someone gets the treatment or has the condition of interest (Foster, 2003). The resulting score is then translated into a type of weighting scheme (and there are a variety of approaches) so that you have a group of program and nonprogram cases that have as close to equal scores as possible (Dehejia & Whaba, 2002). These methods are increasingly being used to handle studies in which data lacked initial random assignment or in which the researchers may wish to examine dose-response effects for subjects who completed more or less of the treatment (Foster, 2003).

Control in quasi-experimental or nonexperimental designs cannot be perfectly achieved, but you can help matters by using statistical control. Recall from Chapter 3 that we introduced the idea of independent variables,

dependent variables, and control variables. Use of control variables in statistics usually requires multivariate statistical techniques. The word *multivariate* simply means using multiple variables. These statistical methods (multiple regression and the like) will tell you how much difference each independent variable makes while controlling for the effects of other variables. The ability to use statistical controls, however, requires two things. First, you need to include the variable in your study. Second, you need a big enough sample. The first requirement is straightforward. If a variable is not in your data set, there is no way to magically include that variable in analysis. The second requirement has to do with the need for statistical techniques for sufficient numbers to run analyses (this issue will be covered in more detail in Chapters 13 and 14). The more factors you control for, the more subjects you need.

Ethical Concerns Associated with Control. True experimental designs can present researchers with a series of ethical issues. There are large numbers of questions that cannot be answered ethically using true experimental designs. Random assignment to conditions is not ethical when either the experimental or control condition is harmful. For example, there are vast numbers of causal questions we would like answered about the effects of a range of harmful things (domestic violence, criminal victimization, parental loss, and the like), but we obviously cannot simply randomly assign individuals to be beaten, to be criminally victimized, or to eat unhealthy diets. In these cases, membership in

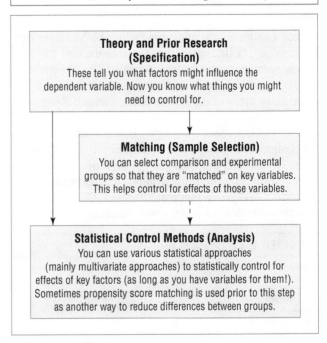

FIGURE 4.5. **Theory, Matching, and Statistical Control in Quasi-Experimental Designs: How They Fit.**

Theory and Prior Research (Specification)
These tell you what factors might influence the dependent variable. Now you know what things you might need to control for.

Matching (Sample Selection)
You can select comparison and experimental groups so that they are "matched" on key variables. This helps control for effects of those variables.

Statistical Control Methods (Analysis)
You can use various statistical approaches (mainly multivariate approaches) to statistically control for effects of key factors (as long as you have variables for them!). Sometimes propensity score matching is used prior to this step as another way to reduce differences between groups.

the experimental condition would be harmful. We apologize if this appears too obvious even to mention, but if you want to understand the effects of a harmful condition, then you can't use a true experimental design to study your question.

There are other conditions where assignment to a control condition may be harmful. For example, if you have a new cancer drug, you would never consider comparing your experimental group to a "no-treatment" group. Instead, you would use a "treatment as usual" group for your control group. Another way out of this problem is to use waiting lists. If an agency can handle only 100 people at a time and gets 200 clients requesting services, they may randomly select 100 and provide services now, while using the 100 waiting people as a control group. This is ethical only in nonemergency situations (for example, it could never be used with actively suicidal clients) and when no other treatment options are available. The most typical use of such a design is when a new intervention is being tested, and a grant provided to test the intervention allows a fixed number of people to be treated. The reasoning is that in the absence of the study, no treatment at all would occur, and the control subjects are benefiting from the study because they get treatment after the initial waiting period.

Ethics and Statistical Control. Statistical control avoids the ethical dilemma associated with random assignment and potential harm. Statistical controls also allow you to examine the control variables in analyses. It is important, however, for the researcher to keep in mind that statistical control is not equivalent to a true experimental design. Researchers are ethically required to be clear about this when disseminating findings. This is particularly true when communicating to agency or policy audiences who may not be familiar with the limits of statistical control. This brings us to our next issue, which involves how we discuss causality in designs other than true experimental designs.

> **Warning!** Never use the word *cause* except in reference to findings from true experimental designs. Only these designs can control for spurious causality. If you do not have a true experimental design, then do not say "*X* caused *Y*." Instead, say "*X* was associated with *Y*." If *X* comes before Y in time, you can also say "*X* predicts Y." There is a fair amount of subtle hypocrisy here, because social scientists routinely use quasi-experimental or correlational designs to test causal theories. They just don't officially admit it. They are very careful to say they are looking for associations, but everyone knows they are really trying to find evidence for a causal relationship. Sometimes even scientists use *cause* incorrectly.

Some examples you undoubtedly encounter commonly are the claims that certain foods "cause" certain medical problems. How do scientists find out what foods cause what problems? Do they randomly assign people to "junk food" and "healthy food" conditions, wait 30 years, and check their health? Of course not. What they do is to ask people what they eat (or have them keep lists) and then check their medical condition. It would be more correct to say "high sugar intake is associated with risk for *X*" than to say "high sugar intake causes *X*." Again, this is because designs of this type cannot rule out spurious causality. Even if you're pretty darn sure of your causal connection, stick with the more conservative language. Scientists use conservative language in reporting findings, and your peers or those evaluating your work may get upset with you if you don't.

SECTION 4.2.3: SUBJECTS AND SAMPLING

Determining who your subjects should be and sampling them properly is one of the trickier parts of the research process. From an empirical standpoint, it is critical because correct selection of subjects from the population is the main factor that provides your study with external validity (generalizability). From an ethical standpoint, sampling is important in evaluating human subjects' protection issues and in understanding how we can fairly make claims about the results of our work. We will discuss issues of subject selection now but will discuss subject assignment to groups later, in the section on groups. Subject selection (from the population) and assignment (to experimental and control/comparison groups) are often confused but are totally different.

CLARIFICATION: SUBJECT SELECTION AND SUBJECT ASSIGNMENT

Selecting Subjects. Who do you pick from the population to be in your study? Good subject selection requires you to pick people who are like the people you want to generalize (apply) your findings to. Good subject selection supports external validity (generalizability).

Assigning Subjects. Once you have your subjects, how do you divide them into ("assign them to") experimental and control conditions in experimental designs? Making sure that subjects are "fairly" distributed into similar groups helps you make sure that the differences between experimental and control/comparison are due to the conditions, not the subjects. Proper subject assignment to conditions supports internal validity.

UNITS OF ANALYSIS

The concept of the unit of analysis has already been discussed in Chapter 3, and we stated that, in general, the unit of analysis is the level at which you sample, score,

TABLE 4.2. Example of Database at the Individual Level Unit of Analysis (Total sample size or $N = 12$).					
KID ID #	NAME	READER TEAM	KIDDIEREADER CURRICULUM?	BOOKS READ	GENDER
1	Bobby	1	Y	3	M
2	Susie	1	Y	4	F
3	Lillian	1	Y	2	F
4	Phillip	2	Y	5	M
5	Margaret	2	Y	3	F
6	Jason	2	Y	4	M
7	Jessica	3	N	1	F
8	Norma	3	N	3	F
9	Sally	3	N	2	F
10	Victor	4	N	1	M
11	Brad	4	N	3	M
12	Boris	4	N	1	M

and analyze. This is sometimes very simple: If you survey 50 people, then the person is obviously the unit of analysis. But what if you want to look at something else, such as classroom performance? You might score each child but also compute classroom means. Which, then, is the unit of analysis, the child or the classroom? Well, it could be either, depending on how you use the data. Often, the easiest way to answer this is to ask yourself the question, "What level will constitute one record in my final database?" or "How many records will be used in the statistics in my study?" Let's do a quick *(fictional)* example. You have four first-grade reading teams of three students each. You decide to use the new "KiddieReader" curriculum. If you want to analyze the data at the child-level unit of analysis, you will have a sample of 12 (four teams of three). Your data might look like Table 4.2.

This is fine. This could be your final data set. On the other hand, you might choose to use the previous data (individual-level unit of analysis) to create a data set at the team-level unit of analysis. The final data from that dataset might look like Table 4.3, with an N of 4.

Neither one is "better"; the choice just depends on what your question is, what is most practical to do, and what the demands of your statistics are (see Chapters 13 and 14). For example, if you already have classroom-level data available on computer, you may want to use that, rather than retesting children individually. As a general rule, however, it is often good to stay at finer levels of analysis (such as individuals) for reasons of statistical power and loss of information that occurs when data are combined.

SUBJECTS

Subjects are the people, organizations, or other entities you study. As with units of analysis, this is usually

TABLE 4.3. Example of Database at the Team-Level Unit of Analysis (Total sample size or $N = 4$).			
TEAM ID #	KIDDIEREADER CURRICULUM?	BOOKS READ	PERCENT MALE
1	Y	9	33
2	Y	12	67
3	N	6	0
4	N	5	100

simple. If your study compares 200 White children to 200 Hispanic children, then you have 400 subjects. We usually use the uppercase letter N to refer to *all* the subjects in the study. We use the lowercase letter n to refer to subgroups (smaller groups within the study, such as all the Whites or all the males in the study). In our example we have White children ($n = 200$) and Hispanic children ($n = 200$), which together give us a study $N = 400$.

POPULATIONS, SAMPLING FRAMES, AND SAMPLES

Populations are sometimes described as being "universal" (everyone), "populations of interest" (the people you are interested in), or "study populations" (the people you are studying). Your sample will be drawn very carefully so that it will match your population of interest as precisely as possible. The better it matches or the more "representative" your study sample is of the population of interest, the more likely it will be that you can say your study results are applicable to the population of interest. The process of selecting this representative group is the art of

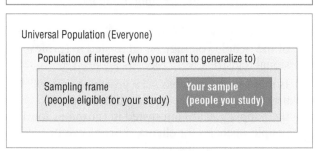

FIGURE 4.6. **Common Sampling Terms.**

Universal Population (Everyone)

Population of interest (who you want to generalize to)

Sampling frame
(people eligible for your study)

Your sample
(people you study)

"sampling." You can overview the relationships between populations and samples in Figure 4.6. We like the following definitions:

■ The **universal population** is everyone.

■ The **population of interest** is those people you are interested in and to whom you want to be able to apply your findings. This can be the same as the universal population (e.g., the census) or can be a very small subset (such as Korean immigrant children with a rare disorder).

■ A **sampling frame** consists of everyone who is eligible to be selected into your sample. These people all must have a fair chance to actually become subjects in your study.

■ Your **sample** is who you actually get. These are the people who are selected from the sampling frame, either randomly or by a particular strategy, such as random sampling, oversampling, or matching. Sometimes your sampling frame will be small enough that the sample and the sampling frame are the same.

Let's look at an example. The United States Census is unusual in that the universal population, the population of interest, and the sampling frame are the same. It is designed to be not only representative but an "actual enumeration" of the population of the United States. Even for the Census, though, the sample will fail to include some people who were just impossible to track down. Attempts are often made to improve known problems with this, such as seeking out homeless persons for survey inclusion.

A more typical example might be a test of a drug meant to reduce birth defects. The population of interest would be pregnant women; the sampling frame might be all women making their first prenatal appointments in a given hospital; and the sample might be a randomly selected subset of these. Here the population of all pregnant women is not the same as the sampling frame because the study is being done at one hospital. A researcher who hopes to discuss implications for the population of interest will have to show why the parti-

cular hospital he or she chose will result in a sample that is fairly representative of the population of interest (all pregnant women). A better approach would have been to use many hospitals, either randomly selected or carefully chosen to be reflective of the nation in general.

ETHICS OF SAMPLING

It is a good idea to introduce ethical issues related to sampling before we discuss ideal processes. We suggest two general areas for consideration. Ethically, you do not want to say something about your results being applicable to a population unless that population is represented in your study. Second, you must consider how vulnerable the population is and how intrusive the study will be. For example, children are a vulnerable population. By reason of their age, they are deemed unable to consent to participate in research and are in need of the oversight and protection of their caregiver. This does not mean you cannot have children as your population of interest, but it does mean that special care and procedures will be needed to access a sampling frame.

The less intrusive the research is, the less problematic the vulnerability of the sample. For example, public access data sets can often provide an option. If there is such a data set available to you (these will have been stripped of identifying information), then you have no need to actually contact a vulnerable population. Obviously, these general priciples apply to all vulnerable populations. You may recall that this was one of the issues that came up in the Tuskegee study (Chapter 2), as the subjects were all members of a population that lacked the information and resources to clearly understand the nature of the research being performed and their role in it.

REPRESENTATIVENESS

It is critical that your sample mirror or "represent" your population of interest as closely as possible. Why? Suppose you want to influence policy regarding access to mental health care. Nationally, the population of interest includes mental health patients in hospitals, persons with mental disorders cared for by family members, persons in private therapy, and persons with mental health needs that go unserved due to lack of funds or access. Ideally, policy regarding access should increase access to services for those who cannot currently obtain services. If you go to hospitals and clinics and sample only from the served population, you will not be able to accurately inform policy makers about the needs of the unserved or underserved groups.

To get a representative sample, you must do several things: (1) clearly define your population of interest, (2) set up a sampling frame that is representative of your population of interest, and (3) get a sample that is representative of your sampling frame.

IDENTIFYING AND OPERATIONALIZING YOUR POPULATION OF INTEREST

The first step is figuring out who your population of interest is and stating who they are in a manner that is highly operationalized (really clear and specific). Students often forget this: You can specify any population you want, but you have to be able to give a good reason why you chose as you did. This reason is usually based on theory, as modified by practical or ethical concerns. You will need to be very clear about the reasons you pick the population you do, because you will have to make this very clear when you write up the study. Good reasons to choose a given population of interest include practicality, theoretical relevance, lack of prior work, or any other compelling reason you can justify.

EXAMPLES OF OPERATIONALIZING A POPULATION OF INTEREST

You might be interested in specific types of gender biases held by mental health therapists. Fine, but "mental health therapists" is not an operationalized group. You may work on it a while and define mental health therapists as "social workers, educational counselors, psychologists, or psychiatrists who are employed full-time in a therapeutic role and hold at least a master's degree in their field." Your reasons for this particular form of operationalization are as follows:

- To cover all four major educational backgrounds (you're not too concerned about other disciplines, because they are relatively few in number, and nobody will get too angry if you ignore them)
- To select only those who are currently practicing full time (you want to look only at people who are doing this as their main work now, not people doing it "on the side")
- To select only those who are working in a psychotherapeutic role. Hmmm . . . This is difficult. There are so many definitions of psychotherapy. This will need to be fleshed out later. Maybe you should select only people who spend at least 10 hours a week in contact with clients around mental health or interpersonal counseling issues? This still sounds a bit fuzzy.
- To select only those people who have levels of education (master's plus) that meet most people's idea of the absolute minimum necessary for a psychotherapist.

Identifying Your Sampling Frame. The next step is deciding how you can identify a set of people who are representative of your population of interest and eligible to be in your study (your sampling frame). This is quite an art

and can be done in many ways. Questions to ask yourself when considering your sampling frame include:

- Is there a good and comprehensive list somewhere of the people you may be interested in (professional registries, birth records, agency records)?
- Is there somewhere you can go where you will meet a reasonably representative sample of the people you are interested in (hospitals for ill people, agencies for clients, sporting events for people who watch sports live)?
- Is there a ready-made sampling frame that is adequately representative? Does an agency need an analysis done of its clients? Is some friendly professor willing to have you piggyback on his or her carefully chosen sample? Is there a preexisting public access data set from another study with the right sample and the right variables?
- What is the level of vulnerability of the population of interest? If you are interested in criminality and the justice system, then a prison might be an obvious location to get a sample. Yet prisoners are a vulnerable population because they may feel compelled to consent or risk being turned down for parole. If your population of interest is considered vulnerable (due to age, cognitive or mental health disability, involuntary nature of confinement, or high degree of trauma), then you will need to develop special processes for protection of their rights.

How you create your sample frame will depend substantially on how you define your population of interest. We might think about the following kinds of populations of interest.

Sampling from the Universal Population. If your population of interest is everyone, which is common in basic research, then you've got trouble. You may want to use a form of random selection (not random assignment as we discussed in the section on control). This means that everyone in the population theoretically has the same chance of being in the sample. Unfortunately, the reality is that there is no way to make absolutely sure your sample is truly representative of the general population, but there are ways to try to get close.

For example, some researchers use random-digit dialing to help them get a random sample of people. Of course, some people have no phones and are excluded from the sample frame. People in lower socioeconomic ranges are probably more likely to not have phones, meaning that your sample may be "biased" toward higher income ranges. This will ultimately limit the generalizability of your results. Second, some people have multiple phones and are thus at higher likelihood of being called. Third, the time of day matters. During daytime hours, persons who are homemakers, retirees, unemployed, and the like are more likely to be contacted. Finally, calling someone is somewhat intrusive and reaching people by phone does not guarantee they will participate. Voluntary participation is a hallmark of ethical research.

There are many other ways to try to get a representative sample of the general population. For example, door-to-door canvassing of random addresses may be used.

Sampling from Diagnostic or Other Specific Groups.

If your population of interest is people with a certain characteristic (say, depression), then you have several choices. You can do a universal population sampling procedure and keep only those with depression. This is rarely done because you will have to go through many, many people to get enough people with depression. A more common approach is to pick somewhere depressive people might go (such as self-help groups or clinics) and select from that sampling frame. This is obviously a compromise, and you will be unable to generalize findings to depressed people who don't go to those places.

Sampling from Agencies or Facilities.

Facilities, such as schools, hospitals, agencies, or similar, provide a ready-made group of people. The strength of this approach is that many times this is precisely the population you are interested in. For example, if you want to improve public school education with a new program, then you want to sample public school students. The fact that private school or home-schooled children are not included is an advantage, because you are trying to generalize to the public school population only. Of course, you will want to make sure that the schools you sample are representative of schools in general, or schools in your state, or whatever level you are hoping to generalize to. You will also need to understand the process required by the agency to gain access to the population. Moving to an agency-based sampling strategy has implications for how you describe your population of interest. If you are looking only at people who attend a given type of agency, you may want to redefine your population of interest to reflect that. For example, instead of studying "maltreated children," you may want to specify up front that your research deals specifically with "maltreated children in the child welfare system."

SELECTING THE STUDY SAMPLE

Once your sample frame is operationalized, you will need to actually recruit the sample. If your sample frame happens to be the same size you wish to include in your study, then take them all. Usually, though, the actual size of your sample will be far smaller than your sample frame. You must therefore pick a subset of the sample frame to be your sample. We will now discuss a number of key concepts that are used in selecting the study sample, which will help you understand more about sampling frames and how samples are derived from them.

Using the Entire Sampling Frame.

On occasion a researcher can simply include the entire sample frame. For example, a child abuse and neglect researcher who is interested in simple case characteristics of children reported for abuse and neglect may be able to get data on the entire sample frame easily from a computerized database. In this example, there is no reason to reduce the sample, since the data already exist, and it is just as easy to download 10,000 records as it is to download 100.

Probability (Random) Samples.

Probability sampling involves random chance. This can be done by assigning a random number to everyone in the sampling frame and then picking the 100 (or whatever) highest or lowest numbers. If everyone in the sampling frame has an equal chance of being in the final sample, then we say the sample is a probability sample from that sampling frame. Probability samples provide strong generalizability (external validity) to the population from which they were selected. This is because the sample, being random, is unlikely to be different from the population along any dimension, even dimensions we can't identify clearly or don't know about at all.

Nonprobability Sampling.

Nonprobablity samples provide weaker generalizability than probability samples but are often necessary for practical or other reasons. Some forms of nonprobability sampling are better than others. **Purposive sampling** occurs when you pick your sample for a reason, not through a process of random chance. **Convenience samples** are purposive samples in which the main criterion is practicality or availability. **Snowball sampling** is often used with hard-to-find groups. The researcher locates a small group of persons that fit the sample criteria (perhaps they have a very rare disease) and then asks them to help him or her make contact with others they know with the same characteristics. In this way, the researcher hopes to gain a large enough group to do a study. The metaphor here is that as a snowball rolls down a hill, it picks up snow and grows larger. Convenience and snowball sampling procedures provide poor generalizability.

Combined Sampling Approaches.

Many, perhaps most, sampling approaches combine random and purposive sampling. This is done using procedures such as cluster sampling, described in Table 4.4.

TABLE 4.4. **Examples of Sampling Frames, Sampling Methods, and Generalizability.**

POPULATION OF INTEREST	SAMPLING FRAME	SAMPLING METHOD	GENERALIZABILITY:
VA Hospital patients	San Diego VA Medical Center	400 randomly selected patients (Random selection from one hospital)	**Good:** San Diego VA Medical Center clients **Fair:** Other VA hospital clients, if you can show they are similar to San Diego clients **Poor:** Hospital clients in general, most of whom differ markedly from VA hospital clients
Hospital patients	All hospitals in the United States	(1) 100 randomly selected hospitals (2) 40 random patients from each hospital (Multistage random selection)	**Good:** U.S. hospital patients in general **Poor:** Hospital patients in unique or unusual types of hospitals
African American men experiencing relationship problems	Participants in a self-help program held in an African American middle-class community	All participants are used in the study (Full program sample, equivalent to random selection from that program)	**Good:** Men seeking help in that particular program in that community **Fair:** Men seeking help in similar programs in similar communities **Poor:** Men experiencing relationship problems in general
Students involved with Yorkville State University's curriculum	All students at YSU	All students in the lunchroom who agree to fill out a survey (convenience sample)	**Poor:** This study cannot generate highly generalizable results except to students who both use the lunchroom and who want to fill out a survey

In sum, for good generalizability you need two things:

1. A sampling frame that represents your population of interest
2. A sample drawn from the sampling frame that represents the sampling frame

If you lack representative sampling (item 2), your study will not have strong generalizability to any population. If your sampling frame does not closely fit your population of interest (item 1), then your generalizability will be limited to your sampling frame and to other subpopulations that are similar to your sampling frame.

THE SAMPLING PROCESS

Now that we understand what sampling is and have briefly discussed probability and nonprobability samples, we'll get into more detail about how we might go about the process of obtaining our samples.

Probability (Random) Sampling. The easiest and often the best way to reduce a large sample frame to a usable sample is to randomly select persons from the frame. The word *random* means that everyone has an equal

chance of being included. Random sampling is very important because it gives you the most statistically representative subset of your sampling frame possible. The laws of chance assure us that any reasonably large (at least 30 or more) subsample will be essentially a smaller copy of the larger one. If we used some other method, we might introduce bias. A biased sample is one that does not accurately represent the sample frame. For example, if we wanted a sample of kids from a school, and we took the first 20 kids who volunteered, then our sample would be biased in favor of enthusiastic kids. If we randomly select, then enthusiasm plays no factor.

Biased Samples. Systematic error, sometimes called bias or systematic bias, occurs when your data are wrong in a particular direction. This is usually discussed as it applies to measurement, but it can also apply to sampling. If your sampling procedures make some people more likely to be included than other kinds of people, then you have a systematic bias in your sampling. This can happen a number of ways. We already discussed how using telephone number sampling can systematically undersample those with no phones and can systematically oversample those with multiple phones. Another way your sample can be biased has nothing to do with whom you approach but instead has to do with who agrees to be in your study. One recent example is presented in the accompanying boxed feature.

RESEARCH DISASTERS: RETICENT REPUBLICANS?

You may recall the afternoon of November 2, 2004, when early exit polls showed dramatically higher support for presidential candidate John Kerry than had been expected. These polls had been conducted by Edison Media Research and Mitofsky International—large, reputable firms. The projections showed Kerry winning by fairly comfortable margins in a number of key states where he (in reality) was losing. OK, so polling is inexact, and mistakes will happen. Interestingly, however, most of the error went the same way, in favor of Kerry. This suggests systematic bias or error in the polling. What happened? Nobody actually knows (which is a very bad thing for future polls), but it is suspected by some that Kerry voters were more likely to participate in polls, while Bush voters often refused to participate, thus skewing the results.

If this is true, then this is a problem of sample selection due to a systematic refusal to participate. The pollsters thought they were getting a random sample, but they were actually getting a very biased one. A usual approach is to approach every fifth or tenth (or whatever) person leaving the poll, to assure an unbiased sample. While some people may refuse to participate, this is a problem only if there is a pattern as to who refuses. In this situation, it might have been that the systematic refusal of Republicans to respond to polling completely invalidated the research (Morin & Deane, 2005).■

How to Select A Random Sample From Your Sampling Frame. If you have a list of the people (or whatever) in your sampling frame, you can easily pull a random sample using the SAS programming in the nearby boxed feature, taking the data set FULLSAMP and reducing it to a smaller number of records (SUBSAMPL). (See program RANDOM.SAS at www.ablongman.com/mysocialworkkit.) If you're computer phobic, you might want to use a random number table (see Appendix) instead. Random numbers can be used to generate a random subsample in a vast number of ways, including the following:

1. Pick a random point on the table. To be honest, we usually just plunk a finger down, but more sophisticated researchers might specify column and row using 1/100 of a second numbers from a digital stopwatch function or some other fairly random method.

2. Using the numbers from that point forward, take the corresponding people from your list (for example if the number is 34, take the 34th person on your list).

SAS EXAMPLE

```
DATA SUBSAMPL; /*creates a new dataset, don't
want to overwrite base data*/
SET FULLSAMP; /*this is where your base data
(full sample) is */
X=RANUNI(1); /* changing the "1" will give
different random #'s in a different order */
RUN;

PROC SORT DATA=SUBSAMPL;BY X;RUN; /* sorts in
random order by x */

DATA SUBSAMPL;
SET SUBSAMPL;
RETAIN COUNTER 0; /*creates COUNTER,
a variable retained across records*/
COUNTER=COUNTER+1; /*increments COUNTER in
ascending order (1,2,3...)*/
DROP X; /*x is now not needed, records are
ranked (1,2,3...) in random order*/
RUN;

DATA SUBSAMPL;
SET SUBSAMPL;
IF COUNTER<=200; /*keeps first 200 records,
you can make it any number.*/
Drop counter; /*we don't need this anymore,
good to keep things cleaned up!*/
RUN;
```

MATCHING

Sometimes you already have one sample and need a comparison group. This is especially common in clinical studies in which you happen to already have 20 people (say, 20 people who just got a new kind of prosthetic hand) and want to recruit a sample of other people to compare them to (a comparison group of 20 people). You might think the best thing to do is just to randomly pick a comparison group from all other people getting regular-type prosthetic hands. The problem is that you have no way to know if these two groups are similar. Are people who get the two types of hands similar to each other? Would these differences bias your results? It is therefore necessary to make sure that the two groups are as similar as possible. One way to do this is through matching. Matching can be done in the following way:

1. *Figure out what key factors you want to match on.* You need to use whatever theory is available to guide you in this. Why? Because theory can tell you what the key factors are. In our case, we want to study how well people can function with the new prosthetic, and factors known to be related to prosthetic functioning might be age (18 to 30, 30 to 40, 40+), gender (male, female), and household socioeconomic status (SES) (under $25K/yr, $25K to $50K/yr, over $50K/yr).

2. *Categorize your current sample on the relevant variables.* You might have a sample as follows:

6 men aged 18 to 30 at $25K to $50K, 1 man aged 40+ at $50K+, 3 women aged 18 to 30 at $25K to $50K, and so on.

3. *Categorize your available comparison subjects on the same variables.* You might have an available set of people as follows: 20 men aged 18 to 30 at $25K to $50K, 13 men aged 40+ at $50K+, 36 women aged 18 to 30 at $25K–$50K, and so on.

4. *Randomly select the needed number of people from the available comparison subjects.* So, to match my 6 men (18 to 30, $25K to $50K), I randomly select 6 of the 20 available men in that category. I then randomly select 1 of the 13 men aged 40+ at $50K, and then 3 of the 36 women (18 to 30, $25K to 50K), and so on.

OVERSAMPLING AND STRATIFICATION

Oversampling happens when a researcher intentionally recruits more of a given type of subject than would naturally occur in a random sample. This is done to be sure of getting enough people of that type. Let's say you want to know about the college experience of different races. Your school has 2,000 people, of whom 100 are Hispanic, 200 are Black, and 1,700 are Caucasian. You want a final sample of about 90. This would mean you will probably get only about 10 Hispanic and 20 Blacks if you select students randomly. This is clearly not enough. You may want to oversample Hispanic and Blacks so that you get, say, 30 Hispanic, 30 Blacks, and 30 Whites. You randomly select your 30 Whites from the 1,700 Whites, then you randomly take 30 of the 100 Hispanic, and finally you take 30 of the 200 Blacks.

CLUSTER SAMPLING AND MULTISTAGE CLUSTER SAMPLING

Cluster sampling takes place when a researcher starts with many clusters of subjects (teachers in particular schools, residents of particular city blocks, etc.) and picks a subset of these clusters for the sample. For example, if you want to know about teachers in Missouri, you may randomly select 100 schools from a roster and then include all the teachers in those schools as your subjects, ending up with, say, about 2,000 teachers. This is best done when you know the size of the clusters, and they are roughly the same sizes. If the sizes of the clusters are different, you will tend to get proportionately more subjects from the smaller clusters, which can introduce bias.

Researchers can also do **multistage cluster sampling** in which the process is repeated. Let's say you want to interview people in the army about their quality of life. You might randomly pick 20 regiments to look at and then randomly pick one battalion within each regiment, and then randomly pick one company within each battalion, and one platoon (about 50 people) within each company, giving you 1,000 participants.

Cluster sampling is generally done for convenience. It is easier if all the teachers you want to study are in one school, for example. A true random sample would be better, and you really should control for clustering effects statistically if you use this kind of sampling.

PURPOSIVE SAMPLING

We will now move to discuss a very different type of sample, purposive samples. Purposive sampling is a form of nonprobability sample very commonly done in qualitative work. The idea is that you know exactly the kind of person you want to find out about, and so you pick people exactly suited to your needs. Purposive samples are often not representative of the general population, and so the research findings from purposive samples cannot be generalized to the general population. This is an absolutely critical point. Why do researchers use purposive samples then? They use them mainly for inductive (using facts to create theory) purposes. Said another way, we usually find out about people who are interesting to us so that we can develop new ideas about them. As an example, we might want to know about how watching reality TV affects children. To get some facts to form ideas, we might purposively select a wide range of children. We might make sure we get some girls, some boys, some smart children, some emotionally fragile children, children with minimal parental monitoring or histories of school violence, whatever we think is relevant. We would then look at those children, often using a qualitative approach, to try to put some ideas about what is happening (theory) together. It is important to remember two things:

1. We can never claim the data are representative of the larger population.

2. We can use the data to come up with theories. This is called *generalizing to theory* by some people. We should then later follow up with a different type of design using probability samples that could help us understand how well the theories we come up with can be generalized to populations.

SAMPLING FROM ADMINISTRATIVE DATA

One final note has to do with administrative, usually computerized, data. Computerized data are becoming more available and are a very good source for many applications, such as researching service trajectories within an agency. Samples can be drawn from administrative data using any of the approaches listed, but often it is perfectly possible to use the entire sampling frame. There are articles based on administrative data using entire sampling frames of 60,000 people or more. Sometimes students get confused, feeling that using their entire sampling frame is somehow not random and therefore not valid. Just remember that the reason you are sampling randomly from the sampling frame is to get the best possible approximation of the sampling frame. It is better to use the entire sampling frame if this is possible. Of course, if you have a labor-intensive aspect to your administrative research, such as hand coding files or interviewing workers or clients, then you will probably have to select out a sample in the normal way.

SINGLE-SUBJECT SAMPLING

Case studies or single-subject designs involve research on a single person or event or system. Fatality review boards are essentially case studies. The space shuttle *Challenger* disaster review was a case study. A biography is a case study. We tend to think that case studies are always qualitative. This is wrong. Go look at any copy of *Behavior Modification,* a journal that publishes behaviorist (think "rats in mazes") research. This journal includes a large number of case studies that use purely quantitative information. For example, they might report results of a therapy course with an anorexic and might include detailed weekly counts of calories consumed, weight, highly operationalized emitted behaviors, and so on. As you look through *Behavior Modification,* you might notice that many articles present data from several patients side-by-side. These are multiple case studies. In multiple case studies, several case studies are done at the same time, in parallel. They are presented together to allow for different cases to be compared. Consistent findings across subjects help give us faith in the strength of the findings. We will cover single-subject design in far more detail in our chapter on clinical single-subject designs (see Chapter 8).

These issues of purposive sampling and single-subject designs will be covered in much more detail in Chapters 6, 7, and 8.

SAMPLE SIZE AND POWER

The number of people you need in your study depends on the numbers needed to include representative subgroups, the number of variables you want to collect, and the statistics you will use. The sample size needed for various statistical approaches will be discussed in Chapters 13 and 14. The key thing is to have enough subjects representing the subgroups of interest so that you can include all the relevant independent and control variables in your analyses.

Sample size also determines your power to detect associations and effects. If you have a very strong association or a very strong causal relationship, your sample does not have to be really large. On the other hand, if you are studying a rare event or the relationship you are studying is weak, you will need more subjects to detect this relationship. Having enough people to do

this is called having adequate "statistical power" or simply, "power." This is discussed in more detail in Chapter 13.

SAMPLING AND EXTERNAL VALIDITY (GENERALIZABILITY)

You have external validity if your findings can extend (generalize) to the larger population. You must always specify your population of interest and your sampling frame so the reader can know what population you expect your findings to generalize to and how well that population was captured by the sampling frame. Random assignment to experimental and treatment groups supports internal validity (it rules out spurious factors), but random selection from your sampling frame supports external validity (you know your sample is representative of your sampling frame). *Example:* I want to generalize findings to all incarcerated criminals. I get a prison sample and randomly draw from it, and I think I am pretty well set. Some people, however, might say I can generalize only to incarcerated criminals in the single prison I drew from. To get away from this, I might do a nationally representative sample of penal institutions instead.

Remember, a sample that supports external validity (generalizability) must include the following features:

- The population of interest must be clearly operationalized.
- The sample frame must be representative of the people in the population of interest.
- Ideally, the sample should be randomly selected from the sample frame or include the entire sample frame.

This process is like a chain in that it is only as strong as the weakest link. There are also criticisms of how generalizable even the best random sample is when we consider issues of how cultural factors may influence results (Vandijver & Leung, 1997; Papadopoulos & Lee, 2002). In other words, just because you sampled a significant number of Latinas in your study does not mean that this is a homogeneous group in terms of values, behaviors, and the like. What does this mean? Well, this is another example of the need for replication in research and the value of combining qualitative with quantitative inquiry.

RESPONSE RATES

You will hear a lot about "response rates." This is the percentage of the people whom you approach to be in your study who complete the study. Some people think that response rates in the 80% plus range are good, while others say 50% plus is acceptable. The problem with low response rates is that if only a few people respond, then there is no way to be sure that those who responded are representative of the population you are drawing from (as with the nonresponsive Republicans). Another good example of this is the famous and profitably best-selling *Hite Report: A Nationwide Study of Female Sexuality,* with a response rate of around 5% and findings that are believed by many scholars to be essentially meaningless. Who were those 1 in 20 people who responded? Do we have any reason to believe that those people were a fair representation of the other 19?

How Can Response Rates Be Increased? Part of this is related to the method you choose to contact the potential subjects. In general, mailed-out surveys get the lowest response rates, and face-to-face interviews get the highest. Keeping your questionnaire short is a good way to improve rates of response and is also a form of being considerate of the burden your study places on the participant. It is considered bad form at the best and unethical at the worst to put a subject through a needlessly long set of questions. As discussed next, cultural competency will improve response rates.

If you are using a mailed instrument, friendly mailed or telephoned reminders are a good way to increase response rates. To avoid having to know who returned the instrument and who didn't, many researchers will send out reminders to everyone, saying basically, "If you returned it, thanks. Otherwise, would you please consider taking the time to return it now?" Inducements are often used. Some researchers include coupons or even money in the initial mailouts as a thank-you to try to bolster rates. You may have received a set of "free" return address labels from a charity requesting a donation. This is an example of using an incentive to encourage response. You will notice these little gifts are not contingent on the survey being returned. That causes ethical concerns, because you might be compelling people to do something they don't really want to do.

Phone surveys and face-to-face interviews are more intrusive and also more likely to yield a response. People are more likely to consent to participate when contacted directly. You, however, may know who the person is (especially if you called him or her from a list with names, such as a phone book) and must be careful not to coerce participation in any way or take undue advantage of situations that may increase participation. For example, an elderly shut-in may be quite lonely and agree to participate not from wanting to be a subject but because he or she needs someone to talk to.

When conversing with someone you may obtain information you don't want. For example, if you know the identity of the person you are talking to and that person begins discussing how he or she maltreats a child, you have an ethical duty to report that maltreatment. While ethical researchers carefully explain this prior to beginning the conversation as a part of the consent process, it sometimes accidentally arises anyway. This can put you in the position of having to file an official report.

Face-to-face interviews have the highest response rates but also have more associated difficulties. You must consider interviewer safety when contacting persons. It is a good idea to have interview teams of two, consider the conditions of the neighborhood, and choose time of day carefully. Sometimes it is necessary to meet at a safe location rather than in the home. Face-to-face interviews often take longer than other formats. Researchers will often pay subjects for their time to offset the inconvenience. In our view, it is most ethical to pay the subject on arrival, not on completion of participation, as this allows more freedom to back out of the study should the subject feel uncomfortable.

SAMPLING IN A CULTURALLY COMPETENT AND ETHICAL MANNER

There is a range of ways in which sampling can be difficult from an ethical standpoint. You need to consider how you can best maximize agreement to participate and make certain that your subjects are treated in an ethical fashion. Dealing with clients from cultures different from yours can be particularly difficult because it can be harder to understand what issues may arise unless concerted efforts are made to understand them. Besides the ethical mandate to treat people fairly and with respect, failure to respect diversity among clients can lead to practical problems, such as low response rates and misunderstanding of instruments or questions.

Cultural competency means that you can work well with people from different cultures and make adjustments to the research process to avoid threats to validity that may stem from cultural differences. This includes knowing how to interact respectfully and genuinely, how to communicate well, and understanding how different people will react to the study. For example, if you wish to study individuals with physical disabilities, you will want to do more than review the literature. You will want to talk with representatives of the population or other experts to get a better understanding of them. You will want to think about how you present yourself and what language you use. This can apply even if you consider yourself a member of a particular population. Your experiences may not be typical. Another issue is that your position as "the researcher" creates a power differential that may make subjects uncomfortable about correcting you once the study begins (Papadopoulos & Lee, 2002).

It is particularly important to understand how to respectfully communicate with a given group (Lum,

2003). For example, in certain cultures it is impolite to enter someone's home without bringing food or a small gift. It may also be impolite if you "get down to business" rather than spend some time making pleasant conversation. Lack of ability to make contact in a way that is perceived as respectful will reduce your response rate and is not part of ethical research practice.

Different cultures may find different issues to be sensitive. For example, some groups find mental health disorders extremely stigmatizing and difficult to discuss. You need to understand how to ask questions about this in a way that minimizes their discomfort. Different cultures may also use different terminology (Boynton et al., 2004). The most extreme and obvious example of this is the need to translate questions for groups that speak a different language (Pan, 2003). A more subtle example is found in a colleague's research on diabetes within a lower-income, urban, African American area. They discovered that residents in the community studied did not use the word *diabetes*, but called it "the sugars." Using the terms used by the community enabled the researchers to obtain the information needed more easily and accurately.

HUMAN SUBJECTS AND INSTITUTIONAL REVIEW BOARDS (IRBs)

Human subjects concerns are central in all social research and go hand in hand with thinking about your sampling process. These concerns cluster around three main issues: privacy, informed consent, and minimizing harm. Specific subtopics that will be addressed include confidentiality versus anonymity and conditions in which confidentiality must be broken, deception, withholding treatment, competence, coercion, special populations, compensation, and financial conflicts.

Privacy is the idea that people have a right to keep personal things to themselves. Because social research commonly involves collecting personal data, the type of data collected and the manner in which they are stored and used are primary concerns. You must not release private information about clients in a way that it can be traced back to them. Privacy therefore applies not only to names but also to other identifying information, such as addresses and Social Security numbers. There are a number of critical concepts within privacy:

- *Confidentiality* means keeping identifying information secret.
- *Anonymity* means that you never obtain identifying information about your subjects, which simplifies privacy concerns dramatically.
- *Informed consent* is the idea that people have a right to know what they are getting into and must agree to it in advance in writing. Researchers must obtain signed consent forms from subjects in their

studies. There are a number of issues that pertain to informed consent. The issue of informed consent can be complicated by the following issues:

Duty to inform refers to the researcher's obligation to inform potential victims of risks to them that may become evident during research. For example, if a researcher is told by a subject of his plans to kill someone, the researcher must inform the potential victim. Similarly, privacy must be violated in cases where the subject is actively suicidal, in which case the researcher may be responsible for informing appropriate individuals of individual's suicide risk.

Mandated reporting is a term that applies to children in all states and elders in some states. Put simply, social researchers are legally compelled to report child and (in some states) elder abuse. There are no exceptions. Failure to report is a crime. This can be a serious consideration in doing research on child abuse and neglect. Some researchers will attempt to avoid this responsibility by using only anonymous data, or data on cases that have already been reported to child welfare authorities.

Deception, necessary in certain kinds of research, must be handled very carefully. Deception occurs when the researcher misleads the subject about the nature of the research being done. For example, if your goal is to measure the effects of praise on task performance, you might not want to tell the client this but might, in fact, simply say your design was about task performance. If you tell the client, "Hey, we're going to see how you react to praise," then the validity of the research will be seriously damaged. In short, you must use deception only when it is absolutely necessary and when it will cause no harm to the client. Deception must be followed by a debriefing, in which the subjects are informed of the nature of the deception (see Chapter 2).

Withholding treatment occurs when you have an experimental or quasi-experimental design and wish to compare a treatment or intervention to an unserved group. In general it is considered unethical to withhold treatment from someone who needs it. There are, however, two exceptions. If nothing is known to work, then it is sometimes possible to get approval to treat one group and leave another untreated. This is because we have no idea if treatment does any good, so there is no harm or benefit known to be associated with being in either group. Of course, problems can occur (from a research perspective) if it becomes obvious midstudy that the treatment group is benefiting, and therefore harm is done by withholding the treatment. A second exception is when there are simply not sufficient resources available for the population. For example, an agency providing nonemergency mental health services might have a substantial waiting list. Sometimes researchers use individuals on the waiting list as the comparison group. This is not considered withholding treatment as these individuals will receive services as soon as they become available. Of course, the waiting list time may vary, which can cause problems with the study. Commonly, a good alternative to withholding treatment is simply to provide the comparison or control group with treatment as usual.

Competence involves the idea that an individual is truly capable of giving consent. In the case of some populations (such as people under 18 or the mentally disabled), it may be necessary to get consent from the parent or legal guardian instead. Many researches will have both parents or guardians and their children sign consent forms. Sometimes the forms signed by the children are called "assent" forms.

Coercion is never acceptable and must be avoided at all costs. Consent must be fully voluntary. Why do we use the word *voluntary?* Of course you wouldn't *force* someone to participate. Even though from your perspective participation is voluntary, the sample group must have the capacity to volunteer (or have a caretaker volunteer for them) *and* they must perceive it as voluntary. For example, let's say a researcher wants to collect information from subjects waiting for service at an income maintenance office. If the subjects somehow perceive that refusal to participate would result in not being granted the sought-after funds, then their participation is not truly voluntary. While it may be easy to avoid obvious forms of coercion, it is also important to be on the lookout for subtle forms of coercion. Individuals who need money, for example, may feel forced to participate in a research program if compensation is not given until after their participation is completed. For this reason, we believe that compensation should be given when the subject arrives. Or if subjects are fearful that a service or benefit may be denied by an agency, then this is considered coercive.

Special or vulnerable populations can be more vulnerable to many of the issues just described. We have already discussed the issue of competence in regard to children and the mentally disabled and the legal necessity of reporting suspected child or elder abuse. In addition, a number of other populations suffer from relatively high imbalances of power between themselves and the researcher and require extra care in assuring their rights. For example, hospital patients may believe that they will please the staff and receive better attention if they engage in a study. It is important that such erroneous beliefs be clearly dispelled. Perhaps the most problematic population is prisoners,

who have had a history of maltreatment by researchers. A number of special guidelines exist when research is performed with prisoners (such as the need to include at least one representative on the IRB). In short, the more disempowered the subjects are, the more strenuously efforts need to be made to assure that this imbalance is not taken advantage of, either overtly or subtly.

Compensation. As stated earlier, sometimes researchers provide incentives or pay participants for their time. This in itself is not unethical and is a way to show that you view subjects' time as valuable. It can be problematic, however, if the compensation is so high that it becomes a possible coercion. For example, if your study sample is from a low-income population and you pay a large amount to participate, it may be seen as bribing rather than a fair incentive. This then has an impact on the subject's willingness to consent. Some researchers are also concerned about possible consequences of compensation. If, for example, you are studying substance abusers, you may wish not to give cash but to give vouchers for groceries instead. Such an approach reduces the risk that clients will use the compensation to harm themselves by purchasing drugs.

Inclusion of Underrepresented Populations. Increasingly there has been an emphasis on inclusion of underrepresented populations as well as their ethical treatment. To some extent this is based on increasing the benefits of research for human subjects. In some areas, like dating violence, almost all the studies have been done on White, middle-class college students. Yet there is no reason to believe that this problem is absent in other ethnic or racial or socioeconomic groups. IRBs may be interested to see if you are including underrepresented populations. Then they will also want to know that you are competent in your approach to working with these populations. Many granting agencies simply will not consider studies that omit women or minorities.

Harm to subjects must be avoided or minimized. Many study designs simply cannot be done due to the risks they pose to subjects. For example, no modern researcher would intentionally poison people to determine how to best treat poisoning.

Balancing risk and benefits is necessary. Some medical procedures that are included in research (such as new forms of chemotherapy or surgical techniques) are very harmful but may represent the best chance for patients with serious diseases. IRB applications require explicit weighing of risks and benefits. More typically, risks in social research are less severe and include psychological reactions to recalling trauma, stress involved in completing tasks, and the like.

Reducing harm through whatever means possible is a key concern. This includes paying attention to the length of the data collection process and the sensitivity of the questions. This also includes paying attention to possible stigma in a given culture attached to being identified. For example, if there is stigma attached to having a mental health disorder in your sample group, then you may wish to plan a means of contacting your participants that does not make it obvious to others in the community that they are being spoken to for this reason.

Plans for dealing with harm to subjects are necessary. IRBs require specific plans for dealing with any harm that might occur. For example, in a survey probing prior experiences of sexual assault, counseling resources should be available to support subjects undergoing unpleasant reactions to the questions.

Researcher Conflicts of Interest. An IRB will also want to ensure that the researcher does not have a conflict of interest. If a researcher has stock interest in a company and then does research that could benefit that company, there may be a concern that the research may somehow be biased. This could result in harm to subjects and potentially harm to others in the future if an intervention or treatment is erroneously thought to be effective.

Human Subjects and Sampling. As you review the elements required for the IRB, it may be that this has an impact on your sampling plan. Recall that the research process is rarely perfectly linear. At any stage you may discover a barrier that causes you to go back and rethink the planning process.

More specific information about human subjects clearance, along with specific examples, will be provided in Chapters 11 and 12.

SECTION 4.2.4: ASSIGNMENT TO GROUPS OR CONDITIONS

In this section, we will discuss the assignment of subjects to groups or conditions. Sometimes beginning researchers become confused about how many groups their study has. True experimental designs always use at least two groups of subjects, randomly assigned. These include one or more treatment (experimental) groups and a control group. Quasi-experimental designs usually use two or more groups but sometimes only use one group with multiple conditions over time (for example, first no treatment, then treatment, then no treatment, and so on). Nonexperimental designs usually do not assign subjects to multiple groups or conditions. The number of groups in a study design depends on the number of conditions you are examining. Examples may help clarify this:

- *Experimental design (many groups):* You want to determine the effectiveness of a range of different types of psychotherapy in reducing anxiety. You randomly assign clients to 10 different groups and provide a different type of psychotherapy to each group, comparing the changes in anxiety levels to see which type is more effective.

- *Experimental design (two groups):* You want to determine if a new police outreach program reduces reported crime. Your unit of analysis is the police patrol area (beat). You randomly assign outreach officers to half the beats and leave the other half alone (control group). You now have two groups, beats with outreach officers (experimental group) and beats without outreach officers (control group). You can track the crime in each beat and see how well your program works.

- *Experimental design (one group):* You want to know if a new law reduces tax evasion in your state. Your dependent variable will be the percentage of IRS audits that resulted in a given outcome (say, charges of tax evasion being brought or assessments of due taxes greater than $1,000 being made). You will check this for the year before the law goes into effect (baseline condition) and then compare it to the same measure the year after the law goes into effect (experimental condition) to see if you can determine any difference.

We hope that seemed simple, but we find that students are chronically confused about this issue. This is because groups are used in so many different ways in research. We have already seen how you can break your sampling frame into different groups for purposes of matching, stratification, or oversampling. We will also see later how important it is to define groups for certain kinds of statistics. Conceptually, every variable you create breaks your sample down into different groups (male versus female, 10-year-olds versus 11-year-olds versus 12-year-olds, etc.). Much of this confusion can be cleared up if you make sure you understand when you are talking about groups in terms of sampling, assignment to conditions, ratings on independent or dependent variables, and so on. We will discuss the many ways in which subjects can be assigned to groups in more detail, under experimental and quasi-experimental designs.

SECTION 4.2.5: INVESTIGATOR MANIPULATION

Sometimes you do things to people to see if something changes. You may give them a drug, show them a particular thing (stimulus), deprive them of sleep, or provide them with a new kind of treatment. True experimental designs always involve manipulation in the experimental condition. Quasi-experimental designs usually involve investigator manipulation but may take advantage of naturally occurring conditions instead. **Natural experiments** provide a common example of experimental designs that lack experimental manipulation. Let's say you want to study the effects of leadership transition (getting a new principal) on the performance of elementary school students. Because it is unlikely that you have the clout to fire or transfer principals, and it would be unethical anyhow, you can't randomly assign schools to "new principal" versus "same old principal" groups. Instead, you would have to go out and find schools with new principals and then contrast these to a comparison group of similar schools with no change in leadership.

INVESTIGATOR MANIPULATION AND ETHICS

Generally, the more investigators manipulate the conditions, the greater the concerns about ethics and group assignment. As mentioned earlier, there are some issues we want to study, like the effect of severe psychological trauma on trust, in which investigator manipulation is simply unethical. Whenever you purposively change what is happening to an individual or group you must carefully weigh the potential harms against the potential benefits of that level of design. If the harms outweigh the benefits, then the method of answering the question must change or the question itself be deferred until a nonharmful alternative can be found.

SECTION 4.2.6: STUDY TIME FRAME

Some of the more common terms dealing with the dimension of time include *cross-sectional, longitudinal, retrospective, prospective, time-series, trend, cohort,* and *panel.* We will look briefly at each.

Cross-Sectional (Point-in-Time) Studies. The simplest and most common type of social research is the **cross-sectional study.** Most surveys are of this type. One simply goes out and collects data about how subjects are at a given time. They are not contacted again.

Longitudinal Studies. Studies that follow subjects over time are called **longitudinal studies.** Data are collected from several different points in time. For example, a study might check the blood of subjects on an ongoing basis to monitor use of illegal drugs. Many Head Start evaluations have followed Head Start graduates for many years to see what long-term effects the program might have had.

Retrospective Studies. Some studies, called **retrospective studies,** look backwards. This can be done either by using records or through asking people to remember. For example, if you want to find out about racial hiring practices at a given agency, the easiest way to do it would be to look

at their hiring records from the last few years. Retrospective designs can collect data over time or from a single point in time. For example, you could ask a subject to recall and rate his self-esteem at different points in his life, or you could ask him to rate his self-esteem at only a single point in his life. Similarly, you could consult arrest records to check if a subject was arrested in a given year, or you could develop a complete history of the subject's arrest record over time. In this way, retrospective approaches can be used to create data representing various points in time.

Unfortunately, retrospective data based on human recall are of questionable value. While many studies use such data, human memory is fallible, and such data can be wrong. The further back subjects are asked to recall, the more dubious such data are. Retrospective data gained from administrative records may be more sound but are vulnerable to the many issues affecting the quality of such data.

SUBJECT RECALL: SOME CAUTIONARY FINDINGS

Many studies rely on subject recall of past experiences or ask subjects to describe themselves as they were when they were younger. There are, unfortunately, a number of studies that suggest that such an approach may result in bad data.

One study involved experienced clinicians interviewing 25-year-old adults to see if they could determine if these adults as had ADHD (attention deficit hyperactivity disorder) as children. The interviewers asked the subjects questions about how they were as children and tried to figure out if they thought the subjects had ADHD when they were younger. The people running the study (not the interviewers) knew very well who was diagnosable with ADHD at 9 years of age and who wasn't, because the subjects were members of a longtitudinal study. The subjects had, in fact, been assessed 16 years previously. Frighteningly enough, when the clinicians assessed the subjects as having had ADHD as children, they were wrong 73% of the time. Note that these judgments about childhood ADHD were made by trained clinicians, not simply by giving the people a paper-and-pencil scale (Mannuzza, Klein, Klein, Bessler, & Shrout, 2002).

Safer and Keuler (2002) reviewed prior studies that tried to evaluate how well psychotherapy clients could recall their own levels of distress. Subjects were asked to rate their distress when they started therapy (distress at start of therapy). At the end of therapy, they were asked again to rate their distress (distress at end of therapy). At the end of therapy they were also asked to remember back and rate their distress as it was when they started therapy (distress at start of therapy as recalled by the subject at the end of therapy). Sorry if that's a bit confusing. The results of two of the three studies reviewed were that subjects overrated their distress when they looked back retrospectively. Worse, certain kinds of clients (those with depression, anxiety, or neuroticism) were more likely to overrate their prior distress than other clients.

Imagine if you were a researcher, and your measure of treatment efficacy was to compare clients' ratings of current distress to their retrospective recall of distress when they entered therapy. Given what we know from the preceding results, your findings might well be that therapy reduced distress and was most effective with certain kinds of clients (the depressed, anxious, or neurotic). Unfortunately, all these findings could simply be the result of clients not being able to accurately recall how distressed they were when they started therapy. The moral is simple: Be suspicious of people's memories.■

_____

Prospective Studies. Studies that begin at a given point and extend into the future are called **prospective studies.** They are longitudinal in nature by definition. If I decide to follow a group of children who had cancer treatment to see how they adjust, and I check them out every month, this would be a prospective study.

Time-series Studies. Sampling at particular points over time is the characteristic feature of a **time-series study.** This design is often used in treatment evaluation. The most typical example would involve a baseline measurement (before treatment), another measurement at the end of treatment, and possibly a follow-up measure later to assess the stability of the treatment effect.

Trend Studies. A **trend study** looks at a given variable from time to time (often year to year). It does not attempt to sample the same people. If you check the public's opinion toward corporal punishment every year, that's a trend study.

Cohort Studies. A **cohort study** is like a trend study but keeps following people born in the same year (or multiyear period). If you track 20-year-old people's views on capital punishment this year and then wait five years and check again (now they're the 25-year-old cohort), then you are doing a cohort study. In cohort studies it is not necessary to track the same subjects, just to track subjects from the same age cohort.

Panel Studies. Just like a cohort study except it keeps the same sample, in a **panel study,** you get information from Bob, Mary, and Joe now, and then later you get information from Bob, Mary, and Joe again.

These are some of the more commonly used terms and types of time frames used in social science

research. Which you use will depend on your question and on how your conceptual framework takes time into account. No one approach is clearly better than the others.

SECTION 4.2.7: DATA TYPE

There is probably an infinite number of ways to get information. The most common ways in social science are observation, use of structured instruments, collecting unstructured data, and collecting secondary or archival data. We will overview these here but will provide far more information, along with examples, in Chapter 5.

Observation involves the researcher tracking and coding behavior. This can be done in many ways: for example, by checklist, by evaluating correctness of task completion, by timing how long it takes to complete a task, or by coding of video or audio tapes. Computers can even be used to observe and record behavior, such as speed and accuracy of typing. Many studies on alcohol impairment, for example, use observation of skill performance (such as driving in a simulator) as a key variable.

Structured instruments are the most common means of collecting information about people. The term *instrument* is normally used to refer to a test or questionnaire. If you fill out a course evaluation form where you rate your professor from, say, 1 to 5, that is a structured instrument. Structured instruments use **closed-ended questions** that require a numerical or categorical response (e.g., "male," or "26," or "more than five per year"). We will go into a great deal of detail about this in the section on survey research. **Standardized instruments** are structured instruments that have been used and checked out enough that most researchers are confident in their validity. The use of standardized instruments supports internal validity and is encouraged. **Normed instruments** are instruments which you can give to find out where someone stands against the general population. IQ tests, for example, are both standardized and normed. As noted in our prior chapter, however, it is important to consider whether a given measure is valid for your particular population (Suzuki, Ponterotto, & Meller, 2000).

Unstructured data include narrative or similar data. Almost all qualitative work uses at least some unstructured data. This type of data can be found archivally (e.g., case notes) or can be generated in response to **open-ended questions** such as, "Describe how you felt the day your child graduated from high school."

Archival or preexisting data can include all of the kinds of information just listed. For example, a school record might include number of times a child has gone to the principal's office for discipline (observation), the child's achievement scores (structured instrument), and notes from the counselor (unstructured data). For practical purposes, the easiest kind of preexisting data to use may be a numeric computerized database, because this requires no transcription by hand. Narrative data, especially case records, are also commonly used. Preexisting data exist in formats you probably haven't considered. For example, newspapers have been used for many studies, because they contain a historical record of all kinds of things (weather, community events, advertisements). If you are interested in the use of sexually explicit advertising, for example, you might compare ads from the same newspaper over time and have independent observers rate their suggestiveness. Preexisting data are often described as archival data if they are stored in a file or record somewhere, as **secondary data** if you are reanalyzing someone else's study, or as **administrative data** if you are using agency or similar data.

Administrative data are an increasingly popular basis for research. This is because of the advent of large computerized databases and increasing agency focus on accountability. Many agencies now use standardized instruments (such as IQ tests or the Child Behavior Checklist) and include those scores in their computerized databases. Administrative data have a number of advantages and disadvantages when compared to other forms of data:

Disadvantages of Administrative Data

- *Administrative databases are of varying quality.* Some are excellent, and some are unusable. The phrase "garbage in, garbage out" applies here. A poor-quality administrative database is simply not useful to the researcher. A high-quality database, on the other hand, is one of the most valuable tools available. In determining the quality of a database, consider the following issues.

  What checks exist to make sure the data entered are correct? Forced-entry screens provide an automatic check for missing data. Many databases are routinely audited, especially databases (like foster care or medical reimbursement) that have money attached to them.

  To what other sources can I compare the data to make sure the data are correct? Can you look at written case files or talk to workers or supervisors to assess how accurate the data are?

- *Sometimes data are obviously wrong.* Sometimes databases will simply lack face validity. Some data sets include obvious errors and impossibilities, such as people receiving medical care after their dates of death. Compare the constructs and the relationships between constructs shown in the database to what is already known. Does the

database agree with other research in key areas? If your data show that most anorexics are male or reveal a spike in pregnancies among 54-year-old women, something's probably not right.

- *Very often parts of a data set are of varying quality.* It has already been mentioned that data sets attached to money are usually more accurate. Key agency decisions and concerns are also more likely to be accurately recorded. You need to carefully evaluate all variables to see which you can have confidence in.

- *It is important that you talk to the people who actually use the system.* You must talk to workers and data-entry people, not just supervisors or administrators. Unfortunately, upper management can sometimes be rather clueless when it comes to what is actually going on in the trenches. Find out from the people who get the data (workers) and enter the data (data-entry or administrative assistants).

- *You have to take what you are given.* Like other forms of secondary data analysis, you don't get to write the questions, you just get to look at the answers. There are two broad exceptions to this. First of all, some researchers are able to supplement archival data with interviews or even convince the agency in question to allow the researcher to add some fields to their database. Similarly, sparse computerized databases can be augmented by researchers themselves hand coding written files. Second, it is sometimes possible to use data management techniques to either create new variables from preexisting data or merge other data sets to the one currently being used. For example, you may have a database giving ages of girls, dates at which they give birth (if any), and their addresses. Based on this, you could easily create a new variable showing their age at the birth of their child. With a little more effort, you could geocode their address, place each person in a specific tract, and include variables from the census that describe their neighborhood (tract-level) environment.

Advantages of Administrative Data

- *Administrative databases often provide immediate access to longitudinal data.* This means that you don't have to wait five years to do a five-year longitudinal study. If the database has been operating for that long, the data exist for your use now.

- *Administrative data are therefore more responsive to immediate needs.* The ability to instantaneously provide truly longitudinal data is unique to administrative data.

- *Administrative data are innately practice oriented.* Agencies generally collect the data that they use and consider important. Using such data constrains the academic researcher to use constructs that people in the field believe to be important.

■ *Administrative data allow for extremely large samples.* This is often the only practical way to longitudinally track rare events. This can be a real asset to the researcher. For example, if you wanted to do a longitudinal study on factors leading to childhood maltreatment fatalities, you would need to sample hundreds of thousands of children to end up with enough fatalities to study. That is simply not practical. Your only other options are to use purely retrospective accounts, relying on the recall of the people who knew the family and the child or to use preexisting administrative data (police, child welfare, and the like) to track the child's and family's prior history.

COMBINING DIFFERENT KINDS OF DATA

Combinations of the previous types of data are also very common. Many surveys use both structured items ("What is your age in years?") and unstructured items ("What is the most important consideration in choosing a health care provider?"). The new SAT has changed from an entirely closed-ended test to one with open-ended (essay) components. To get back to an earlier example, the course evaluations you are familiar with probably also had both structured and unstructured items. It is also very common to use preexisting data, such as medical records, to support other forms of data. A study that is mainly focused on administrative archival data ($N = 10,000$) may use interviews for a subset of cases (perhaps $n = 100$) to add some context to the administrative data.

When designing your study, choose your data type based on the research questions, operationalization of constructs, and accessibility. The data type may also be constrained by resources (e.g., interviews tend to be expensive compared to surveys) and the vulnerability of the population (e.g., preexisting or administrative information may be chosen when direct access to a given sample is impossible or unethical).

Whatever type of data is chosen, the main objective is that it includes variables that are valid representations of the research constructs and are reliably recorded. For example, a teacher report that a child acts "odd" is unlikely to be accepted as a valid measure of the presence of a mental health disorder, as it is difficult to know what "odd" means. On the other hand, a variable that accurately identifies the DSM-IVR diagnosis for a subject would be accepted as a valid measure of mental health disorder. Alternately, a score on a construct measured by a standardized instrument, such as the externalizing behaviors scale of the Child Behavior Checklist (CBCL) is likely to be seen as valid. It is also important that the data are reliably or consistently recorded. The presence of a question on a survey or variable in the data set may be a very valid measure, but it's useful only if it is reliably recorded for all the subjects.

ETHICAL ISSUES

There are potentially serious ethical problems associated with selection of instruments. This can be especially true for instruments that may yield misleading results that can hurt or help stigmatize vulnerable populations. For example, we happen to know many people who study mental health issues among Hispanics. This results in their frequently having to translate instruments into Spanish. Translation must be done very carefully, in a way sensitive to specific terms used by this population. Selection of terms that may carry stigma can result in the study overstating or understating the prevalence of mental health issues in the Hispanic community. The practical and ethical implication of such work are obvious.

Better known are the ongoing controversies over intelligence testing and ethnic minorities. Is a given IQ test improperly biased against members of certain races? Sometimes the issue can be even more subtle. Let's say, for example, you want to look at mental health issues among high school students. You pick a depression screener and call it your measure of mental health. This is a foolish but surprisingly common practice. You will certainly overstate the prevalence of mental health problems among females relative to males. Why? Because you have chosen a measure that focuses on the kind of mental health problems more likely to be experienced by girls and have chosen not to test for those mental health issues (addictions, conduct problems) more commonly found among males.

Other ethical issues involve harm to subjects. Are the instruments chosen likely to cause harm to the subjects? Are they age appropriate? You obviously don't want to give children instruments with vignettes (stories) featuring explicit sex or violence. Overall, the key here is to use common sense. Is the instrument something that fits your population and won't hurt the subjects? Has it been used successfully before?

SECTION 4.3
INTERNAL VALIDITY AND RESEARCH DESIGN

If a study really measures the constructs and variables it says it is measuring, then it has **internal validity.** Memorize that last definition. Your instructor will almost certainly test you on it. Now that you have some ideas about your design, you should review to see if the following threats to internal validity may be a problem.

Section 4.3.1: Some General Terms Used when Discussing Internal Validity

These are very general terms that can apply to constructs, to the instruments that measure the constructs, or to your model as a whole. These terms are not defined the same way by everyone, and some of these ideas overlap. We are simply attempting to give you what we see as a representative idea of how they are most commonly used:

■ **Face validity:** Face validity is synonymous with "it looks right" or "it makes sense." This is a big one in our view. You have common sense for a reason. Do the instruments seem as if they would measure the construct they intend to measure? Does the full research model make sense, or does it seem tortured? Trust your judgment here. There are a lot of studies out there that are very questionable. For example, a study might claim to tell you about "long-term" outcomes among children but may only follow them for three months. That's just silly. Other studies claim to measure "mental health" and do so by looking only at a score from an instrument measuring depression. Not only is that ridiculous, but it will have nasty unanticipated effects, such as making females (who are more prone to depression) look less mentally healthy than males.

■ **Content validity:** Are all key factors included in the instrument or model? This matters because failing to include a key construct can cause designs, especially nonexperimental designs, to come to very wrong conclusions. For example, one of the most frequently overlooked variables in social research is income. Controlling for income will often completely change apparent relationships between variables. Many apparent associations between race and other factors (such as child abuse reporting) will be reduced or entirely eliminated if poverty is considered. As another example, we might ask if Asians earn more than Whites in the United States. We've seen statistics saying they do, but we've also seen studies reporting that if you control for years of education, they actually make less. In this case, forgetting to include years of education is a serious breach of content validity.

■ **Construct validity:** Are we measuring the constructs in our study correctly? Are they correctly reflected in the variables we create? This is often checked by seeing if the construct/variables behave in the model the way we expect them to. This obviously overlaps with the next type of

validity. In our experience, construct validity is most useful as a term describing how well your constructs function in a model as theory predicts they should. It is a way of seeing if your measurements and your theory seem to be getting along well and supporting each other. If they don't, you've got some explaining to do.

■ **Criterion validity (concurrent, predictive, discriminant):** These forms of validity are most commonly referred to when trying to figure out if a particular measure or instrument is working right (see Chapter 5). A good instrument should agree with other indicators of the construct. When you check to see if an instrument agrees with other measures or behavioral observations (or whatever) taken at the same time, that's *concurrent validity.* For example, if you have a new instrument measuring depression, it should agree with other measures taken at the same time (such as other depression measures or evaluations of trained psychologists). *Predictive validity* is similar, except the question is how well the measure can predict *future* events. For example, a measure intended to determine your heart health could be checked by seeing if people who score poorly on the measure actually do get heart attacks at higher rates over the next several years. *Discriminant validity* is a little bit trickier. Discriminant validity is how you show that your instrument is *not* measuring some specific other thing. For example, let's say that you have a good theoretical reason to believe that "depression" and "hopelessness" are different constructs. You want to measure "hopelessness." You design "The Hopelessness Scale." Unfortunately, nasty, critical people keep saying, "Hey, you're just measuring depression." How do you show that your measure of "hopelessness" is not just measuring "depression"? You administer your hopelessness scale to a bunch of people and also give them a scale measuring depression. If the scores are very highly correlated, then it looks as though your critics are right, and you are just measuring depression. If the scales are not highly correlated, then you say, "Look here, my scale does not measure just depression—it measures something else."

Section 4.3.2: Some Specific Threats to Internal Validity

We will now turn to a discussion of some particular ways in which a design's validity can be compromised. Again, these terms are not always used the same way by everyone, but we hope this will give a sense of how they are often used.

THREATS TO INTERNAL VALIDITY

- *Measurement (or Instrumentation) **Error:*** We see these terms often used interchangeably. Basically, the threat here is that your instrument changes the person and how he or she is likely to respond, thus biasing your results. For example, you ask parents a bunch of questions about bullying. They think about all the different aspects of bullying you ask them about, they imagine lots of things happening, and the more they think about it the more worried they get. Asking them how worried they are about bullying *after* grilling them on the subject may well give you a different response than if you asked them how worried they were about bullying *before* you subjected them to your questions.

- *Lack of Treatment Fidelity:* You might do an intervention wrong or inconsistently. This is a real problem in evaluating new treatments. Frequently, if an independent researcher finds that a new treatment is ineffective, the people who like the treatment (or designed it, or get paid to deliver the treatment) will simply say, "You didn't do it right, your conclusions are worthless." Treatment fidelity must be monitored by researchers to make sure they are doing the intervention right. This can be done by randomly taping sessions and having neutral trained raters evaluate what is being done. If you don't demonstrate you did a good job in providing the treatment with a high degree of fidelity, nobody will have confidence in your results.

- *History:* The world changes, and your subjects change. Let's say you are doing a study on how enrollment in an ethnic diversity class changes participant's xenophobia (fear of things foreign) over time. If some important historic event occurs during the class that relates to that issue (such as the attack on Pearl Harbor or 9/11) it poses a massive, possibly fatal, threat to your study. How can you know that the effects you measure aren't just due to the event? Control and comparison groups can help with this problem to some degree.

- *Maturation:* Your subjects change (mature) as time goes by. People grow and have new experiences. You may notice a shift toward political conservatism over time in a longitudinal study, but it may have nothing to do with any variables in your study—it may just be people getting older. This is especially problematic with studies of children. Again, however, if you have random assignment in an experimental design or a quasi-experimental design with equal numbers of children of the same age range, this threat should be less of a problem, because they are all getting older together.

- *Contamination across Groups:* Sometimes people talk too much. Let's say you have a group of therapists you train to give a special kind of treatment, which you evaluate by comparing their clients to those of other therapists whom you don't train. What's to stop the trained ones from telling the untrained ones about these neat new ideas? What happens if everyone, including your comparison therapists, starts using the new model? You've got to monitor this and try to prevent it in advance.

- *Sample **Attrition** or **Mortality:*** If you lose many people from your sample, then you may have a problem. If the people leave randomly (for example, if your budget is slashed and you randomly remove half your subjects), then this will not effect the representativeness of your sample. If, however, people left for a reason (such as if the ones who had lower frustration tolerance got sick of your boring treatment and left), then your remaining sample is biased and no longer representative of your sample frame. This is especially problematic in a long-term longitudinal study. A variety of things are done to prevent attrition, such as maintaining subject contact through update cards between surveys, ensuring that the research process is not too burdensome, and providing incentives for participation.

- *Regression to the **Mean:*** This is a tricky one, and an example might help. If I have a new treatment for people in crisis, I might get 100 people who call the crisis hotline, and I might use my treatment on them. No matter how effective my treatment is, the people will *certainly* get better. Why? Because if you nab a bunch of people on their worst day, then they have nowhere to go but up. Any sampling process that takes people in a special condition or time in their lives is likely to be subject to this effect. Similarly, you will usually note that individuals within your sample who score very high or very low also tend to moderate when retested. This is because you probably just caught them on a bad or good day, and they are just returning to normal. This really isn't very complex, just remember that "returning to average" is English for "regressing to the mean."

- *Social desirability bias:* Sometimes people say things to look good. It is important to avoid questions that subjects will feel uncomfortable answering in a given way. For example, don't ask, "Do you hit your child?"; ask something like, "How often do you use physical punishment with your child?"

- *Subject and Investigator **Expectation effects:*** People often can influence outcomes through their expectations. The famous "Hawthorne" effect was discovered when researchers found that subject productivity increased even when the researchers did *nothing.* People were simply responding to the researcher's attention. Some crafty guys once set up a study where they gave out a bunch of rats to students, half of which were supposed to be genetically good at running mazes, while the other half were supposed to be poor at it (Rosenthal & Lawson, 1964). The "good" rats did better, even though the researcher was deceiving the students, and the rats were really all the same. The student's expectation was what made the difference. To get rid of expectation effects, "blind" designs are often used. In **single-blind experiments** you don't tell the subject what condition he or she is in. The use of sugar pill placebos is a form of single-blind experiment. This removes the threat of the subject's expectations changing the outcome. In **double-blind experiments,** neither the subject nor the persons who deal directly with the subject know what condition the subject is in. If sugar pills and real pills are given, and even the person giving the pills doesn't know which pills are fake, then this is a double-blind study. This removes the threat of both the subject and the researcher influencing the outcomes with their expectations.

SECTION 4.4
FINALIZING THE DESIGN

In this section we will describe how the dimensions discussed fit into overall study designs. We will start with experimental and quasi-experimental designs. We will then cover nonexperimental designs.

SECTION 4.4.1: DESIGN MEETS REALITY

In addition to the consideration of the dimensions with the following designs, the researcher must also consider real-world constraints. We have mentioned things such as difficulty with random assignment, difficulty accessing certain subject groups, and response rates. There are also other practical concerns that may alter the design, such as sufficient financial resources to conduct the study, the political atmosphere of agencies, or facilities that must allow access to the subjects, and time constraints.

COST IS IMPORTANT

While all research projects require human and monetary resources, some methods are more expensive than others. For example, interviewing subjects may provide more depth to the information, but it takes longer and is thus expensive to implement. You must have enough

resources to serve sufficient persons in the treatment group to have a large enough sample size to use statistical control. This is why so much of social science is funded by outside grants; the universities, colleges, and partner agencies lack the resources to mount large-scale and/or expensive studies.

ORGANIZATIONAL CONTEXTS CAN ALSO HAVE AN IMPACT ON STUDIES

For example, to do a quasi-experimental design at the local clinic, the clinic administration and staff must buy into the project. Sometimes agencies are reluctant to participate in research because they fear losing funding if their services turn out to be less effective. Service staff may be too burned out to follow a study protocol that involves extra record keeping. Or they may be nervous about possible consequences if their own clients fare worse than others. Finally, there may be policy constraints from higher levels that affect their willingness to participate. For example, the Health Insurance Portability and Accountability Act of 1996 (HIPAA) places stringent requirements on protecting medical and mental health information (www.hhs.gov/ocr/hipaa). A largely unintended consequence of this policy is new restrictions on researcher access to data. This is why it is important to have willingness to participate from any agency involved in the study prior to finalizing your plan. Even if you do this, however, be aware that administrations can change, and sometimes previously granted approval must be reestablished again during the study itself.

TIME CAN DICTATE WHAT DESIGNS ARE AVAILABLE TO YOU

For example, in an evaluation study, an agency may have to provide results within a year. Thus the researcher must alter the "ideal" design to fit within the needs of the agency. For example, follow-up times may be shorter than is ideal. Similarly, if a researcher wants to affect contemporary policy, it may be impossible to do a 10-year longitudinal study because by the time the study is over the findings are no longer relevant to policy. This is one reason why some researchers use administrative data or secondary analysis. Sometimes these data types provide sources of longitudinal data without having to wait 10 years.

THE NEEDS AND VALUES OF THE CONSTITUENT COMMUNITY ARE FACTORS

Sometimes cultural issues or the needs of a community can alter the choice of design (Israel, Eng, Schulz, Parker, & Satcher, 2005; Van Dijver & Leung, 1997). It is unethical to impose an approach to data collection that is not acceptable to a community. It is also likely to result in poor response rates.

Unless you work in a well-funded laboratory environment, the real-world context of your research is likely to moderate the design process. Even if you do work in a laboratory setting, you may wish to consider the field context because it may be hard for others to translate your findings to the field later. This is a major concern in the area of mental health research (Burns & Hoagwood, 1999).

SECTION 4.5
TRUE EXPERIMENTAL DESIGNS IN DETAIL

True experimental designs (sometimes called "equivalent group designs" or "randomized designs" or "randomized clinical trials") are very common in medical and psychological disciplines and are considered by many to be the best or "gold standard" form of research. This is because true experimental designs allow maximum control over spurious causality and therefore are the best designs for really nailing down causal relationships between variables. Most researchers will think badly of you if you say something "causes" something else unless you use a true experimental design. You will also be committing a faux pas (French for "embarrassing boo-boo") if you use the term *control group* for anything but a true experimental design. For other designs, use the term *comparison group* instead.

SECTION 4.5.1: NECESSARY FEATURES OF TRUE EXPERIMENTAL DESIGNS

True experimental designs always have all these features:

- They include one or more **experimental groups** that experience the experimental or treatment conditions.

- They include a **control group** that experiences either nothing, a placebo, a treatment-as-usual, or some other similar condition.

- Subjects are randomly assigned to experimental and control groups. Without random assignment, you do not have a true experimental design.

- True experimental designs always test the hypothesis that the experimental group(s) will differ from the control group on an outcome variable.

- True experimental designs are deductive (our theory predicts factual outcomes; we then design an experiment to see if the results are as the theory predicts).

The purpose of a true experimental design is to test a causal theory. This theory will take the general form

of "if I do something different to the experimental group, then they will have different outcomes than the control group." The associated hypothesis will be that "the experimental group will have a different outcome than the control group." As an example, I might theorize that ice will melt faster when it is in a cubic quart container of 75°F water (experimental condition) than when it is on a Formica countertop at 75°F (control condition). I get 20 ice cubes, I number them and use coin flips to randomly assign them to the experimental condition (I throw them in a tub of 75° water) or the control condition (I put them on a countertop at 75°). I then note when each ice cube finishes melting. If the 10 cubes in water melt in an average of 1.5 minutes, and the cubes on the countertop take an average of 13.9 minutes, then I say my hypothesis was supported. If both groups take around 4 minutes to melt, then I say my hypothesis was not supported. If my hypothesis is supported, I now have empirical evidence for my theory that ice in water melts faster than ice on a countertop. This evidence was derived deductively (theory predicted a fact; we tested for that fact). As this example shows, experimental designs can be very simple in their general nature. They are probably the easiest kind of design to understand and implement, at least conceptually. As with most things, of course, details can rise up and bite you (sample attrition, treatment fidelity, and so on).

SECTION 4.5.2: IMPORTANT LANGUAGE ISSUE: PHRASING RESULTS OF HYPOTHESIS TESTING

Hypotheses are formally written in pairs. For each hypothesis (ice will melt faster in water) there is a corresponding "null" hypothesis (ice will not melt faster in water). The hypothesis that there will be a difference is formally called the "alternative hypothesis" (shorthand is "H1, H2," and so on). The hypothesis that there will be no difference is the "null hypothesis" (shorthand is "H0"). You should know the following language:

- If you *did find* the effect your hypothesis stated would occur: *Technically correct language:* "We rejected the null hypothesis." *Common language:* "Our hypothesis was supported."

- If you *did not find* the effect your hypothesis stated would occur: *Technically correct language:* "We failed to reject the null hypothesis. *Common language:* "Our hypothesis was not supported."

The weakness of using the technically correct language is that only scientists will understand what on earth you are talking about. The term "fail to reject the null" is, in fact, a triple negative and is appalling English. The strength of using the technically correct language is that it is, well, technically correct, will appeal to formal scientists, and reflects the following very good thinking: One experiment cannot ever prove that the alternate hypothesis will always happen, so you can never totally support the alternative hypothesis. However, one experiment can prove that the null hypothesis did not happen at least once. This is why, in a technical sense, we never "accept" the alternative hypothesis, but we only "reject" the null hypothesis.

When do you use each type of language? Base it on your audience. If you are applying to the National Science Foundation (NSF) for a grant, use the technical language. If, however, you are talking to a room full of politicians, practitioners, or others who are not expert researchers, use simple terms. A good deal of this is at your discretion, and there is no established firm practice out there. We have seen top researchers use very informal language at conference presentations, and we have seen new researchers use completely formal language in presenting their first work to laypersons.

We will now review the seven dimensions of research with regard to experimental designs.

DIMENSION 1: PURPOSE IN TRUE EXPERIMENTAL DESIGNS

In simple terms, the purpose of a true experimental design is to test theory. The theory to be tested takes the form of an assertion of an expected (usually causal) relationship ("Intervention X increases self-efficacy in clients"). Grand or midrange theories rarely stand or fall based on single experiments. Usually the theories tested are lower level and are what we have termed "models." It might be technically more accurate to say that the purpose of a true experiment is to test a relationship or outcome that a theory says will happen, as expressed in a model. If we find what the theory says we will find, then we add empirical support to the theory. If enough empirical support builds for a theory, then the theory is said to be well supported and will be accepted by more people. Figure 4.7 may make this more clear.

This process is often recursive. If your hypotheses are not supported, you may well want to go back and figure out what happened. Were your methods sound? Was the theory sound? Should you change something and try again?

DIMENSION 2: CONTROL IN TRUE EXPERIMENTAL DESIGNS

As previously stated, true experimental designs use random assignment to experimental and control groups to make sure that the subjects in each group are, for all practical purposes, identical. This means that the only differences that will show up between the groups will happen based on the real differences between the experimental and control conditions. Be warned that even in true experimental designs, there remain many threats to internal validity, which will be discussed in the next section.

DIMENSION 3: SUBJECTS IN TRUE EXPERIMENTAL DESIGNS: WHO AND HOW MANY?

Your sample frame for any design should match your population of interest as closely as possible. Frequently, this will be impossible or too difficult, and sample frames with the advantage of convenience (such as undergrad psychology majors) will be used. This then becomes a limitation of your study and must be described as such, with you clearly acknowledging that your findings can generalize only to a particular populaton. Your subjects should be pulled randomly from the sample frame. Again, this often borders on the impossible, and other methods (random digit dialing) may be used. This is also a limitation to generalizability. The main issue is as follows: Can you make a logical case that your sample frame and subjects allow you to generalize to a useful target population?

True experimental designs require random assignment to groups so that you have enough subjects in each group to give you the statistical power needed for the effect size you expect to find. If you have only two groups and expect to find a large difference, this may mean that

FIGURE 4.7. **The Relationship of Theory to Experimental Design.**

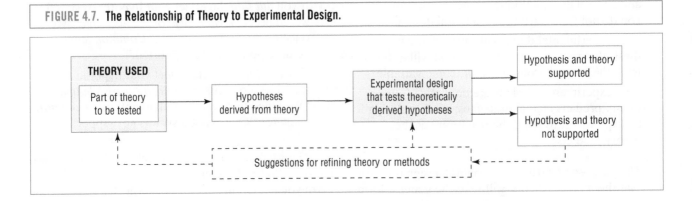

you can get away with as few as 20 or 30 people per group. If, however, you are looking for a smaller difference, if you have many different kinds of groups (for example, see "dosage" designs), or if you want to include many control variables, you may need hundreds (or, rarely, thousands) of subjects. See the section on "Power" in Chapter 13 for more information.

DIMENSION 4: GROUPS IN TRUE EXPERIMENTAL DESIGNS

Combinations of the following types of groups may be used, but at least one experimental group and a control group must be included.

Experimental groups are groups that receive the experimental treatment (for example, they get the drug, they get the new training module, etc.). There can be different types of experimental groups used in the same study (that is, multiple drugs or treatments can be tested in different experimental groups simultaneously).

Control groups are groups that do not receive the experimental treatment. It is usually a bad idea to simply do nothing with the control group, because the mere act of doing anything (regardless of what it is) to the experimental group may make a measurable difference from a group that had nothing done to it. For this reason, a placebo is often used in the control group. The classic case is giving the control group sugar pills. As a more dramatic example, if you want to shoot up rats with a new drug and see if they run a maze faster, you will also want to shoot up the control rats with a neutral solution (saline). Otherwise, how would you know if the drug or the simple act of getting a shot makes them run faster? Often, for ethical reasons, we cannot simply do nothing or give a placebo. For example, a new cancer treatment will generally be compared to a **treatment as usual** group, because comparing a new treatment to a placebo is totally unethical (how would you like to be in the placebo group?). For this reason, the control group is

often a treatment as usual group. Blind and double-blind formats, as just described, are commonly used in experimental designs whenever possible to avoid expectation and experimenter effects. Some examples might be handy. Note that by "no treatment," we mean "no experimental treatment." This might be nothing, a placebo (better), or treatment as usual.

Use the model in Table 4.5 when you want to test the differences between the different conditions (A, B, C) and the control group. Use the model in Table 4.6 when two new approaches are to be compared to each other. This is rarely used, because there is no way to compare the effects of the new treatment to a prior treatment or other control condition. We know we said earlier all true experimental designs need a control group. While some people would probably call this a true experimental design, others might say that this is not a true experimental design at all, because it lacks a control group.

More Groups (Blocking). Sometimes, you will want to understand how different subjects respond to experimental conditions. Blocking accomplishes this and also serves as a control for that characteristic. Let's say you want to test a new psychotherapy but are concerned that it may have different effects based on subject age. You might assign people to age groups (20 to 29, 30 to 39, 40 to 49, 50+). You would then randomly assign these people to experimental or control conditions, giving a total of eight conditions (20- to 29-year-old people with treatment, 20- to 29-year-old people with no treatment, 30- to 39-year-old people with treatment, and so on). This is essentially the same idea as using a stratified sample, but it also determines who gets assigned to which group. In common practice, you might select a stratified sample, and then you make sure that you randomly assign to experimental and control conditions from each strata separately. In the fictional example in Table 4.7, we see that the treatment

---

TABLE 4.5. Experimental Design with Multiple Experimental Conditions.

Experimental Group	Pretest	Treatment A	Posttest	Follow-up #1	Follow-up#2
Experimental Group	Pretest	Treatment B	Posttest	Follow-up #1	Follow-up#2
Experimental Group	Pretest	Treatment C	Posttest	Follow-up #1	Follow-up#2
Control Group	Pretest	Placebo	Posttest	Follow-up #1	Follow-up#2

TABLE 4.6. Experimental Design with No True Control Group.

| Experimental Group | Pretest | Treatment A | Posttest | Follow-up #1 | Follow-up#2 |
| Experimental Group | Pretest | Treatment B | Posttest | Follow-up #1 | Follow-up#2 |

TABLE 4.7. Blocking by Age.

BLOCKING GROUP	GROUP AGE (Blocking Variable)	NUMBER OF SUBJECTS	PRETEST	TREATMENT? (Independent Variable)	POSTTEST
	20–29	20	Pretest	Yes	Posttest
1	20–29	20		Yes	
		20		No	
2	30–39	20		Yes	
		20	Given to all subjects	No	Given to all subjects
3	40–49	20		Yes	
		20		No	
4	50+	20		Yes	
		20		No	

seems to work better with people under 40, especially with those under 30, and it doesn't seem to work much at all with those over 40 (see table below). In this example, age is the blocking variable.

Mean Pretest/Posttest Change for Different Groups

	Tx	No Tx
20–29-year-olds	+17 pts	−1 pt
30–39-year-olds	+8 pts	+1 pt
40–49-year-olds	+2 pts	−1 pt
50+ year-olds	−1 pt	+1 pt

In this example, it appears that treatment is most effective for younger people and ineffective for people over 40. Remember, blocking is done on characteristics of the subjects and does not represent new experimental conditions or treatments. When you vary the levels of the treatments, we call that a factorial design.

Groups in Factorial Designs. Factorial designs include multiple factors (independent variables) with multiple levels (values of the independent variables), for example:

■ Factor 1: Music volume. Levels: Low, Medium, High.

■ Factor 2: Difficulty of reading task. Levels: Easy, Hard.

Factorial designs are meant to test each level of each factor against every other level of the other factor. In the previous example, we would have three levels of

music volume and two levels of task difficulty, yielding six conditions:

Experimental Group 1: Low volume, easy task

Experimental Group 2: Low volume, hard task

Experimental Group 3: Medium volume, easy task

Experimental Group 4: Medium volume, hard task

Experimental Group 5: High volume, easy task

Experimental Group 6: High volume, hard task

You can think of it as a grid, if you like:

	Easy Task	Hard Task
Low Volume	Group 1	Group 2
Medium Volume	Group 3	Group 4
High Volume	Group 5	Group 6

Sometimes it is important to know how things work either alone or in combination. You might have a country that is considering implementing one or both of two policies designed to reduce poverty. This calls for a factorial design with two factors (policy A and policy B), where each factor has two levels (1 = policy present, 0 = policy not present). This might look as follows:

Experimental Group 1: A1, B0: Policy A (only) is instituted.

Experimental Group 2: A1, B1: Policy A and policy B are instituted.

Experimental Group 3: B1, A0: Policy B (only) is instituted.

Control Group: A0, B0: No new policy is instituted.

Factorial designs can test every possible combination to see which works best. They can have more than two dimensions (variables), but these designs can get out of hand fast. For example, if you are testing three levels of one factor against four levels of another factor and two levels of a third factor, this will be $3 \times 4 \times 2$ groups, for 24 groups. Even if you had only 20 people per group, that's 480 subjects you need to test.

Dosage Designs. Sometimes it is important to know how much of something it takes to get a given effect. This situation may call for a **dosage design.** This may require that there be many experimental groups. We might believe that our new form of aspirin works better, but we aren't sure how much it takes to be effective. We would create a series of groups, getting pills with different levels of the new aspirin (sugar, or 0 mg; 150 mg; 300 mg; 450 mg; 600 mg). Let's say (hypothetically) the results look like this, with higher scores indicating more pain:

Group	Pain Rating
Sugar placebo	7.8
150 mg	6.3
300 mg	3.3
450 mg	3.3
600 mg	3.2

We now know not only that the new aspirin works, but also that 150 mg works a bit, and that it never really helps much to take more than 300 mg. Studies like this can be done on things that don't use drugs at all. For example, you may want to find out how many weeks long your summer remedial reading sessions should be. You could use a similar design to try to see how different lengths of session produce different gains in reading level.

Crossover Designs. Crossover designs give subjects exposure to different experimental conditions over time. For example, you might have the design shown in Table 4.8.

TABLE 4.9. Partial Crossover Design.

Group 1	Test	Treatment	Test		
Group 2	Test	No treatment	Test	Treatment	Test

Advantages of crossover designs are their efficiency (someone is always going through a condition, you can keep running all three conditions with full membership) and the fact that they can tell you if the time order in which the treatments are given matters. Designs of this type are fairly rare, because sequencing of treatment is rarely an issue of theoretical interest.

Far more common are partial crossover designs (Table 4.9). They are common not for any purely methodological, scientific, or practical reason, but because partial crossover designs reduce the ethical problem of refusal of treatment.

This very common design allows you to bring subjects in, have a standard true experimental design (boxed area), and then serve your control group. In this way, the ethical concern that some of your subjects will fail to receive needed help can be dealt with. Typically, control group subjects are given the option of participating in the treatment condition, often after having been informed of the benefits received by the treatment group. Of course, if the treatment turns out to be harmful, then it would not be offered. This is the same as using a waiting list. Remember, you can never ethically refuse or delay needed treatment if the time delay is likely to cause harm to the subject.

DIMENSION 5: INVESTIGATOR MANIPULATION IN TRUE EXPERIMENTAL DESIGNS

This issue is at the heart of experimental designs. Experimental designs compare one group of subjects who receive the condition (treatment) of interest and one group that does not. What the experimenter does in the experimental condition can be pretty much anything you can imagine. We'll look at a couple of examples to give you an idea of the range of possibilities.

TABLE 4.8. Crossover Design.

Group 1	Test	Treatment A	Test	Treatment B	Test	Treatment C	Test
Group 2	Test	Treatment A	Test	Treatment C	Test	Treatment B	Test
Group 3	Test	Treatment B	Test	Treatment A	Test	Treatment C	Test
Group 4	Test	Treatment B	Test	Treatment C	Test	Treatment A	Test
Group 5	Test	Treatment C	Test	Treatment A	Test	Treatment B	Test
Group 6	Test	Treatment C	Test	Treatment B	Test	Treatment A	Test
Control	Test	Placebo	Test	Placebo	Test	Placebo	Test

An Obvious Example of Investigator Manipulation. You may want to know if a new form of aspirin works better than the old, or than nothing. You would randomly assign your subjects who have pain (chronic headache sufferers, for example) into three conditions (old aspirin, new aspirin, sugar pill placebo). You would then give them the pills and ask them to rate their levels of pain before and after. The manipulation is obvious: You are giving either the old drug, the new drug, or no drug.

A Subtle Example of Investigator Manipulation. Some clever person (Loftus, 1975) wanted to better understand if leading questions could change memories. She divided up her sample into several groups, all of which saw the same short film which did *not* include a barn. The investigator manipulation came in the form of different questions asked of the three groups immediately after the film was shown. Two groups got questions that included references to a (nonexistent) barn in the film; the other group did not. One week later, everyone was questioned about the presence or absence of a barn in the original film. The two experimental groups (who had been asked questions about a barn) had much higher rates of (erroneously) reporting that they actually saw a barn in the film. This was hailed as a major study showing that memories are fallible and can be intentionally manipulated. As can be seen, sometimes the experimental manipulation can be so subtle as to be completely unnoticeable by the subject.

DIMENSION 6: TIME FRAME IN TRUE EXPERIMENTAL DESIGNS

Experimental designs are often thought of as being point-in-time studies where the subject walks into a lab somewhere and gets messed with by someone in a white coat, and then everyone goes home. While it is correct that true experimental designs cannot be retrospective, they can certainly be prospective, and the subjects can be followed longitudinally. One of the main criticisms of many experimental designs that test new psychological or social interventions is that they do not follow the subjects for long enough to get a sense for what is really happening.

The time frame in Table 4.10 illustrates an ideal case. You find out how the people are doing before and after the intervention (which allows you to show degree of improvement), and you find out how well the intervention effect (assuming you got one) persists at 90 days and a year. Your theory should guide you in determining if and how many follow-ups you need to do. A program that theoretically makes a long-term difference, such as Head Start, needs a multiyear follow-up period. The aspirin study described, on the other hand, is designed to have only a short-term effect, and a follow-up of months or years would make no sense whatsoever.

Should You Always Pretest? Pretesting is a good idea in almost all cases. You will want to know where your subjects scored before the intervention for two reasons:

1. You can use these data to determine the degree of change (change = time 2 score − time 1 score).
2. You can verify that your groups were similar at start with respect to variables of interest. But—"Hey," you say, "doesn't random assignment guarantee that the groups will be similar? Isn't that the whole point of random assignment?" Yes, it is mathematically true that sufficiently large groups that are randomly selected will not vary from each other appreciably, *but* a pretest allows you to nail it down for sure. This is especially true of small groups, where the "law of large numbers" (things average out given big enough numbers) may not apply as well.

DIMENSION 7: DATA TYPE IN TRUE EXPERIMENTAL DESIGN

Direct observation and structured (often standardized) instruments are the most commonly used ways of gathering data in experimental designs. Data used can be very simple or very complex. Our aspirin example used a closed-ended question (pain rating number) as its outcome data. This is a very simple rating of pain on a scale of 1 to 10, which is often called a SUDS (subjective units of distress scale) score. Those who have been to the hospital lately may well remember people asking them to rate their pain using this method. Other experimental designs use testing protocols that involve blood tests, videotaping, or written examinations that

TABLE 4.10. Experimental Design with Follow-Up.

	PRETEST	INTERVENTION	POSTTEST	FOLLOW-UP I	FOLLOW-UP II
Experimental Group	Test given right before intervention	Experimental intervention administered	Test given right after intervention	Test given 3 months later	Test given 12 months later
Control Group	Test given right before intervention	Placebo intervention administered	Test given right after intervention	Test given 3 months later	Test given 12 months later

take hours. Animal experimental designs commonly use autopsies, as have some extremely unethical human studies (such as the Nazi medical studies).

Which Type of Data Should You Use? The data you will use will depend almost entirely on your theory and your question. If your question has to do with behavior (for example, domestic violence) then the best choice of data type will be some direct measure of violence. If this is unavailable, then an instrument measuring something similar, such as ways of resolving problems, or ratings of anger, or client self-reported violent acts, may be your best option. Try to keep as close as possible to your question when you select your means of data collection. You may want to use separate and reinforcing types of data. For example, an experimental design that explores a new form of marital therapy might measure not only marital satisfaction but also relationships with children, blood pressure, and other health indicators. Any indicator that might be theoretically related to your experimental condition is fair game.

SECTION 4.6
QUASI-EXPERIMENTAL DESIGNS IN DETAIL

Quasi-experimental designs are probably the most common form of social research. They lack random assignment and are therefore often called "nonequivalent group" designs.

DIMENSION 1: PURPOSE

Quasi-experimental designs also attempt to assess theoretically derived relationships between variables (usually cause and effect) and must have experimental and comparison groups, or, in the case of time-series designs, experimental and comparison conditions.

DIMENSION 2: CONTROL

The main weakness of quasi-experimental designs is that unlike true experimental designs, they lack random assignment and so cannot completely rule out

spurious factors. Because ruling out spurious causality is one of the three conditions of demonstrating causality, these designs are weaker with regard to questions that seek to test hypotheses that something *causes* something else. Quasi-experimental designs can best be thought of in several types depending on how they deal with the issue of control.

Multigroup quasi-experimental designs with experimental and comparison groups are very common, particularly in research that occurs in the field (outside the lab). Most agency-based research is done this way and, except for the lack of random assignment, these studies are exactly like true experimental designs. The reason that so many such studies are done is simple practicality. It is often not possible to randomly assign people to control and experimental conditions without considerable expense and trouble. So groups getting different interventions are compared or intervention groups are compared with waiting list groups, and so on. The example in Table 4.11 is quasi-experimental and uses cluster sampling.

Time-series quasi-experimental designs with comparison *conditions* provide for some control. Time-series designs involve switching the same group (or individual, see Chapter 8) between experimental and comparison conditions. One common, if informal, example involves the standard medical practice for determining which drugs work best for which patients. A doctor might track a client's psychotic behaviors to get an initial sense for the client's normal (baseline) functioning. She might then try different drugs to see which has the best effect. She then compares the first (baseline) levels of psychotic behavior to later levels on different drugs to see which drug works best. The term *baseline* is commonly used in time-series designs to refer to the way things were before the experimental condition went into play. For this reason, time-series designs often include an initial period where no experimental intervention is applied, simply so a baseline can be established.

Very weak designs without comparison groups or comparison conditions also exist but should be avoided. Most people would say these are not experimental designs at all. One example is the single-group posttest-only design. If you run an antisuicide intervention and

TABLE 4.11. **Example of Multigroup Quasi-Experimental Design.**				
	SAMPLE	PRETEST	CONDITION	POSTTEST
Treatment Group	326 subjects seen in five agency offices. These offices got the new computer-assisted treatment program.	Pretest given	All subjects get computer-assisted treatment.	Posttest given
Comparison Group	875 subjects seen in 15 other agency offices that do not have the new program.	Pretest given	All subjects get treatment as usual.	Posttest given

only 1% of your subjects kill themselves within a year, you may say, "Wow, this works great!" Unfortunately, you don't really know anything at all about how effective your treatment was. Is this outcome better than would have happened without your treatment? Worse? How do you know? Such designs are basically a waste of time.

CRITICISMS OF EARLY FAMILY PRESERVATION RESEARCH

Many years ago, it was hypothesized that a crisis-intervention model (lots of services over a brief time at a critical point) would be a great way to help families with serious problems who came to the attention of child protective services. More specifically, the idea was that if you gave these services (Family Preservation Services, or FPS) to families who would otherwise have children placed in foster care, you could help them out and avoid foster placement. This made political liberals happy (services got provided), and it made political conservatives happy (family intrusion was limited), and it made child welfare service providers very happy (it was considerably cheaper than foster care, if it worked). Much of the initial research was very positive and showed that FPS was very effective. It seemed perfect. All 50 states adopted it, and the federal government approved $623 million in 1993 (GAO, 1997) for states to use. Unfortunately, new research demonstrates that FPS certainly doesn't work as well as the early research showed. In fact, for many populations, it may not work at all. How did this happen?

Early research used the following logic: (1) FPS will be used only for children who are appropriate for it and who workers say would otherwise be placed in foster care. (2) A comparison or control group is not needed, because 100% of children would have been placed in foster care if not served (the workers said so). (3) Any child avoiding placement in an FPS program is therefore one who would have otherwise been put in foster care. The following design was used: (A) Get a sample of children referred to FPS and (B) see how many end up not going into foster care. Any child who avoids foster care is counted as a success for FPS. You will immediately notice that this design lacks multiple groups or conditions. Many of the children avoided foster care, and the program was declared effective.

Subsequent research used true or quasi-experimental designs. The children who were presumably going to be placed were given either FPS or another condition (usually normal child welfare services). Foster care rates were tracked. The results were that FPS kids and non-FPS kids looked pretty much the same. Some studies even showed a negative effect. For a nice review, see Littell and Shuerman, 1995, available online at http://aspe.os.dhhs.gov/hsp/cyp/fplitrev.htm.

The moral of this story, of course, is that control and comparison groups are really important.■

Natural experiments happen when the world creates a quasi-experimental design for you, and you take advantage of it. Naturalistic experiments can happen in an almost infinite number of ways. For example, you might compare 20 different communities that have had a large employer leave town to 20 other communities that were otherwise similar but did not lose a major employer. In this case, you can't ever do a true experimental design, because you can't randomly assign communities to "lose major employer" or "not lose major employer" conditions.

Naturalistic experiments can also be historical time-series designs. One simple example of a naturally occurring time-series design might be as shown in Table 4.12.

In such cases as this, the researcher needs simply to gather the data and report them. This data (if real) would be interpreted as failing to show any large surge of reports during a local Super Bowl win or loss. Natural experiments often are not time-series designs but involve experimental and comparison groups that occur naturally. For example, if you want to understand the effect of child death on marriages, you would go out and interview a number of people from two groups (those experiencing child death and those not), and do a two-group posttest-only design. Of course, the researcher would have to try very hard to minimize or statistically control for differences between the groups to try to minimize the role of spurious causality. In short, naturalistic experiments are very common in the social sciences and are, in fact, the best way to study many kinds of issues that cannot be approached with a true experimental design.

TABLE 4.12. **Homicides in St. Louis Metro Area during Super Bowl Weeks (Fictitious Data).**

WEEK OF SUPER BOWL XXXIII	WEEK OF SUPER BOWL XXXIV	WEEK OF SUPER BOWL XXXV	WEEK OF SUPER BOWL XXXVI	WEEK OF SUPER BOWL XXXVII
St. Louis not in Super Bowl	St. Louis wins Super Bowl	St. Louis not in Super Bowl	St. Louis loses Super Bowl	St. Louis not in Super Bowl
13	10	9	12	11

DIMENSION 3: SUBJECTS

The lack of random assignment to groups makes these designs a little harder on the researcher, because you have to do your best to convince your audience (and yourself) that differences you observe in your study are not just because your two groups started out different. You must do everything you can to show that the experimental and comparison groups are alike. This can be done in the following ways:

■ Recruit them from the same or very similar sampling frames.

■ Recruit them in similar ways.

■ Consider using matching (as we have discussed).

■ Make sure you measure all subjects with regard to any variables that could, for theoretical or practical reasons, influence your dependent variables.

■ Present statistics to show that the groups do not differ on these variables and/or control for them statistically.

Your goal is to make a compelling case that your experimental and comparison groups are alike. If you can do this well, people will feel more comfortable that you have ruled out spurious factors and will have more faith in your findings.

DIMENSION 4: GROUPS

The number and construction of groups in a quasi-experimental design can be identical to those used in true experimental design. If you use any of the designs described in the section on true experimental designs and do not use random assignment, then you have a quasi-experimental design. There are a number of other quasi-experimental designs, however, that involve single groups, which we have not mentioned. The simplest is the "one shot" design in which an individual or group is tested, exposed to the experimental condition, and then retested.

One Group, Single Treatment Pretest/Posttest Design

Pretest (Baseline)	Treatment	Posttest

Obviously, this is a weak design because there is no comparison group. Any noted change may be due to the treatment, or it may be due to regression to the mean, the Hawthorne effect, history, or other things. Unfortunately, many studies with important policy implications are done this way. For example, most studies of the impact of new policies are based on measurements under the old policy (baseline) compared to measurements after implementation of the new policy. A more complex and somewhat stronger example might involve tracking how many disruptive behaviors occur (average per child) in a group of children in different treatment conditions. This is a form of time-series design, as illustrated in Figure 4.8.

The graph in Figure 4.8 shows a number of interesting things. First of all, the baseline was stable at around 60 disruptive behaviors per day. Second, the disruptive behaviors dropped almost to nothing when treatment A was in place. Unfortunately, the behaviors bounced right back after treatment A was discontinued. Treatment B dropped the problem behaviors, too, although maybe not quite as much as treatment A. Fortunately, however, the gains made in treatment B seem to have continued even after the treatment ended. B seems to have a longer-lasting effect. Alternate guesses about what happened are also possible. Is treatment B really more enduring, or is it just that it had the benefit of coming after a prior intervention? Would treatment A have had an equally enduring effect the second time it was offered? We can't say. A wide variety of different such designs can be imagined.

The design is stronger than the prior example for several reasons. First of all, measurements are made on a continuing (daily) basis. This allows us to get a sense for the trends over time within each period and helps us be sure we didn't just get one faulty measurement.

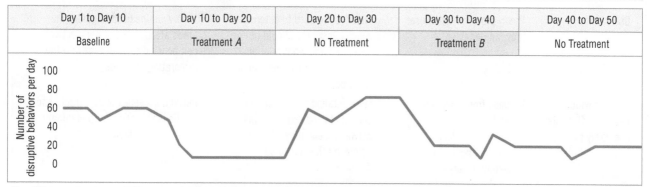

FIGURE 4.8. **Time-Series Design (Two Sequential Treatments).**

Day 1 to Day 10	Day 10 to Day 20	Day 20 to Day 30	Day 30 to Day 40	Day 40 to Day 50
Baseline	Treatment A	No Treatment	Treatment B	No Treatment

Another strength of the design is that there are more periods we can refer to, including three "no treatment" periods, allowing us more information. This design also tests two different interventions (*A* and *B*), allowing us to draw inferences about each.

DIMENSION 5: INVESTIGATOR MANIPULATION

Because questions in quasi-experimental studies still seek to understand cause, there is often some sort of investigator manipulation, and it is handled in the same way as in experimental designs. Quasi-experimental designs can also occur with naturally occurring groups, as explained in the naturalistic experiment section. In this case, no investigator manipulation occurs.

DIMENSION 6: TIME FRAME

Again, the time frame of the data collection process can be very similar to an experimental design. Longitudinal studies (beyond pre- and posttest) are somewhat more common, however, particularly in the case of naturalistic experiments. For instance, in the example regarding homicides and Super Bowl events (Table 4.12) the study actually occurs over multiple years to capture the desired events. The investigator is not manipulating the situation but just following events as they unfold in a naturally occurring time-series design.

DIMENSION 7: DATA TYPE

Any type of data may be used in a quasi-experimental design. The selection of the type of data should be based on maximizing internal and external validity in

attempting to answer the research question(s). For example, if you are studying how grades of children in a divorce support group at school compare to grades of children who experienced divorce but did not choose to participate, then you might rely on the school's computer system to look up student grades. If you are measuring a change in attitude among high school students following diversity training compared to the attitude of high school students at a comparison school, then you are likely to use interviews or some sort of survey.

SECTION 4.7
NONEXPERIMENTAL DESIGNS IN DETAIL

We will now turn to nonexperimental designs. Nonexperimental design can be broken down into three types: correlational, descriptive, and exploratory. Correlational designs test theoretically derived relationships. Exploratory and descriptive designs are similar to each other in many ways, differing mainly in the degree to which the constructs that will be studied are specified in advance. Descriptive studies start with identified constructs, which they seek to gather data about. Exploratory studies start with the intent of describing constructs as they develop in the course of the research.

DIMENSION 1: PURPOSE

As previously discussed, the three types of nonexperimental design differ in their purpose and the role of theory (Table 4.13).

TABLE 4.13. **Theory and Non-Experimental Designs.**

	CORRELATIONAL	DESCRIPTIVE (often includes qualitative data)	EXPLORATORY (often includes qualitative data)
Type of theory normally used	Detailed and developed theories and models that predict specific relationships between variables	Broad theories that can provide a background context for the research	Extremely broad theories or specified perspectives that guide exploration
Use of theory	Theory provides hypotheses that can be tested.	Theories are used to determine which constructs should be described and what relationships between constructs need to be explored.	Theory can be used to guide what areas are explored or perspectives can be used to determine how the exploration proceeds.
Ways in which research findings are likely to influence theory	Findings from research support or fail to support hypotheses, thus strengthening or weakening theory.	More detailed specification of constructs and relationships between them allows for more advanced theories to be developed.	Initial discoveries of constructs and relationships allow for preliminary theory development.

The Role of Theory in Correlational Designs. Correlational designs use nonexperimental means to test theoretical models. Their greatest weakness is that they cannot fully control for issues of spurious causality and thus cannot prove causation. Their advantages over true experimental designs are that they are often easier to do and that they can often be accomplished in more naturalistic settings, which enhances generalizability. It is important to realize that correlational and experimental designs share a similar goal: to test relationships as predicted by theory. To do a correlational design, you must start with a clear model of the relationships your theory says should exist. Correlational designs are therefore always deductive, starting with theory, figuring out what that theory says will happen in the real world, and then gathering facts to see if the world really is as the theory says it is. As an example, we could use the theory of learned helplessness to predict that people's job-hunting motivation would decline in periods of scarce employment opportunities. This is a specific theory that yields a specific hypothesis, which can be tested in a correlational design.

The Role of Theory in Descriptive Designs. Compared to correlational designs, these designs use theory very differently. Instead of using theory to describe expected relationships and then test for them, descriptive designs use theory to frame what constructs (and relationships between constructs) need further exploration, description, and definition. Hypotheses are therefore not appropriate for descriptive analyses, because there are not theoretically based relationships between constructs that are being tested. Despite this, theory remains critical in descriptive designs. Theory is used to select the constructs that will be examined and to guide how that examination is done. There should be sound reasons, either theoretical or practical, why these particular constructs require attention and for the ways they are examined. Because the role of theory is to frame and guide the research, not to generate specific hypotheses, theory used in descriptive designs is often at a much more broad or abstract level than is the theory used in correlational designs. As an example, we may want to describe discipline problems in public schools. We could pick one or several broad theoretical orientations to guide our research. It might be a good idea, for example, to use a grand theory such as behaviorism, perhaps in conjunction with theories about child development, to help us in making sense of how to describe the subject at hand. Modeling (Bandura) is a theory that says that people do what they see others doing. If we use this theory, then we will be very careful to try to describe not only the delinquency behaviors themselves, but the relationship between one student demonstrating such behaviors and other students copying those behaviors.

The importance of theory in descriptive designs should not be underestimated. A behaviorist describing school discipline problems will look at emitted behaviors and construct tables of specific actions (rate of talking out of turn, rate of pushing, etc.). A psychodynamically oriented researcher would be much more interested in looking at more abstract and interpersonal things, like student–teacher relationships, self-esteem, and so on. The researcher might even try to describe the problem through a series of qualitative case studies. You need to understand and be in charge of the theoretical stance you're taking, even in the most exploratory research.

The Role of Theory in Exploratory Designs. Exploratory designs can take many forms. Exploratory designs may be entirely quantitative or entirely qualitative. The goal can be deductive (to see if what's out there matches our theory) or inductive (to see if we can create a meaningful theory from what we find out there). Many inductive exploratory designs can be classified as "grounded theory." Grounded theory is not a theory in itself; it is an approach to generating theory and is pretty much just plain induction. The researcher intentionally starts with no specified theory (as far as that is possible) and lets a new theory "emerge" through an inductive process, using a method of "constant comparison" to check to see if the data observed seems to fit the emerging theory. If the comparison between data and emerging theory is poor, then the theory is modified. We will discuss this in more detail in Chapter 13.

While most people think of exploratory research as entirely qualitative, this is not the case. It is entirely appropriate to use purely numerical data (income, crime, household composition, and the like) in trying to understand and develop ideas about different kinds of neighborhoods, for example.

DIMENSION 2: CONTROL

Control in Correlational Designs. Control is normally handled through careful sample selection or through statistical means. How you select your sample can help limit the influence of known factors. If you know some factors may affect your dependent variable, you may exclude people with those factors. For example, you may limit a study of the progression of heart disease to nonsmokers. Multivariate regression and similar techniques also allow the researcher to account for the influence of known factors by using statistical models. We will discuss this in more detail in Chapters 13 and 14, but for the time being, it is enough to know that multivariate methods allow you to control for the effects of other variables in your study. Obviously, factors that are not measured cannot be controlled for because they cannot be entered into the equations.

Control in Descriptive and Exploratory Designs. Descriptive and exploratory researchers are usually less interested in control because their first task is simply to try to document what is. Descriptive and exploratory researchers do document observed relationships and may propose theories about those relationships. They may even use statistical controls to try to determine the unique contribution of one variable to another. Detailed testing of these relationships, however, is more normally left to experimental or correlational designs.

DIMENSION 3: SUBJECTS

Subjects in nonexperimental designs are recruited using essentially the same conventions described for experimental designs. This is because the logic behind sampling is meant to support generalizability (external validity), something of importance to all studies. A few things are worth noting, however:

- Correlational designs will often have only one group. For example, if we want to analyze the relationship between weight and exercise, we might get 100 people of various weights and see how much they excercise.

- Descriptive and exploratory designs that are intended to generate data for inductive purposes (theory building) often try to include as many different types of subjects as possible, so that the resultant theory can be as broad as possible. This means that samples drawn for inductive purposes will sometimes try to emphasize the diversity of a population, instead of representing the actual distribution of characteristics within a population. This is done so that the theory can take into account all the various differences that are likely to occur in the general population. As an example, if you are doing an exploratory study on women's reactions to divorce and you want to develop a theory that will have the best chance of covering a wide range of reactions, you might be very careful to make sure you include women who had divorces for different reasons, some who have children and some who don't, and so on. Of course, if your goal is simply to develop theory around a specific subset of divorced women (perhaps women who have suffered domestic violence), then you would sample only those women. Once again, it all depends on your original question. These sampling issues will be covered in much more detail in Chapter 6, as they are often an issue in inductive, qualitative designs.

DIMENSION 4: GROUPS

Few issues are as confusing as the issue of "groups" in nonexperimental designs. We prefer not to use the term when talking about such designs. However, you will often have nonexperimental designs that are described as including several groups. This may be due to sampling from different populations, stratification by subject characteristics (e.g., gender), or other reasons.

Usually, correlational designs are thought of as having one group. In a correlational design, we would typically look at a bunch of people, and then compare them on two or more variables. For example, we might look at 100 college freshmen (freshpeople?) and ask them how many hours they volunteered to community service in the past year. We might then provide them with a scale to measure altruism, to determine if people who score high on altruism actually volunteer more service.

On the other hand, we might want to look at altruism across the lifespan. What if we get another 100 students at the high school level, and we complete another analysis on these people to see if the same relationships hold, or if relationships vary by age cohort? This design clearly has two "groups" from a sampling perspective, and you may well choose to analyze each group separately. Instead of calling this a "two group correlational design," we would favor saying something like "we completed correlational analyses on two different samples, one at the high school level, and one at the college level, to see if the relationships looked similar."

The same principle applies to exploratory and descriptive designs. If you want to describe Hispanic acculturation in different contexts (rural, suburban, inner-city, etc.) you might purposively sample from each of these different areas. We feel it is easiest to think of these as separate samples, not as if they are groups in an experimental design. We apologize if this section seems overly semantic. We just hope that you restrict your use of the term *groups* mainly to experimental designs so that confusion can be avoided.

DIMENSION 5: INVESTIGATOR MANIPULATION

There is not usually investigator manipulation of subjects in nonexperimental designs.

DIMENSION 6: TIME FRAME

The time frame in nonexperimental designs can be virtually anything you can imagine. All of the various time frames reviewed earlier this chapter can be employed in nonexperimental designs. There are vast numbers of correlational and descriptive studies that use retrospective archival or administrative data. Studies of crime, poverty, and other social ills are frequently based on a review of data that may encompass decades. A few examples might be useful to show how different time frames can be used. For simplicity, we'll use the same subject matter, video game viewing, as an example:

- *Retrospective Example:* You might find a number of teenagers, ask them (or check records for) how many times they have been in trouble at school for violence since age 5, and then also ask how long ago they started playing video games and how often they play. Of course, you are trusting their recall, which places you on fairly shaky ground.

- *Point-in-Time Example:* You might track how many violent behaviors a child emits in a given period (a day, a week) and also track his or her video game usage during that time.

- *Prospective Example:* You might ask parents to monitor their child's video game use and also fill out monthly ratings of the child's violent behaviors. You might keep this up for a few days or a year or more.

- *Combined Example:* You might track prior records of violence and get a history of video game use but also follow the children for several more years, tracking video game use and violence periodically.

As previously discussed, trend, cohort, and panel studies are also popular forms of nonexperimental research and provide the researcher with ways of tracking trends within populations, cohorts, or samples over time.

DIMENSION 7: DATA TYPE

Again, nonexperimental designs afford the researcher almost complete flexibility in regard to the type of data used to measure constructs. We discussed a series of data types prior, including observation, structured instruments, unstructured data, preexisting data, and combinations of these types. There will be far more information on this in Chapter 5.

Observational Data in Nonexperimental Designs. A large number of nonexperimental designs use observations. Observations can be done using complicated laboratory instruments that measure things like galvanic skin response, or they can be simple checklists filled out by a researcher.

EXAMPLE: PARK USE STUDY

One of the authors consulted on a study of the uses of a large urban park. This study had a large number of components, including two that were purely observational. In one component, a researcher parked his car at an intersection and simply noted the number, type, and direction of vehicles passing through. This was done to get a sense for the flow of traffic through the park. The researcher showed up at different times and different days and at different intersections according to a rotating schedule, so that the best overall

picture of park traffic flow could be obtained. In another component of the same study, the researcher drove through the park, which had been broken down into a number of subareas, and noted what pedestrians were doing (running, dog walking, picnicking, and the like). Again, times and locations were rotated, so he could track rates of different use at different points in the park at different times.■

The key thing is to use a method that is clearly structured and that can be replicated. Those people actually doing the recording must be carefully trained and must be tested with simulations or real subjects to assure consistency of recording or "inter-rater-reliability" (see Chapter 5).

Structured instruments in nonexperimental designs can take the form of standardized instruments (see above) or instruments that are not standardized but are created by the researcher. Most structured instruments are filled out by the subject, but many are not. For example, the Home Observation for Measurement of the Environment (HOME) is an instrument that has a number of items that are filled out by a researcher based on what he or she sees in a child's home. As mentioned in earlier chapters and sections, cultural sensitivity is critical. A good reference for constructing and conducting survey research with diverse communities is *Cross-Cultural Survey Methods* (Harkness et al., 2002).

The park use study also sampled park users using a specific sampling plan for when and where they would be selected, so as to get the best representation of the park users. On the instrument were questions like the following:

EXAMPLE: PARK USE STUDY, PART II

I would use the park more if I felt safer in the park.

[1]	[2]	[3]	[4]	[5]
Strongly disagree	Disagree	Neither agree nor disagree	Agree	Strongly agree

How often do you go to the park?

[ ] Every day
[ ] Less than every day but more than once per week
[ ] About once per week
[ ] Less than once per week but at least once per month
[ ] Less than once per month■

If standardized instruments exist for the constructs you wish to study, then using them will make it easier for you to demonstrate instrument reliability and validity.

Unstructured Data in Nonexperimental Designs. Unstructured data can be found in preexisting narratives or can be recorded by researchers doing interviews on tape or in writing. Much of the unstructured data used in social science research come in response to open-ended questions. It is very common for open-ended questions to be combined with closed-ended questions on the same form, typically with the open-ended questions coming last.

EXAMPLE: PARK USE STUDY, PART III

What change or changes do you think would make the park a better place for you?

What things (if any) about the park make you less likely to come here?■

In addition to this form of written unstructured data, narrative or similar data are very commonly used in qualitative designs and in content analyses. Typically such data will take the form of a series of audiotaped subject responses to open-ended researcher questions. In some qualitative approaches, this can be even less structured.

Preexisting Data in Nonexperimental Designs. Preexisting data are an increasingly available and detailed source of data. Earlier we briefly discussed archival data, which simply means "data stored somewhere"; secondary analyses, where you use data from a prior study to answer your own questions; and administrative data, which are those kept by organizations. All are perfectly appropriate for nonexperimental designs.

Secondary analyses are easier to do now than in the past, because so many high-quality computerized data sets are now available. These cover areas of poverty (Panel Study on Income Dynamics), drugs (National Household Study on Drug Abuse), Mental Health (Epidemiological Catchment Area study), and many other areas. Many grants require that you archive your data and allow other researchers to use them after you are finished with them. Combine this increasing availability of data with the fact that the number of articles that can be written on a large data set are virtually limitless, and you can see why secondary analyses are becoming increasingly popular. There exist a number of sites where such data can be accessed, including ICPSR at the University of Michigan (http://icpsr.umich.edu) and, in the author's area, the NDACAN at Cornell (http://ndacan@cornell.edu). These organizations both hold many data sets, and people work there who can help you gain access to them.

The advantage of using such data sets is that you don't have to go out and collect new data. The biggest disadvantage is that you don't have the chance to decide what questions get asked. Nonetheless, if your field of study includes a large preexisting data set that can be used to effectively answer your questions, this should be your first choice for a data source. Why collect new data if you don't need to?

SECTION 4.8

IMPLEMENTATION PLAN AND TIME LINE

It is important to have a written plan for what will happen and when it will happen. This is most commonly done through the use of a time line. A time line shows when each phase of the research is planned to happen. There is a fairly common format for doing time lines, which is shown in Figure 4.9.

Note that tasks may overlap in time. For example, much of the report writing involves introductory, literature review, and methods sections, all of which can be written before data are obtained, or at least before they are analyzed. We will go into much greater detail about implementation in the next chapter.

FIGURE 4.9. Time Line for Hypothetical Experimental Design.

Tasks	September	October	November	December	January	February	March	April	May
Obtain list of subjects from agency and assign to groups	▓								
Pretest		▓							
Implement experimental and control conditions			▓	▓	▓				
Posttest						▓			
Data Management						▓			
Data Analysis							▓		
Report Writing							▓	▓	▓

When you are done with your design work, you should have the following things down in a written plan:

1. Your question

2. Your hypotheses (deductive research only)

3. How your question and hypotheses are grounded in theory

4. The type of design you will use, which will either be experimental (true or quasi) or nonexperimental (correlational, descriptive, or exploratory). This will include how you intend to deal with the issue of control.

5. Your population of interest, units of analysis, sampling frame, and sampling strategy, including number of groups and plans for matching (if used)

6. What constructs will be looked at and exactly how they turn up as measurable variables in your study

7. An implementation plan and time line for implementing your research

8. An understanding of the relevance of your study to the field

9. Strengths and limitations of your design

10. A completed IRB application that includes complete consideration of all ethical issues involved

You may also want some idea of how you plan to manage and store the data. This will be covered in more detail in Chapter 11. The elements listed are sufficient for you to begin a research project or even submit a grant application. As we have said before, one key issue is how well these various parts mesh together. Your theory should lead to your research question, which should mesh well with your design. That's the core of your work, and if you can show that clearly, you're in better shape than most people we know.

This chapter has covered a lot of ground. Because of the amount of content, we have divided the review questions into two sections, general research design questions and questions relating to specific kinds of designs.

★ ★ ★

EBP MODULE

The third step in EBP involves critically evaluating the studies you find. You need to review the research to find out how useful it is for your own purposes. In this process,

the main questions you will ask will center around issues of design, sampling, and external validity, as well as issues of internal validity.

DESIGN

All kinds of design, from exploratory to true experimental designs, can be useful in EBP. As we have seen, they all serve different purposes and answer different questions. The type of designs that will be most useful for you will be determined by the questions you ask.

True or Quasi-Experimental Designs. If your question is about causality or treatment effectiveness, a true experimental design will provide you with the best possible data. Of course, such designs are often not available and may not even be ethical to conduct. In such cases, we often rely on quasi-experimental designs. The more rigorous the design, the better. For example, a quasi-experimental design using blind conditions and a carefully matched comparison group would be much preferred over a simple one group pretest-posttest design.

Correlational Designs. Many questions that we ask, however, are less focused on causality or treatment effectiveness. You may want to find out what risk factors are associated with different types of maltreatment. You may want to find out about locus of control and how it is associated with academic performance. To answer such questions, you will need to consult correlational designs. Such designs are more common than experimental designs. Be careful not to draw undue conclusions about causality.

Descriptive Designs. Sometimes you just want to know about a given group or event or other social phenomenon. You may need information on characteristics of people using emergency rooms for nonemergency care. You might need to know more about problems commonly encountered by immigrants from Mexico. Do you need to know how much money the government spends on child maltreatment services each year? Descriptive designs, which tell you about the characteristics of a given group or thing, would be what you need in this case.

Exploratory Designs. Sometimes you need help thinking about some new population, issue, or other entity. Perhaps you want to start thinking about something that hasn't been studied much, and you don't even know where to begin. Exploratory designs, which seek to begin to understand new areas or phenomena, can be useful in this case.

Of course, the trick is to find quality studies that use the right kinds of designs to answer the questions you want answered.

When you ask a practice-relevant question, you mean to apply the results to someone or some group. If the study you find does not relate to that kind of person or group, then you have trouble. Put simply, you want to see if the final sample used in the study appears to be similar enough to the people you want to apply the results to.

In particular, you will need to look at sample attrition. The following points may be important to consider:

- *Attrition:* Did the final sample include a reasonably high percentage of the original sampling frame? If not, then the results may be questionable. This can be tricky. Some articles will report that they were able to contact, say, 80% of targeted individuals, that 90% of these gave consent, and that they were able to follow 70% of them for the whole study period. While these are all high numbers, the actual percentage of the original sampling frame who were followed is actually 80% times 90% times 70%, which is only 50.4%, a far less impressive rate.

- *Small sample size:* Was the sample large enough to confer adequate power? This issue is addressed more in Chapters 13 and 14, but you want to make sure that there were enough people in the study to allow findings to emerge. If you find strong relationships, but these strong relationships fail to reach statistical significance, you need to ask yourself if this seems to be due to inadequate sample size. Nonsignificant findings should always be treated very skeptically.

- *Large sample size:* Was the sample so large that even trivial differences reached statistical significance? Don't just notice asterisks and get all happy about them. How strong was the association? A highly significant yet practically meaningless difference (like a change of GPA of .05 points, for example) is meaningless. Remember: "A difference that makes no difference is no difference."

- *Similarity to your client:* This may be the most important consideration. Did the final sample used look enough like the people you want to apply the results to? This is a judgment call on your part to some degree. Ask yourself if they were similar enough on theoretically meaningful dimensions. Such dimensions might include social class, gender, race/ethnicity, or a number of other factors.

As we have seen, to be useful, studies must show several general types of validity. These include face validity (does it look right?), construct validity (do the constructs perform as they should in the model?), and criterion validity (do measures match up right against other measures?). You will have two main tasks, evaluating the research as a whole and evaluating specific constructs as they are measured.

In general, and perhaps most importantly, what do you think of the face validity of the design? Does it make sense, or does it look stupid? Many years ago, one of the author's professors recounted a story about a school of psychology that wanted to study behavior in bars. In order to achieve a highly controlled setting, they actually built a fake bar in the basement of a psych building on a college campus. In the professor's view, this was just plain nuts. People would obviously know they weren't in a real bar, no matter how realistic it appeared. For him, the study lacked face validity because the setting was so contrived.

Content validity is also critically important. We read a lot of articles, both in support of our own research and as reviewers for journals. This problem is among the most common we encounter. Are all the necessary things measured? Does omission of those things render the research useless? For example, if you read an article about educational success among children from single-parent homes, and there is no mention of social class, then you have a problem. Is the educational success (or lack thereof) due to single-parent status or the fact that single-parent families are far more likely to be poor? If the study doesn't tell you, you can't know, and you can't have too much faith in their findings.

Construct validity can be harder to appraise. We like to step back from the article we're reading and say, "What should these variables be doing?" Think about relationships that should occur due to theory or based on past findings from other articles. If the article finds what others find, or what theory says, then that supports the article's validity. If it doesn't find what should be found, then one of two things is happening. Either they've bumped into something interesting and special, or they screwed up. For example, if I found a study showing that 50-year-old males were equally as likely to engage in violent crime as 20-year-old males, then I'd conclude that either the sample was very unique and interesting (unlikely) or the study was not very valid (very likely).

Criterion validity is useful in assessing the validity of measures used. Many articles will use standardized measures that have been subjected to tests of criterion validity. If the measures used are not standardized, then you might be able to evaluate criterion validity by comparing measures to things they should be associated with or predictive of. Superior articles will provide several measures of key constructs so that these measures can be checked against each other. If you have an article measuring academic success, and the measure used correlates highly with GPA, high school completion, or SAT scores, then you have more confidence in that measure.

There are other threats to validity. After assessing these general categories, you should look at the specific threats listed earlier. Measurement or instrumentation error should be assessed. Instruments and use of instruments should be clear enough for you to determine if you think risks exist. If the study evaluates a treatment, is treatment fidelity addressed? The researchers must provide clear evidence that they implemented the treatment as intended. While less commonly an issue, sometimes history can be important. This is particularly important in very long-term studies. Changes in attitudes or behaviors over many years may simply be artifacts of external things happening in the world in general. For example, let's say you are evaluating a violence reduction program that cut rates of assault by 40% during the 1990s. That seems swell, except that the whole country experienced a substantial drop among many forms of violence during the 1990s. The program may have had no effect at all. Maturation is always worth considering. People change over time. Children tend to change more rapidly. Does the study take this into account? For example, a longitudinal study looking at voting patterns among a group of people should consider that people tend to vote in a more conservative fashion as they age and not necessarily attribute such shifts to other causes. Like treatment fidelity, cross group contamination should be directly addressed when multiple groups are used in an evaluative study. Is there any way at all that there could have been "bleed over" from one group to another? How do the authors assure you that it didn't happen or was minimal? Another serious problem, particularly in studies using clinical populations, is regression to the mean. People come for help when they're feeling bad. If you catch someone on a day they feel unusually bad, then it is likely that in the future they will feel better, even if you do nothing. Controlling for this normally requires a control group or rigorously established comparison group. Social desirability

bias can be hard to evaluate. How likely is it that subjects said what they thought would make them look good? Does the article address how this was dealt with? What about investigator and subject expectation effects in experimental studies? These are best handled by blind or double-blind designs. If the study was not blind, what reasons are given by the researcher?

TIME

One final point we'd like to emphasize is time. When you read a study, always be aware of how long the subjects were followed. If you are interested only in achieving short-term effects or understanding relationships at a point in time, then this is not so important. However, if you are trying to pick a treatment method that will have enduring effects, then you really need to try to find studies that have long follow-up periods. This can be hard to do. Follow-up periods in clinical evaluations are often as short as one to three months. You can't change what's available in terms of current research, but you should at least be aware of this as an area of limitation.■

REVIEW

GENERAL REVIEW QUESTIONS

1. What is meant by the word *operationalize?*
2. Briefly define *aims, questions,* and *hypotheses.* Highlight how they are different.
3. What are directional hypotheses, and when would you use one?
4. What kinds of designs should have hypotheses? What kinds of designs should not have hypotheses?
5. What is an exploratory design, and when would you use one?
6. What is a descriptive design, and when would you use one?
7. What is a correlational design, and when would you use one?
8. What is an experimental design, and when would you use one?
9. How are true and quasi-experimental designs different?
10. What three things do you need to show causality?
11. Describe spurious causality. What is the best way to avoid it?
12. What is the difference between random assignment and random selection?

13. What is control by matching? Is it as good as random assignment?

14. What is a unit of analysis?

15. How are *N* and *n* different?

16. Define the following terms: *universal population, population of interest,* and *sample frame.*

17. Find a journal article that uses either an experimental or a quasi-experimental design and identify the three populations in that article as listed in question 16.

18. How does random selection support generalizability?

19. Give one reason you might use a nonprobability sample. Explain.

20. Define: *snowball sampling, purposive sampling, convenience sampling, matching, oversampling,* and *stratification.*

21. How are cluster sampling and multistage cluster sampling different?

22. How are case studies and multiple case studies different?

23. Describe external validity.

24. What is the relationship of sampling to external validity?

25. Why are response rates important?

26. Give two ways you can increase response rates.

27. Define: *privacy, confidentiality,* and *anonymity.*

28. When can deception be used?

29. What is informed consent?

30. Can you ever withhold treatment? If so, under what circumstances?

31. Give an example where compensation may be unethical.

REVIEW QUESTIONS SPECIFIC TO PARTICULAR RESEARCH DESIGNS

32. What is a natural experiment?

33. Explain what these terms mean and how they are similar or different: *cross-sectional, longitudinal, retrospective,* and *prospective.*

34. Explain how the following time-series designs differ: cohort, panel, and trend.

35. Are *structured* and *standardized* synonyms with regard to instrumentation? Explain.

36. What is a "normed" instrument?

37. What is meant by the terms *archival, administrative,* and *secondary* as applied to data?

38. Describe two really serious mistakes you might make with hypothetical secondary data.

39. Give two ways administrative data can be more useful than other kinds of data.

40. What are "single-blind" and "double-blind" designs for?

41. Give at least three of the five key elements of a true experimental design.

42. Translate "failed to reject the null hypothesis" into English.

43. What is meant by treatment as usual?

44. What are factorial designs?

45. What is blocking?

46. Give a hypothetical example of a dosage design.

47. What is meant by a crossover design?

48. Describe a situation where you would not need to do a follow-up measurement in an experimental design.

49. What is a comparison group?

50. What is a comparison condition?

51. Briefly describe how theory is used in correlational designs.

52. Briefly describe how theory is used in descriptive designs.

53. Briefly describe how theory is used in exploratory designs.

54. You want to know if a cognitive behavioral training program reduces the reoffense rate in a sample of juvenile delinquents. What type of design will you need to answer this question and why?

55. Jane wants to interview female inmates in a state mental health facility for the criminally insane. What types of human subjects issues will she need to consider when preparing her IRB application?

56. Name at least one advantage and one disadvantage of the following methods of control: random assignment, matching, statistical.

57. Sally does a nonexperimental study to understand the association of reported alcohol use with days absent from the job within a large corporation over the course of a year. Identify and explain the threats to internal validity that are most relevant to her study.

58. Think of a topic you are interested in that would involve human subjects. Can you think of any real-world concerns that might affect your study design? If yes, explain what they are and how you might address them. If no, explain why not.

59. A researcher is interested in whether or not education of female day care providers is associated

with child development. His research question is: Does education affect child development? Help the researcher revise the question so that it is clearly operationalized.

60. Find an article reporting an empirical study in an area that interests you. Identify the type of design the researchers used. Now read the discussion section. Did the authors mention any limitations? If so, what specific elements of the design were affected by these limitations (for example, sample/subjects, internal validity, external validity)? How would you design a study to answer the same question but not encounter the same problems?

SUPPLEMENTAL READINGS

- Byrne, D. (2002). *Interpreting Quantitative Data.* Thousand Oaks, CA: Sage. This book is hip and interesting but probably too advanced for a casual reader. It is not purely about interpretation but more about social science in general.

- Denzin, A., & Lincoln, Y. (2005). *The Sage Handbook of Qualitative Research* (3rd ed.). Thousand Oaks, CA: Sage. Another backbreaker of a book, this compendium has a lot of very interesting topics—for example, a section on the politics of funded qualitative research.

- Gubrium, J., & Holstein, J. (2002). *Handbook of Interview Research: Context & Method.* Thousand Oaks, CA: Sage. This massive and expensive book should quench anyone's desire for detail on how to do research using interviews.

- Shaddish, W., Cook, T., & Campbell, D. (2002). *Experimental and Quasi-Experimental Designs for Generalized Causal Inference.* Boston: Houghton-Mifflin. This should provide you with all the details you might need to run experimental and quasi-experimental designs that are more complex than those described in this book.

- Van de Vijver, F., & Leung, K. (1997). *Methods and Data Analysis for Cross-Cultural Research.* Thousand Oaks, CA: Sage. This book is a good reference for specific methodological considerations for cross-cultural research.

CHAPTER

5

MEASUREMENT

This chapter will focus on types of data and instruments used in quantitative research. Data used in qualitative research will be covered in Chapter 6. It is important to note that we will discuss questionnaire and survey development, but we will stop short of discussing the process of developing a new, standardized scale from scratch. This is because the process of development, testing, norming, and the like is a field of study unto itself and is beyond the scope of this text. Scholars often devote their entire career to the development, modification, and use of a particular instrument.

SECTION 5.1
MEASUREMENT AND DATA TYPES

SECTION 5.1.1: PREEXISTING DATA

Some studies use data from preexisting studies (we call this "secondary analysis") or from administrative data sources. Although this type of information has many advantages, the researcher is usually not in control of the measurement process. We say "usually" because in some instances a researcher may have collaborated on the prior work or may have collaborated on the development or alteration of an administrative data system (Jonson-Reid, Kontak, & Mueller, 2001).

When using preexisting data, it is important to check out the variable definitions given and data collection procedures used to assess possible sources of error. Is the variable really defined the way you think it was? Was it consistently put into the computer? For example, as a student, one of the authors decided to use an administrative data set that captured information about juvenile offenders. Educational achievement is associated with delinquency in the literature, so the author was hoping to use a "reading level" variable as a control variable to represent educational achievement. Unfortunately, on meeting with the person in charge of the data set, she discovered that this information was frequently not forwarded from the assessment center to the central data center. So, the data were collected, and the definition was accurate; but the data were not consistently entered into the computer. Sometimes missing information in preexisting data can be recaptured from hard-copy files, a proxy can be developed by combining other variables that are valid and present, or, if the data are missing at random, they can be replaced with statistical techniques. Sometimes you're just out of luck and have to change your plan.

When using preexisting data, the review of the data and the data collection and entry process should take place while you are planning the study design, not later when you are running the analyses. You don't want to put yourself in the position of making a lot of promises about what you will do with preexisting data before you check the data out carefully.

We frequently have students come to us who want to use variables in preexisting data which are, well, stinky. These variables may be coded sloppily, may not make sense, or may contain many missing values. Students often get blinded by their desire to capture a particular construct. A kind of mania seems to take over, and they become willing to overlook obvious and serious problems. There's an old saying in computer programming, often abbreviated as GIGO. It means "garbage in, garbage out," and serves to remind us that no matter how cool something is, or how many complicated statistics you apply, or how much you massage something, if you start with invalid data, you will reach invalid conclusions. We feel that this is one of the reasons that administrative data analysis has such a bad reputation in some places. While we are strong advocates of the utility of good administrative data, we stress the word "good," and hope that you remember that it is your responsibility to make sure any variables you employ are usefully capturing the constructs they are intended to represent.

SECTION 5.1.2: STANDARDIZED AND UNSTANDARDIZED MEASURES

By definition, a standardized measure should measure what it says it measures (validity) and do so consistently over time (reliability). This is supported by the process of development, use, and revision. Some instruments are "normed" on populations, meaning your subjects' results can be compared to general (usually national) populations. Few standardized instruments have been through extensive field testing with all populations. So, it is possible to have a perfectly valid measure of posttraumatic stress disorder for White female U.S. citizens that is totally inappropriate for Rwandan refugees. Using such an instrument without modification could likely lead to measurement error (Suzuki et al., 2000). If the researcher does not understand this about the instrument prior to use, he or she risks reporting incorrect results.

It is also possible that an existing standardized measure is simply too long for your use. Sometimes researchers modify instruments by using selected subscales or reducing the number of questions. Be aware that if you do this, the validity and reliability of the measure may change. Even though the source is standardized, you should go through the process of checking the instrument as if you were creating an unstandardized measure for the first time. At a minimum, you should check subscale reliability, discussed in Section 5.2.2.

Unstandardized measures may include those you develop yourself or instruments that already exist but have not had sufficient field testing to be standardized. In the case of preexisting unstandardized measures, the researcher should ask the following questions:

■ Who developed the instrument? Is that person an expert in the field with training in instrument development?

■ What type of assessment of the validity and reliability of the measure (discussed in detail later in the chapter) has been done? Are these measures acceptable?

■ Is the instrument theoretically compatible with what you're doing? In other words, is it based on the same kinds of ideas that underlie your work (construct validity)?

■ Does it measure all (or most) of the constructs you hope to measure (content validity)?

■ Do the questions make sense (face validity)?

■ Has it been used with a sample that has similar characteristics to the one you intend to use?

If the answer to the last question is no, it is possible that the instrument can still be used with your population, but it may require modification, such as translation into a different language or rewriting questions so that they can be easily understood by a 10-year-old.

If you decide that you need to create a new instrument, try to enlist the assistance of someone experienced in instrument design. We will review the

construction of questions and process of development, but it really is a course in itself. Students are encouraged not to use this chapter as the sole guide through such a process. In addition, you should enlist the assistance of a person or persons with substantial expertise in the area to review the instrument. Finally, you should make a thorough list of the constructs and related independent, control, and dependent variables you hope to measure. This will help make sure you don't inadvertently omit an important question.

SECTION 5.1.3: OBSERVATIONAL DATA

One very common source of data is observation of events, behaviors, or situations. Observations can be done on almost anything you can imagine, such as the number of people entering a particular agency or performing certain acts, the duration and intensity of specified behaviors, or the length of time it takes someone to respond to a victim in an experimental situation. For observational data to be valid and reliable, they must meet the same criteria as any other data. Do different raters come up with reliable answers? Do the observations apply to the intended construct? Do the observations of the construct agree with data from other sources? This is simply our old friend operationalization rearing his head again. Observational data are valid only to the degree that the procedures for obtaining them are clearly operationalized. Observers must be trained to high standards to assure that these criteria are met. They generally use formalized checklists or other means of recording data in a structured way. Observers are typically tested to see if they agree with each other. This is called "interrater reliability" and is covered below. If raters do not agree, protocols are changed, or more training is provided.

One potential problem with observational techniques is that you may interpret the data from your own perspective, and you may jump to inappropriate conclusions about what the observations mean. This is obviously a problem in cross-cultural work. It can also occur with populations you may be familiar with. A friend had the following experience as an elementary school child: He was referred by the teacher to the school psychologist because he was drawing in black all the time. The teacher felt this might be a signal of emotional problems. The teacher referred the child to a psychologist solely based on this observation. When the psychologist questioned the child, there seemed to be nothing wrong. Finally, exasperated, the psychologist asked my friend why he was drawing in black. He told the psychologist that the crayons were shared and placed in a single box in his classroom. He was the smallest in the class and the last to reach the crayon box. By the time he got there, all the other colors were usually taken. He didn't want to color in black but was not assertive enough at that age to complain. The moral here is that you should make every attempt to contextualize your observations by understanding and talking to the people being observed.

SECTION 5.2
RELIABILITY AND VALIDITY

Before proceeding, we need to spend some time nailing down the tricky concepts of reliability and validity. We have already gone over validity in Chapter 4, but we will now describe validity in more detail as it specifically relates to measurement. When you do research, you will have to show both that your design is valid and that your measurements are reliable and valid.

SECTION 5.2.1: ARE RELIABILITY AND VALIDITY THE SAME?

Reliability is synonymous with "repeatability." *Valid* is synonymous with "correct." For a measure to be valid (correct) it must be reliable (repeatable with the same result). Validity requires reliability. If a measure is valid, it must first be reliable. The opposite is not true. Reliability can easily exist in the absence of validity. If you give the same wrong answer repeatedly, then you are reliable in what you will say and also wrong. If you ask someone what page in this book a certain subject is on, that person might say, "page 36." If the person always says "page 36" no matter how many times you ask, then that person is certainly reliable. If "page 36" is the right answer, then they are reliable and their answer is valid. If "page 36" is the wrong answer, then they are reliable, but they are not giving a valid answer. Of course, if they give you a different (incorrect) page number every time you ask, then they are neither reliable nor valid. A more visual way to think about this is the classic target example. As far as we can tell, this picture is contractually required to exist in all research methods textbooks, so here it is, as Figure 5.1.

FIGURE 5.1. **The Classic Target Example.**

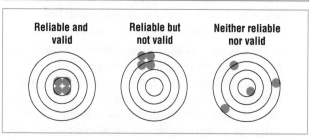

Reliable and valid   Reliable but not valid   Neither reliable nor valid

---

SECTION 5.2.2: RELIABILITY

Reliability is having a measuring tool or instrument that produces the same result every time. A normal ruler is reliable. A stretchy rubber ruler is unreliable. A calculator that always returns an answer of "2.5" no matter what you enter is totally reliable and totally useless. Often reliability is established through **test-retest reliability,** which involves giving the measure twice and checking statistically to see if you get the same result. Another type of reliability is **interrater reliability.** If a researcher is using other persons to help with data collection using case file review for example, you want to make sure that each person collecting the data is doing so in the same way. You do this by pretesting the procedure with the raters and measuring the agreement on items on the same subjects.

Instruments are rated according to something called the **coefficient alpha,** which is a measure of internal reliability. For example, items in subscales must agree with each other. This is called having **subscale reliability.** The idea is that if all items in a subscale are measuring the same construct, they ought to agree with each other. For example, the items in each of the three subscales of the Maslach burnout inventory have been shown to hang together within the subscales (Maslach, Jackson, & Leiter, 1997). Coefficient alpha is the statistical measure reported that researchers use to assess this. We will find out how to do this in Chapter 13. For now, it is enough to know that you want to find coefficient alphas of around .8 or higher ($\alpha \geq .80$) for a scale to be considered to have strong internal reliability.

If the items are all measuring the same thing, why not ask just one question? Well, one reason we ask multiple questions is that we may assume that the construct is complex or perhaps difficult for the subject to interpret. Asking multiple questions allows us to avoid being misled by one confused answer and get a more stable response from averaging many similar answers.

SECTION 5.2.3: INTERNAL VALIDITY

If a study really measures the constructs and variables it says it is measuring, then it has internal validity. As we saw in the last chapter, the four most commonly described broad types of validity issues are face validity, content validity, criterion validity, and construct validity. We will revisit these forms of validity here, so that we can see exactly how they may apply to measurement issues in a little more detail:

- *Face validity:* You have face validity if your instrument makes sense. *Example:* An instrument that measures individual life success by a single point-in-time measure of income lacks face validity because most people think there is more to having a successful life than earning money and because people's wealth changes over time. An instrument that rates how liked a supervisor is by asking the supervisor himself would also lack face validity because many people would question the validity of the supervisor's judgment on this issue.

- *Content validity:* A measure that includes all the necessary issues to be studied has content validity. *Example:* An instrument trying to rate child well-being that asks questions only about child abuse lacks content validity. There's more to doing well as a child than not being abused. An instrument not including obvious and critical questions lacks content validity.

- *Criterion (concurrent, predictive, discriminant) validity:* We've seen each of these terms used in many different and interesting ways. As we saw in Chapter 4, *concurrent validity* means your measure agrees with other simultaneous instruments, or expert judgments, or behavioral indicators, or whatever. Predictive validity means that your instrument correlates with something that happens in the future (e.g., a risk assessment accurately predicts the problem it is trying to predict). Discriminant validity exists when your instrument should not be highly correlated with another measure and actually isn't. For example, if internal locus of control and psychological aggressiveness are theoretically distinct constructs, then measures of them should not be highly correlated.

- *Construct validity:* Does the measure being used do what it is supposed to do in your design according to theory? Do the parts of the model relate to each other the way they are supposed to? *Example:* My theory says A causes B, and B causes C. I find or work up instruments to measure constructs *A, B,* and *C.* If I find positive relationships from *A* to *B* and from *B* to *C,* I have construct validity. We know that this is sort of circular logic, in that you will simultaneously be saying, "My theory is good because my measures prove it," as well as, "My measures are good because they do what the theory says." Nonetheless, if your instruments, model, and theory don't perform as planned, you have serious issues. Obviously this kind of validity always relates to both measures and designs.

There is a range of other factors that bear on the validity of measurement, which we discussed in Chapter 4. These include measurement (or instrumentation) error, treatment fidelity, history, maturation, regression to the mean, social desirability bias, and subject and investigator expectation effects.

Standardized instruments must show strong internal validity and usually have the following qualities:

- Good test-retest reliability, meaning they will get the same answer twice
- Good reliability of components in scales and subscales
- Good criterion validity as shown by comparing their results to other measures of the same construct
- Good construct validity in that the variables they produce behave as theory would predict
- Good content validity as demonstrated by the agreement of experts that key aspects of the variable to be measured are reflected in the instrument

SECTION 5.2.4: INTERNAL VALIDITY AND MEASUREMENT ERROR

Measurement is key to the valid study of an issue or relationship or outcome of interest. One source of variability that researchers try to prevent is measurement error. Measurement error occurs when you do not measure what you want to measure accurately because your instrument or procedure is wrong. This can come in many forms:

- *Asking about the wrong construct:* Measurement error can occur due to an erroneous assumption that questions being asked are related to the construct. Researchers need to have a thorough understanding of the topic being studied, how it has been studied, measures available, and limitations of measures available.

- *Asking the question in a way that invites a specific response (social desirability bias):* You want to avoid asking loaded questions that are likely to make the subject want to answer a certain way. For example, you might believe that adolescent males are uncomfortable being perceived as weak or vulnerable, so you might avoid questions like, "Were you afraid when . . .?" instead asking, "Were you uncomfortable when . . .?"

- *Not being specific enough about your construct:* Measurement error can occur due to lack of specification. For example, a researcher may ask a question about how a person feels about school when he was really trying to understand how people feels about their ability to succeed in school.

- *Asking questions your subject doesn't understand:* Measurement error can also occur when a subject misunderstands a question or the response categories. This can be related to language, reading ability, poorly worded questions, ambiguous response categories, or poorly worded directions.

■ *Subjects will sometimes not answer all questions:* Measurement error can occur when a subject fails to answer all questions. The longer and more complicated the instrument, the greater the risk it will not be completed. Sometimes subjects avoid very personal or sensitive questions. Sometimes mistakes can be made in duplicating the instrument, such as accidentally using a one-sided copy setting for a two-sided original. This can also happen due to complicated directions such as **skip patterns,** in which the test taker moves to a different place in the test based on how he or she answers. For example, you will often see directions like, "If you answered *'no,'* please go directly to question 45b."

■ *Researchers can make mistakes while asking questions or observing:* Measurement error can occur due to errors made in observation, file review, or interview implementation on the part of the researcher or research team. It is important to make sure the entire data collection team is thoroughly trained on the instrument and how to administer it.

SECTION 5.2.5: LEVELS OF MEASUREMENT—THE ECOLOGICAL FALLACY AND CLUSTERING

It is important that you measure the constructs at the appropriate level. In Chapter 4 we discussed unit of analysis. The **ecological fallacy** is associated with this concept. The ecological fallacy occurs when you take the average value for a group and assign this value to all members of the group. For example, if you know that the average height for adult White males in the United States is 5'10", and you therefore say that all White males in your study are 5'10", then you are committing the ecological fallacy. This does not mean you cannot use a proxy at one level to help control for a missing variable at another level (see Chapter 13), but you cannot equate the two.

Further, if several subjects share a characteristic based on being clients of the same therapist, or workers in the same organization, or residents in the same community, you must account for this in your analysis. This is called "clustering" (see Chapter 14, Section 14.9). Students using this type of data will need to pursue techniques such as hierarchical linear modeling, controlling for clusters in time series, or generalized estimating equations.

Another problem is collecting information at the wrong level. For example, if you are interested in organizational issues, you may get radically different information by measuring a construct among administrators compared to line staff. You must consider what level (or levels) of measurement best answers your research question. Usually this has to do with who your subjects are, to whom you are generalizing, and who has the best and least biased information to give you.

Instruments can be self-administered, administered to a subject by a member of a research team, or be completed through observation of various aspects of the subject without contact with the subject. Each method of administering an instrument has advantages and disadvantages.

SECTION 5.3.1: SELF-ADMINISTERED INSTRUMENTS

These have typically been paper-and-pencil surveys, but technology is changing this. Some instruments are being created for or adapted to laptop computers or administered on the Internet. Computers can deliver questions visually or through auditory means, making them accessible to individuals with lower-level reading levels or visual or auditory disabilities. Computerized instruments may also be more appealing to certain populations, like children, who commonly use computers in school and for entertainment.

One advantage of using paper or network-based self-administered surveys is that they allow the subject more privacy and can be used in situations where the researcher wants to let the answers be completely anonymous. This method also allows for flexibility in the method of delivery of the instrument. Such instruments can be mailed, placed on the Internet, or administered in group or individual settings.

Disadvantages include the inability to monitor the subjects' progress. If subjects inadvertently skip a question, misunderstand something, or begin to show fatigue, there may be little opportunity to correct this. These instruments also produce limited depth of information. Sometimes a self-administered instrument will incorporate open-ended or fill-in responses to encourage elaboration, but subjects often fail to use these.

SECTION 5.3.2: RESEARCHER-ADMINISTERED INSTRUMENTS

These can be unstructured (open-ended), semi-structured, or completely structured. Less structured instruments are almost always administered by phone or face-to-face. Researchers can follow up on questions or probe unexpected areas of interest when performing such interviews. Besides face-to-face contacts, telephone interviews are another very common way researchers administer instruments to subjects. Researchers will commonly read standardized instruments to subjects over the phone, recording the subject's responses. We have an entire suite of little cubicles in the basement of our building just for this purpose.

Even when subjects are available in person, sometimes instruments will be administered by the researcher directly, instead of using paper forms. The subject may need assistance due to age, incapacity, language difficulties, or other factors. If there are language or communication barriers, the researcher may be assisted by an interpreter who is also trained on the instrument. Another advantage of administering an interview directly is the ability to include skip patterns, which can be followed by the interviewer, instead of making the subject figure them out.

SECTION 5.3.3: INSTRUMENTS COMPLETED BY A RESEARCHER OR THIRD PARTY

These instruments do not involve eliciting answers from the subject. A researcher may have raters observing playground behavior in children, or a teacher may complete a behavior checklist about a student. These instruments are the least intrusive, but the researcher's activities can be misinterpreted. You don't want to be identified as a potential child predator while observing schoolchildren, and obviously, these kinds of observation raise a host of ethical issues which must be considered (see Chapter 2.)

It is critical that the guidelines for the observations and/or meanings of the questions on third-party scales be clear and applicable to the population being studied. It is also important that observers be well trained prior to the observation. A check for interrater reliability is also important to make sure that there is no need to refine the instrument or retrain the observers.

SECTION 5.4
STRUCTURE OF INSTRUMENTS

Broadly defined, an instrument can be structured or semi-structured. Some interviews may be so loosely organized or directed that they could be called unstructured, but this rarely happens in quantitative work. For more information about relatively unstructured qualitative instruments, see Chapter 6.

SECTION 5.4.1: THE STRUCTURE OF STRUCTURED INSTRUMENTS

Structured instruments are a key part of social science research. We therefore need to look at them in particular detail. First we will look at the individual types of questions that one might find.

TYPES OF QUESTIONS

Virtually all structured instruments are made up of a series of items. These items usually have closed-ended responses, which most commonly are in the form of yes/no items, numeric or categorical response items, true/false items, Likert scale items, semantic differential

items, or list-selection items. We will provide descriptions and examples of each:

- Yes/no items are very simple:

  Example: Have you ever been in prison or jail?
  Yes [ ]   No [ ]

- True/false items are also familiar:

  Example: I brush my teeth at least twice a day.
  True [ ]   False [ ]

- Numeric response items are common and simply request a numeric response:

  Example: How many people aged 17 or under live in your home? [__]

- Categorical response items are also common but are tricky. They are not really closed ended and may result in unanticipated responses. They should be avoided if other options exist:

  Example: What is your religion? [_____]

- List-selection items are also common and involve the subject selecting from a list of possible responses:

  Example: How many people aged 17 or less live in your home?   [1] [2] [3] [4 or more]

  Example: What is your gender?   Male [ ]   Female [ ]

  Sometimes list-selection items leave room for the respondent to insert his or her own item. This may be necessary when all possibilities cannot be put on the list.

  Example: What is your religion? (*check only one*)

  [ ] Buddhist
  [ ] Catholic
  [ ] Hindu
  [ ] Jewish
  [ ] Muslim
  [ ] Mormon
  [ ] Protestant
  [ ] Other (please specify below):
  [_____]

  List-selection items sometimes allow multiple responses, commonly asking the respondent to "check all that apply."

- **Likert scale** items are probably the most common type of item on standardized instruments, and usually include four to seven numeric choices along an agree/disagree (or similar) continuum. Some researchers prefer using an even number to avoid the possibility that people will just pick the middle choice:

  Example: I feel as if these examples will never end.

[1]	[2]	[3]	[4]	[5]
Strongly disagree	Disagree	Neither agree nor disagree	Agree	Strongly agree

■ **Semantic differential** items usually come in groups and are similar to Likert items, except that they list opposite characteristics as a continuum instead of using the agree/disagree continuum. Care must be taken to make sure the terms used are truly opposite ends of a single continuum. Sometimes semantic differential items that invite the respondent to complete a sentence are termed **phrase completion** items:

Examples: I would describe the new "EXCITEMENT!" cable television channel as

Informative	[5]	[4]	[3]	[2]	[1]	Uninformative
Entertaining	[5]	[4]	[3]	[2]	[1]	Not entertaining
Thrilling	[5]	[4]	[3]	[2]	[1]	Boring
Morally sound	[5]	[4]	[3]	[2]	[1]	Morally unsound

■ **Grounded scale** items are another option. Grounded scales are similar to Likert or semantic differential scales, except that every possible response is "grounded" or "anchored" in a detailed description. Grounded scale items take longer to fill out, because the respondent has to read each description. They can be hard to administer by phone for this same reason. The advantage is that interpretation of the item is easier because the researcher can look at the box to get a feel for exactly what the respondent meant. This provides more meaning than "Agree" on a Likert scale or "4" on a semantic differential. Instructions on grounded scales sometimes ask the reader to start with the boxes from the side with the highest rating for the variable and move to less severe items, checking the first box that fits.

Example: Check the box that best describes your assessment of the family situation. Begin at the left and check the first box that fits the situation well:

[4]	[3]	[2]	[1]
The child is in immediate risk of harm and must immediately be removed to custody.	The child is at risk of harm, but immediate removal is not necessary.	The child may be at risk of harm. Removal is not appropriate for this child.	The child is not at risk of harm and removal should not be considered.

SECTION 5.4.2: SUBSCALES

Many structured instruments include a number of subscales within them. For example, the Maslach burnout inventory is an instrument that includes 22 questions, but these are broken down into three separate subscales. Nine of the items assess "emotional exhaustion," five items assess "depersonalization," and eight items assess "personal accomplishment." These items are mixed together in the instrument but are summed into their separate subscales later. People who should know better often make the mistake of mixing subscales inappropriately. We have seen papers reporting the results of the MBI as a single score for burnout. This is wrong and downright silly because it mixes up the three very different theoretical constructs (mental fatigue, treating clients as things, feeling you're doing something worthwhile).

Other scales are designed both to create separate subscale measures and to allow for a summative overall score. There is no substitute for a thorough understanding of the instrument you are using and what its intended uses are. This can best be arrived at by reviewing the instructions and documentations on the publisher's Web site or provided with the instrument, through reviews of the instrument in sources such as *Mental Measurements Yearbook* and *Tests in Print VI*, or through articles or Web sites that use or review the instrument and its qualities.

SECTION 5.4.3: SKIP PATTERNS

Sometimes questions are meant to be answered only by certain subjects. For example, if one of your variables is the type of illicit drug used, then only subjects who admit to using illicit drugs can have valid answers for this question. Rather than create different instruments for different groups of subjects, researchers will create skip patterns in their instruments. Using our example, a person who responded negatively to the general question about drug use would be instructed to skip all the questions related to types of drugs. It might look like this:

#29: Have you used an illegal drug in the last year?   Yes [ ]   No [ ]
(If "Yes," continue to next item. If "No," skip to item #35 on page 5).

Because skip patterns can be confusing, they are more common in instruments that are administered by a researcher rather than self-administered. Computers can handle this process automatically, so the user need not pay attention to the issue. The computer can track prior responses, and items that need to be skipped will simply not be shown.

SECTION 5.4.4: SEMI-STRUCTURED INSTRUMENTS

Semi-structured instruments are similar in form but include questions without predetermined responses. Sometimes these are follow-up questions to structured questions. For example, you might ask if the person was satisfied with his or her treatment by the agency receptionist (yes or no). This could be followed by a question that asks the person to say why he or she was satisfied or unsatisfied. In other cases, the open-ended question stands alone. Most college course and instructor evaluations are of this type, with both Likert scale items and sections for the students to write their opinions down in narrative form.

SECTION 5.4.5: UNSTRUCTURED INSTRUMENTS

An unstructured instrument consists solely of a open-ended question or questions, such as, "Tell me about your family." These questions will focus on constructs of interest, but they do not provide guidance for an answer. They may also allow the researcher discretion in asking follow-up questions. This method is more likely to be associated with grounded research and qualitative methods as the responses are probably going to be narrative and the goal of the research is likely to be inductive. This is covered in detail in the next chapter.

SECTION 5.4.6: MEASUREMENT AND CULTURAL COMPETENCE

As stated earlier, just because a measure of something (say, posttraumatic stress disorder) is valid with one population does not mean it can be used with another population. It is not enough to know about the issue and constructs you wish to study as they occur in general. You must know how these issues manifest themselves and are described within the various groups you hope to include in your study. This includes understanding:

■ Language and dialects used

■ Slang or colloquial expressions used to describe constructs of interest

■ The perception of the constructs with the cultures in the sample (i.e., what topics are sensitive)

■ Comfort level with talking to others outside their culture

TRANSLATING INSTRUMENTS

Not everyone is an English speaker. You must carefully assess not just the primary languages spoken but also the dialects present in the sample group. As part of the translating process, you need to find someone who is both bilingual and from the specific population the instrument is intended for. Such a translator is more likely to understand the nuances of the language. Once the translation is complete, it should be back-translated into English to double check the terms.

Evaluating respondent sensitivity and comfort is as important as getting language right. Some cultures, ethnicities, and religions, for example, are less well-disposed toward gays and lesbians than are others.

If you are asking some populations questions about same-sex marriage, you may find that you need to promise anonymity and provide the subjects complete privacy to avoid social desirability bias.

SECTION 5.5
CHOOSING A MEASURE

If possible, it is best to find a standardized instrument for your study. Why? These instruments, as aforementioned, tend to have high validity and reliability. They also typically have the advantage of more common use, meaning that you will be able to more directly compare your results with prior work. From a purely practical perspective, it also means you won't spend half your time and effort evaluating and defending the instrument you created.

SECTION 5.5.1: LOCATING INSTRUMENTS

Locating instruments is easier than you might think. We would suggest that you try the following approaches:

■ Review your literature and see what instruments were used. This is often the easiest and best approach.

■ Ask people (professors, other researchers) in your area what instruments are available.

■ Check articles using a computerized search engine (like PsycINFO) to find reviews of instruments either by name or in a given area.

■ Check your library catalog to see if any books exist in your area that include either reviews of instruments or that include the instruments themselves (e.g., Corcoran, K., & Fischer, J. (2000). *Measures for Clinical Practice, A Sourcebook* [3rd ed.]. London: The Free Press.)

■ Check to see if your university (or one nearby) has a hard-copy collection of the instruments. This can be a wonderful way to actually see and get a feel for what's available.

■ Use books or computerized databases that are designed to allow you to find and review instruments, such as *Test Critiques*, the *Mental Measurements Yearbook*, or the ETS Test Collection.

As we imply above, there are differences between finding out that an instrument exists, finding reviews of the instrument that comment on its validity, finding out how commonly it is used, learning whether it is well regarded, and finally, actually getting your hands on the darn thing. In some cases, you may have to spend money to purchase an example of an instrument.

Sometimes there simply isn't a good preexisting validated instrument that can be used with your population. You have two choices: modify an existing measure or create your own.

SECTION 5.5.2: MODIFYING EXISTING INSTRUMENTS

Common reasons for modification include the need to:

- Translate into a different language
- Change due to age or cognitive ability
- Shorten the measure

You cannot assume that the validity and reliability assessment from the original instrument will be the same for the modification. It is important to redo assessments like the coefficient alpha (subscale reliability) and compare them to the original scale.

SECTION 5.5.3: CREATING NEW INSTRUMENTS

Perhaps you will create an instrument from scratch based on careful review of the study constructs. Creating valid standardized scales and measures is no joke; it requires substantial expertise in item creation and statistics and repeated pilot testing of the instrument and can end up taking years.

So what do you do? For practical purposes, any instrument you are likely to create is most likely to have variables represented by single items, not by scales. In other words, instead of using a standardized many-item scale to assess something, you just ask about it. If you are interested in learning whether people feel that TV commercials are too racy, you might just ask a single question. That question could be a grounded scale, a semantic differential, a Likert item, or whatever. There is nothing wrong with this, and many published articles use this approach. Although it is better to use standardized scales if they are available, sometimes you just have no choice.

WRITING GOOD QUESTIONS

Good questions are simple and clear and generate useful data. The following general rules should be adhered to and will reduce biased responses:

- Make your physical presentation visually simple and pleasing. Confused or tightly packed questionnaires can result in bad data.
- Use very simple language. Aim for the lowest possible level of respondent in terms of vocabulary and sentence structure.

- Avoid negatives, especially double negatives, whenever possible. This is another way to make sure you use simple language.
- Pretest your questions on the same type of people who will be answering the questions for real.
- Avoid emotionally loaded terms. For example, we initially wrote "morally corrupt" instead of "morally unsound" in the semantic differential presented several pages back. We realized this was a loaded term, and changed it to "unsound."
- Avoid leading questions. Do not ask questions that encourage a given response. For example, do not ask, "Should the school district adopt the improved, scientifically proven plan *X?*" Instead, ask, "Should the school district adopt plan *X?*"
- Try to go from the general to the specific whenever possible. If you want to know how someone feels about something or someone in general, ask that first. Why? Because if you ask a lot more specific questions early, especially negative-sounding ones, you may lead people to respond in the way they think you want them to, not the way they really feel.
- Consider reverse-scoring some questions. Reverse scoring is a way to avoid "yea-saying" bias, where respondents have a general tendency to say either "yes" or "no," regardless of how they really feel. Reverse scoring can be illustrated with the following Likert scale example:

1) I feel like crying most of the time.				
[1]	[2]	[3]	[4]	[5]
Strongly disagree	Disagree	Neither agree nor disagree	Agree	Strongly agree

2) I am a very happy person.				
[1]	[2]	[3]	[4]	[5]
Strongly disagree	Disagree	Neither agree nor disagree	Agree	Strongly agree

3) I enjoy life.				
[1]	[2]	[3]	[4]	[5]
Strongly disagree	Disagree	Neither agree nor disagree	Agree	Strongly agree

4) There is nothing I really care about.				
[1]	[2]	[3]	[4]	[5]
Strongly disagree	Disagree	Neither agree nor disagree	Agree	Strongly agree

Items 1 and 4 appear to be measures of unhappiness, while items 2 and 3 are measures of happiness. We can create a simple measure of happiness by "reverse scoring" items 1 and 4, by making 5s equal 1s and 4s equal 2s. In SAS, we might simply write "ITEM2 = 6-ITEM2; ITEM3 = 6-ITEM3;." In SPSS, we would use "TRANSFORM," "RECODE." From this point forward, we will occasionally intersperse computer code when we feel it may be helpful. For more information on getting started on computers (SAS, SPSS, Excel, and InVivo) see Chapter 10.

SECTION 5.5.4: PILOTING INSTRUMENTS

After developing your questions, you should find a person with expertise in the same area to review the instrument for face validity. Next, it is important to pilot the instrument. This will help you identify awkward questions and translation difficulties and estimate the time it will take subjects to complete the instrument. We suppose you could just go ahead and administer your instrument. The problem with this approach is that it almost always provides bad data. You need to make sure your instrument is actually doing what you want. We suggest the following steps:

1. Preliminary (very informal) piloting should take place first. Bother a friend or go to the library or commons and find some poor fellow student with too much time on her hands. Ask the person to do the instrument, and then ask what the person thought each item meant. After revising (and rechecking) any altered items, repeat. When you stop getting surprises, you can move to the next phase. At this very preliminary level, you are just looking for really major problems. The main goal is just to make sure the instrument you are about to more formally pilot is not totally awful.

2. Now it's time for formal piloting. Go and find people of the group on which you will eventually use the instrument. Have them do the instrument. After they are done, ask some (or all) of them about the instrument, what they thought the items meant, if anything was unclear, and the like. Incorporate their suggestions. Check for the following issues:

   - Are some items commonly unanswered? This is bad. Why? How can you fix it?

   - Is there sufficient variability in each response? In English, this means you had better make sure that everyone didn't answer a given question the same way. It may sound obvious, but a "variable" has to "vary." If everyone answered "yes" or "5," then you need to redo and try to stretch those responses a little.

   - Do the answers make sense? If not, you need to talk to the people answering the questions, and make sure you and they are on the same page (metaphorically, that is).

   - If subscales are used, is the coefficient alpha high enough ($\geq$.80)?

3. Next, revise the instrument based on the pilot. Did everything go fine at the first pilot? Ha. You wish. You now need to redo the instrument. If major changes were made, do more formal piloting. If only minor changes are made, such as type font size, you may want to be brave and move directly into full-scale administration of the instrument.

CONCLUSION

As you can see, measurement is a complex and tricky issue. Some professors spend their entire careers just being measurement experts. What you need to do is create a defensible measurement strategy. We often suggest to our PhD students that they imagine themselves presenting their research at a conference to a room full of fellow researchers—hostile fellow researchers. What would they ask? Is your measurement strategy good enough that you can comfortably respond to their questions? Another way to look at it is to think about writing up the research. How will you describe the strengths and limitations of your work? Will you have clear reasons that make sense for why you did what you did? Can you write your methodology section without wishing you were someplace, anyplace, else? These little mental exercises can be a pretty good way of trying to review the quality of your measurement plan.

★ ★ ★
EBP MODULE

In the third step of EBP, we are required to critically evaluate the best available evidence. We'll try to give a few tips from the perspective of the field practitioner using EBP.

EVALUATING INSTRUMENTS

If a study relies on data generated by a measurement tool, then you will need to check out that instrument before you can have faith in the findings. How can you do this quickly and easily in a practice context? First, if the study is in your area, then you may already know all you need to know about it. After you have been consulting the available evidence in a given area relevant to your practice (e.g., parenting) for a while, you will be familiar with most of the commonly used measures. This is one of the ways that EBP gets easier as you go forward. Second, you can consult reviews of the instrument. You can do this through the means listed above, or you can simply PsycINFO or Google the instrument name. For most instruments, this is a pretty easy task. You will, of course, have to use your own judgment. Even well-validated instruments may not work with new populations or in circumstances different from those under which they have been validated. There is no substitute for your own common sense.

EVALUATING OTHER MEASURES

Frequently, studies use behavioral measures or data from other sources, such as case files or computerized databases. Good articles will carefully explain their data sources and give you an idea of the strengths and limitations of the data. In most cases, you will be again reliant on your own judgment here. One way to proceed is by recalling the general categories of validity. Does what they did make sense (face validity)? Did they include key things that should have been measured (content validity)? Do the measures "behave" as they should according to theory or prior work (construct validity)? Do measures in their study line up with other measures as they should (criterion validity)?

WHICH ARE BETTER? STUDIES USING STANDARDIZED INSTRUMENTS OR STUDIES USING BEHAVIORAL, ARCHIVAL, OR OTHER MEASURES?

All of the above. In the best of all possible worlds, you will find studies using well-validated instruments on an appropriate population, and you will also find studies using behavioral or other measures. This is good. If something is studied *the same way* over and over again, using the same approach over and over again, and we get the same results over and over again, then this is replication, and that is nice. If a study is replicated successfully, it means that we can have more confidence that a given research design will reliably produce the same results. If something is studied over and over again *using different approaches* and we get the same results over and over again, then this is "triangulation," and that is also nice. Triangulation gives us more confidence that the results are not just happening due to some mistake in one particular design. Of course, ideally,

you would have a wealth of articles showing both replication and triangulation. For some well-researched areas, this will be true. ■

REVIEW

1. Find a standardized instrument (cite at least two articles describing the instrument, you don't have to get a copy of the instrument). Explain why you think it is standardized.
2. What are "test-retest," "interrater," and "subscale" reliability?
3. What are "face," "content," "construct," and "criterion" validity?
4. Find an article that you think fails with regard to one of the four types of validity mentioned above. Explain why.
5. What is the "ecological fallacy"?
6. Make up a Likert scale item.
7. Make up a semantic differential item.
8. Make up a grounded scale item.
9. What are "skip patterns"?
10. What is a "semi-structured" instrument? When would you use one?
11. What is an "unstructured" instrument? When would you use one?
12. Give three ways you might find a standardized instrument.
13. Give four mistakes that people make in writing questions.

SUPPLEMENTAL READINGS

■ Devellis, R. (2003). *Scale Development: Theory and Applications.* Thousand Oaks, CA: Sage. If you really want to get into creating and validating your own valid and reliable scales, this is a good place to start.
■ Eid, M., & Diener, E. (2005) *Handbook of Multimethod Measurement in Psychology.* Washington, D.C.: APA. Another large desk-reference-type book, this work provides an overview of many different types of measurement and data gathering strategies.
■ Harkness, J., Van de Vijver, F., & Mohler, P. (2002). *Cross-Cultural Survey Methods.* Hoboken: Wiley-Interscience. This covers certain aspects of measurement specific to the construction of surveys with other cultures.

■ Hawson, C., Yule, P., Laurent, D., & Vogel, C. (2002). *Internet Research Methods: A Practical Guide for the Social and Behavioural Sciences.* Thousand Oaks, CA: Sage. This could be a nice reference for those of you who might be interested in doing your research online.

■ Psychometrics (entry in Wikipedia) http://en. wikipedia.org/wiki/Psychometrics. This is a very nice section with lots of useful links. We'd recommend this as a general location to learn more about a range of issues regarding measurement.

■ Suzuki, L., Ponterotto, J., & Meller, P. (Eds.). (2000). *The New Handbook of Multicultural Assessment: Clinical, Psychological, and Educational Applications* (2nd ed). San Francisco, CA: Jossey-Bass. This massive text does a great job of not only discussing cultural sensitivity in measurement but also reviewing many common measures.

QUALITATIVE RESEARCH

Qualitative research is possibly the most confused and potentially misleading phrase used in social science. There is no bright line separating qualitative and quantitative research, and there is much disagreement about where one starts and the other begins. Frankly, we feel uncomfortable even separating out qualitative research into a different chapter. Many studies combine both qualitative and quantitative methods in the same study, and these designs are known as "mixed-methods" studies. This is an increasingly common way to do research.

This section will overview qualitative research generally, with specific focus on those aspects of qualitative methods that lend themselves to inclusion in mixed-methods designs. It is not the purpose of this textbook to be a stand-alone handbook of qualitative methods, but we hope we can introduce you to the area and give you the tools you need for smaller-scale qualitative work. You will want to refer to Chapter 10, which introduces NVivo, a qualitative software package. You may also want to look at Chapters 9, 12, and 15, where you can follow our example of John's qualitative research through design, implementation, and analysis.

Although we will spend time describing some of the background and traditions that underlie qualitative methods, our emphasis will be mainly on how to do it. Students reading the qualitative literature may be surprised by the dozens of different approaches to thinking about and doing research. It is true that qualitative researchers use literally hundreds of different terms to describe how they view their work and how they do it. We believe, however, that when it actually comes down to doing the work, most qualitative researchers use fairly similar methods.

┌───┐
│   **SECTION 6.1**   │
│   **QUALITATIVE RESEARCH DEFINED**   │
└───┘

The best way to begin to understand what qualitative research is and what it isn't is to overview the dimensions of research that we have been following throughout the book. We will do this briefly, our main goal being to give the reader some sense of what the boundaries of qualitative research are.

DIMENSION 1: PURPOSE AND ROLE OF THEORY IN QUALITATIVE RESEARCH

Qualitative designs are generally exploratory, sometimes descriptive and are occasionally used in correlational or experimental designs. The average person who imagines doing qualitative research thinks about the (inductive and exploratory) process of observing the world, interpreting meaning, and using that infor-

mation to come up with ideas (theories) about what is being observed. What most people don't know is that qualitative methods can also be used deductively. In the following examples, the first two questions are inductive (looking at facts to get to theory), while the second two are deductive (using theory to predict what facts you will find).

BRIEF EXAMPLE QUESTIONS SUITABLE FOR QUALITATIVE RESEARCH

Exploratory (inductive): What prevents male victims of domestic violence from seeking help?

Descriptive (inductive): Which interpersonal communication styles (information provision, debate, compliance-oriented) are used by instructors in direct practice, human diversity, and research methods courses in schools of education?

Correlational (deductive): Is there an association between the party affiliation (Republican versus Democratic) of the subject of a story and favorable versus unfavorable reporting (ratio of positive versus negative statements) in front-page articles in the *New York Times*?

Experimental (deductive): Does an empathy-based multicultural training format produce different empathic responses to vignettes when compared to a standard, non-empathy-based multicultural training model?■

To repeat, many people believe that qualitative methods are only exploratory and inductive. This viewpoint is in error. Qualitative methods can also be used to see if theoretical predictions are consistent with qualitative observations (*English translation:* You can see if the qualitative data supports the predictions you make based on your ideas). For example, qualitative studies have been carried out in an attempt to validate the accuracy of Elisabeth Kubler-Ross's stages of reaction to dying (denial, anger, bargaining, depression, and acceptance). Do these stages occur? Is the order consistent? These are completely appropriate qualitative questions.

EXAMPLE: MULTIMETHOD TRUE EXPERIMENTAL DESIGN

EMDR is a technique used to help people to resolve trauma symptoms. A friend of ours, Tonya Edmond (Edmond, 1997), performed a true experimental design in which subjects received either treatment as usual or EMDR. She measured their symptoms after treatment and again later at a follow-up. She also collected qualitative data about how the subjects described the value of the treatment. Her quantitative findings were as follows:

1. At end of treatment, the two groups looked fairly similar.
2. At follow-up, the EMDR group had continued to improve, whereas the treatment-as-usual group had not.

The quantitative data alone provide no clues as to *why* this is so.

Fortunately, her qualitative data did provide her with some clues. The treatment-as-usual people said that the therapy had been helpful in teaching them how to live with the trauma more successfully. The EMDR people, on the other hand, said that the treatment had largely taken away the distress resulting from the trauma. The strong differences in the qualitative responses from the two groups allowed Dr. Edmond to triangulate and feel more secure about the quantitative data and also provided a means of interpreting them.■

DIMENSION 2: CONTROL IN QUALITATIVE RESEARCH

One of the biggest differences between quantitative and qualitative research is the greater difficulty of exercising control in qualitative work. On the whole, qualitative designs are not characterized by strong attention to issues of control. In exploratory designs, of course, the idea of control can run contrary to the goal of the research, which is to find out as much as possible about all the various factors bearing on the subject. In short, you may be looking for as many factors as possible, not trying to reduce them.

A sort of control in qualitative studies has to do with setting the sampling frame. Extraneous factors can be excluded from the study through carefully specifying the population of interest. For example, a qualitative study looking at the experiences of the homeless might factor out (eliminate the issue of) substance abuse by prescreening subjects and not using individuals with substance abuse problems. Occasionally, experimental formats can be used, providing some control. For qualitative methods that produce numeric data, such as content analysis, it is conceivable that statistical controls could be employed. In such cases, the line between qualitative and quantitative research becomes impossible to draw.

DIMENSIONS 3 AND 4: SUBJECTS, SAMPLING, AND GROUPS IN QUALITATIVE RESEARCH

Case studies are studies of a single individual, event, group, organization, social body, or whatever. Case studies are defined by the fact that you are looking at only *one* individual, event, or social entity. For example, a study of one person or one NGO (nongovernmental organization) would be considered a case study. Case

studies can also be framed around single events. For example, if you wanted to research how a particular political decision was made, you could do a case study of that event. Case studies can be entirely qualitative, entirely quantitative, or a mixture of both. For example, a case study of "White flight" in a neighborhood could be done entirely by interviewing community members, or it could be done entirely from numerical records of home sales and other demographic data, or it could be a mix.

One of the more common types of qualitative study is the multiple case study. This is just simply a series of case studies done by the researcher and presented together. Looking at many individuals, events, or organizations can help the researcher to understand a broader range of case characteristics, dynamics, and other factors than can be understood from a single case. As an example, someone studying the stresses faced by couples after the birth of their first child might follow a number of couples rather than just one. If you follow just one couple it would be easy to miss very important things that just don't happen to show up in those two people.

It is important to remember that not all qualitative designs are case studies. For example, **focus groups** are an increasingly popular method, and the use of surveys that generate unstructured (narrative) data has always been common. Qualitative work is also very commonly archival, with publicly available sources such as newspapers being a popular source of data.

THEORETICAL SAMPLING

In inductive qualitative work, where building theory is the goal, the most common kind of sampling is theoretical sampling. This is the idea that you should pick subjects who can help you to cover the whole range of ideas that you want to study. For example, if you were studying long-term adjustment of crime victims, you would want to sample some people who seemed to be doing well and some who seemed to be doing poorly, and you'd also want to sample across other dimensions, such as severity of the crime. The whole idea is to cover a broad enough range of people so that you don't miss key ideas that might emerge from the subjects and help guide you toward theory.

Figure 6.1 shows two different approaches to studying test anxiety. One way is to just sample everyone randomly and see what you can find out about people in general. This allows you to generalize back to the sample frame very well. Of course, most of the people you sample will have middle-of-the-road levels of test anxiety, so you may not get very many (maybe not any) people who are extremely calm or extremely tense. Unfortunately, studying these extreme cases may not be the best thing if your goal is to figure out why

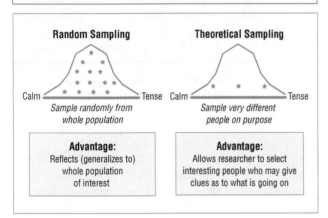

FIGURE 6.1. Two Different Approaches to Selecting Participants: Study of Emotional Reactions to Test Taking.

some people are more tense than others. This is why qualitative (and sometimes quantitative) researchers will often use theoretical sampling. You may decide in advance to study only very calm, very tense, and very average people to try to find out how these groups differ. Results from this kind of sampling will be useful in qualitative studies when developing theory is the goal.

Of course, theoretical sampling (a kind of purposive sampling, which you recall from Chapter 4) is also often used quantitatively. For an example, see Drake and Pandey (1996) in which the poorest, least-poor, and most middle-of-the-road zip codes in a state were selected to learn more about social class and child abuse.

Some qualitative designs do break subjects up into groups. For example, you might want to look at reactions to the death of a spouse in different cultures and might sample several cases from each of a series of ethnic populations. Although this is sometimes done, most qualitative research does not expressly conceptualize subjects as members of separate groups.

Correct sampling is absolutely vital to all forms of social research, including qualitative research. As with quantitative research, sampling decisions must be driven by your theory, your question, and how you hope to generalize your results. The test is this: Can you explain clearly to someone why you sampled as you did?

DIMENSION 5: INVESTIGATOR MANIPULATION IN QUALITATIVE RESEARCH

Investigator manipulation in qualitative research does occur but is not the norm. Most qualitative researchers want to immerse themselves in the subject's world to understand it better. One example of the use of qualitative methods in a design including investigator manipulation was experienced by one of the authors. A film production company was trying to figure out which ending to a film worked better. People were given yellow or blue tickets (we assume at random)

and were invited to attend a free movie. The yellow-ticket holders went to one screen at the theater, while the blue-ticket holders saw the movie on a different screen. The films were shown with different endings, and after each film concluded, participants from each theater filled out a questionnaire. After this, people were invited to participate in focus groups to determine their liking for each version of the film.

We assume that this was an experimental design, with two groups each being shown similar versions of a film with a different ending. We might guess that there were at least two research questions: First, which ending caused people to express more liking for the film? If this were the only question, though, the easier (and cheaper) paper questionnaire rating would have been sufficient. Why do the focus groups? Maybe the filmmakers were interested in *why* one ending was preferred or exactly *what* about the ending was liked. Such questions would justify the extra time spent in running the focus groups and qualitatively analyzing the data.

DIMENSION 6: TIME FRAME IN QUALITATIVE RESEARCH

Most qualitative research is conducted "in vivo" (in real life) over a period of weeks or months. Often, subjects are contacted only once. Some qualitative researchers spend long periods of time with their subjects and so are able to generate longitudinal data and insights that apply over time. Retrospective accounts are also very common in qualitative research, with many studies being focused on accounts subjects give of their past experiences.

DIMENSION 7: DATA TYPE IN QUALITATIVE RESEARCH

Many people (incorrectly) define qualitative research by its use of narrative data. *Narrative data* means words written or spoken, usually in sentences. While most qualitative data are in the form of the written or spoken word, not all of them are. For example, the investigator may notice a range of nonverbal cues or other data and may base parts of her analysis on things such as where people sit, what their physical mannerisms are, and the like. This is one reason why videotape is preferred by some qualitative researchers to the more traditional audiotape. Qualitative data analysis can be done in an extremely large number of different ways. A few examples may help illustrate the range and complexity of different means of qualitative analysis.

Content analysis involves identifying the occurrence of specific words or ideas in a narrative. Sometimes called **conceptual analysis,** this can be as easy as counting the times a given word is used. This can be done automatically by many computer software packages such as

NVivo. It is more difficult, but still fairly simple, to try to track the number of times a given idea or theme is expressed. More involved forms of content analysis **(relational analysis)** may look at the relationships between concepts, attempting to understand how two or more concepts are related in the narrative. As one extreme example, content analysis can be completely numeric and not very (if at all) different from quantitative methods (e.g., counting the number of times women are referenced in history books). The argument could be made that this type of content analysis is not qualitative research at all because no interpretation of meaning is attempted. On the other hand, more involved relational analyses can make full use of the researcher's human judgment and can be more clearly distinguishable from quantitative approaches.

At the other end of the spectrum, a number of qualitative approaches, including qualitative work done from a postmodernist perspective, are expressly and purely subjective and interpretivist their approach, meaning they look only at the meanings that people express and discount objective measures. In research of this nature, attempting to understand the nature of what is being communicated is far more important than developing schemes to accurately count words.

In summary, qualitative research includes the same basic dimensions that exist in quantitative research. There is no single clear definition of what qualitative research is, and there is a large gray area between quantitative and qualitative methods. The best and most accurate way to describe any given research project would be through reference to its theory, purpose, questions, and design, not as qualitative or quantitative. If a brief definition of *qualitative research* is demanded, however, it might best be phrased as follows: "Qualitative research emphasizes meaning."

We will now look at how qualitative research is conceptualized and done in more detail. We will break our discussion down into two parts. First, we will discuss philosophical orientations and frameworks that are used in qualitative research. Second, we will discuss qualitative methods and specific tools.

SECTION 6.2

PARADIGMS AND FRAMEWORKS IN QUALITATIVE RESEARCH

In this section, we will begin with general ideas that underlie most qualitative research (ethnography, social constructionism) and will move to some of the more specific orientations (e.g., postmodernism). These descriptions are meant to be broad introductions only. Those interested in learning more about each approach should consult the indicated references.

SECTION 6.2.1: ETHNOGRAPHY

A commonly used term for understanding and studying culture is **ethnography.** It has been taken to mean any qualitative approach designed to understand a culture or group, generally from the point of view of its members. As such, *ethnography* is a term used very broadly by some and can incorporate most of the specific forms of qualitative research described in the following section. While early ethnographic work was often done with other cultures, such as Pacific Islanders (Mead, 1928), much modern ethnographic work is done on subpopulations within the researcher's own society. Key principles of ethnographic research include:

- A detailed, rich description of the culture
- Drawn from the perspectives of members of that culture
- By a researcher who has substantial firsthand contact with the culture.

One of the best-known examples of ethnographic research is *Street Corner Society.* Based on observations taken between 1937 and 1940, this work explored the complex social organization of an impoverished Italian American neighborhood (Whyte, 1993). The work was typical of ethnographic research in its qualitative nature, the complexity of the data generated, and the close association between the researcher and the culture being investigated. For a painless and practical introduction to ethnography see Fetterman (1998).

SECTION 6.2.2: SOCIAL CONSTRUCTIONISM

One of the most influential books ever written in the social sciences is *The Social Construction of Reality, A Treatise in the Sociology of Knowledge* (1966) by Peter Bergman and Thomas Luckman. A fundamental aspect of this work is the claim that human beings cannot exist apart from their social context. It is asserted that human beings are best understood through their constructed and shared social reality. The way we view ourselves, each other, and the nature of all social institutions can be understood only as constructs (created subjectively by the observer), not as objective realities. *Note:* The meaning of the word *constructs* here is not the same as when we used *constructs* to describe things we study (less operationalized variables) in Chapter 3.

It is likely that you have already been exposed to this book in sociology or psychology courses. A **social constructionist** view is, of course, entirely compatible with an ethnographic approach to knowledge. The point is to develop a rich understanding of people, interactions, and institutions. Aspects of social constructionism, combined with an ethnographic approach, are present in the vast majority of qualitative works.

SECTION 6.2.3: ETHNOMETHODOLOGY

One part of sociology that works with how people understand their world is **ethnomethodology.** Harold Garfinkel's (1967) *Studies in Ethnomethodology* is often cited as the early prime work in the area; the book describes a sociological method that emphasizes exploring people's ways of understanding and making sense of their social environment. Ethnomethodologists are likely to study meaning in very small elements of human interaction, attempting to understand how people bring order out of confusing contexts. In this way, ethnomethodology is strongly empirical, basing conclusions on observations of a series of carefully analyzed interactions between people.

SECTION 6.2.4: GROUNDED THEORY

Grounded theory is a fairly basic form of induction (Glaser & Strauss, 1967). Grounded theory starts with empirical (real-life) observations of the subject matter. It then uses a method called "constant comparison" (Figure 6.2). In constant comparison, different cases are compared to each other with the goal of figuring out how to look at and think about the data. This is done through the development of coding schemes and theories that fit the data better as each new case is considered. For a very nice and detailed online overview of grounded theory from Southern Cross University in Australia, see www.scu.edu.au/schools/gcm/ar/arp/grounded.html.

OTHER PERSPECTIVES

Feminist, postmodern, and participant action research perspectives are also commonly seen in qualitative work. Because we reviewed these in Chapter 1, we will not reiterate the information here. To varying degrees, such qualitative approaches are characterized both by the value on subjective meaning and the explicit involvement of the researcher. Both feminist and PAR studies often seek to involve their participants in a larger political process to end oppression and/or seek social justice.

FIGURE 6.2. Grounded Theory.

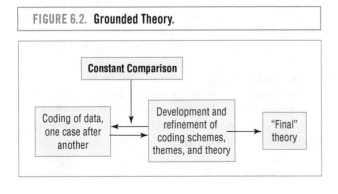

People tend to think of qualitative data as coming entirely from interviews. This is not the case. While detailed interviewing of subjects (which we will call "in-depth interviewing") is the most common source of data, other researchers may gain information from various forms of unobtrusive observation or through direct involvement as participants **(participant observation).** Increasingly, focus groups are seen as economical and efficient means of producing qualitative data. In addition, there exist many millions of preexisting text sources, from newspaper articles to agency records to personal correspondences, all of which can be subjected to qualitative analysis.

SECTION 6.3.1: IN-DEPTH INTERVIEWING

Most qualitative research involves talking to people and asking them questions. The hallmarks of qualitative interviewing include:

- *The use of open-ended questions:* Open-ended questions allow the clients to provide information from their own perspective in their own words. Qualitative studies from a constructivist or ethnographic tradition almost always use open-ended questions, so as not to force the researcher's perspective too strongly upon the subject.

- *The use of very general questions early in the interview:* While very specific questions are often used, they should come later in the interview. This is to avoid guiding the subject along particular lines of thought. As we discussed in Chapter 5, this can bias your results. If you want someone's genuine views of a broad issue, then it is best to ask these questions first, before the subject gets a clearer idea of what you might be looking for or getting at. For example, if you want to know about views on the death penalty, the fairest thing to do is to first ask a question such as, "What are your thoughts about the death penalty?" Later questions ("How do you feel about the fact that we know from new DNA evidence that innocent people have been executed?") may betray a focus or bias to your study that may change what responses you get.

- *The ability to follow up in areas of interest:* Qualitative researchers are constantly making decisions during the interview process. One of the most important and difficult decisions is how much to follow up on ideas or streams of thought that were not clearly what you expected to discuss.

While it is important to allow subjects to present information in their own way and from their own perspectives, it is equally important not to allow the discussion to become so off-topic that it is irrelevant to the research question. This is related to the issue of time management during an interview. It is important that you get a chance to get to the issues you need covered. Our suggestion in dealing with these issues is to move away from your intended questions only after making a conscious choice to do so. We believe it is appropriate to divert from your intended questions so long as you do so intentionally and for good reasons. It is equally important, however, to avoid unintentionally drifting away from your topic of interest and then failing to cover the key points you need covered.

- *Pursuit of rich detail:* Another of the hallmarks of qualitative research involves gathering detail. In general, you want to make sure that you get both understandable information that conveys main points or "big ideas" and that you are recording illustrative quotes. In the rare instances when audiotaping is not available, notetaking should focus on these two aspects: big ideas and illustrative quotes.

Like all other forms of research, in-depth interviews require planning. You must carefully select participants. Even "unstructured" interviews require that the researcher consider many issues in advance:

- *What questions will be asked, at what level of specificity?* The degree of structure in qualitative interviews can range from high to very low. It is mainly based on how detailed your underlying theory and questions are. For example, if you have a clear theory about how people respond to parental death, you may ask many questions specifically informed by your theory. If, for example, your theory holds that the early relationship with the parent is critically important to understanding the grief process, you may have a number of questions specifically about different aspects of that. On the other hand, if you are doing inductive work (building theory), then your questions may be less focused and extremely broad in nature. In general, the more exploratory and inductive, the broader and less structured the questions. While some researchers simply specify a subject area or ask a single question, it is more common to have a written list of several questions or topics to ask the subject about. In the accompanying boxed example, a social service agency has put together a set of very basic questions to begin to try to understand how clients view their experiences at the agency and to get input for how the agency could do a better job.

EXAMPLE OF INTERVIEW QUESTIONS

Questions for Client Experiences Study

1. How would you describe your experience at this agency?
2. What were some of the better things that happened to you here?
3. What were some of the worst things that happened to you here?
4. In what ways did the staff make your time here better or worse?
5. If you could change one thing about our agency to make your time here better, what would that be?
6. What else could be done differently to make things better?
7. What else can you tell us about your experiences here? ■

- *What is the most appropriate setting for the interview?* Choice of setting can be determined by practicality or happenstance, but it is best to put the subject's comfort first in deciding where to hold the interview. Interviews are often done in the subject's own neighborhood or home. This can provide the researcher with additional opportunities to observe the subject's surroundings and to see the subject in a natural context. Neutral settings such as parks, recreation centers, or diners are often used. These settings are generally preferable to having the subjects come to you, as visiting imposing or unfamiliar environments can be distracting or intimidating and can reduce the quality of the data you are given. Sometimes, serious ethical concerns will intrude. If you are interviewing domestic violence victims, for example, extreme measures may be necessary to make sure your contact with them does not put them at risk.

- *Will the client be paid or otherwise reimbursed?* Many projects will pay subjects for their time. It is a way to promote participation in the project, and the reimbursement cost is usually not that large when compared to other project costs (such as transcribing audiotapes). Ethical concerns may arise if payment is made to individuals who may use the money in ways that might hurt them (e.g., buying drugs). This concern can be lessened by providing clients with coupons to supermarkets or similar forms of payment instead of cash.

- *How long will the interview last?* Depending on who is being interviewed and what the questions are, interviews can last from a few minutes to many hours. As a very general rule, 90 minutes can be a reasonable amount of time to budget for interviews with adults. Less time will not allow for details to be covered, while more time can sometimes be too fatiguing to the subjects.

■ *How will data be recorded?* Most researchers use audiotapes, which are then transcribed to computer text files. Obviously, the client's knowledge of and permission for taping is necessary. In some situations, particularly participant observations, this may not be possible. In these cases, the researcher should take hand or audio notes as soon as possible after the observations. Note taking should focus on key ideas and should also include illustrative quotations if possible. Sometimes people do studies in which groups are involved, and it is necessary to be able to record who says what to whom. In this case, it may be necessary to use video cameras to capture a visual record of the interviews. To cover all participants, three cameras are often used. Video recordings are also commonly used when key data are nonverbal. For example, parental interaction with infants is largely nonverbal and requires the researcher to visually observe parent and child actions to produce meaningfully coded data.

SECTION 6.3.2: PARTICIPANT OBSERVATION

Participant observation is an extremely time-intensive means for gaining a deep understanding of the lives and experiences of subjects. Due to the time and effort involved in formal participant observation work, it is not commonly done by students, and we will therefore only overview the subject here. In short, participant observation includes the following steps:

1. Determining a question, population, or area of interest

2. Locating a context or group where the researcher can participate in the social context being studied

3. Gaining trust, joining, and participating in that context

4. Continuing to make structured recordings, often in the form of notes taken after observations

5. Analyzing the recordings.

Advantages of participant observation include the fact that it is possibly the most immersive and fully involved form of social research, yielding a depth of data that might be unavailable through other means. This can yield insight and richly textured data. Potential disadvantages are many and include the risk of the researcher losing any semblance of objectivity. The participant-observer attempts to strike a difficult balance, being engaged both as a (partly detached) observer and a more fully engaged participant. Some

researchers have recently suggested doing participant observation in teams, with one member being focused on a more objective form of observation and one being more focused on pure participation (Hong & Duff, 2002). In this way, one researcher can allow him- or herself relatively complete abandon to become part of the situation, while another researcher monitors the situation from a more objectivist perspective.

Another issue is that ethical considerations generally dictate that the subjects be informed of the researcher's identity and goals, as discussed in Chapter 2. This may inhibit the subject's ability to behave in a natural fashion. In addition, it is usually impossible for the researcher to inform all individuals who might be contacted of his or her researcher status. Furthermore, a large number of issues cannot easily be studied through participant observation. Criminality, violence, and similar subject areas pose real challenges to the researcher using participant observation.

In summary, participant observation is an intensive research method that promises richness of data and insight but poses a series of practical, ethical, and personal challenges. For further information on participant observation, see Spradley (1997).

SECTION 6.3.3: FOCUS GROUPS

Focus groups are a very common means of generating data for qualitative analysis. For an outstanding and readable introduction to focus group methods, see Kruger and Casey (2000). Focus groups are becoming one of the most common and important forms of qualitative inquiry (Linhorst, 2002). Focus groups are relatively quick and easy to do. They tend to generate very clean and useful text, as participants have a chance to think out their answers before responding to questions. In addition, this method provides a good way to get the views of many people quickly. Focus groups are held with between 4 and 12 participants (about 8 is best) and usually two facilitators. Focus groups usually last about 90 minutes and are composed of people who have experience with the issue being researched (e.g., group of consumers of medical services). If groups are to be held with both providers and consumers of services, then these individuals should not be mixed together in a single group. Participants should not know each other well or have any strong past history together because these factors can inhibit or distort disclosure. Focus groups are *not* intended to reach consensus, only to evoke a full range of views from all participants. This is an important point and requires some emphasis. Most groups we attend are meant to come to agreement or formulate a plan or a product. Focus groups are just the opposite; they are a place where you want to get as many views as possible. This must be stressed to subjects. The heart of a focus group is the "questioning route," a set of questions designed to prompt responses on specific topics from the participants. The facilitators' role is to serve as a neutral force, moving discussion forward along the questioning route and ensuring that all members have a chance to contribute. The facilitators also take notes.

ONE EXAMPLE OF FOCUS GROUP RESEARCH

As part of a larger research project (DHHS Grant #90cw1006/01), information was needed on what child protection workers and child protection clients saw as key worker competencies. This work was needed to inform a new federally funded training program at a university. As such, this study was basically exploratory and descriptive, the goal being to develop a list of competencies from the points of view of workers and consumers. Separate focus groups were held with consumers and providers, and different versions of a questioning route were used with each. The worker questioning route looked like this:

1. What are the most important skills a beginning worker can have?
2. What are the most important skills or qualities in making a good assessment?
3. What are the most important skills or qualities in good intervention?
4. What other skills or task competencies are most important for a children's services worker?
5. What skills are important in dealing with agency or organizational tasks or demands?
6. What about job-related stress? How do you deal with this?
7. What skills or tasks are the hardest to learn?
8. In what areas do you feel you need more education or training?

Nine groups in all were held, four with workers and five with consumers. Audiotapes were transcribed, and eight major themes were identified. These included skills involving the worker–client relationship, diversity skills, skills in dealing with special populations, intraorganizational and interorganizational skills, self-management skills, assessment skills, and intervention skills. Each of these major categories was further defined into subcategories. For example, one specific relationship competency was the worker's ability to express an appropriate attitude to the client. Each specific competency was arranged under its major heading, and the source of each item (worker, consumer, or both) was indicated. The final published report on this study (Drake, 1996a) presented this outline of major themes and subcategories and also included a large number of direct quotations from workers and clients to provide the reader with a better feel for the participants' perspectives.∎

Transcripts from focus group sessions are then analyzed using typical qualitative methods. One special consideration in any group-based qualitative data is that it can be hard to determine who says what on a tape. Do you have many people saying something or one person repeating a point of view over and over? This can be addressed by using multiple videocameras (usually three), which allow the person making the transcript to number or otherwise identify respondents and then note who says what in the transcripts. When doing focus group text analysis ourselves, we tend to downplay the presence of multiple occurrences of a given theme, looking for how many different groups identify given issues rather than how many times an issue may come up in any single group.

SECTION 6.3.4: ARCHIVAL SOURCES

Qualitative research is commonly done on preexisting data. Massive amounts of narrative or text data exist in easily available forms. These range from the public (e.g., newspaper articles, commercials, children's cartoons, court records) to the private (correspondences, medical records, etc.). Preexisting data are appropriate for qualitative analysis to the extent that the narrative content is responsive to the questions being asked. In other words, if it answers your question, use it. One example of a qualitative analysis done on archival sources (Heron, 2004) used students' assignments at the start and end of their educational programs to determine if they showed increased antiracist content in their writing. Student assignments (which were not specifically about racism) were selected and coded for antiracist content. In this way, the researcher was able to use preexisting data as material, and new interviews did not need to be done.

SECTION 6.3.5: HOW MANY SUBJECTS SHOULD I INTERVIEW?

The number of subjects depends on the complexity of the issue being studied and the degree to which people are giving you similar or different information. Many qualitative researchers involved in exploratory work keep interviewing subjects until they reach **saturation.** This is a key concept in qualitative research. Saturation occurs when you no longer get new information from additional subjects. An informal gauge for identifying when you have reached saturation is that conducting the groups or interviews becomes boring and repetitious, no longer fun or interesting. In focus groups, this often occurs after four or five groups. With individual subjects, it may be necessary to interview anywhere from a half dozen to several dozen to achieve saturation. *Warning!* The term *saturation* here is very different from the term *saturation* used to describe a model that is not parsimonious (see

Chapter 3). Saturation in a theoretical model is bad. Saturation in qualitative analysis is good.

SECTION 6.4
ANALYSIS IN QUALITATIVE RESEARCH

After qualitative data have been collected, the researcher faces the task of analyzing that data. We will focus on the analysis of narrative data because this comprises the vast majority of qualitative work. We will assume that the data have been transcribed into electronic document form (MS Word, WordPerfect, etc.). We will describe a general approach to qualitative data analysis that is commonly used by most researchers. Most researchers would describe the system described below as a form of content analysis. Different researchers have different terms for different parts of the process, but the primary approach is fairly consistent among most qualitative researchers. For a more detailed example of the analysis of qualitative data, you can see Chapter 10, which introduces you to NVivo, or the portions of Chapters 9, 12, and 15 that deal with John's project.

SECTION 6.4.1: SHOULD YOU USE A QUALITATIVE ANALYSIS PROGRAM?

Qualitative research can certainly be done by hand, with no help from computerized qualitative analysis packages. In a study with only a very small qualitative component, this may be appropriate. In studies with large numbers of files or in studies using more complicated qualitative approaches, such as relational analysis, you really need a computer package. Commonly available computer analysis programs include NVivo, Qualrus, Ethnograph, "N6" (the program formerly known as "NUD * IST"), HyperRESEARCH, and Atlas. For a very nice overview of specific characteristics of these and other programs, see Lewins and Silver "Choosing a CAQDAS Software Package" (http://caqdas.soc.surrey.ac.uk). Specific information on N6 and NVivo, along with demo downloads, can be found at www.scolari.co.uk/frame.html?http://www.scolari. co.uk/qsr/qsr_nvivo.htm. All these programs include the ability to bring text into the program, code text, retrieve text based on codes or other means, explore the text interactively, and output information into other electronic formats.

SECTION 6.4.2: STEPS IN QUALITATIVE ANALYSIS

REVIEWING THE DATA AND IDENTIFYING THEMES

Most qualitative analysis starts with the researcher reading the transcripts. This allows the researcher to gain familiarity with the data and begin to get ideas

about how the coding will proceed. Generally, readers will notice several recurring themes, and these form the basis for the "coding scheme." A coding scheme is simply a set of categories or labels that can be attached to different sections of text. Most often, these coding schemes include several major categories, each of which may have subcategories. For example, a major theme might be "stressors" and subcategories might be "family stressors," "financial stressors," and the like. During the initial review of the data, you will begin to get ideas about how to construct your coding scheme.

YOUR CODING SCHEME

The next step involves writing out your coding scheme. A coding scheme is not set in stone and may be modified as more data or different ideas emerge. Nevertheless, it is important to get it down on paper. Depending on what analysis software (if any) you are using, you may want to use a simple number/letter tag for each code, or not. For example, in a study of stressors on first-year medical school students, you might come up with the coding scheme shown in the following boxed example.

EXAMPLE OF SIMPLE CODING SCHEME FOR STUDY OF MEDICAL STUDENT STRESSORS

Workload (W)

1. Insufficient time (W1)
2. Difficulty of work (W2)
   a) Technical difficulty of readings (W2a)
   b) Difficulty of learning practice skills (W2b)
   c) Difficulty with amount of memorizing (W2c)
3. Other workload issues (W3)

Personal and social (P)

1. Self-esteem issues (P1)
2. Loss of prior relationships (P2)
3. Other personal and social issues (P3)

Financial (F)

1. Current financial difficulties (F1)
2. Concern over future indebtedness (F2)■

Notice that this is a three-level coding scheme. You can have as many subcategories as the data require, but three or four levels are common.

CONTENT UNITS

To code qualitative data, you need a coding scheme and data that are separated into content units. A content unit is a bit of narrative that contains an idea.

These content units can then be given a code word, phrase, or letter/number sequence from your coding scheme (see the accompanying boxed example).

EXAMPLE OF SIMPLE CODING
(*FICTIONAL DATA*)

Source Narrative

"I get stressed every time I think about money, I can barely make my payments. Another thing: I don't know how I'm ever going to earn my way out of all this student loan debt! What else do you want to know about? I'm not sure what else to say . . . I guess the good thing is that I'm so overwhelmed with schoolwork that I don't have that much time to even worry about other things."

Coded Content Units:

(F1) I get stressed every time I think about money.

(F1) I can barely make my payments.

(F2) I don't know how I'm ever going to earn my way out of all this student loan debt!

(W1) I guess one good thing is that I'm so overwhelmed with schoolwork that I don't have that much time to even worry about other things.■

As previously stated, coding can be done by hand or electronically. For examples of electronic coding, see Chapter 10. In Chapter 10, we use John's data and run it through NVivo so that you can see how a software package can be used in qualitative analysis. In the above example, you will notice that some of the narrative is essentially meaningless filler ("What else do you want to know about? I'm not sure what else to say . . ."); you need not feel compelled to include every word of the narrative into a content unit. Also notice that the first sentence has been separated out into two separate content units. You need to base content units on the ideas given, not on the sentence structure. Frequently you will code single sentences under multiple codes. This is perfectly legal.

CODING SCHEMES IN DETAIL

Validity. When developing **coding schemes,** it is common practice to have several people independently create coding schemes. These people can then meet and see if their schemes are similar or different. If the schemes are different, they can decide together how to combine them to create the strongest possible scheme. Is each theme brought up in the content units represented in the coding scheme? This is similar to the

general idea behind content validity, as more eyes on the work will help assure that all key issues get coded for. More people's judgment can also enhance face validity, making the coding scheme more logical and understandable.

Construct validity is also important. Does your coding scheme fit with your theoretical orientation? Will it allow for interpretation of your data under the theory or paradigm being employed? It may be necessary to alter your coding scheme somewhat to allow you to better interpret your findings under a given framework.

Reliability. Particularly worrisome when there are multiple coders, intercoder reliability can be enhanced in the following ways:

- All individuals doing the coding should be trained on exactly how to code.

- These people can be tested by coding a set of content units. Individuals failing to correctly code a certain percentage of content units (say 90%) could be retrained until they can reach an acceptable level of consistency.

- Individuals coding the data should be tested in an ongoing way. One way to do this is to have several people code the same data periodically and to check to make sure that high levels of agreement are achieved.

Coding "Up" and Coding "Down." People often talk about "coding up" and "coding down." They can be described as follows.

Coding up is done when you are doing exploratory work using grounded theory. As we said, grounded theory rises up out of the data (induction). Put simply, you look at the text and say, "Hey, that chunk of text (content unit) is about *X*," and you make "*X*" your coding category. Building codes, you put together a coding scheme, which has risen "up" from the data. For example, if you know nothing about what people think of a new policy, you might talk to people and find out what ideas come up. You would code each idea (and subidea), creating a coding scheme. In case you're wondering, "induction," "coding up," "grounded theory" and "exploratory" are pretty synonymous in this context.

Coding down happens when you are doing non-exploratory work and you already start with an idea of what your coding scheme is. For example, you may be testing a theory that says that political articles in newspapers become more negative the closer you get to an election. You would have preexisting coding categories. These categories might just be "positive," "negative," and "neutral," or they might be much more complex. In any case, you start with the coding scheme and then look "down" at the data from that point.

INTERPRETATION AND PRESENTATION OF MANIFEST CONTENT

Following coding, the researcher will have a clear understanding of the text's manifest content. **Manifest content** is what the data say directly. Much qualitative work focuses entirely or almost entirely on manifest content. Manifest content can be understood and reported very easily, simply through summarizing your coding scheme and reporting what was said under each section. This can be done simply, by presenting your scheme and main findings in a figure (see below).

WORKLOAD ISSUES FOR MEDICAL STUDENTS

Insufficient time was available for studying, personal tasks, and other necessary functions.

Difficulty of work was an issue, particularly in three areas:

1. Readings were difficult due to language, new concepts, and complexity.
2. Practice skills were hard to learn and apply on a consistent basis.
3. Difficulty with amount of memorizing was reported by all students.

Other workload issues included difficulty of finishing required volunteer work and antiquated school computer and library systems wasting valuable time. ■

Manifest content can also be presented in a narrative fashion, using the coding scheme as an outline for your writing, spiced up by relevant and interesting quotes. Manifest content can be presented numerically. For example, a content analysis could be performed identifying the use of researcher-identified sexist terms on television over time. Hypothetical tabular data from such a study is presented in Table 6.1. From this (hypothetical) data, we would conclude that there might have been an improvement in sexist terms in the news, that it appears worse in situation comedies, and that there appears to be little change in drama programs.

INTERPRETATION AND PRESENTATION OF LATENT CONTENT

Latent content is information that is less objectively identifiable but is subjectively identified by the researcher. Such content is often more abstract and

---

TABLE 6.1. Sexist Terms in News, Sitcoms, and Drama Programs, 1984 and 2004 (*Fictional Data*).

	1984	2004
# of Type I Sexist Terms per hour (News)	6.9	0.5
# of Type I Sexist Terms per hour (Sitcoms)	17.9	32.4
# of Type I Sexist Terms per hour (Drama)	10.9	11.2

---

may be theoretically based. For example, Freudian researchers are commonly interested in identifying latent themes in narratives. These latent themes are generally consistent with Freudian theory and its focus on the unconscious mind and unconscious motivations. Latent content of interest to a Freudian researcher may include themes of general paranoia in how subjects describe their world or may be based on consistently emerging sexual themes that give clues to underlying repressed issues.

Identification of latent content requires that the researcher make a subjective judgment about particular content units or, more commonly, about each subject's narrative as a whole. This is obviously tricky to do reliably, so the reliability of latent content coding should be checked by the use of multiple coders, with their conclusions compared. Validity of identified latent content can also be checked through triangulation. Do other data sources (e.g., behavior, administrative records, subject history) agree with your interpretation? In short, latent content can be more interesting than manifest content, especially from a theoretical point of view, but the trade-off is that issues of reliability and validity become more troublesome (see nearby boxed example).

DESCRIPTION OF LATENT CONTENT FROM MEDICAL STUDENT DATA

Overall, the comments we received suggested two underlying themes. First, there was a consistent sense of students feeling overwhelmed by their experience as first-year medical school students. This was true in both practical as well as psychological terms. Our quantitative findings support this conclusion, showing that time spent on school-related tasks exceeds 80 hours per week. Second, there was a strong determination on the part of the students to survive this overwhelming process. Students appeared to have very high ego strength, and few students seemed to genuinely believe that the tasks they faced would defeat them. Subsequent review of school records indicated only 2 of the 35 students in the study dropped out in their first year. ■

CONCLUDING A QUALITATIVE RESEARCH PROCESS

As a final step, many qualitative studies present theoretical conclusions derived inductively from the data. How this is done will vary radically based on a number of factors. More theoretically advanced areas will likely include detailed discussions of how existing theories can be better understood, applied, or modified. Exploratory work in newer areas may simply include suggestions for new theoretical constructs that can serve as a basis for further exploration.

Mixed-methods work will incorporate the qualitative findings into final products, ideally showing triangulation between findings derived through different methods and supporting the validity of the study as a whole. Discussion sections of mixed-method studies will commonly use qualitative findings as a way of adding depth or color to more quantitative results.

SECTION 6.4.3: DUTY TO REPORT

Members of all helping professions are mandated to report child maltreatment in all states. Many of us are also mandated to report other risks to clients, such as elder abuse. In addition, failure to report threats of violence to potential targets can make you vulnerable to criminal or civil action. If you become aware of such issues, you have no choice but to make a formal report to the appropriate agencies or individuals. This responsibility is with you just as strongly in quantitative work, but the issue is probably more likely to arise unexpectedly in deep qualitative studies. Ethics always come first, and you cannot decide to ignore such information or delay mandated reporting. It is necessary to inform all study participants of your duty to report in advance. This could possibly be difficult in some forms of research. For example, in participant observation, people may come and go quickly, with no real opportunity for you to advise everyone you contact of your mandated reporter status.

★ ★ ★

EBP MODULE

The use of qualitative studies in evidence-based practice has not received the attention it deserves. We believe that qualitative studies are a vital resource for the evidence-based practitioner in the social services and that their use can improve practice in a number of ways. We will discuss the utility of qualitative studies using the familiar three-part framework for applying evidence, which includes

using the best available evidence, being aware of client factors, and using your own best professional judgment.

QUALITATIVE STUDIES AS EVIDENCE

Qualitative studies can supply evidence directly. Evidence-based practice always begins with a practice-relevant question. It is clear that exploratory or other very general questions dealing with meaning might be answered qualitatively. As we are writing this, we have an MSW student confronted with the practice-relevant question, "What factors account for low participation in social services among some Native American groups?" We suggested that she look for whatever quantitative analyses may be available but also that she pay particularly close attention to existing qualitative research. Why? As you recall, qualitative research is often defined by its focus on meaning. Our student's question is all about meaning. She wants to know, in human terms, how Native Americans feel about services so that she can work on ways to solve any problems. When you need rich data, qualitative methods are generally the approach of choice.

Qualitative studies can help us evaluate the value of quantitative research. One simple example is the EMDR example discussed earlier. The qualitative component of the study helped us to both understand and have more faith in the quantitative component. There are a range of particular ways in which reading qualitative research can help you be a better consumer of quantitative research. One of the most obvious ways this can happen is with regard to face validity. If the quantitative articles you read are consistent with the qualitative work, then that's a good thing. Do the quantitative designs, measures, and samples make sense, given what we read in qualitative studies? Do the constructs and relationships explored in the quantitative works fit well with what people tell us in more human terms? A closely related issue has to do with content validity. Some familiarity with qualitative work will help you get a feel for the important dimensions of any situation. This will help you to see if the quantitative studies you read include all the key concepts. Similarly, qualitative studies can help you assess construct validity in quantitative works. If constructs in a quantitative study operate in a way consistent with relationships as portrayed in a qualitative work, then you can have more faith in the value of both studies.

When studies that use different methods come to similar conclusions, we achieve triangulation. The more different two approaches are, the more impressive it is when they find the same thing. Given the substantial differences between many quantitative and qualitative designs, triangulation between such research models can be very compelling.

THE UTILITY OF QUALITATIVE STUDIES IN UNDERSTANDING CLIENT FACTORS

By now, we've told you many times that you must consider client factors. The clients' values, preferences, culture, situation, and other factors are all key determinants in how you provide services. Of course, this will often center around asking questions of your particular clients and being alert to their responses as well as to unspoken or indirect cues.

Qualitative studies can be of assistance in helping you to better understand clients. Let's say that you are a teen counselor who often encounters bullying in your practice. Qualitative studies examining the victims or the perpetrators of bullying can provide you with important insight into the clients you serve. What kinds of themes are commonly found? Do victims tend to blame themselves for what happens? What do bullies get out of their behavior? Rich qualitative data can give you starting points in assessing these questions. Sources such as focus groups, in-depth interviews, participant observation, or case studies can be amazingly rich sources of contextual data that you can use in helping you to understand the person sitting in front of you.

In a more general sense, qualitative works may help you to explore alternative paradigms for considering your clients and your practice. An obvious class of examples can be found in qualitative work done from a feminist perspective. Is thinking about the societal subordination of women a viewpoint that will help you better understand the woman in front of you? Will you see the client differently if you are familiar with such a perspective?

THE UTILITY OF QUALITATIVE STUDIES IN DEVELOPING PROFESSIONAL JUDGMENT

The final component of EBP involves professional judgment. In this area, case studies can be particularly useful. A clinician who writes a case study usually puts a lot of thought into explaining what he or she did and why, explaining the reasoning and how particular clinical situations were dealt with. This gives you a way to review your own practice and compare notes. Would you have done the same thing? Could or should you have done something different? We would encourage you to read as much as you can in case study literature related to your area of practice. We do not suggest by any means that you uncritically adopt conclusions or practices found in these works, but we do suggest you use them as a chance to grow and reflect upon your own practice.■

REVIEW

1. Assume you meet someone who knows nothing about research. Describe the difference between qualitative and quantitative research in 30 words or less.

2. Give a hypothetical example of using control in qualitative research.

3. What is a "case study"? Describe in detail.

4. What are "focus groups"? Describe in detail.

5. Give a hypothetical example of a sampling strategy that is "theoretical," not random.

6. What is a "content analysis"? In your opinion, are content analyses always qualitative? Why or why not?

7. How are "relational" and "conceptual" analyses different?

8. What is "ethnography"?

9. What is "ethnomethodology"?

10. How are the two terms in questions 8 and 9 different?

11. Define "grounded theory." Explain how it is or is not different from induction.

12. Define "social constructionism." Is it different from postmodernism (see Chapter 2)? If so, how?

13. What is "in-depth" interviewing? Why do it?

14. What is "participant observation"?

15. Describe a hypothetical study that is entirely qualitative and in which you never meet, see, or hear another human being.

16. What is "saturation" in qualitative research? How do you know when you have achieved it?

17. What is a "coding scheme," and why do you need one?

18. What are "content units"? Give a short text example.

19. How are "coding up" and "coding down" different?

20. What is "manifest content"?

21. What is "latent content"?

SUPPLEMENTAL READINGS

■ Denzin, A., & Lincoln, Y. (2005). *The Sage Handbook of Qualitative Research* (3rd ed.). Thousand Oaks, CA: Sage. We know we recommended this text in Chapter 4, but we thought it should be referenced here, too. It's a bit on the more radical side.

■ Elliott, J. (2005). *Using narrative in social research: Qualitative and quantitative approaches.* Thousand Oaks, CA: Sage Publications. This book is a nice general overview of narrative research focusing on quantitative aspects as well as qualitative ones; it's practical.

■ Hammersly, M., & Atkinson, P. (1997). *Ethnography: Principles and Practice.* London: Biddles. Simple and straightforward, this text attends to many of the practical aspects of doing ethnography.

■ Strauss, A., & Corbin, J. (1998). *Basics of Qualitative Research: Techniques and Procedures for Developing Grounded Theory.* Thousand Oaks, CA: Sage. This book is a nice guide to inductive qualitative research.

■ Yin, R., & Campbell, D. (2003). *Case Study Research: Design and Methods* (2nd ed.). Thousand Oaks, CA: Sage. We recommend this simple and understandable book.

CLINICAL MULTISUBJECT RESEARCH

This chapter looks at the many kinds of clinical research done with groups, also typically discussed as program evaluation. Agencies need to know about their clients, how they are doing, and what can be done better. This is often done using multiple-subject designs. Even individual workers may want to know about how their caseload is doing as a whole, and so they too may study many subjects at a time. Finally, this work may also inform policy. We have already learned a lot about how to do this kind of study in Chapters 4 and 5. We will now look at how we can apply the skills we have learned in prior chapters to clinical situations. It should be noted that this chapter serves as a mere overview of an area about which there are many excellent texts available. A few of these are listed at the end of the chapter to further guide students in evaluation research.

SECTION 7.1

INTRODUCTION

SECTION 7.1.1: WHY DO RESEARCH ON AGENCIES AND CASELOADS?

Agencies or practitioners do evaluation research for several reasons, which are all pretty much interconnected. The main reasons are:

- To improve our practice
- To demonstrate accountability
- To be able to report back to your client; your agency; and funding, accrediting, or other oversight agencies
- To serve as a basis for making applications for grant funding

Obviously, improving practice is the most important reason to do research on practice. You do research to find out what is needed, what works best and for whom, and to answer other questions, such as, "Do benefits of treatment stay or just fade away?" If you don't really know what's going on, or base your estimate of what's going on simply on guesswork, then you don't have as good a chance of doing a better job in the future, either as an agency or as an individual practitioner. As reviewed in our section on values and ethics, helping professions strongly endorse competent practice.

CLINICIANS ARE ETHICALLY REQUIRED TO BE ACCOUNTABLE

This means that there needs to be some evidence that what you do works. There are many ways you can be accountable, such as selecting interventions that have been shown to work before (evidence-based practice).

One of the best ways to be accountable is to measure and be able to report exactly how successful your interventions are. Do your interventions work? Are they making people worse? Are they worth the client's time? Are they worth the funder's investment? These are important questions you need to be able to answer.

Part of assessing whether or not the interventions are worth a client's time is about whether or not they are culturally appropriate. Many intervention studies have been limited to White, English-speaking participants (Royse, Thyer, Padgett, & Logan, 2006). Translating this research to populations of differing cultural and ethnic backgrounds can be problematic without replicating evaluative research with the particular group served by the agency in question.

REPORTING ABOUT THE OUTCOMES OF YOUR WORK IS MORE COMMON AND NECESSARY THAN YOU MIGHT THINK

You should be able to tell incoming clients about your agency's success in achieving outcomes. Agencies often publish outcomes in annual reports. Many funding agencies, such as the United Way, require yearly research on outcomes in agencies they serve. Failure to do so can cut off your funding. Many agencies are accredited, and most accrediting bodies require that you evaluate the work you do and give them numbers on outcomes. This working with and reporting back to the stakeholder is also a key tenet of cultural competence in community-based participatory research (Israel et al., 2005).

Applying for funding is much easier if you can report on exactly what you do, why you need money, and how successful your agency has been in the past. Ideally, you might even have piloted a new program and can provide some data from the pilot to show that the new program you want money for is worth the investment. Further, most funding sources now require that a formal evaluation of the services or treatment provided is conducted.

SECTION 7.1.2: PERSPECTIVES ON EVALUATION

It is important to note that there are different approaches or frameworks that guide how evaluation research might be done. These approaches can generally be thought of on a continuum from a more agency-controlled to a more researcher-controlled situation. For example, on one end of the continuum, a researcher using an empowerment evaluation perspective might think of herself as a coach helping the agency actually design, implement, and interpret the results (Fetterman, Kaftarian, & Wandersman, 1996). Or a researcher may act as an outside party who designs, implements, and interprets the information and then provides a report to the agency (Royse et al., 2006). A thorough treatment of these approaches is beyond the scope of a single chapter, but the references at the end of the chapter can be consulted for more detail.

In real-world settings, the choice of perspective may well depend on the purpose and consumer of the evaluation. In a more academic research project, one identifies appropriate questions and theory and then relates the design to those. In an agency, an evaluation may be a required component of funding, and the funder may dictate much of the design. Real-world limitations such as time and resources also influence one's ability to restrict evaluation practice to a fixed perspective (Bamberger, Rugh, & Mabry, 2006). The goal becomes to collect the best possible information that comes closest to answering the need for the evaluation.

SECTION 7.1.3: GENERAL IMPLEMENTATION ISSUES

Many of the implementation issues faced in doing evaluation research are the same no matter what the question is. Almost all of these issues relate to you as a researcher thoroughly understanding the context of the evaluation. In other words, you must understand something of the desire for evaluation and resources on the part of the agency as well as the likely access to and willingness of participation on the part of those answering questions. The following are some typical issues faced by any evaluation project that impact the design independently of the research question and optimal methodology.

Cost is a big issue for any sort of evaluation. While an agency may be fully aware of the desirability of a full-scale experimental design investigation of their counseling services, that same agency may lack the resources to implement such a venture. Unlike some better funded laboratory research or grant-funded efforts, you need to aim for the best possible information given the limitations.

Agencies and organizations and communities are composed of different people. Not all members may find evaluation equally intriguing or important. For example, the executive president of a foundation may be very enthusiastic about evaluation, whereas the line staff may not be. Sometimes this is due to lack of understanding of the value of evaluation, and sometimes it is merely due to staff burden. For example, one author has done work with helping school social workers evaluate aspects of their practice and has found the time involved in the data entry to be an enormous barrier for the workers despite their desire to have the evaluation done (Jonson-Reid et al., 2001).

The evaluation researcher must also know something about the intended target population. Errors in this area can cause fatal flaws. For example, if you do a phone survey at 1 p.m., who is likely to be home?

Well, in most communities you are likely to reach retired older persons, homemakers, and the unemployed. If you want to survey working parents, then an early afternoon time frame for contacting your sample is a very bad idea. In another example, one author recalls a needs assessment that was conducted in a particular neighborhood. Unfortunately, the agency neglected to consider the language background of the residents. So, all surveys were in English, despite the fact that there was a substantial proportion of Hispanic residents who could not read English. At the end of the day, this means that the information they obtained was useful in guiding services for only a subgroup of the target area.

Evaluation researchers must keep in mind respondent burden. The workers or clients or community members surveyed are busy people, thus the shorter the survey the better. Generally people are happier to respond to brief well-stated questions that do not require a lot of their time. This is likely to improve your response rate as well as the completeness of the data.

Like any other researcher using human subjects, evaluation researchers should be careful to follow the ethical protocols outlined in Chapter 2. Sometimes agencies will have a review committee that addresses human subjects. In other cases, it is incumbent on the researcher to understand how to ethically conduct the work. For example, even if the agency does not require it, one should still seek informed consent.

In the next three sections, we will overview the most common types of clinical multisubject or agency-level evaluation research. While we have divided various forms of evaluation research into three general different types, this is a somewhat arbitrary division. For example, a satisfaction survey is thought of as part of program monitoring, but there is also often a needs assessment aspect included when we ask clients to identify changes or additional services that would improve agency capacity to serve them. Each section touches on major considerations related to implementing that type of evaluation. Human subjects treatment was mentioned earlier and is not repeated in each section as it is the same no matter what type of evaluation one is attempting.

SECTION 7.2

NEEDS ASSESSMENT AND CASELOAD ANALYSIS

SECTION 7.2.1: ISSUE—"WHO AM I SERVING?" AND "WHAT DO THEY NEED?"

As Rossi, Freeman, and Lipsey (1999) explain, you need to understand the "size, distribution, and density of the problem" (p. 126). This helps you know *who* needs services, *how much* services are needed, and *where* they should be targeted. If you are looking within your existing clients and trying to understand them and their needs better, you might call this a "caseload analysis." If you are trying to gain a better understanding of a broader group of people, such as a community or a set of potential clients, this would more commonly be labeled a "needs assessment."

Sometimes caseload analysis and needs assessment are thought of as being only a part of program development, but these activities really should be an ongoing process (Royse et al., 2006). Human beings and society are dynamic. Populations change, social conditions change, available treatments change, and people change across the life span. This means that the problem you identify in a needs assessment today may not be at all the same next year. Further, a needs assessment is not limited to a client population. For example, there may be needs among staff in an organization that are the focus of a study.

Section 7.2.2: Basic Concepts in Needs Assessment or Caseload Analysis

Unless you are doing a limited assessment of your own caseload, it is important to involve a variety of stakeholders in the assessment process (Bleyer & Joiner, 2002). This will help insure that you correctly identify whom you need to survey and what type of focus is most useful. This can also help identify agency barriers, such as resources and staff time, that can affect what is possible to accomplish.

Typically we are interested in identifying needs and the scope of those needs. The number of people with a need or a disorder or whatever at a point in time is called **prevalence.** The number of people who pick up that thing over a certain period of time is called **incidence.** If 40 million people in the United States are currently depressed, and there are 5 million new cases per year, then the current prevalence is 40 million, and the incidence of new cases is 5 million people per year. Sometimes people talk about "lifetime prevalence," which is the proportion of people who will get something over their entire life span, usually expressed as a percentage (e.g., the lifetime prevalence of depression is about 15% [Kessler and Zhao, 1999]). Obviously both prevalence and incidence are important and also require different types of data. If you want to understand prevalence, you can do a cross-sectional survey of the target group; but if you want to understand incidence, then you will need to follow subjects over time.

Another issue is one of relevance to the situation. For example, persons in a community can have a multitude of needs related to a multitude of problems or issues. Needs assessments and caseload analyses are typically done by a particular agency to better tailor or alter or expand services that are relevant to that agency. It is therefore important not to "cast your net" so broadly that the information collected is not useful to the intended audience. For example, if you ask an open-ended question about needs and everyone lists child care, but your agency serves elders and wanted to know about aging issues, then your assessment will not be useful.

Finally, real-world clinical research often faces limits due to time, resources, and even availability of data. These are important considerations when setting aims. For example, a door-to-door survey might be an ideal way of interviewing residents about needs. This, however, is an expensive, time-consuming, and relatively invasive form of research. If you can't afford in-person approaches, you may have to adjust the aims of the study.

Section 7.2.3: Data Collection

In needs assessment or caseload analysis, you are typically doing some form of survey of a group or description of administrative agency or government data rather than attempting to assess causality. In other words, you are describing "what is." There are a variety of approaches that can be used, including interviews, mailed surveys, phone surveys, computer-assisted surveys, or administrative data kept by agencies to track clients or by government agencies to track population characteristics. Your goal is to use data that will maximize the relevant information obtained about the right people. It is therefore key that you are sure the concepts or ideas you are asking about are defined and worded in the same way the population of interest would word them (Pan, 2003; Thompson-Robinson, Hopson, & SenGupta, 2004).

We have already covered generalizability in prior chapters, but this is also important here. For example, if your needs assessment is done as a part of an exit interview after the close of services, you will not capture the opinions of clients who did not complete the program. If you are interested in expanding services or targeting underserved populations, you need to consider how best to gain access to the individuals you wish to serve.

Section 7.2.4: What Do You Measure?

This really boils down to careful consideration of the questions you will ask. We will not review survey techniques here (see Chapters 4 and 11), although the same issues apply. We will highlight only two major points. First, don't forget demographic information! It is often the case that different subgroups of our target population will have differing needs or opinions. If your agency services more than one population (e.g., elders and children), it's likely that you will have needs identified that are specific to a given group. Unfortunately, if you omit demographic questions such as age, race, and gender, this information will be impossible to break down by group.

Closed-ended multiple-choice questions are often ideal for needs assessments. Don't be overly vague and hope that the respondent will read your mind and clarify the issue for you. For example, if you need to know if transportation is a barrier to attending group sessions, then ask that or include transportation on a list of potential barriers. If you also want to elicit new ideas then sprinkle some open-ended questions in certain key areas.

Section 7.2.5: Ethical Considerations

In general the same ethics issues that apply to other forms of research apply to needs assessment and caseload analysis. There is, however, an additional consideration beyond that of respondent burden discussed earlier. In many cases, we are interested in the needs of very vulnerable populations (e.g., low income, mentally ill, children, etc.). Sometimes communities or client populations have been the subjects of multiple surveys only to feel that this information is never used. In the opinion of these authors, needs assessments should be limited to those things the agency intends to act on, and the results should be made available to the participants.

Why limit the questions? Let's look at an example. A community needs assessment identifies five priorities: child care, affordable housing, activities for older persons, jobs, and better transportation. The agency that does the needs assessment serves only children. By letting residents make any needed request, however, the agency has essentially (albeit unintentionally) raised the hopes of residents that these other issues will be addressed when they cannot be.

Why is it unethical not to make results available? In an earlier chapter, we discussed the ethical need not to harm or needlessly invade people's lives. No agency has funding to do everything it wants to do—even within its priority areas. By making the results available to the participants, the need to prioritize can be discussed and the participation of the subject is validated. In other words, even if I don't get my particular first choice, I know the agency valued my input and will try to do something at a later time or notify another agency.

SECTION 7.3
PROGRAM MONITORING

Section 7.3.1: Issue—"What Am I Doing?" or "What's Going on Here?"

Agencies and organizations need to understand certain basic aspects of their operation to continue to function appropriately. Monitoring questions include: How many total persons have been served? How long does

our staff stay here? How satisfied are the clients? How are financial resources disbursed relative to services? Are treatment protocols being followed?

This is an important aspect of understanding outcomes as well. Why? Well, let's say our researcher Yuan finds that the new treatment for domestic violence perpetrators is not effective. One might conclude that cognitive behavioral therapy just doesn't work for this problem. That is possible, but it seems unlikely given the wealth of research supporting CBT. It is more likely that, because of staff turnover, inadequate training, or client dropout, the CBT was never offered as planned in the manner that is needed to be effective. This is obviously related to the concept of treatment fidelity.

Section 7.3.2: Basic Concepts in Monitoring

One of the keys to a monitoring evaluation is a thorough understanding of the operation of the agency. This includes the decision-making structure, the way resources are allocated, the way data are or are not archived, the way employees are trained and supervised, and so on. For example, some agencies computerize basic aspects of client information. If so, tracking numbers served and perhaps key characteristics and even time spent in services is relatively easy. If not, such information must be captured from case files. The quality of this information is dependent on the recording practices of the staff.

Client satisfaction is one type of those gray areas that sometimes crosses evaluation boundaries. Some agencies see their client satisfaction measures as equivalent to an outcome assessment. Clearly we want our clients or target population to be happy with the services, right? The problem is that satisfaction does not always prove you have good outcomes. Let's take an extreme example to illustrate the point. An older individual is homebound and is rarely visited by family. The person is therefore lonely and also has physical therapy needs to recover from a hip operation. An incompetent case manager (who also happens to be very nice and talkative) is assigned. The manager never successfully arranges for the correct physical therapy but is given a glowing satisfaction evaluation by the client. This is because the client also really needs and values the human relationship and therefore ignores whether or not the other need is met. So, while satisfaction may be one type of outcome, it is best cast as a part of program monitoring.

Staff trust is another potential dilemma in a monitoring evaluation separate from consideration of time burden. It can feel threatening to have someone looking at who exactly is getting what type of service or how many minutes a person is spending on a given task. It is key here that the organization has in mind a clear purpose of improving services rather than "cleaning house." In other words, the staff must understand that if problems in service delivery are revealed that this information will be used to talk about improvements rather than to fire people. On the other hand, the researcher must realize that, if a serious breach in ethical behavior or practice is uncovered, this may still be an outcome.

SECTION 7.3.3: DATA COLLECTION

Program monitoring data often come from administrative data sources (case files or computer records), staff or client surveys, or time studies. Unless the administrative data source is highly detailed or designed specifically to capture evaluation information, a general rule is that mandatory data are the most reliably present. In other words, if certain data items *must* be recorded for an agency to receive funding, these items are likely to be more complete. Second, information used by the service provider is also likely to be complete. For example, a blood test will be recorded by the physician who is treating someone for HIV.

Anonymity is often key to staff or client surveys regarding agency function. I may be more likely as an employee to express my honest opinions about the work climate if I am sure that my supervisor cannot identify who made the comment. Likewise, it is important not to have the service provider for a client administer the satisfaction survey. Even if there is no name on the form, the client may fear that a negative comment will influence the ability to continue services or gain access to other services.

While we have discussed time burden related to surveys, the time study deserves special mention here. Sometimes we are examining how many hours a client is receiving a set group curriculum. We know how long the group is and have no need to document what the worker is doing on a minute-by-minute basis. In other cases, however, a staff person may provide a wide range of services to a given client from counseling to case management. If we want to understand why some clients do better than others, it becomes necessary to better understand what service configuration was given to a client. Sometimes merely asking a worker to check all the services provided is enough, but sometimes more detail is needed to track funding streams and target program improvements. A time study asks workers to record what they are doing for specified time intervals throughout the day. Such a study is normally done over several days or at random intervals to provide a picture of typical practice. This can be a significant recording burden and strong buy-in by the staff is critical. At the end of the day the evaluator must have confidence that times are being consistently and accurately recorded. In the past, such research was

done on hard copy forms, but handheld and computer programs are available specifically for such studies (e.g., Accustudy, Workstudy, and VMTPlus, etc.). Such technology may be out of reach for small agencies, but may greatly improve results for larger organizations.

SECTION 7.3.4: WHAT DO YOU MEASURE?

What is measured really depends on the purpose of the evaluation. Program monitoring may focus on numbers of clients, on time and services, or on more subjective measures of employee culture and climate or client satisfaction. Perhaps the most basic question to ask is, "Am I using this information in conjunction with an outcome evaluation?" If the answer is "yes," then it is absolutely necessary to think about all the program processes that are theoretically important in producing that outcome. So, in Yuan's study we would need to know if the staff were all well trained in the use of cognitive behavioral theory (CBT); we would need to know whether or not there was a difference in the experience levels of staff in the treatment and control group; we would want to carefully record the practice of assigning clients to groups to insure that there was nothing systematically different about the two groups that could explain outcomes; we would want to monitor staff turnover and client dropout.

If the study is not being used in conjunction with outcome measures then it is important to explore why the agency wants the information as well as what it thinks are key questions. Sometimes a question is more complex then it seems. For example, agency A wants a study of who is served to project caseload numbers for the following year for budgetary reasons. The answer to their question is going to depend on how and when you measure the caseload. An intake list may include many clients who never participate in services; certain proportions of clients may end services midway; certain funding sources may be triggered only by clients who meet a certain income requirement. It is an unfortunate event when an evaluation is carried out only to find that the information cannot be used for the reason the agency had hoped. Patton's text (1996) does a particularly nice job of discussing how to identify and clarify stakeholder needs for information.

SECTION 7.3.5: ETHICAL CONSIDERATIONS

We will not review the issue in detail again, but issues of confidentiality tend to be particularly sensitive in program monitoring evaluations. It is important that neither staff nor clients feel compelled to participate to continue employment or receive services. Likewise, it is important that data are collected so that respondents feel they can be honest about their perceptions without risking jobs or services. Having said this, a study of staff perceptions of supervisors in a very small agency has greater potential for someone knowing who said what. This is another reason that a clear understanding of the purpose, data collection method, and ultimate use of the information be outlined between the agency management and the researcher.

The next issue is one of interpretation and also exists for outcome evaluations. As aforementioned, some individuals may incorrectly associate satisfaction with efficacy or caseload numbers served with evidence of effective outreach. It is important that the researcher clearly outline what the monitoring data do and do not say. Although it is impossible for the researcher to completely control the use of information after a study is done, careful use of wording, and clearly labeled figures and highlighted findings can go a long way in preventing misuse of information.

SECTION 7.4
OUTCOME EVALUATION

In the world of evaluation research, the term *impact* is sometimes used instead of *outcome*. We will use the term *outcome* here and break it into two major categories: (1) understanding the effect of a service, program, or treatment; (2) understanding differential effects for different subgroups. The first question typically implies an experimental design, while the second question is typically more correlational.

SECTION 7.4.1: BASIC CONCEPTS IN OUTCOME EVALUATION

One of the most fundamental requirements of an outcome evaluation is a clear theory of program effect (Rossi, et al., 1999, have a nice discussion of program theory). In other words, to test whether your program works, there should be a clear connection between the problem to be addressed and the service or treatment provided. There should also be a clear connection between the service and measures of the outcome of interest. If you cannot create a basic flowchart of how the problem is associated with the service and the measures available to assess success, then it will be difficult to assess results even if they are positive. Our outcomes must be of import, but they must also be realistic given the population, issue, resources, and setting (Bamberger et al., 2006; Rossi et al., 1999). Before you even think about how to deal with data, you want to answer the "who," "what," "how," and "where" of your situation so that the measured outcomes make sense.

Immediate outcomes are different from maintenance of the effects of a program. For example, one might see very positive results with serious delinquents during an intensive outdoor therapeutic program, but this impact may be temporary (MacKenzie, 1997). When the youth return to their typical environment, the likelihood of returning to offending behavior may be high. So, an evaluation researcher must also consider how long it is reasonable to expect an effect to endure, given the program and whether or not to measure maintenance of effect.

The level of surety about the impact of the program is tied to the research design. If you absolutely want to establish cause and effect, then you must do a good true experimental design. If you want to look at impact but are satisfied with not being absolutely sure that the results can't be explained for some other reason, then a quasi-experimental design will do. Real-world settings often find experimental designs difficult or impossible to do because of resource limitations or the inability to deny services to one group. This does not mean that nonexperimental designs are worthless; one just has to be careful about the level of confidence in the reason for the outcome and clear about possible alternative explanations. We strive to obtain the most rigorous assessment possible and can sometimes be creative about maximizing resources to do so (Bamberger et al., 2006).

An outcome evaluation really cannot be done without program monitoring components. Even if one has a true experimental design, implementation issues can alter the outcome separate from the effect of the services. So a structure needs to be in place to monitor "treatment fidelity" or the actual delivery compared to the plan.

Not all services are equally effective for all clients or groups. This issue is different from that of confounding factors and is not addressed by simple randomization. For example, let's say a hospital randomly assigns its bipolar patients to a new treatment compared to a control (usual care) treatment. If the new mental health treatment protocol works great for females with bipolar disorder but is totally ineffective for males, there could be a null result if the results are not stratified by gender. It is important to consider what aspects of the target population should be measured so that major differences in treatment effectiveness by client characteristic can be examined.

Finally, outcomes in social science can take a long time. For example, it may be years before the outcome of an empowered or high-capacity community results from intervention (Jonson-Reid, 2000). In fact, a given program may have to end before it is realistic to expect the ultimate goal to be obtained. Thus it is important to think about proximal versus distal outcomes. If you have a year before an evaluation report is due, then the measurable outcomes should be realistic to expect within that year.

SECTION 7.4.2: DATA COLLECTION

Data used for outcome evaluations may be quantitative or qualitative and come from almost any source. The main considerations are ethical access to the participants in the service or program prior to and following the service; the resources the agency has to devote to data collection; and the reliability and validity of the data source. One must also consider whether or not to measure immediate effects only (pretest, posttest) or conduct a longitudinal study that can capture maintenance of effect.

To understand a program's total impact, one needs to have baseline data. Now this may seem confusing in light of the contention that outcome evaluation should not be done until a program has been well established. This recommendation is made because people realize that early in a program's initial implementation various changes occur, and it can take a while for implementation to be complete as described. While this is a valid point, a researcher must be cautious. If a program has multilevel effects, the initial operation may have already altered the initial conditions that were related to the problem. If possible, it is important to collect pre-program data even if one is going to wait for full implementation prior to conducting assessment of individual outcomes. This will help consumers of the results understand whether or not the individual outcomes may also have been affected by a change in the environment.

Another key data collection issue is one of confidentiality compared to anonymity. One of the authors taught an evaluation course and had the following occur. A student was asked to analyze a pre- and post-knowledge survey following a presentation. The data had already been collected. Part of the class assignment was to submit the data collection instrument. When this was reviewed, it was obvious that the survey was totally anonymous. Although a total pre- and post- score could be obtained for the entire group, it was impossible to provide feedback about results by subgroup because it was not possible to match a given person's pretest survey to the posttest survey. Oops. Typically, in outcome evaluation work, the data cannot be anonymously collected because the individual's final results need to be compared to the individual's baseline results.

SECTION 7.4.3: WHAT DO YOU MEASURE?

Whether you are assessing an individual client or a group, the first step is determining the best means of measuring the initial problem and later change. If the issue of interest is emotional or behavioral, then one might use a standardized scale to assess change. Or perhaps you are interested in reducing repeat service use, and then the measure is simply whether or not the client returns.

Sometimes the context of the evaluation dictates a compromise in how something is measured. For example, studies of child maltreatment recurrence (Drake et al., 2003) often use administrative data records of child abuse reports. A limitation of this method is the inability to actually be present with the family to be sure that maltreating behaviors are not present. In other words, one cannot tell whether undetected maltreatment is occurring from agency reporting data. On the other hand, it is a useful system measure, it is arguably impossible to follow families in their home 24 hours a day for several years, and it does allow for answering questions about system services to known maltreating families. You should strive for using the best known measure for the particular outcome(s) of interest.

If you want the information to be used (Patton, 1997), then you should also consider the audience for the results when planning the evaluation. For example, a school service worker will want to show that the program is valuable to the host agency that funds it (Jonson-Reid, 2006). Perhaps the school service worker is interested in self-efficacy, but the school really wants to have ways of improving test scores. If the increase in self-efficacy might reasonably affect test scores, then it's a good idea to also measure those test score changes.

Finally, it is important to remember to measure program implementation. For example, if Yuan wants to test the CBT model against usual care, he must have a clear description of what is included in *both* groups, he must monitor how the services are delivered to make sure they match the desired description, and he must account for client attrition, staff turnover, and perhaps unique events (e.g., an earthquake occurs midway through the study that has a profound impact on the clients' behavior).

SECTION 7.4.4: ETHICAL CONSIDERATIONS

One of the biggest dilemmas in outcome evaluation is what happens to bad news. Most of the time funding of programs is tied to effectiveness. This seems rational, right? Unfortunately, sometimes this hampers the ability to tweak partially effective projects to try again to improve results. Furthermore, jobs may be contingent on the project funding. Or there may be a side benefit to the program that the host agency doesn't want to lose even if the intended effect is not there. For example, DARE research has generally not shown long-term reductions in drug use related to this very large school-based program (Rosenbaum & Hanson, 1998). Most schools, however, want to maintain the relationship with the police department and may even be benefiting from more on-site security. In other words, there can be a lot of pressure to produce positive results. This is best handled by proactive discussions with agency leaders prior to the evaluation so that the handling of the outcome information can be addressed. What will happen if the results are not as expected? How will the agency react? Find out first.

Finally, it is critical that you document the evaluation design as well as the program itself. Ideally, evaluation research is done to build knowledge about how to better help people. Consumers need to understand clearly how generalizable the results you found are to their situations. For example, just because one program had excellent results with smoking cessation among Latina teenagers does not mean that the same program will be as effective with Bosnian refugees. Understanding program, population, and evaluation characteristics helps the next program operator know if the program can be applied as is or if careful thought to alterations or at least replicating the evaluation must be considered.

CONCLUSION

There are many nuances to evaluation research that go beyond the scope of a single chapter. Hopefully this introduction provides some food for thought about how the research skills discussed in this text are applied in this unique practice context. Readers are encouraged to seek further information. There are many texts in this area. The readings suggested here are those commonly used by one of the authors and *not* the results of a comprehensive comparison of all available material.

★ ★ ★
EBP MODULE

As you recall, the first two steps in doing EBP include formulating an empirically answerable question and finding relevant literature. Chapter 3 has already dealt with these two issues as they relate to forming a research question and searching literature to support research. Within the area of program evaluation, the process of forming the question is also related to the particular stage in program development, the feasibility of answering the question given available resources, and its import to program stakeholders. At each program stage we ask questions, access available research, and think about its applicability given our client characteristics and the resources/context of the program. This process leads us to form the particular question we will answer in our evaluation.

For example, let's say your agency wishes to do a better job addressing the needs of the homeless and mentally ill population. Your agency provides case management services. Drawing on Bamberger and colleagues' "theory of programs" and Chen's "taxonomy of program stages," let's look at how the program theory and research interact with program development using EBP.

STAGE 1: NEEDS

We have a target population: homeless and mentally ill persons.

- *Question:* What are the characteristics of our target population and their needs?
- *Research:* What is known about the target population generally?
- *Critique:* How valid is the available research; is it generalizable to our situation?

    If nothing is available or if we are not confident that the available information generalizes well to our local program population, then our first question is formed:

- *Possible evaluation question:* What are the characteristics and needs of our target population?

    If adequate information is available regarding target population needs, then we can proceed to program theory development. If not, then we may need to engage in a needs assessment to find out more about our prospective clients

STAGE 2: PROGRAM THEORY AND PLANNING

Let's say our agency focuses on case management. Now we need a theory about how this fits or doesn't fit with the needs of the population and the available resources:

- *Question:* How can this population be effectively served under a case management model?
- *Research:* What is known about effective case management with mentally ill homeless populations or similar populations? What resources are needed to run an effective program?
- *Critique:* How valid and generalizable is the available research?

    After we identify the factors needed to move from needs to positive client outcomes, we have to assess whether or not we have the program components needed. We may ask one or both of the following questions:

- Do resources in the community exist to serve the client needs? (i.e., case management assumes there are services and programs to refer the clients to . . .)
- Do the resources exist in our agency (staffing, staff expertise) to implement the program?

If we know whether or not we have the resources to mount the program indicated in the research or, if not, research what is logically needed based on needs, then we can move on to beginning implementation. If we do not know, we must gather evidence from the local community to determine where we stand.

STAGE 3: BEGINNING IMPLEMENTATION STAGE

Now we have identified client needs, available referral resources, and staff expertise. Let's assume that needs include housing, stabilizing mental health symptoms, and some sort of employment training. We now believe, based on the prior stages, that case managers can meet the needs of the target population. We have also evaluated whether needed resources exist. At this point, we may have more focused questions about how our agency should operate:

- *Research:* What is known about effective referrals? What client and case manager factors influence follow-through? How will we know if it's working?
- *Critique:* How valid and generalizable is the available research?

At this stage we need a way of monitoring how services are provided and whether or not things are working the way we envision. We need to answer the following evaluation questions:

- Are we reaching the intended population?
- Are case managers actively making referrals that match identified needs?
- Are clients getting access to services they are referred to?
- Are clients satisfied with the staff and services?

Answering these questions requires that the above concepts be clearly operationalized and that research mechanisms are in place to measure them. If we have the answers or at least the processes are in place to answer these questions, then we are ready to move on to outcome evaluation.

STAGE 4: SHORT- AND LONG-TERM OUTCOMES

Now we have set up the program and the program monitoring system. We can therefore ask: Are we achieving the desired outcomes? First, we need to operationalize our outcomes. What outcomes are reasonable for such a program? How have others measured these outcomes? Are there both shorter-term and longer-term outcomes? What factors other than program services can influence outcomes?

Once we have operationalized our outcomes, we may ask one or more of the following evaluation questions:

- How satisfied are clients with services?
- Short-term: At what level are clients successfully accessing services (remembering we have to define *successfully*)?
- Long-term: Are clients achieving stable housing, mental health care, and employment?

We hope this example shows you how the evidence-based decision-making process is compatible with and can be used in tandem with various stages in a program's development and implementation.■

REVIEW

1. Assume you are trying to convince an agency to do evaluation research. Give three reasons you would use in your arguments.
2. How are "prevalence" and "incidence" different?
3. What is the difference between a "needs assessment" and a "caseload analysis"?
4. What is "program monitoring"? Why is it usually done?
5. What is meant by "outcome evaluation"? What kinds of research designs (exploratory, descriptive, etc.) would be most commonly employed in outcome evaluations? Why?
6. Give three reasons why it is necessary for needs assessment/caseload analysis, program monitoring, and outcome evaluations to be done on a continual (or at least periodic) basis.

SUPPLEMENTAL READINGS

- Bamberger, M., Rugh, J., Mabry, L. (2006). *Real world evaluation: Working under budget, time, data and political constraints.* Thousand Oaks, CA:

Sage Publications. A practical but sufficiently detailed text that focuses on impact (or outcome) evaluations. It is one of the few texts with an international approach and examples. The book concentrates on making the most of an evaluation given considerable real-world constraints.

- Fetterman, D. , Kaftarian, S., Wandersman, A. (Eds). (1996). *Empowerment Evaluation Knowledge and Tools for Self-Assessment & Accountability.* New York: Guilford. This text does a good job of outlining both the philosophical approach to evaluation known as "empowerment" evaluation and the provision of examples.

- Patton, M. (1997) *Utilization Focused Evaluation* (3rd ed.). Thousand Oaks, CA: Sage. This book is very readable and really focuses on doing evaluation work that is effectively used by the organization or group being evaluated. It has a very good review of the rationale and theory (and debate) regarding different approaches to evaluation and has a nice chapter on reporting results.

- Rossi, P. F., Freeman, H. W., & Lipsey, M. (1999). *Evaluation: A Systematic Approach* (6th ed.). Newbury Park, CA: Sage Publications, Inc. This is a nicely done overall text on program evaluation that is one of the few to dwell on thoroughly identifying the question to be asked and evaluating

program theory (e.g., what the program does that is likely to impact the issue and why). This text goes into more detail on the various types of evaluation (e.g., needs assessment, specific research designs, and so on) than the text that follows.

- Royse, D., Thyer, B., Padgett, D., & Logan, T. (2006). *Program Evaluation: An Introduction.* (4th ed.). Belmont, CA: Thomson/Brooks Cole. This nicely done overall text on program evaluation is readable and concise. It contains material on single system design and guide for write-up of results.

- Thompson-Robinson, M., Hopson, R., & SenGupta, S. (Eds.). (2004). In search of cultural competence in evaluation: Toward principles and practices. *New Directions for Evaluation, 102* (entire issue). This journal issue is one of the few resources dedicated entirely to the issue of cultural competence in evaluation research.

- Yuen, P., & Terao, K. (2003). *Practical Grant Writing and Program Evaluation.* Pacific Grove, CA: Brooks/Cole. This is a very practical and concise book that links evaluation directly to grant writing. It is not a good stand-alone resource for understanding the field of program evaluation, but it is a great applied supplement. It contains a very useful sample outline of a grant proposal and a typical review and has several practical "how-to" tips throughout.

CHAPTER

8

CLINICAL APPLICATIONS: SINGLE-SUBJECT DESIGNS

This chapter is designed to help you do research in clinical practice situations involving single clients ($N = 1$ designs), so that you can be sure that you are achieving what you mean to achieve. In one psychotherapeutic approach, behaviorism, very tightly operationalized single-subject research is pretty much built in to the process. For other treatment approaches, such as humanistic or psychodynamic approaches, single-subject designs can be a little more tricky, requiring careful operationalization of fairly abstract concepts, such as "anxiety."

SECTION 8.1
WHY STUDY INDIVIDUALS IN YOUR PRACTICE?

There are a lot of reasons you should study your clients using formal methods. These include the following:

■ *You are ethically required to be accountable for your practice.* If you don't know what's going on, then you are not accountable. Your "feeling" for how things are going is certainly important. It is better and more professional, however, to help inform those feelings with some hard data. Your clients have a right to expect you to be able to tell them how they are doing, and it's nice to say something better than "I think that . . ."

■ *Coming up with outcome measures forces you and the client to come to a very clear understanding about treatment goals.* This exercise is tremendously helpful in and of itself. It is surprising and troubling how few therapists actually have clear treatment goals. This strikes us as irresponsible practice.

■ *Recording the client's progress helps both you and the client to know how the therapy is going.* People have an unfortunate tendency not to remember things clearly. One of the authors recalls a particularly intelligent client he was treating for anxiety-related vomiting. The client had made tremendous gains in therapy but was convinced he hadn't. It was very useful to be able to check the recorded data and say to the person, "Hey, when you got here, you were throwing up five times a week, and now you're only doing it about once a month." The change had occurred over about six months, and the client simply didn't notice the change. Of course, the opposite can also happen. Many people (and their therapists) are convinced that progress is being made when the person's complaint is actually not improving or getting worse.

■ *Formalized research on client outcomes can not only help you with individual clients but can be used over time to determine strengths and weaknesses in your whole practice.* Have you done better with some types of clients than with others? Are there places your skills need refining? Keeping track of which of your clients do better and worse can be used as a way to support your own plans for professional development.

SECTION 8.2
REVIEW OF KEY TERMS IN SINGLE-SUBJECT DESIGNS

Before we get too far in, let's go over some terms that we'll be using constantly in this chapter:

■ *Baseline:* The word *baseline* means "the level of functioning before treatment." *Baselining* is getting a measure of the outcome variable before treatment begins. Ideally, you will be able to get several days or weeks of measurement on the outcome variable before you begin your intervention. Why do this? If you don't know where you are starting from, you won't know how much the treatment has helped (or hurt!) the client. There is no substitute for a good baseline measure.

■ *Intervention:* By *intervention,* we simply mean the specific treatment the client is getting. You may use one intervention, or you may use several interventions simultaneously or one after the other. For example, you may start one treatment, notice it is worsening the behavior, and then switch to something else. It is also very common to use multiple interventions at the same time. You may try treatment *A,* find it works a little, then supplement it by adding treatment *B.*

■ *Outcome:* For the purposes of this chapter, *outcome* is the same as *dependent variable* and means "the thing we're trying to change." Outcomes must be operationalized. One way to look at it is that an outcome is an operationalized treatment goal. An outcome could be a score on a scale or instrument measuring anxiety. It could be the commonly used SUDS (subjective units of distress scale) on which the client rates his or her distress on a scale of 1 to 10, 1 to 100, or whatever. It could also be specific behaviors or events recorded by the client (how many calories eaten each day) or someone else (number of minutes in time-out each day).

■ *Follow-up:* Follow-up occurs when you stop treatment but come back later to see how the outcome is holding up. Many therapists include a follow-up visit (or sometimes a phone call if a visit isn't possible) a month or several months after treatment ends so that they can check in, see how the client is doing, and make sure treatment gains haven't gone away. If you want to see how durable treatment changes are, there is really no other way to do it. If you are trying to create a lasting change, you should do a follow-up.

SECTION 8.3
TREATMENT GOALS AND OUTCOMES

As in all things, to succeed you need to know what you're trying to do. You and the client must agree on why treatment is happening and what the desired outcome or outcomes are. Although this is usually a team effort, sometimes this isn't the case. A student, for example, may not want to stop fighting at school, but everyone else (the school, parents, etc.) may require that the behavior changes. Usually, however, goals come from the client with the help of the therapist. Good goals reflect the client's needs, are clear to both the client and the therapist, are achievable, and fall within the therapist's area of expertise. These same qualities are reflected in the outcomes we will be discussing in this chapter: Note that you certainly may have several outcomes in play at once. If there are multiple treatment goals, then each should have at least one associated outcome. Each goal (such as increased social engagement), may be measured one way or several ways (contact with friends, family, etc.).

■ *Outcomes must be helpful to the client.* Choosing an outcome because it is something the therapist just learned about or just because it is easy to study isn't OK. This sounds obvious, but many therapists don't really listen to their clients and end up moving away from what the client wants and needs. Don't do that.

■ *Outcomes must be clearly operationalized.* Operationalizing means taking a construct (such as "depression") and changing it into a measurable variable (such as a score on a depression scale). Similarly, you could operationalize "disruptive classroom behavior" as "the number of times per hour that the teacher has to tell Bobby to stop his behavior." Some treatment goals, especially vague ones, are hard to operationalize. It's hard to measure "just feeling better in general." There's nothing so frustrating as trying to help someone and having only very diffuse and general goals. We suggest you do your best to pick outcomes that can be clearly operationalized. If you can't operationalize an outcome, you probably don't have a very clear or very useful idea of what you're doing.

■ *Outcomes must be measurable.* The good news is that anything you can operationalize is measurable. You can put literally anything on a Likert, semantic differential, or grounded scale. More good news is that most common problems, such as depression, general anxiety, and so on, already have nice, short standardized instruments available that you can use. In general, we have the following preferences for how to measure things, listed in order, best to worst:

1. Objective measurement of real events is often best.

2. Using standardized scales *that fit your client* is good.

3. Creation of specific measurement tools to fit your client may be necessary and may work well.

Some problems, such as disruptive classroom behaviors, are easy to track using objective measurement. Other problems, such as generalized anxiety, may be harder or even impossible to measure objectively. Although some physical symptoms (for example, cold sweats) may be countable, you may need to rely on scales, other tools, or more subjective measures. It really depends on what the issue and desired outcome are. We have already mentioned one such measure that is commonly used, the SUDS. The subjective units of distress scale is indeed pretty subjective. It works like this: You say, "On a scale of 1 to 10, with 1 being no distress, and 10 being the most distress you can imagine, how much distress did you feel around this issue this week?" The client says "6," and you write that down. This may sound silly, but it is very commonly used. We suggest you avoid such measures if there is any way to get a more objective read on what's happening.

■ *Outcomes must be achievable.* You should pick things that can reasonably be expected to change in the desired time frame. Often, a series of outcomes of increasing difficulty are included. For example, let's say you have a child who is not doing her homework. You may have several outcomes that are quite modest, leading to your final desired result. An initial outcome might be remembering to bring her books to study hall. Another outcome might be that she turns something in to the teacher in a particular class every day, while a final outcome may be that she receives at least a B on her homework each day. This last outcome may take a while to achieve and may be reasonable only for phased treatments that can be expected to continue for a long time. If you have just the toughest outcome, then it will be easy for you and the client to lose hope and give up. Picking achievable intermediate outcomes is a way to help keep people happy and feeling good about the work being done.

■ *You should know something about the behavior you are trying to change and approaches that have worked with other clients, and you should have a specific plan for how to achieve the outcome with this particular client.* These things are clinical skills and knowledge that are not really part of this book, but the point is that your choice of outcomes isn't just made up out of air. As with choosing a treatment approach, choosing outcomes depends largely on your clinical knowledge, skills, and judgment.

SECTION 8.4
CHOOSING A WAY TO MEASURE OUTCOMES

There are a large number of ways to measure outcomes. We break these into the following four broad areas: observing behaviors directly, using already existing scales, creating scales, and using other forms of existing data. Each has advantages and disadvantages.

SECTION 8.4.1: OUTCOMES AS OBSERVED BEHAVIORS

The simplest and often the best way to operationalize an outcome is as an observed behavior. Whereas many of us are more used to thinking of research as including the use of standardized instruments, there is certainly a place for direct observation.

ADVANTAGES

Real behaviors are being observed; conditions are not inferred from instruments that may or may not work well with your client. Clients can easily understand the practicality of measuring real things. Error involved in measurement is minimized. Risks to validity such as faulty recall or bias are reduced.

DISADVANTAGES

Some problems (e.g., anxiety, dysthymia) are more difficult to describe in terms of observable behaviors. Some normed instruments have useful features such as diagnostically relevant cutoffs (scores above which the client is likely to be experiencing serious problems).

Certain principles apply to any attempt to observe behavior.

■ *The behavior must be clearly operationalized.* It is not easy to observe each time a child "looks distracted," but it is easy to observe each time

a child "speaks in class without first raising his hand." Great care must be taken to make sure the way the behavior is recorded is reliable. This is especially true if multiple raters are used who may interpret their task differently.

■ *The behavioral outcome must be clearly related to the goal.* Sometimes it is tempting to pick something as an outcome that is easy to measure even if it isn't really that closely tied to the real goal. For example, you might want to get a nursing home resident to interact with other residents more. Is it reasonable to use "Hours per day spent out of own room" as a measure? If time spent out of the room is spent interacting with others, then this might be a good measure. If the person is just sitting alone in the hallway, then maybe it isn't.

■ *Pick the best available person to observe the behavior.* High-functioning clients may well be able to observe and track their own behaviors. Children's behaviors can be tracked by parents or teachers. A therapist doing play therapy with a child may track behaviors herself during the play period in each session. Basically, you want to pick the person who will give you the most valid and reliable recording of the behavior in question.

■ *The behavior must be measured in the right place and at the right time.* If a problem occurs at a given place or time, then that should be when the measurements occur. It can often be very helpful to measure many different places and times. For example, if you are changing a child's behavior at school, you might worry that the problem behavior might displace to another location, like home. It would be good to measure behavior in both places. That way, when someone comes up to you later and says, "Yeah, but you're not fixing anything, Johnny's just waiting till he gets home to create a mess" you can say, "Ah, but we have been watching that, and his disruptive behavior at home has actually lessened by 12.7%." The authors have a mutual friend, a researcher who is fond of wearing a button that reads, "We have charts and graphs to back us up, so lay off." Actually, the second-to-last word in that sentence was changed to make it suitable for our more delicate readers, but the idea still comes through.

WAYS OF OBSERVING BEHAVIORS DIRECTLY

Behaviors must not only be observed, they must be recorded. This is best done on paper (or maybe electronically for you techie types out there with those tiny portable computer things).

FIGURE 8.1. **A Simple Observational Log.**

Swear words used, week of [_____]

	Mo	Tu	We	Th	Fr	Sa	Su
At work							
At home							
Other places							

A simple observational log might look like Figure 8.1. On this log, the client would record a hash mark each time she swore that day. (As an unrelated clinical side note, the simple act of attending to things such as this will often work very effectively in reducing the frequency of the behavior.) Notice that this log not only tracks swearing, but it tracks where the swearing occurs and what day. Of course, "Swear words" would have to be clearly operationalized on a list (see George Carlin). If it is unrealistic for the client to whip out her log every time she swears, you might let her complete a log at the end of the day that looked like Figure 8.2. There are limitless ways you can do this. The trick is to make it totally clear and idiot proof. Remember, the easier it is to use the more likely it will get done.

FIGURE 8.2. **The Client's Log.**

Swear words used, week of [_____].
Circle best answer:

	Mo	Tu	We	Th	Fr	Sa	Su
At work	0 1–2 3+	0 1–2 3+	0 1–2 3+	0 1–2 3+	0 1–2 3+	0 1–2 3+	0 1–2 3+
At home	0 1–2 3+	0 1–2 3+	0 1–2 3+	0 1–2 3+	0 1–2 3+	0 1–2 3+	0 1–2 3+
Other places	0 1–2 3+	0 1–2 3+	0 1–2 3+	0 1–2 3+	0 1–2 3+	0 1–2 3+	0 1–2 3+

INTERVAL RECORDING

Sometimes, you will be able to get someone to observe a behavior, but he or she won't be able to do it all the time. Something called "interval recording" can be used. The basic idea is you specify a time in advance for someone to look at something. If you let that person choose the time, he or she may pick a particularly good or bad time on purpose, and this is a validity and reliability problem. That time can be either an exact point in time (like 10:30 a.m.) or a period of time (like 10:30 a.m. to 10:35 a.m.). Interval recording can work several ways:

- You can observe the behavior at the moment specified and see if it is happening or not. Let's say a teacher is supposed to look at a kid and see if he is doing his work (clearly operationally

defined and labeled "on task"). A recording for doing that may look like this:

Time	10:30	10:50	11:10	1:20	2:00
On task?	Y N	Y N	Y N	Y N	Y N

- You can also observe the behavior over periods of time. A recording for doing that may look like this:

Time	10:00–10:05	10:50–10:55	11:10–11:15	1:20–1:25	2:00–2:05
On task? (all/some/none)	A S N	A S N	A S N	A S N	A S N

As another example, you might want to count a particular behavior more exactly. You might have a stopwatch and record the total time between 10:00 and 10:05 a child is on task. In this example, the log entry might be "35." You might record the number of times the child talks without being called on with a number (such as "3"). Pretty much anything you can imagine that makes sense (is valid) and can be done reliably is appropriate. One of the totally cool things about interval recording is that one recorder can switch from person to person in a group and thus record multiple people simultaneously. A form for that might look like the one in Figure 8.3.

This example shows how you can track multiple subjects at once. It also shows that you can track multiple behaviors at once. The rater would use hash marks on the first three items. Notice that the last behavior is a judgment call rather than a specifically countable behavioral event. This is permissable, but like all items, it is only as reliable and valid as the training that the rater gets. Try to stay with more concrete observations if possible. One nice thing about this type of recording is that it can be done from videotapes after the fact. Obviously, ethical concerns and agency policy would have to be considered and addressed before such technology is used.

FIGURE 8.3. **Logging Multiple Clients.**

| | 10:00–10:05 | 10:05–10:10 | 10:10–10:15 | 10:15–10:20 | 10:20–10:25 | 10:25–10:30 |
	Johnny	Megan	Timmy	Johnny	Megan	Timmy
Talked out of turn						
Out of seat						
Touched another student						
Appeared attentive > ½ the time (Y/N)	Y N	Y N	Y N	Y N	Y N	Y N

HAVE YOU LICKED YOUR RAT TODAY?

You can really be creative with observational measures. One study (Zimmerberg & Gray, 1992) had the objective of finding out if cocaine hampered mothering in rats. How do you know if a rat is a good mother? You don't just look at a rat and say, "Yeah, that rat looks like a good mom to me." It turns out that rat-studying types agree that rats who lick their pups more and who sniff their pups more are better moms (and dads). Zimmerberg and Gray used interval recordings of the frequency of rat pup licking at 60 minutes after rats were injected (cocaine or placebo) and again at 24 hours later. They also rated nest quality. In case you're wondering, the above article concludes that "cocaine impaired the parenting ability of both male and female rats, with and without previous parenting experience" (p. 379).■

We hope we've given you some ideas about how you can create observational logs for use with your clients. Just remember that the key is to make the items both relevant to the treatment goal and to make sure that they can be recorded in a valid and reliable fashion. Of course, there is nothing unique about these measures that applies only to clinical practice. These same techniques are often used in regular old research. Many studies, such as the Zimmerberg & Gray study cited in the nearby box, use logs in observing behaviors in nonclinical settings.

SECTION 8.4.2: ASKING THE CLIENT OR SOMEONE ELSE (FINDING AND USING EXISTING MEASURES)

We've already spent a lot of time talking about standardized tests and where to find them in the section in Chapter 5 called "Choosing a Measure." To be useful for clinical practice, a test should be simple to administer. Because the test will be given more than once, there ideally should be some evidence that the test can be given repeatedly without affecting how the subject responds. For example, if a test of attention is the ability to do a puzzle fast, then that test will work only once, because the client will learn how to do the puzzle. Examples of commonly used clinical scales include the Beck Depression Inventory and the Maslach Burnout Inventory. One very commonly used, very simple, and very general scale is the Global Assessment of Functioning Scale, where the clinician assigns a single score based on a grounded range. This scale is presented in the DSM-IV-TR (American Psychiatric Association, 2000, page 32) and will be familiar to most clinicians.

GLOBAL ASSESSMENT OF FUNCTIONING SCALE

91–100 Superior functioning in a wide rage of activities, life's problems never seem to get out of hand, is sought out by others because of his or her many qualities. No symptoms.

90–81 Absent or minimal symptoms, good functioning in all areas, interested and involved in a wide range or activities, socially effective, generally satisfied with life, no more than everyday problems or concerns.

80–71 If symptoms are present, they are transient and expectable reactions to psychosocial stresses; no more than slight impairment in social, occupational, or school functioning.

70–61 Some mild symptoms *or* some difficulty in social, occupational, or school functioning, but generally functioning pretty well, has some meaningful interpersonal relationships.

60–51 Moderate symptoms *or* any moderate difficulty in social, occupational, or school functioning.

50–41 Serious symptoms *or* any serious impairment in social, occupational, or school functioning.

40–31 Some impairment in reality testing or communication *or* major impairment in several areas, such as work or school, family relations, judgment, thinking, or mood.

30–21 Behavior is considered influenced by delusions or hallucinations *or* serious impairment in communications or judgment *or* inability to function in all areas.

20–11 Some danger of hurting self or others *or* occasionally fails to maintain minimal personal hygiene *or* gross impairment in communication.

10–1 Persistent danger of severely hurting self or others *or* persistent inability to maintain minimum personal hygiene *or* serious suicidal act with clear expectation of death.■

Even though this is "just" a single-item grounded scale, it is still among the most commonly used clinical tools we have. Full examples of several other tests can be found in Chapter 12 under Abigail's project. These are representative of the kinds of short, usable instruments that would work well in measuring clinical goals. No matter what test you use, there are several things you should think about. These include the following:

■ *Who will fill out the test?* Lots of tests are filled out by the client. Others are done by the therapist, particularly tests like the GAF, which require clinical judgment. Other tests are filled out by people who know the client. This last kind of test is especially common when the functioning of young children is being studied.

■ *How often will the test be given?* Most of the time, you don't have to give the test each week. Giving a test every week may even cause the client to get bored with the task and may result in poor measurement. Long-term goals may be best assessed on a monthly or even quarterly basis. You may even want to limit your use of tests to the beginning and end of treatment, although this will make the tests much less clinically useful to you and your client during treatment.

■ *Is one test enough?* You may well have a client with multiple problems, goals, and outcomes and may want to use several tests to measure progress. If you do this, the tests should be short and easily administered. Nobody likes paperwork.

SECTION 8.4.3: ASKING THE CLIENT OR SOMEONE ELSE (CREATING MEASURES)

If you don't have access to a sourcebook, and if your agency does not have appropriate tests it uses, and you can't find any valid tests that you can use, then it may be necessary to create a test of your own. This will be particularly true when clients come to you with specific complaints or concerns. You can feel free to use all the various approaches you have learned about in Chapter 5. Some examples might help clarify what might be possible.

Let's say you work for an agency that houses and provides parenting support to teen mothers. One particular client has a 2-year-old child who is a little slow developing verbal skills. The staff noticed that the client is an unusually quiet person who rarely talks to her son. You are working with the client for an hour a week to give her ideas and encouragement around being more verbal around the toddler. How should you measure how much Mom speaks to her child? Just watching her in the therapy session may not give a good read on what she does outside therapy. You could use an observational rating log, which might be the best choice, but the staff won't agree to do it. The staff are willing to fill out a short form each day when they chart the client. You work up the form in Figure 8.4 using a Likert scale, a yes/no item, and an open-ended question.

This little three-item form may seem trivial, but it can make a lot of difference. The ability to have relatively solid input on a person's behavior is a big upgrade over asking, "How do you think you did this week?" You are welcome to use more involved and complex instruments, either filled out by the client or someone else. We would remind you again to keep it as simple and usable as possible.

FIGURE 8.4. Form to Measure Mother–Child Interactions.

How much did Jesse talk to her son today?

		About half	Most of	Almost all of
Not at all	Occasionally	the time	the time	the time
[1]	[2]	[3]	[4]	[5]

If Jesse did talk to her son, did it appear to be at the right level to help the child in his language development?

Yes [___]   No [___]   She did not speak to her son. [___]

Can you tell us anything about where or when Jesse was more or less likely to speak to her son?

SECTION 8.4.4: CHECKING THE RECORD (ADMINISTRATIVE OR SIMILAR DATA)

It's the Information Age. If you work for a school or certain other kinds of institutions, there is a good chance you have access to all kinds of data that you never bother to check. One of the first questions you should ask yourself is, "Are any of my outcomes reflected in already available data?" If so, use them. This sounds simple, but often eludes people. Available administrative or other data may include:

■ Achievement (grades, tests, homework completion)

■ Behavior problems (fighting, poor attendance, how often a person wanders off his or her ward at a geriatric facility, how often a person returns after curfew)

■ Daily ratings on token economy or similar reward systems. Many places such as residential facilities use reward systems to encourage good behaviors. These may be relevant to treatment goals.

Administrative data are often very useful because they generally measure real things (like suspensions) that are important to people's lives. They are already recorded for you, and that saves you effort. Sometimes, administrative data can be used to baseline things retrospectively. In plain English, you can use already existing records to get your baseline measure over the past few weeks, months, or even years. This is done in the example on page 168.

SECTION 8.5
CHOOSING AND IMPLEMENTING A DESIGN

Now you know how to set outcomes and how to measure them. It's time to figure out what design we're going to use. Most single-subject designs are quasi-experimental. They are never true experiments, because you can't randomly assign one person to both treatment and control groups. The next few sections will introduce the basic approach most often used, sometimes called "pretest/posttest " or "baseline/treatment" or "*AB*." Later sections will get more complicated, but none of this material is really all that difficult to grasp.

SECTION 8.5.1: THE BASIC QUASI-EXPERIMENTAL PRE/POST APPROACH (*AB*)

The most basic way to see if a treatment reduces a problem is to try it out and see. You have four tasks:

1. *You must know what the problem is and how you will measure it.* Clearly operationalized outcomes must be determined before anything else can happen. We covered this in the last section.

2. *You must measure the problem before the intervention (baselining).* Without knowing this, you can't tell if later measurements show improvements or steps backward.

3. *You should measure the problem during the intervention.* Without doing this, you get no feedback on progress during therapy.

4. *You must measure the problem at the end of the intervention.* If you don't do this, you don't know if the problem got better or worse.

The practical details usually fall out like this:

Step 1: Specifying goals and outcomes. During the first meeting (or two) with a client you decide on treatment goals and operationalize them into measurable outcomes.

Step 2: Baselining. Once the outcomes are operationalized, you have the client (or whoever) log them for a week or more. This does not usually require a delay of treatment because usually treatment does not start the first session anyway. In some cases, such as acutely suicidal clients, it is obviously unethical to do anything except immediately start treatment, so true baselining may not be possible.

Step 3: Providing interventions and observing outcomes. Intervention will usually take from a few weeks to several months. Ideally, outcome measures will be available on an ongoing basis to help assess the intervention as it proceeds. Outcome measures may show several kinds of trends:

- *If outcomes are progressing:* This suggests that the intervention is working and should continue.

- *If outcomes are not progressing or are worsening:* The therapist and client may decide to stick with the intervention, hoping for improvement. Some kinds of interventions commonly produce a brief, initial worsening of symptoms. Alternately, unexpectedly bad outcomes may require changing the intervention or supplementing it with a different intervention.

- *If outcomes are fully met:* The focus of treatment can change to maintaining those outcomes, to working on new outcomes, or treatment can be discontinued.

Step 4: Final measurement of outcomes. In any case, outcomes should be measured at the end of treatment. Sometimes symptoms can reappear near the end of services because some clients will get nervous around termination. In cases such as this, it is helpful to have had an ongoing log of outcomes so that this dip can be seen in context.

That's really all there is to it. As we said, it isn't rocket science. Perhaps a couple of short examples will help.

EXAMPLE: MORE RATS

Sara is afraid of rats. How afraid of rats is she? She is so afraid that she can't even be around fur of any kind, because it reminds her of rats. This fear is becoming so serious that she is getting into embarrassing situations at work (she's a fashion designer). She comes to you for help. Being a good behaviorist, you decide to create a "hierarchy of fears" ranging from 1 to 7, with 1 being an unthreatening stimulus and 7 being a very threatening stimulus. This is a standard practice in the treatment known as "systematic densensitization." The hierarchy looks like this:

1: Thinking about a fur coat
2: Being 5 feet away from a fur coat
3: Touching a fur coat
4: Being 20 feet away from a rat
5: Being 5 feet away from a rat
6: Touching a rat
7: Picking up and holding a rat

Every week, you see how far Sara can go up the hierarchy, creating a weekly score from 1 to 7. Sara is very motivated and wants to reach level 7 to prove to herself that she's got this thing licked. The weekly progress log you keep may look like this:

Week	1(B)	2(B)	3	4	5	6	7	8	9	10	11	12	13
Score	1	1	1	2	3	6	*	2	6	5	6	7	7

*Missed appointment: fashion show in New York.

Weeks 1 and 2 were baseline measures, taken at the end of session 1 and the beginning of session 2. All subsequent measures were taken at the beginning of the session. It is interesting to note that week 8 showed substantial backsliding, after the missed session and the trip to New York. Week 9 showed resumption of treatment gains, though, and they held steady through week 13. Treatment was originally supposed to be for 15 weeks, but you and Sara decided the last two weeks were not needed.■

That was too easy. We had only one treatment goal/objective, which was simple to operationalize. The next examples will get a little more complex, and show how you can approach more complicated or "fuzzy" situations.

SECTION 8.5.2: QUASI-EXPERIMENTAL APPROACHES WITH FOLLOW-UP (ABA)

The previous section showed us the following steps:

1. Operationalize
2. Baseline
3. Measure during treatment (if possible)
4. Measure at end of treatment

We now add a "follow-up":

5. Wait a while, then recontact the subject and measure again.

A follow-up is just a remeasurement done weeks, months, or (rarely) years after treatment ends. It is done for one reason: to see if treatment gains continue over time. This kind of design is sometimes called an *ABA* design, but you can also call it a pretest/posttest design with follow-up, or an *AB* design with follow-up, or a baseline/treatment design with follow-up.

WHEN SHOULD YOU DEFINITELY DO A FOLLOW-UP?

Follow-up designs are particularly important when not doing so may result in clients being at risk:

■ When trying a new intervention
■ When trying an intervention that you might worry has negative long-term effects
■ When working with clients who may be very isolated or you feel may be at risk over time (e.g., suicide risk)

It is always a good idea to do follow-up contacts and measurements, but in cases such as these, doing a follow-up becomes ethically important.

HOW DO YOU DO A FOLLOW-UP?

Generally, follow-up measurement is done the same way it was done before. Sometimes this will involve a paper instrument being mailed to a client, sometimes a phone contact will be made. The best way is to arrange a follow-up visit with the client; when work begins, so it is a normal and expected part of treatment.

EXAMPLE: BOB MEASURES FRED'S DEPRESSION

Client Fred is referred to Therapist Bob for depression and stress. Before Fred arrives for his first meeting, Bob decides he needs a way to objectively measure the problem. How should he measure depression and stress? Therapist Bob had learned about the Beck Depression Inventory at school, but his agency didn't have any copies, and he couldn't get his hands on one quickly. It also doesn't measure stress directly. Instead of ordering that scale, he decided to do a Web search and see if there were any good scales freely available. He entered "public domain anxiety scale" ("public domain" is legalspeak for "anyone can copy and use for free") into Google. The third entry was the "Victim's Web," a Web site hosted by the University of New South Wales in Sydney (www.swin.edu.au/victims/resources/assessment/affect/dass42.html). This site had links to a site describing the DASS, or "Depression Anxiety Stress Scales." Bob had hit the jackpot. The DASS had scales measuring not only depression, but also anxiety and stress. There is a 42-item version (two pages) and a shorter 21-item version for handy administration.

Of course, Bob didn't want to grab things off the 'Net uncritically: This is both unprofessional and, well ... stupid. Some research on the reliability and validity of this scale was needed. Fortunately, the Web site included resources, including citations of articles from quality journals (Brown, Chorpita, Korotitsch, & Barlow, 1997). A quick review of some of these studies suggested that this scale was adequately researched, had sound psychometric qualities, and would be good to use with Client Fred. Bob decided to use the shorter version, the DASS21. Bob was now very happy that he had paid such close attention in his research methods class, so that he could locate and assess the quality of a tool he needed to help his client. The instrument is shown on the next page.

DASS21   Name: Date:

Please read each statement and circle a number 0, 1, 2, or 3, which indicates how much the statement applied to you over the past week. There are no right or wrong answers. Do not spend too much time on any statement.

The rating scale is as follows:

0   Did not apply to me at all
1   Applied to me to some degree, or some of the time
2   Applied to me to a considerable degree, or a good part of time
3   Applied to me very much, or most of the time

1	I found it hard to wind down	0	1	2	3
2	I was aware of dryness of my mouth	0	1	2	3
3	I couldn't seem to experience any positive feeling at all	0	1	2	3
4	I experienced breathing difficulty (e.g., excessively rapid breathing, breathlessness in the absence of physical exertion)	0	1	2	3
5	I found it difficult to work up the initiative to do things	0	1	2	3
6	I tended to overreact to situations	0	1	2	3
7	I experienced trembling (e.g., in the hands)	0	1	2	3
8	I felt that I was using a lot of nervous energy	0	1	2	3
9	I was worried about situations in which I might panic and make a fool of myself	0	1	2	3
10	I felt that I had nothing to look forward to	0	1	2	3
11	I found myself getting agitated	0	1	2	3
12	I found it difficult to relax	0	1	2	3
13	I felt down-hearted and blue	0	1	2	3
14	I was intolerant of anything that kept me from getting on with what I was doing	0	1	2	3
15	I felt I was close to panic	0	1	2	3
16	I was unable to become enthusiastic about anything	0	1	2	3
17	I felt I wasn't worth much as a person	0	1	2	3
18	I felt that I was rather touchy	0	1	2	3
19	I was aware of the action of my heart in the absence of physical exertion (e.g., sense of heart rate increase, heart missing a beat)	0	1	2	3
20	I felt scared without any good reason	0	1	2	3
21	I felt that life was meaningless	0	1	2	3

Adding up items 1, 6, 8, 11, 12, 14, and 18 gives the client's stress score. Items 3, 5, 10, 13, 16, 17, and 21 give the depression score, and 2, 4, 7, 9, 15, 19, and 20 give the anxiety score. Therapist Bob can now track three different outcomes at once using one simple scale.

Fine; so Therapist Bob knows how to measure the problem now. Client Fred shows up and does indeed seem to have issues around depression and stress. Treatment is scheduled for ten sessions (the current assessment session, eight sessions, and one follow-up, which is what Fred's insurance will cover). Bob asks Fred to fill out the 21-item form every week and bring it in to therapy. Work goes well, and Fred shows steady improvement. Bob then has Fred come in three months later (this is the "follow-up") part. Fred is still doing well, and contact is terminated.

Fred's progress on the three subscales of the DASS21 is shown in the accompanying graph. The first two measurements represent baseline measures before the CBT was started in week 2. The final measurement was done 13 weeks later. Remember, on the DASS, high scores show the presence of symptoms and are bad. The chart shows relatively steady

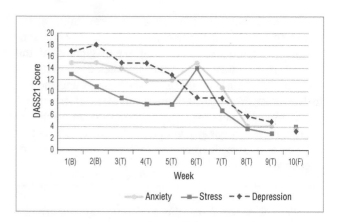

progress, apart from a little blip around week 6 on the stress and anxiety scales. The follow-up scores are similar to, perhaps slightly better than, the scores at the end of treatment. This would be considered a very successful treatment.■

SECTION 8.5.3: MULTIPLE BASELINE MODELS

Let's say you really need to be sure if a treatment works for a client. To do this, you might stop the treatment and then restart the treatment again. This is called an *ABAB* design (no treatment/treatment/no treatment/treatment). Some people call the second *A* a second baseline, but we find it less confusing to call it a no-treatment condition.

Warning! ABAB designs make sense only for those treatments that are not expected to have lasting benefits. Why? Because if the first treatment solves the problem (first *B*), then the no-treatment score afterward (second *A*) will not return back to pretreatment, and the second treatment (second *B*) cannot be expected to produce effects.

Another warning! ABAB designs may pose ethical problems. You will discover this the first time a parent asks you, "Why did you stop helping my little Suzy?" and you have to say, "Because I just wanted to see if the therapy was really working."

Ideally, the outcome of an *ABAB* design would look like Figure 8.5 (if you were measuring good behaviors and higher on the chart meant "better"). Such a result would show that the client improves during treatment and gets worse without treatment. We

FIGURE 8.5. **Outcome of an *ABAB* Design.**

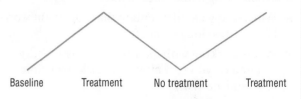

won't spend any more time on this approach, mainly because it is not commonly used and can be ethically questionable. Notice also that we are assuming that the client will get better only while the treatment is being administered, and that treatment effects will wear off.

SECTION 8.5.4: MULTIPLE INTERVENTION MODELS

You don't always know in advance what will work and what won't. Most experienced counselors or therapists will have backup plans ready in case their first attempt fails. Being forced to go to your backup plan may look like this: baseline/first treatment/second treatment. This is an *ABC* design. Sometimes *ABC* designs occur after the *B* part fails. At other times, you may intend to use multiple treatments from the beginning. Perhaps two different approaches have been found to work with a given problem, and you plan to try both out to see if they help. Of course, it would be nice to slap a follow-up on any such design, causing it to be an *ABCA* design or, as we would call it, an *ABC* design with follow-up.

EXAMPLE: HAZEL LOVES ICE CREAM

Let's say you are a school counselor who is called in to help third-grade teacher Jim out with student Hazel. The problem is that Hazel is throwing stuff, yelling in class, and generally not keeping her hands to herself. You decide to have Teacher Jim use time-outs when Hazel acts up. You teach Teacher Jim how to do it and have him record the outcome (disruptive behavior by Hazel) by simply making a hash mark each time Hazel throws something, gets out of her seat, touches another student, or talks out of turn. You baseline for three days and then implement the time-outs for a week. It looks like this:

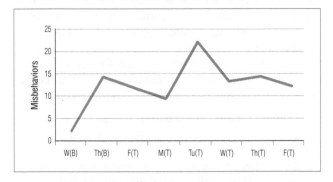

After some initial good behavior when the baseline observation started (Hazel knew about what was going on), she pretty much lost it again, averaging around 10 to 15 misbehaviors per hour throughout the rest of the baseline and through a week of treatment. It was decided to scrap the time-out thing completely, mainly because for some reason Hazel seemed to be, if anything, enjoying it. Obviously, another treatment was needed.

The next plan was to use a reward system (labeled "T2" for "Treatment 2" in the graph below). It was decided that during the next week, if Hazel committed fewer than 10 bad

behaviors, she could have an ice cream after school. The technical term for this is a "reinforcement contingency," which sounds better than "bribery." The next week went like this:

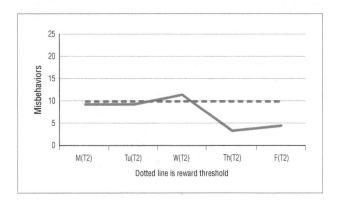

Well, that worked better. Hazel has shown she can control her behavior with the help of dairy products. Ideally, Teacher Jim would like to get Hazel's bad behaviors down to zero. You therefore move the reward threshold down to five the next week and zero the following week. Results can be seen below. At this point, you, Teacher Jim, and Mom decide to leave well enough alone. Mom keeps coughing up the ice cream money, and everyone's happy.■

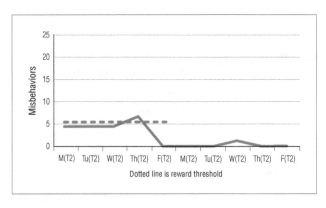

SECTION 8.5.5: COMBINED INTERVENTION MODELS

Sometimes you need to do two things at once. For example, you might try a less expensive, immediately available, or easier intervention first and then supplement it, if necessary, with something else. One way to write this is as an *ABB+C* design. As with all designs, following up would not be a bad idea, making it an *ABB+CA* design. Combining treatments is very common in psychotherapy, with drugs and talk therapy being commonly combined. Of course, you could just as easily do an *AB+CA* design, in which neither treatment (*B* or *C*) is given alone. The only advantage to running *B* alone is to see if it works without the help of *C*. Or, as in the below example, it just might work out that way.

EXAMPLE: DON'T DO THE CRIME . . .

It's December 2006, and you work at a local community agency and are particularly interested in helping your community to reduce street crime. You are lobbying for improved streetlighting to be installed, but this won't happen for about a year. You are thinking of starting up a citizen's watch program to see if that will help. Your goal is to reduce assaults and robberies that occur in your zip code. Fortunately, the police publish quarterly crime rates by zip code in your area, so you have a nice outcome measure all ready for your use. Because they have been publishing yearly reports for a long time, you can look at the past year (2005) to get a baseline measure. Your time line looks like this:

Dec. 2005: Baseline on 2005 by consulting last year's records: Go back and get reports on rates of robberies and assaults in your zip code.

2006: Implement citizen watch: Check crime levels to see if it helps.

2007: Keep up citizen watch. Streetlights come in. Check crime levels.

In this case, 2006 is the baseline *(A)*, 2006's citizen watch program treatment is 1 *(B)*, and the next year (2007) we see treatment 1 plus treatment 2 (streetlights), which we'll call *B+C*.

As time goes on, rates of crime can be tracked easily by just getting the most recent police data. Police records are broken down by quarter, and might look like this:

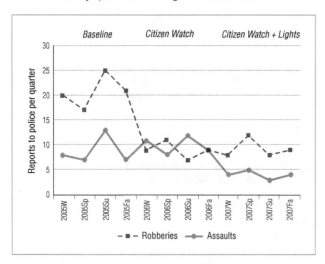

What does this tell us? First of all, the number of robberies seems to be getting lower from winter 2006 onward. That corresponds to the implementation of the citizen's watch program. There appears to be no additional drop from winter 2007 on, suggesting that the streetlights gave no extra help in reducing robberies. Just the opposite happened with rates of assaults. They did not seem to drop when citizen's watch started but did seem to drop when the streetlights came in. It looks as if it might be a good idea to continue both the

citizen's watch program and the streetlights. It is worth noting that there is no way to tell if the streetlights would have had any effect if the citizen's watch had not been there. To find that out, you'd have had to have a different design, such as baseline/watch only/lights only/watch+lights. This would be an *ABCB+C* design.

In an even stricter scientific sense, you'll recall that quasi-experimental designs such as these never prove causality. Sure, there is pretty nice evidence that your program is working, but you can't say you've "proven" that the programs caused the reduced crime without a true experimental design. Nonetheless, I'd keep up the citizen's watch and streetlights.■

Basically, you can do anything you want that is ethical and makes sense. If you keep trying new interventions, you may have to use even more letters. For example, if you baseline *(A)*, try an approach *(B)* that fails, and then try two more approaches together *(C+D)* that also fail, and then finally try an approach that looks as if it is working *(E)*, and then you follow up *(A)*, you might be said to have an *ABC+DEA* design. Many social interventions work this way. One thing gets tried, then something else, then two things together, then nothing is done for a while . . . You are likely to find that practical concerns and client needs drive what you do as much as your initial plan does, and you may end up with a very messy set of letters. Nobody said clinical practice is simple.

SECTION 8.6

TIME FRAMES

As a clinician, you have to deal with reality. Sometimes you just have to do things a certain way, no matter how they interfere with the quality of your research. For example, you can't tell a person at high risk of suicide, "Hey, go off somewhere and chart your feelings for a month." The issue of time frames therefore becomes one you will need to consider, and you may face the following questions:

■ *How long should I baseline?* You want to baseline long enough to get a clear picture of what's going on. How can this be done without delaying therapy? Sometimes an initial screening visit will occur several weeks in front of the start of therapy. This may be your best chance to get some baseline data and even to start the client (or the client's parent or teacher or whomever) logging. If that doesn't work, you will usually have an introductory session before any real work begins. Do not lose the opportunity of baselining during that week. If you work in a school or similar agency, you may be able to start baselining before the client even knows she is getting treated. You will want to check on the ethics and agency guidelines regarding this. While simply charting a child's disruptive behavior would probably not be an ethical concern, a company tracking an employee's behavior prior to offering EAP (Employee Assistance Program) services might well be unethical. If you can use existing records for your outcome measure, do that. In such cases, baselining is done for you and you won't have to worry about it.

■ *How long should I treat?* This is a clinical, not a research question, and is covered in one of your other classes. Obviously, from a research perspective, if you don't treat long enough to expect an effect, you shouldn't expect an effect to show up, and your findings won't pan out the way you want them to.

■ *Should I do a follow-up?* Yes. Unless there is some reason not to, you should. As we said, it is especially important when you feel the client may be at risk after treatment (e.g., suicide risks, people with very up-and-down histories). You certainly want to know if your work is "sticking," no? The only way to figure that out is to do the follow-up.

■ *How long should the follow-up time be?* Clinical sense is required here. How long are you trying to have the change last? If you want to see if your work holds up for years, then why not do a few follow-ups two, three, even five years later? More typically, you'll wait a few months.

SECTION 8.7

ANALYSIS, INTERPRETATION, AND DISSEMINATION

We suggest the following rules of thumb in what can only be called the art of interpreting clinical data:

■ *Graph the data visually:* See the preceding examples. You can use bar graphs, lines on a page, little sticky-stars, whatever. Try to get something you can look at. This is especially true in looking at progress over long periods of time.

■ *Look at the graphs and ask yourself, "Do these changes look consistent and real?"* Changes that are real should be *big and stable* and should *make sense.* Did the change occur when it logically should have? Is the change consistently maintained? Little blips shouldn't worry you too much, but trends that persist over time and are large need consideration, even if (especially if) they are bad trends.

■ *Try to use objective measurements of the actual problem whenever possible.* Who knows what moving down two points on a SUDS really

means except that, "You're doing better"? On the other hand, in the preceding example with Hazel, we can say, "Well, she went from about a dozen misbehaviors a day to zero on most days." That's much easier to interpret.

SECTION 8.7.1: ONE FINAL NOTE ABOUT DISSEMINATION

You've done your work; you've formalized outcomes, intervened, graphed, and interpreted. At a very minimum, you have probably used this information to help your client to do better. You may also have used the information to improve as a clinician, as we discussed at the beginning of this chapter. Good.

It is also likely that you will be called on at some point to present your cases to colleagues or even at conferences or similar venues. Having done the kind of research we describe here can make case presentations much easier. It is far more difficult to stand up and say, "In my clinical judgment . . . ," than it is to say, "Here we can see the client's progress as shown by . . ." It is also possible to publish case studies of interventions. There are entire journals dedicated to this. For example, *Clinical Case Studies, The Innovation Journal, The Journal of Psychiatric Practice,* and *The Journal of Applied Behavioral Analysis* all publish case studies. We strongly suggest you browse these and other journals at the library and see what others have published. Does it look as though you could do the same? If so, why not do it? It looks good on the résumé.

★ ★ ★

EBP MODULE

So far, our discussion of EBP has focused on looking at other people's research. In the original (evidence-based medicine) model, this was a primary focus. However, there was also an exhortation for physicians to track their own practice in a more structured way, so that they could gain important evidence about what was and wasn't working well with their clients. The skills covered in this chapter were meant to help you do that.

The main point we'd like to make with regard to EBP that you will have to consciously think about when referring to the scientific literature it will be adequate to meet your needs and when you may have to develop data by yourself. We would suggest that there are basically two kinds of questions you will ask about individual clients. The first kind of question has to do with finding out what social and medical science knows about your client's problem, his or her situation, or whatever. Questions such as these may take the form, "What works to treat X?" or, "Will X go away if left untreated?" or, "Does treatment effectiveness for X vary by culture/age/and so on . . .?" Questions such as these should be answered by going to the research literature. The following example may help.

Example 1: Relying on Other People's Research

Let's say that you want to decide on a course of treatment for a person who compulsively pulls out her hair. The practice question is, "What treatments have been shown effective in getting people to stop pulling their hair out?" You've never encountered anything like this before. Finding that there are no experts you can refer to (or even consult) in your area, you decide to treat the person yourself and learn all you can about the problem. You use Google and PsycINFO as usual, using search terms such as "hair pulling," and find out that this problem is a diagnosable mental disorder defined in the DSM and that it has a name (trichotillomania). You find a keen Web site from the Trichotillomania Learning Center (www.trich.org/index.asp) with lots of information. You decide to look for specific practice guidelines that will suggest courses of action you can use with your new client. You remember reading about the National Guideline Clearinghouse earlier in this book (www.guideline.gov), and you go there. They suggest behavioral interventions and medication. Throughout your search process you are able to find a number of primary articles that further increase your understanding of the problem.

Of course, sometimes your question will take a far more focused form, such as, "Is this client improving?" or, "Does treatment completion among the people I serve vary by race?" These questions can be addressed only by engaging in your own research. The next example might help clarify this.

Example 2: Generating Your Own Research

Let's say that you decide to treat the client using a combination of behavioral (reward system, situational avoidance) and cognitive behavioral (reframing, attention diversion) approaches. You start treating your client with trichotillomania. Being a good therapist, you want an objective measure of how well your client is doing. This means you need to know the answer to the question, "Is my client pulling her hair less?" You would set up your own single-person case study to track treatment success or failure. Hopefully you would have several ways of tracking hair pulling. These might

include your own observations of hair pulling in session, your client's answers on a daily hair-pulling log, or your own observation each week of the amount of hair visible to you in a given area. We'd even consider taking some photos as time goes by if this would not be overly distressing to the client. First, you do a week's baseline measurement, and then you start weekly recording. Let's say that your initial behavioral or CBT interventions do not seem to be achieving any success over the first two months. You may, on the basis of your data, decide to change what you are doing. You would continue to collect data in hopes of seeing more success with the new approach. This is essentially an *ABC* design, in which *A* is the baseline, *B* is the first (failed) approach, and *C* is the new approach.

We hope this module has been at least somewhat helpful. We want to make sure we are communicating that searching the literature cannot always replace the need to engage in your own original research.■

REVIEW

1. What does "$N = 1$" mean?
2. What is a baseline, and why do you need one?
3. List three things that make for good outcomes.
4. List two advantages of observing real-world outcomes instead of relying on paper instruments.
5. What is a behavioral log?
6. Make up an example of an $N = 1$ study using entirely administrative data.
7. Give a hypothetical example of an *ABA* design.
8. What is a multiple baseline model?
9. Give an example of a design using all the following letters: *ABC & D*.

SUPPLEMENTAL READINGS

■ *Journal of Applied Behavioral Analysis* (any issue or volume). This journal includes interesting examples of mainly quantitative case studies. It's a wonderful source of examples of how to do the work.

■ Todman, J., & Dugard, P. (2001). *Single-Case and Small-N Experimental Designs: A Practical Guide to Randomization Tests.* Mahwah, NJ: Lawrence Earlbaum Associates. This very advanced book is really for the serious small-sample researcher who wants to publish at an academic level.

CHAPTER

DESIGN EXAMPLES

This chapter will overview the five example projects. We will see how each person handled the issues covered in Chapters 3 and 4, including:

- Aim, question, and hypotheses
- Type of design
- Population of interest, unit of analysis, sampling frame, and sampling
- Constructs and variables
- Control
- Strengths and limitations of design
- Time line
- IRB issues

SECTION 9.1

PROFESSOR KATHY

SECTION 9.1.1: AIM, QUESTION, AND HYPOTHESES

Professor Kathy's aim is to determine whether classical background music (CBM), easy-listening background music (ELBM), or no background music (NBM) produces faster and/or more correct coding. She does not believe that the theory and research are sufficiently developed to use directional hypotheses. Her independent variable is presence and type of music (classical versus easy-listening versus none), and her dependent variable is speed of coding (Question 1), and accuracy of coding (Question 2). Her questions and hypotheses are:

QUESTION 1: DOES BACKGROUND MUSIC AFFECT SPEED OF CODING?

- Q1: Do CBM, ELBM, and NBM coders have different speeds of coding?
- H1: CBM, ELBM, and NBM coders will have different rates of files coded per hour.

QUESTION 2: DOES BACKGROUND MUSIC AFFECT ACCURACY OF CODING?

- Q2: Are CBM, ELBM, and NBM coders equally accurate?
- H2: CBM, ELBM, and NBM coders will have different accuracy rates as determined by file review.

SECTION 9.1.2: TYPE OF DESIGN

Professor Kathy has chosen to use a true experimental design with three groups (CBM, ELBM, and NBM). Her question is clearly causal, so the true experimental design is her strongest approach. Furthermore, her question is one where the artificiality of the experimental setting will not be an issue because she is not trying to create findings that are generalizable beyond the coding room.

SECTION 9.1.3: POPULATION OF INTEREST, UNIT OF ANALYSIS, AND SAMPLING

Again, Professor Kathy is unusually fortunate. The point of the study is to help researchers to improve their coders' performance, so her population of interest is people who code for university researchers. She works at a typical public university and uses undergraduate work-study students for her coding, like many other researchers, so she has good confidence that her population of interest will be well represented in her sample. She will, in fact, simply recruit coders as usual. Her procedure for assigning subjects will be as follows: Professor Kathy uses about 60 new coders per year (she has a large ongoing project), and they are trained in September. Each coder is trained using a standard procedure. Coders must pass a test showing they have reached at least 90% agreement with precoded training files. Following training, she will randomly assign students to one of her three conditions (CBM, ELBM, NBM). Students will code during timed sessions lasting one hour. Only files completed before the hour expires are counted.

Each file represents one day of client care. Entries are made every half-hour. If a client has needed assistance with an activity of daily living, such as washing or going to the bathroom, the care provider enters a description of the service provided, prefaced with the word "Assist." The coders use a coding sheet broken down into half-hours (48 entries) for each daily file and make a check mark during each half-hour block in which an "Assist" code is recorded in the file.

SECTION 9.1.4: CONSTRUCTS AND VARIABLES

One construct (music) will be used to divide the subjects into three groups. The first variable used will be number of coded files per hour (measured by the number of files completed in an hour-long coding session). Professor Kathy knows from experience that this number should be between about two and eight for most students, a large enough spread to show sufficient variability. The second variable used will be number of mistakes made per coded file. This will be done by having senior coders (students who did coding last semester) check each of the coded files for errors and then totaling the errors. Although it is possible for a coder to make up to 48 errors in an average-sized file, past experience suggests that the number of errors will be about 2 per file. Again, she

has sufficient variability in her variable. Senior coders will be randomly assigned to check files and will be blind to which coder did the file and what group the coder is from to avoid any bias. Each subject will be tracked over 10 sessions. Only the first hour of each student's coding session will be used from each session, so that the possibility of fatigue having an impact on the findings can be minimized.

As we have seen, Professor Kathy finally decided to assign students to different groups for the duration of the study. She could have chosen different approaches. For example, she could rotate each student through each condition. While this would be a valid approach, it would have introduced other factors that would have needed to be considered, such as the order in which students experienced different conditions. Professor Kathy decided to follow the old "KISS" rule ("Keep It Simple, Stupid") and instead opt for the cleanest, most simple design as the most compelling.

SECTION 9.1.5: CONTROL

Professor Kathy feels very good about her level of control in this study. Subjects are randomly assigned, accuracy checking is determined by raters who are "blind" and randomly assigned. Each coder will occupy his or her own cubicle in which the appropriate type of background music will be playing, and the kind of music in each individual cubicle will be randomly rotated daily to assure that differences between conditions are not due to differences in each room (temperature, other subtle differences). Professor Kathy is as confident as she feels she can be that she has done all that anyone could do to rule out spurious factors.

SECTION 9.1.6: STRENGTHS AND LIMITATIONS OF DESIGN

The strength of the design is superb internal validity. The study also has very strong external validity, as it relates to other professors and their coders who are engaged in similar coding tasks. It is unclear, however, how well the findings from these coders doing this kind of coding might generalize to other coders doing other kinds of coding. In this way, the study's external validity may be limited in scope. The study is also somewhat limited in power. While the study will be able to detect large differences with 20 subjects per condition, very small differences might not be detectable.

SECTION 9.1.7: TIME LINE

This study is basically simple, is done by an experienced researcher, and Professor Kathy anticipates it will go quite quickly (Figure 9.1).

FIGURE 9.1. **Professor Kathy's Time Line.**

	Week number													
	1	2	3	4	5	6	7	8	9	10	11	12	13	14
IRB clearance	X	X												
Obtain music, prepare coding cubicles	X	X												
Recruit subjects	X	X	X											
Train subjects				X	X									
Assign to groups					X									
Coding						X	X	X	X					
Coding checking							X	X	X	X				
Database creation							X	X	X	X				
Database cleaning and checking										X	X			
Coder debriefing										X				
Analysis											X	X		
Write-up													X	X

SECTION 9.1.8: IRB ISSUES

This study is rather difficult from a human subjects perspective. On one hand, there is clearly little risk of harm, and the only experimental manipulation is the playing of background music (or not). The question is whether informed consent is required at all. Professor Kathy is concerned that if her students know that they are in a research project, this may contaminate the findings (remember the Hawthorne effect?). This would be especially bad if students knew that the type of music they were listening to made a difference. Professor Kathy had three choices with regard to the IRB. She can:

- Claim she didn't need to do consent forms and hope the IRB agrees. In this case she will be doing something very unusual—research without informed consent.

- Do consent forms that tell people that they are being studied in some way without telling them about the music. This involves mild deception.

- Tell them exactly what is going on. This involves no deception.

Professor Kathy went to her school's IRB and argued for the first option above, and they said "no." They did, however bite on the second option. Professor Kathy therefore had her students fill out consent forms that said that information about their performance might be used in research (Figure 9.2). It did not mention the differing conditions or the fact that music was involved.

FIGURE 9.2. **Professor Kathy's Consent Form.**

File Coding Study

You are invited to participate in a research study conducted by Kathy Doe, PhD. The overall purpose of this project is to understand more about the process of coding files. Your participation will involve coding files and will not go beyond your regular role as a file coder. There will be no additional work or burden on you. There are no known risks or benefits to you associated with your participation in the study. Your participation is voluntary, and you may choose not to participate in this research. If you choose not to participate, it will not affect your employment as a coder in any way. We will do everything we can to protect your privacy. As part of this effort, your identity will not be revealed in any publication that may result from this study. In rare instances, a researcher's study must undergo an audit or program evaluation by an oversight agency (such as the Office of Human Research Protection) that would lead to disclosure of your data as well as any other information collected by the researcher. If you have any questions, concerns, or complaints about the research please contact Professor Kathy Doe, PhD, at (555) 555-5555. If you cannot reach anyone at the above number or if you wish to talk to someone else, have questions or concerns about the study or your rights as a research participant, feel you were pressured to participate, or believe you have been harmed in any way as a result of this research, call Bob Brown at (555) 555-5556. Mr. Brown is an employee of Washington College but is not part of the research team. You can call before, during, or after you take part in the research study. Everything you say will be kept confidential.

I have read this consent form and have been given a chance to ask questions. I will also be given a signed copy of this form for my records. I agree to participate in the research project above, titled "File Coding Study."

_____

Participant's Name Here

_____

Signature of Project Director

Professor Kathy will debrief her students after the data collection and tell them the details of the experiment.

SECTION 9.2

MARIA

SECTION 9.2.1: AIM, QUESTION, AND HYPOTHESES

Maria wants to know if higher residential density and poverty are associated with increases in homicide and suicide rates in zip codes in San Diego. Her questions and hypotheses are as follows.

QUESTION 1A: IS HIGHER RESIDENTIAL DENSITY ASSOCIATED WITH HIGHER HOMICIDE RATES?

- Hypothesis 1A: Higher residential density (2000 Census) will be correlated with a higher homicide rate (2000–2001) in San Diego zip codes.

- Hypothesis 1B: Lower income (2000 Census) will be correlated with a higher homicide rate (2000–2001) in San Diego zip codes.

QUESTION 2A: IS HIGHER RESIDENTIAL DENSITY ASSOCIATED WITH HIGHER SUICIDE RATES?

- Hypothesis 2A: Higher residential density (2000 Census) will be correlated with a higher suicide rate (2000–2001) in San Diego zip codes.

QUESTION 2B: IS LOWER INCOME ASSOCIATED WITH HIGHER SUICIDE RATES?

- Hypothesis 2B: Lower income (2000 Census) will be correlated with a higher suicide rate (2000–2001) in San Diego zip codes.

The above questions and hypotheses are theoretically derived, but Maria also wants to do a little exploring on her own, and see:

QUESTION 3: WHAT OTHER COMMUNITY FACTORS ARE ASSOCIATED WITH HOMICIDE RATES?

QUESTION 4: WHAT OTHER COMMUNITY FACTORS ARE ASSOCIATED WITH SUICIDE RATES?

SECTION 9.2.2: TYPE OF DESIGN

Maria's choice of design is driven by her data. She already has the dependent variable (homicide and suicide rates in San Diego zip codes). She downloads her census data, which give her even more information (see "Constructs and Variables" and "Control," following). Maria is clearly not doing an experimental design, because she is not assigning zip codes to different groups or conditions. Her one-group design means that she must be doing a nonexperimental design. She is, however, testing a theoretically derived relationship with her first two questions, which means that the kind of nonexperimental design she is doing must be a correlational design. She will look at all the zip codes in San Diego and test for the relationships her theory says will show up. Her last two questions are more exploratory and have to do with identifying which other factors seem to be associated with homicide and suicide in San Diego. These questions are more descriptive or exploratory in nature, and thus do not require hypotheses.

SECTION 9.2.3: POPULATION OF INTEREST, UNIT OF ANALYSIS, AND SAMPLING

Maria's population of interest is everyone. Her sampling frame is all zip codes in San Diego County, and her sampling strategy is to use all of them. Maria's unit of analysis is the zip code. Each zip code will be one record in her study. She has suicide and homicide data for two years and will combine them into a single number. This is because the rates of homicide and suicide are very low, and Maria believes that combining two years will give her higher, more stable rates, which will make her models more stable. While there is a good chance that any one year of data on such a rare event could be high or low due to random luck, this chance of misleading data is lower when two years are combined. If more years of data were available, Maria would probably have folded them in too.

Maria will not use the raw numbers of homicides and suicides directly in her analysis. She will be calculating rates of homicide and suicide by dividing these events into the (census-derived) population of each zip code. On this same issue, Maria has one lingering concern. Some zip codes may have very small populations, only a few hundred people. Small zip codes will either have no homicides or suicides (in which case they will look very good, with a rate of 0), or they will have one or two (in which case they will look very dangerous because the events will be divided into a very small population, and the rate will look huge). For this reason, Maria is thinking she may have to exclude zip codes from the analysis if they have less than some set number (5000?) of people. Probably she should talk to a statistics person about this.

SECTION 9.2.4: CONSTRUCTS AND VARIABLES

For hypotheses one and two, Maria will need the following variables:

1. Number of homicides per 10,000 residents
2. Number of suicides per 10,000 residents
3. Residential density in zip code
4. Poverty in zip code

HOMICIDE AND SUICIDE RATES

To create variables 1 and 2, she needs to know the population of each zip code. She already has the number of homicides and suicides from the coroner's Web site (see Chapter 2).

RESIDENTIAL DENSITY

The residential density variable could be done a couple of different ways:

- She could create a number of average (mean) people per residence by dividing the number of housing units in the zip code by the number of residents.

- She could create a variable showing the percentage of people who live alone. To do this, she would divide the number of single-resident housing units into the population.

Maria doesn't know what to do. She has noticed that one professor in an adjacent building has all kinds of census maps and analyses plastered all over his door. She checks his office hours and goes to visit. She explains what she is doing and asks which variable he thinks she should use. He says, "What does your theory tell you to do?" She says that she thinks that the theory says that people who live alone are more likely to kill themselves (Jarvis et al., 1982; McCullough et al., 1967) and has heard population density (people per square mile) leads to homicide rates increasing. She realizes that she really has to track both variables. She therefore decides to use the following variables:

- Percentage of all residences that are single-person occupied
- Number of people in zip code divided by square miles in zip code

This requires a change in her hypotheses. Hypotheses 1A and 2A go away and are replaced by the following:

- H1A1: More residents per square mile (2000 Census) will be correlated with a higher homicide rate (2000–2001) in San Diego zip codes.
- H1A2: Higher percentages of single-person residences (2000 Census) will be correlated with a higher homicide rate (2000–2001) in San Diego zip codes.
- H2A1: More residents per square mile (2000 Census) will be correlated with a higher suicide rate (2000–2001) in San Diego zip codes.
- H2A2: Higher percentages of single-person residences (2000 Census) will be correlated with a higher suicide rate (2000–2001) in San Diego zip codes.

She could have tested only residents per square mile against homicides and single occupancy against suicides, but it seems more elegant and symmetrical to test both against both. Why not? She has to collect the data anyhow. Maria feels a little silly, because on reflection, this should have been obvious to her sooner from a close reading of the Jarvis et al. article. What she doesn't realize is that this is typical of how research projects go.

INCOME

Maria decides to measure income by median income in the zip code.

OTHER VARIABLES

Maria has found references to age and race as other factors that could influence suicide rates. She will therefore track the age of residents in each zip code and will also look at race. Race, of course, is a categorical variable, and San Diego is one of the most diverse communities in the world. She therefore will have to track percentages of Whites, Blacks, Hispanics, and Asians separately.

SECTION 9.2.5: CONTROL

Maria hasn't thought that much about control. She just planned on doing simple correlations, univariate for H1 and H2 and then a correlation matrix for H3 and H4. This would do the following important things:

- It would tell her the bivariate relationship between her independent and dependent variables (H1 and H2).
- It would tell her what other factors (H3 and H4) would be associated with the dependent variable.

But none of this provides any control for spurious causality. What Maria decides to do is to have even more hypotheses (H5 and H6) to test her associations while using statistical controls:

- H5A1 (multivariate version of H1A1): More residents per square mile (2000 Census) will be correlated with a higher homicide rate (2000–2001) in San Diego zip codes *while controlling for other factors that are associated with homicide rates.*
- H5A2 (multivariate version of H1A2): Higher percentages of single-person residences (2000 Census) will be correlated with a higher homicide rate (2000–2001) in San Diego zip codes *while controlling for other factors that are associated with homicide rates.*
- H5B (multivariate version of H1B): Lower income (2000 Census) will be correlated with a higher homicide rate (2000–2001) in San Diego zip codes *while controlling for other factors that are associated with homicide rates.*
- H6A1 (multivariate version of H2A1): More residents per square mile (2000 Census) will be correlated with a higher suicide rate (2000–2001) in San Diego zip codes *while controlling for other factors that are associated with suicide rates.*

- H6A2 (multivariate version of H2A2): Higher percentages of single-person residences (2000 Census) will be correlated with a higher suicide rate (2000–2001) in San Diego zip codes *while controlling for other factors that are associated with suicide rates.*

- H6B1 (multivariate version of H2B1): Lower income (2000 Census) will be correlated with a higher suicide rate (2000–2001) in San Diego zip codes *while controlling for other factors that are associated with suicide rates.*

SECTION 9.2.6: STRENGTHS AND LIMITATIONS OF DESIGN

Maria has now moved from testing four hypotheses to testing ten hypotheses. The good news is that Maria now feels more comfortable and assured in what she is doing and feels that she can do a better job linking her hypotheses to the literature (H1 and H2) and can now make some claim to be providing at least some control for spurious causality (H5 and H6). Her study has the strength of being clearly based on prior work and of having a good theoretical basis. She has the unavoidable limitation of being able to test only association and not causality (not a true experimental design). Her only being able to sample a rare event over a two-year timespan may present her with difficulties around a few random events throwing off her findings. The fact that her findings will result from a decently large number of zip codes will help with this. Another limitation is that she can't be absolutely sure that the suicides and homicides occurred in the zip code in which the person lived. Maria did some research on this and found that most suicides and homicides occur near the home, so she plans to include that information in her write-up in an attempt to forestall criticism.

SECTION 9.2.7: TIME LINE

Maria's time line is informal, but looks something like Figure 9.3. Notice that Maria has budgeted herself a fairly long time for the write-up (three months). She understands that she is new at this and may need to make some fairly radical changes to her plan. She is therefore building in some "cushion time" toward the end.

SECTION 9.2.8: IRB ISSUES

Maria files an IRB request under "exempt" status. She is using publicly available information. She therefore outlines her project, explaining that no identifying data is used, and gives this to her IRB. Maria knows that most researchers wouldn't even do this much, but she wants to be completely safe and confident that she is doing the right thing.

FIGURE 9.3. Maria's Time Line.

	Dec	Jan	Feb	Mar	Apr	May	Jun
IRB clearance	X						
Get census downloaded	X						
Get dataset completed, including created variables and load into SAS		X					
Do bivariate and correlational analyses (H1–4)			X				
Do multivariates (H5–6)				X			
Do rough write-up for class project					X		
Get feedback from class and others if possible					X		
Rewrite. Final class project due May 21!						X	
Redo based on comments and submit to journal							X

SECTION 9.3
ABIGAIL

Abigail wants to see what environmental factors are associated with the impact of client death on child protective services workers. The theory she has found suggests that positive work communication styles and support from friends and families should reduce the negative impact of client fatality on the worker.

SECTION 9.3.1: AIM, QUESTION, AND HYPOTHESES

Her aim is to find out the degree to which work climate factors (supportive and conflictual communication) and nonwork supports (family and friend emotional support, social support, and advice/guidance) are associated with the impact of client death on workers (postevent intrusive and avoidance experiences). She has the following questions.

QUESTION 1: ARE ORGANIZATIONAL FACTORS (SUPPORTIVE COMMUNICATION, CONFLICTUAL COMMUNICATION) ASSOCIATED WITH THE IMPACT (INTRUSIVENESS, AVOIDANCE) OF CLIENT FATALITIES?

- Hypothesis 1A1: Organizational supportive communication will be associated with lower levels of worker-reported postfatality event intrusive experiences.

- Hypothesis 1A2: Organizational conflictual communication will be associated with higher levels of worker-reported postfatality event intrusive reactions.

- Hypothesis 1B1: Organizational supportive communication will be associated with lower levels of worker-reported postfatality event avoidance experiences.

- Hypothesis 1B2: Organizational conflictual communication will be associated with higher levels of worker-reported postfatality event avoidance reactions.

QUESTION 2: ARE NONWORK SOCIAL SUPPORT FACTORS (EMOTIONAL, SOCIAL, ADVICE/GUIDANCE) ASSOCIATED WITH THE IMPACT (INTRUSIVENESS, AVOIDANCE) OF CLIENT FATALITIES?

- Hypothesis 2A1: Emotional support by friends will be associated with lower levels of worker-reported postfatality event intrusive experiences.

- Hypothesis 2A2: Emotional support by friends will be associated with lower levels of worker-reported postfatality event avoidance reactions.

- Hypothesis 2A3: Emotional support by family will be associated with lower levels of worker-reported postfatality event intrusive experiences.

- Hypothesis 2A4: Emotional support by family will be associated with lower levels of worker-reported postfatality event avoidance reactions.

- Hypothesis 2B1: Social support by friends will be associated with lower levels of worker-reported postfatality event intrusive experiences.

- Hypothesis 2B2: Social support by friends will be associated with lower levels of worker-reported postfatality event avoidance reactions.

- Hypothesis 2B3: Social support by family will be associated with lower levels of worker-reported postfatality event intrusive experiences.

- Hypothesis 2B4: Social support by family will be associated with lower levels of worker-reported postfatality event avoidance reactions.

- Hypothesis 2C1: Advice and guidance by friends will be associated with lower levels of worker-reported postfatality event intrusive experiences.

- Hypothesis 2C2: Advice and guidance by friends will be associated with lower levels of worker-reported postfatality event avoidance reactions.

- Hypothesis 2C3: Advice and guidance by family will be associated with lower levels of worker-reported postfatality event intrusive experiences.

- Hypothesis 2C4: Advice and guidance by family will be associated with lower levels of worker-reported postfatality event avoidance reactions.

QUESTION 3: WHAT OTHER PERSONAL CHARACTERISTICS ARE ASSOCIATED WITH INCREASES IN THE IMPACT OF CHILD FATALITIES?

Abigail will test association of each personal characteristic with intrusive experiences and avoidance separately, to determine which have statistically significant associations.

QUESTION 4: DO EFFECTS FOUND IN Q1 AND Q2 PERSIST IN THE PRESENCE OF CONTROLS FOR PERSONAL CHARACTERISTICS?

Abigail will retest H1 and H2 elements in multivariate equations including controls from Question 3.

SECTION 9.3.2: TYPE OF DESIGN

Abigail's design is nonexperimental and correlational. She is testing anticipated relationships using statistical methods. She has only one group and therefore is not doing an experimental design. Although there is a descriptive flavor to her work (especially in Q3), she is mainly testing theoretically derived hypotheses and so, like Maria, is doing a correlational study.

SECTION 9.3.3: POPULATION OF INTEREST, UNIT OF ANALYSIS, AND SAMPLING

Abigail will work with her state's child protection agency, but she isn't quite sure of how she will draw her sample. She's a little worried because there might not be enough workers with client fatalities to make for a reasonable sample size. For a start, she is planning on using fatality review commission files to identify how many children who died in the last year had been open for services. She then plans to locate their workers and administer the survey packet to them. She will therefore be sampling the entire population of interest in her state.

SECTION 9.3.4: CONSTRUCTS AND VARIABLES

Her main independent constructs are the impact of the fatality, organizational communication, support by friends and family and other worker factors (i.e., age, experience, and the like). The variables she will use are either descriptive (worker factors) or are drawn from the subscales of the instruments she is using, with the IES providing her dependent variables (intrusiveness and avoidance).

SECTION 9.3.5: CONTROL

Abigail will control for worker characteristics in the multivariate model in Q4. She is not planning any other form of control.

SECTION 9.3.6: STRENGTHS AND LIMITATIONS OF DESIGN

Strengths of the design include that she has an entire state to draw her sample from, that she has measures that appear to be good matches to her constructs, and that she is studying an important and underexplored area. Abigail is concerned about several things, however.

SAMPLE SIZE

Will she get enough people?

RESPONSE RATE

Will the packages get returned? Should Abigail call people to make sure they got the packages?

RECEIVING ACCOUNTS OVER DIFFERENT TIME FRAMES

Abigail will probably have to look at all fatalities in the past year or longer. There will therefore be differences in how long ago the death occurred. Her measures of organizational and support factors will therefore sometimes be given to subjects soon after the client death and will sometimes be given to subjects several months later. Ideally, she'd measure all of these things at the same time for each person (say, climate and support one week after the event and impact of event one, six, and twenty-four months after the event). Unfortunately, she will be sending out her surveys to some people for whom the fatality was a year ago and to others for whom it only recently happened.

CONTENT VALIDITY

Is Abigail studying all the key issues? She is not, for example, looking at PTSD, which some people might find to be an omission.

SECTION 9.3.7: TIME LINE

Abigail plans to do the study rather quickly (see Figure 9.4).

SECTION 9.3.8: IRB ISSUES

Obviously, bringing up something so sensitive might well trigger negative emotions. Abigail is planning to send the survey out by mail, and so she won't be there to monitor reactions and provide support if needed. She's not exactly sure how to proceed. Maybe she should have a phone counselor available? Apprise them of their own internal counseling resources on the consent form? Her consent form is generally like Kathy's, but altered to fit her study.

FIGURE 9.4. Abigail's Time Frame.

	Sept	Oct	Nov	Dec	Jan
IRB clearance	X				
Identify subjects from fatality files	X				
Complete package layout, copy and mail survey packages	X				
Telephone subjects to see if they got the package and to encourage package completion		X			
Receive returned packages and enter into database		X	X		
Statistical analysis				X	
Write-up					X

SECTION 9.4

YUAN

Yuan wants to determine if cognitive behavioral therapy (CBT) is more effective than standard therapy (ST) in reducing male domestic violence.

SECTION 9.4.1: AIM, QUESTION, AND HYPOTHESES

Yuan is working with a local agency that runs a large number of groups serving males who batter. That agency has been using "regular" treatment for a long time, but wants to try out CBT and see if it works better. This is his aim, to see which works better. The agency serves court-mandated clients and has a close relationship with local law enforcement. Part of that arrangement is that the police department reports to them any domestic violence reports made against the clients before, during, and for two years after treatment.

QUESTION 1: DO SUBJECTS RECEIVING CBT AND ST SHOW DIFFERENT CHANGES IN AS SUBSCALE SCORES?

- Hypothesis 1A1: Subjects receiving CBT and ST will show different levels of change in the AS avoidance subscale from pretest to posttest (change during treatment).

- Hypothesis 1A2: Subjects receiving CBT and ST will show different levels of change in the AS avoidance subscale from posttest to six-months posttreatment (change following treatment).

- Hypothesis 1B1 and hypothesis 1B2 mirror the above, except the AS empathy subscale is the DV.

- Hypothesis 1C1 and hypothesis 1C2 mirror the above, except the AS forethought subscale is the DV.

- Hypothesis 1D1 and hypothesis 1D2 mirror the above, except the AS usefulness subscale is the DV.

QUESTION 2: DO SUBJECTS RECEIVING CBT AND ST SHOW DIFFERENT RATES OF REPORTED VIOLENCE?

This would yield the following hypothesis:

- Hypothesis 2: Subjects receiving CBT and ST will show different rates of recidivism during the six months following treatment.

Yuan is also considering adding new hypotheses, to see if the AS subscales predict recidivism rates. Those two new hypotheses would be under a new question and would look like the following.

QUESTION 3: DO EMPATHY AND ARGUMENT AVOIDANCE PREDICT RECIDIVISM?

- Hypothesis 3A: People with higher AS avoidance scores at posttest will have lower rates of recidivism.
- Hypothesis 3B: This is the same as 3A, except the empathy subscale is used.
- Hypothesis 3C: This is the same as 3A, except the forethought subscale is used.
- Hypothesis 3D: This is the same as 3A, except the usefulness subscale is used.

SECTION 9.4.2: TYPE OF DESIGN

We will see below that Yuan was not able to do random assignment. He is, however, following the standard experimental design in every other way, and so he is doing a quasi-experimental design.

- H1A1, H1B1, H1C1, and H1D1 reflect a simple "pretest/posttest" design, with measures at start and end of treatment to see if the treatment group does better over the course of therapy than the comparison group.
- H1A2, H1B2, H1C2, and H1D2 relate to a standard follow-up design, with measures at end of treatment and six months later. These are designed to see if the treatment has any durability (if it "sticks").
- H3 is a correlational design looking at the relationship between two variables. Note that the group format is not needed for this design, but each group should be tested separately to see if the effect occurs for both the experimental and comparison samples.

SECTION 9.4.3: POPULATION OF INTEREST, UNIT OF ANALYSIS, AND SAMPLING

You could argue that Yuan is interested in how treatment works with all batterers. This would ideally be based on a random sample of all men who have battered. Unfortunately, this is not what he has. It is doubtful that such a sample is ever possible, because many batterers are unidentified except to themselves and their silent victims. What Yuan has are court-referred batterers. This will limit the generalizability of his findings to other court-ordered batterers. The more Yuan thinks about this, the more comfortable he becomes, because there is a strong need to know what works with court-ordered batterers, and so his work should be generalizable to a broad and important population. He will have to check later to see if his court-ordered batterers are similar to state or national norms for court-ordered batterers (assuming that data are available somewhere). The more his people look like the "average" court-ordered batterers, the more generalizability he can claim.

Yuan was hoping to be able to randomly assign subjects to groups, but that didn't work out. The agency has a computer-based system of assigning people to openings in groups as they become available, and they were unwilling to change it. Subjects were therefore assigned to groups in the order in which they signed up, which is not random. What Yuan was permitted to do was to alternate treatment (CBT) and comparison (ST) groups, with comparison groups being the first, third, fifth, and so on groups assigned and the CBT being the second, fourth, sixth, and so on groups assigned. Each of the groups will be taught by a different facilitator who was randomly assigned to CBT or ST groups. All five of the facilitators using the CBT technique are being sent to a three-day training session by a behavioral institute specializing in the application of CBT to batterers.

In terms of actually getting the data, there will be three steps. First of all, the agency files will be examined to get the subject's dates of birth, marital status, number of prior reports, and the like. Second, the pretests and posttests (argument scales) will be given at the first and final meetings of the treatment and comparison groups. Third, the agency files will be checked again six months following the last group meeting to see if there were any recidivism reports. All of this data will be entered into an electronic (.XLS) dataset. Yuan plans to physically take his laptop into the agency and simply enter variables into his database straight from the files.

SECTION 9.4.4: CONSTRUCTS AND VARIABLES

Yuan's variables are as follows:

- *Independent variable:* CBT versus ST treatment group membership (Q1 and Q2); subscale scores (Q3)
- *Dependent variables:* AS empathy, avoidance, forethought, and usefulness scores at posttest and follow-up (Q1); Recidivism (Q2 and Q3)
- *Control variables:* Age, marital status, prior reports to police

SECTION 9.4.5: CONTROL

Control will be achieved by the use of a comparison group and the inclusion of control variables in multivariate models. Yuan will check to make sure members of the control and experimental groups look similar with regard to demographics and initial subscale scores.

SECTION 9.4.6: STRENGTHS AND LIMITATIONS OF DESIGN

As in all quasi-experimental designs, there are limitations as well as strengths. First of all, Yuan lacks random assignment. It is possible, for example, that a different judge may work one week and may refer substantially less severely battering subjects for treatment. This may introduce systematic bias into who gets into which groups. Yuan hopes to compensate for this lack of control by including control variables, such as prior reports.

Another serious limitation is that Yuan is having trouble categorizing what "standard treatment" is. It seems to be pretty much whatever the therapist wants to do. This is not so good because it is hard to say exactly what Yuan will be comparing CBT to. Yuan sees no way to solve this problem. An advantage is that there are five separate therapists in each condition. If one therapist did all the CBT groups and another therapist did all the ST groups, it would be impossible to say if the differences between groups would be due to the CBT/ST difference or if one therapist was just plain better than the other. On the other hand, if the same therapist were doing all 10 groups, you would have serious problems being sure that the therapist wasn't contaminating the ST groups with her

new CBT skills. This brings us to another couple of concerns. Yuan is worried that his internal validity will be compromised by the therapists talking to each other, with the ST therapists learning some of the skills the CBT therapists use (the dreaded "cross-group contamination"). Yuan is also worried about treatment fidelity. Will the therapists really use the CBT interventions? Yuan decides to add a treatment fidelity component. He will tape two sessions at random from each therapist. He will then pay a fellow graduate student who is well versed in CBT to note each time a therapist uses a (specifically operationalized) CBT intervention. In this way, he will compare the degree to which CBT is used in CBT and ST groups. The rater will be kept blind to the nature (CBT versus ST) of each group. Yuan realizes that this is a somewhat weak approach and that it would be better to put more work into this part of the design. For example, he could have multiple raters using more highly formalized rating criteria and then test them against each other to assure reliability. Unfortunately, he just doesn't have the resources to do that. Another problem is that the CBT therapists will have more training than the ST therapists. Yuan wanted to send the ST therapists to some kind of general training workshops so everyone would be comparable, but the agency didn't have the money.

SECTION 9.4.7: TIME LINE

Yuan is probably compressing his analysis and writing time into too small a space (Figure 9.5). He plans to do preliminary analyses on groups 1 through 4 to get his models working and then add data from the

---

FIGURE 9.5. **Yuan's Time Frame.**

	2005						2006									
	J	A	S	O	N	D	J	F	M	A	M	J	J	A	S	O
Final meetings with agency to work out logistics	X															
Training of therapists		X	X													
Groups 1–4*				T	T	T					F					
Groups 5–8					T	T	T					F				
Groups 9–10						T	T	T					F			
Receive follow-up data from police							X	X	X	X	X	X	X	X		
Data entry and management							X	X	X	X	X	X	X	X		
Data analysis												X	X	X	X	
Report writing													X	X	X	X

*T = Treatment, Boldfaced means AS will be administered.

other groups as they become available. He plans to begin writing his introductory sections as early as June, three months before his final data come in. His September and October look as if they're going to be busy.

SECTION 9.4.8: IRB ISSUES

Yuan is using a well-recognized treatment protocol with subjects who are mandated to receive treatment anyway. The fact that he is studying involuntary clients raises some concerns. In talking with his IRB, they require that he allow subjects in the groups to opt out of his study (he just won't collect data on those participants). Yuan hopes that this will be only a few people. The consent form will not state which group is the experimental or control group because this would risk compromising his validity, with the "new" treatment group possibly feeling more motivated to do well.

His consent form is very much like the one on page 174 and is not shown here in order to save space. The only exception is that there was a line added stating "I give my consent for the researchers to consult my files at Family Support Agency for the next year, including any data provided to the agency by law enforcement." This is simply to assure that consent is given for the researcher to collect the follow-up data.

> ### SECTION 9.5
> #### JOHN

SECTION 9.5.1: AIM, QUESTION, AND HYPOTHESES

John has a clear aim, which is "to determine what strengths Bosnian refugees report to be helpful to the acculturation process." He intends to allow his subjects to define what their strengths are (grounded theory). Even though he will let subjects tell him about strengths with little guidance, he will use Berry's model as an orienting framework for understanding the acculturation process. Of course, if the acculturation experience related by his subjects does not match that model, this may change. He is interested both in current strengths and in past strengths that may have been helpful to the refugees. John will not test specific questions or hypotheses, although he would not be surprised if he finds what others had found before, for example, that strengths in social skills and English language skills seem to predispose people to assimilation and integration outcomes and away from marginalization or separation outcomes. John was hoping to use focus groups to generate data because they are relatively fast and inexpensive and can generate rich data. The more he thought about it, however, the

more he realized that wouldn't work. It might become important for John to be able to categorize people (and their strengths) by their adaptation type, so he would need to know what comments came from what person. This is hard to do in a focus group unless the sessions were to be videotaped. Videotaping seemed to be an intrusive procedure with people who may be fleeing political persecution. For these reasons, John chose to do individual interviews instead.

SECTION 9.5.2: TYPE OF DESIGN

John is doing an exploratory design, guided by Berry's ideas. His goal is to use narrative data from individual interviews inductively to generate new ideas about refugee strengths and their relationships to acculturation outcomes. This could be considered use of grounded theory.

SECTION 9.5.3: POPULATION OF INTEREST, UNIT OF ANALYSIS, AND SAMPLING

John is going to use Bosnian refugees as his subjects. His population of interest would be all Bosnian refugees, particularly those who have been in the country long enough to have clear adaptation outcomes. He is particularly interested in finding people with different adaptations and determining what relationships individual strengths had to those adaptation outcomes. John will therefore use theoretical sampling to recruit subjects with a wide range of adaptation outcomes. He is going to set up his sampling frame as Bosnians using services or attending events at the Resettlement House, an agency providing services to this population. John is doing an exploratory study and wants to sample a broad a range of people who have had different types of outcomes. He has a two-step plan. First, he intends to recruit in a way that will get him a broad array of people. He hands out flyers at the Resettlement House asking for volunteers for interviews and offering a $20 reimbursement (John has been able to get a small amount of seed money from his school). The only limitation on the flyer as to who can attend is that the person must have been in the United States for at least a year. John will also put up flyers in the community, in businesses, and in public areas frequented by Bosnian refugees. Second, he will attempt to determine if he has managed to gather a sufficiently broad sample by discussing the preliminary findings with agency staff who have experience with the Bosnian refugees served by the agency. If the agency staff can identify particular themes or types of clients with whom they are familiar but who do not appear represented in the data, John will attempt to gain the agency's help in purposively recruiting individuals who can stand as examples of these missing types of people.

John does not speak Bosnian. He therefore plans to have an interpreter present at the interviews who can interpret from Bosnian to English and vice versa. Because of John's growing relationship with the agency, and because of the agency's interest in the subject matter, Resettlement House has been kind enough to provide him an interpreter free of charge (although John will have to work around the interpreter's schedule at the agency).

John's main design task is putting together his questionnaire (Figure 9.6). He includes both a structured section with closed-ended questions and a section with open-ended questions. The structured questions are mainly to get a sense for the people he is interviewing and to help with later analysis. John reviewed the questions with the interpreter and with individuals at the agency, resulting in some slight changes in wording and focus, and the addition of a new question (item 3).

John has kept the questions few in number because he expects the interpreter to slow the interviews considerably. Fortunately, his core questions are fairly simple and easily covered. The opening questions are very brief and intended to capture only the most important demographic information about the subject. The next three (open-ended) questions are broad "grand tour" questions. The fourth through sixth questions use a systems or ecological framework to elicit specific responses across the ecological spectrum. Questions 7 through 9 are attempts to gain further specific information, while question 10 is a "backstop" question intended to get anything that might have been missed. Question 3 is a little bit "double-barreled," but John considers people and their pasts to be intertwined, so he decided to put these ideas together. John is planning to do about 20 interviews to start, and he will then reassess to see if he needs more interviews or needs to add other kinds of people. This is a sufficiently large number to allow John to get a sense for responses and to let him see if he is reaching saturation in the data.

FIGURE 9.6.   **Questions for John's Bosnian Immigrant Study.**

Date: _____   Time: _____   Location: _____
Subject Age [18–24] [25–29] [30–39] [40–49] [50–59] [60–69] [70+]
Years in United States [   ]
Subject Gender [M] [F]
Married or living with partner? [Y] [N]
How many children in family? _____
Subject describes English skills as: Good [   ]   Some English [   ]   Little or No English [   ]
Highest educational level achieved in Bosnia (grade level/years of college): _____
Highest educational level achieved in U.S. (grade level/years of college): _____
Employment: [ ] Not currently   [ ] Specify: _____

Question #1:   How would you describe your adaptation to life in the United States?
Question #2:   What were the most important things that made a difference in how you adapted to life here?
Question #3:   What can you tell me about your decision to leave Bosnia?
Question #4:   What things about yourself or your past experiences were important in your adjustment to life in the United States?
Question #5:   What role did your family play in how you adjusted to adaptation to life in the United States?
Question #6:   What things about your neighborhood or community were important in your adjustment to the United States?
Question #7:   What was most helpful in your adjustment to the United States?
Question #8:   What was least helpful in your adjustment to the United States?
Question #9:   What abilities or strengths were most important to you in helping you adapt to the United States?
Question #10:   Is there anything else that you can tell us that would help us understand your adaptation to the United States?

[Author's note: In actuality, this route would be printed with two questions per page, using one-sided copying, allowing space on each page (and on the back) for notes to be taken.]

SECTION 9.5.4: CONSTRUCTS AND VARIABLES

John is asking questions about experiences, circumstances, strengths, and adaptations from an ecological framework. Because he is doing an inductive study, he expects his constructs and variables to emerge during the process of the interviews.

SECTION 9.5.5: CONTROL

Control is not a focus of this exploratory design.

SECTION 9.5.6: STRENGTHS AND LIMITATIONS OF DESIGN

John is trusting to luck, to some degree, to make sure his sample is adequately broad. Ideally, a more structured approach to getting a wider range of participants would be good. Obviously, he is also limited to Bosnians getting services at the Resettlement House. This can be a substantial weakness because he may miss altogether certain groups of assimilated people who no longer use immigrant-specific services.

SECTION 9.5.7: TIME LINE

John is hoping to do his interviews within a month and then to determine if further interviews are needed. He then hopes to spend an additional month in data analysis and interpretation and a final month in writing up the project. This is an ambitious schedule that he may well have trouble meeting.

SECTION 9.5.8: IRB ISSUES

John does an IRB application including the above questions, a description of how he will perform the study, and what the risks and benefits to subjects are.

He stresses that there will be a counselor on call in the agency to immediately intervene should recollection of past traumatic events cause such intervention to be needed. His consent form is also included and follows the same format as the one on page 174 with only minor modifications. The consent form stresses that the tapes will be destroyed after they are transcribed and that there will be no names or other identifying information transcribed. The questions were left specifically vague in some regards (e.g., age, number of children) to avoid any possibility that the data could be backtracked to the subject.

REVIEW

1. For each of the five examples above, list the weakest aspect of the design.
2. For each of the five examples above, list the strongest aspect of the design.
3. Rank the five studies above in order of their internal validity. Explain.
4. Rank the five studies above in order of their external validity. Explain.
5. Pick one of the examples above and change all the instruments. Justify your choices for new instruments.
6. Write up why you might reject the IRB application of one of the above studies. What changes would be needed for you to grant permission to do the work?

COMPUTERS IN RESEARCH

SUPPLEMENTAL READINGS

It is hard to imagine doing social research without computers. Without the ability to store and use large amounts of data and perform analyses with lightning speed, modern social research could not exist. If you want to learn research, you simply have to learn to do it on computers.

SECTION 10.1
WHAT ARE COMPUTERS USED FOR IN RESEARCH?

Computers have the following uses:

- Data input for quantitative data (Excel) or qualitative data (word processors, NVivo)
- Data management for quantitative data (Excel, SAS, SPSS)
- Data management for qualitative data (word processors, NVivo)
- Data analysis for quantitative data (SAS, SPSS)
- Data analysis for qualitative data (NVivo)

SECTION 10.1.1: WHICH COMPUTER PROGRAMS ARE COVERED IN THIS BOOK?

We have chosen to focus on one spreadsheet (Excel) and one qualitative program (NVivo) because these programs are both easy to use and very commonly used. If you are a student, it is likely you have access to them, as students at our university do. We have chosen to focus on two statistical programs, however, because both are very commonly used. In our opinion, SAS is more powerful, better at data management, and more commonly used by advanced researchers such as Ph D students or professors. It is also, in our opinion, not user friendly. Most programming in SAS is done by typing in commands, not through the use of windows. Many people find SPSS

easier to use. It has a very nice window-driven interface. While somewhat more limited than SAS, master's-level students may find it to be better for their needs. There are a range of other programs available, but we simply could not cover them all. If you have a basic understanding of SAS and SPSS, the other programs should look pretty similar.

SECTION 10.1.2: WHAT WILL I LEARN IN THIS CHAPTER?

You will be introduced to four programs. Each of these programs has literally hundreds of options and special features. Learning any of them completely would take forever and is not necessary. Instead, you will now learn the following things:

- How to start each program
- How to input data into each program
- How to manage data in each program
- How to save your work in each program
- How to do very basic analyses in SAS, SPSS, and NVivo

Really mastering these programs will be useful only if you pursue a research career. Most people we know teach themselves what they need to know. Once you finish this chapter, you can stop, learn on your own, or pick up one of the many excellent how-to books we reference at the end of the chapter. We also provide much more detail on how to use these programs for data management and analysis later in the book (Chapters 11–15). There are whole categories of computer programs we aren't even going to address. Perhaps the most important of these are GIS (geographic information systems) programs such as ArcView. Such programs allow analysis of data linked to maps. Again, there are excellent books available to you, and we try to reference a few below.

Before we get to that material, however, let's look at an Excel spreadsheet.

SECTION 10.2
SPREADSHEETS (EXCEL)

One of the oldest kinds of programs for personal computers is spreadsheets. Spreadsheets are basically "living" tables. They do two main things:

1. They store data in boxes (cells) in a two-dimensional grid (sheet).

2. They let you calculate values for some cells on the sheet based on other cells. That sounds more confusing than it is. Basically, you pick a cell and tell the computer to use it to give the answer of a math computation involving other cells. For example, cell Y4 (column Y, row 4—easy, huh?) might be the sum of the numbers in cells Y2 and Y3. You would do this by typing "=Y2+Y3" into the Y4 cell.

All this is surprisingly easy to do, and many of you probably have been using spreadsheets for years.

HOW TO START EXCEL

Double-click on the icon, and you'll see the screen shown in Figure 10.1. That's the sheet, actually, "Sheet1," as you can see at the bottom of the screen. Note that each box, or cell, is at the intersection of a lettered column and a number. The top left box is A1, and the box in the lowest right is L25. This sheet goes on pretty much forever right and down, and you can move around using the scrolling bars on the side and bottom.

FIGURE 10.1. A Blank Excel Spreadsheet.

SECTION 10.2.1: INPUTTING DATA IN EXCEL—HOW TO DO IT

We suggest you take data from paper and type them directly into Excel. We suggest the following steps:

1. Use Row 1 to label your variables. Just highlight a box and type in a label for what's going to go underneath.

2. Use columns for your variables. Every variable should have a column.

3. Type in the values.

INPUTTING DATA IN EXCEL—AN EXAMPLE

Let's say you have a survey of male prisoners. You want to find out about their involvement in prison violence. You think that people who are planning to get out soon and are future oriented may not be as likely to be involved in violence. You put together the survey shown in Figure 10.2.

FIGURE 10.2. A Hypothetical Survey.

Neville River Institute Survey

1) What is your age in years? [_____]

2) What is your race or ethnicity? (check one)
☐ Asian or Pacific Islander   ☐ Black/African-American
☐ Hispanic/Latino   ☐ White   ☐ Other

3) What crime are you serving time for?
[_____]

4) How many years have you served on your current sentence? [____]

5) How many years until you expect to be released? [_____]

For the items below, check either "Yes" or "No."

6) Have you seen a prisoner injuring another prisoner on purpose in the last year? (check one)
YES ☐   NO ☐

7) Have you yourself been injured by another prisoner in the last year? (check one)
YES ☐   NO ☐

8) In the past year, have you gone to the prison hospital because you were hurt by another prisoner? (check one)
YES ☐   NO ☐

For the items below, check the box that best answers the question for you.

9) How much do you think about what you will do when you get out of jail?
☐ Never ☐ Rarely   ☐ Sometimes   ☐ Often   ☐ Very Often

10) How much do you think about what job you will get after jail?
☐ Never ☐ Rarely   ☐ Sometimes   ☐ Often   ☐ Very Often

11) How much do you talk to other inmates about what you will do when you get out of jail?
☐ Never ☐ Rarely   ☐ Sometimes   ☐ Often   ☐ Very Often

THANK YOU FOR COMPLETING THIS FORM.

The form in Figure 10.2 requires some explanation:

■ The "What crime are you serving time for?" question was coded later as 1 if the crime was violent (such as murder or assault) or 0 if the crime was not violent (drugs, burglary).

- Items 6 through 8 are the PVS, the Prison Violence Scale (a fictional scale for this example only), which measures involvement in prison violence.
- Items 9 through 11 are the FOS(PV), the Future Orientation Scale Prisoner Version (a fictional scale for this example only), which is a measure of the degree to which people are looking forward to and planning for the future.

The sheet in Figure 10.3 shows the data from the form in Figure 10.2 after it has been typed in to Excel. The variable names are along the top, the ID numbers of each respondent are along the left side, and the values from their responses are in the cells. Note that prisoners serving life terms were indicated as having "99" years left on their terms (cell E8). This will have to be remembered later if calculations are made about average time left to serve. The labels for each column were selected to be simple and easy to understand. The PVS and FOS items were labeled with their question number on the survey and what scale they belonged to, for clarity.

FIGURE 10.3. A Spreadsheet with Data from the Survey in Figure 10.2.

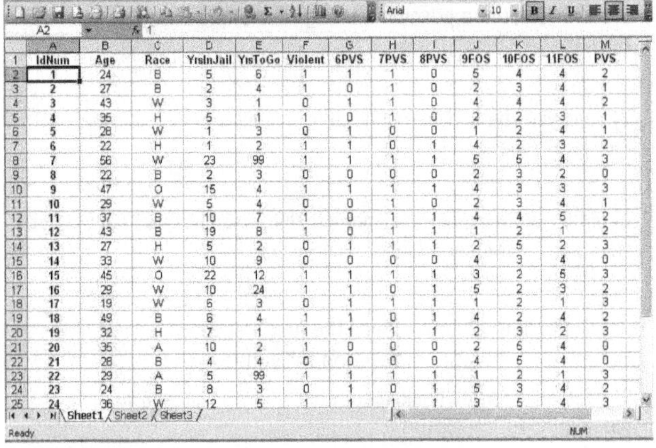

	A	B	C	D	E	F	G	H	I	J	K	L	M
1	IdNum	Age	Race	YrsInJail	YrsToGo	Violent	6PVS	7PVS	8PVS	9FOS	10FOS	11FOS	PVS
2	1	24	B	5	6	1	1	1	0	5	4	4	2
3	2	27	B	2	4	1	0	1	0	2	3	4	1
4	3	43	W	3	1	0	1	1	0	4	4	4	2
5	4	35	H	5	1	1	0	1	0	2	2	3	1
6	5	28	W	1	3	0	1	0	0	1	2	4	1
7	6	22	H	1	2	1	1	0	1	4	2	3	2
8	7	56	W	23	99	1	1	1	1	5	5	4	3
9	8	22	B	2	3	0	0	0	0	2	3	2	0
10	9	47	O	15	4	1	1	1	1	4	3	3	3
11	10	29	W	5	4	0	0	1	0	2	3	4	1
12	11	37	B	10	7	1	0	1	1	4	4	5	2
13	12	43	B	19	8	1	0	1	1	1	2	1	2
14	13	27	H	5	2	0	1	1	1	2	5	2	3
15	14	33	W	10	9	0	0	0	0	4	3	4	0
16	15	45	O	22	12	1	1	1	1	3	2	5	3
17	16	29	W	10	24	1	1	0	1	5	2	3	2
18	17	19	W	6	3	0	1	1	1	1	2	1	3
19	18	49	B	6	4	1	1	0	1	4	2	4	2
20	19	32	H	7	1	1	1	1	1	2	3	2	3
21	20	35	A	10	2	1	0	0	0	2	6	4	0
22	21	28	B	4	4	0	0	0	0	4	5	4	0
23	22	29	A	5	99	1	1	1	1	1	2	1	3
24	23	24	B	8	3	0	1	0	1	5	3	4	2
25	24	36	W	12	5	1	1	1	1	3	5	4	3

Section 10.2.2: Managing Data in Excel

Calculating Cell Values Based on Other Cells

You will often want to create cells that show numerical calculations. For example, if you have a list of different times it took a person to do a task, you might want the average time. You can get this in SPSS or SAS, but you can also do it in Excel. To do this, you pick any cell and type in an equals sign (=) and then the calculation. In the above example, let's say the person's times are stored in C4, C5, and C6. The average would be (C4+C5+C6)/3. To get this value in cell C7, simply go to that cell and type in =(C4+C5+C6)/3. Hit <Enter>, and the value appears.

Formatting Cells

In the above example, you might get a result such as 5.342528, but maybe you want only the first two decimal places (5.34). This is easily solved. Go to the cell (or drag-highlight a bunch of cells) and right click. Select "Format Cells." Under the "Number" tab, select "Number" and tell it how many decimal places you want it to recognize. That's it. This same general approach can get you text, percentages, date formats, and other things. Play around with it and you'll get a feel for it.

Example

Our example includes two scales, both of which need to be summed. We will do this in columns M and N. In the example in Figure 10.4, we have already formatted the value for the PVS variable in column M. We typed =G2+H2+I2, hit <Enter>, and then copied and pasted to the rest of the column. We have just typed =J2+K2+L2 into cell N2. We are about to hit <Enter> and then copy and paste to the rest of the N column. Notice that Excel helpfully outlines the cells being used in the current calculation.

FIGURE 10.4. Performing Calculation with Excel.

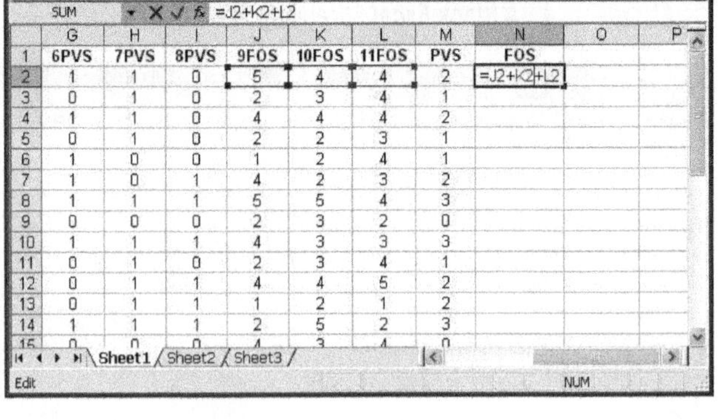

	G	H	I	J	K	L	M	N	O	P
1	6PVS	7PVS	8PVS	9FOS	10FOS	11FOS	PVS	FOS		
2	1	1	0	5	4	4	2	=J2+K2+L2		
3	0	1	0	2	3	4	1			
4	1	1	0	4	4	4	2			
5	0	1	0	2	2	3	1			
6	1	0	0	1	2	4	1			
7	1	0	1	4	2	3	2			
8	1	1	1	5	5	4	3			
9	0	0	0	2	3	2	0			
10	1	1	1	4	3	3	3			
11	0	1	0	2	3	4	1			
12	0	1	1	4	4	5	2			
13	0	1	1	1	2	1	2			
14	1	1	1	2	5	2	3			
15	0	0	0	4	3	4	0			

Saving Work in Excel

Go to the top and hit "File" and then "Save as." This feature works just like a word processor.

Section 10.2.3: Other Features of Excel—Graphs and Charts

Excel is very useful for making graphs and other visual presentations of data. This is done as follows:

FIGURE 10.5. **Creating a Bar Graph in Excel.**

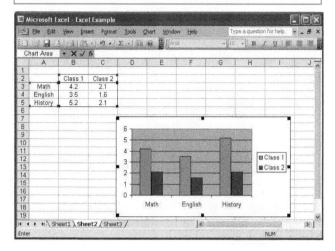

- Type in a table that you want the graph or chart to use.
- Highlight that area.
- Select the bar graph icon at the top of the screen.
- Follow the instructions.

Again, Excel provides an easy and user-friendly package. Mess around with this a bit and you will easily figure it out. It uses almost exactly the same controls as a word processor. In the example in Figure 10.5, we have created a table showing average scores for Class 1 and Class 2 in Math, English, and History. You can select the table, copy it ("Edit/Copy") and then paste it into a word processor such as Microsoft Word, if you like. We do this all the time for our journal articles. This is also how most of the graphs in this book were made.

The graph in Figure 10.5 is the basic default version, without any options. Play around and discover how to do such things as change the look of the graph, add the actual numerical values to the graph, and so on.

That's really all you need to enter data and do some basic data management in Excel. Next, we'll look at SPSS, which is a bit more challenging.

SECTION 10.3
STATSTICAL ANALYSIS SOFTWARE (SPSS)

SPSS is a relatively user-friendly software but is not as powerful (can't do as much) as SAS in some areas. While both SAS and SPSS have the capability of point-and-click analyses, this is the primary means of using SPSS, whereas SAS users tend to rely on programming statements (lines of typed commands). You can use programming statements in SPSS, but few people do this. It is really set up to be a windows point-and-click

approach to data management and analysis. It also uses a visual spreadsheet (very much like those in Excel) to display your data. Partly because of this, SPSS is not an optimal choice for working with very large data sets (such as those with tens of thousands of cases). It is also not the best way to go when data management is the primary task you are facing. We will only cover the menu-driven approach to SPSS. Our favorite "getting started" guide for SPSS can be found online at www.und.ac.za/users/clarke/support/click_spss_feb_2003.pdf. That site, however, refers to version 11.5. Our text examples and these instructions use the similar but updated SPSS version 14.0 for Windows.

SECTION 10.3.1: GETTING READY TO LEARN: PREPARE YOUR COMPUTER FOR A FUN INTERACTIVE EXPERIENCE

First, SPSS must be loaded into your computer or on your department's network. Locate the icon and click on it to activate the program. On your computer, you will see a screen like the one in Figure 10.6 on top of a spreadsheet and SPSS window. We highly recommend that you take the time to do the tutorial. We are providing only a minimal introduction here.

FIGURE 10.6. **An SPSS Screen.**

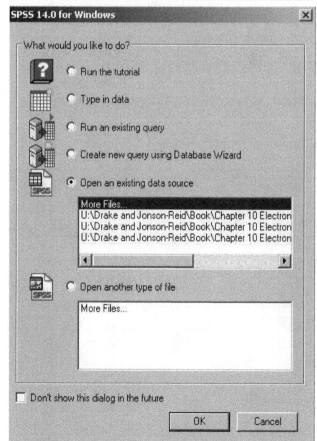

The program will default to (put you at) "Open an existing data source." This works fine for inputting most kinds of data. In this case, we will input a file called "SPSS Example.DBF," a Database (.dbf) file that includes Professor Kathy's data (access at www.ablongman. com/mysocialworkkit). This file can be found in the electronic example material associated with this book if you'd like to follow along on your own computer. There are also several example files that come with SPSS.

After you click "OK," SPSS will bring the data into a spreadsheet environment. It may also show you an output screen (not shown), which you can close. This screen just tells you how SPSS understood your data. The "Data View" tab will let you visually inspect the data. If we look at the "Data View" tab located toward the bottom of the SPSS screen, we see a spreadsheet displaying Kathy's data. Across the top are the command areas—very much like any other Windows program. Under "File" you will find import and export commands for data, save, print, page setup, and so on. Under "Edit" you find the typical cut-and-paste commands. Under "View" you can request different toolbars or screen appearances (see Figure 10.7).

First take a brief look at the "Variable View" tab below the spreadsheet. When we click on this view, we find the variable list and variable characteristics. This "View" area allows you to alter variables through a point-and-click method instead of using format statements in programs that require actual data programming. In other words, we can use this view screen to alter variable characteristics.

In the first column of the variable view (see Figure 10.8), one sees a listing of the variables with whatever names they currently have. After this, the columns indicate various attributes of those variables.

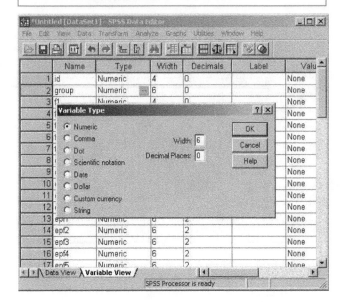

FIGURE 10.8. "Variable View" in SPSS.

These can be altered for a specific variable by going to the cell that corresponds to a given variable in the column that describes the attribute of interest. For example, we have clicked on the cell corresponding to the "type" column for the variable called "group." Currently, the variable type is "numeric," but if we wanted SPSS to treat it as a character value, we could click on the circle in front of the word *string* instead. In "computerese" the word *string* and the word *character* both mean the same thing relative to the type of data entered. A string or character variable cannot be treated as a number (even if it looks like a number). As you can see, this same screen also allows you to decide the width (how many spaces you have to store this variable) and the number of decimal places. Another commonly used column is the "Label" column. You can select any cell and change the label for that variable. This is then included in the printout of results.

Now, let's go back to our "Data View" by clicking on the tab. Let's look at the command row at the top of the screen. The "File," "Edit," and "View" menus include commands similar to those you see in most computer programs (save, delete, and the like). We will not spend time on these menu areas, except to point out the import function of SPSS. When we opened SPSS, we selected a data set to open, but you can also do this within SPSS by going to the "File" menu and selecting "Open," and "Data." This allows you to browse for and open files. Make sure you are looking for the right type of file (see "Files of type" window).

Now, we will turn to the four menu areas we will focus on for the remainder of the SPSS section: "Data," "Transform," "Analyze," and "Graphs."

FIGURE 10.7. **SPSS Spreadsheet.**

	id	group	f1	f2	f3	f4	f5	e1
1	1	1	6	8	4	5	7	
2	2	1	6	6	10	6	7	1
3	3	1	4	6	4	5	11	
4	4	1	4	4	8	6	4	
5	5	1	4	7	6	8	5	
6	6	1	7	3	5	3	5	1
7	7	1	7	8	7	5	4	
8	8	1	2	6	7	4	7	
9	9	1	5	5	4	6	7	
10	10	1	4	6	5	5	6	
11	11	1	7	7	4	9	8	1
12	12	1	6	3	3	6	3	1
13	13	1	7	5	5	7	10	1
14	14	1	4	6	5	1	6	
15	15	1	6	3	6	10	4	
16	16	1	5	5	1	6	5	

FIGURE 10.9. The "Data" Menu in SPSS.

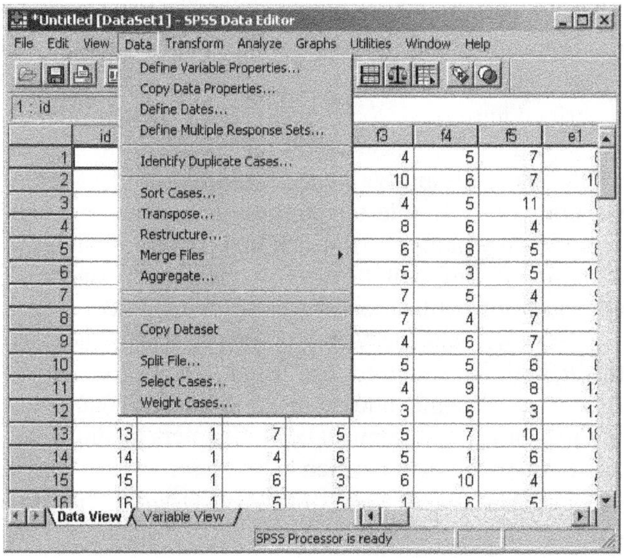

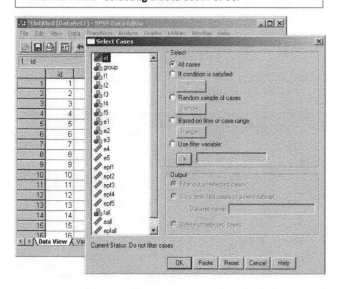

FIGURE 10.11. The "Transform" Menu in SPSS.

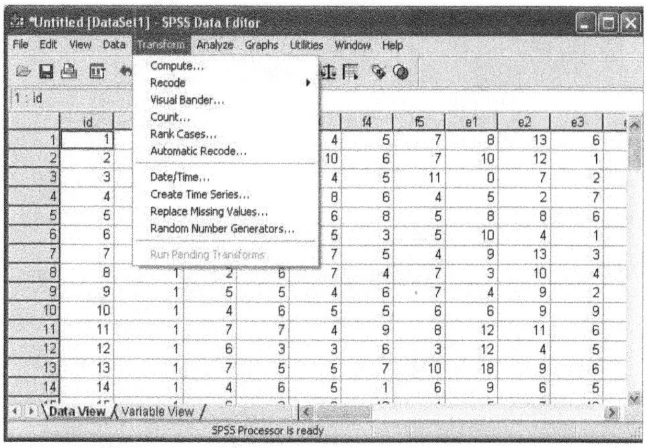

The "Data" menu (Figure 10.9) allows you to manipulate the variables or data files. For example, if we click on "Select Cases," we can select a portion of the data set we are interested in (see Figure 10.10). This is very useful if we have a large data set that we wish to analyze by subsample.

Again, the idea of this chapter is just to give you a flavor for working with the program, so we won't go through every command here. Let's move on to the "Transform" menu (Figure 10.11).

SPSS lets you mess with and change ("recode") existing variables. This is handy if you want to create new variables that are modified from prior ones. For example, let's say Professor Kathy decides she wants to

recode how her groups are labeled. In her design, Group 1 is the classical music group, Group 2 is the easy listening group, and Group 3 is the no music group. Let's say she wants to combine Groups 1 and 2 into an "any music" group and leave Group 3 as "no music." She may want to recode members of Groups 1 and 2 as "1" (music), and members of Group 3 as "2" (no music). This is how she does it:

Professor Kathy goes to "Transform," then to "Recode" and finally to "Into Different Variables" (Figure 10.12). You will usually want to use the "Into Different Variables" option, as this will create a new variable instead of overwriting an old one. Overwriting is rarely a good idea, because you will usually want to be able to refer back to your source variables.

Now Professor Kathy sees the "Recode into Different Variables" screen (Figure 10.13). She first selects the "group" variable from the left side by

FIGURE 10.10. Selecting a Data Set in SPSS.

FIGURE 10.12. Using the "Recode" Command in SPSS.

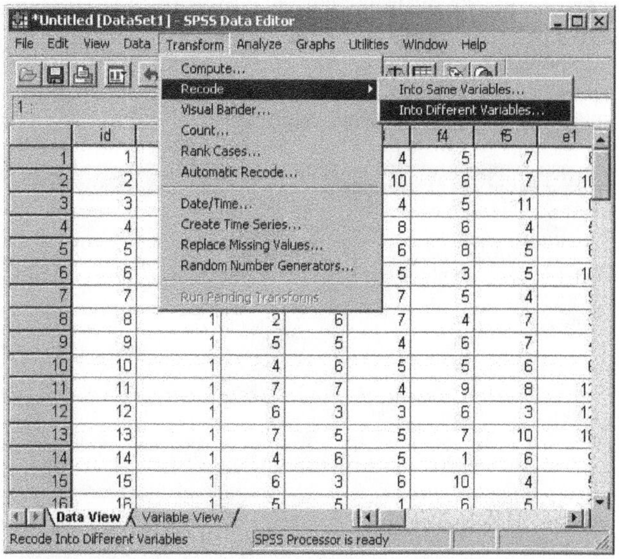

FIGURE 10.13. **Recoding a Variable in SPSS.**

FIGURE 10.13. **Recoding a Variable in SPSS.**

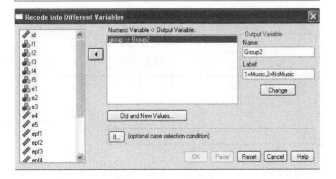

highlighting that variable and hitting the right-pointing triangle button. Under "Output Variable" she puts "Group2" in the "Name:" window and "1=Music, 2= NoMusic" in the "Label" window. She then hits "Change."

Now that she has identified which variable will be used, and what the new variable will be called and labeled, she has to tell the computer how to change it. To do this she hits the "Old and New Values" button and sees the screen shown in Figure 10.14. First, she has to make sure that a "Group" value of 3 (no music) becomes a value of 2 (no music) in "Group2." She does this by using the "Value" window under "Old Value" and entering "3." Then under "New Value" she hits the "Value" window and enters "2." Next, she wants to change values of "1" or "2" in "Group" to a value of "1" (music) in "Group2." On the left side, she clicks the dot by "Range" and puts in a value of "1" in "Range, LOWEST . . ." and a value of "2" in "Range, HIGHEST. . . ." On the right side, under "New Value," she hits the dot by "Value" again, entering "1" (this is the screen condition as shown in Figure 10.14). After hitting "Add," the numeric phrase "1 thru 2 → 1" will appear in the Old→ New window, right under "3 → 2" (this is not pictured in a figure, take our word for it). "Continue" gets her back to the "Recode into Different Variables" screen and "OK" gets her fin-

ished with the data recoding altogether, dumping her back to her data editor screen.

The previous example is only a taste of what SPSS can do in recoding, and you will find that you'll pick up other capabilities pretty fast just by using the screens described here.

Just a final quick note on the "Transform" menu. SPSS has a missing value replacement ability, but it uses only very simple techniques, such as using mean values (see Chapter 13), which may suffice for a class assignment but will not be a sufficiently rigorous approach for publication or a broader audience.

Next, we have the "Analyze" menu. This is where all the statistical techniques are listed. You will probably need to spend some time exploring this area to figure out where a particular test might be. In Chapters 13 and 14 we guide you to the right location for the tests covered in this text. For example, for a t-test, our text will guide you to do the following: Go to Analyze ⇒ Compare Means ⇒ and then select the particular type of test.

Basically the first two options in the "Analyze" menu provide descriptive information and the remainders relate to statistical tests—but this is not always the case. For example, chi-square statistics are located in the "Crosstab" submenu of the "Descriptive Statistics" option.

As an example, we're going to continue using Professor Kathy's data and we will do a t-test to see if the mean number of errors (epfall) is significantly different for music (Group2="1") and no music (Group2="2") conditions.

From the Data Editor screen, hit "Analyze," "Compare Means," "Independent-Samples T-Test" (see Figure 10.15). Don't worry about what test you will be using on your own data right now (we'll cover that in Chapters 13 and 14). In this case, you're going to have to decide what value the t-test will be testing (in this case it is errors per file, "epfall") and scoot that variable into the "Test Variable(s)" window using the right-pointing triangle button. Next, you need to tell the computer who is in which of the groups you are comparing. Scoot "Group2" (which identifies who is in the no music and

FIGURE 10.14. **Old and New Values.**

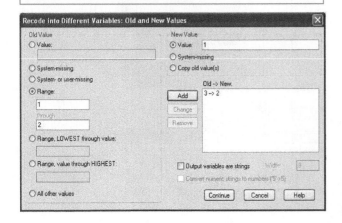

FIGURE 10.15. **SPSS Data Editor.**

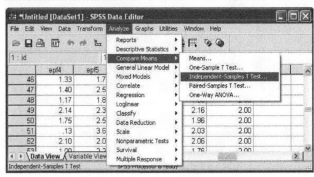

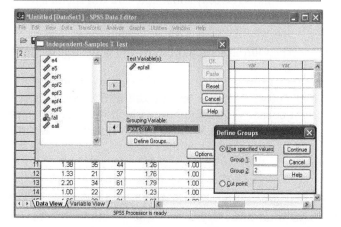

FIGURE 10.16. **Independent-Samples T Test.**

only to provide enough of an introduction to allow you to follow the later text in the analysis chapters. Further, later in the analysis chapters you will note that certain techniques we present in SAS do not have a counterpart in the SPSS menus. It may be possible for more advanced SPSS users to use programming statements with the Syntax Editor to call for these procedures. As stated earlier, our intent is only to provide instruction in how to access SPSS in the windows menu version.

For a more detailed guide for SPSS, check out the following resource:

Clarke, P. (2003). Click-Start Guide: SPSS 11.5 for Windows. http://www.und.ac.za/users/clarke/support/click_spss_feb_2003.pdf

Einspruch, E. (2005). *An Introductory Guide to SPSS for Windows*. Thousand Oaks, CA: Sage Publications Ltd.

Note that the first resource refers to an older version of SPSS, but many of the suggestions are still applicable.

music groups) into the "Grouping Variable" window (triangle button time again). You will see a weird (?,?) thingy, which is OK; this just means you still have to tell the computer how to understand the "Group 2" variable. To do this, click "Define Groups" and you will see a new screen pop up (Figure 10.16). Tell the computer that people with a Group2 value of "1" will be "Group 1:" and that people with a Group2 value of "2" will be "Group 2:" Hit "continue" and "OK" and you're done.

Now you can see the nifty output screen (Figure 10.17). This screen is larger than you can see in Figure 10.17, the part you can't see (below) giving you lots of other information (such as statistical significance). The part you can see tells you that the no music people appear to have made fewer errors per file (about 1.61) compared to the music people (about 1.85).

In the graphics menu we find various chart commands that are very similar to those in Excel. This is also where we find graphic tools for assessing distribution of variables (such as boxplot), linear relationships (such as scatter/dot), or even predictive utility of a logistic regression model (such as ROC curve). We will cover some of these in Chapters 13 and 14.

Of course, this brief introduction cannot do justice to the full range of SPSS capabilities. We are attempting

SECTION 10.4
STATSTICAL ANALYSIS SOFTWARE (SAS)

SAS is very powerful but not very user friendly. It can be learned only by doing it, and most people find that they spend a lot of time typing in and repeating language that they really don't understand, at least until they get more experience. That's OK. We're going to teach SAS by providing you with the exact code (or "programming," or "language," or "words") that you need to do what you need to do. There are also many SAS programs provided to you in electronic form accompanying this book. Stick with it; don't try to make too much sense of it at first; and see if you can get the darn thing to run. Unfortunately, some of the most confusing things about SAS are the first things you need to do: loading data and making data sets.

SECTION 10.4.1: WHAT DOES SAS DO?

SAS provides superior ability to manage data and analyze data statistically. It can show you your data in a large number of ways, including a limited graphic ability.

SECTION 10.4.2: GETTING READY TO LEARN: PREPARE YOUR COMPUTER FOR A FUN INTERACTIVE EXPERIENCE

Make a folder on your C drive named "statproject." To do this, double-click "My Computer," then "Local Disk (C:)," then "file" (at top left), then "new," then "folder." Make sure you title the folder "statproject." Now copy

FIGURE 10.17.

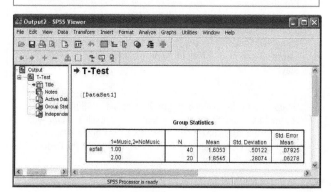

the files "Scores" SASExample from the website www. ablongman.com/mysocialworkkit. Paste them into C:\statproject\. You are now ready to go.

HOW TO START SAS

Do either of the two startup procedures below:

1. Go to the C:\statproject directory under "My Computer" and "Local Disk (C:)." Double-click on the SAS program "SASExample." This opens SAS and loads the program.

2. Go to the C:\statproject directory under "My Computer" and "Local Disk (C:)." Double-click on the SAS program "SASExample." Hit the SAS icon, which should be on your desktop or under "Start," then "All Programs," then "SAS." This opens SAS but does not load a program. To load a program, hit "File" at the top of the screen, then "Open Program," then browse to your directory (C:\statproject) using the window to the right of "Look in:.." Once you get there, click on "SASExample" in the big center screen.

Either of these procedures loads SAS and places you on the basic screen. If you use the second procedure and hit "New Program" instead of "Open Program," you start a new program (a blank editor with no program loaded). Assuming you loaded SASExample, you will see the screen shown in Figure 10.18.

Look at the bottom of Figure 10.18; there are three gray buttons. These are as follows:

■ The Editor is where you type in programs. It is the only screen you can type into. You will spend 90% of your programming time here. The Editor button will carry the name of the program being seen; here it is "SASExample."

■ The Log tells you how the program ran and what mistakes (errors) you made. You will spend a lot of time here looking for red or green text showing you what you did wrong.

■ The Output screen presents you with your findings.

You can keep all three screens up at once if you like, but we generally maximize (hit the icon in upper right corner of active panel) whichever screen we're viewing at the time. We also usually minimize the vertical "Explorer" panel on the left.

GETTING ORIENTED TO SAS: LIBNAMES

Libnames (think of them as "library names") just tell SAS what directory to use when looking for data or making permanent data sets. This is done using the "Libname" statement. An example is shown in Figure 10.19. This means "When I type 'Statp,' please look at the C:\statproject directory." You are allowed to use multiple libnames at the same time, just type additional statements with different names. To review:

■ "Libname" is the command, it is always typed like this.

■ "statp" is our chosen label for the library. It can be anything legal to SAS, but we'd keep it short and start with a character. It could be "project," your name, or even "a" (we use that "a" quite a bit to reduce finger fatigue).

■ "C:\statproject" is the directory (folder) name (not the file name) of the directory that will be your library. Just put in the address of the folder/directory where your file is. *Tip:* Go to the directory using your browser and then copy that

---

FIGURE 10.18. **Getting Started in SAS.**

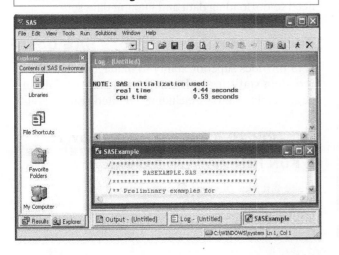

FIGURE 10.19. **The Libname Statement.**

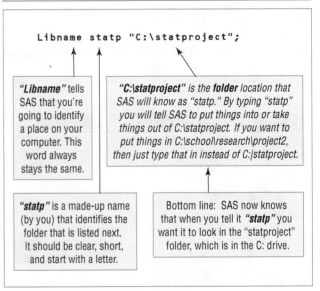

directory location from the browser window and paste it into SAS. This way you avoid any possible spelling mistakes.

■ The ";" tells SAS that the command line is over. You must always do this. Virtually everything you type into SAS will end with a ";". Failure to do this results in confusing error messages.

After you do this, SAS will give you a message saying the libname was "successfully assigned." You have to go to the Log (gray button) to see that message. You should probably check this to make sure it ran. You can now use the libname (statp) in the future.

INPUTTING DATA TO SAS FROM EXCEL (*WARNING!* RUN LIBNAME STATEMENT FIRST)

We're assuming you are going to put your data in Excel first and then move it into SAS. You can use the procedure below for almost any kind of spreadsheet format, not just Excel. You're going to hit "File/Import Data." This will bring up a series of screens as follows:

■ *The first screen:* You go to the white window and hit the little downward-pointing triangle to the right. Select from the options available. For us, this will be "Microsoft Excel 97, 2000, or 2002 Workbook." This tells the computer what type of file you are importing. Hit "Next."

■ *The second screen:* "Connect to MS Excel." Browse and find the location of your source file on your hard drive or wherever. We'll go to "c:\statproject\scores.xls." Hit "OK."

■ *The third screen:* This one asks you what table you want to import. Usually you will have just one table on the spreadsheet, so just hit "Next."

■ *The fourth screen* (part one): This screen asks you where to put the imported stuff. Go to the white

window under "Library" and find the libname you just created. In the example above, this was "statp."

■ *The fourth screen* (part two): Here you must also put in a name for the dataset you are importing. Pick a name and type it in under "Member." Let's say we pick "mydata01."

■ *The fifth screen:* Although this screen isn't necessary, you really should use it. In the white area, type in "C:\import.txt" (or whatever you want, so long as you can find it later). This will copy the commands you just gave into SAS language as a textfile at C:\import.txt. Minimize SAS (yes, you actually have to go do something outside the SAS program here, but it isn't too hard). Go to C:\ using "my computer" and "C:" on your desktop. Open the import.txt file, highlight all the text, and copy it. Go back to SAS and paste the text right into SAS. By the way, you can use ALT-DELETE and ALT-INSERT to cut and paste in just about any program, including Word and SAS. The program editor will look like Figure 10.20.

If you leave that material starting with "PROC IMPORT" and before "RUN;" in your program, it will import data from C:\statproject\scores.xls each time you run the program. This will be a good thing because any changes you make in scores.xls will be updated into your SAS work each time. You should also check the Log again, to make sure everything worked out. Basically, you should check the Log often.

We've come a long way. We've now assigned a libname and imported data into SAS. Those data reside as a permanent SAS data set at C:\statproject\mydata01. You can look at your data as they exist in SAS by typing in "PROC PRINT;RUN;". There will be more about that later, in the analysis chapter.

FIGURE 10.20. Importing.

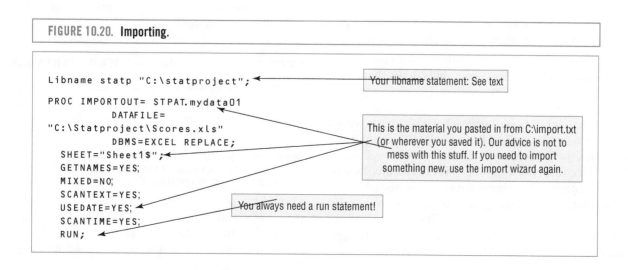

```
Libname statp "C:\statproject";          ◄──  Your libname statement: See text

PROC IMPORT OUT= STPAT.mydata01
          DATAFILE=
"C:\Statproject\Scores.xls"
          DBMS=EXCEL REPLACE;             This is the material you pasted in from C:\import.txt
    SHEET="Sheet1$";                      (or wherever you saved it). Our advice is not to
    GETNAMES=YES;                         mess with this stuff. If you need to import
    MIXED=NO;                             something new, use the import wizard again.
    SCANTEXT=YES;
    USEDATE=YES;        ◄──  You always need a run statement!
    SCANTIME=YES;
    RUN;
```

You still need to learn several more things, though:

- How to run programs
- How to create and access permanent data sets and temporary data sets
- How to do simple calculations in SAS
- How to save programs
- How to save data sets

SECTION 10.4.3: HOW TO RUN PROGRAMS IN SAS

You type in your program and hit the little running man icon at the top of your screen. If you only want to run part of a program, highlight that part and hit the running man. Only that part will run. The program (or part) you run will have to end with a "run;" statement, or it won't run. *Do this:* Hit the button and see what happens. Hit the Log button at the base of the screen. You should see this:

```
NOTE: STATP.MYDATA01 was successfully
created.
NOTE: PROCEDURE IMPORT used (Total process
time):
      real time        1.91 seconds
      cpu time         0.45 seconds
```

That tells you your data set was "successfully created," and everything is OK.

SECTION 10.4.4: PERMANENT DATA SETS AND TEMPORARY DATA SETS

SAS has two kinds of ways of remembering things. You can create permanent data sets at locations (by using a libname), or you can create temporary data sets (by not using a libname):

- Permanent data sets are files stored on your disk. They will still be there when SAS shuts down.
- Temporary data sets exist only in SAS's own memory. When the program shuts down these data sets go away forever.

Permanent data sets always have two parts with a dot in the middle. "STATP.MYDATA01" is a permanent file. It is located at C:\statproject\mydata01. Why? Because the libname STATP means "go to C:\statproject\". Permanent data sets are always in the form [libname].[datasetname]. If you do not specify the libname, or if you use the libname "WORK" (which we never do), then you have created a temporary data set.

Temporary data sets are usually referred to just by the data set's name, with no libname and no dot. *Example:* The following language opens a permanent data set and stores a copy of it as a temporary data set called "TEMP01." Temporary data sets just float around in SAS's brain and disappear forever when SAS is turned off. This is a bad thing if you meant to keep it, but it is a very good thing if the data set is just something temporary that you don't want residing on your computer and cluttering it up.

THE *DATA* AND *SET* TERMS

You no doubt noticed the terms *data* and *set* and wondered what they were for. They are how you bring in and spit out data for each part of your programming. We find the terms confusing, so the way we think about this is "Data is *destination*, Set is *source.*" Almost always when you do something, you need to get data from somewhere and put them somewhere. Some examples are shown in Figure 10.21. We know this is a lot of repetition, but in our experience, students have lots and lots of trouble with this. In our opinion, it is the single hardest thing to learn about SAS.

You can also use SAS to overwrite the current data set instead of creating a new one. To overwrite a file, simply use the same file in the DATA and SET commands, as in Figure 10.22.

In the example in Figure 10.22, we go and get a temporary data set (MYDATA01), and we create a new variable TOTTIME, which is TIME1, TIME2, and TIME3 added together. We then save the data set back again under the old name. This erases the old data set (the one with no variable TOTTIME) and replaces it with the new data set containing TOTTIME. We have just created a new variable in MYDATA01.

What you do between the "SET" and the "RUN" statements is entirely up to you. The example above is just one of many kinds of things that you will do. This is where you do your data management and your analysis. These will be covered in much greater detail in this and following chapters.

SECTION 10.4.5: MAKING NEW VARIABLES

We just saw how you can add a variable to a data set using a simple equation. This is very common. There are other ways you can create new variables too.

MAKING A NEW VARIABLE BASED ON A CALCULATION USING OTHER VARIABLES OR NUMBERS

This is what we saw above. We just did an equation using the new variable name (TOTTIME), putting in an equals sign, then using other variables with plus signs between them. We could have also used minus (−),

FIGURE 10.21. Data Sets.

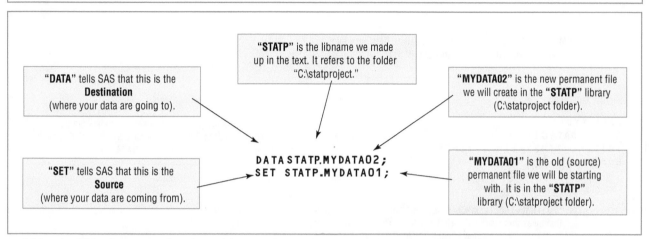

"DATA" tells SAS that this is the **Destination** (where your data are going to).

"STATP" is the libname we made up in the text. It refers to the folder "C:\statproject."

"MYDATA02" is the new permanent file we will create in the **"STATP"** library (C:\statproject folder).

"SET" tells SAS that this is the **Source** (where your data are coming from).

DATA STATP.MYDATA02;
SET STATP.MYDATA01;

"MYDATA01" is the old (source) permanent file we will be starting with. It is in the **"STATP"** library (C:\statproject folder).

(a) Starting With a Permanent Data Set and Creating Another Permanent Data Set

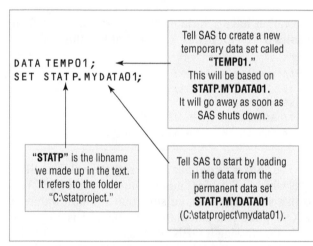

DATA TEMP01;
SET STATP.MYDATA01;

Tell SAS to create a new temporary data set called **"TEMP01."** This will be based on **STATP.MYDATA01.** It will go away as soon as SAS shuts down.

"STATP" is the libname we made up in the text. It refers to the folder "C:\statproject."

Tell SAS to start by loading in the data from the permanent data set **STATP.MYDATA01** (C:\statproject\mydata01).

(b) Starting With a Permanent Data Set and Creating a Temporary Data Set

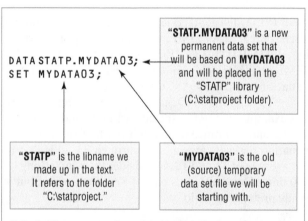

DATA STATP.MYDATA03;
SET MYDATA03;

"STATP.MYDATA03" is a new permanent data set that will be based on **MYDATA03** and will be placed in the "STATP" library (C:\statproject folder).

"STATP" is the libname we made up in the text. It refers to the folder "C:\statproject."

"MYDATA03" is the old (source) temporary data set file we will be starting with.

*Notice that the permanent and temporary data sets in the above example are both called **MYDATA03**. We could have used different names if we had wanted. The above code basically just takes a temporary data set and copies it someplace on the hard drive (C:\statproject) using the same file name.*

(c) Starting with a Temporary Data Set and Creating a Permanent Data Set

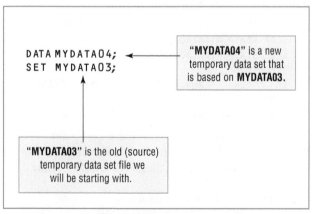

DATA MYDATA04;
SET MYDATA03;

"MYDATA04" is a new temporary data set that is based on **MYDATA03.**

"MYDATA03" is the old (source) temporary data set file we will be starting with.

(d) Starting with a Temporary Data Set and Creating Another Temporary Data Set

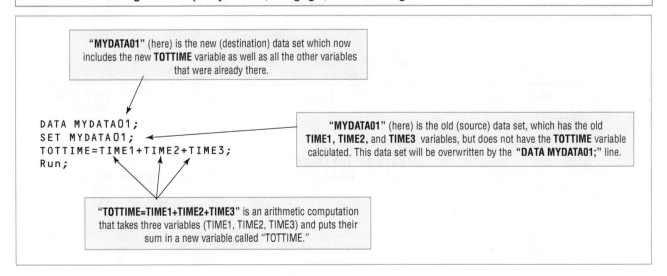

FIGURE 10.22. **Starting with a Temporary Data Set, Changing It, and Overwriting It.**

times (*), or division(/) operators. *Example:* If we hadn't already created AVTIME, we could do so just by typing in "AVTIME=TOTTIME/3;" or "AVTIME=(TIME1+ TIME2+TIME3)/3;". *Another example:* More complex equations such as "SCORE = (((S1+S2+S3)/3) + ((T1+T2)/2))) / (100*Denom23);" are perfectly fine. In this example, SCORE is the new variable, and S1, S2, S3, T1, T2, and Denom23 are already existing variables. The equation basically averages S1 through S3, adds that to the average of T1 and T2, and divides the whole thing by 100 times Denom23. This part of SAS looks scary, but is really pretty easy to do.

Warning about Variable Names. SAS won't let you use a number as a variable name or as the first character in a variable name. TEST3 is acceptable for a variable name, but 3RDTEST is not. "34" is also not acceptable, but "Thirty4" or "Var34" is.

MAKING A NEW VARIABLE AND GIVING EVERY OBSERVATION THE SAME VALUE

Let's say you want everyone in your data set (every observation) to have a variable called "indata" which reads "1" for every observation. The language for that is this:

```
DATA STATP.MYDATA01;
SET  STATP.MYDATA01;
INDATA=1; Run;
```

That's it. Everyone now has a variable INDATA with a value of 1.

MAKING NEW VARIABLES USING "IF / THEN" STATEMENTS

This is also very common. Right now, we have the variable GENDER coded as either "M" or "F." Let's say

we'd rather have a variable "Sex" that is either "1" for females or "0" for males. You do that like this:

```
DATA STATP.MYDATA01;
SET  STATP.MYDATA01;
SEX=.;
IF GENDER="F" THEN SEX=1;
IF GENDER="M" THEN SEX=0; Run;
```

The "Sex=." command just sets the value of SEX to "." which is SAS for "missing numeric variable." You do this so that you make sure that the new value of SEX is what you calculate it to be and is correctly labeled as missing if GENDER is neither "F" nor "M."

More complex calculations are also possible. Let's say you want a variable marking individuals who are both fast (AVTIME = 25 seconds or less) and female (GENDER="F"). You could do this:

```
DATA STATP.MYDATA01;
SET  STATP.MYDATA01;
SPEEDYF=0;
IF GENDER="F" AND AVTIME <= 25 THEN SPEEDYF=1;
RUN;
```

This first gives everyone a SPEEDYF value of 0. It then finds those females who have an average time of 25 seconds or faster and gives them a SPEEDYF value of 1.

GETTING RID OF VARIABLES

To get rid of a variable (say, "score21"), you need to do this:

```
DATA STATP.MYDATA01;
SET  STATP.MYDATA01;
DROP SCORE21;RUN;
```

If you'd prefer, you can substitute "KEEP" for "DROP," in which case SAS keeps only the variables you list. For example, "KEEP ID V1 V2 V3;" would kill off everything in the data set except those four variables.

CHARACTER AND NUMERIC VARIABLES

Let's take a step back and learn a bit about character and numeric variables. If you want to know which of your variables are which, type in this:

```
PROC CONTENTS DATA=STATP.MYDATA01;RUN;
```

This will show you the variables in STATP. MYDATA01. Of course, using a different data set name (either temporary or permanent) will tell you what's in that different data set. PROC CONTENTSDATA= TEMP01; RUN; will tell you what's in the temporary data set TEMP01. The boxed code above will generate this:

ALPHABETIC LIST OF VARIABLES AND ATTRIBUTES

#	Variable	Type	Len	Format	Informat	Label
3	Age	Num	8			Age
7	AvTime	Num	8			AvTime
2	Gender	Char	1	$1.	$1.	Gender
1	IdNum	Num	8			IdNum
4	Time1	Num	8			Time1
5	Time2	Num	8			Time2
6	Time3	Num	8			Time3

This shows all the variables you have, their type (*Num*eric or *Char*acter), how long the character variable(s) are (1 character long, in this case), and what they are labeled (more about that later; what you see above are default labels assigned by SAS based on the variable names). The length of the numeric variables is confusing and won't matter unless you use very very long numbers.

Numeric variables are stored as numbers and are not referenced in quotes. All the variables above except GENDER are numeric.

Character variables are strings of letters, numbers, and other characters. If you want to do something like the above if/then statement, you must refer to the value of the variable in quotation marks.

Warning about Referencing Values in Character Variables. You can't say IF GENDER=F THEN SEX=1;—you must say IF GENDER="F" THEN SEX=1;. SEX does not get quotations because it is numeric.

Warning about Lengths of Character Variables. The length of a character variable is set the *first time* you create it. If you type NAME="A" ; with only one

character between the quotations, then all future NAME variables will be limited to one character long. Why do you care? For example, let's say you type this:

NAME="A";

NAME="Bob";

What happens is the first NAME= sets the length of the character variable to one character long. When you do the second NAME= command, you will end up with "A" being overwritten by "Bob." This is OK, but only the first character of "Bob" will fit in NAME, and the value of NAME will actually be "B." The "ob" fades away into electronic na-na-land.

To avoid this, make sure you put the right number of spaces in the first time you create a character variable, like this:

NAME="   ";

In that example, we put 12 spaces in. If you are copying another variable like this NEWNAME= NAME; then the new variable NEWNAME will have the same length as the source variable NAME, and so you won't usually have a problem.

SECTION 10.4.6: REVIEW—SIMPLE CALCULATIONS IN SAS

As we have seen, SAS can be used to do calculations and create new variables, either using simple computations

```
avscore = (score1 + score2 + score3 +
score4) / 4;
or conditional statements
If Gender="F" and Race="B" then RaceGen=
"BF";.
```

This ability to do quick and easy manipulation of data is possibly SAS's best quality and makes for very easy data management. Sometimes, you will do a calculation based simply on a single variable. For example, if you have a time in hours, you could convert it to minutes like this: **Time=Time*60;**.

SECTION 10.4.7: MAKING NOTES IN YOUR SAS PROGRAM—DOCUMENTATION AND LABELING

Documenting your program is very important. You will probably go back to the program later, and you will probably not remember what each line does. We suggest you use the SAS documentation feature. Basically, any text after a forward slash–asterisk [/*] and before an asterisk–forward slash [*/] is ignored by the computer (becomes green on the SAS editor screen). How you document is a matter of personal style. Anything is

```
/*********************************************************************/
/** Add new variables TOTTIME and SEX, make temporary dataset TEMP01 **/
/** to use while programming.                                       **/
/*********************************************************************/
DATA TEMP01;
SET STATP.MYDATA01;
TOTTIME=TIME1+TIME2+TIME3; /*make TOTTIME as sum of Time1-3*/
IF GENDER="F" THEN SEX=1; /*convert GENDER into SEX (numeric)*/
IF GENDER="M" THEN SEX=0;
LABEL TOTTIME = "Summed total of Time1-3"
      SEX     = "1=Female, 2=Male";
RUN;
```

acceptable so long as it would be clear to anyone. For example, you might do this:

DOCUMENTATION

The code above includes the two kinds of documentation that we use. It includes a top header (the block in asterisks) for the particular part of the program that tells what is going on. We use the asterisk border to make it stand out visually. It also includes side comments on the right showing what each key line does. This may seem silly with such a simple example, but it will be very important as the length and complexity of your programming grow.

LABELING

The above section also includes an example of the "Label" command. Labels are little tags attached to your variables that show up when the computer uses the variable (like in a PROC CONTENTS, PROC PRINT, PROC FREQ, or any statistical test). The label is your chance to tell yourself what is in the variable, so that later on it won't get confusing. Labels should always be given and should be clear to anyone who reads them. Notice that the term "LABEL" only needs to go in once; also notice that the only ";" is at the end of the last variable labeled.

SECTION 10.4.8: HOW TO SAVE PROGRAMS

You must always remember to save your program ("File/Save As"). This is one of the easier features of SAS. However, make absolutely sure that you save *from the program editor*. If you save from the output or log, it will save the output or log instead, and you will lose your program forever. We periodically save extra copies of our program under other names. For example, if we are saving a program backup for a program called "Povanalysis.sas", we might call our backup save "PovanalysisBAK.sas" and save it alongside "Povanalysis.sas" in the same directory.

SECTION 10.4.9: HOW TO SAVE DATA SETS

Any permanent data set (for example, STATP .MYDATA01) is saved when you run the program.

Any temporary data set (such as TEMP01 or WORK. TEMP01) dies when the program shuts down. Follow the instructions above to create permanent data sets.

SECTION 10.4.10: MANAGING DATA IN SAS

This is covered in detail in Chapters 11 and 12. You will find large amounts of sample SAS code there.

SECTION 10.4.11: QUICK SAS FAQ

DO UPPERCASE AND LOWERCASE MATTER?

Here's a two-part answer: First, while programming it does not matter. "DATA TEMP01;" is exactly the same as "Data Temp01;" or "data temp01;". However, there's an exception: While performing operations on character variables, case does matter. *Example:* "IF GENDER="F" then SEX=1;" will make SEX=1 when GENDER is "F" but not when GENDER is "f."

WHAT HAPPENS IF I FORGET TO USE A SEMICOLON AT THE END OF A COMMAND LINE?

The short answer is: Very bad things. You will get confusing error messages. Basically, when you get errors you don't understand, check to make sure you got all the semicolons in the right places. To quote Geena Davis's character in *The Fly*, "Be afraid. Be very afraid." This is another irritating thing about SAS.

CAN I PUT MULTIPLE COMMANDS ON THE SAME LINE?

Yes; the following are exactly the same to SAS:

```
DATA MYDATA;SET MYDATA;DROP VAR02;RUN;
```

or

```
DATA MYDATA;
SET  MYDATA;
DROP VAR02;
RUN;
```

Most people use the second option most of the time to make programming easier to read and debug.

CAN I PUT SPACES ANYWHERE I WANT?

Yes, you can put spaces most places except between quotes. We often do this to line things up. In the example above, there is an extra space after the [SET] so the [MYDATA] text lines up. This makes debugging and cutting and pasting easier.

CAN I DO A VERTICAL CUT-AND-PASTE IN SAS?

Yes; you can highlight and cut-and-paste vertical blocks of text by holding the "Alt" key, just as in Word. If you don't get this, try messing around with highlighting while holding the "Alt" key down and then hitting "Delete," and you'll figure it out.

CAN I SWITCH A VARIABLE FROM CHARACTER TO NUMERIC FORMAT?

Yes, but this can be tricky. First, make sure every value in the variable is really a number. Then execute the following commands. In this example, "areacode" is the variable that starts as a character and that you want to turn into a number called "tempvar":

```
Data INFO; Set INFO;
tempvar=areacode*1;drop areacode;run;
Data INFO; Set INFO;
areacode=tempvar ;drop tempvar ;run;
```

The reason you need two steps is that so long as the old **AREACODE** variable exists, SAS seems to want to stick with the old format. You have to drop the variable altogether, and SAS then forgets it ever existed (computers are pretty stupid) and lets you respecify it as numeric.

CAN I SWITCH A VARIABLE FROM NUMERIC TO CHARACTER FORMAT?

Yes; let's say you have a data set (INFO) with a variable "areacode," which is numeric, and you want it to be character. Do this:

```
Data INFO; Set INFO; a="";tempvar=areacode||a;drop
areacode; run;
Data INFO; Set INFO; areacode=tempvar;drop a
tempvar;run;
```

WHY WOULD I EVER USE A TEMPORARY DATA SET?

We suggest the following:

1. Load in your data and save raw data in a permanent data set.
2. Copy your data to a temporary data set while programming.

3. Resave your data under a different permanent file name when you're finished and the data is how you want it to be.

If you do this, you will never overwrite your original raw data.

WHAT ARE THE MOST IMPORTANT THINGS TO REMEMBER WHILE PROGRAMMING?

Remember to keep it simple, to document well, and to make the program visually easy to read. Why? Because most people spend most of their SAS programming time debugging. Simplicity and good documentation are your best ways to minimize the necessary but unpleasant task of getting rid of errors.

I'M GOING NUTS. I CAN'T FIND THE PROBLEM. HELP!

Did you check to see if your semicolons are in the right places?

Well, that's a brief intro to SAS. There will be much more on SAS later in the book. *Some advice:* The only way to learn is by doing; don't get discouraged. SAS is hard to pick up, and you will probably do a fair amount of messing about until you get a clear sense of what's going on. The authors use SAS at least 10 hours per week, and we still make dumb mistakes.

SECTION 10.5
QUALITATIVE ANALYSIS PACKAGES (NVIVO)

Qualitative data analysis has been done for a very long time, but it has only really been easy to do on computer for the last decade or so. New programs such as NVivo allow much faster and better qualitative analysis in a handy, windows format. This section will provide you with the information you need to input files into NVivo, code those files, and take a preliminary look across the files you coded. More examples in NVivo will be given in the sections on John's project in Chapters 12 and 15.

SECTION 10.5.1: OUR EXAMPLE

We will learn NVivo by using the set of interviews John did for his project. These text files are available to you online at www.ablongman.com/mysocialworkkit in "NVivo test examples," "John's uncoded data," and are titled "Subject01" through "Subject12." We're going to assume you can use a word processor and are likely to start your analysis with transcribed notes or verbatim transcripts. We suggest you load these files into NVivo (we tell you how below), and we suggest you play around with the coding and analysis as you read this. Our examples and what you do won't be exactly the

FIGURE 10.23. **The NVivo Launchpad.**

FIGURE 10.23. **The NVivo Launchpad.**

if you want to open an already existing project? Hit "Open a Project" from the launchpad and browse to wherever the project is by hitting the "Choose" button. Find the folder the project is in and hit "OK." We have found we need to hit "OK" twice.

SECTION 10.5.3: KEY TERMS IN NVIVO— SIMPLE VERSION USING OUR OWN (UNAPPROVED BY QSR) LANGUAGE

- *Documents* are basically text files.
- *Nodes* are lots of things, and we find the term very confusing. For now, you need to know that nodes are used mainly as codes. Each code you enter will be a node. If you code a text as "Intrusive Memory," then you will do that by creating an "Intrusive Memory" node, which remembers where each bit of text marked by you as "Intrusive Memory" is to be found.
- *Attributes* are labels (we think of them as sort of like variables) attached to either documents or nodes. We will discuss attributes only as they apply to documents.
- *Sets* are ways to group documents. If you have 50 interviews from five different locations, it may make sense to keep them in five different sets. We won't focus a lot on sets because they aren't necessary for simple analyses.

same, because you will undoubtedly choose to apply different codes and create different coding schemes.

SECTION 10.5.2: HOW TO START NVIVO

Hit the QSR NVivo icon, and you will see the "launchpad." It looks like Figure 10.23.

From here, you can use the tutorial or create or open a project. Mostly, you'll already have a project going and will hit "Open Project." Right now, though, we need to create a project. Hit that button. Do "Custom" on the next screen (if you don't, your work will be saved in a default location in the QSR directory). The steps here are very simple. Just tell the computer where you want your work stored, what you want to call your project, stuff like that. You have now created a project, even though there is nothing in it. You will now see the "Project Pad," possibly the most important NVivo screen. It looks like Figure 10.24.

You will notice that there are two main tabs, "Documents" and "Nodes." Within each, you can find blue subcategories about "Attributes" and "Sets." What

SECTION 10.5.4: HOW TO LOAD DOCUMENTS (IMPORT TEXT FILES) INTO NVIVO

From the project pad, under "Documents," hit "Create a Document." Use the default on the next page—"Locate and import readable external file(s)." Next, you browse to where your documents are. It is good practice to have already made a folder with the source documents in them so you can easily get to them. NVivo will notice only rich text documents (.rtf) at first, so if your documents are in some other format (the examples used following are just plain text [.txt] files), then you need to go down to the bottom of the screen and adjust the "Files of type" for your format. For this example, we will use the raw .txt files from John's work. You can find these at www.ablongman.com/mysocialworkkit. Highlight the files you want to put in your project. You should see a screen like the one in Figure 10.25.

Hit "Open," use the default (top option) on the next screen, and you're done. You get helpfully bounced back to the project pad.

SECTION 10.5.5: HOW TO ASSIGN VARIABLES (ATTRIBUTES) TO EACH DOCUMENT

Our example data are 12 interviews done by John. These are fairly short text interviews that begin with

FIGURE 10.24. **The NVivo Project Pad.**

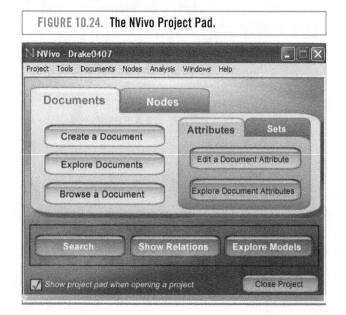

FIGURE 10.24. **The NVivo Project Pad.**

FIGURE 10.25. Loading a Document in NVivo.

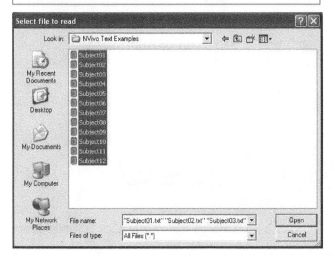

FIGURE 10.26. Assigning Attributes in NVivo.

some information about each subject (such as age, gender, and the like). We will want to attach these variables to each document, and we will do that using document attributes. Warning! Nodes also can have attributes; don't get confused.

What attributes do we want to attach to our documents? We suggest you include any descriptors that you think might be helpful, which might include demographic characteristics (age, sex, etc.), time and place of interview, and the like. You can always add more later, so don't panic.

In our case, at the start of each interview, a number of questions were asked and responses noted at the top of the transcript. These include Age, Education in Bosnia, Education in the United States, English Skills, Who the Person Lives With, Sex, Time in the United States, and Employment. These would be good attributes to start with. You enter them as follows.

From the project pad (documents tab) hit the blue "Attributes" tab and then "Explore Document Attributes." We now need to add our first attribute. Go to "Attribute" (top gray bar) and hit "New Attribute." Next you "Type the new attribute name:". Then hit the <Enter> key and enter another attribute. When you are done, hit "Close."

The documents are listed on the left, and the attributes are over them. You have now assigned attributes, but they are all blank. To fill in each box, just right-click on that box. You can click "New Value" to type in a value, but first look at the top of the little pull-down box. It will list all the values already entered, and you can just click on the one you want. In the screen in Figure 10.26, we have already entered the age and sex values to document "Subject01," have put in the age of "Subject02," and are just about to put in her sex.

That's about all there is to it. You can do such other things as sort, invert the table, delete and add stuff, but all that is pretty easy, and you can figure it out for yourself. You

can look at John's finished attribute table by opening his NVivo project at www.ablongman.com/mysocialworkkit and using the "Explore Document Attribute" button as we described above.

SECTION 10.5.6: HOW TO CODE DOCUMENTS

You will probably spend most of your time coding. Coding is the act of labeling bits of text (content units) with a word or phrase (code). Coding in NVivo is easy and, well, kind of fun. To code, do this:

GETTING THE DOCUMENT BROWSER READY TO CODE

- Open your project in NVivo from the launchpad and "Explore Documents."
- Highlight a document, right-click it, and "Browse/Edit/Code a Document."
- We suggest you maximize this screen so you can see more.
- We suggest you always go to the top gray bar and use the "View" / "Coding Stripes" option. If you don't do this, you won't be able to see what's coded and what isn't.
- Pull up (click on) the "Coder" at the bottom of the screen.

ACTUALLY CODING: CODING IS SIMPLE

- Bring up the "Coder" at the bottom of the screen.
- Highlight some text with your mouse.
- Do **one** of the two options below:
  1. *To create a new code,* type the code name in the little window in the coder and hit the <Enter> key. The highlighted text will be coded (see right side of screen), and the new code (called a node, specifically a purple-ball-like "Free Node") will appear in the large window.

FIGURE 10.27. **A Document Browser in NVivo.**

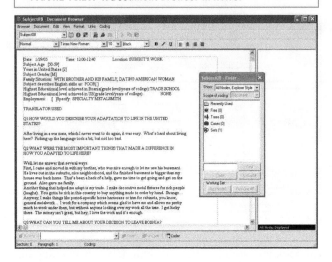

FIGURE 10.28. **Coding in NVivo.**

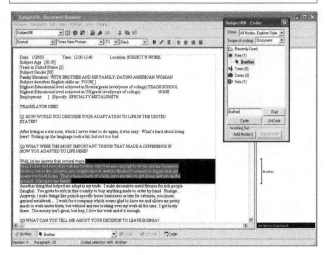

2. *To use an already existing code,* click on the code you want in the larger window, either under purple-ball "Free" nodes or under the "Tree" nodes (see below for how to set up tree nodes). Then hit the "Code" button, and the code will be assigned.

We're going to do an example in a little more detail to help you get this down. We're going to use uncoded data from John's project that we used above when we practiced opening a project. You need to go to wherever you stored that project and click on it. If you didn't do that, just go back to the start of this section and create an NVivo project. Anyway, click on the NVivo icon where you stored the project, and the project pad will pop up. Now go to "Explore Documents," highlight one (we picked Subject08), right click on the highlighted document, and "Browse/Edit/Code Document." Do "View," "Coding Stripes," and pull up (click on) "Coder" at the base of the screen, and you're ready to go. You should see a screen that looks like Figure 10.27.

Let's say we want to code this text, focusing especially on social contacts. We might highlight the part under "Q2" where the guy talks about his brother. We highlight that text with the cursor, go to the coder, type "brother" in the little window above "code," hit the enter key, and hit the code button. We now see the screen pictured in Figure 10.28, with "Brother" added on the right as a code. You might notice that under "Q3" brother comes up again. This time you don't have to type "Brother" in the window, just click on the word "brother" to the right of the purple dot, and NVivo will type the code for you. This saves time and assures that you don't get mixed up by misspelling coding terms. Next, the Ex-Wife emerges, so we enter her by typing her in as a new code. We suggest you keep going, coding other social contacts as you see fit. This will get you used to how the coder works.

For our example, we went ahead and did some coding (see Figure 10.29). This shows that we have developed seven coding items (dots, starting with "Brother" and going down to "Wife and Family"). Right now "Wife and Family" is selected and those parts of the text are highlighted on the left. On the right, you can see all the coding that was done.

Arranging Codes into Trees (Coding Up)

Let's see how we can take these seven purple-dot codes and put them into a logical structure. NVivo calls these structures "Trees" (trees are just hierarchical coding structures or coding schemes—see Chapter 6). Back at the project pad, hit "Nodes" and "Explore Nodes." Right now the purple-ball-question-mark icon "Free" says "(7)," meaning you have seven "free" (unassigned) codes. Click on that purple ball, and you should see what is pictured in Figure 10.30. These are the seven codes we created a couple paragraphs back. We want to take them and put them into a tree. We can see that

FIGURE 10.29. **Coding Examples in NVivo.**

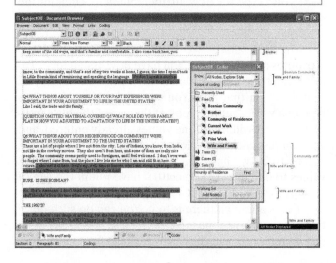

FIGURE 10.30. **Arranging Codes into Trees.**

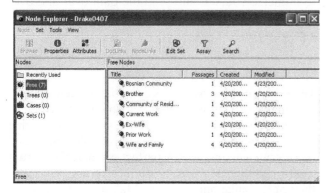

FIGURE 10.31. **Creating a Coding Scheme.**

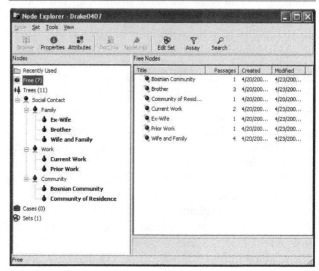

right now we don't have any trees, because the cute little tree icon says "(0)," meaning you have no trees. We'd like a tree that captures the "social contact" construct. We look at our seven items and it looks as if they could be collapsed into three categories: family, work, and community. We need to make a "tree" with those three subcategories. We do it like this:

- Right click on "Trees" near the tree-shaped icon.
- Do "create tree node."
- Click on the text to the right of the blue ball "tree node" and rename it "Social Contact."
- Right click on "Social Contact" and hit "create," then "child node." Rename this "Family." This creates a node (coding term) "Family" under the node (coding term) "Social Contact."
- Right click on "Social Contact" and hit "create," then "child node." Rename this "Work."
- Right click on "Social Contact" and hit "create," then "child node." Rename this "Community."

We have now created a coding scheme (tree) with one main category (social contact) and three subcategories (Family, Work, Community). Now we just have to assign the codes we did (now under "free") to their rightful place in the tree. We do this by clicking on the purple "free" ball. You will see the codes come up to the right. Now for the fun part—just go to the right, grab the purple ball you want (for example, "Brother") and put it where you want to in the tree (for example, "Family"). It's that easy. When you are done, things should look like they do in Figure 10.31. You have now successfully told NVivo how you want your coding scheme arranged.

We now have a set of categories (blue balls with three legs at their bases) and a set of codes within those categories (blue balls with no legs). If you want to read the text that was coded under any particular coding

term, just right-click on it and select "browse/code node." That will show you all the text coded with that term. In Figure 10.32, we have shown what happens when you right click on "Wife and Family" and pull up "browse/code node." This is a great way to look at the whole project and see all the text for that code across all your subjects.

MAKING TREES BEFORE YOU CODE (CODING DOWN)

Coding down can be a little different but very easy. You can create your trees before you even start to code at all. The first time you enter a new code in the coder, it will show up in the coder as a purple "Free Node." Just grab it and move it to where you want it in a tree structure. From then on, it will show up in the tree right where you want it.

FIGURE 10.32. **Node Browser.**

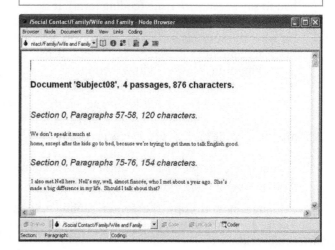

CODING THE NEXT DOCUMENT

As long as you're in the same project, all the coding terms and the tree you created will be ready and waiting to go right there in the coder. In fact, you can do most of what we talked about above directly from the coder.

SECTION 10.5.7: HOW TO ANALYZE CODED DOCUMENTS

You've already done a lot of the analysis. How? Putting things into a coding scheme has already formed the outline of your work. If you were to describe your results, you probably would simply use the coding scheme as the outline of your write-up. You could then describe responses in each part of the scheme, and you'd have done a good job explaining what your subjects had to say. Now that you have material coded and put into a scheme, you might want to use more of NVivo's capabilities. We're going to cover only a tiny part of that here. NVivo offers a lot, and we're going to teach you how to do just two things, looking at the responses as they fit into your coding scheme and using the search tool to look at responses across categories of subjects using a matrix. *Note:* You may want to open John's project at this point so you can follow along with the text below. Get back to the launchpad (we usually just restart NVivo). Hit "Open A Project," click on "Choose," and navigate to PROJECTS/JOHN/NVIVOPROJECT/JOHN/ DATABASE.NV1. This will bring up John's project.

USING THE NODE EXPLORER TO ANALYZE CONTENT UNITS ACCORDING TO YOUR CODING SCHEME (OR "TREE")

You already learned how to open the node explorer (project pad to "Nodes" to "Explore Nodes"). Just move through the tree. You may have to click on the little "[+]" icons to expand the tree out. As we said, right-clicking on a coding term (blue ball without legs) and selecting "Browse/Code Node" will bring up all the things coded with this term. By doing this you can:

- Get a better understanding for what the subjects had to say about *each issue* (coding term). It is absolutely essential that you develop a good feel for what the subjects had to say in each area. Was there agreement or disagreement? What surprised you? What things have obvious theoretical, methodological, policy, or practice implications?

- Look for *general trends and themes* across the data. Are there general things that hold across areas of coding? Are respondents generally optimistic about the issue being studied? Do they appear to feel helpless? Do cultural issues seem to be popping up everywhere?

We suggest you copy the folder "John" under "Projects" to your computer (www.ablongman.com/ mysocialworkkit).

The only way to really find out about your data is to immerse yourself and read the data over and over again. Bouncing around the tree in the node explorer is a great way to do this.

USING A MATRIX

The other function we feel is essential for new qualitative analysts to know about is NVivo's ability to generate matrices. This is important when you are comparing subgroups within a study. Let's say you ask women and men about what makes the perfect partner. You'd want to arrange their responses side by side and see where they were similar and different. Making a matrix allows you to do this. John, for example, is very interested in four different outcomes for his immigrants. Do they experience assimilation, integration, separation, or marginalization? His whole project is all about finding out about how these groups differ in terms of strengths and issues. John wants to create a matrix that allows us to look at subjects' responses by their status in Berry's theory (marginalization, separation, assimilation, integration). We have already given each document (person's response) one of these labels under an attribute called "BerryStatus." So put technically, he wants to split out content units under each code based on their status in Berry's theory. The computer can display what looks like the screen in Figure 10.33.

HOW DID HE DO THAT?

- Click "Search" on the project pad. This will bring up the "Search Tool."

- Under "Find" hit "Boolean." This will bring up the "Boolean Search" screen.

- Under "Operator," hit "Matrix Intersection." *This is very important.*

- In the first big window, hit "Choose Nodes" and specify the codes you want to look at (blue balls without legs). Hit "OK." John has chosen to look

FIGURE 10.33. **Using Matrices in NVivo.**

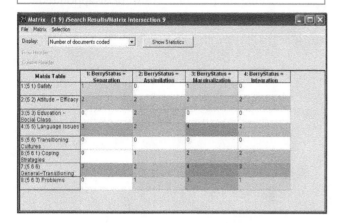

FIGURE 10.34. An NVivo Matrix.

only at the nodes under the general category "Issues" so that he won't clutter up the screen.

■ In the next big window, select "Choose Attribute Values." On the left, double-click on "Document Attributes." Expand-out "BerryStatus" and select the four categories Assimilation, Integration, Separation, and Marginalization.

■ Hit "OK" and you're back to the "Search Tool" screen. Hit "Run Search," then when the "Search Completed" screen comes up, hit "OK." This should bring up a screen that looks like Figure 10.34.

■ Hit "OK," then "Run Search," and you'll get the neat matrix.

What do you do with the matrix?

1. You can see different things. You can look at the data using word count, number of documents coded, and the like. We suggest using "Number of Documents Coded." This tells how many documents (subjects) had at least one of the specified codes in their document. Using total numbers of references or words can be misleading because even single documents with many repetitive codes can really mess up the numbers.

2. You can look at how the responses are spread across categories to get a sense of the data. *Warning!* This can be misleading if you don't bother to carefully read the coded text in each box (see immediately following).

3. You can right click on each box and "Browse/Code Node." This will bring up every code at that intersection point (for example, everyone with "BerryStatus" of "Separation" who had an entry under "Language Issues"). In our view, this is the single best way to analyze themes across dif-

ferent groups. You can quickly look at each code for each group, and similarities or differences should immediately become apparent. For example, John finds pretty strong differences between "Marginalization" and the other groups under the "Attitude– Efficacy" variable, with the responses from the marginalized people being much more negative.

By now you've probably noticed there's a lot of reading and thinking involved in qualitative data analysis. In our view, this is one of the reasons people don't do more qualitative research. It's hard. We hope this section has helped you to see some of the many capabilities you can get in qualitative packages in general and with NVivo in particular.

REVIEW

There are no review questions for this chapter. We hope you were able to execute the above programs and that you are feeling more comfortable with them.

SUPPLEMENTAL READINGS

EXCEL

■ California State University at Northridge has a nice Web site introducing people to Excel at www.csun.edu/itr/guides/excel/2000/beg.html

■ Harvey, G. (2003). *Excel for Dummies.* Hoboken, NJ: Wiley

SPSS

■ Dr. Clarke's Web site at the University of Natal has a "click start" guide available at www.und.ac.za/users/clarke/support/.

■ Field, A. (2005). *Discovering Statistics Using SPSS for Windows* (2nd ed.). London: Sage.

SAS

■ SAS provides a nice Web site with a number of example programs and links to other interesting resources at http://support.sas.com/documentation/onlinedoc/code.samples.html.

■ Cody, R. P., & Pass, R. (1995). *SAS® Programming by Example.* Cary, NC: SAS Institute Inc.

■ Der, G. & Everitt, B. (2001). *Handbook of Statistical Analyses Using SAS* (2nd ed.). Boca Raton, FL: Chapman & Hall.

NVivo

■ A wonderful set of references for using NVivo, including a "click start" guide, can be found at Patsy Clarke's Web site at the University of Natal (www.und.ac.za/users/clarke/ support/). This was the primary source we used in learning the program. We were disappointed with the several hard-copy introductions we reviewed.

IMPLEMENTATION

The design of a research project is very much like a blueprint produced by an architect or a recipe used by a cook. In this chapter, we will talk about how that plan gets turned into a research project. The content of this chapter includes getting ready to do the research, doing the actual research, getting your data, and managing that data until they are ready for analysis. It would be impossible to discuss everything that could possibly occur during the implementation of the full range of research designs. Instead, we will try to cover basic themes that pop up a lot and provide some ideas about how to deal with some of the most commonly encountered issues.

SECTION 11.1

THE RELATIONSHIP OF DESIGN TO IMPLEMENTATION

A finished design is a plan for how you are going to attack your research problem. Napoleon is reported to have said that "No battle plan survives contact with the enemy." It would be equally true to say "Few research designs survive contact with reality." In rare cases, a design may be implemented with no changes or with minimal changes, but normally, designs have to be revised once implementation begins. Sometimes these revisions are minor and may include such small changes as dropping a few variables that didn't work out or adding a few subjects to get more power. Sometimes, however, major changes are needed, and the revised design may look very little like the original design. For example, sampling strategy may need to be radically changed to get enough respondents, or a program you are analyzing may change a key policy in the middle of your analysis. The degree to which your design will need to be modified has to do with how simple and practical your design is to begin with. Simpler designs tend to need less modification. Seasoned researchers may need to make fewer changes because their past experience helps them to anticipate problems in advance and account for them. Good luck also helps. The main thing to remember is that there is no firewall between design and implementation. You aren't cheating if you have to make some adjustments to your design.

SECTION 11.2

PILOT STUDIES

SECTION 11.2.1: BRIDGING DESIGN AND FULL-SCALE IMPLEMENTATION

This preliminary section will discuss the nature and use of pilot studies. Pilot studies can range from small informal testing to very sophisticated trial runs of large studies.

Pilot studies are a common way to make sure your design makes sense before you get in over your head. The best way to see if something works is to try it. Pilot studies are simply small trial runs to see if you can implement your design the way you think you can. Many funding agencies are far more likely to give you support (money) if you can show that the project you propose has been tested at the pilot level. Pilot studies differ from full studies in the following ways:

- The goal of a pilot study is usually to see if the design can be implemented, not to answer the research question.

- Pilot studies are often done with very small samples. Even running five or ten subjects will help you get a feel for how things are going. Because you are probably not going to do a full analysis of the data, sample size is not that important.

- Pilot studies are a good way to test sampling strategies. If you find, for example, that your sampling strategy has only a 30% response rate, then you will need to go back and try another method.

- Pilot studies are a good way to test instruments. Did your subjects understand the items? Did things get done in the allotted time?

- Pilot studies are sometimes a good way to get feedback from participants. There is no reason you can't talk to subjects about their experiences after they participate. Try to get a feel for how the subject was thinking, feeling, and responding. This can help you make changes that will increase the validity of your work. For example, if your subjects felt that the experimental condition you set up was completely unrealistic, then you may have generalizability issues.

- Pilot studies will help you get a more realistic idea of how much effort and expense the full study will require.

- Pilot studies should be done so as to not contaminate the main study. For example, if your main study is going to be done in five high schools in a given district, you would want to run your pilot in a different school in that same district. In this way, you keep as close to your designed sample as possible (same district), but you do not "muddy the water" with any of the schools you plan to use for real.

- Pilot studies should go as far as possible through the research process. You should collect the data and do data management and even do preliminary analyses. Although the results from the analyses will probably be meaningless (sample size issues), it is a good idea to make sure your analysis plan can work. For example, you may have made an error in selecting your statistical approach, and this can often become apparent when you try to run the program.

Pilot studies sometimes come about unintentionally. If you implement your project, and some fatal problem occurs (such as an unacceptably small response rate) then you may have to go back and start over. We think of studies like these as "unplanned pilots." Make sure you gain all the help you can from your experience, just as you would have done in a planned pilot.

When should you do a pilot study? These guidelines may be useful:

- Large or complicated designs should always be piloted. There are just too many things that can go wrong.

- Pilot studies are easier to do if you have a long time before the actual study has to start. Try to give yourself several months to run and figure out what you got out of the pilot.

- Sometimes your available study sample is so small that you don't want to lose sample size by piloting.

- New scales or similar instruments should always be piloted in advance.

- Projects that require use of reviewer ratings (such as rating behaviors on videotapes) must include training of raters, which can sometimes be done using data gained in the pilot, although you will want to retest later using real data.

- If you feel as if you are lost, you probably need to pilot. Often the act of piloting will spark creativity or will help you pinpoint that nagging concern that's been bothering you.

- Replications of your own or other people's studies are probably less likely to need a pilot because the work has already been done and the problems fixed.

- Working with new people or situations is a very good reason to do a pilot, no matter how often the instrument or approach might have been tried in the past. For example, let's say you are using a family relationships survey package that has never been used with a Hispanic population. You may have theoretical reasons to believe that there are some differences between Hispanic and non-Hispanic families that could affect your instruments. It would be a good idea to test it out with some Hispanics first to make sure it works well with them.

A couple of examples of pilots might be helpful; see below.

PILOT STUDIES: TWO EXAMPLES

Example 1: A $60 million federal research project has been mandated by Congress. It will be managed by the Centers for Disease Control and will occur simultaneously in all 50 states. It will use both preexisting standardized instruments and also new instruments. Such a study might have a pilot phase that occurs in all states, costs hundreds of thousands of dollars, and includes many hundreds of participants. While it might seem silly to call such a study a "pilot," that's what it is. Although expensive, it is cheap insurance against the possibility of catastrophic failure when the real study goes online.

Example 2: A PhD student is surprised by an RFA (request for applications) for a grant that is due in a very short (45-day) time frame. She is going to try to collect data in an area that has caused researchers a lot of trouble in the past. Her biggest worry is that the grant reviewers will not believe that her methods will be practical. She decides to quickly collect data from ten subjects so that she can show that her data collection methods produce usable data. It will also help her fine-tune her application and will provide some very preliminary data, even if the sample size will be too small to draw any conclusions.■

SECTION 11.3
IMPLEMENTATION TASKS

We will now look at the tasks that need to be done during the implementation of a project. Some of these steps apply to almost all projects (creating codebooks), while some of these steps occur only in special cases (monitoring fidelity). We break the implementation process down into three phases (Table 11.1). "Getting ready" occurs before data collection; "monitoring the process" occurs during data collection; and "data management" occurs after at least some of the data are collected. While we do not list pilot studies as a step in the process, we encourage you to do pilot work.

We will now describe each of these areas in more detail in the following three sections.

SECTION 11.3.1: GETTING READY

Getting ready actually starts during the design phase. Designs should not be created in isolation from the real world. Program evaluation studies, for example, cannot be designed without the researcher having already developed a relationship and a set of agreements with agency partners. In this section we will overview a number of critical steps that the researcher must take before beginning a study. This list is not exhaustive but is designed to

TABLE 11.1. **The Implementation Process.**

	KEY ELEMENTS OF TASK
TASK	GETTING READY
Getting agreements with partners	• Partners may include coinvestigators, agencies, consultants, or others. • Agency partners are more likely to cooperate if they believe that the research serves their own needs directly. • Clear descriptions of who will perform what tasks and when are necessary. • Clear communication about which partners will assume any costs and workload burdens must occur.
Getting access to subjects or sample	• Samples are frequently drawn from agencies, in which case agreements with agencies must be worked out down to the smallest detail. • Samples may be drawn from the general population, in which case subject contact and recruitment protocols must be carefully worked out. Pilot trials are usually necessary. • In secondary analysis, this step is best thought of as "gaining access to your data" and may be as simple as downloading a file. • Many studies piggyback on already existing studies, using samples that have been already recruited for other purposes.
Getting formal IRB clearance	• Human subjects approval must be obtained from your institution and frequently from the institutions you will be partnering with.
Getting money	• Funding for activities (if necessary) can come from the government, foundations, nongovernmental organizations, partner agencies, or from your institution.
Getting materials ready	• The things you need for the research must be made ready. In survey research, this often includes obtaining needed scales and preparing and copying questionnaires. • Experimental designs may require the physical creation of a testing environment. • Necessary supplies must be obtained. These will sometimes be very simple but may involve such tasks as purchasing complicated hardware or software packages.
Getting personnel	• Many studies require the use of assistants, raters, or similar skilled people. These must be located and recruited.
Formalizing data collection (codebooks)	• For many kinds of data collection, you need to develop a specific set of instructions regarding how to do it. For example, coding case files requires a specific process to assure it is done reliably.
Training	• Once recruited, project staff must be trained.
	MONITORING THE PROCESS
Monitoring data collection	• Data are often gathered by different people. It is necessary to assure that they are collecting data the same way. • Specific procedures (such as testing how raters score sample videos) must be put in place to assure that data are being collected in a uniform manner.
Monitoring contamination	• Between-group contamination can occur and must be avoided. Procedures used with treatment groups must not bleed over into comparison groups. This is best done through making sure that groups stay separate from each other throughout the study and through monitoring fidelity.

Monitoring fidelity	• It is important to make sure that the conditions in groups continue to be as you claim they are. • In treatment evaluation, you must monitor what is being done in treatment and control/comparison groups to make sure that what is happening is what you claim is happening.
Monitoring other potential problems	• You must remain closely connected with the process and be constantly alert for problems that might arise. • In large studies, weekly or monthly project meetings are absolutely necessary to identify issues which may arise.
Monitoring when to stop	• Sometimes researchers must use judgment about when to terminate data collection or when to stop recruiting subjects. In rare cases, ethical concerns may arise that may require that the project be shut down.
DATA MANAGEMENT	
Steps	• Data must be moved from whatever source they came from (paper records, surveys, electronic databases, and so on) into a usable data format (Excel, SAS, Word, and the like). • Once in electronic form, new variables necessary for your analysis must be created.
Data quality and cleaning	• Data quality must be carefully checked at *every point* for completeness, accuracy, and outliers. This must be done at each of the following steps: raw data, initial electronic data, final electronic data (with new created variables). • Completeness: Missing data must be identified and dealt with. • Accuracy: All variables must be checked to see if they appear to be valid. This includes checks against original (raw) data and commonsense reviews to see if data are clearly invalid (e.g., age coded as 300 years, people receiving services before they are born, males who are coded as pregnant, and the like). • Outliers: Some observations may be radically different from all (or most of) the others. These must be examined and decisions made regarding what to do with them.
Codebook creation and updates	Virtually all projects require a codebook in which variables are listed and their nature is explained. This should minimally include: • Where the variable came from • How the variable is scored • What the variable represents

address many of the key early implementation issues that beginning researchers are likely to face. Before moving to that stage, however, let's look at the terms that are used for roles held by people in the research process. Smaller efforts are likely to be done entirely by a single individual, who may hold no formal title. Larger projects, however, can involve many people, for whom the terms shown in Table 11.2 are sometimes used.

SECTION 11.3.2: GETTING AGREEMENTS WITH PARTNERS

ACADEMIC PARTNERS

While a few researchers do their work completely alone (Maria is one example), most researchers deal with a number of other people in their work. Research partners and consultants may already be familiar to the researcher and can be approached informally. Newer researchers who may not have an established network can identify potential research partners through their publication records or their positions in academic or other research-oriented agencies. Once identified, such potential partners can be approached directly. We find that buying individuals lunch is a nice, informal way to learn more about them and see if they might be interested in partnering (or might know someone who is).

AGENCY PARTNERS

Gaining agreements with agency partners can be more intimidating and require more care. Agencies exist to perform their missions, which generally are centered on helping their clients (individuals, families, communities, and the like).

TABLE 11.2. Who's Who in a Research Project.

RESEARCHERS AND CONSULTANTS	
Principal Investigator (PI)	Principal investigators have overall responsibility for the project and get most of the credit for the work that's done. Usually each project may have only one principal investigator.
Co-principal Investigator (CoPI)	Co-principal investigators share responsibility for the research endeavor with principal investigators. They may direct parts of the project.
Investigator	Investigators are typically researchers involved in one aspect of the project but not holding overall responsibility for the project as a whole.
Project director	This term is sometimes synonomous with principal investigator. In other cases it refers to someone more like a research coordinator, or someone in between.
Consultant	Consultants commonly provide expertise in particular substantive areas (child development, economic theory) or in technical areas (statistics, questionnaire construction). Consultants are often paid on a per diem (daily) basis.
PROJECT STAFF (MORE COMMON IN LARGER, FUNDED STUDIES)	
Research coordinator	Research coordinators do the daily work of keeping a project running, but leave most decisions to the PI or CoPI.
Agency or community liaison	Liaisons are sometimes hired to maintain communication with partner agencies, communities, or other groups and to assist in tasks such as dissemination of findings to those groups.
Research assistant	Research assistants are the line workers of many projects. Telephone interviewing, survey administration, coding of videotapes, or similar tasks are frequently done by research assistants, often under supervision of an investigator, project director, or the research coordinator. Research assistants may also be used for other tasks, such as literature reviews or maintaining a reference library.
Data manager	Data managers change data into more usable forms by cleaning, reducing, merging, and other means. Archival analysis often includes more data management tasks than data analysis tasks.
Data analyst	Data analysis is frequently done by an Investigator, but in larger projects a dedicated person may be hired to fulfill this function.
Web site manager	Some projects hire technically skilled individuals to manage Web sites, online databases, or similar electronic resources.
Administrative assistant	Administrative assistants are sometimes hired by large projects with extensive word processing, paperwork, or other administrative tasks.

Why should an agency work with you? Agencies are typically not receptive to researchers who want to impose a rigid plan of action on them but are often very receptive to working with researchers who will help them to achieve their agency's goals. The core principle of effective researcher–agency collaboration is that the research must be designed in such a manner that the agency gets something out of it. There are a number of ways in which agencies can benefit from involvement in your project:

■ *Establishing accountability:* In the last 30 years there has been a radical increase in the degree to which agencies are required by funding agencies or clients to show empirical evidence that their services work. For example, in St. Louis, the

United Way requires empirical self-evaluation as a precondition for continued funding. Agencies may even approach you to help them meet such requirements. Agencies will often want you to help them set up a evaluation system that will allow them to monitor their services in a scientific manner.

- *Generation of required reports:* Many agencies need yearly reports developed for funders, accreditation boards, or other oversight agencies, and they may be very happy to let you help with this (or do this for them).

- *Answering questions of interest to the agency:* Agencies often have questions they need answered on a wide range of issues, such as who their clients are, what their needs are, how they can best be served, and how they are doing after they leave the agency. The authors are somewhat embarrassed to mention that often agency-generated questions are more important and interesting than the questions we bring to agencies.

How do you go out and gain support of agency partners? Your question or research task may be very compatible with agency needs, or it may not. The art of successful researcher–agency collaboration is based on your ability to meet both your needs and the needs of the agency. There are several ways you might try to do this:

- *Select a topic that is practically relevant and is already known to be of interest to agencies.* While this approach assures that your research question will be very interesting to the agency, it may restrict you too much in following your own area of interest. On the other hand, if your research isn't very interesting to anyone in the field, you may want to question why you are doing it at all.

- *Include both topics mainly of interest to you and topics mainly of interest to the agency in the research.* This hybrid approach has the advantage of meeting your needs as well as the agency needs but may require a project of larger scope than is easily manageable.

- *Select a topic of interest to you and try to convince the agency that it matters to them.* We advise against this. This sometimes works, but if the research really turns out to be of little interest to the agency, you are likely to face issues of noncompliance and just plain lack of effort on the agency side.

- *Spend time before the design is finalized to carefully listen to agency ideas, needs, and input and see if that leads to natural refinement of your ideas.* In our view, this is often the best course of action. Agencies know more about their work, personnel, procedures, and context than you do. Researchers often tend to be arrogant and domineering in their contacts with the community. One way to get away from this potential problem is to spend time listening. Talking to people in the field early in the process lets you get their ideas about how to improve your design and make it more relevant to the real world. A question and design that is closely relevant to real-life situations has two advantages. It is going to be more attractive to your agency partner, and the findings are more likely to be practically useful and relevant to the field. So do some creative thinking somewhere other than at the university and with someone else besides other researchers.

- *Minimize the labor the agency must contribute.* A project that simply requires an administrative data download from an agency will require far less agency buy-in and enthusiasm than a project in which each worker has to spend two hours per week extra on paperwork. Many researchers will use strategies such as outposting a research assistant at the agency to minimize agency burden.

- *Provide other concrete benefits to the agency.* For example, if you are doing a case-file review of people using the agency's services, you may help the agency refine its forms and information retrieval system to make it more efficient, something that will help your work too. As another example, if computer data entry at an agency is required, a computer purchased by the project for data entry purposes may be left with the agency after the project terminates.

Establishing clarity regarding roles is critical in any partnering endeavor. One way to do this is through a written contract or letter of agreement. These are usually required from research partners as part of any formal grant submission. Such documents generally state who will do what. Such written agreements can be either general or specific. Another good way to formalize who will do what is through the use of a formal description of personnel and tasks or through a time line that specifies who will be involved in which task.

SECTION 11.3.3: GETTING ACCESS TO YOUR SAMPLE

Gaining access to a good sample can be simple or difficult. How you get access to your sample depends entirely on your design. Table 11.3 gives a range of

---

TABLE 11.3. **Gaining Access to a Sample.**	
APPROACH	ISSUES IN ACCESS
Survey	IRB clearance, contacting a representative sample, consent forms from subjects
Agency-based survey	Permission of agency, IRB clearance, consent forms from clients
Agency-based archival	Permission of agency, IRB clearance, data transfer, interpretation and management issues; consent of clients in some cases
Experimental	IRB clearance, recruiting a representative sample, consent from clients, getting subjects to experimental situation (or vice versa)
Secondary data analysis	Obtaining permission from data holder (if not public domain), obtaining precise data documentation, downloading and managing file

examples as to how you might need to gain access to your sample.

In survey research, problems typically revolve around having access to enough of the right subjects and gaining an acceptably high response rate from those subjects (see Chapters 4 and 5). Opinions as to adequate response rates vary, but most researchers agree that response rates below 60% or 70% are seriously problematic (bad). This is because you don't know why so many people did not respond, and there might be something special about them that causes the remaining respondents to be systematically biased and unrepresentative. You may hear people say such things as, "We got a response rate of 35%, and that's good for an Internet survey." Unfortunately, the fact that their unacceptable response rate is higher than other people's unacceptable response rates does not make it acceptable. In other words, a 35% response rate is bad, no matter how "good" it is for the substandard approach used.

As we saw in Chapter 3, people have tried many different ways of obtaining samples in survey research. Mail and Internet approaches typically have low response rates. Telephone or face-to-face interviews will often have higher response rates but will be more expensive and time-consuming. Sometimes populations can be accessed by physically going to where they are. For example, if you want to study school teachers, you can physically go to schools, get permission to drop by during their faculty meetings, and distribute your survey then. This sort of approach can assure a high response rate and will save time in the long run.

In agency-based survey research, your population is usually already in a set physical location and may be easier to access. Careful coordination with the agency is necessary. In some cases, you may be able to take advantage of data already collected by the agency on clients. Many agencies are beginning to use standardized instruments such as the Beck Depression Inventory or the Achenbach Child Behavior Checklist

(CBCL). Preexisting data on your subjects can be used to supplement any original data you may collect.

Secondary data analysis occurs when you analyze data someone else has already collected, for research or other purposes. In the case of data collected for research purposes, you might think that you just get the data, pop them into your computer, and start analyzing. It often does not go like that. Data are useless without complete documentation that allows you to get a thorough understanding of the variables. Many data sets are confusing or lack documentation. Even well-documented data sets can give trouble. For example, in Census data, many fields are at the household level, while other records are at the individual, family, or sub-family unit. Some data are full-sample, while other data are imputed. A careless researcher who doesn't understand the nature of such data could easily produce incorrect and embarrassing results. Even a careful researcher is likely to make serious errors the first few times he or she tries to use such data. Availability can also be an issue. While some data are freely available, some other data sets are held by individuals or clearinghouses, and access may be gained only through applying to that person or clearinghouse. Secondary data analyses based on data not expressly collected for scientific purposes are often called "archival data analyses."

Archival data are increasingly popular and have drawbacks and advantages. While you cannot specify the variables that are measured, sometimes it is possible to combine preexisting data sets to be able to address your questions without collecting your own data. For example, Maria has combined an archival source (coroner's records) with a secondary data source (Census) to create a new and unique data set. Obtaining archival data from agencies usually requires contracts with participating agencies that specify exactly how the data will be used. When confidential data are obtained, strong protective measures (such as stripping off identifiers) must be used.

Experimental research can be problematic in terms of gaining access to a sample. Many experimental designs require the use of highly controlled and prepared contexts (such as rooms with particular equipment). Because of this, experimental designs are sometimes carried out with convenience samples that do not provide optimum generalizability, such as college students. Often, experimental research takes the form of randomized clinical trials, in which the experimenter will set up his or her study at a hospital or similar facility, and these people will draw their sample from and access subjects at that facility. This can limit generalizability.

SECTION 11.3.4: OBTAINING HUMAN SUBJECTS (IRB) CLEARANCE

Human subjects clearance is required for most social research done under the authority of a school, hospital, or other entity. The intent is to prevent harm to subjects through oversight of proposed projects. Funding agencies will frequently require that clearance be approved before a grant will be considered. Many social service agencies also have their own IRBs, which may have to give additional consent. A large project may require many clearances. The need for review boards has been highlighted by a number of unethical studies. We have reviewed many of these in Chapter 2.

PROCEDURES

Human subjects clearance is generally granted by an institutional review board (IRB) at the agency sponsoring the research, such as a university. Many universities handle this partly through their Web sites, providing instructions and forms for the researcher's use. There are often several different types of review that can be sought. For example, a project can be "exempt" or can be given an "expedited" or "full" review. Exempt studies are those posing no real risk of harm to subjects, while expedited reviews are done on more potentially risky projects, and full reviews are reserved for those requiring the most detailed review. The instructions in Figure 11.1 apply to individuals filing for full reviews at our university. They will give you some idea of exactly what goes into a human subjects proposal.

Generally, the researcher will fill out a fact sheet and do a proposal such as that described in Figure 11.1, supported by other key materials (instruments, procedures, etc.). There is usually a hearing, which may include community representatives, and then approval can either be given immediately, be given contingent on requested study modifications (common), or be denied. Human subjects protection is as much a protection for the researcher as the subjects. We will frequently request full reviews even when we qualify

for lesser levels of review, simply to make sure our work meets ethical standards.

SECTION 11.3.5: OBTAINING FUNDING

Your project may require little expense, perhaps copying, materials, and local travel, which you might pay out of your own pocket. Some research using preexisting data may require no funding at all. Larger projects may require modest or very substantial funding. Where does all this funding come from?

Intramural (within-school) grants are often available to professors and students. Very limited funds can be obtained through application to the university and will help smaller projects to cover costs associated with travel, purchasing instruments, copying, and so on. Sometimes intramural funding is set aside particularly to help master's or doctoral students.

Governmental grants are given by a large number of different local, state, and federal agencies. These range from small agency or dissertation grants to large multibillion dollar cross-university efforts such as the Human Genome Project. Such grants are generally competitive and are announced online and in the *Federal Register* (www.gpoaccess.gov/fr/). Federal funding agencies use very different criteria in awarding grants based on the purpose of the grant and the mission of the funding agency. For example, NSF grants (National Science Foundation, www.nsf.gov/home/grants.htm) are judged mainly on how well they contribute to scientific knowledge building (basic science) while DHHS grants (Department of Health and Human Services, www.hhs.gov/grants/index.shtml) may be heavily focused on knowledge building, practical implementation (applied science), or a combination of both.

Foundation grants support many projects. Foundations generally exist for a certain specific purpose, such as enhancing education in inner cities, and applications to such agencies must conform closely to the agency's goals. Foundations are typically more applied in their interests, and applications to these bodies usually should stress how the research will help people "on the ground."

Other funding opportunities may include agencies bidding out evaluation projects, professional associations that provide dissertation support, and the like.

THE GENERAL PROCESS OF OBTAINING FUNDING

Although substantial variation can occur, the following steps are typical of how money is made available:

1. A request for proposals (RFP) or request for applications (RFA) is released. Some of these are ongoing, with applications due every four or six months. Some are one-time-only, with specific due dates. Sometimes, there is a step that occurs even

---

FIGURE 11.1. **Example of Template for IRB Approval.**

PROJECT TITLE
Project Director Name and Faculty Advisor (for nonfaculty members)

OVERVIEW
  Be sure to include the following four items as subheadings.
  Brief background/history (Be succinct.)
  Rationale (This should be extensive when deception will be used.)
  Research hypothesis and/or objective(s) (Be succinct.)
  Potential contribution to literature/field (Be succinct.)

METHOD
  Participants and recruitment
    Number of subjects: Provide an estimate.
    Population: Specify approximate age ranges.
    Recruitment: Provide details for each group to be included.
      (include two copies of any advertisements or flyers)
        Note: Whenever possible, recruitment should be designed to
        permit the potential participant to actively seek information
        about volunteering for a study (e.g., a flyer with a contact
        phone number provided as a tear-off strip). Also, to reduce
        the possibility of coercion, asking friends or acquaintances
        to participate should be avoided whenever this is feasible.
    Remuneration: If applicable, specify the amount or value.
  Design
    Number of groups:
    If applicable, total number of variables (factors):
    If applicable, number of conditions (levels) associated with
      each variable:
  Time line
    Provide an estimate of when the project should be completed (the
    estimate should include the amount of time needed for all of the
    following: recruitment, data collection, and data analysis).
  Procedure
    Please provide a brief overview of the complete procedure
    including an estimate of how much time is required per
    participant. In addition, include any of the following information
    that applies:
      1) For studies that involve experimental methods such as
        those often used to study cognition, decision making,
        emotions, game theory, language, perception, psycho-
        physiology, and sensation:
        >> Please provide a detailed description of the
        procedure(s) that includes sample stimuli (nonverbal
        stimuli can be provided in pictorial or digital format).
      2) For studies that involve any deception:
        >> Please provide a complete verbal script of what the
        participants will be told throughout the course of the
        study.
      3) For studies using surveys or questionnaires that were
        developed by the investigator:
        >> Please provide one copy of the instrument(s). (Note,
        however, that standard, published surveys or question-
        naires such as those used for assessment or diagnostic
        purposes do not need to be sent to the HHSC unless
        specifically requested.)

(continued)

---

      4) For studies using interviews or focus groups:
        >> Please provide a list of questions and/or topics that
        will be covered in the interview.
      5) For studies that will recruit children in a school setting:
        >> Please provide an original letter from any school where
        you will be recruiting and/or testing children stating that
        you have the permission of the principal and school
        district (if applicable) to recruit and/or conduct the study
        on the schools' premises.

INFORMED CONSENT
  Indicate whether you will be obtaining written informed consent or
  seeking either a waiver of written documentation or a waiver of
  consent.
    a) Provide one copy of each consent document, verbal or assent
    script or document, and/or any waivers that are requested.
    b) If deception will be used in the study, you *must* also request
    that informed consent be waived and include a copy of the waiver
    request. In addition, please provide a complete copy of the
    debriefing script.
  When an informed consent document will be used, indicate at what
  point it will be discussed and signed. (For example, some studies
  may send out a document to participants prior to an initial interview
  and then discuss what is in the document along with obtaining a
  signature on the day of the study, whereas others may simply
  discuss the study and obtain a signature just before data is
  collected.)
  >> Be sure to include an assent document (or script) if you plan to
  recruit children (i.e., anyone under the age of 18 years) along with
  the appropriate minor form (for minimal risk studies or greater
  than minimal risk studies).

PROCEDURES FOR MAINTAINING CONFIDENTIALITY
  1) Indicate how the data will be treated to ensure confidentiality
  (e.g., data to be kept on a computer that is not used to access the
  Internet, anonymous completion of surveys).
  2) Include information that describes whether and, if applicable,
  when names and data will be separated. If the data will be
  identifiable only via code numbers or fictitious names, please state,
  if applicable, at what point any existing key to the codes will be
  destroyed.

ASSESSMENT OF RISKS AND BENEFITS
  Keep in mind that most Social Behavior Research (SBR) has very
  little risk outside of the possibility of mild boredom or fatigue
  (*except when participants may be exposed to negative emotional
  distress either directly as part of a procedure or indirectly by virtue
  of being deceived during participation*). In addition, SBR has very
  little (if any) direct benefits (other than those derived either from the
  educational experience or from the knowledge that one's efforts may
  help to advance science).

(Washington University in St. Louis, http://hhsc.wustl.edu)

before this step, where the funding agency, often the government, issues a request for comments about how the RFP should be structured. This allows the scientific community some input into how the RFP is oriented.

2. The researcher will read the RFP and write and submit a proposal. Some agencies will be willing to discuss the proposal with the researcher in advance of submission; some will not.
3. The funding agency will review applications and give feedback to successful and unsuccessful applicants. This may take from two months to a year.
4. Unsuccessful applications frequently are revised in accordance with reviewer comments and resubmitted.

Many agencies have a multilevel funding process. For example, NIH (National Institute of Health) often funds pilot "R03" projects that later evolve into full "R01" projects.

SECTION 11.3.6: GETTING MATERIALS READY

Many research designs require that you prepare some kind of physical materials for use in the study. Survey designs require that your instrument(s) be finalized, copied, and prepared for use. Experimental designs may require anything from the preparation of a simple questionnaire to the construction of a specialized testing area. You may need to purchase computers or other resources. These tasks can take longer than you might think, so adequate time must be budgeted for these efforts.

SECTION 11.3.7: GETTING PERSONNEL

While some small projects can be done by individuals, it is often necessary to bring in others to help you. This is particularly true for funded projects headed by professors or other professional researchers. Students or other paid workers are often used for tasks such as survey administration, coding, or rating videotapes. Student workers can be recruited at universities, sometimes using mechanisms such as work-study. For larger projects, more technically skilled individuals are often needed for data management or analysis tasks, and these will normally have to be recruited in a more formal and time-consuming manner.

SECTION 11.3.8: FORMALIZING DATA COLLECTION (CODEBOOKS)

Your data is useful only if it can be used in an analysis. It is therefore a very good idea to think early on about how your data will eventually be used. Care at this point will avoid substantial problems later. Studies using observation should have clear ways of recording responses. This can be audio- or videotape or computer records of performance that can be analyzed later. Often observers will use checklists or rating forms. A typical observer checklist might look like the one in Figure 11.2.

FIGURE 11.2. A Typical Observer Checklist.

(1) Subject ID Number: ___________

(2) Hour observation taken [9am] [10am] [11am] [1pm] [2pm]
[9] [10] [11] [13] [14]

(3)Time block observed :00 to :15 :15 to :30 :30 to :45 :45 to :00
[1] [2] [3] [4]

(4) Type A aggression events observed:

[01]	[02]	[03]	[04]	[05]	[06]	[07]	[08]	[09]	[10]
[11]	[12]	[13]	[14]	[15]	[16]	[17]	[18]	[19]	[20]
[21]	[22]	[23]	[24]	[25]	[26]	[27]	[28]	[29]	[30]
[31]	[32]	[33]	[34]	[35]	[36]	[37]	[38]	[39]	[40]
[41]	[42]	[43]	[44]	[45]	[46]	[47]	[48]	[49]	[50]

(5) Type B aggression events observed:

[01]	[02]	[03]	[04]	[05]	[06]	[07]	[08]	[09]	[10]
[11]	[12]	[13]	[14]	[15]	[16]	[17]	[18]	[19]	[20]
[21]	[22]	[23]	[24]	[25]	[26]	[27]	[28]	[29]	[30]
[31]	[32]	[33]	[34]	[35]	[36]	[37]	[38]	[39]	[40]
[41]	[42]	[43]	[44]	[45]	[46]	[47]	[48]	[49]	[50]

(6) Type C aggression events observed:

[01]	[02]	[03]	[04]	[05]	[06]	[07]	[08]	[09]	[10]
[11]	[12]	[13]	[14]	[15]	[16]	[17]	[18]	[19]	[20]
[21]	[22]	[23]	[24]	[25]	[26]	[27]	[28]	[29]	[30]
[31]	[32]	[33]	[34]	[35]	[36]	[37]	[38]	[39]	[40]
[41]	[42]	[43]	[44]	[45]	[46]	[47]	[48]	[49]	[50]

In the example in Figure 11.2, Sections 4, 5, and 6, the observer simply checks off boxes, left to right, and the last box checked shows the total number of observations of that type. You will notice that in this example small numbers have been added to the form; for example, under the "time block" entries. This is to help the person who will be doing the data entry from the forms. It is a good idea to do this on any written instrument so that you can increase the accuracy of your data entry. Another example from a survey form might look like Figure 11.3. In this example, the coder

FIGURE 11.3. Example from a Survey Form.

Name: ______________________________________
EQ1

Has anyone at school hit you with their fist this week? Yes [ ] No [ ]
EQ2: 1 2

How many times have you been hit at school this month? [ ]
EQ3: #

TABLE 11.4. **A Codebook.**

NAME	SOURCE	DESCRIPTION	VALUES AND RANGE	MISSING VALUE INDICATOR	FORMAT	COMMENTS
EQ1	Elem. School Survey, Q #1	Name of respondent	Up to 30 characters of any type	"MISSING"	Character	Field must be deleted after data are merged.
EQ2	Elem. School Survey, Q #2	Hit w / fist last week?	1= Yes 2= No	9999	Numeric	
EQ3	Elem. School Survey, Q #3	Number of times hit in last week	0+	9999	Numeric	

can easily see that on question EQ2 she is to enter a "1" or "2" corresponding to "Yes" and "No" and that she is to enter a number as given for EQ3. Such simple tricks can help you to make sure you are getting the data transcribed correctly.

Codebooks (also called data dictionaries) are commonly used to keep formal track of variables. A codebook might look like the one in Table 11.4.

A codebook normally includes the variable name and a description of the variable. It includes the numeric or character values and the possible range of responses. It also includes a specific value that is to be used when the data are missing. This value must be so clearly different from normal values as to be easily identified. The format (character, numeric, SAS date, etc.) should be included, and there should be a space for any comments. For data from questionnaires, you may want to include the actual question in the codebook, instead of the more general "description" given in Table 11.4.

In survey research, it is a good idea to do a codebook as you put together your survey instrument. This can help you identify possible problems in how you are collecting and recording the data. In secondary analysis, you will ideally have someone else's codebook to refer to. In archival analysis, you will need to construct a codebook based on the data you extract. This can be very tricky and may require that you consult with many people (workers, data entry people, administrators, etc.) to figure out what the data really mean.

SECTION 11.3.9: TRAINING PERSONNEL

People who help you do the research must be trained to the point where you are satisfied that they are doing the work the way you want it done. People who give surveys, either in person or on the phone; people who code narratives or other data sources; or people who administer experimental situations—all require training and monitoring. The reason for this is that people who do not do

what you want them to do will hurt the internal validity of your study. If, for example, you have one telephone interviewer who tends to lead subjects toward particular responses, then you will have that bias in your data.

Training personnel requires the creation of manuals or other materials that tell the people what to do. If you are having people watch videos and count the number of times a parent compliments a child, then the idea of complimenting the child must be operationalized to the point where people can agree on when it is happening. If your study involves telephone interviewing, then the interviewer's words must be carefully scripted, and there must be information for the interviewer about how to respond to likely contingencies. Similarly, people running experimental designs or confederates (pretend subjects meant to fool real subjects) must be tested in simulations until their performance meets explicit guidelines.

Interrater reliability is an issue in many studies. Raters or coders are often given practice situations that are meant to show that they can do the task in a correct and reliable way. For example, a person trained to record the number of a certain kind of advertisement occurring in a newspaper might be given five newspapers that are also coded by his fellow coders. The degree to which the coders agree with each other is assessed to determine if there is adequate interrater reliability. If raters do not agree, then that team of raters can't be considered a reliable measure of the construct.

Validity of ratings is a separate issue. Raters must not only agree (interrater reliability) but they must be right (validity). This can be assessed by having an acknowledged expert (or group of experts) process the data and have that person's responses compared to those of the experts.

Be warned, the entire process described above must be carefully documented because it will be necessary to describe how you did it when you write up your methodology for publication or use by the target audience. Trying to piece together what you did a couple of years ago can be a virtually impossible enterprise.

SECTION 11.4
MONITORING THE PROCESS

This phase is a continuation of the getting-ready phase and mostly consists of keeping track of how your plans and preparations actually play out.

SECTION 11.4.1: MONITORING DATA COLLECTION

You can't just tell people what to do and then ignore them. If you have several different people collecting data, you must make sure that they are continuing to do what you trained them to. Two problems must be checked out:

1. *Are different people continuing to do the same thing?* This can often take the form of periodic testing, where each person is given a sample case or situation to assure that his or her ratings continue to be reliably similar to other raters.

2. *Are people changing what they do over time?* More experienced people may start to change what they do or "cut corners." It is important that what they do and what they create be checked periodically. There is an old military saying that "soldiers do well only those things that the commander checks." How you do this depends on the situation. Sample cases can be used; or simple monitoring of what experimental assistants or confederates do can help.

SECTION 11.4.2: MONITORING CONTAMINATION

In experimental designs, you usually have two or more groups. It is sometimes possible that the subjects or the people administering care in the two groups may contact each other. This can be bad, because often what goes on in one group may "bleed" into another group. For example, clients in a comparison group may learn about the treatment condition and may react to that knowledge in any number of ways. Another serious problem, particularly in evaluation work, can occur when agencies are introduced to a new treatment program. What happens if one of the treatment group therapists shares the wonderful new treatment with a control group therapist? You can easily have the treatment intervention contaminate the control conditions.

How can contamination be avoided? The best situation occurs when different group members cannot have contact. The next best solution is to try to minimize such contact by telling agency staff what the concern is and then monitoring fidelity, which we will discuss next.

SECTION 11.4.3: MONITORING FIDELITY

Any time you test something, you need to make sure that the thing you are testing is what you say it is (internal validity). The two nearby boxed examples might help point out exactly what this issue is about, what problems it can cause, and how it can be monitored.

Example 1: We want to test neotherapy (NT) against cognitive behavioral therapy (CBT). We randomly select half the therapists in an agency (which currently has all therapists trained in CBT) and give them a week's training in NT. We tell them to stop using the old CBT and start using the new NT, and then we find out how their clients do. There is no difference, and so we conclude that NT and CBT are equally effective. This is a rather awful way to do a study.

Example 2: We want to test neotherapy (NT) against cognitive behavioral therapy (CBT). We randomly select half the therapists in an agency and give them a week's training in NT. We then do the following:

- Devise a rating system so that a blind rater (no knowledge of which type of therapist he is rating) can tell how much NT content and how much CBT content is going on during a videotaped 50-minute therapy session.

- Do baselines on every therapist's NT and CBT behaviors before anyone is trained.

- Right after training, do the rating again.

- Every month, do the rating again.

Depending on what you find, several courses of action may be appropriate:

1. If there is no difference between baseline and right-after-training, then the training did not help the NT therapists do anything different, they are not doing NT therapy, and the research is not valid. *Solution:* More training.
2. If there is an initial difference, but that decays, then the NT training is not holding up over time, and again, your design is not valid. *Solution:* Booster training sessions.
3. If both groups start doing more NT behaviors in therapy, then you have contamination between experimental and control groups, and the research is not valid. *Solution:* Keep those people from talking to each other!
4. If the therapists are really doing different things, then you have a fair test. If there is a difference in outcomes, then you can say that NT is more (or less) effective than CBT. If there is no difference in outcomes, you have failed to detect a difference using a fair test.■

As can be seen in the accompanying example, it is important to measure the degree to which your people are doing what you say they are doing. In addition, you will have to do these measurements on an ongoing basis. Without such measurements, there is no way for you to defend your internal validity.

Some readers may note that many studies do not bother to do this. This is true. However, it is difficult to have much confidence in such work, and it is harder to procure funding without some way to assure the funder that you are checking for treatment fidelity. Many students simply will not have the resources to do the complicated blind rating we describe above and may have to accept some weaknesses in their design along this dimension. It will also be noticed that this mechanism can be used to check for the cross-group contamination, thus getting rid of two key threats to validity at the same time.

SECTION 11.4.4: MONITORING OTHER POTENTIAL PROBLEMS

You don't know what you don't know. If you are doing all the work on a research project, you will see problems as they arise. However, if you are running a large project, things may be going on that are simply not correct, and you may have no clue. For this reason, it is vital to keep closely in touch with everyone doing work on the project. Weekly project meetings are one of the best ways to do this. Everyone doing work on the project must be supervised and must have the ability to bring potential problems to your attention. Once again, if you don't check it, you don't know if it's being done right. Possible problems might include:

■ *Low response rate.* Solutions: Rethink your approach to subjects. Is a different incentive needed? Are people being approached in a professional way? Do you need to rethink your sampling frame?

■ *Personnel problems.* Solutions: Retrain or replace people who are not doing adequate work. Often, people not doing well in one part of a large study can be shifted to tasks in another area.

■ *Equipment problems.* Solutions: Change physical or procedural parts of your study. This is usually the easiest kind of problem to solve.

■ *Unusable data being generated.* Solution: Redo data collection/recording techniques.

This last issue is especially serious. You must start doing data input and management as early as possible. It is amazing how many problems can hide until you see the data on a spreadsheet or an SAS Proc Print output. You must move your data (or at least a part of your data) through the process as early as possible, so you can find problems in time to fix them.

SECTION 11.5
DATA MANAGEMENT

Data management is the term for the process of turning raw data into data that can be analyzed. Much of the time, this process requires very little work. Other times, the data management phase of a project is the most complex and time-consuming part. Data management basically includes the steps shown in Figure 11.4.

The data management process requires lots of attention to detail and lots of data cleaning. Data must be cleaned (checked for completeness and accuracy) at every stage of the process. What most new researchers do is to race through the process without checking anything, and then they find themselves doing statistical analyses where 60% of their data are missing or nonsensical. This causes them to have to go back and do everything over. Be smart, and check your product at every step. Ask yourself the following questions:

FIGURE 11.4. **The Data Management Process.**

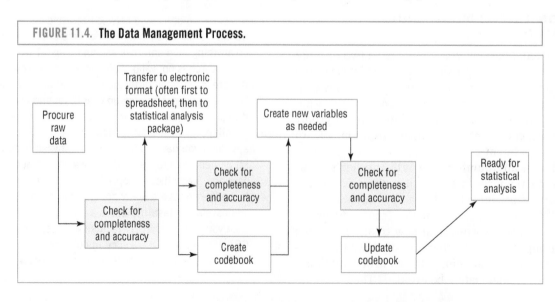

- How many data are missing? Do the raw data and the managed data have the same amount of missing data?

- Do the variables all make sense? If the data don't make sense, is that because of the raw data being wrong or because I made a mistake in managing the data?

Formatting problems can often be to blame for messed-up data. Make sure that shifts from program to program (Excel, SAS, Word, etc.) do not result in your data being changed. One common problem is that numeric or character variables are truncated. The only way to look at this and get it right is to compare data before and after each step, side by side.

As you continue to manage your data, you must make sure your codebook stays current. Did you modify the codebook to reflect the new missing data codes you are using? Did you add in a line for that new variable you created? Data management is rather more difficult and more of an art than you might think, so follow the diagram in Figure 11.4, take your time, and don't get discouraged if you make a mistake or two. It is far better to find problems now than to spend weeks trying to figure out why you are getting some bizarre statistical result that is due to a simple data management error.

SECTION 11.5.1: DATA PROCUREMENT

Data are procured in many ways. Most researchers collect their own data, using paper forms that must be distributed, collected, checked, and transformed into electronic data. Other researchers use computerized instruments, where the interviewer inputs data directly onto screens during the interview process. Still other researchers use existing data. Sometimes existing data are already cleaned and require little checking. Census data are like this. Other times, existing data and input tables may require extensive cleaning. Handwritten agency records are frequently in this category. Even computerized records are often of poor quality and require extensive checking and cleaning. Obviously, data must be stored in a manner consistent with ethical concerns and as described in your human subjects clearance.

Data cleaning at the procurement level is an ongoing process, as shown previously. Data must be examined as they are collected. Many researchers make the mistake of waiting until their data collection is finished to check data quality. This is a serious mistake because the researcher loses the chance to make corrections to the data collection process on the fly. He or she also may miss the chance to go back to subjects and try to collect missing data. The first data collected for any project should be considered to be essentially a pilot phase and treated accordingly, even if not officially described as a

pilot. It is sometimes helpful to have a gap of several days or weeks in your data collection schedule following the first data collection effort, to allow changes to be made to your instrument or process if necessary. This is especially important if formal piloting is not done.

If your data are archival or secondary data, you face the same issues. It is important to check the data as you receive them. Are the expected number of cases present? Are the variables all there? Are the data complete?

SECTION 11.5.2: TRANSFERRING DATA TO AN ELECTRONIC FORMAT

As you begin to move your data to a more usable, electronic format, you will need rules for how to do this. For this reason, data transfer and codebook creation must occur at the same time. Do not put it off and attempt to do a codebook when the project is nearly finished. This will almost always result in more work and poor-quality data. It can be difficult to do the boring work of codebook construction right when you're all excited about finally getting your data, but try to stay in control of yourself and do it right. You'll thank yourself later.

Paper forms such as filled-out questionnaires are perhaps the most common form of data. Such forms must be entered into a computer to be made useful. The standard way to do this is to type data directly from forms into a spreadsheet program, such as Excel. A questionnaire might look like the one in Figure 11.5, and the subsequent entry of three of these completed forms into Excel might look like Table 11.6.

In Table 11.6 we see that each line includes an ID number to distinguish each case (often written on the survey form by the researcher after the questionnaire is turned in), a letter value to indicate gender (Q1), a numeric age value (Q2), a letter indicating "yes" or "no" (Q3), the number of days per week the person watches TV (Q4), the hours per day the person watches TV (Q5), a numeric (Likert scale) response (Q6), and a letter indicating a categorical response (Q7). The final question elicits a text response, which is put into the computer in text form.

The first way to avoid errors in the data is to establish a way of assuring quality data input. Errors will always creep in. If you are rushed or pressed for time, then many errors will occur and probably go undetected. At the very least, data can be double-checked by the same person or a different person. Greater accuracy can be gained by double entry, with each line entered twice by different people and compared (usually by a computer) for mistakes.

We have been discussing data entry for paper data. Other kinds of data will begin as electronic. Computerized secondary or archival records, or surveys done directly with the aid of a computer, will generate data already in an electronic format. This does

1) Sex: M[ ] F[ ]

2) Age in years: ____

3) Do you have a television in your home? Y[ ] N[ ]

4) How many days a week do you watch TV? _____

5) On the days you do watch TV, how many hours do you usually watch? _____

6) I worry that I watch too much television.

[1]	[2]	[3]	[4]	[5]
Strongly disagree	Disagree	Neither agree nor disagree	Agree	Strongly agree

7) Which one of the following best describes you (mark only one response):
   A) I watch television mainly for fun.
   B) I watch television mainly for educational value.
   C) I watch television mainly for the news.
   D) None of the above

8) What is the title of your favorite TV show?

_____

not mean you don't have to check the data. Other people are just as likely to have made mistakes as you are.

Data cleaning and codebook creation are very important at this step. First, make sure you save copies of the raw data and the original spreadsheet file just in case. Next, look at the spreadsheet visually. In the example in

TABLE 11.5. **Data from Figure 11.5 in Excel Format.**

ID	Q1	Q2	Q3	Q4	Q5	Q6	Q7	Q8
1	M	24	Y	7	6	3	A	12 Hours
2			Y			2	C	
3	F	31	y	5	0.5	5	D	Celebrity Annihilation
4	M	36	Y	5	8.42	5	B	Dial 911
5	F	19	Y	7	12	4	C	The Bob Show
6	F	56	y	7	8.9		B	Flyfishing Weekly

Table 11.5, there are six obvious missing elements (questions 1, 2, 4, 5, and 8 from ID#2, question 6 from ID#6). In addition, question 3 has both "Y" and "y" entered to signify "yes." You will have to start making decisions about what kinds of data are acceptable and how to note missing data. These decisions must be written down in the form of a codebook. Let's say you want to denote missing data as "." (a standard practice for numeric data in SAS, missing character variables are generally coded as no character [""]), and that you want to use capital values only for variables (see Table 11.6).

The fields shown represent the minimum required for a codebook. The codebook must show the variable name, what the variable means, if the variable is a character or numeric, what the allowable values are (range), how missing data are indicated, and exactly where the value came from.

You can make corrections now, at the spreadsheet level, or you can make them later, once the data have been moved into a data format for a statistical analysis program. If the data set is small, it will be easier to do it by hand at the spreadsheet level. For larger programs, however, common errors can be cleaned automatically by writing programming code to do this. For example, you could either change all "y" responses to "Y" responses in the spreadsheet, or you could include a line in your program such as this SAS example:

```
If Q3="y" then Q3="Y";
```

MORE DATA CLEANING: DO THE DATA MAKE SENSE?

Data cleaning can be done in either your spreadsheet or your statistical analysis package. It is important to look not only for formatting errors but also to begin to get a "feel" for your data. Do the data appear to do what you expected? Are there results that are just plain strange? It is frightening how many researchers will become slaves to their data and abandon all human judgment.

TABLE 11.6. **Example of a Codebook for Figures 11.5 and 11.6.**

VARIABLE	DESCRIPTION	TYPE	RANGE	MISSING DATA CODE	SOURCE
ID	Subject ID number	Num	1+	Should never be missing	Written on form by researcher
Q1	Gender of respondent	Char	M or F	" "	Q1 (check boxes) from form
Q2	Age of respondent	Num	18–99*	"."	Q2 (fill-in) from form
Q3	Television in home	Char	Y or N	" "	Q3 (check boxes) from form
Q4	Days watched per week	Num	0–7	"."	Q4 (fill-in) from form
Q5	Hours watched per day	Num	0–24*	"."	Q5 (fill-in) from form
Q6	Worry about watching too much	Num	1,2,3,4,5	"."	Q6 (Likert scale) from form
Q7	Self description	Char	A,B,C,D	" "	Q7 (checked letter) from form
Q8	Favorite TV show	Char	Text	" "	Q8 (Fill-in) from form

* Round to nearest tenth

There is no substitute for actually looking at your data, using your brain, and coming to understand them. This can be done at the spreadsheet level by using the spreadsheet's computational features to calculate average scores and the like. It can be done in statistical programs such as SAS by using routines such as PROC PRINT, or PROC FREQ, or PROC UNIVARIATE.

TRANSFERRING FROM SPREADSHEETS TO STATISTICAL DATA SETS

The next step for most researchers is moving data into data sets. In SAS, this is a very easy process, using an "import wizard" available at the upper-left corner of the screen (click on "File"). This wizard both will pull in the data and will actually write the SAS code for you so that you can include the code in your program for future use. If you are using a different program, a similar system will probably exist. It may be necessary to transfer the database into a simpler format (ASCII, .RTF, or the like) in some cases.

The SAS program in Figure 11.6 uses the data set discussed in the preceding paragraphs and gives examples of the programming we've been discussing.

The PROC PRINT output looks like Figure 11.7.

The PROC FREQ output (in part) looks like Figure 11.8.

The PROC UNIVARIATE output (in part) looks like Figure 11.9.

The PROC UNIVARIATE applies only to numeric variables. It provides many univariate statistics, such as mean and kurtosis, and also tracks outliers under the heading "Extreme Observations." If you want to restrict your PROC FREQ to only a few variables, you can do that easily in this format:

PROC FREQ;TABLES Q1 Q2;

The above code would provide frequencies of variable Q1, then frequencies of variable Q2. To do a cross-tabulation, you would need to use an asterisk:

PROC FREQ;TABLES Q1*Q2;

The above code would provide a matrix or table, showing each value of Q1 crossed with each value of Q2. Taken together, these simple procedures should help you get a good "feel" for your data.

FIGURE 11.6. **SAS Program.**

```
/*****************************************/
/****MYNEWDATA1.SAS *******************/
/** DATA MANAGEMENT PROGRAM*************/
/*****************************************/

/**********libname statement tells computer where files are ***/
LIBNAME mydata "c:\aaaawork\school\courses\method03\book";

/*****PUT INTO SAS DATASET*****************************/
/**** this was written by SAS import wizard (click on "file") ***/
PROC IMPORT OUT= WORK.MYNEWDATA
    DATAFILE= "C:\AAAAWork\SCHOOL\COURSES\Method03\Book\MYDATA.xls"
    DBMS=EXCEL2000 REPLACE;
    GETNAMES=YES;RUN;

/***********See what's in the dataset******/
proc contents data=mynewdata;run;

/***********Label the variables in SAS dataset*********/
data mynewdata;
set mynewdata;
label id = "ID number assigned by researcher"
      Q1 = "Sex (M or F)"
      Q2 = "Age in Years (whole number)"
      Q3 = "TV in home? (Y/N)"
      Q5 = "Hours watched/day (nearest tenth)"
      Q6 = "Worry too much TV (1-5)"
      Q7 = "Which decribes me (A=Fun,B=Ed,C=News,D=oth)"
      Q8 = "Favorite show (text)";run;

/****************change values to match codebook*****/
Data mynewdata;
set mynewdata;
if Q3="y" then Q3="Y";  /*change q3 to caps*/
Q4=ROUND(Q4,0.1);      /***round q4 to the nearest tenth**/
run;

/***********************Review Variables***********/
PROC PRINT;run;/*************look at the whole dataset***/
PROC FREQ;RUN;/*****check frequencies of all variables**/
PROC UNIVARIATE;VAR Q2 Q4 Q5;RUN;/****check numbers**/
```

FIGURE 11.7 **PROC PRINT.**

Obs	ID	Q1	Q2	Q3	Q4	Q5	Q6	Q7	Q8
1	1	M	24	Y	7	6.0	3	A	12 Hours
2	2		.	Y	.	.	2	C	
3	3	F	31	Y	5	0.5	5	D	Celebrity Annihilation
4	4	M	36	Y	5	8.4	5	B	Dial 911
5	5	F	19	Y	7	12.0	4	C	The Bob Show
6	6	F	56	Y	7	8.9	.	B	Flyfishing Weekly

FIGURE 11.8. **PROC FREQ.**

TV in home? (Y/N)

Q3	Frequency	Percent	Cumulative Frequency	Cumulative Percent
Y	6	100.00	6	100.00

Hours watched/day (nearest tenth)

Q5	Frequency	Percent	Cumulative Frequency	Cumulative Percent
0.5	1	20.00	1	20.00
6	1	20.00	2	40.00
8.4	1	20.00	3	60.00
8.9	1	20.00	4	80.00
12	1	20.00	5	100.00

Frequency Missing = 1

FIGURE 11.9. **PROC UNIVARIATE.**

TV in home? (Y/N)

Q3	Frequency	Percent	Cumulative Frequency	Cumulative Percent
N	3	50.00	3	50.00
Y	3	50.00	6	100.00

Hours watched/day (nearest tenth)

Q5	Frequency	Percent	Cumulative Frequency	Cumulative Percent
0.5	1	20.00	1	20.00
6	1	20.00	2	40.00
8.4	1	20.00	3	60.00
8.9	1	20.00	4	80.00
12	1	20.00	5	100.00

Frequency Missing = 1

SECTION 11.5.3: CREATING NEW VARIABLES

Many times, researchers will want to study variables that are changed from their raw format. This is done either to aid statistical analyses or to create new variables of interest. The simplest created variable is called a "dummy" variable.

Dummy variables are created when a researcher changes a binary nominal variable (e.g., "hospitalized" versus "not hospitalized") to numeric form. For example, in our study, the researcher may want to change sex from "M" or "F" to "1" or "2."

Created categorical variables can be made from preexisting data. For example, in our data, we have five (fictional) TV shows listed. Let's say that *12 Hours* and *Dial 911* are "reality TV" shows; *The Bob Show* and *Celebrity Annihilation* are comedies; and *Flyfishing Weekly* is a sports program. We may want to categorize these with numeric codes (1=Reality TV, 2=Comedy, 3=Sports). This is a great way to change text variables into a format that can be easily examined.

Collapsed categorical variables can also be made from preexisting data. If your theory says that you need to look specifically at the behavior of people under 30 compared to the behavior of people over 30, you might want to give all under-30s a value of "1" and all over-30s a value of "2." There is a real cost to collapsing data,

however, in that you lose statistical power (the ability to detect differences).

Computed variables are often needed to draw from more than one source variable. For example, we might want to know how many hours per week our subjects watch TV. Because we have the number of days they watch TV and their estimate of the average number of hours watched per day, we can multiply these to get a figure for hours watched per week.

SAS code for accomplishing these transformations is shown in Figure 11.10.

Of course, new variables require new codebook entries (see Table 11.7). At this point, you should have the data you need to begin analysis. The next chapter will discuss how you can move through that part of the process.

We hope this chapter has been useful. In the next chapter we will see how the file example projects are done.

FIGURE 11.10. SAS Code.

```
/*********** Create New Variables **********/
data mynewdata;
set mynewdata;
if Q1="M" then GENDER=1; if Q1="F" then GENDER=2;
if Q8="Dial 911" or q8="12 Hours" then SHOWTYPE=1;
if Q8="The Bob Show" or q8="Celebrity Annihilation" then SHOWTYPE=2;
if Q8="Flyfishing Weekly" then SHOWTYPE=3;
if Q2 ne . and Q27<30 then OVER30=0;
if Q2 ne . and Q27>30 then OVER30=1;
HRSPERWK= Q4 * Q5;
label GENDER=    "1=M,2=F"
      SHOWTYPE=  "1=Reality,2=Comedy,3=Sports"
      HRSPERWK=  "Total hours watched per week"
      OVER30=    "0=under 30, 1=30 or over";
run;
```

TABLE 11.7. Codebook with New Variables.

VARIABLE	DESCRIPTION	TYPE	RANGE	MISSING DATA CODE	SOURCE
GENDER	Gender of subject in numeric form (1=M, 2=F)	Num	1 or 2	"."	CREATED VARIABLE from Q1
SHOWTYPE	Type of favorite TV show: 1=Reality TV 2=Comedy 3=Sports	Num	1 to 3	"."	CREATED VARIABLE from Q8
HRSPERWK	Total number of hours watched per week	Num	0 – 168	"."	CREATED VARIABLE (Q4 * Q5)
OVER30	Subject over or under 30 years old: 0=under 30, 1=30 or over	Num	0 or 1	"."	CREATED VARIABLE from Q2

1. Give three reasons why it is a good idea to run a pilot.

2. Give three circumstances that might reduce the need to run a pilot.

3. What's the difference between a principal investigator, a coprincipal investigator, and an investigator?

4. Give three different ways you might try to get an agency to work with you.

5. Using a hypothetical research project, locate and fill out the human subjects IRB paperwork from your university, school, or department.

6. Using a hypothetical research project, create an Excel spreadsheet codebook. See Chapter 10 if you have problems using Excel.

7. Why is it absolutely necessary to begin to check and clean data as soon as the data come in?

CHAPTER

IMPLEMENTATION EXAMPLES

This chapter will overview the five example projects. We will see how our people deal with their implementation issues, focusing on the issues of:

- Getting ready
- Monitoring the process
- Data management

We do not describe how the projects are analyzed; that will be covered later, in Chapter 15, after we learn some introductory statistics.

All of the files in this chapter are available to you electronically at www.ablongman.com/mysocialworkkit. Each person has a separate folder, which includes his or her programming, data sets, and final projects. You are encouraged to use these programs and data to develop your own programming skills or to use them as "templates" should you find that your project requires similar programming (and it probably will). *Warning! You will have to adjust the libname statements in the programs so that they point to wherever you have the project data files on your computer (see Chapter 6).*

SECTION 12.1

PROFESSOR KATHY

Professor Kathy decided not to do a pilot study because she essentially already had. In her prior work she had recruited students and had them code files, so she knew how this works. The only difference this time would be the presence of the music. Her first step, of course, would be to install speakers in the coding areas. There were no switches or other electronics to install because the music would be on all the time. Kathy selected the music from CDs that she procured from royaltyfreemusic.com, a commercial supplier of background music (cost = $200). She was careful to pick CDs with well-known music that everyone would agree really do constitute easy- listening and classical music. There is probably a cheaper way to do this, but Professor Kathy just wanted to get going, and besides, what are faculty research funds for?

Professor Kathy was very experienced and knew exactly what variables she would be using and how they would be created. She therefore developed the codebook in Figure 12.1 in advance (for more

---

FIGURE 12.1. Professor Kathy's Codebook.

VARIABLE	DESCRIPTION	TYPE	RANGE	MISSING DATA	SOURCE
CoderID	Coder ID number	Num	1–60	.	Assigned at start
Group	Group (1=Easy Listening, 2=Classical, 3=No Background Music)	Char	"ELBM" or "CBM" or "NBM"	" "	Randomly assigned at start
Files1	Number of files coded session #1	Num	0+	.	Session 1
Error1	Number of errors coded session #1	Num	0+	.	Session 1
Files2	Number of files coded session #2	Num	0+	.	Session 2
Error2	Number of errors coded session #2	Num	0+	.	Session 2
Files3	Number of files coded session #3	Num	0+	.	Session 3
Error3	Number of errors coded session #3	Num	0+	.	Session 3
Files4	Number of files coded session #4	Num	0+	.	Session 4
Error4	Number of errors coded session #4	Num	0+	.	Session 4
Files5	Number of files coded session #5	Num	0+	.	Session 5
Error5	Number of errors coded session #5	Num	0+	.	Session 5
Below variables are created by the researcher, using simple math from above variables					
EPF1	Number of errors per file session #1	Num	0+	.	Error1/Files1
EPF2	Number of errors per file session #2	Num	0+	.	Error2/Files2
EPF3	Number of errors per file session #3	Num	0+	.	Error3/Files3
EPF4	Number of errors per file session #4	Num	0+	.	Error4/Files4
EPF5	Number of errors per file session #5	Num	0+	.	Error5/Files5
FilesAll	Total number of files coded	Num	0+	.	Files1+2...+5
ErrorAll	Total number of errors	Num	0+	.	Error1+2...+5
EPFAll	Total number of errors per file coded	Num	0+	.	ErrorAll/FilesAll

FIGURE 12.2. **Professor Kathy's SAS Code 1.**

```
/*********************** KATHY1.SAS ********************************/
/*********************** KATHY1.SAS ********************************/
/* THIS FILE TAKES LIST OF NAMES (KATHYNAMES.XLS) AND PUTS THEM IN**/
/* RANDOMLY ASSIGNED GROUPS (1, 2 or 3)  AND OUTPUTS AS          **/
/* KATHYDATA01.XLS                                              **/
/*****************************************************************/
libname Music "u:drake and jonson-reid\book\projects\kathy";
/******************BRING LIST OF NAMES FROM EXCEL INTO SAS **/
/**created with import wizard ***/
PROC IMPORT OUT= WORK.kathylist
    DATAFILE= "u:drake and jonson-reid\book\projects\kathy\KathyNames.xls"
    DBMS=EXCEL2000 REPLACE;
    GETNAMES=YES;RUN;

/***********RANDOMLY ASSIGN INDIVIDUALS TO GROUPS******************/
data kathydata;set kathylist; /*source(kathylist)names 60 coders  */
x=ranuni(1);run;                 /* gives each a random #        */
proc sort data=kathydata; by x;run;  /* sorts randomly (by number) */

/*********GIVE EVERYONE A PROJECT ID AND GROUP NUMBER ************/
data kathydata;set kathydata;        /*keep using same dataset    **/
by x;           /* SAS needs this to do the RETAIN command      */
retain ID 0;    /* the retain statement allows you to "remember" */
                /* values of a variable from one record to the next.*/
ID=ID+1;        /* each coder gets an ID # based on their random #  */
if     ID<=20 then group=1;    /***take first 20 for group 1      */
if 20<ID<=40 then group=2;    /***take next  20 for group 2      */
if 40<ID<=60 then group=3;  run;/***take next  20 for group 3    */

data music.kathykey;set kathydata;
keep name id group;run;      /*keep separate key to link ID and names*/

data kathydata;set kathydata;drop name x;run;  /*dump unneeded stuff*/
proc sort data=kathydata; by group id;run;        /*put in order*/
proc print;run;                 /*outputs list with ID# & Group # */

/************* Send back to Excel for data coding ***/
/**created with export wizard ***/
PROC EXPORT
 DATA= WORK.KATHYDATA
 OUTFILE= "U:\drake and jonson-reid\Book\projects\Kathy\Kathydata01.xls"
 DBMS= EXCEL2000 REPLACE;RUN;
```

information on codebooks, see Chapter 11). She recruited her coders as usual and put their names in an Excel spreadsheet (see Kathynames.xls. She then wrote an SAS program "KATHY1.SAS," which imported that spreadsheet into SAS and randomly assigned the coders to groups using the SAS code shown in Figure 12.2. That program then exported the file back to Excel for data entry.

Professor Kathy now had an Excel file listing the ID numbers and group numbers for the coders in her study. She did not bring forward the names of the coders because it is always a good idea to leave identifying information out of the data whenever possible. If she needs to link names to ID numbers later she can do so by consulting the SAS data set (KATHYKEY. sas7bdat) that she has kept. The current .XLS file (KATHYDATA01.XLS) will serve as the spreadsheet on which data will be entered.

Kathy took the finished files as the coders completed them and gave them to other student research assistants to check. She randomly assigned the files to her quality-assurance coders for checking. The random assignment is done to prevent bias from creeping in this way. The files are marked with the original coder's ID number and not his or her name. This is another attempt to make sure they are checked in a fair and unbiased manner. Following this second coding, the ratings were compared by yet a third reviewer. If the first two coders agreed on a file, then the file was classified as correctly coded. When differences between the raters arose, this third rater went back to the original file to determine whether the original coder was in error. As the last coders finished each file, they entered the number of files completed and the number of errors onto a sheet of paper, which Professor Kathy entered herself into the Excel spreadsheet changing the name to KATHYDATA02.XLS. Although a series of minor problems emerged, the coding got done, and Professor Kathy was now ready to reimport the Excel spreadsheet back into SAS. She also wanted to compute the number errors per file coded in each session (EPF1, EPF2 . . .). She also wanted to know the total number of files coded over all five sessions (FALL), the total number of errors over all five sessions (EALL), and the average number of errors over all sessions (EPFALL). Finally, she wanted to make sure she had good labels on the variables. The SAS code in Figure 12.3 did this and also printed

---

FIGURE 12.3. **Professor Kathy's SAS Code 2.**

```
/*******************************************************************/
/*********************** KATHY2.SAS *******************************/
/*******************************************************************/
/****** DATA MANAGEMENT PROGRAM FOR KATHY'S PROJECT **************/
/*******************************************************************/
/* Takes entered scores from kathydata02.xls and data manages them */
/*******************************************************************/

libname Music "U:\drake and jonson-reid\book\projects\kathy";

/******************BRING DATA FROM EXCEL INTO SAS ***/
/* below from input wizard */
PROC IMPORT OUT= WORK.kathydata
 DATAFILE= "U:/drake and jonson-
reid/book/projects/kathy/Kathydata02.xls"
 DBMS=EXCEL2000 REPLACE;
 GETNAMES=YES; RUN;

/*** DATA MANAGEMENT: CREATION OF NEW VARIABLES *************/
data kathydata;set kathydata;
/****calculate errors per file for each of the five sessions**/
/****errors per file (EPF) = errors / files coded (E/F)     **/
/****round to nearest thousandth to make output cleaner     **/
epf1=round (e1/f1,.001); /** for session 1 **/
epf2=round (e2/f2,.001); /** for session 2 **/
epf3=round (e3/f3,.001); /** for session 3 **/
epf4=round (e4/f4,.001); /** for session 4 **/
epf5=round (e5/f5,.001); /** for session 5 **/
fall=f1+f2+f3+f4+f5; /*calculate total # files  */
eall=e1+e2+e3+e4+e5; /*calculate total # errors */
epfall=round (eall/fall, .001); /*round to .001*/
/***  LABELING SO I'LL KNOW WHAT THE VARIABLES MEAN     ********/
label f1   = "Files coded (session 1)"
      e1   = "Errors made (session 1)"
      epf1 = "Errors per file (session 1)"
      f2   = "Files coded (session 2)"
      e2   = "Errors made (session 2)"
      epf2 = "Errors per file (session 2)"
      f3   = "Files coded (session 3)"
      e3   = "Errors made (session 3)"
      epf3 = "Errors per file (session 3)"
      f4   = "Files coded (session 4)"
      e4   = "Errors made (session 4)"
      epf4 = "Errors per file (session 4)"
      f5   = "Files coded (session 5)"
      e5   = "Errors made (session 5)"
      epf5 = "Errors per file (session 5)"
      fall = "All files coded (all sessions)"
      eall = "All errors made (all sessions)"
      epfall = "Errors per file (all sessions)"
      group  = "Group (1=CBM, 2=ELBM, 3=NBM)"
      id     = "Individual ID number"; run;
/********put in logical order and review**********/
      proc sort data=kathydata;by group id;run;
      proc print;   run;
      proc freq;    run;
/*********output as final dataset*********/
data music.kathydata;set kathydata;run;
```

out some basic numbers (PROC FREQ, PRINT, and UNIVARIATE) so that she could look at her data. She therefore wrote KATH2.SAS to do her data management tasks.

Things looked very much as they should, and Professor Kathy was now ready to begin her analysis.

SECTION 12.2
MARIA

Trouble started early for Maria. Getting Census data wasn't easy. She had difficulty using "American Fact Finder" at the U.S. Government Census Web site because it would show only a few numbers at a time, and she needed hundreds. She couldn't figure out how to download spreadsheets or other kinds of data files. After many hours, and a series of e-mails to the Feds, Maria got frustrated and tried looking for other sources. Finally, she noticed that the Census data are also on DVD (Census 2000 Summary File 3), and her university had a copy. They even let her take the disk home and install the data on her computer. This disk also included all the documentation in a .pdf file, so she could see what each variable was all about. Unfortunately, she couldn't figure out where to get data on how much land there was in each zip code. She needed this so that she could figure out a measure of population density. More surfing got her to California and to SANDAG (San Diego Association of Governments), which got her to "Resources and Other Data," which eventually got her to "Data Warehouse," where she was able to find data on how many developed acres there were in each zip code in San Diego. They also had a measure of median age, something she couldn't find directly in the zip code data. According to the Web site, these data are apparently also Census data, but Maria never quite figured out how to get them directly from her Census disks. Maria felt confident that SANDAG was a reliable source because it is the governmental regional planning agency for San Diego, so she was willing to trust their data. If Maria were writing for publication, she'd have to call up the Feds and find out how to gain access to the data directly. For her purposes, however, citing SANDAG is fine.

She downloaded the Census data into an Excel (.xls) file, printed out the acreage and coroner data, and entered these by hand into the .xls file. Maria knew that she would need to do a lot of data management in her programming later. For example, the number of people per developed acre required her to divide the number of persons (Census data) by the acreage of land in San Diego (SANDAG data).

ISSUES WITH UNITS OF ANALYSIS

Census data are collected at a large number of different "universe" levels. These are essentially units of analysis. For example, poverty might be collected at the "universe: households" level, telling you how many households are poor, or it might be collected at the "universe: individuals" level, telling you how many individuals are poor.

Maria had trouble finding data about income and poverty at the level of the individual. Maria's unit of analysis was the zip code, but her outcome variable measured people who die. Because of this, Maria tried to collect Census data at the level of the person, but many fields were at the household or family level. Although she wanted a measure of median individual income, the only median income numbers she could find were at the family and household levels. She found the following options:

- There is a measure of individual mean income at the individual level (Census variable P082001). She worried about this because means are subject to skewing by a few outliers (such as very rich persons in this case).

- A measure of household median income (P053001) is also available. Maybe she could use the household median income number? This made some sense because an individual might be best characterized by how much money his or her household earns, but it would also make very large households appear richer than they really are on a per-person basis. Could this bias the data if some zip codes had larger average household sizes? Maria wasn't sure.

- She found the percentage of persons in each zip code who were in poverty. This could be found by taking the number of people in poverty (P087002), dividing this by the total number of people (P087001), and multiplying by 100. These numbers are not exactly based on the total population, but on the "population for whom poverty status is determined." This is why she needed to use P087001 as the denominator and not just use P001001. Reviewing the documentation (Summary File 3, Technical Documentation, U.S. Bureau of the Census, p. B-35, 2000), she learned that this is everyone except people in institutions, colleges, military barracks, and some people under 15 years old. This seemed OK.

Maria figured she'd download all the variables into her data set. Which one would she use? Her professor always told her to base her decisions on theory, and theoretically she was really trying to get at how many people had their lives influenced by true financial hardship. This implied the percentage of persons in poverty might be the most useful.

SECTION 12.2.1: CODEBOOK CONSTRUCTION

Perhaps the most important phase for Maria was careful codebook construction. She had variables all over the place and had to keep a tight lock on where she got

them from. She therefore created the codebook shown in Figure 12.4.

Note that Maria's codebook tracked both her variable name and also the source variable code (e.g., P001001) found in the technical documentation. This would save time if Maria (or anyone else) had to go back and refer to the original data or documents later. Note also that Maria chose to list each created variable twice, once telling about the source, range, and missing data codes for each variable and once listing a more

---

FIGURE 12.4. Maria's Codebook.

Census Data

(Census 2000 Summary File 3, Census of Population and Housing (on DVD), V1-D00-S3ST—08-US1, U.S. Census Bureau, 2003)

My Variable Name	Data Description	Census Data Field	Range	Missing Data
People	People in Zipcode	P001001	0+	.
PovPoor	People in Zipcode* in poverty	P087002	0+	.
PovAll	People in Zipcode*	P087001	0+	.
IncomeI	Individual Mean Income	P082001	0+	.
IncomeH	Household Median	P053001	0+	.
AloneM	Males in 1-Person Households	P009019	0+	.
AloneW	Females in 1-Person Households	P009022	0+	.
TotalHH	Total people in households	P009001	0+	.
RaceHISP	Hispanics (all)	P007010	0+	.
RaceBIRA	NonHispanic Biracial	P007009	0+	.
RaceAMIN	NonHispanic Amerindian	P007005	0+	.
RaceAS1	Nonhispanic Asian	P007006	0+	.
RaceAS2	Nonhispanic Hawaiian	P007007	0+	.
RaceBLAC	Nonhispanic Black/Af.American	P007004	0+	.
RaceWHIT	Nonhispanic White	P007003	0+	.
RaceOTHE	Nonhispanic Other	P007008	0+	.
Over24	People 25 years old and up	P037001	0+	.

Coroner Data

(www.sdcounty.ca.gov/cnty/cntydepts/safety/medical/stat/2000mestats.pdf)

(www.sdcounty.ca.gov/cnty/cntydepts/safety/medical/stat/2001mestats.pdf)

My Variable Name	Data Description	Range	Missing Data
Ho2000	Homicides in 2000	0+	.
Su2000	Suicides in 2000	0+	.
Ho2001	Homicides in 2001	0+	.
Su2001	Suicides in 2001	0+	.

Data From SANDAG (http://cart.sandag.org/dw/)

Acres	Total Developed Acres	0+	.
Age	Median age	0+	.

Created Variables (Sources, Range, and Missing Values)

Variable	Source Variables	Range	Missing
Homicide	(Ho2000+Ho2001) / 2	0+	.
Suicide	(Su2000+Su2001) / 2	0+	.
Density	People/acres	0+	.

Variable	Source Variables	Range	Missing
Suicide	1000*Homicide/people	0+	.
Density	1000*Suicide/people	0+	.
PCTpoor	100 * (PovPoor/PovAll)	0–100	.
PCTalone	100 * ((AloneM+AloneW)/People)	0–100	.
PCThispa	100 * (RaceHISP/people)	0–100	.
PCTasia	100 * ((RaceAS1+RaceAS2)/people)	0–100	.
PCTblack	100 * (RaceBLAC/people)	0–100	.
PCTwhite	100 * (RaceWHIT/people)	0–100	.
PCTother	100 * ((RaceOTHE+RaceAMIN +RaceBIRA)/people)	0–100	.
PCT25up	100 * (over24/people)	0–100	.

Created Variables (Definitions)	
Homicide	Average homicides per year (2000–01)
Suicide	Average suicides per year (2000–01)
Hrate	Homicides per 1000 people per year
Srate	Suicides per 1000 people per year
Density	people per acre of developed land
PCTpoor	percentage of people below poverty line
PCTalone	percentage of people living alone
PCThispa	percentage Hispanic
PCTasia	percentage Asian
PCTblack	percentage African-American / Black
PCTwhite	percentage White
PCTother	percentage Biracial, Other, or Amerindian
PCT25up	percentage of population over 24

* For whom poverty status is determined.
Note: All variables are numeric.

heuristic (humanly understandable) definition. Notice the codebook is designed so that every variable can be traced back to the original source data easily.

Maria wrote an SAS program (Figure 12.5) to input the data from her codebook and transform them into the variables she needed. Maria then reviewed the output,

FIGURE 12.5. Maria's SAS Program.

```
/***************maria.sas***************/
/***************maria.sas***************/
/***************maria.sas***************/
/***************maria.sas***************/
/***************maria.sas***************/
/****   manages maria's.data       ****/
/****************************************/
libname maria "u:drake and jonson-reid\book\projects\maria";run;

PROC IMPORT OUT= WORK.CENSUS
 DATAFILE= "U:\drake and jonson-reid\Book\projects\Maria\census.xls"
 DBMS=EXCEL4 REPLACE;GETNAMES=YES;RUN;

/***************data management section ********************/
/*************   rename and relabel   ********************/
data census;
set census;
People   = P001001;PovPoor    = P087002;PovAll   = P087001;
IncomeI  = P082001;IncomeH    = P053001;AloneM   = P009019;
AloneW   = P009022;TotalHH    = P009001;RaceHISP = P007010;
RaceBIRA = P007009;RaceAMIN   = P007005;RaceAS1  = P007006;
RaceAS2  = P007007;RaceBLAC   = P007004;RaceWHIT = P007003;
RaceOTHE = P007008;Over24=P037001;
```

(Continued)

FIGURE 12.5. (Continued)

```
drop P001001 P087002 P087001 P082001 P053001 P009019
     P009022 P009001 P007010 P007009 P007005 P007006
     P007007 P007004 P007003 P007008 P037001;
label
People    = "People in Zipcode                 P001001"
PovPoor   = "People in Zipcode* in poverty      P087002"
PovAll    = "People in Zipcode*                 P087001"
IncomeI   = "Individual Mean Income             P082001"
IncomeH   = "Household Median                   P053001"
AloneM    = "Males in 1-Person Households       P009019"
AloneW    = "Females in 1-Person Households     P009022"
TotalHH   = "Total people in households         P009001"
RaceHISP  = "Hispanics (all)                    P008010"
RaceBIRA  = "NonHispanic Biracial               P008009"
RaceAMIN  = "NonHispanic Amerindian             P008005"
RaceAS1   = "Nonhispanic Asian                  P008006"
RaceAS2   = "Nonhispanic Hawaiian               P008007"
RaceBLAC  = "Nonhispanic Black/Af.American      P008004"
RaceWHIT  = "Nonhispanic White                  P008003"
RaceOTHE  = "Nonhispanic Other                  P008008"
Acres     = "Acres of developed land in Zip"
ho2000    = "Homicides in Zip (2000)"
su2000    = "Suicides in Zip (2000)"
ho2001    = "Homicides in Zip (2001)"
su2001    = "Suicides in Zip (2001)"
over24    = "People 25 And Over";run;

/**************data management section *********************/
/************* create new variables ***********************/
data census;set census;
Homicide = (Ho2000+Ho2001) / 2;
Suicide  = (Su2000+Su2001) / 2;
Density  = People/acres ;
PCTpoor  = 100 * (PovPoor/PovAll);
PCTalone = 100 * ((AloneM+AloneW)/People);
PCThispa = 100 * (RaceHISP/people);
PCTasia  = 100 * ((RaceAS1+RaceAS2)/people);
PCTblack = 100 * (RaceBLAC/people);
PCTwhite = 100 * (RaceWHIT/people);
PCTother = 100 * ((RaceOTHE+RaceAMIN+RaceBIRA)/people);
PCT25up  = 100 * (over24/people);
label
 PCT25UP  = "Percentage of people 25 and over"
 Homicide = "Average homicides per year (2001-02)"
 Suicide  = "Average suicides per year (2001-02)"
 Density  = "people per acre of developed land"
 PCTpoor  = "percentage of people below poverty line"
 PCTalone = "percentage of people living alone"
 PCThispa = "percentage Hispanic"
 PCTasia  = "percentage Asian"
 PCTblack = "percentage African-American / Black"
 PCTwhite = "percentage White"
 PCTother = "percentage Biracial,other,or Amerindian";
 run;
/******** take out very low population zipcodes
 which could produce unstable results*********/
data census;
set census;
if people<3000 then delete;run;

/***Calculate rates per year*****************/
data maria.maria2;set census;
HRate=round((homicide*1000)/people,.0001);
SRate=round((Suicide*1000)/people,.0001);
label HRate="Homicides per 1000 people per year";
label SRate="Suicides per 1000 people per year";
  run;
/************* examine the data *************/
proc freq;run;
proc univariate;run;
proc print;run;
```

which looks as she expected. She was now done with her basic data management and was ready for analysis.

SECTION 12.3
ABIGAIL

Abigail started by looking at her state child welfare agency's annual report. She found that there were 110 child fatalities the prior year. This is, of course, a serious tragedy, but for Abigail's purposes, higher numbers are better, providing a larger potential sample and more statistical power. She made an appointment to talk with a representative of the research division of the state agency and got to work putting together her mailout packet and her human subjects application. She decided to do a mailout that included the three instruments she would use, the Social Support Behaviors Scale (SSB), the Impact of Events Scale (IES), and the Organizational Climate Scale (OCS). She decided to front these with a letter introducing the project and with a short questionnaire to get basic demographic information from the respondents. She talked with her human subjects committee about how to handle the difficult issue of having workers react to the memory of the child fatality and got some initial ideas about how to do that. Her packet included the following items:

- Cover page
- Consent form
- General information form
- SSB
- OCS (items 21 through 30 only: other subscales were not needed)
- IES

Abigail met with a representative of the state child welfare agency, who was enthusiastic about the project. She also met with the director of a local crisis hotline, "WeCare," who agreed to allow her to put their number in the consent form. It was decided that the questionnaires would be mailed directly to the worker's workplace using a list supplied by the agency. This list included 110 workers who had suffered fatalities on their caseloads in the last 12 months. It was further decided that Abigail would telephone the workers a week after the forms were mailed to answer any questions the workers may have. Abigail hoped this might increase the response rate. The packet included a stamped, self-addressed return envelope and looked like the materials in Figure 12.6.

Abigail submitted an IRB packet to Washington College's oversight committee, describing her work and providing a copy of the instrument, and was granted approval. She mailed 110 packets to the list of workers

---

FIGURE 12.6. Abigail's Packet.

a. Abigail's Cover Page

September 9, 2005

Hello,

My name is Abigail Smith, and I am a PhD student at Washington College. I am interested in finding out about how workers do after they have fatalities in their caseloads. I would like to ask you to fill out the accompanying forms and return them to me so that we can learn more about this very important subject. You have the option not to participate, but we hope you can take a few moments from your workday so that we can better understand this issue and possibly learn to help others better in the future. If you do agree to participate, please fill out the enclosed consent form. Someone may telephone you in the next few days to see if you have any questions.

Thank you for your cooperation.

Abigail Smith

Abigail Smith, MSW,
Washington College

b. Abigail's Consent Form

Worker Coping Study

You are invited to participate in a research study conducted by Abigail Smith, MSW, and Joe Advisor, PhD. The overall purpose of this project is to understand more about how child welfare workers do after suffering a fatality in their caseload. Your participation will involve filling out the below forms. There are no known risks or benefits to you associated with your participation in the study, except that recalling the events may trigger some emotional reactions. Your participation is voluntary, and you may choose not to participate in this research. If you choose not to participate, it will not affect your employment in any way. The State Child Welfare Agency will not even be informed of your participation or nonparticipation. The data you supply will be anonymous, meaning your name will not be on any of the forms provided, and all forms will be kept confidential and will be destroyed after data entry. Although your consent form does include your signature, it will be kept separately from your response form and there will be no way of linking your name to the responses you provide. We will do everything we can to protect your privacy. As part of this effort, your identity will not be revealed in any publication that may result from this study. In rare instances, a researcher's study must undergo an audit or program evaluation by an oversight agency (such as the Office of Human Research Protection) that would lead to disclosure of your data as well as any other information collected by the researcher. If you have any questions, concerns, or complaints about the research please contact Abigail Smith, MSW at (555) 555-5555. If you cannot reach anyone at the above number or if you wish to talk to someone else, have questions or concerns about the study or your rights as a research participant, feel you were pressured to participate, or believe you have been harmed in any way as a result of this research, call Bob Brown at (555) 555-5556. Mr. Brown is an employee of Washington College but is not part of the research team. You can call before, during, or after you take part in the research study. Everything you say will be kept confidential.

(Continued)

FIGURE 12.6. (Continued)

If you experience discomfort or emotional distress while filling out this form and feel you need help or wish to talk to someone, you may contact the Child Welfare Agency internal helpline (555) 555-5557 or the "WeCare" crisis hotline at (555) 555-5558.

I have read this consent form and have been given a chance to ask questions. I will also be given a signed copy of this form for my records. I agree to participate in the research project above, titled "Worker Coping Study."

_____
Participant's Name Here

_____
Signature of Project Director

c. Abigail's General Information Form

Worker Coping Study
General Information Form

First we'd like to get some basic information to help us understand you. Please fill in the below items.

1) Please select one: I am Male[ ] Female[ ]

2) What was your age at the time of the most recent child fatality in your caseload?
[_____] years

3) What was the age of the child who died (select the youngest if more than one died in the most recent fatality case)?
[_____] years

4) Was the case with the fatality active in your caseload at the time?
[ ] Yes [ ] No

5) How long ago did the most recent fatality occur (enter "0" if less than one month)?
[_____] months

6) How long was the child's case active in your caseload (enter "0" if less than one month)?
[_____] months

7) How many years have you worked for the State Child Welfare Agency?
[_____] years

SSB

People help each other out in a lot of different ways. Suppose you had some kind of problem (were upset about something, needed help with a practical problem, were broke, or needed some advice or guidance). *How likely* would (a) members of your *family*, and (b) your *friends* be to help you out in each of the specific ways listed below? We realize you may rarely need this kind of help, but *if you did* would family or friends help in the ways indicated? Try to base your answers on your past experience with these people. Use the scale below, and circle one number under family, and one under friends, in each row.

1 = *No one* would do this
2 = *Someone might* do this
3 = *Some* family member/friend would *probably* do this
4 = *Some* family member/friend would *certainly* do this
5 = *Most* family members/friend would *certainly* do this

		(a) Family					(b) Friends				
1	Would suggest doing something, just to take my mind off my problems	1	2	3	4	5	1	2	3	4	5
2	Would visit with me or invite me over	1	2	3	4	5	1	2	3	4	5
3	Would comfort me if I was upset	1	2	3	4	5	1	2	3	4	5
4	Would give me a ride if I needed one	1	2	3	4	5	1	2	3	4	5
5	Would have lunch or dinner with me	1	2	3	4	5	1	2	3	4	5
6	Would look after my belongings (house, pets, and the like) for a while	1	2	3	4	5	1	2	3	4	5
7	Would loan me a car if I needed one	1	2	3	4	5	1	2	3	4	5
8	Would joke around or suggest doing something to cheer me up	1	2	3	4	5	1	2	3	4	5
9	Would go to a movie or concert with me	1	2	3	4	5	1	2	3	4	5
10	Would suggest how I could find out more about a situation	1	2	3	4	5	1	2	3	4	5
11	Would help me out with a move or other big chore	1	2	3	4	5	1	2	3	4	5
12	Would listen if I needed to talk about my feelings	1	2	3	4	5	1	2	3	4	5
13	Would have a good time with me	1	2	3	4	5	1	2	3	4	5
14	Would pay for my lunch if I was broke	1	2	3	4	5	1	2	3	4	5
15	Would suggest a way I might do something	1	2	3	4	5	1	2	3	4	5
16	Would give me encouragement to do something difficult	1	2	3	4	5	1	2	3	4	5
17	Would give me advice about what to do	1	2	3	4	5	1	2	3	4	5
18	Would chat with me	1	2	3	4	5	1	2	3	4	5
19	Would help me figure out what I wanted to do	1	2	3	4	5	1	2	3	4	5
20	Would show me that they understood how I was feeling	1	2	3	4	5	1	2	3	4	5
21	Would buy me a drink if I was short of money	1	2	3	4	5	1	2	3	4	5
22	Would help me decide what to do	1	2	3	4	5	1	2	3	4	5
23	Would give me a hug or otherwise show me I was cared about	1	2	3	4	5	1	2	3	4	5

		(a) Family	(b) Friends
24	Would call me just to see how I was doing	1 2 3 4 5	1 2 3 4 5
25	Would help me figure out what was going on	1 2 3 4 5	1 2 3 4 5
26	Would help me out with some necessary purchase	1 2 3 4 5	1 2 3 4 5
27	Would not pass judgment on me	1 2 3 4 5	1 2 3 4 5
28	Would tell me who to talk to for help	1 2 3 4 5	1 2 3 4 5
29	Would loan me money for an indefinite period	1 2 3 4 5	1 2 3 4 5
30	Would be sympathetic if I was upset	1 2 3 4 5	1 2 3 4 5
31	Would stick by me in a crunch	1 2 3 4 5	1 2 3 4 5
32	Would buy me clothes if I was short of money	1 2 3 4 5	1 2 3 4 5
33	Would tell me about available choices and options	1 2 3 4 5	1 2 3 4 5
34	Would loan me tools, equipment, or appliances if I needed them	1 2 3 4 5	1 2 3 4 5
35	Would give me reasons why I should or should not do something	1 2 3 4 5	1 2 3 4 5
36	Would show affection for me	1 2 3 4 5	1 2 3 4 5
37	Would show me how to do something I don't know how to do	1 2 3 4 5	1 2 3 4 5
38	Would bring me little presents of things I needed	1 2 3 4 5	1 2 3 4 5
39	Would tell me the best way to get something done	1 2 3 4 5	1 2 3 4 5
40	Would talk to other people to arrange something for me	1 2 3 4 5	1 2 3 4 5
41	Would loan me money and want to "forget about it"	1 2 3 4 5	1 2 3 4 5
42	Would tell me what to do	1 2 3 4 5	1 2 3 4 5
43	Would offer me a place to stay for awhile	1 2 3 4 5	1 2 3 4 5
44	Would help me think about a problem	1 2 3 4 5	1 2 3 4 5
45	Would loan me a fairly large sum of money (say the equivalent of a month's rent or mortgage)	1 2 3 4 5	1 2 3 4 5

d. Abigail's OCS

	Please read each statement below and decide to what degree each describes your workplace:	False	Mostly False	Mostly True	True
21	We confront and embarrass each other in meetings.	0	1	2	3
22	We are respectful of each other's feelings.	0	1	2	3
23	We are not open and honest with each other.	0	1	2	3
24	We work hard to be sure colleagues/coworkers are not offended or hurt emotionally.	0	1	2	3
25	We walk away from disagreements and heated discussions feeling frustrated.	0	1	2	3
26	We affirm each other's opinions and viewpoints, even when we may disagree.	0	1	2	3
27	We make matters more difficult by getting emotionally upset and stirring up old problems.	0	1	2	3
28	We take the time to hear what each other has to say or feel.	0	1	2	3
29	We work to be calm and talk things through.	0	1	2	3
30	We get upset, but we try to end our differences on a positive note.	0	1	2	3

she got from the agency, telephoned them to see if they had any questions (which resulted in her resending several packets), and was fortunate enough to receive 78 completed forms back in the mail, giving a response rate of 78/110 or 71%, a good rate for a mailed survey.

She entered her data into Excel and then imported it into SAS, using the import wizard. Her codebook for her data looks like Figure 12.7. Apart from inputting the data from Excel and labeling commands, the only SAS code Abigail had to run was to create the subscale totals (Figure 12.8). To see the full program, refer to "ABIGAILDATAMGMT.SAS." Abigail had now done her data management and was ready for the next step.

SECTION 12.4
YUAN

Apart from his consent form, Yuan had to distribute only one form, the argument scales. He would administer these himself at the first and last sessions of the groups. He didn't simply let the group leaders do it because he wanted the administration of the instrument to be as uniform as possible. (*Author's note: unlike the other scales used in this book, this is a purely fictional scale for purposes of this example project only.*) The argument scales are a set of four subscales, the avoidance scale (1r*,15,4,21,9r,24), the empathy scale (14,5,19r,8r,22,11r), the forethought scale (2,3r,7,13r,18r,20), and the usefulness scale (6,10r,12,16,17r,23r). Items are scored 1 to 5 ("never" to "always").

FIGURE 12.7. **Abigail's Codebook.**

Variable	Description	Type	Range	Missing Data	Source
		Subject General Information			
active	1=active case at time of fatality	Num	0 or 1	.	General Information Form
age	age of worker at time of fatality		20-70		
childage	child age at time of fatality (0=<1yr old)		0-17		
female	1=female worker, 0=male worker		0 or 1		
jobyears	years in this job (0=<1)		0 to 50		
monthago	number of full months between fatality and survey (0=<1 month)		0-12		
timeopen	time case open to worker in months (last spell, 0=<1month)		0		
		IES Item Data			
IESAV002	IES avoidance subscale item #02	Num	0,1,3,5	.	IES
IESAV003	IES avoidance subscale item #03				
IESAV007	IES avoidance subscale item #07				
IESAV008	IES avoidance subscale item #08				
IESAV012	IES avoidance subscale item #12				
IESAV013	IES avoidance subscale item #13				
IESAV015	IES avoidance subscale item #15				
IESAV019	IES avoidance subscale item #19				
IESINT01	IES intrusiveness subscale item #01				
IESINT04	IES intrusiveness subscale item #04				
IESINT05	IES intrusiveness subscale item #05				
IESINT06	IES intrusiveness subscale item #06				
IESINT10	IES intrusiveness subscale item #10				
IESINT11	IES intrusiveness subscale item #11				
IESINT14	IES intrusiveness subscale item #14				
		IES Subscale Totals (Created)			
IESAVO	IES avoidance subscale total	Num	0-40	.	IES (summed)
IESINT	IES intrusion subscale total	Num	0-35	.	IES (summed)
		OCS Item Data			
OCSCON21	OCS Conf. Subscale, ITEM 21	Num	0,1,2,3	.	OCS
OCSCON23	OCS Conf. Subscale, ITEM 23				
OCSCON25	OCS Conf. Subscale, ITEM 25				
OCSCON27	OCS Conf. Subscale, ITEM 27				
OCSCON29	OCS Conf. Subscale, ITEM 29				
OCSSUP22	OCS Supp. Subscale, ITEM 22				
OCSSUP24	OCS Supp. Subscale, ITEM 24				
OCSSUP26	OCS Supp. Subscale, ITEM 26				
OCSSUP28	OCS Supp. Subscale, ITEM 28				
OCSSUP30	OCS Supp. Subscale, ITEM 30				
		OCS Subscale Totals (Created)			
OCSCON	Full score from OCS conflictual communication subscale	Num	0-15	.	OCS
OCSSUP	Full score from OCS supportive communication subscale	Num	0-15	.	OCS

SSB Item Data					
SSBAD10A	SSB advice/guidance (family) subscale item # 10A				
SSBAD10B	SSB advice/guidance (friend) subscale item # 10B				
SSBAD15A	SSB advice/guidance (family) subscale item # 15A				
SSBAD15B	SSB advice/guidance (friend) subscale item # 15B				
SSBAD17A	SSB advice/guidance (family) subscale item # 17A				
SSBAD17B	SSB advice/guidance (friend) subscale item # 17B				
SSBAD19A	SSB advice/guidance (family) subscale item # 19A				
SSBAD19B	SSB advice/guidance (friend) subscale item # 19B				
SSBAD22A	SSB advice/guidance (family) subscale item # 22A				
SSBAD22B	SSB advice/guidance (friend) subscale item # 22B				
SSBAD25A	SSB advice/guidance (family) subscale item # 25A				
SSBAD25B	SSB advice/guidance (friend) subscale item # 25B				
SSBAD28A	SSB advice/guidance (family) subscale item # 28A				
SSBAD28B	SSB advice/guidance (friend) subscale item # 28B				
SSBAD33A	SSB advice/guidance (family) subscale item # 33A				
SSBAD33B	SSB advice/guidance (friend) subscale item # 33B				
SSBAD35A	SSB advice/guidance (family) subscale item # 35A				
SSBAD35B	SSB advice/guidance (friend) subscale item # 35B				
SSBAD39A	SSB advice/guidance (family) subscale item # 39A				
SSBAD39B	SSB advice/guidance (friend) subscale item # 39B				
SSBAD42A	SSB advice/guidance (family) subscale item # 42A				
SSBAD42B	SSB advice/guidance (friend) subscale item # 42B				
SSBAD44A	SSB advice/guidance (family) subscale item # 44A	Num	1-5	.	SSB
SSBAD44B	SSB advice/guidance (friend) subscale item # 44B				
SSBEM03A	SSB emotional (family) subscale item # 3A				
SSBEM03B	SSB emotional (friend) subscale item # 3B				
SSBEM08A	SSB emotional (family) subscale item # 8A				
SSBEM08B	SSB emotional (friend) subscale item # 8B				
SSBEM12A	SSB emotional (family) subscale item # 12A				
SSBEM12B	SSB emotional (friend) subscale item # 12B				
SSBEM16A	SSB emotional (family) subscale item # 16A				
SSBEM16B	SSB emotional (friend) subscale item # 16B				
SSBEM20A	SSB emotional (family) subscale item # 20A				
SSBEM20B	SSB emotional (friend) subscale item # 20B				
SSBEM23A	SSB emotional (family) subscale item # 23A				
SSBEM23B	SSB emotional (friend) subscale item # 23B				
SSBEM27A	SSB emotional (family) subscale item # 27A				
SSBEM27B	SSB emotional (friend) subscale item # 27B				
SSBEM30A	SSB emotional (family) subscale item # 30A				
SSBEM30B	SSB emotional (friend) subscale item # 30B				
SSBEM31A	SSB emotional (family) subscale item # 31A				
SSBEM31B	SSB emotional (friend) subscale item # 31B				
SSBEM36A	SSB emotional (family) subscale item # 36A				
SSBEM36B	SSB emotional (friend) subscale item # 36B				
SSBS001A	SSB social (family) subscale item # 1A				

(Continued)

FIGURE 12.7. **(Continued)**

SSBS001B	SSB social (friend) subscale item # 1B				
SSBS002A	SSB social (family) subscale item # 2A				
SSBS002B	SSB social (friend) subscale item # 2B				
SSBS005A	SSB social (family) subscale item # 5A				
SSBS005B	SSB social (friend) subscale item # 5B				
SSBS009A	SSB social (family) subscale item # 9A				
SSBS009B	SSB social (friend) subscale item # 9B				
SSBS013A	SSB social (family) subscale item # 13A	Num	1–5	.	SSB
SSBS013B	SSB social (friend) subscale item # 13B				
SSBS018A	SSB social (family) subscale item # 18A				
SSBS018B	SSB social (friend) subscale item # 18B				
SSBS024A	SSB social (family) subscale item # 24A				
SSBS024B	SSB social (friend) subscale item # 24B				
SSBS0A	SSB Total, Social Subscale (Family)				
SSBS0B	SSB Total, Social Subscale (Friends)				

SSB Subscale Totals (Created)

SSBADA	SSB Total, Advice/Guidance Subscale. Family items 10+15+17+19+22+25 +28+33+35+39+42+44		12–60		
SSBEMA	SSB Total, Emotional Subscale. Family items 3+8+12+16+20+23 +27+30+31+36		10–50		
SSBS0A	SSB Total, Social Subscale. Family items 1+2+5+9+13+18+24	Num	7–35	.	SSB
SSBADB	SSB Total, Advice/Guidance Subscale. Friend items 10+15+17+19+22+25 +28+33+35+39+42+44		12–60		
SSBEMB	SSB Total, Emotional Subscale. Friend items 3+8+12+16+20+23 +27+30+31+36		10–50		
SSBS0B	SSB Total, Social Subscale. Friend items 1+2+5+9+13+18+24		7–35		

FIGURE 12.8. **Abigail's Subscale Totals.**

```
DATA BOOK.ABIGAIL1;
SET BOOK.ABIGAIL1;
/************* Sum up values of subscales ****/
/*** OCS ***/
OCSCON=OCSCON21+OCSCON23+OCSCON25+OCSCON27+OCSCON29;
OCSSUP=OCSSUP22+OCSSUP24+OCSSUP26+OCSSUP28+OCSSUP30;
/*** IES ***/
IESINT=IESINT01+IESINT04+IESINT05+IESINT06+IESINT10+IESINT11+IESINT14;
IESAV0=IESAV002+IESAV003+IESAV007+IESAV008+IESAV012+IESAV013+
IESAV015+IESAV019;
/*** SSB ***/
SSBEMA = SSBEM03A+SSBEM08A+SSBEM12A+SSBEM16A+SSBEM20A+SSBEM23A+SSBEM27A
+SSBEM30A+SSBEM31A+SSBEM36A;
SSBEMB = SSBEM03B+SSBEM08B+SSBEM12B+SSBEM16B+SSBEM20B+SSBEM23B+SSBEM27B
+SSBEM30B+SSBEM31B+SSBEM36B;
SSBS0A = SSBS001A+SSBS002A+SSBS005A+SSBS009A+SSBS013A+SSBS018A+SSBS024A;
SSBS0B = SSBS001B+SSBS002B+SSBS005B+SSBS009B+SSBS013B+SSBS018B+SSBS024B;
SSBADA = SSBAD10A+SSBAD15A+SSBAD17A+SSBAD19A+SSBAD22A+SSBAD25A+SSBAD28A+
SSBAD33A+SSBAD35A+SSBAD39A+SSBAD42A+SSBAD44A;
SSBADB = SSBAD10B+SSBAD15B+SSBAD17B+SSBAD19B+SSBAD22B+SSBAD25B+SSBAD28B+
SSBAD33B+SSBAD35B+SSBAD39B+SSBAD42B+SSBAD44B;
RUN;
```

The study appeared to be going along well, and Yuan was able to get his pretest data. Unfortunately, the therapists running the ST groups became unwilling to participate in the posttest and followup portions of the project, feeling it an unnecessary intrusion. Yuan never really understood the details of how this happened, and he approached the agency director, who was of the opinion that he should not push the issue. Given Yuan's position, he felt there was little he could do about it. He did have to revise his questions and hypotheses to reflect the reduced amount of data he would receive:

Q1: Do subjects receiving CBT show changes in AS subscale scores from pretest to posttest? This question is meant to address changes during treatment.

H1A: Subjects will show change in the AS avoidance subscale (pretest–posttest).

H1B: Subjects will show change in the AS empathy subscale (pretest–posttest).

H1C: Subjects will show change in the AS forethought subscale (pretest–posttest).

H1D: Subjects will show change in the AS usefulness subscale (pretest–posttest).

Q2: Do subjects receiving CBT show changes in AS subscale scores from posttest to follow-up? This question is meant to see if the changes persist.

H2A: Subjects will show change in the AS avoidance subscale (posttest–follow-up).

H2B: Subjects will show change in the AS empathy subscale (posttest–follow-up).

H2C: Subjects will show change in the AS forethought subscale (posttest–follow-up).

H2D: Subjects will show change in the AS usefulness subscale (posttest–follow-up).

Q3: Do subjects receiving CBT and ST show different rates of reported violence?

This would yield the following hypothesis:

H3: Subjects receiving CBT and ST will show different rates of recidivism during the six months following treatment.

Unfortunately, only Question 3 now uses the comparison group. The study is now essentially correlational with regard to questions 1 and 2, and quasi-experimental with regard to Question 3. A copy of the AS can be seen in Figure 12.9.

Yuan has reverse-scored items in his data set, so he has to switch the values, so that 5s=1, 4s=2, 2s=4 and 1s=5. This can be done with the code shown in Figure 12.10.

The rest of Yuan's data management program does labeling and subscale summing in a way very similar to the prior programs you have seen in this chapter. For the full program, see YUANDATAMGMT.SAS.

Yuan's codebook is quite long and not dissimilar to Abigail's. Yuan's full codebook is too large to present here but is appended as YUANCODEBOOK.DOC and is available online at www.ablongman.com/mysocialworkkit. Yuan was now ready for data analysis.

<hr>
SECTION 12.5
JOHN
<hr>

Recruitment posed some problems for John. He received five responses to his posted flyers within the first week. He was initially concerned about this, and did some repostings in other locations, getting an additional three responses. All the respondents appeared appropriate to the study, being the right age and having been in the United States for at least a year. After completing the first eight interviews, John became troubled by his inability to attract a particular type of respondent. Many of his interviewees mentioned friends of theirs who had more or less left the Bosnian community. John decided to ask some of them for the names and telephone numbers of their friends so that he could interview them. This is a form of snowball sampling and required John to make a revision to his human subjects proposal, which was approved. All of these people had good English skills, and so the interpreter was not needed in the additional interviews. Four new people were recruited in this way. John would very much have liked more respondents but decided to go forward with twelve.

NOTE: We have intentionally restricted this study to 12 respondents to keep it manageable for this book. The number of cases involved is probably not sufficient to reach saturation (see Chapter 6), especially because John wants to look at four subgroups. In a real study, John would have at least three to five times this number of subjects.

The usefulness of the questionnaire was examined. After doing the initial three interviews, John discussed the questions with his interpreter, and they also discussed how the interviews were going. They decided that there were no changes needed.

Each participant's tape-recorded session was transcribed by John. Uncoded versions of the transcript can be viewed in the files subject01.txt through subject12.txt, which can be accessed at www.ablongman.com/mysocialworkkit. John was now ready to begin analysis using NVivo.

FIGURE 12.9. Yuan's Argument Scales (AS) *(fictional example).*

Please indicate how often the statement applies to you by filling in the box by the best answer.

ITEM 1   I am sometimes just in the mood to argue.
☐ Never ☐ Rarely ☐ Sometimes ☐ Often ☐ Very often

ITEM 2   I will usually stop and try to think it over before I argue.
☐ Never ☐ Rarely ☐ Sometimes ☐ Often ☐ Very often

ITEM 3   I don't care about what happens next when I argue.
☐ Never ☐ Rarely ☐ Sometimes ☐ Often ☐ Very often

ITEM 4   I try to avoid topics that will get me into arguments.
☐ Never ☐ Rarely ☐ Sometimes ☐ Often ☐ Very often

ITEM 5   I pay attention to how people feel when I am arguing with them.
☐ Never ☐ Rarely ☐ Sometimes ☐ Often ☐ Very often

ITEM 6   Good things often come out of arguments.
☐ Never ☐ Rarely ☐ Sometimes ☐ Often ☐ Very often

ITEM 7   I pretty much know how an argument is going to go before I get into it.
☐ Never ☐ Rarely ☐ Sometimes ☐ Often ☐ Very often

ITEM 8   Winning an argument always makes me feel good, no matter what.
☐ Never ☐ Rarely ☐ Sometimes ☐ Often ☐ Very often

ITEM 9   Sometimes I can't help it, I just need to tell someone what I think.
☐ Never ☐ Rarely ☐ Sometimes ☐ Often ☐ Very often

ITEM 10 Arguing doesn't help anybody.
☐ Never ☐ Rarely ☐ Sometimes ☐ Often ☐ Very often

ITEM 11 How the other person reacts to what I say is no concern of mine.
☐ Never ☐ Rarely ☐ Sometimes ☐ Often ☐ Very often

ITEM 12 Arguing is often the best option to make something happen.
☐ Never ☐ Rarely ☐ Sometimes ☐ Often ☐ Very often

ITEM 13 I tend to argue first and think about the consequences later.
☐ Never ☐ Rarely ☐ Sometimes ☐ Often ☐ Very often

ITEM 14 I feel bad when an argument turns nasty.
☐ Never ☐ Rarely ☐ Sometimes ☐ Often ☐ Very often

ITEM 15 When I get into an argument, I try to win at any cost.
☐ Never ☐ Rarely ☐ Sometimes ☐ Often ☐ Very often

ITEM 16 Arguing helps people to get things done.
☐ Never ☐ Rarely ☐ Sometimes ☐ Often ☐ Very often

ITEM 17 Arguing stops things from getting accomplished.
☐ Never ☐ Rarely ☐ Sometimes ☐ Often ☐ Very often

ITEM 18 I never think about if I should get into an argument in advance.
☐ Never ☐ Rarely ☐ Sometimes ☐ Often ☐ Very often

ITEM 19 I worry only about how I feel when I am arguing with someone.
☐ Never ☐ Rarely ☐ Sometimes ☐ Often ☐ Very often

ITEM 20 I usually try to figure out if arguing is a good idea or not.
☐ Never ☐ Rarely ☐ Sometimes ☐ Often ☐ Very often

ITEM 21 I feel like I can stop myself from arguing if I want to.
☐ Never ☐ Rarely ☐ Sometimes ☐ Often ☐ Very often

ITEM 22 When I hurt someone's feelings in an argument, it really bothers me.
☐ Never ☐ Rarely ☐ Sometimes ☐ Often ☐ Very often

ITEM 23 I find that arguing makes things worse.
☐ Never ☐ Rarely ☐ Sometimes ☐ Often ☐ Very often

ITEM 24 I try hard to keep discussions from turning into arguments.
☐ Never ☐ Rarely ☐ Sometimes ☐ Often ☐ Very often

FIGURE 12.10. Code to Reverse Yuan's Scores.

```
DATA YUANDATA;SET YUANDATA;
/** REVERSE THOSE ITEMS NEEDING REVERSE SCORING **/
PRE1A    = 6-PRE1A ;  PRE9A    = 6-PRE9A  ;
PRE8E    = 6-PRE8E ;  PRE11E   = 6-PRE11E ; PRE819E    = 6-PRE19E;
PRE3F    = 6-PRE3F ;  PRE13F   = 6-PRE13F ; PRE18F     = 6-PRE18F;
PRE10U   = 6-PRE10U;  PRE17U   = 6-PRE17U ; PRE23U     = 6-PRE23U;
POST1A   = 6-POST1A ; POST9A   = 6-POST9A  ;
POST8E   = 6-POST8E ; POST11E  = 6-POST11E; POST819E   = 6-POST19E;
POST3F   = 6-POST3F ; POST13F  = 6-POST13F; POST18F    = 6-POST18F;
POST10U  = 6-POST10U; POST17U  = 6-POST17U; POST23U    = 6-POST23U;
FOLL1A   = 6-FOLL1A ; FOLL9A   = 6-FOLL9A  ;
FOLL8E   = 6-FOLL8E ; FOLL11E  = 6-FOLL11E; FOLL819E   = 6-FOLL19E;
FOLL3F   = 6-FOLL3F ; FOLL13F  = 6-FOLL13F; FOLL18F    = 6-FOLL18F;
FOLL10U  = 6-FOLL10U; FOLL17U  = 6-FOLL17U; FOLL23U    = 6-FOLL23U;
```

REVIEW

We assume you are working on a project of your own for these questions. Please do the following:

1. If you are doing interview or observational research, show the package of tools or instruments that you will use.

2. If you are doing secondary research, show the data and supporting materials (original documentation) that you will be using.

3. If you are doing qualitative research, show at least three transcripts.

4. Create an electronic database for your findings.

5. Create a codebook.

13

Quantitative Analysis

Now it feels as though as you have been planning forever. You have been reading and copying and reading and writing until you thought it would never end. You now have that burning question . . . or two or three. You have just got to have the answer! So, unless you are doing purely qualitative research (Chapter 6), you must enter the magical world of statistics.

If you are like many folks entering the social sciences, this may be the dreaded moment where you are forced again to consider the role of math in your life. If not, wonderful! If so, be of good cheer; the world of computer analysis programs no longer requires that you be able to evaluate complex algebraic equations. You must simply know what type of statistic has what requirements and be able to answer certain questions. You will need to know how to tell the computer to do what you want and how to interpret the output. Of course, each computer program is a little different, particularly the output, and it's not possible for us to show you how each works. Generally, however, the names of the procedures are similar, and once you learn one it's often not too hard to move to another format with the

help of a "how to use program X" book. It is rather like moving from one word processor to another. The most common programs you are likely to encounter in your course work are STATA, SAS, and SPSS. We will focus on SAS and SPSS in this text, as they seem to be more frequently used programs. Generally, we will provide programming language for SAS but describe the programmer interface (windows-driven) methods in SPSS. This is because, in our experience, most SAS users type in commands ("code") line by line, but most SPSS programmers use the windows-driven interface.

The next two chapters will provide you with the basic tools to answer questions using bivariate (two variable) approaches and a few multivariate (more than two variable) techniques. We will discuss why and how these tests are used, as well as provide SAS and SPSS examples. (In some cases these programs use slightly different algorithms or rounding procedures, so on occasion the output for the same data will vary between the two programs though the conclusions will be the same.) We assume that you have had a basic introduction to statistics in the past (i.e., understanding the normal curve, what probability is, etc.), and therefore these issues are only briefly reviewed prior to discussing univariate and bivariate statistics in this chapter. The chapter then covers the basic tools that a master's-level student might be expected to use. Chapter 14 goes beyond this to provide an introduction to multivariate techniques with interval/ratio data, categorical data, and longitudinal data. Following these chapters, we will see how our five researchers use some of the techniques covered to complete their analyses.

These chapters are not meant to be an advanced statistical resource. Like the rest of this text, we are focused on what you need to know—not necessarily all there is to know. We will not be dwelling on the mathematical formulas underlying the statistics, as found in most statistics texts, but will focus on how to choose a test statistic, use it appropriately, and understand its limitations.

SECTION 13.1
IMPORTANT TERMS

There are a few basic and indispensable terms you must understand to use statistics correctly. We will begin by briefly reviewing (or introducing) these terms and providing practical definitions. You will encounter other terms along the way as we introduce specific techniques, but you need to have a good grasp of these first:

- Probability
- Statistical significance
- Distributions
- Normality
- Measures of central tendency
- Variability
- Nominal, ordinal, and interval/ratio data
- Parametric and nonparametric statistics
- Power
- Degrees of freedom
- Assumptions

SECTION 13.1.1: PROBABILITY

You'll recall early on that we reminded you that you never "prove" a hypothesis; you just fail to accept the "null." So for example, if you think there is a relationship between X and Y, your null hypothesis is that no relationship exists. If you find a relationship between X and Y in your data, then you can't accept the null hypothesis. Why such weird word salad? Well, part of it is just the nature of science being conservative, but it's also because statistics is about **probability.**

Usually this is illustrated by a six-sided die in textbooks, but we will take a more everyday approach. Each day the weather forecast is based on a certain probability

that the weather will behave a certain way. Sometimes satellites provide the knowledge that there are no clouds for thousands of miles, and the weather forecaster can say with almost a 100% certainty that it will be sunny. More often, however, there is activity that might result in rain or might not. Perhaps on Monday this pattern produces rain. If we could see the same weather pattern a hundred times and then wait to see what would happen, we could calculate a probability (or likelihood) that rain will occur given that same pattern. If this pattern has occurred 100 times, and it rained 40 of those 100 times, we say the chances of rain are 40/100, or 40%. In other words, there is more uncertainty when we only see the outcome 40 times out of 100. In social science research, we do not expect to have a 100% probability that the relationship exists. We don't prove anything; we just increase the likelihood that we "know the answer" if our probability is high. This is one reason that replicating results is such an important part of science.

Probability can be hard to estimate because of other factors, too. When you measure something, there is usually some variability involved in that measurement. If you ask someone how much he watches television per day, his answer may vary slightly each time he is asked. Quite frankly, we also learn new techniques in statistics that sometimes replace old methods (better math or even more powerful computers that allow more complex procedures to be accessible to a broader audience). You can use the very best in current statistical approaches only to find out a year later that the technique you used has more error in it than the new one does. Most times it won't make any practical difference—but sometimes it does. Once again, that's how science moves forward.

SECTION 13.1.2: STATISTICAL SIGNIFICANCE

A concept related to probability is the idea of significance. You have by now all seen something that looks like this: $p <= .05$ or $p <= .001$, etc. Generally, any value of .05 or less is considered significant. The p stands for probability. In the first case it means that you will see a different result in 5 or fewer cases out of 100; in the second case, you will get a different result in 1 or fewer case in 1,000. The lower the number on the other side of the "$<=$" sign, the more confidence you have in the statistical significance of your result.

The following statements all mean *exactly* the same thing:

$p <= .05$

This is statistically significant at the $p <= .05$ level.

There is a 5% or less chance that this difference is due to luck.

There is a 95% or more chance that this difference is a "real" difference.

The chance of a Type I error occurring in this result is less than 5%.

Remember these important issues: (1) None of these statements tell you how large or how important the difference is; and (2) Very large samples will show significance for small, unimportant relationships.

But beware . . . statistical significance is not the same as practical significance. Please say that again to yourself: "Statistical significance does not equal practical significance." This is an important language issue for scientists. We believe that to avoid confusion, you should use the word *significant* only as part of the phrase *statistically significant.* When you mean to say *important,* or *meaningful,* or *interesting,* you should use those words or a synonym instead. To repeat, never say *significant* unless it immediately follows the word *statistically.* Some prominent authors have gone so far as to suggest that that professional style guides prohibit the use of the term *significant* in any way in all psychological publications (Meehl, 1998). Although we think this is a good idea, we doubt it will happen.

How can a statistically significant result be unimportant or not practically meaningful? This is because *p* values are *very* sensitive to sample size. We have done studies with more than 30,000 cases and can get a significant *p* value for gender, for example, when there was only a 2% difference between boys and girls. It is not that the *p* value is lying. It should be clear, however, that it might not be wise to change a multimillion-dollar service program to focus on gender if there is only a 2% difference—unless that 2% difference has an extraordinary value. For example, if it's a life-or-death matter. Having a 2% reduction in cancer deaths nationally would clearly be very important.

INSIGNIFICANT SIGNIFICANCE

About 30 years ago, the nation of Holland decided to do intelligence tests on all adult males at a certain age. They ended up testing 350,000 people (Zajonc & Markus, 1975). A third of a million subjects is a *large* sample. It was found that younger siblings had lower IQs than their older siblings. Before you go out and hire a tutor for your youngest child, you should know that the difference between older and next-oldest siblings was around one IQ point or less. Now, IQ scores have a mean score of 100 and a standard deviation of 15. In a few pages, you will learn that this means that the difference is 1/15 of a standard deviation or less (basically, nothing). If this study had been done with a typical sample size (say, a few hundred), there certainly would have not been any statistically significant difference detected at all. For a nice overview and criticism of this study, see Hock (2004). ■

The second reason that you should not be slave to the *p*-value master is that sometimes a nonsignificant result is still important. Perhaps you have a tiny sample for a pilot program (15 cases split into two groups). You have a fairly large difference in success rates, but the sample is so small that the *p* value is not significant. This is because you lacked power (see Section 13.1.9). Clearly, even though the *p* value may be nonsignificant, this pilot program may be worth testing again but with a larger group. When presenting the pilot findings you would say something like "given the small sample size, we don't know if the relatively large difference we detected was a real difference, or may simply be due to chance." Then you ask for more money to get a bigger sample.

SECTION 13.1.3: DISTRIBUTIONS

Sometimes when the word **distribution** is used it means how your actual data is arranged. Sometimes it refers to the theoretical distribution of a statistic that is used to determine significance. Most commonly used distributions underlying statistics are not single curves like the normal curve, but rather what Rosenthal (2001) calls a "family of distributions." Each statistical test you use has an accompanying *p* value or probability that you got your answer. This *p* value is based on the family of distributions that accompany that test statistic.

SECTION 13.1.4: NORMALITY

You probably encountered the normal curve when you received some grade in a class, as in "grading on a curve." **Normality** means that a variable is distributed along the normal curve with the middle of the hump being the mean and the distance from the mean measured in standard deviations. Many statistics require that data be distributed normally in order to produce accurate results.

SECTION 13.1.5: MEASURES OF CENTRAL TENDENCY

The **measures of central tendency** are the **mean, median,** and **mode.** Not only are these useful statistics themselves, but looking at these can tell you if your data are "normal" or not. The mean is also called the "average" or "μ." It is the sum of the individual values of something divided by the total number of those values you measured. It is not always the middle value, though, because it is sensitive to what we call outliers—values that are really big or really tiny—particularly in a smaller data set, where they can move the mean off-center. The median is always the midpoint or 50% mark and is not sensitive to outliers. The mode is simply the value that occurs most often. Taken together, they are indicators of normality.

EXAMPLE OF MEAN, MODE, AND MEDIAN

Let's say you have 12 people who take a short math test. They get the following scores: 60%, 70%, 70%, 70%, 80%, 80%, 80% 80%, 90%, 90%, 90%, 100%. You could show the scores in a bar graph as follows, with the percentage correct scored as the bottom line (*x*-axis) and the number of people scoring at that level as the vertical measure (*y*-axis):

You could draw a line around the bars, and you would then see something like the familiar bell curve, showing a relatively normal distribution:

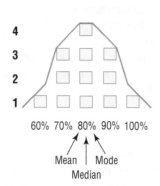

In this case, the mean is (60 + 70 + 70 + 70 + 80 + 80 + 80 + 80 + 90 + 90 + 90 + 100) / 12 = 80%. The median is 80% because the middle location is between the sixth and seventh highest-ranked scores, both of which are 80%. The mode (most frequent result) is also 80% because there are four of them, more than any other value.

Let's look at another set of scores (50%, 60%, 60%, 60%, 60%, 70%, 70%, 70%, 80%, 80%, 90%, 90%, 100%). This is no longer a normal distribution, but has a "tail" pointing toward higher numbers:

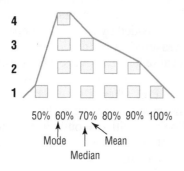

We say this is "positively skewed." Now the mean is (50 + 60+ 60 + 60 + 60 + 70 + 70 + 70 + 80 + 80 + 90 + 90 + 100) = 940 / 13 = 72.31. The median is 70% (seventh place out of 13, six on either side). The mode is 60%, the only value with more than three respondents.∎

SECTION 13.1.6: VARIABILITY

Variability refers to the degree to which individual values in your variable are dispersed from some central or average value. When you think of variability, the most commonly thought-of measure is the "standard deviation." This is typically used in description of data. The variance is just the square of the standard deviation. This form of variability is used by many statistical tests. How much values vary from other values in your data influences the ability to test statistical significance.

SECTION 13.1.7: NOMINAL, ORDINAL, AND INTERVAL/RATIO DATA

As we stated previously, numbers can come in different forms in statistics. It might be helpful to review that again, though, highlighting how these different types of data influence statistical approaches. Numbers can be **nominal** (named), as when 0="no" and 1="yes." These are numbers that are essentially standing for nonnumerical categories of something (gender, hair color). There is no smaller number between them, and there is no particular order. These data are often called categorical. Next we have **ordinal** (ordered) data. These data also stand for categories (first, second, third). These data differ from nominal data because the order of the numbers means something. Statistically, we often treat these as categorical variables, and at other times we are able to use parametric approaches (see next section). Finally we have **interval** or **ratio** data. Not only is the order meaningful (there are larger and smaller values), but also we can potentially divide the data into smaller measures in between. For example, your study may measure age in years, but it is also possible to measure age in smaller units such as days or months. These data are typically analyzed using parametric procedures unless they do not meet the standards of normality. The difference between interval and ratio data is that in ratio data, a value of "0" is a "true zero," meaning "none present." For practical purposes, ratio and interval schedules are generally the same in statistics.

SECTION 13.1.8: PARAMETRIC AND NONPARAMETRIC STATISTICS

Many statistical procedures (in fact, most of those you were exposed to in any introductory statistics class earlier in your training) are based on the normal curve. We call these **parametric.** The problem is that unless you have a very large sample or are lucky enough to be measuring something that is normally distributed, variables in social science often don't look like this. Your data may be skewed, which means they look like a ramp instead of a symmetrical hill, or they may be really strange and have two humps like a Bactrian camel or some other shape. Sometimes this can be fixed by altering a variable mathematically to force it to be normal (we'll look at that later). In other cases, you need to move into the land of categorical or **nonparametric** procedures. We'll discuss more about that later.

SECTION 13.1.9: POWER

In statistics we do not use the term **power** to explain someone's ability to control others. Instead, having enough power means that you have enough subjects in the study to detect differences between subjects.

Power is related to your sample size. If your sample is too small, the statistical test you are trying to use may not be powerful enough to detect a difference. In short, the more subjects you have, and the bigger the effect that you're trying to find, the more power you have. There are many ways to calculate power based on the type of data and type of test you hope to run. SAS has made this easier by integrating approaches to calculate power for many of the commonly used statistics. You will be introduced to a few of these options in this class.

SECTION 13.1.10: DEGREES OF FREEDOM

When you begin using statistics or begin reading research articles, you will see **degrees of freedom** listed with the particular test used. The term *degrees*

A SLIGHTLY SILLY EXAMPLE ABOUT POWER

Let's say you want to know which is taller, a Great Dane or a Toy Poodle. Let's also say you live on Mars and have never seen either. What do you do? You go out and find a Great Dane and a Toy Poodle and look at them. The Great Dane looks much bigger. Being a cautious, scientific Martian, however, you decide to get more information. Maybe one of the dogs you saw had a hormone imbalance or something. You go look at a couple more Great Danes and a couple more Toy Poodles. At this point, you may feel pretty confident that Great Danes are bigger than Toy Poodles. You think this because it is almost impossible that such a freakishly big difference might occur due to luck three times in a row.

Obviously smaller   **Obviously bigger**

But what if you want to decide if Toy Poodles are taller than Chinese Crested dogs? (*FYI: AKC standards are not too different, with Toy Poodles being up to 10 inches at the shoulder, and Cresteds being 11 to 13 inches at the shoulder: see www.akc.org/breeds.*) You go look at your first Poodle and Crested, and they look pretty similar. You go look at a couple more, and the difference is still small. Is this a real difference or did you just happen to find three slightly small Poodles?

Maybe smaller????   **Maybe bigger????**

What do you do? Well, you get a lot of dogs. If the small difference you are noticing keeps appearing time after time after time, then you become pretty sure that the difference you are seeing is a real difference, even though it is small.

Most probably slightly smaller   Most probably slightly bigger

In short, you need more subjects to be sure of a difference if the difference is small. Having more subjects, or looking for a bigger difference, gives you more power to be sure of that difference.■

---

of freedom relates to how much information is free to vary. Degrees of freedom are associated with the sample size and the number of variables you are examining. Some texts discuss degrees of freedom as solely related to the number of variables analyzed, which can lead to the idea that one simply needs more variables. As Yu (2005) cautions, it is important to consider both how many observations you have and how many variables you measure per observation. Yu provides the following helpful illustration: "In regression, the working definition of degrees of freedom involves the information of both observations and dimensionality: $df = n - k - 1$, where n = sample size and k = the number of variables. Take the 3 observation and 2 variable case as an example. In this case, $df = 3 - 2 - 1 = 0!$" (Yu, 2005). Without some degrees of freedom, it is impossible to appropriately build a statistical model of something.

SECTION 13.1.11: ASSUMPTIONS

By the time you have entered your advanced research program, someone at some point has probably told you "never assume anything" or something to that effect. Statistical tests ignore this social warning. Each has a set of assumptions that may include such things as (1) normally distributed data, (2) a certain sample size, (3) independence of observations, or many others. These assumptions are the basic criteria or rules for using that test. If you violate them, the computer may still run the procedure, but the results may be invalid. We say "may" because in some cases, tests are robust against certain violations. In other words, you can often get away with certain small violations of the assumptions and still get valid results. Caution is needed here. As Helberg (1995) states, "The robustness of statistical

techniques only goes so far—'robustness' is not a license to ignore the assumption." Always check to see what the assumptions are and find out which ones are critical to using the procedure. We'll get into this in much more detail later.

SECTION 13.2
CHECKING YOUR DATA

SECTION 13.2.1: A BRIEF REMINDER ABOUT COMPUTER APPLICATIONS

Having reviewed some basics, we are now ready to look at numbers. As stated earlier, this chapter and the next chapter are designed to complement the use of SAS or SPSS to conduct analysis. As we move through topics and statistical tests, we first discuss the area or test of interest and then provide information on how to use SAS or SPSS to provide the desired results. For SAS this will mean that we provide the programming language statements. For SPSS, we provide a set of directions for selecting the various menu and submenu commands within the windows-driven part of SPSS. We will also provide examples of the output from both programs as they do differ in appearance. Finally, as you may recall from Chapter 10, some of the procedures we run in SAS are not available through the menus in SPSS. The reader will be warned that this is the case, and only SAS output is included in such instances.

SECTION 13.2.2: BACK TO THE TOPIC AT HAND!

Being an eager and curious researcher, you may be tempted to jump right to the bivariate or multivariate statistic that you determine will answer your question.

You must viciously suppress this desire at all costs! Why? Data that are missing, obviously wrong (e.g., age of 143), or miscoded can lead you to bad conclusions that will be embarrassing to have to explain later. We discussed this in Chapter 11 in a general way. We will now describe how to check your data more completely to make sure they will work for purposes of statistical analysis. You must go through the following steps:

1. Understand what data are missing.
2. Make sure that no values are obviously wrong.
3. Make sure that variables vary.
4. Determine if your data are normally distributed.
5. Recode (and sometimes discard) data as necessary.

Well, first of all, you need to know your data better. You need to know exactly what is there and what is not. If you don't have a "feel" for your data, you need to get one. For example, say you receive your survey results or your secondary data set and you, of course, know what variables were collected. But . . . you may not be aware of the amount of missing data. Some subjects may not have answered all the questions, or data entry errors might have occurred. Unless you have a very small data set that you can just eyeball, the only way to get the full picture is to run frequencies on all the variables. Do this. Failure to do this will result in later suffering. When you get those frequencies, you will also have to check to make sure that your variables are not obviously wrong. Do things make sense? Do you have four different values for your "Pregnant? [Y] [N]" question? Do you have people with negative years of college? You'd be surprised how often things like this happen.

As a next step in familiarizing yourself with your data, make sure that variables that you expect to vary do, in fact, vary. If everyone's score on a measure were within a very narrow range, this could make that measure useless. Remember that we learned that various statistics have their own assumptions. A lot of the most common assumptions are that your dependent variable is "normally distributed." Unfortunately, just because you choose a continuous measure doesn't mean that the results will be normally distributed for your sample. This can be checked only by looking at the univariate distribution. If it is not normal, and it needs to be, you can decide to try manipulating the variable through transformations or switch to a categorical or nonparametric approach to analysis.

Finally, there is often the need to recode. For example, perhaps you have five racial categories, but on further inspection only two have sufficient numbers by themselves. Univariate analysis can help you identify that so you can make decisions to collapse or eliminate categories of a specific variable. In the above case, you may go with two races and an "other" category.

We will describe and give examples of the code you will use to do the things listed above. SAS offers a variety of helpful visual plots that can help you identify issues like outliers. **Outliers** are values for a variable that are way off the general trend in your data. For example, suppose you survey 200 people about chocolate bar consumption. The typical range may be from 0 to 15 bars a week, but one person claims to consume 100 bars a week! Many of our statistics, like the mean, are sensitive to being pulled off the true course by such unusual responses. In most cases, we are trying to understand the typical or most normative response to something so that we can think about group-level policies or intervention. This data point may need to be eliminated from later analyses to give us a more accurate picture of 99% of the sample. As a general rule, remove outliers only when you have a sound logical reason to do so. In the above case, you would state that your sampling frame is meant to include only individuals with relatively normal rates of chocolate consumption (say, <=40 bars per week), and that the few people with higher consumption rates (1/200 or .5% of the population sampled) can therefore be excluded.

SECTION 13.2.3: SAS APPROACHES TO CHECKING DATA

In SAS there are a few different procedures that are useful in checking your data.

PROC PRINT AND PROC FREQ (OR PROC UNIVARIATE)

The first thing you should do is run both a PROC PRINT and a PROC FREQ (a frequency) of all the variables in your data set. Why run both? Well, a PROC PRINT gives you a direct visual printout of your data—it is especially useful in identifying problems with data that should be sequenced. For example, if you run only a PROC FREQ of a TIME 1 date and a TIME 2 date, it will give you two separate frequency tables. You can see if data are missing or strange, but you can't tell if TIME 1 is consistently before TIME 2. With PROC PRINT, you can see the time values for each record and see if they make sense.

PROC PRINT also lets you identify which cases in your data appear to have either data entry problems that can be fixed or other problems that must be handled separately. If you have a large number of variables you may wish to use "PROC PRINT; VAR x y z etc.; run;" so you can print smaller groups of specific variables at a time.

We could go to Professor Kathy's data set (KATHYDATA) with SAS command:

```
PROC PRINT; var group epfall; run;
```

FIGURE 13.1. **Output from Professor Kathy's Data Set.**

FIGURE 13.1. **Output from Professor Kathy's Data Set.**

The SAS System		
obs	group	epfall
1	1	0.70000
2	1	0.78261
3	1	0.86364
4	1	1.04167

FIGURE 13.2. **The FREQ Procedure.**

The FREQ Procedure

Group (1=CBM, 2=ELBM, 3=NBM)

group	Frequency	Percent	Cumulative Frequency	Cumulative Percent
1	20	33.33	20	33.33
2	20	33.33	40	66.67
3	20	33.33	60	100.00

Taking out the "var group epfall;" would give you all variables.

This produces the output in Figure 13.1 (only the first four observations are shown to save space). There is one line per observation, so every value on that row belongs to the same person in the data. This shows us the first four observations (people) and that they are all in group 1; it also gives their values on the "epfall" variable.

Next, it is important to run PROC FREQ on your variables (Figure 13.2). This is the primary means of looking at nominal and most ordinal variables to examine sample and subsample size. This will also help you identify weird things like a value of "8" in the gender column when the values should be "M" or "F." If you're lucky, you will be able to go back and fix such errors (maybe from the original paper survey forms); if not, these become missing data elements. This procedure will also help you identify missing data that are truly absent (not just an error). Sometimes when looking at a lot of variables you miss things about individual variables that are easier to see with a PROC FREQ. Now to request specific variables with PROC FREQ, you use TABLES rather than VAR in the next line, like this:

```
PROC FREQ data = kathy; TABLES group; run;
```

If you are running frequencies on a lot of continuous variables, you can also use the PROC UNIVARIATE command with the FREQ or VAR options (Figure 13.3). This will provide summary information for continuous variables such as highest, lowest, mean, and so on (which we will discuss later) and also print a frequency table. The difference is that this procedure prints the table in more than one column saving a lot of page space. Once again, you must use the VAR statement to identify the variable(s) of interest.

Why did they make PROC PRINT and PROC FREQ variable commands different? We suppose it's because PROC FREQ can actually produce multiway tables, but it's still a hassle to get used to, and you will invariably get an error message on occasion because you said VAR instead of TABLES or vice versa. It's irritating, but most programs have some aspects that are like that.

SECTION 13.2.4: SPSS APPROACHES TO CHECKING DATA

In SPSS, one first opens the data set as indicated in Chapter 10. Then, select the "Analyze" pull-down menu option from the command bar at the top of the screen. From among the options provided, select "Descriptive Statistics." Here you will find several options. The command we are interested in now is "Frequencies." Within the "Frequencies" menu you select the variables from the variable list shown on the left and then click on the arrow to move them to the variable box on the right. So:

Analyze ⇒ Descriptive Statistics ⇒ Frequencies ⇒ select variables from list and click on arrow to move to "variables" box ⇒ click 'OK.'

The output in Figure 13.4 for the same variable we just looked at in SAS. Because SPSS displays the data in a spreadsheet form in full view as a default, the

FIGURE 13.3. **PROC UNIVARIATE FREQ data=kathy; var group; run;**

Frequency Counts

		Percents				Percents				Percents	
Value	Count	Cell	Cum	Value	Count	Cell	Cum	Value	Count	Cell	Cum
1	20	33.3	33.3	2	20	33.3	66.7	3	20	33.3	100.0

FIGURE 13.4. SPSS Output.

Frequencies:

Statistics
Group (1=CBM, 2=ELBM, 3=NBM)

N	Valid	60
	Missing	0

Group (1=CBM, 2=ELBM, 3=NBM)

		Frequency	Percent	Valid Percent	Cumulative Percent
Valid	1	20	33.3	33.3	33.3
	2	20	33.3	33.3	66.7
	3	20	33.3	33.3	100.0
	Total	60	100.0	100.0	

PROC PRINT command we had to use in SAS is not necessary. You can simply review the data by scrolling down and across as you would with an Excel spreadsheet.

MISSING DATA

Often, even when you are sure the data are complete, there are a few missing values. There are several ways of handling missing information. We will take time to review some of these issues before moving on.

Can I Delete Observations with Missing Values? Sure, if the numbers of missing data are small and those with missing values are not unique in some way. In other words, if you delete the data and the data elements are not "missing at random," you may bias your results. For example, let's say you are analyzing a satisfaction survey and all the unhappy people refuse to answer the last two questions. If you delete these observations, you will have a biased assessment of client satisfaction. "Missing at random" (MAR) means there is no systematic pattern to observations with or without missing values that can't be predicted by other variables. It doesn't mean that the data has to be random in the sense of a random number—this is called "missing completely at random" (MCAR). Sometimes data are missing due to the design of the study—for example, if your data end before certain subjects are old enough to have a value for this variable. The MAR assumption is met if the values are missing for cases by design. Even if you can delete data you may not wish to because you may lose too large a portion of your sample if you delete these cases.

Can I Replace Missing Values? Yes, assuming that you have enough information, that values are not missing for everyone of a given class (type), and that the data

are MAR (missing at random). For example, if none of the females in your study answered question 5, there will be no way to estimate a value for question 5. The data are not MAR or by design. If your data are MAR, then there are the following basic types of approaches.

> **NOTE:** There are actually many procedures nested within these categories. See *Missing Data* by P. Allison (2002) as a good place to start.

- *Old way:* Just put in the mean values of the missing variables. This is not really a good idea because it messes with things like the distribution of the variable. We suggest you not do this although SPSS has a menu option for this under "Transform => Replace missing values."

- *Better way:* Use multiple regression or logistic regression to replace values. You need enough data to model the value. If too many values are missing, this doesn't work well. This method is better than mean values but can still introduce bias because statistics are about probability, so a single model of the missing element may be an under- or overestimate. See Allison (2002) for details.

- *Even better way:* Multiple imputation (complicated and not covered in this book) can handle large amounts of missing data because it creates multiple data sets (many many data sets) and uses those to estimate missing values. You can then take the average of the multiple data sets to get the best estimate. SAS can do this for continuous-level variables (PROC MI). For categorical and mixed data sets, either you need S-plus *or* you will need to use SAS and round the imputed variable to the closest legitimate code. If you are interested in doing this, see the PROC MI documentation in SAS help or *Analysis of Incomplete Multivariate Data* by John Schafer (1997).

Is There Anything Else I Can Do? Yes, depending on the type of data you have and the sample size, there are various statistical procedures that will run with missing data without deleting those cases. In other words, they use the nonmissing values for a subject and essentially ignore the missing values (for examples, see *Generalized Estimating Equations* [Hardin & Hilbe, 2003] or *Mixed Model Regression* [Hedeker, 2005]). These procedures are more advanced than this text will cover. As many of these still lack user-friendly explanations for the nonstatistician, it is a good idea to consult with a statistician or colleague knowledgeable in this area if you think you might be using such an approach.

SECTION 13.3

UNIVARIATE STATISTICS

Now that you have looked at the quality of your data and identified missing or strange values, it is time to look at univariate statistics. We are interested in measures of central tendency, distribution, variability, and outliers.

SECTION 13.3.1: SAS APPROACHES TO UNIVARIATE STATISTICS

In SAS you can use PROC MEANS and get basic statistics to look at your data characteristics for interval/ratio numbers. In this case, you actually need to customize the command procedure to get more than just the means so we add options called "var skewness kurtosis" in the command line (put your variable names in where "x y z" are):

```
PROC MEANS data=X statistics var skewness
kurtosis;
    var x y z; run;
```

But—you can get much more information including an array of plots using PROC UNIVARIATE (our personal favorite). Put your data set name in where "X.X" is, put your variables in where "X Y Z" are, and put your variable name for your ID number variable in where "name" is:

```
PROC UNIVARIATE Data= X.X NORMAL PLOT;
    VAR X Y Z;
    ID name;
    run;
```

This procedure provides means, variance, kurtosis, skewness, measures such as the Shapiro-Wilk test of normality, and a listing of outliers. In addition, the preceding plot command will provide a box plot that gives you a visual way of assessing normality, skewness, and outliers. If you include the "ID" statement and the name of your ID number after the "VAR X Y Z," then it will print the ID number of the case by its listing of outliers. PROC UNIVARIATE can also be used to look at subsets, for instance, describing the age distribution for boys compared to girls. This is done by sorting by the subset indicator and including "by variable name;" after the VAR portion of the statement. We will look at various parts of this output, starting with the main measures of central tendency and distribution (see Figure 13.5).

SECTION 13.3.2: SPSS APPROACHES TO UNIVARIATE STATISTICS

In SPSS you also have some choices. You can use the

1. Analyze ⇒ Descriptive Statistics ⇒ Frequencies selection; or
2. Analyze ⇒ Descriptive Statistics ⇒ Explore option

The first option will provide basic descriptive statistics by clicking open the "statistics" option button at the bottom of the "Frequency" screen (see Figure 13.6). Then one selects the various measures of interest by checking the boxes, clicking "Continue" and then "OK." The second option, as with PROC UNIVARIATE in SAS, allows you to get more information.

FIGURE 13.5. The UNIVARIATE Procedure.

```
                    The UNIVARIATE Procedure
              Variable: epfall (Errors per file (all sessions))
                            Moments

N                   60          Sum Weights              60
Mean          1.68829682        Sum Observations   101.297809
Std Deviation 0.45289901        Variance           0.20511752
Skewness      -0.0622163        Kurtosis           -0.4747298
Uncorrected SS 183.122702       Corrected SS       12.1019335
Coeff Variation 26.8257933      Std Error Mean     0.05846901

                  Basic Statistical Measures

        Location                      Variability

    Mean    1.688297       Std Deviation        0.45290
    Median  1.760952       Variance             0.20512
    Mode    2.000000       Range                1.99565
                           Interquartile Range  0.67949
```

FIGURE 13.6. **SPSS Statistics.**		

Errors per file (all sessions)		
N	Valid	60
	Missing	0
Mean		1.6883
Median		1.7610
Mode		2.00
Std. Deviation		.45290
Skewness		−.062
Std. Error of Skewness		.309
Kurtosis		−.475
Std. Error of Kurtosis		.608
Range		2.00
Percentiles	25	1.3141
	50	1.7610
	75	2.0000

FIGURE 13.7. **SPSS Output.**

```
Errors per file (all sessions) Stem-and-Leaf Plot
  Frequency        Stem & Leaf
     3.00          0 . 778
    19.00          1 . 0000111222333444444
    22.00          1 . 5555667777888888889999
    14.00          2 . 00000011122444
     2.00          2 . 56
Stem width:        1.00
Each leaf:         1 case(s)
```

UNDERSTANDING UNIVARIATES

Kurtosis is found on the right side of the SAS output and about two-thirds of the way down on the SPSS output. The number indicates the shape of a curve, not the direction of the tails. A high-mountain-peak-looking curve with thick tails is leptokurtic, and the value for kurtosis will be greater than 0. A plateau appearance is platykurtic, and the value will be less than 0. The following analogy might help:

> Platykurtic curves like platypuses are squat with short tails. Leptokurtic curves are high with long tails, like kangaroos, noted for lepping (Lomax & Moosavi, 1998).

Most tests are robust (will still work) when it comes to high or low kurtosis. Thus, we won't dwell on fixing the problem. There are cases, however, where kurtosis is too extreme. *Warning*: SPSS uses a different formula to calculate kurtosis. They should result in identical practical meaning but the actual numbers will vary.

Skewness. Found on the left side of the top portion of the SAS output and above kurtosis on the SPSS output, skewness is more of a problem child for data analysis than kurtosis. The number indicates whether or not one of the tails of the distribution is too long. If the tail is too long toward the high value, we say that it is positively skewed. If the tail is too long toward the low value, we say that it is negatively skewed. In the PROC UNIVARIATE output, a skewness value of "0" means there is no skewness. A positive skewness value indicates positive skewness, and a negative value indicates negative skewness. If you have a very large sample, the tests may still be robust (meaning they will work anyway without biasing results). Sometimes, however, the skewness is just too great. How much is too much?

Our skewness value was not 0 but was low (−0.622163). In addition to the skewness value, there are other ways to assess how far off the data are from normality. We can reexamine our measures of central tendency (recall above that the mean = 1.68 and the median was 1.76 in the portion of the PROC UNIVARIATE printed above) and look at our stem leaf and box plots from SPSS or SAS (displayed below). *Note*: In SPSS, the plots are easiest to obtain by selecting: Analyze ⇒ Descriptive statistics ⇒ Explore option and selecting the graphs desired under the "Plots" button options. In SPSS, the stem leaf plot is printed separately from the box plot. SAS prints out the box plot alongside the stem leaf plot. In the interest of space we have chosen to display only the SPSS stem leaf and the combined plots from SAS in Figure 13.7.

We know the mean and median are not exactly in the same place. On the other hand, the stem leaf plot does not resemble a one-way ski slope. We know this because the "leaf" column (they are numbers really, not leaves like a tree) shows the shape of the distribution, and it does look sort of like a normal distribution (on its side). In SAS the stem leaf and box plots are side by side. In the box plot from SAS, the "+" in the middle of the box is below the midline, indicating that the mean and median are not in the same place (Figure 13.8). The box, however, is fairly symmetrical, and the area marked with dashes on either side is of relatively similar length. If there were extreme outliers we would see asterisks and "0" replacing the dashes.

For some people, it feels too "artsy" to be making a judgment call based on pictures and vague guidelines. The following provides a more exact formula for assessing skewness.

Values of two standard errors of skewness (*ses*) or more (regardless of sign) are probably skewed to a significant degree. The *ses* can be estimated roughly using the following formula (after Tabachnick & Fidell, 1996):

$$\sqrt{\frac{6}{N}}$$

. . . let's say you are using Excel and calculate a skewness statistic of −.9814 for a particular test administered to 30 students. An approximate estimate of the *ses* for this example would be:

$$ses = \sqrt{\frac{6}{N}} = \sqrt{\frac{6}{30}} = \sqrt{.20} = .4472$$

Since two times the standard error of the skewness is .8944 and the skewness statistic is −.9814, which is greater (in "absolute" terms—plus and minus don't matter) than .8944, you can assume that the distribution is significantly skewed. Since the sign of the skewness statistic is negative, you know that the distribution is negatively skewed. (Brown, 1997)

Applying this formula to our data gives us an *ses* of 0.3162. Twice the *ses* is 0.6324. Our value is much lower than that, so we will consider the "epfall" variable close enough to normally distributed to use parametric statistics. What can you do if your data are too skewed? First, we look at the possibility of outliers and remedies.

Outliers. If you'll recall from our overview of measures of central tendency, these measures are sensitive to outliers—values that are at the extreme range for a few subjects. What do you do?

1. First, you find the outliers.
2. Then, are they recording errors? If so, correct them.
3. If they are not errors or cannot be corrected, run simple analyses with and without the outliers. Do you get similar results? If yes, leave them in.
4. If the results differ, and the outliers come from a different population than what you are hoping to study, exclude them. If there is some other logical reason to exclude them then do so.
5. If you cannot exclude them, go to a nonparametric method or do analyses with and without them and report both.

Let's look at how SAS and SPSS output can help us find outliers. In SAS, information on outliers is automatically provided as part of PROC UNIVARIATE output (Figure 13.9). In SPSS (Figure 13.10) we use our second option to get the outlier information by going to:

Analyze ⇒ Descriptive Statistics ⇒ Explore ⇒ click on the "Statistics" button and then check the "outliers" box from among the options ⇒ Click "Continue" when done ⇒ click "OK"

Notice that only 1% of all the observations are above 2.695652. (SPSS rounds up to 2.70.) Later, under

FIGURE 13.8. Partial Display from SAS PROC UNIVARIATE.

```
Stem Leaf              #       Boxplot
27 0                   1          |
26                                |
25 4                   1          |
24 016                 3          |
23                                |
22 39                  2          |
21 069                 3          |
20 000336              6       +------+
19 01666               5       |      |
18 0336668             7       |      |
17 3669                4       *------*
16 29                  2       |  +   |
15 0478                4       |      |
14 455778              6       |      |
13 013                 3       +------+
12 367                 3          |
11 0179                4          |
10 467                 3          |
9                                 |
8 6                    1          |
7 08                   2          |
   ----+----+----+----+
   Multiply Stem.Leaf by 10**-1
```

FIGURE 13.9. SAS Output from PROC UNIVARIATE.

Quantile	Estimate
100% Max	2.695652
99%	2.695652
95%	2.433894
90%	2.258242

Extreme Observations

Value	ID	Obs	Value	ID	Obs
0.700000	3	1	2.40000	40	37
0.782609	6	2	2.40625	47	60
0.863636	16	3	2.46154	31	38
1.041667	20	4	2.54286	37	39
1.062500	17	5	2.69565	26	40

FIGURE 13.10. SPSS Output.

Extreme Values

		Case Number	Individual ID Number	Value
Errors per file (all sessions) Highest	1	40	26	2.70
	2	39	37	2.54
	3	38	31	2.46
	4	60	47	2.41
	5	37	40	2.40
Lowest	1	1	3	.70
	2	2	6	.78
	3	3	16	.86
	4	4	20	1.04
	5	5	17	1.06

TABLE 13.2. SAS Codes for Common Transformations*.

TRANSFORMATION	SAS CODE
Logarithm (most common)	newvariablename = log(variablename);
Square	newvariablename = variablename* variablename;
Square root	newvariablename = sqrt(variablename);

*Various problems can occur with negative values for variables. For example, when you square a variable, it will become positive, even if it started as a negative number. An observation of "−2" will be squared to "4," just the same as an observation of "2." One way to fix this is to change your variable values so that they are all positive values before transformations are done.

"Extreme Observations" we see that this value belongs to ID # 26. This isn't very extreme. Very high outlier values (e.g., "10.345252") would be more likely to catch our attention.

To return to our problem of skewness: If handling outliers doesn't resolve the problem with skewness, we can try to use a transformation from the list in Table 13.1.

Table 13.2 shows SAS codes for common transformations. SPSS procedures follow.

SPSS TRANSFORMATIONS

In SPSS, transformations can be done in two ways. From the top menu bar select:

1. Transform ⇒ select "Recode" ⇒ select "Into different variables" and type in the desired statement by hand; or

2. Transform ⇒ select "Compute" ⇒ create a new variable name in the "Target variable" box ⇒ go to the "Function Group" list and select "Arithmetic" for the log or square root functions ⇒ click on the arrow

pointing up ⇒ then type in the variable name for the list in the parentheses to replace the "?" mark next to the function ⇒ click "OK." If you wish to use the square function, you can ignore the function group list and simply add the variable name from the list on the left, then click on the multiplication sign from the little calculator and then repeat the variable name again ⇒ click "OK."

After transforming a variable, you need to run your univariate statistics again to see if you have fixed the problem. There are two potential issues: You will probably need to untransform any variables you changed after running analyses to interpret the results easily. Further, transformations do not always work. All is not lost, however. You can still recode a continuous variable and use a different approach. For example, let's say your age variable is horribly skewed, and you just can't fix it. You can recode age (for example) into categories by doing the procedure shown in Figure 13.11. By recoding the variable we can turn "age" into a categorical variable (0–5 or 5–10 years). We highly recommend labeling variables (particularly when the number stands for another value). You'll be surprised how easy it is to forget what you're doing once you're trying to interpret output. This can result in your reporting things that are totally wrong.

If none of the above "fixes" take care of the normality issue, and the problem variable is a dependent variable in your study, you will now be thinking of a nonparametric analytic approach. In some cases there are direct nonparametric alternatives to the typical parametric test as shown in Table 13.3. In other cases, one moves to an entirely different approach using categorical data analyses such as chi-square. These alternatives are available in SAS and SPSS.

TABLE 13.1. Ladder of Powers (Tukey).

Severe negative skewness	Cube it (X^3)
Mild negative skewness	Square it (X^2)
Mild positive skewness	Square root
Positive skewness	Logarithm
Severe positive skewness	Negative reciprocal root
Very severe positive skewness	Negative reciprocal

FIGURE 13.11. **Recoding into Categories.**

```
In SAS

        Data X;
        Set X;
        Age2=0; /*create a new variable and initialize it to zero*/
        If 0<=age< 5 then age2=1; /*recode the old variable */
        If 5<=age<10 then age2=2; /*more recoding...*/
        Label age2 = "1=young children, 2=elementary"; Run;
In SPSS

        ⇒Transform
        ⇒select "Recode"⇒Select "Into different variables"
        ⇒select "Age" from the variable list and click the arrow
        ⇒create a new variable name "Age2" in the output variable box
        ⇒select "Old and New Values" button
        ⇒select "range" circle under old values, enter "0" through "5"
        ⇒go to the "New value" box and enter "1"
        ⇒click the "Add" button
        ⇒repeat for all values of the old variable
        ⇒click "Continue"⇒click "OK"
```

TABLE 13.3. **Parametric Tests and Some Nonparametric Alternatives.**

PARAMETRIC	NONPARAMETRIC
Independent *t* test	Mann-Whitney U
Paired *t* test	Wilcoxon Signed-Rank
ANOVA	Kruskal-Wallis
Pearson correlation	Spearman correlation

SECTION 13.4

HOW WE EXPLORE DATA AND TEST HYPOTHESES

Before moving on to bivariate statistical tests, the issues of error and power deserve greater attention.

SECTION 13.4.1: ERROR

Because statistics are based on probability, there is always error or "unexplained stuff" in a given estimate. In social science we are often explaining less of the particular outcome or issue than we would like because there are simply so many variables involved in people's behavior. We want to decrease error as much as possible so that we can more accurately answer our research question and any hypotheses. There are many sources of error that can have an impact on statistics and many ways we use the word *error*. For example, *sampling error*

is about who or what is in your sample; *measurement error* is about how well you are able to assess a given variable.

We tend to be more familiar with discussing error related to specific variable estimates. The error you may be most familiar with is called the standard error ('e'). This is used to construct confidence intervals for specific variable coefficients (typically 95% confidence intervals). A 95% confidence interval means essentially that the computer is 95% certain that the number you get next time you or someone else runs similar analyses, the variable coefficient will fall in that range.

Later when we talk about multivariate statistics or modeling the data, there is always an error term in a model equation though some statistics texts do not discuss it much. This error term has to do with the residual or variability that is not explained by the variables you entered in the model. Although this term is not always explicitly described in articles and studies, it does exist. The larger the error term, the less the model explains. We touch on some issues related to this in the next chapter but don't talk about this very much as it is a complex area. Entire classes could be devoted to handling error terms in statistics.

Error can also occur in relation to interpretation of statistics. In Chapter 4 you learned how to phrase a hypothesis for your research questions. We think of them slightly differently in statistics. First, you can have a unidirectional (one-tailed) or a bidirectional (two-tailed) hypothesis. A one-tailed hypothesis suggests that you know enough about the issue of interest to test only one possible outcome. Suppose you are interested in students' happiness following orientation. A one-tailed hypothesis would mean choosing one possible outcome (e.g., student happiness will increase). While in practice, we sometimes know enough to make an educated guess with words, when it comes to statistics we usually look at both possible directions, and most procedures print both. Why? Well, if you're wrong, it's nice to know whether the relationship is significant in the opposite direction. For example, let's say you think that your program will decrease depression among senior citizens, so you choose to test only whether there is a significant decrease (a one-tailed test). You can find out whether it decreased this way, but not whether it increased.

Of course, rejection of the null hypothesis (e.g., no relationship or no effect) occurs when your test result is significant. This depends at least, in part, on power. Before going over power, however, let's review another form of error related to interpretation: type I and type II error. Type I error means claiming a difference when none really exists—a false positive. Type II error means missing a difference when one actually does exist—a false negative.

You set the type I error probability in advance by setting the p value, or alpha, or significance level. In practice, most people use a p value of .05, meaning that they want to be 95% sure that they did not make a type I error. If you have a very large sample (e.g., 10,000), the chances of making a type I error would be greater for small effect sizes, so some people will choose a more conservative p value or alpha (e.g., $p < .0001$). The default in most statistical programs is $p < .05$. Many programs or statistical procedures within programs print out the actual p value for a given statistic, so technically you don't need to worry about it until after you see the results. For other statistical procedures, you need to set the p value or alpha in advance of running the program.

The probability of a type II, a false negative, error is "beta." (A test's power is $1 -$ beta.) Now, ideally you want both type I and type II errors to be minimized, but there is generally an inverse relationship between the two. If you make the alpha level too restrictive, your type II error rate goes up. Also, if your sample is not big enough, your power to detect a difference goes down, and the type II goes up. We must be careful not to oversimplify though. The probability of making a type II error can also be decreased by using a more powerful statistic, improving measurement, increasing sample size, and improving effect size.

SECTION 13.4.2: POWER

So what is power, and how do I deal with it? All statistical tests have a certain level of sensitivity. The power of a test is affected by the sample size and effect size, as well as measurement accuracy. Usually one checks for whether or not the sample is big enough to have enough power to detect significance prior to the study to make sure one collects enough subjects. Sometimes, though, you are using secondary or administrative data and are checking to see how power issues may limit your analyses. Let's use the paired t test formula as an example of how sample size and effect size might alter power. This is the formula we might use to test whether or not a posttest mean was different from a pretest mean. The bigger the t statistic is, the more likely it is to be significant. By inserting some numbers into the following example you can see how you can alter the t value:

$$t = \frac{\mu 1 - \mu 2}{s / \sqrt{n}}$$

$\mu 1 - \mu 2 =$ your effect size (difference in means)

$s \quad =$ your variability (standard deviation of the difference scores)

$n \quad =$ your sample size

1. We can make t bigger with a bigger effect size.
2. We can make t bigger with less sample variance.
3. We can make t bigger with a larger sample.

How can you guess what your effect size will be? Mainly, people look at prior studies, see how big the effect sizes were that others found, and then make a guess as to what they will find. If you can make guesses about your effect size and variability and you know your sample size, then you can calculate your anticipated power:

$$\text{Power (omega)} = (t^2 - 1) / (t^2 + N - 1)$$

Power values of approximately .80 (80% chance or greater of not missing an effect that is really there) or better are considered adequate to excellent. In general, parametric tests have greater statistical power. Why? Well, let's say we measure a person's IQ using a well-standardized instrument that we assume offers a certain level of precision. If I have to recode the data into categories (like high, medium, or low), then I lose some of that precision and some of the variation. When you give up some precision you also give up some power to detect significance; but this is heavily influenced by sample size. Statisticians suggest that you need about a 10% bigger sample to have the same power with a nonparametric test. Another way to maximize power is to use a one-tailed hypothesis. If the distribution of the data is symmetric, then the p value for a one-tailed test is half the value of the p value for the two-tailed test. This means one needs a bigger sample for a two-tailed test.

What does this mean practically when I am conducting a study? Well, if I don't have a big enough sample size relative to the size of the effect or association I expect, then I won't get a significant p value. If you want to study something rare or something where a small actual difference has huge implications, or if you are running a small pilot test of a program, then too little power is going to be an issue for you. You may adjust the alpha or just accept and report a lower p value. Adjusting the alpha to greater than $p => .05$ is sometimes done, with people occasionally reporting significance at the $p <= .10$ level, but this is generally frowned upon.

How do I figure out how much power I have? Formulas for power vary by statistic and get increasingly more complex for more advanced statistics. Fortunately, there are various computer programs that can help you assess power. SAS will do so in the "analyst" window for t tests and ANOVA. An SAS macro program called UnifyPow has been integrated into SAS 9.1 and has a wider range of power tests it can perform, including nonparametrics such as chi-square (but not logistic regression). These power tests can be accessed using the command PROC POWER. The "help" section of your SAS program will tell you what type of statistics PROC POWER can handle and the specific syntax. There are also numerous programs you will find on the Internet to do this. Use a search engine to look for "statistical power calculator." Most of these will require that you have some sort of estimate of the values you wish to test in your study. Prior studies can be used to guess at effect sizes. You can also sometimes start with a sample size and ask for the effect size needed to identify statistical significance given that sample size. An example of an easy-to-use, window-driven online power calculator is the UCLA School of Education program at http://calculators.stat.ucla.edu/powercalc/normal/n-2-equal/index.php.

SECTION 13.5
BASIC STATISTICAL TESTS

Once you have gotten to know your data and fixed problems that could be fixed, you will probably be looking at moving on to statistical tests. You can basically divide statistical tests into "tests of difference" and "tests of association." Tests of difference are designed to understand how one group is different from another or how a pretest differs from a posttest (t tests, ANOVAs, and the like). Tests of association are intended to find out how one set of variables is associated with either one or more other variables (chi-square, correlation, multiple regression). There are also hybrids that allow you to test whether the association between variables is the same across

groups (e.g., ANCOVA). The analyses chapters in this text introduce you to practical approaches to using the t test, ANOVA techniques, ANCOVA correlation and coefficient alpha, chi-square techniques, multiple regression, logistic regression, principal components, and survival curves. In this chapter we will review bivariate techniques that provide the foundation for commonly used multivariate approaches. In Chapter 14, we will overview commonly used multivariate approaches and introduce the idea of controlling for time elapsed in a study. These chapters are intended to provide you with the tools necessary to begin using the techniques. References for further study and more in-depth explanations of the techniques are provided at the end of Chapter 14.

We will start with bivariate tests, those that look at differences between groups or pre- and posttests and those that look at whether two variables are associated with each other. We will start with common tests of association, chi-square and correlation.

SECTION 13.5.1: TESTS OF ASSOCIATION

In many introductory statistics texts, nonparametric tests such as chi-square are typically covered near the end. So much of social science data, however, is categorical in nature (e.g., male /female, yes/no, graduated/not graduated) that we prefer to get students oriented to thinking about these types of data early. Chi-square tests look at the association of nominal or limited ordinal variables. They also provide a weaker measure of magnitude and no information about direction. We actually have to use additional measures like risk ratios and odds ratios to provide that information. In Section 13.5, we examine the Pearson chi-square, the Trend test for ordinal variables, the McNemar, and the Fisher Exact (not a chi-square test but an alternative for small samples). Next, we will cover two forms of correlation tests, correlation of continuous (interval/ratio) variables (Pearson) and correlation with ordinal (Spearman) variables. We will also provide a brief discussion of some special forms of correlation such as the phi, biserial, and partial correlation.

SECTION 13.5.2: BIVARIATE CATEGORICAL TESTS

Often our questions relate to proportions of something, individual values that are grouped into cells. The data are nominal or limited ordinal values. For example, trying to figure out if gender and asking for directions were related would compare two categorical variables: Male/Female and Asked/Didn't. You could think about it in a box or table format. In these boxes, you can get a distribution where the values are spread evenly with regard to the dependent variable (see Table 13.4).

TABLE 13.4. **Nonsignificant Distribution in Chi-Square.**

	ASKED	DIDN'T ASK
Male	25	15
Female	24	16

TABLE 13.5. **Significant Distribution in Chi-Square.**

	ASKED	DIDN'T ASK
Male	10	**30**
Female	**26**	14

Alternately, you could get a table where the dependent variable ("Asked") looks very different for men and women, such as Table 13.5. This is what a chi-square looks for. Tables like Table 13.5, where 75% of men didn't ask but only 35% of women didn't ask, will give you a significant *p* value. Tables like Table 13.4, where men and women ask at about similar rates, will not be statistically significant.

There are many different tests used to examine these kinds of associations. You have probably heard of chi-square before, though there are many variants of this. We will explore Goodness of Fit, Pearson, Cochran-Mantel-Haenszel chi-square for ordinal or stratified data, and McNemar's chi-square for paired data. For small samples we will explore a Fisher's Exact Test (not a chi-square test but often included in the same sections in texts). For trends in proportions across an ordinal outcome we will discuss the Cochran-Armitage trend test.

CHI-SQUARE

Chi-square can be used to test whether a single set of responses to a categorical question is distributed as expected. For example, let's say you were doing a study of political party affiliation. Your null hypotheses might be that a given set of respondents are equally likely to be Democrats or Republicans. If this is true, one might "expect" there should be about 50% in each group. This "expectation" is the basis of chi-square statistics. This "expected value" is compared to your actual data, the "observed" data (see SAS example Figure 13.12). If the observed data are sufficiently different from the expected data, then the chi-square test will be significant (which means the null hypothesis can be rejected, see Chapter 4). In SPSS this output can be obtained by selecting:

Analyze ⇒ Nonparametric Tests ⇒ Chi-Square ⇒ select variable ⇒ select "OK"

See Figure 13.13 for SPSS output.

In this example, the chi-square is significant. Looking at the frequency we can see that there are a lot more Republicans responding than Democrats. In other words, there was a significant difference between the equal groups expected and the actual data collected. SAS labels this the chi-square test for equal proportions. This test is also sometimes called a goodness-of-fit chi-square. This is sometimes called a "1 by 2" or "1 × 2" chi-square because we have essentially only two boxes people can fall into (Democrat or Republican).

A more common use of the chi-square is the chi-square test of independence, which tests a bivariate association in a "2 × 2" or "*r* × *c*" (meaning whatever # of rows by whatever # of columns) table of information. How does it do this? The "marginals" or row and column

FIGURE 13.12. **SAS Chi-Square.**

```
Proc Freq; tables variable / chisq; run;
                        The FREQ Procedure
                                        Cumulative    Cumulative
democrat     Frequency     Percent      Frequency      Percent
*****************************************************************
     0          1995        79.14          1995         79.14
     1           526        20.86          2521        100.00


                        Chi-Square Test
                      for Equal Proportions
                  ***************************
                  Chi-Square     855.9940
                  DF                    1
                  Pr > ChiSq       <.0001
                  Sample Size = 2521
```

FIGURE 13.13. **SPSS Chi-Square.**

democrat

	Observed N	Expected N	Residual
0	1995	1260.5	734.5
1	526	1260.5	−734.5
Total	2521		

Test Statistics

	democrat
Chi-Square(a)	855.994
Df	1
Asymp. Sig.	.000

a 0 cells (.0%) have expected frequencies less than 5. The minimum expected cell frequency is 1260.5.

■ There are at least five expected (not observed) frequencies per cell.

We do not dwell on formulas in this text, but sometimes it is helpful to understand how the computer works out a mathematical approach "behind the scenes" to solving a problem. Obviously there is no substantive value in between two nominal categories, so some sort of number that can vary must be calculated in order to develop a statistical test. First the computer finds the "expected values" (numbers by chance based on the row and column totals in the sample) for the cells in Table 13.6. Cell expected=row*column totals / total. (*Note:* Some texts call these totals "marginals.")

1. $((1209 * 1946) / 2467) = 953.67$
2. $((1209 * 519) / 2467) = 254.35$
3. $((1258 * 1946) / 2467) = 992.32$
4. $((1258 * 519) / 2467) = 264.65$

Then the computer asks, "How different are the actual (observed) numbers from what I expected them to be?"
Cell chi-squares = (observed − expected)^2 /expected

1. $((883 − 953.67)^2 /953.67) = 5.24$
2. $((326 − 254.35)^2 /254.35) = 20.18$
3. $((1065 − 992.32)^2 /992.32) = 5.32$
4. $((193 − 264.65)^2 /264.65) = 19.40$

Finally, the computer determines an overall association between the two categories:

Final chi-square = sum (also shown by Σ) of cell chi-squares
Chi-square = 50.14 df = $(r-1)(c-1) = 1$

The computer compares the final chi-square with values of chi-square distributions to determine if this chi-square is significant. If it is, then you reject the null.

You can ask SAS to give you a cross-tabulation by merely altering the PROC FREQ statement to include a "*" between variables you want in the cross-tabulation. Then you can request the chi-square test after a forward slash and before the semicolon:

```
PROC FREQ data= libname.dataset;
TABLES gender*party /chisq; run;
```

SPSS for Chi-Square Test of Independence. In SPSS, a chi-square test of independence is obtained by selecting:

Analyze ⇒ Descriptive Statistics ⇒ Crosstabs ⇒

values are used to help the chi-square procedure figure out what value would be expected in a cell if there were no association between the rows and columns. This is called the "expected" value. Let's say you want to know if gender is associated with political party (we'll limit it to Republicans and Democrats to stick with an easy example; see Table 13.6):

■ *Research question*: "Is gender (male=1; female=0) associated with voter preference (Democrat=1; Republican=0)?"

■ *Null hypothesis*: Gender is not associated with voter preference.

■ *Alternative hypothesis*: Gender is associated with voter preference.

Now, although chi-square is a nonparametric test, it does require certain things. Assumptions of chi-square include:

■ Both variables should be measured on a nominal scale.

■ Cell entries are independent (each subject needs to be in one cell in that table—think of it as putting subjects in "boxes").

TABLE 13.6. **Example 2 × 2 CHI-SQUARE Table.**

	Republican	Democrat	Total
Male	883 (1)	326 (2)	1209
Female	1065 (3)	193 (4)	1258
Total	1948	519	2467

then select the row variable desired and click the arrow to select the column variable required and click the arrow to select the "Statistics" button, then select "chi-square" from within the statistics menu, select "Continue," then select "OK."

FIGURE 13.14. **SAS Output.**

```
Table of female by democrat
female(1=female)
            democrat(1=yes)
Frequency,
Percent  ,
Row Pct  ,
Col Pct  ,         0,        1,   Total
*********^*************^********^
    0 ,         883 ,      326 ,    1209
      ,       35.79 ,    13.21 ,   49.01
      ,       73.04 ,    26.96 ,
      ,       45.33 ,    62.81 ,
*********^*************^********^
    1 ,        1065 ,      193 ,    1258
      ,       43.17 ,     7.82 ,   50.99
      ,       84.66 ,    15.34 ,
      ,       54.67 ,    37.19 ,
*********^*************^********^
Total          1948        519      2467
               78.96      21.04    100.00

    Frequency Missing = 54

  Statistics for Table of female by democrat
Statistic          DF      Value      Prob
*********************************************
Chi-Square          1     50.1335    <.0001
Likelihood Ratio
Chi-Square          1     50.5217    <.0001
Continuity Adj.
Chi-Square          1     49.4363    <.0001
Mantel-Haenszel
Chi-Square          1     50.1132    <.0001
Phi Coefficient           -0.1426
Contingency
Coefficient                0.1411
Cramer's V                -0.1426
```

Both SAS and SPSS will print the cross-tabulation table and then the chi-square statistics (Figure 13.14 and 13.15). The first one, also called the Pearson chi-square, is the one normally reported for a 2 × 2 table. You'll use the Likelihood Ratio Chi-square in modeling more complex associations. You can also request the "measures" option to obtain an odds ratio. We will cover that as we begin to look at logistic regression in Chapter 14.

In the preceding fictitious example, we would conclude that gender does appear to be associated with political party affiliation. We would also note, however, that 54 cases have missing data. With such a large sample, it is not likely that these values would change the result if present, because 54 cases is only about 2% of the total sample. Still, we always want to be careful about checking this.

FIGURE 13.15. **SPSS Output.**

Case Processing Summary

	Cases					
	Valid		Missing		Total	
	N	Percent	N	Percent	N	Percent
1=female; * democrat	2467	97.9%	54	2.1%	2521	100.0%

1=female; * democrat Cross-tabulation

Count

		democrat		
		0	1	Total
1=female;	0	883	326	1209
	1	1065	193	1258
Total		1948	519	2467

Chi-Square Tests

	Value	df	Asymp. Sig. (2-sided)	Exact Sig. (2-sided)	Exact Sig. (1-sided)
Pearson Chi-Square	50.133(b)	1	.000		
Continuity Correction(a)	49.436	1	.000		
Likelihood Ratio	50.522	1	.000		
Fisher's Exact Test				.000	.000
Linear-by-Linear Association	50.113	1	.000		
N of Valid Cases	2467				

a Computed only for a 2 × 2 table
b 0 cells (.0%) have expected count less than 5. The minimum expected count is 254.35.

When you write up your findings, the formal notation is: X^2 (df, N size) = value, $p < .05$. In practice, if you are referencing a table that identifies the n size anyway, people will often limit the notation in the text to (X^2 = value, df $p < .05$). A simple table might look like Table 13.7.

Note that SAS also automatically provides the phi coefficient, contingency coefficient, and Cramer's V in

TABLE 13.7. **Gender and Party Affiliation.**

VARIABLES	N	% DEMOCRAT
Gender		
Female	1258	15.3%
Male	1209	26.9%*

*Chi-square significance indicated for the difference of the proportions.

the output. (You can request these under "Statistics" options from SPSS.) What are these? These are correlation calculations for nominal variables. The phi is limited to a 2 by 2 table, so the others are used when there are more rows and/or columns. Why do this? Well, chi-square tells you whether the association is significant but doesn't give a measure of the magnitude of the association. You won't see these in social science much because they are sensitive to unequal row and column totals *and* because most people will choose to use odds ratios instead. What are these? We will learn about these in the next chapter, but for now suffice it to say that these also provide a way of understanding magnitude and are not as limited by design assumptions as these quasi-correlations are.

Small Samples. When your expected value in a cell dips below 5, the regular chi-square is no longer appropriate. Now this can be confusing, because sometimes your actual data may drop below 5 in a cell, but the expected value the computer generates based on the row and column totals is still above 5, or vice versa. How can that happen? Let's say that 9% of your total sample experiences a relapse, and you have 200 people in your sample. Let's say that your total sample is half male and half female. This means that you would expect there to be 9 relapses among the 100 males and 9 relapses among the 100 females. This means you have expected values of 5 or more in every cell (91 nonrelapsed males, 9 relapsed males, 91 nonrelapsed females, 9 relapsed females). What you actually find is shown in Table 13.8. This distribution does not violate the "5 or more expected per cell" rule, because you expected 5 or more (actually 9 or more) per cell, even though you actually got a lower number in one cell (female relapses).

The Fisher exact test is used in place of the chi-square when your expected count dips below the magic number 5. It computes exact probabilities from a hypergeometric distribution. This means it is not dependent on the marginals, so it does not have the same frequency requirement.

If your data do not meet the cell size requirements for chi-square, SAS and SPSS will still print out the regular chi-square output (Figure 13.16 and 13.17). They will, however, include a warning underneath the typical chi-square output saying that a certain percentage of the cells have less than 5 as an expected value. Fortunately, both SAS and SPSS already provide you an extra piece

FIGURE 13.16. **SAS Output.**

```
              Fisher's Exact Test
**************************************************
Cell (1,1) Frequency (F)                      883
Left-sided Pr <= F                       8.490E-13
Right-sided Pr >= F                         1.0000

Table Probability (P)                    4.379E-13
Two-sided Pr <= P                        1.295E-12

Effective Sample Size = 2467
Frequency Missing = 54
```

of information with the regular chi-square output that takes care of this issue. In SPSS, it's included in the middle of the chi-square output (refer back to the preceding discussion). In SAS you will see an extra table called the "Fisher's exact test" underneath the table that prints out the chi-square statistics. When you see the warning, you should use the two-sided value in this table under the exact test instead of the chi-square value. This value adjusts for the low cell counts.

Fisher's exact test has no formal test statistic and no critical value (Simon, 2005). Simon recommends noting that the results in text include either listing the proportions, then the *p* value (*x*% versus *x*%, *p* value, Fisher exact test), or just the *p* value (*p* value, Fisher exact test). Some form of an "exact" test exists for many statistical procedures to handle small sample or rare event issues.

E-GAD! THERE ARE E'S IN FIGURE 13.16

Just what do those little "E−12" thingies mean anyhow? This is the scientific notation you learned in high school or as an undergraduate. $4.379E-13$ means "4.379 times ten to the negative 13th power. In normal writing, this means "0.0000000000 004379," a very small number, and definitely less than .05 (which is $5.000E-2$, of course). Positive E numbers are positive powers of ten; that is, $3.5677E4$ equals 35,677. SAS will use these too sometimes. If you never learned scientific notation, just move the decimal point one space to the left for each "E−" or to the right for each "E+," adding zeroes as necessary.■

TABLE 13.8. **Working with a Small Sample.**

	RELAPSED	NOT RELAPSED
Male	17	83
Female	1	99

FIGURE 13.17. **SPSS Output (row taken from SPSS table in Figure 13.15).**

Fisher's Exact Test	.000	.000

r × *c* **Tables.** Chi-square can also be used to assess associations between variables with multiple levels. *Warning:* Here is our first case that SPSS has no window selection to handle, so only SAS is included here.

The regular Pearson chi-square (or general association chi-square) will provide you with a test of whether or not the row variable is associated with the column variable. This is OK, but it is not sensitive to order, so if one or more of the variables is ordered, then this won't evaluate that variable. If one variable is ordinal, you can compare mean responses between cells for group levels. This is done by assigning "scores" (computers do this for you) to the ordinal categories. This is a chi-square for the "mean scores differ." Significant chi-squares again mean that you reject the null. Finally, if both levels are ordinal then nonzero correlation or CMH chi-square tests a "linear" relationship between the ordered categories of the two variables. Instead of looking at a case where both variables are ordinal, though, let's look at an example using three race categories and voter frequency. For the sake of space we will omit the cross-tabulation output and just review the statistics (see Figure 13.18).

Notice that the general association statistic is nearly identical to the Pearson chi-square, and the nonzero correlation is identical to the Mantel-Haenszel chi-square in the table we are now used to seeing. This will not be the case later when we discuss stratified tables in the next chapter. Recall, the Pearson chi-square is not sensitive to ordering. There is no order to race, so the nonzero correlation is not appropriate either. The row means scores differ, however, can be used. It is statistically significant, which tells us that the race distribution is different in the differing levels of voting frequency.

Also notice a statistic called "Cramer's V" in the regular chi-square table portion of the output. If you will recall, earlier we mentioned that a phi coefficient was a correlation statistic for the dichotomous variable cross-tabulation. The phi cannot handle more than a 2×2 table, so for more than two rows or more than two columns, the Cramer's V can be used. "Cramer's V corrects for the fact that this correlation often cannot reach 1 in nonsquare and larger tables" (Losh, 2004, Guide 5).

Trend Test. Sometimes your question relates to a dose-response effect in treatment or at least variation in some ordinal outcome compared to group membership (see Chapter 4, Sections 5 and 6). Using our same two gender groups, suppose you measure voting frequency on an ordinal scale (never votes, rarely

---

FIGURE 13.18. SAS Commands and Output.

```
PROC FREQ; tables race*votes/ cmh chisq; run;

           Statistics for Table of race by votes

Statistic                         DF          Value        Prob
***************************************************************
Chi-Square                         8         79.0734      <.0001
Likelihood Ratio Chi-Square        8         79.4543      <.0001
Mantel-Haenszel Chi-Square         1         57.5968      <.0001
Phi Coefficient                              0.1796
Contingency Coefficient                      0.1768
Cramer's V                                   0.1270

              Effective Sample Size = 2452
              Frequency Missing = 23


                  The FREQ Procedure
            Summary Statistics for race by votes
      Cochran-Mantel-Haenszel Statistics (Based on Table Scores)

Statistic    Alternative Hypothesis       DF       Value      Prob
******************************************************************
    1        Nonzero Correlation           1      57.5968    <.0001
    2        Row Mean Scores Differ         2      74.3044    <.0001
    3        General Association            8      79.0411    <.0001
              Effective Sample Size = 2452
              Frequency Missing = 23
```

TABLE 13.9. Gender by Voting Frequency Category.			
	MALE	FEMALE	N
Never votes	37.2	21.9	726
Rarely	18.1	27.6	566
Sometimes	13.6	10.9	302
Often	13.2	18.5	393
Always	17.8	21.1	480
Total Responding	1258	1209	2467

votes, sometimes votes, always votes; Table 13.9). The data are not at the interval or ratio level, but you want to know if the frequency is associated with gender. The Cochran-Armitage trend test actually combines tests of proportions with components of a regression analysis. The null hypothesis for the Cochran-Armitage test is that there is no trend, which means that the proportion of the dependent variable is the same for all levels of the explanatory variable (Agresti, 1990).

There is no windows menu item for this analysis in SPSS. If we add the TREND statement along with the CHISQ command in SAS, we can get an assessment of the trend among the ordinal values as well as whether or not there is an association between the variables (Figure 13.19).

FIGURE 13.19. **SAS Command.**

```
PROC FREQ data= libname.dataset;
TABLES gender*votes / trend chisq; run;
```

Partial SAS Output for Trend test

```
Statistic             DF    Value    Prob
******************************************
Chi-Square             4   91.0763   <.0001
Likelihood
Ratio Chi-Square       4   91.7932   <.0001
Mantel-Haenszel
Chi-Square             1   29.4452   <.0001

        Cochran-Armitage Trend Test
************************************
Statistic      (Z)          -5.4274
One-sided     Pr < Z         <.0001
Two-sided     Pr > |Z|       <.0001

Effective Sample Size = 2467
Frequency Missing = 54
```

The trend test is equivalent to the Mantel-Haenszel statistic if the dichotomous variable can be considered "ordered" (e.g., good versus bad instead of female versus male). This test also tells you if the subject's gender is associated with voting frequency. The trend test seems to be the test of choice in biomedical research and was specifically designed to test a trend hypothesis. The trend test is based on a z distribution instead of the chi-square distribution, but they are related statistics. The trend test is related to the Mantel-Haenszel chi-square for linear association: X^2 trend = (Armitage Trend)^2. If both the column and row variables are ordinal, then either statistic may be used. Technically, if either the row or column is nominal, then the trend statistic should be used.

While in this example, the test of general association and the trend test are both significant, that will not always be the case. You can have a nonsignificant general association and still have a significant dose-response or ordinal trend. How can this happen? Let's look at Table 13.10.

Such data can result in there being no association between gender and response category because the distribution of gender is not significantly different for each response level. There are always more females in each voting category, but within gender categories there are trends. A greater proportion of the males appear to be in the "always" category, and a greater proportion of the females appear to be in the "never" category.

Paired Data and Chi-Square. Sometimes we have pairs of subjects, meaning that the regular chi-square test cannot be used because we lack independence. In such a case we use McNemar's chi-square. This is used when comparing proportions with paired samples, for example, husband and wife responses to a quit-smoking campaign or pre- and posttest responses to a group of subjects who have participated in a group to stop using physical punishment with their children. The quit versus did not quit proportions for each are compared (see Table 13.11).

TABLE 13.10. Gender by Voting Frequency Category.		
	MALE	FEMALE
Never votes	5	30
Rarely	7	28
Sometimes	8	26
Often	9	24
Always	10	23

TABLE 13.11. **Physical Punishment with Children.**

TIME 1	TIME 2		TOTAL
	USE	**DON'T USE**	
Use	20	5	25
Don't use	10	10	20
Total	30	15	45

Our research question: Is the proportion of people who use physical punishment in time 1 the same as in time 2? This test uses diagonals to look for association:

$$\text{Chi-sq} = (5 - 10)^2 / (5 + 10)$$
$$= 1.67 \text{ with 1 degree of freedom}$$

SAS for McNemar's Chi-Square. Our SAS commands are as follows:

```
PROC FREQ; tables time1 * time2 /AGREE; run;
```

Instead of asking for the CHISQ after the forward slash, we type in AGREE. This provides the McNemar's statistic.

SPSS for McNemar's Chi-Square. In SPSS, this test can be run by choosing:

Analyze ⇒ Descriptive Statistics ⇒ Crosstabs ⇒ select variables ⇒ select "statistics" box ⇒ check "McNemar" ⇒ select "Continue" ⇒ select "OK"

A significant test indicates that there is a difference in proportions between the pairs. If there is no difference, then we conclude that subjects' use of physical punishment is similar at time 1 and time 2. An extension of this approach can produce kappa statistics for inter-rater reliability to assess when raters agree on categorizations of subjects into nominal categories at higher levels than the 2 × 2 table. We won't go over this in this text, but so that you can interpret kappas reported in articles, a kappa of .4 to .80 indicates moderate agreement, and over .8 indicates excellent agreement.

SECTION 13.5.3: CORRELATION

A typical bivariate (also called zero-order) correlation assesses a relationship between two variables measured at the interval/ratio level instead of the nominal or ordinal level. This means it can tell you whether two continuous variables are correlated (associated). You will see some people argue that correlations can also be used with ordinal data instead of the CMH chi-square

we just discussed, but we are going to stick with the more strict interpretation of use here. Compared to the chi-square, the correlation provides us extra information about the direction and magnitude of that association without having to ask for additional statistics. Not only are correlations useful analysis tools, they are also a part of checking assumptions for other tests that require variables to have a linear association.

You always run correlations, for example, before you run any test such as multiple regression that is the multivariate extension of correlation. While this is a first step in understanding whether or not one variable might cause another using more advanced tests, you must always remember that correlation does not prove causation. You remember from Chapter 3 that we need three things to show causation: time order, association (correlation), and lack of spurious causality. A correlation test demonstrates only the second. There are many forms of correlation. Indeed, we introduced two that accompany chi-square in the last section. Now we'll talk about the Pearson r, probably the most commonly used correlation measure. Assumptions of the Pearson r include:

1. It requires interval or ratio data.
2. Data are approximately normal and have sufficient numbers of observations.
3. It also assumes a linear relationship.

The research question for a correlation might read:

- Is age (0–99) associated with depression scale scores (3–60)?
- Null hypothesis: Age is not associated with depression.
- Alternative hypothesis: Age is associated with depression.

If your data are not shaped like a line, what do you use? If your data are ordinal rather than interval or ratio you can use the Spearman ("rho"), which we will get to in a minute. Some slight variations or curvature in the data can also be handled by Spearman, but if it's shaped like a U or a camel (see the nearby box), then Spearman is not appropriate. You have to enter the realm of polynomials, which we will not cover in an introductory text.

CURVILINEAR DATA: WHAT IS IT?

Mostly, we think of linear relationships. In other words, we think about patterns where as one thing goes up (self-efficacy), another thing goes up, too (academic achievement). Basically, the two variables make a kind of line (linear relationship) when graphed against each other.

Some things, however, don't come in lines. For example, the association between test preparation time and test results might look like this:

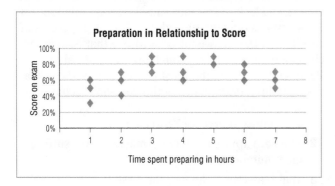

In these data, the people who prepared for a moderate amount of time (about 3 to 5 hours) seemed to do better than those who spent more or less time preparing. Notice how the dots make a curved arc, rather than a straight line. A curvilinear relationship can be many shapes, and we often hear of U, J, L, or ∩ -shaped associations.■

The easiest way to assess a linear relationship between two variables is by using a graphic plot with your interval/ratio data. Weird shapes cannot be analyzed using a Pearson *r*. It won't be a perfect line usually, so think roughly of a line, not whether or not it looks like someone drew it with a ruler.

SAS for Scatterplot

In SAS, the code to get a line plot or scatterplot for Maria's data is:

```
PROC GPLOT data = x; Plot murder * poverty;
run; [Note: the order you list the variables
will determine which one is the x-axis and
which one is the y-axis.]
```

See Figures 13.20 and 13.21.

FIGURE 13.20. **SAS Scatterplot.**

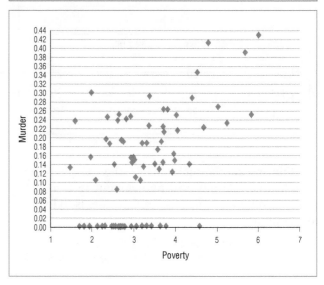

SPSS for Scatterplot

To get an SPSS scatterplot for Maria's data:

Go to Graphs ⇒ Scatter/Dot. . . ⇒ select "Simple Scatter" ⇒ Click on "define" ⇒ select murder for the *y*-axis and poverty for the *x*-axis ⇒ click "OK"

See Figure 13.21.

In the two graphs, we see two variables. The straight line you see in both graphs is merely the result of there being several areas that have a "zero" murder rate. This kind of a picture can happen when you have a relatively small *n* size (there are 77 zip codes in Maria's data) and a rare event (murder). Once the rate begins to vary, then we can see that there is a rough line that indicates an increasing murder rate with increasing poverty. We also have some points that seem to be hanging in space by themselves, such as zero murders for a poverty rate of 40%. We would want to look over

FIGURE 13.21. **SPSS Scatterplot.**

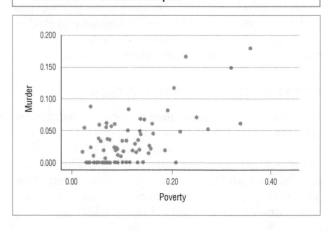

our descriptive statistics to see if there are outliers that need to be dropped. Anyway, the relationship looks roughly linear without odd and obvious curves or a flat line that would indicate no association at all. So, we would likely proceed with our correlation.

Of course, we also assessed for normality, right? We used univariate descriptive statistics and found that both poverty and homicide rate were mildly skewed. We created new variables using a square root transformation for both variables. So in Maria's raw data it is homicide rate and PCTpoor, but now we have a variable called murder = sqrt(homicide rate) and poverty = sqrt(PCTpoor).

SAS AND PEARSON CORRELATION

In SAS we ask for:

```
PROC CORR; var murder*poverty; run;
```

And we'd get this:

```
     Pearson Correlation Coefficients, N=77
          Prob > |r| under H0: Rho=0
                      murder        poverty
     murder         1.00000        0.52820
                                    <.0001
     poverty        0.52820        1.00000
                    <.0001
```

If you do not specify the variables in the SAS command it will try to run correlations on everything, including your ID numbers. You can enter as many variables as you like, and it will do bivariate correlations with each against the other.

SPSS AND PEARSON CORRELATION

In SPSS we do the following:

Go to Analyze ⇒ Correlate ⇒ Bivariate. . . ⇒ specify the variables 'murder' and 'poverty' ⇒ Under Correlation Coefficients, check 'Pearson' ⇒ select 'Two-tailed' under Test of Significance ⇒ click "OK"

And our SPSS output will look like Table 13.12.

You will notice that SAS did not print out the n size for each correlation, but SPSS did. SAS will include the n sizes if they vary for combinations of variables. What does this mean? Well, let's say you are doing several bivariate correlations at once with different variables. The statistical packages will throw out missing values. So if we have nonmissing values for murder and poverty, but we have five missing values for another variable called vacancy, then our n size for the correlation between poverty and murder would be 77, but our n size for a correlation between murder and vacancy would be

TABLE 13.12. Correlations.

		MURDER	POVERTY
murder	Pearson Correlation	1	.528(**)
	Sig. (2-tailed)		.000
	N	77	77
poverty	Pearson Correlation	.528(**)	1
	Sig. (2-tailed)	.000	
	N	77	77

** Correlation is significant at the 0.01 level (2-tailed).

only 72. Therefore it is important to look at the sample sizes associated with correlations if you have not already taken care of missing data for the whole data set.

The results tell us that there is a moderate to strong positive association ($r = .528$) between these two variables. How do we know that? Correlation coefficients occur between -1 and 1. A positive correlation means that both variables are moving up or down together. A negative correlation means that as one variable increases, the other is decreasing. The greater the absolute value, the greater the magnitude of the relationship. In other words, a correlation of $r = .20$ indicates a weaker relationship than $r = .80$. How big is big enough? Generally a correlation of .20 or less is considered weak, even if it is statistically significant, and a correlation of .75 or more is very strong. What's the exact rule? Well, there really isn't one, and you will see a variety of descriptions of magnitude in the articles you read. The discussion below, however, will help you understand why a correlation of .20 is not very strong.

First it is helpful to go "behind the scenes" with Mr. Computer. Obviously income and murder rate are not really on the same scale. Herein lies one of the uses of the z score. Deep inside your computer, its little chips are busily converting your data to z scores so that one variable is directly comparable to another. Correlation tests think in pairs. The basic formula is the sum of the multiplied and paired z scores divided by the sample size -1 ($r = \Sigma z \times zy \,/\, N - 1$); or another way to represent the formula for the Pearson r is:

$$\frac{\Sigma XY - (\Sigma X)(\Sigma Y) \,/\, N}{\sqrt{[\Sigma X^2 - (\Sigma X)^2 \,/\, N]\,[\Sigma Y^2 - (\Sigma Y)^2 \,/\, N]}}$$

The resulting r gives an unadjusted measure of association, but for actual magnitude it is most appropriate to use the r^2, or coefficient of determination. This provides an absolute measure of the variability of Y accounted for by X. So an $r = .20$ would be an $r^2 = .04$. This illustrates why a correlation of only $r = .20$ is considered weak. "Variability accounted for" or "variability explained" means that a certain percentage (4% in the above example) in the differences in scores in the second variable are explained by their relationship to the first variable. It does not mean that variable *A* caused variable *B*, only that they share some unique amount of variation.

Format Examples for Correlations. In text one usually reports correlations as $r = -.30; p < .05$; or some journals still prefer ($r = -.30; p < .05$) or $r(n \text{ size}), p \leq .05$.

A correlation table will look like Table 13.13. The numbers in the table are the *r* for each paired correlation. The diagonal is left out, as the correlation between a variable and itself is understood to be 1. The lower left part of the table is left out because it just repeats the upper right part of the table. Table 13.13 shows several moderate correlations (variable 1 with variables 2, 4, and 5; variable 2 with variable 3; a stronger correlation of 4 with 5; and a weak correlation of 2 with 5).

SPEARMAN

Now, when both variables are ordinal (with enough categories that we really don't think our categorical CMH trend alternative is the best), or one is ordinal and the other interval/ratio, then you will want to use the Spearman correlation. This method is also useful when one or both of the variables are sufficiently skewed to worry about normality. It can also be used for some forms of curvilinear data. It is not as powerful as the Pearson when data are normal, however, so it isn't just used as a default for any type of data.

The formula for the Spearman correlation is:

$$\text{rho} = 1 - 6\sum D^2 / n^3 - n$$

You rank both sets of data (*X* and *Y*) from lowest to highest; ties can be split by assigning each a fraction. For example, if you have two values for 6 for variable *X*, you might assign them both a 6.5. Subtract the ranks to get *d*. Square each value of *d*, then sum the square values to get $\sum D^2$; n = the number of ranks.

SAS and Spearman Correlation.

```
PROC CORR SPEARMAN data=libname.x; var x y;
run;
```

SPSS and Spearman Correlation.

Go to Analyze $\Rightarrow$ Correlate $\Rightarrow$ Bivariate. . . , $\Rightarrow$ specify the variables 'murder' and 'poverty' under Variables $\Rightarrow$ under Correlation Coefficients, check 'Spearman' $\Rightarrow$ select 'Two-tailed' under Test of Significance $\Rightarrow$ click "OK"

The output is identical to the Pearson *r* except that the heading will indicate that it's the Spearman, and the relationships are likely to be weaker. Here we looked at the untransformed (skewed) variables of Hrate and PCTpoor instead of poverty and murder. The way you interpret the results is the same as the Pearson. To conserve space we have provided only the SAS output for the Spearman (Figure 13.22).

Indeed, we see that the correlation between poverty and homicide rate is still significant using a nonparametric method with the original skewed values, but the magnitude of the association has declined.

COEFFICIENT ALPHA

There are other uses for correlation as well. You may have already come across an article reporting on a scale's reliability or "coefficient alpha." This is really another way of using correlation. The coefficient alpha you see reported is really measuring how individual items on the scale correlate with each other. An alpha of .70 or above is considered good, whereas less than .60 is moving into the unacceptable range. The coefficient alpha will be high when there are lots of items and they are highly correlated with one another.

SAS and Coefficient Alpha.

```
PROC CORR data=x ALPHA NOMISS; VAR list of
items in scale goes here; run;
```

Partial SAS output is shown as Figure 13.23.

FIGURE 13.22. SAS Output for Spearman.

```
Spearman Correlation Coefficients, N = 77
                Prob > |r| under H0: Rho=0
                                    HRate          PCTpoor
HRate                               1.00000        0.44699
Homicides per 1000 people per year                 <.0001
PCTpoor                             0.44699        1.00000
percentage of people below poverty line  <.0001
```

TABLE 13.13. **Pearson Correlation Coefficients and Significance for Study Variables.**

	VARIABLE #1	VARIABLE #2	VARIABLE #3	VARIABLE #4	VARIABLE #5
Variable #1	--	.25**	.07	.41***	.40***
Variable #2		--	.26**	.11	.15*
Variable #3			--	.14	.09
Variable #4				--	.54***
Variable #5					--

*$p <= .05$; **$p < .01$; ***$p <= .0001$

SPSS and Coefficient Alpha.

Go to Analyze $\Rightarrow$ Scale $\Rightarrow$ Reliability Analysis . . . ,
$\Rightarrow$ select the variables of interest from the list on the left
$\Rightarrow$ move to under 'items' by using arrow $\Rightarrow$ select 'Alpha'
for the Model $\Rightarrow$ click on "Statistics. . ." button $\Rightarrow$ under
"Descriptives for," check 'Item,' 'Scale' and 'Scale if
item deleted' $\Rightarrow$ under "Inter-Item," check 'Correlations'
$\Rightarrow$ click "Continue" $\Rightarrow$ click "OK"

Partial SPSS output is shown in Figure 13.24.

SPSS provides somewhat different-looking output than SAS. Basically, in SAS you are interested in the columns under "raw data." These are equivalent to columns 4 and 6 of the SPSS table. SPSS rounds the numbers, and SAS does not. Your output will also contain summary descriptive statistics of the items and regular correlations. We have not shown these to conserve space.

So what does it mean? Well, our overall alpha is pretty good at about .77. Next we check out the items and look for possible problems. We look at the correlation with the total scale and then the alpha if that item was deleted (SAS columns 1 and 2 and SPSS columns 4 and 6). For example, item m4 does not appear to correlate with the total too well ($r = .135$). Indeed, it looks like the overall alpha would improve if you dropped that item (from .770 to .771). Your next decision is whether to retain that variable or get rid of it. Now in this example, deleting m4 would not lead to an earth-shaking improvement in the overall alpha. Your decision about whether or not to retain a variable should depend on theory as well as statistics. Sometimes there is a reason to retain an item like m4 because it belongs to a subscale or the question itself is important. If you choose to delete this item or others, you must do so one at a time and then rerun the procedure to see if your coefficient alpha improves. Why can't you just delete

FIGURE 13.23. **Partial SAS Output.**

```
                    Cronbach Coefficient Alpha

           Variables                Alpha
           * * * * * * * * * * * * * * * * * * * * * * * * * *
           Raw                      0.769941
           Standardized             0.753937


           Cronbach Coefficient Alpha with Deleted Variable
                    Raw Variables              Standardized Variables
                 Correlation                      Correlation
     Deleted     with Total      Alpha            with Total      Alpha
     Variable
     * * * * * * * * * * * * * * * * * * * * * * * * * * * * * * * * * * * * * * * * * * * * *
        m1       0.588730        0.745482         0.564972        0.726449
        m2       0.585759        0.745705         0.560006        0.726813
        m3       0.561670        0.743604         0.540636        0.728230
        m4       0.134665        0.770889         0.163260        0.754648
```

FIGURE 13.24. **Partial SPSS Output.**

Reliability Statistics

Cronbach's Alpha	Cronbach's Alpha Based on Standardized Items	N of Items
.770	.754	22

Item-Total Statistics

	Scale Mean if Item Deleted	Scale Variance if Item Deleted	Corrected Item-Total Correlation	Squared Multiple Correlation	Cronbach's Alpha if Item Deleted
m1	68.53	166.947	.589	.694	.745
m2	68.36	167.100	.586	.713	.746
m3	69.13	162.396	.562	.689	.744
m4	67.74	184.320	.135	.254	.771
m5	71.44	172.453	.392	.519	.757
m6	70.26	165.143	.513	.562	.748
m7	67.94	187.802	.019	.296	.777
m8	69.42	159.856	.611	.689	.739
m9	68.84	188.592	−.028	.489	.784
m10	70.23	167.091	.397	.665	.756
m11	70.32	162.220	.502	.674	.747
m12	69.03	193.868	−.148	.429	.790
m13	68.56	166.602	.567	.571	.746
m14	68.93	167.520	.485	.423	.750
m15	71.62	176.946	.348	.489	.760
m16	70.88	166.574	.537	.606	.747
m17	67.82	188.892	−.006	.273	.777
m18	69.45	190.317	−.064	.420	.784
m19	69.28	187.459	.002	.493	.781
m20	70.57	161.332	.649	.606	.739
m21	67.86	189.723	−.039	.236	.779
m22	69.40	174.447	.278	.333	.765

---

them all at once? Well, the alpha is based on intercorrelations, and when you remove one item, it can have an impact on other items.

The table format for reporting item values is somewhat different than for correlations; an example is shown as Table 13.14.

OTHERS TYPES OF CORRELATION

There are certainly other forms of correlation you will encounter in the literature that this book simply lacks the time to cover sufficiently. As aforementioned, there are correlations that apply to categorical data, such as the phi correlation (which is printed out with the chi-square output).

Another form of correlation called the biserial correlation can be used when one variable is interval/ratio and the other is dichotomous. You use the dichotomous variable to split the continuous variable into 2 groups

(M_0 and M_1); see the chart on page 275. The formula for correlation coefficient is:

$$r_{xy} = \mu_1 - \mu_0 \div \sigma_y(\sigma_x)$$

TABLE 13.14. **Example of Correlation Table Format for Article.**

ITEMS	MEAN	SD	1	2	3
Item 1			(alpha)		
Item 2			r	(alpha)	
Item 3			r	r	(alpha)

N = Reliability estimates appear on the diagonal
The alphas for the table are taken from the Correlation with Total column on the output. The alpha value if that item were deleted is estimated in the next column.

Cases	X	Y	
Allen	0	1	
Becky	0	2	$M_0 = 1.5$
Cathy	1	3	
Debra	1	4	
Edgar	1	5	$M_1 = 4$
μ	3/5	3	
σ^2	6/25	2	

—example taken from (Visual Statistics with Multimedia, 2003 www.visualstatistics.net/Visual%20Statistics%20Multimedia/ point-biserial_coefficient_of_correlation.html).

First- and *higher-order* correlations are other terms you commonly hear. While we don't cover their use in this text, it is helpful to know what they are. The basic bivariate correlation is also known as the zero-order correlation. When we move beyond that to control for a third variable, we then move to a partial correlation known as a first-order correlation. This helps tease out the unique association of *x* and *y* while controlling for a third variable that is related to both *x* and *y: z*. This type of controlling for another variable is *not* identical to an interaction term in a regression equation! We'll cover interaction terms later. The goal of the partial correlation is to try to identify the "pure" relationship between two variables, assuming you have the awareness of and ability to measure other variables that are involved in that relationship.

SAS and Partial Correlation.

```
PROC CORR; var X Y; PARTIAL z; run;
```

SPSS and Partial Correlation.

Go to Analyze ⇒ Correlate ⇒ Partial . . . , ⇒ specify the *x* and *y* variables under "Variables" and the *z* variable under "Controlling for" ⇒ select 'Two-tailed' under Test of Significance ⇒ click "OK"

SECTION 13.5.4: BIVARIATE ASSOCIATION SUMMARY

So far we have explored two forms of tests of associations that span parametric and nonparametric techniques. These tests form the basis of more advanced techniques such as logistic regression and linear regression. Before going on to more advanced topics related to association, we will now cover some basic tests of group differences to round out our understanding of bivariate tests.

Tests of difference look at mean group values and try to see if there are significant differences in mean values according to various group designations. We will look at the *t* tests, ANOVA, and factorial ANOVA in this chapter. A repeated measures ANOVA is introduced in the next chapter.

All *t* test and ANOVA procedures look for group differences in means of some criterion or outcome variable. All such tests are based on the ability to group the sample according to some (1) nominal value, such as males or females; or (2) a nominal grouping variable that represents different time periods like pre/post or pre/post/follow-up or time1/time2/time3 test-taking events. In other words, you need to have two groups (usually defined by a nominal variable like "male/female" or "before/after") that you want to compare to do this stuff. As we will see, you will also need something to compare them on, a dependent variable such as a test score.

SECTION 13.6.1: *T* TESTS

There are essentially three forms of the *t* test: the single sample that compares a value to a known prior value (rarely used in social science), the single-sample pre-post *t* test (or paired samples *t* test), and the independent samples *t* test. We will focus on the paired samples and independent samples tests, as these are the most common. The single-sample *t* test is used only when comparing a sample to a larger population for which the mean value of the variable of interest in the population is known.

INDEPENDENT SAMPLES *T* TEST

Let's say you are curious about whether or not men have higher GRE scores than women among applicants to social work PhD programs:

- *Research question:* "Is the mean score on the GRE different for male than it is for female applicants to social work PhD programs?"
- *Null hypothesis:* The mean value of the GRE is the same for male and female applicants.
- *Alternative hypothesis:* The mean value of the GRE will differ between male and female applicants.

Assumptions for the independent samples *t* test include:

1. There will be an interval or ratio level dependent variable and a nominal predictor variable.

2. Independence of observations—one subject cannot have scores in both groups, nor can one subject's score influence another subject's score within the same group.

3. The dependent variable should be normally distributed (although if you have at least 30 subjects in each group, you can tolerate some deviation from normality).

First, you should go back to basics and look at the distribution of the dependent variable. The easiest way to do this is by sorting your data by the criterion or predictor (in our example, gender): The "BY" statement tells the computer to look at the distribution for the predictor variable for each gender.

SAS and Assumptions for *t* Test.

```
PROC SORT data = libname.data; by gender;
run;
PROC UNIVARIATE data = NORMAL PLOT; VAR GRE;
BY gender; run;
```

Sorting the data by the grouping variable is important. SAS cannot execute the next procedure if the data are not sorted by the "BY" variable.

SPSS and Assumptions for *t* Test.

Go to Analyze ⇒ Descriptive Statistics ⇒ Explore ⇒ specify the "Dependent variable" (GRE score) and the nominal variable under "Factor list" (gender) ⇒ select 'both' under Display (so that you get the univariate statistics and the plots) ⇒ click "OK"

You also need to look at the variance of both groups. If it's equal, you run an equal variance test; and if it's unequal, you run an unequal variance test. SAS and SPSS automatically look at this, so all you have to do is know how to read the output. You also want to think about your "power," that is, your sample size. If you have met your three assumptions and you have a big enough sample, you proceed to the *t* test.

What is a *t* test? The *t* test sets up a sampling distribution of differences with a mean of zero. The *t* test calculates if your difference between the means ($\mu 1 - \mu 2$) is far in the tails of the sampling distribution or far away from zero. The *t* score is made a relative score by dividing the difference between the means by the standard error of the difference:

$$t = \frac{\mu 1 - \mu 2}{s / \sqrt{n}}$$

$\mu 1 - \mu 2$ = the difference in means (or effect size)

s = your variability
n = your sample size

SAS and Independent Samples *t* Test.

```
PROC TTEST data= libname.x; CLASS gender;
VAR GRE; run;
```

SAS happens to call the grouping variable "CLASS" instead of using the "BY" command we saw in PROC UNIVARIATE.

SPSS and Independent Samples *t* Test.

Go to Analyze ⇒ Compare Means ⇒ Independent-Samples T Test ⇒ specify the test variable or dependent variable and the nominal variable as the grouping (independent) variable from the list on the left of the window ⇒ use arrows to move variables to boxes ⇒ Click "Define Groups" ⇒ define the levels for the groups (e.g., 0=. . . ;1=. . .) so the output will label them ⇒ click "Continue" ⇒ click "OK"

This procedure will print out a table of the measures of central tendency and variability for GRE for each gender. Then it provides two different *t* tests: one for equal variances and one for unequal variances. But which one do you use? In SAS, we look under the *t* tests where you will find an *F* value and significance. If the test is significant, you report the unequal variance *t*-test results above it. If the test is not significant, you report the equal variance *t* test. Let's use Abigail's data to look at gender and one of her social support scale measures. SAS output is shown in Figure 13.25. In SPSS, the *F* test is slightly different, but it does the same thing. It is labeled "Levene's" and is found in the second column of the output table shown in Figure 13.26.

In both cases, we see that our *F* test is not significant. This is a good thing. Why don't we want statistical significance, as we usually do? Well, when we are running tests to see whether our data meet assumptions, then a significant result means that our data vary from what we want. So, in general, whenever you see a test that is run to check assumptions, you want that test to be nonsignificant (or a *p* value above .05).

Because our *F* value is not significant, we refer to the equal variance *t* statistic, which is rounded to $t = -.86$, $p = .3919$ on the SAS output and $t = -.861, p = .392$ in SPSS. This *t* test was not significant (.3919 is greater than .05), so we cannot reject the null hypothesis, or in other words, the relationship between gender and the family social support score in Abigail's sample is not statistically significant.

When you report a *t* test in text, the typical format is:

$$t(76) = -0.86; \quad p = .39$$

This means, "*t*(degrees of freedom)= *t* value; *p* value." If your *t* test is significant, do not forget to tell your reader (in a table or in the text) what the mean for each value was. The *t* test only tells whether there was a

```
                              The TTEST Procedure
                                  Statistics
                         Lower CL        Upper CL   Lower CL         Upper CL
Variable   female    N    Mean    Mean    Mean   Std Dev  Std Dev  Std Dev Std  Err
SSBSOA     0        22   10.154  12.409  14.664  3.9133   5.0865   7.2689      1.0844
SSBSOA     1        56   12.132  13.536  14.94   4.4203   5.2431   6.445       0.7006
SSBSOA     Diff (1-2)     -3.733  -1.127  1.4794  4.4888   5.2003   6.1818      1.3085
                                  T-Tests
           Variable    Method          Variances    DF      t Value   Pr > |t|
           SSBSOA      Pooled          Equal        76       -0.86     0.3919
           SSBSOA      Satterthwaite   Unequal      39.6     -0.87     0.3881

                           Equality of Variances
           Variable    Method       Num DF   Den DF   F Value   Pr > F
           SSBSOA      Folded F       55       21      1.06     0.9117
```

significant difference but does not tell how they were different. If all you report is the *t* test, no one will be able to determine whether women had higher scores than men or vice versa. They will also not be able to look at the difference between the mean scores for men and women and tell how big the difference was.

The *t* test is not typically used as a causal test in social science. On the other hand, if we have a sample randomly assigned to two groups and the independent variable is manipulated in an experiment, we may be interested in the variability of the dependent variable *A* explained by group membership. This can be done by calculating yet another Greek letter:

$$\varphi^2 = \frac{(t_{obt}^2 - 1)}{(t_{obt}^2 + N - 1)}$$

Group Statistics

		N	Mean	Std. Deviation	Std. Error Mean
SSB TOTAL, SOCIAL SUBSCALE (Family)	0	22	12.41	5.086	1.084
	1	56	13.54	5.243	.701

Independent Samples Test

	Levene's Test for Equality of Variances		*t* test for Equality of Means						95% Confidence Interval of the Difference	
	F	Sig.	t	df	Sig. (2-tailed)	Mean Difference	Std. Error Difference		Lower	Upper
SSB TOTAL, SOCIAL SUBSCALE (Family) — Equal variances assumed	.060	.808	-.861	76	.392	-1.127	1.308		-3.733	1.479
Equal variances not assumed			-.873	39.559	.388	-1.127	1.291		-3.737	1.484

This is really an adjusted R^2. The variable t_{obt} is the obtained value from your *t* test squared to get rid of the positive or negative. *N* is the total of both groups. This will give you an estimate of the percent of the variability in the outcome explained by your independent variable. It implies only cause in a controlled true experimental design. Could you use this in a non-experimental context? Well, yes, but then you have to remember that its meaning is analogous to the *R* in the correlation—it is merely a measure of association.

What if my data aren't normal? Is there an alternative? Yes, the nonparametric alternative to the independent samples *t* test is called the Wilcoxon rank sum test (also known as the Mann-Whitney U—they are technically different calculations, but they are identical in usage, and the rank sum is easier to compute). SPSS will output both tests. This test assigns rank scores across the two groups (adjusting for ties). It is similar in approach to what we saw for the Spearman correlation, but the data are lumped together for the ranking, and then the group ranks are compared separately. It can be used for ordinal variables or for continuous variables that depart from normality. The formula for the Kruskal Wallis test for ANOVA (which is similar to the Wilcoxon) is provided in a later section. This test does not allow you to test for differences in situations where the two groups have radically different distribution shapes. In other words, if the skewness of one group is radically different than the other group, then this test may be inaccurate. It is robust against minor to moderate violations.

SAS and Wilcoxon. There are two ways to arrive at the Wilcoxon using SAS, but we favor:

```
PROC NPAR1WAY WILCOXON; CLASS gender;
VAR SSBSOA; run;
```

This command is easier than the special options for PROC FREQ, and it's the same command you will use for the nonparametric alternative to the ANOVA. SAS output is shown in Figure 13.27.

SPSS and Wilcoxon. In SPSS there is no way to select only the Wilcoxon, but it will be output with the Mann-Whitney U:

Go to Analyze $\Rightarrow$ Nonparametric Tests $\Rightarrow$ 2 Independent Samples. . . $\Rightarrow$ specify the test variable (dependent variable) and the grouping (independent) variable from the list on the left of the window $\Rightarrow$ move with arrows to appropriate box $\Rightarrow$ Under "Test Type" select Mann-Whitney U $\Rightarrow$ click "OK"

SPSS output is shown in Figure 13.28.

FIGURE 13.27. SAS Output.

```
        Wilcoxon Scores (Rank Sums) for Variable SSBSOA
                  Classified by Variable female

                 Sum of      Expected      Std Dev       Mean
female    N      Scores      Under H0      Under H0      Score
************************************************************************
1        56      2281.50      2212.0      89.856296     40.741071
0        22       799.50       869.0      89.856296     36.340909
                Average scores were used for ties.

                    Wilcoxon Two-Sample Test
                 Statistic           799.5000
                 Normal Approximation
                 Z                    -0.7679
                 One-Sided Pr < Z      0.2213
                 Two-Sided Pr > |Z|    0.4426

                 t Approximation
                 One-Sided Pr < Z      0.2224
                 Two-Sided Pr > |Z|    0.4449

            Z includes a continuity correction of 0.5.

                    Kruskal-Wallis Test
                 Chi-Square            0.5982
                 DF                         1
                 Pr > Chi-Square       0.4393
```

FIGURE 13.28. SPSS Output.

Ranks

	N	Mean Rank	Sum of Ranks
SSB TOTAL, SOCIAL 0	22	36.34	799.50
SUBSCALE (Family) 1	56	40.74	2281.50
Total	78		

Test Statistics(a)

	SSB TOTAL, SOCIAL SUBSCALE (Family)
Mann-Whitney U	546.500
Wilcoxon W	799.500
Z	−.773
Asymp. Sig. (2-tailed)	.439

a Grouping Variable: 1=female worker, 0=male worker

The practical interpretation is the same as the *t* test except there is a *z* value and a *t* approximation rather than a *t* value. The *p* values for the two-sided *t* approximation and normal approximation are both nonsignificant. Because SAS prints out the *z* test statistic, this is normally the one used. Other statistical packages may default to the *t* approximation, which uses a *t* distribution table. Either *p* value is correct. The SPSS *p* value actually defaults to the Kruskal-Wallis test statistic used in SAS. We will revisit the Kruskal-Wallis as a nonparametric alternative to the ANOVA later.

THE PAIRED-SAMPLES *T* TEST

Let's say you want to evaluate a group training session. You have developed a psychoeducational approach to reducing anxiety among graduate students. You have a group of 30 students and give an anxiety test prior to the training session and then again six months later. If your approach works, the students should have a lower anxiety level the second time you give them the scale:

- *Your research question:* "Is there a difference in mean anxiety scores between time 1 and time 2?"
- *Null hypothesis:* There is no difference in mean anxiety scores.
- *Alternate hypothesis:* There is a difference in mean anxiety scores (nondirectional).

Of course, your observations are not independent—in fact, they are correlated to some degree because the values are taken from the same person each time. You therefore need a different kind of *t* test to see if the

pretest means are significantly different from the posttest means. This is the paired-samples *t* test.

Assumptions of the paired-samples *t* test include:

1. There is an interval or ratio level dependent variable and a nominal predictor variable that identifies the two time periods.
2. Paired observations can be created by comparing the same subject's scores at time 1 and time 2 or by a matching process.
3. Even though the scores of the same subject will be correlated, the scores of different subjects should be independent.
4. The distribution of the difference scores (D1−D2) must be normal.
5. The variances of the dependent variables in the two time periods should be equal.

The statistical formula is as follows:

$$t = \frac{D1 - D2}{S_D / \sqrt{N}}$$

$D1 - D2$ = the difference in scores
S_D = standard deviation of the difference
N = number of difference scores

The degrees of freedom for this test are $N-1$, where N = number of pairs.

SAS and Paired *t* Test. To request the procedures in SAS you have two options.

For the first method if you use the old-fashioned way, you must first create a difference score, DIFF = pre − post. We also include a means of the raw pre- and posttest scores to check assumptions and to be able to report the test means:

```
DATA x;
Set libname.yuan:
DIFF=posta-prea; run;

PROC MEANS; VAR prea posta; run;
PROC MEANS N MEAN STDERR T PRT; VAR DIFF; run;
```

The second method does not require the variable creation step and provides a confidence interval with the output—a nice benefit! The SAS code for this method is as follows using Yuan's pre- and posttest for the avoidance scale:

```
PROC MEANS data=libname.yuan; VAR prea posta;
run;
PROC TTEST; PAIRED prea*posta; run;
```

FIGURE 13.29. SAS Output (for the second method only).

```
                              The MEANS Procedure

Variable   Label                                  N      Mean      Std Dev     Minimum
****************************************************************************************
PREA       PRETEST    score on AVOIDANCE subscale  200  17.8250000  5.0767353  8.0000000
POSTA      POSTTEST   score on AVOIDANCE subscale  100  18.0800000  4.8402354  9.0000000
****************************************************************************************

                    Variable    Label                                  Maximum
                    ************************************************************
                    PREA        PRETEST score on AVOIDANCE subscale    29.0000000
                    POSTA       POSTTEST score on AVOIDANCE subscale   27.0000000
                    ************************************************************

The TTEST Procedure
                                      Statistics

                 Lower CL                  Upper CL  Lower CL           Upper CL
Difference   N    Mean      Mean            Mean      Std Dev  Std Dev   Std Dev   Std Err
PREA - POSTA 100  -1.151    -0.61          -0.069     1.7379   2.0592    2.5123    0.2059

                                      T-Tests
                    Difference        DF     t Value    Pr > |t|
                    PREA - POSTA      99      -2.96       0.0038
```

FIGURE 13.30. SPSS Output.

Paired Samples Statistics

		Mean	N	Std. Deviation	Std. Error Mean
Pair 1	PRETEST score on AVOIDANCE subscale	17.47	100	5.004	.500
	POSTTEST score on AVOIDANCE subscale	18.08	100	4.840	.484

Paired Samples Test

		Paired Differences					t	df	Sig. (2-tailed)
		Mean	Std. Deviation	Std. Error Mean	95% Confidence Interval of the Difference				
					Lower	Upper			
Pair 1	PRETEST score on AVOIDANCE subscale – POSTTEST score on AVOIDANCE subscale	-.610	2.059	.206	-1.019	-.201	-2.962	99	.004

SAS output is shown in Figure 13.29. Notice that the descriptive statistics output by SAS remind us that Yuan started with 200 subjects, but only 100 subjects completed the posttest. Thus the paired *t* test is limited to the 100 subjects with nonmissing data on the pre- and posttest. The SAS values for the descriptives are not going to be valid unless you limit the sample before asking for the PROC Means. In contrast, the descriptive statistics included in the SPSS output in Figure 13.30 are already limited to the 100 subjects.

SPSS and Paired *t* Test.

> Go to Analyze ⇒ Compare Means ⇒ Paired-Samples *t* Test ⇒ specify the pair of variables to be tested by selecting the first and second variable of interest from the list on the left of the window ⇒ click "OK"

SPSS output is shown in Figure 13.30.

We have a significant *t* test, so we reject the null hypothesis that there is no difference between pre- and posttest scores on this variable. Reporting the results of this type of *t* test in the text is the same as the independent samples *t* test. But remember to report the means of each group. Why? Well, the reader of your brilliant article cannot tell what the implications of your findings are from just a *t* test. For example, you could have a significant value for your *t* test if the posttest condition did better or worse than the pretest. Also remember that difference between practical and statistical significance. It is quite possible to get a statistically significant value where the difference between means in inconsequentially small. In Yuan's data, the pretest mean is about 17.5, and the posttest mean is about 18.1. It will be important to determine whether this represents a practically meaningful change in the avoidance scale.

What if the descriptive statistics show that the data aren't normal? Welcome to real-world research! Fortunately, once again there is a nonparametric alternative to the rescue. This time it is the Wilcoxon Signed-Rank Test. This method uses the difference of the ranking of difference scores and does not require

normally distributed data. It can even handle bimodal data.

SAS and Wilcoxon Signed-Rank. The easiest way to do this in SAS is to create the difference score (as you did for the preceding example in the first method) and then request the following:

```
PROC UNIVARIATE data = x NORMAL; VAR DIFF; run;
```

SAS output is shown in Figure 13.31.

After the basic descriptives you are used to using from the PROC UNIVARIATE output, you will find a statistic called "SIGNED RANK" in the "Tests for Location" section and corresponding *p* value. This is the nonparametric version of the paired sample *t* test.

SPSS and Wilcoxon Signed-Rank. In SPSS we request the statistic directly from a menu:

> Go to Analyze ⇒ Nonparametric Tests ⇒ 2 Related Samples. . . , ⇒ specify 'PREA' as the first variable and 'POSTA' as the second variable as the "Test Pair" ⇒ Under "Test Type," select "Wilcoxon" ⇒ click "OK"

SPSS output is shown in Figure 13.32. Note that SPSS again uses a somewhat different test statistic, but the interpretation is identical. In both cases we have found a significant result, meaning that the mean of the avoidance scale is different at time 2 than it was at the pretest.

SECTION 13.7
ONE-WAY ANOVA

So *t* tests are great for evaluation of two group differences, but what if you have more than two groups? This is the wonderful world of the ANOVA. Don't sigh; you know this already from the last section. It isn't too different. See the comparison in Table 13.15.

ANOVA uses an *F* test (this is similar to, but not the same as, the *f* statistic that tests for equal variances for your *t* test) to examine statistical significance. If you have only two groups, then your ANOVA *F* test = $(t)^2$.

FIGURE 13.31. SAS Output.

```
Tests for Location: Mu0=0

            Test          -Statistic-      ----p Value----
            Student's t   t  2.962316      Pr > |t|    0.0038
            Sign          M     9.5        Pr >= |M|   0.0503
            Signed Rank   S   670.5        Pr >= |S|   0.0024
```

FIGURE 13.32. SPSS Output.

Ranks

		N	Mean Rank	Sum of Ranks
POSTTEST score on AVOIDANCE subscale – PRETEST score on AVOIDANCE subscale	Negative Ranks	33(a)	35.06	1157.00
	Positive Ranks	52(b)	48.04	2498.00
	Ties	15(c)		
	Total	100		

a POSTTEST score on AVOIDANCE subscale < PRETEST score on AVOIDANCE subscale
b POSTTEST score on AVOIDANCE subscale > PRETEST score on AVOIDANCE subscale
c POSTTEST score on AVOIDANCE subscale = PRETEST score on AVOIDANCE subscale

Test Statistics(d)

	POSTTEST score on AVOIDANCE subscale – PRETEST score on AVOIDANCE subscale
Z	–2.976(e)
Asymp. Sig. (2-tailed)	.003

d Wilcoxon Signed-Ranks Test
e Based on negative ranks.

TABLE 13.15. Comparing *t* Test with ANOVA.

	DEPENDENT	INDEPENDENT (class)
***t* test**	Grouped by class variable interval/ratio data Independence of obs Normal/Equal variance	**Two** groups nominal categories
	DEPENDENT	INDEPENDENT (class)
ANOVA	Grouped by class variable interval/ratio data Independence of obs Normal/Equal variance	**Three or more** groups nominal categories

In ANOVA we are still looking for differences in the means, just as with a *t* test. Why not just run multiple *t* tests? Because if we did that, we could inflate the error. In other words, if you run gazillions of *t* tests, you're going to hit statistical significance just through random luck because $p<=.05$ means a randomly significant result 1/20 of the time. If a table includes 28 comparisons, you're going to have a very high chance of getting at least one of them to hit the $p<=.05$ level. The ANOVA fixes this so you have a real *p* value, not a *p* value inflated because it had so many chances to reach the $p<=.05$ level. So the *F* test uses the variance of the data across multiple groups for hypothesis testing. This way, one *F* test allows for one overall computation of the difference between more than two groups:

- *Research question:* "Are the mean GRE scores different among any of these three groups?"

- *Null hypothesis:* There is no difference among the mean GRE scores among three groups of PhD students.

- *Alternative hypothesis:* There is a difference among the mean GRE scores among three groups of PhD students.

Notice we don't specify between which pairs of groups, we'll get to that later.

Assumptions of ANOVA include:

1. There is an interval or ratio level dependent (or criterion) variable and a nominal predictor variable that identifies the three or more groups.

2. Observations are independent.

3. Distributions are normal. (*Note:* Groups of 30 or more mean that your data will be robust [meaning "pretty much OK"] with regard to violations of this rule.)

4. There is homogeneity of variance. This means that if the largest group variance is no more than 1.5 times bigger than the smallest, the test will be robust. You can check this using a variety of tests; Levene's is generally well thought of.

Let's look at an example (Figure 13.33). Here we have three groups of PhD students. Did the mean GRE scores differ by treatment type (a 3-level nominal variable of "None [group 1]," "Training only [Group 2]," and "Shot [Group 3]")?

Each of our groups has some variability within the group. In other words, some students in Group 1 had higher or lower GRE scores than the mean of 800. In ANOVA, this variability within a group is called "within sum of squares." Now there is also variability between group means. This is called "between sum of squares." We want the between sum of squares to be sufficiently large compared to the within sum of squares so we can detect a difference in the means. If the variability within a group is too large, then the

group can run into another group, like too-thin pancake batter in a pan.

A significant *F* test tells us that we can reject the null hypothesis. The *F* test considers the two types of variability—the variability that occurs within a group (within SS) and the variability that occurs between groups (between SS). Its value is based on a ratio of the variability between groups over the variability within groups. Of course any significant difference between any combination of the groups can result in a significant *F* test. That's why the test hypothesis is just about "any" difference rather than a specific one. Obviously you will want to pinpoint which groups are different, and ANOVA does this with post hoc tests. First, however, let's go over the main part of the ANOVA model. The *F* test can be given as:

$$F = \frac{MS_b}{MS_w} = \frac{\text{mean square between groups}}{\text{mean square within groups}}$$

or

$$\frac{\text{error variability} + \text{variability in means}}{\text{error variability}}$$

or

$$\frac{S_b^2}{S_w^2}$$

We'll use the last notation to look at the formula (taken from Pagano, 2001) more closely for a three-group ANOVA in which X = an observed value; n = group size; and N = total sample size:

```
SS_b = [(Σx_1)²/n1 + (Σx_2)²/n2 + (Σx_3)²/n3]
     - (Σxall)²/N
SS_w = (Σx_all) - [(Σx_1)²/n1 + (Σx_2)²/n2
     + (Σx_3)²/n3]

df_b = # groups - 1
df_w = Total N - number of groups
S_b² = SS_b/df_b
S_w² = SS_w/df_w
F = S_b²/S_w²   p value <.05?   Reject the null.
```

The SS_w is also known as your error variability. You can see that a large value for within group error will lead to a smaller *F* value. You can also see that by increasing your total *N* you are increasing the S_b^2 value. Again, the power of a test is linked to effect size (S_b^2), variability (S_w^2) and your sample size (*N*).

An ANOVA will also provide us with a R^2 as part of the regular output:

R^2 = % of variance accounted for by the independent variable

R^2 = SS between/corrected total SS (in social science, .30 or above is pretty good)

FIGURE 13.33.   GRE Scores for PhD Students

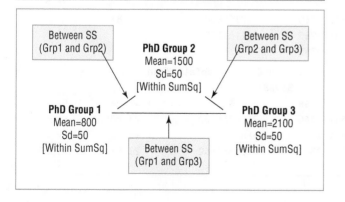

SECTION 13.7.1: SAS AND ANOVA

The SAS code to produce the ANOVA output is either PROC ANOVA or PROC GLM. We suggest you forget the use of PROC ANOVA unless you have equal group sizes. PROC GLM can handle cases in which the group sizes differ, so this is generally a better way to go:

```
PROC GLM data =mouse.kathy; CLASS group;
MODEL epfall=group;
MEANS group /TUKEY;
MEANS group; run;
```

Warning: If you use the point-and-click option in the SAS analyst screen, it will give you the PROC ANOVA result.

SECTION 13.7.2: SPSS AND ANOVA

In SPSS we have a similar issue. If you use the ANOVA command, then you need equal groups. So we again prefer the GLM method:

Go to Analyze ⇒ General Linear Model ⇒ Univariate . . .
⇒ specify the dependent variable 'epfall' and the independent variable 'group' under Fixed Factor(s) ⇒ If post-hoc tests are required, click on "Post Hoc" ⇒ specify the factor(s) to run the post-hoc tests for ⇒ check the desired post-hoc test(s) (e.g., Tukey) ⇒ click "Continue" ⇒ click "OK"

We'll get to the post hoc tests in a minute after we look at the overall results. First review the major SAS output in Figure 13.34. In SAS, the value for "Model" = between sum of squares, and the value for "Error" = within sum of squares. The R square is given directly below the ANOVA table. Students frequently ask, "Why does SAS output a type I and a type III summary,

and why is type III the one we use in class?" The "type" portion of the output refers to a form of hypothesis test about the influence of the independent variable on the criterion. The type I form assesses the incremental improvement in the SS error (the within group portion of the SS) as each independent variable is added. It is sensitive to the order in which you add variables and does not partial out the effect of independent variables that follow. In our one-way ANOVA, we have only one grouping variable, and the type I and type III are identical. Later when we move to the factorial ANOVA we will have more than one independent variable, and the type III will differ from the type I. So it's best to get in the habit of looking at the type III.

In SPSS the output is more intuitively labeled, but it also lacks the automatic output of the R-square (see Figure 13.35). The results give you a significant F and a decent R^2 (in the SAS output). So what's the bad news? We don't know which group is significantly different from which group. How do we find out? It depends on your research design.

We already know how to look for normality by using the **PROC UNIVARIATE** command. Like the *t* test, we sort by the group variable and then do:

FIGURE 13.35. SPSS Output.

Errors per file (all sessions)

	Sum of Squares	df	Mean Square	F	Sig.
Between Groups	5.517	2	2.759	23.879	.000
Within Groups	6.585	57	.116		
Total	12.102	59			

FIGURE 13.34. SAS Output.

```
                              The GLM Procedure

Dependent Variable: epfall    Errors per file (all sessions)
                                    Sum of
        Source              DF      Squares      Mean Square    F Value    Pr > F
        Model               2      5.51713360    2.75856680      23.88     <.0001
        Error              57      6.58479985    0.11552280
        Corrected Total    59     12.10193345

                R-Square     Coeff Var     Root MSE      epfall Mean
                0.455889     20.13191      0.339886        1.688297

        Source              DF      Type I SS    Mean Square    F Value    Pr > F
        group               2      5.51713360    2.75856680      23.88     <.0001

        Source              DF     Type III SS   Mean Square    F Value    Pr > F
        group               2      5.51713360    2.75856680      23.88     <.0001
```

```
Proc univariate; var epfall; by group; run;
```

Because the one-way ANOVA is fairly robust, some departure from homogeneity of variance is fine—particularly if the group n sizes are equal. By the way, in case you wish to impress your friends, this is also called "homoscedasicity." As we mentioned earlier you can use a rough estimate of the ratio of the smallest group variance to the largest, but there are also tests available. We will just present Levene's test here as it is the least sensitive to violations of normality (see Ender, 2002 for a nice comparison of four different approaches).

In SAS we just add Hovtest=Levene after the forward slash in the means statement:

```
PROC GLM data=mouse.kathy; CLASS group;
MODEL epfall=group;
MEANS group / TUKEY Hovtest=Levene;
MEANS group; run;
```

This produces the following SAS output in addition to the ANOVA on previous page:

The GLM Procedure					
Levene's Test for Homogeneity of epfall Variance ANOVA of Squared Deviations from Group Means					
Source	DF	Sum of Squares	Mean Square	F Value	Pr > F
group	2	0.0667	0.0333	1.89	0.1607
Error	57	1.0063	0.0177		

SPSS (not shown) will print out a tabular row that lists the dependent variable in the first column, the Levene statistic in the second column, the DF for the group and then the error, and finally the significance level.

Go to Analyze $\Rightarrow$ General Linear Model $\Rightarrow$ Univariate ... $\Rightarrow$ specify the dependent variable 'epfall' and the independent variable 'group' under Fixed Factor(s) $\Rightarrow$ If post-hoc tests are required, click on "Post Hoc" $\Rightarrow$ specify the factor(s) to run the post-hoc tests for $\Rightarrow$ check the desired post-hoc test(s) (e.g. Tukey) $\Rightarrow$ click "Continue" $\Rightarrow$ click "options" and click on "Descriptives" and "Homogeneity-of-variance" $\Rightarrow$ click "OK"

Here we can see that the F statistic is not significant, which is good because the null hypothesis for the test is that our variances are equal. If it was significant we have a couple of options. If our data otherwise fit parametric assumptions, then we can request the Welch option (type "WELCH" after the forward slash in SAS), which weights data of very unequal group sample sizes with homogeneity of variance issues. This produces an F test that is interpreted exactly the same way as the regular ANOVA F test for practical purposes. If the data are really not normal nor of equal variance or they are ordinal, etc., then we need to move to nonparametric alternatives.

SECTION 13.7.3: DETERMINING DIFFERENCES BETWEEN TWO SPECIFIC GROUPS IN ANOVA

A PRIORI DESIGNS

If you design a multigroup comparison with a clear hypothesis about one group varying from the others, that is called an a priori design. Basically, this is where you say, "I want to test for differences between group A and group B and between group A and group C" (or whatever) based on theory in advance. For example, let's say that we give a shot to group 3, and that leads us to believe that it will be different from either group 1 or group 2. We then test group 3 against group 1 and group 3 against group 2. We do not test group 2 against group 1. In this situation you use a hybrid t test:

$$t = \mu 1 - \mu 2 / \mathrm{sqrt}\, (S_w^2\, [1/n + 1/n])$$

$$S_w^2 = SS_w / df_w$$

(We get the S_w^2 by running the ANOVA procedure first $= MS_{\mathrm{between}}$.)

The difference between this t test and the ones we learned about in the two-sample or paired-sample tests is that this t test includes the variance within groups for all the class groups rather than just two. A regular t test written using ANOVA sum of squares terminology looks like this:

$$t = \mu 1 - \mu 2 / \mathrm{sqrt}\, ([SS_1 + SS_2 / n_1 + n_2 - 2][1/n_1 + 1/n_2])$$

POSTERIORI OR POST HOC DESIGNS

When you have no clear single theoretical relationships you are testing, you have a posteriori or post hoc design. You are not saying, "Among all possible outcomes, I expect this one (or these few) to be significant because of theory." Instead, you might say, "Hey, I don't have a clue what I'm looking for, so let's check everything against everything and see what pops up." This is fine in descriptive or exploratory work (see Chapter 4), but is mightily frowned on in correlational or experimental designs.

If you design a study using an ANOVA without a clear a priori hypothesis about the groups, you cannot use the t test above. Why? It's our old friend type I error. Without specifying prior to running the test, we would have to test all possible interrelationships. This inflates type I error. As you increase the number of hypothesis tests with the same sample, you inflate the alpha. In other words, look at enough relationships with a 5% chance of error, and you're bound to find something just through luck.

If we extend this logic to testing the differences between means, a scenario might look like this. Let's say you have 10 means from the same sample to compare. That's $10(10 + 1)/2 = 45$ total comparisons. Each comparison has .05 probability of error. As you continue to compare means from the same sample, it's like rolling the same die. You increase the chances of being in that .05 error area more than once. It is not an additive increase but an exponential one. In this case, the chance of finding at least one erroneous (5% likely) error is: $1 - (.95)^{45}$, or 90%. You have a 90% likelihood of making a type I error when making this many comparisons.

Never fear! There is a solution (you probably guessed that). There are special tests designed to do multiple comparisons without inflating the type I error. How? The tests are based on sampling distributions based on multiple samples. There are many choices that all do slightly different things. For example: The Tukey HSD compares all possible pairs of means while maintaining the type I error for the complete set of comparisons. The Newman-Keuls does the same thing but maintains the type I error for each pair rather than the whole set. Both use a Q statistic that is the same as the modified t test except that the group means change each time and the test statistic has a different distribution. The Tukey maintains the same critical value for each pair. The critical value for the Newman-Keuls has a different critical value for each pair based on the number of groups having means encompassed in the numerator. Generally the Tukey HSD is considered the more conservative test. You will have a higher type II error rate. The Newman-Keuls has a higher type I rate overall but a lower type II rate with individual comparisons.

There are several other multiple comparison tests including the Bonferroni, Dunnett's, and the Scheffe (see "multiple comparison procedures" www2.chass.

ncsu.edu/garson/pa765/anova.htm for a nice description). However, the Tukey test performs the best in simulation studies, holds a more conservative alpha value, and can also be used to calculate confidence intervals. So, we will use the Tukey in this text. Other texts will differ, and it becomes a matter of choice and whether or not you are particularly concerned about type II error and the like. If you refer back to the SAS code and SPSS directions you will note that we asked for the Tukey (see Figure 13.36).

When you read the output, SAS will put the same letter in front of groups that are not different from each other. SPSS output is in tabular form and the significance values refer to the comparison in that particular row (Figure 13.37). So, row 1 is testing group 1 against group 2.

What did we learn? In Professor Kathy's data, groups 1 and 3 were different, and groups 1 and 2 were different, but 2 and 3 were the same. Once again we look at the raw means to interpret this practically—this is a little easier to do in SAS because the means are included with the Tukey. In SPSS the means are output in a third table (not shown to conserve space) labeled homogenous subsets. The errors per file were lower in group 1 (mean=1.26) than either group 2 (mean=1.95) or group 3 (mean = 1.85).

An ANOVA table in an article looks like Table 13.16.

In the text it should appear as: $F (2, \#) = F$ value; $p <$ value. Then (similar to the t test) if your F test is significant, be sure you provide the results of your post hoc (Tukey) tests so your reader knows where the differences are. Do not interpret the post hoc tests if your F test in the ANOVA is nonsignificant.

OK, so you're getting fancy now; you can drop that old descriptive stuff, right? But wait—didn't that strange professor keep babbling on about how important the

FIGURE 13.36. SAS Output Post Hoc.

```
Tukey's Studentized Range (HSD) Test for epfall
NOTE: This test controls the Type I experimentwise error rate, but it generally has a higher Type II
                          error rate than REGWQ.
                  Alpha                                    0.05
                  Error Degrees of Freedom                   57
                  Error Mean Square                     0.115523
                  Critical Value of Studentized Range   3.40320
                  Minimum Significant Difference          0.2586
          Means with the same letter are not significantly different.
              Tukey Grouping        Mean       N      group
                         A        1.9474       20      2
                         A
                         A        1.8546       20      3
                         B        1.2628       20      1
```

FIGURE 13.37. **SPSS Output.**

Multiple Comparisons

Dependent Variable: Errors per file (all sessions)
Tukey HSD

(I) Group (1=CBM, 2=ELBM, 3=NBM)	(J) Group (1=CBM, 2=ELBM, 3=NBM)	Mean Difference (I-J)	Std. Error	Sig.	95% Confidence Interval	
					Lower Bound	Upper Bound
1	2	−.68463(*)	.10748	.000	−.9433	−.4260
	3	−.59181(*)	.10748	.000	−.8505	−.3332
2	1	.68463(*)	.10748	.000	.4260	.9433
	3	.09282	.10748	.665	−.1658	.3515
3	1	.59181(*)	.10748	.000	.3332	.8505
	2	−.09282	.10748	.665	−.3515	.1658

* The mean difference is significant at the .05 level.

TABLE 13.16. **ANOVA Table in an Article**

SOURCE	DF	SS	MS	F	R^2
Label for Groups	2	Sum of squares	Mean squares	F value*	R^2
Within Groups	#	Sum of squares	Mean squares		
Total	#	Sum of squares			

$N = X$. *$p <$ value

SAS AND NONPARAMETRIC ANOVA

The SAS code is the same as the other WILCOXON procedure we requested:

```
PROC NPAR1WAY WILCOXON; CLASS group; VAR
epfall; run;
```

SAS output is shown in Figure 13.38.

SPSS AND NONPARAMETRIC ANOVA

Go to Analyze ⟹ Nonparametric Tests ⟹ K Independent Samples . . . , ⟹ specify the dependent variable 'epfall' under "Test Variable" and the independent variable 'group' under "Grouping Variable" ⟹ define the range for the grouping variable by clicking on "Define Range. . ." and entering the appropriate values ⟹ under "Test Type" select Kruskal-Wallis H ⟹ click "OK"

SPSS output is shown in Figure 13.39.

FIGURE 13.38. **SAS Output.**

```
       The NPAR1WAY Procedure

  Wilcoxon Scores (Rank Sums) for Variable
    epfall Classified by Variable group

               Sum of  Expected   Std Dev   Mean
  group   N    Scores  Under H0   Under H0  Score
  ***********************************************
  1      20    272.0    610.0    63.765992  13.600
  2      20    805.0    610.0    63.765992  40.250
  3      20    753.0    610.0    63.765992  37.650

  Average scores were used for ties.

        Kruskal-Wallis Test

     Chi-Square        28.3184
     DF                      2
     Pr > Chi-Square    <.0001
```

basic descriptives were? Why, yes! If you didn't run them, then how do you know if your data meet the assumptions of the ANOVA? If your data do not meet the assumptions of the ANOVA, then you need the Kruskal-Wallis nonparametric test. This is a generalization of the Wilcoxon test you learned as a nonparametric alternative for the t test.

Once again we create ranks of scores—the ranks cross over each group. So if we had a total of 60 observations in three groups we would create ranks from 1 to 60 sequentially based on the order of the values. If the lowest value is in group 1, that is where rank score 1 goes. If the next lowest value is in group 2, that is where rank 2 goes. Each group will have a list of 20 rank scores that all fall somewhere between 1 and 60. The sum of the rank scores for each group is completed and the Rs (or rank sums) are entered into the following formula:

$$H = [12/N(N+1)] [(R_1)^2/n1 + (R_2)^2/n2 + (R_3)^2/n3] - 3(N+1)$$

FIGURE 13.39 **SPSS Output.**

Ranks

Group (1=CBM, 2=ELBM, 3=NBM)		N	Mean Rank
Errors per file (all sessions)	1	20	13.60
	2	20	40.25
	3	20	37.65
	Total	60	

Test Statistics(a,b)

	Errors per file (all sessions)
Chi-Square	28.318
Df	2
Asymp. Sig.	.000

a Kruskal Wallis Test
b Grouping Variable: Group (1=CBM, 2=ELBM, 3=NBM)

This procedure gives you the Kruskal-Wallis result, which is roughly equivalent to the *F* test. It also prints out the means and variances for the groups. Once again your results should be identical to the parametric ANOVA with the exception that a nonparametric test's power is lower. The bad news is that you don't have post hoc tests available in SAS or SPSS, so you have to make a visual determination based on the group output as to where the differences are. Some people are working on this problem now, and within the next few years, post hoc tests for the nonparametric test will likely be available.

SECTION 13.8
FACTORIAL ANOVA OR TWO-WAY ANOVA

Sometimes we are interested in controlling for another factor when looking at the differences in group means. Remember we reminded you earlier that as we get "fancy," we are really just building on concepts you have learned and introducing a few new twists. At this point, we begin to think about statistical models that have more than one independent variable. In a factorial design in experimental research you may manipulate two (or more) separate variables. Just like the regular ANOVA, however, you can also use this technique to analyze two or more independent variables that are descriptive in nature. These two or more independent variables are nominal (or limited ordinal). Technically you can use many independent variables, but realistically you will rarely see more than three in a

published study that uses a factorial ANOVA because the results become more difficult to interpret (understand and explain) the more variables you add.

SECTION 13.8.1: TYPE I OUTPUT

Before diving into this technique, recall the discussion about type I and type III output earlier. We can now illustrate the problem. The type I form assesses the incremental improvement in the SS error (the within group portion of the SS) as each independent variable is added. It is sensitive to the order in which you add variables and does not partial out the effect of independent variables that follow.

For example, if you enter three independent variables in a factorial ANOVA:

- *Gender:* The result for this variable would include effects of race and happiness.
- *Race:* The result for this variable would be independent of gender that is already partialed out (controlled for) but would still be contaminated by the effect of happiness.
- *Happy (yes/no):* The result for this variable would include only the effect of happiness, after controlling for gender and race.

Type III asks, "What is the net effect of each variable uncontaminated with the effects of other variables?" In plain English, this means they are considered simultaneously, and the order doesn't matter. This test is also called a "partial sum of squares" and is based on a separate underlying matrix. As we run the factorial ANOVA, the SS in the type III model will typically not add up to the one in the initial summary table in models with more than one variable.

OK, so let's say we are interested in the mean unit of services difference according to treatment (level) and gender. It is now more helpful to think of our means as present in a cell rather than in a group. So if we have three treatment levels and two levels of gender, we have a total of six cells, each with its own mean units of services.

- *Research question:* "Does the mean unit of service given to clients vary according to treatment group and gender?"
- *Null hypothesis:* There is no difference in mean units of service
- *Alternative hypothesis:* At least two cells will have differences from each other in mean units of service.

We now have two independent variables: treatment and gender. These independent variables can have significant main effects—this is what we are used to.

But they can also interact with each other. What does this mean? In simplest terms, this means that the effect of variable *A* on the outcome depends on the value of variable *B*. Without an interaction, looking at the factorial ANOVA is pretty much like interpreting a one-way ANOVA. If there is an interaction term, however, things get interesting.

Assumptions for factorial ANOVA include:

1. The criterion (dependent, outcome) measure is interval/ratio. Independent or predictor variables should be nominal or possibly limited ordinal.

2. Observations must be independent (subjects are unrelated to each other).

3. Distributions are normal; if each cell has 30 or more subjects, this test is robust against moderate departures from normality.

4. There must be homogeneity of variance; if the largest cell variance is less than 1.5 times the smallest cell variance, then the test is robust.

Consider our example of PhD students and GRE scores from the prior section. Let's say we are interested in testing a drug that improves GRE scores. Before, we had a simple ANOVA where we asked whether the mean GRE scores differ by treatment type (a three-level nominal variable of "none," "training only," and "shot"). Let's pretend we are still interested in whether there is a difference in the mean scores of the three groups of PhD students, but now we also want to know if gender has a unique effect on GRE scores or interacts with the treatment groups. We now have a 2 (male/female) by 3 (none/training/shot) or "2 × 3" ANOVA.

Now instead of just the sum of squares within and the sum of squares between, we have a "column SS" (or block), a "row SS" (or treatment), and a "row and column SS" (or interaction). We are also dealing with means and standard deviations within cells not by group (see Table 13.17).

F ratios are used to test the effects of the independent variables (see Figure 13.40).

TABLE 13.17. Example of Cells for a Two-Way ANOVA.

	FEMALE	MALE	
No Tx	Mean GRE score	Mean GRE score	Mean row 1 (n)
Training	Mean GRE score	Mean GRE score	Mean row 2 (n)
Shot	Mean GRE score	Mean GRE score	Mean row 3 (n)
	Mean column 1(n)	Mean column 2(n)	TTL cell mean (N)

FIGURE 13.40. Testing with *F* Ratios.

For Treatment variable (also known as the group variable):

SS row = Row 1 n size* (Row GRE mean for NO TX – TTL cell mean)^2 +
Row 2 n size* (Row GRE mean for Training – TTL cell mean)^2 +
Row 3 n size* (Row GRE mean for Shot – TTL cell mean)^2

$Fobt_{row}$ = Row variance/Within cell variance *Or* Mean square row/Mean square error

For Gender variable (also known as the block variable):

SS column = Column 1 N* (Column GRE Mean for Females – TTL cell mean)^2 +
Column 2 N* (Column GRE Mean for Males – TTL cell mean)^2

$Fobt_{column}$ = Column variance/within cell variance *Or* Mean square column/Mean square error

For Interaction:

SS interaction = (Row – Column N) * (cell mean – TTL cell mean)^2 +
Repeat above for each cell

$Fobt_{int}$ = Row-column variance/within cell varience *Or* Mean square interaction/Mean square error. If significant then the means of at least 2 of our cells were different.

R-square:

Total variance in GRE scores explained by the gender and the test preparation condition as well as any interaction between those two variables.

An overall *R* square is output for the procedure, but we can also calculate an *R* square for each term by dividing the SS for the effect by the corrected total sum of squares (from GLM ANOVA summary table).

You may be asking, "What exactly will an interaction mean?" Well, if our interaction term is significant, it means that the effect of our treatment on GRE scores varies by gender. Males will have different means than females between at least two of the treatment groups. Mechanically, a significant interaction term means that you actually have to go back and divide your data set by one of the independent variables and run one-way ANOVAs to get accurate assessments of mean differences. Let's go back to our research question relating to some fictitious treatment data.

- *Research question:* "Does the mean unit of service given to clients vary according to treatment group and gender?"
- *Null hypothesis:* There is no difference in mean units of service.
- *Alternative hypothesis:* At least two cells will have differences from each other in mean units of service.

SAS AND CHECKING ASSUMPTIONS FOR TWO-WAY ANOVA

First I can create two terms in my data to help me test assumptions in SAS by creating some new variables that will allow me to look at descriptive statistics for each cell:

```
Data temp;
Set temp;
treatgend=treatment*gender;
newtreat=0;
if gender=0 then do;
newtreat=treatment; end; run;
```

Then we run a PROC UNIVARIATE by "newtreat" (treatment when gender = 0) and "treatgend":

```
PROC SORT data=temp; by newtreat; run;
PROC UNIVARIATE; var services; by newtreat;
run;
PROC SORT data=temp; by treatgend; run;
PROC UNIVARIATE; var services; by treatgend;
run;
```

I check the variance and normality assumptions for all possible cells. You would look at the variance for treatgend = 1, 2, and 3 and newtreat = 1, 2, and 3 to check the variance assumption and the skewness and Shapiro-Wilk for normality. We ignore the output for the zero value of the variables as this is just everybody else lumped together.

SPSS AND CHECKING ASSUMPTIONS FOR TWO-WAY ANOVA

In SPSS we will also create these variables to assess all possible cells by using the "transform" menu.

To create "treatgend":

Go to Transform ⇒ Compute ⇒ make up new variable name (treatgend) in "target variable" box ⇒ select first variable (treatment group) then select multiplication sign on calculator (*) and then select the second variable (gender) ⇒ click "OK"

To create "newtreat":

Go to Transform ⇒ Recode ⇒ Into Different Variables ⇒ select the variable "treatment" and click arrow to place in box ⇒ click the "If" button ⇒ select the "include if case satisfies condition" circle ⇒ type in "gender=0" in condition box ⇒ click "Continue" ⇒ type in the new variable name "newtreat" in the "Output Variable" box ⇒ click "Old and New Values" button ⇒ for each value of treatment in the "Old Value" box type in the same value in the "New Value" box and click on "Add" each time ⇒ click "continue" ⇒ click the "Change" button ⇒ click "OK"

Next:

Go to Analyze ⇒ Descriptive Statistics ⇒ Explore ⇒ select the dependent variable ⇒ select our new variables ("newtreat" and "treatgend") as factors ⇒ click "OK"

Because we have looked at univariate output before, we have not displayed it again to conserve space. We do find that the service unit variable is skewed. This makes sense, as most people would have smaller numbers of service contact, and a few intensive cases might require a lot of contacts. So we take the logarithm of the old variable to correct for skewness (refer back to page 259 for computer instructions in SAS and SPSS) and now our variance for "logserv" by cell looks fine! (In other words there was never a variance for one of the levels of treatgend or newtreat that was over 1.5 times larger than the variance of another level.) So, after we decide if we have met the assumptions we continue with the ANOVA.

SAS AND TWO-WAY ANOVA

To request the factorial ANOVA in SAS, the code is:

```
PROC GLM;
Class treatment gender;
Model logserv = gender treatment*gender /SS3;
Means treatment gender treatment*gender
/tukey;
LSMEANS treatment gender; run;
```

Notice the little SS3 after the forward slash in the model statement? This tells SAS not to bother printing out the type I SS table. The LSMEANS statement tells SAS to include a listing of our cell means with our output. This is handy for interpreting the interaction terms. SAS output is shown in Figure 13.41.

SPSS AND TWO-WAY ANOVA

Go to Analyze ⇒ General Linear Model ⇒ Univariate . . . , ⇒ specify the variable 'logserv' as the Dependent Variable and the variables 'treatment' and 'gender' as the Fixed Factor(s) ⇒ If you click on the "Model" button you can select a specific Type for Sum of Squares (the Type III is typically the default) ⇒ click "Continue" ⇒ click "OK"

There is no simple way to get the means for cells printed in SPSS so you'll need to keep your output from your descriptive statistics handy (see Figure 13.42).

Now there are some annoying differences between SAS and SPSS output that you have to get used to. In SAS we have two class levels identified and the total number of observations used compared to observations read. If they are the same, there were no missing data for class or the dependent variables. The SAS output does an overall ANOVA table, the *r* square output, and then prints the type III sum of squares for the factors and interaction.

In SPSS, there is a between factors table that provides the *n* size for each level of the independent or factor variables. You can add these up and figure out whether or not the total seems right. SPSS then prints out the entire table at once according to the type box selected. The *F* tests will be the same, and the interpretation is the same, but the sum of squares values will be different because of the way SPSS outputs the information.

FIGURE 13.41. SAS Output.

```
                    The GLM Procedure
                  Class Level Information

              Class         Levels      Values
              treatment        3         1 2 3
              gender           2         0 1

          Number of Observations Read      2481
          Number of Observations Used      2481

                    The GLM Procedure
Dependent Variable: units

                              Sum of
Source              DF        Squares       Mean Square    F Value    Pr > F
Model                5      116.454458       23.290892      20.64     <.0001
Error             2475     2792.215497        1.128168
Corrected Total   2480     2908.669955

              R-Square    Coeff Var    Root MSE    units Mean
              0.040037    51.16188     1.062152    2.076062

Source              DF     Type III SS     Mean Square    F Value    Pr >F
gender               1     10.34992412     10.34992412      9.17     0.0025
treatment            2     17.04616766      8.52308383      7.55     0.0005
treatment*gender     2     12.99079123      6.49539561      5.76     0.0032

   Level of      Level of                  ------------units------------
   treatment     gender        N            Mean          Std Dev
      1             0          895        2.26693714      1.01119138
      1             1          182        2.19787231      0.99644525
      2             0          379        2.13344285      1.05536105
      2             1           66        2.43184090      1.15138060
      3             0          866        1.79043694      1.12299357
      3             1           93        2.17412764      1.04430803
```

FIGURE 13.42. SPSS Output.

Between-Subjects Factors

		N
1=cbt; 2=usual; 3=other	1.00	1077
	2.00	445
	3.00	959
1=female;	.00	2140
0=male	1.00	341

Tests of Between-Subjects Effects

Dependent Variable: units

Source	Type III Sum of Squares	df	Mean Square	F	Sig.
Corrected Model	21.965(a)	5	4.393	20.645	.000
Intercept	877.164	1	877.164	4122.288	.000
Treatment	3.215	2	1.608	7.555	.001
Gender	1.952	1	1.952	9.174	.002
Treatment * gender	2.450	2	1.225	5.757	.003
Error	526.645	2475	.213		
Total	2565.471	2481			
Corrected Total	548.609	2480			

a R Squared = .040 (Adjusted R Squared = .038)

What does it mean? Your *F* value is interpreted the same as with a one-way ANOVA. We have a significant difference in means between at least two cells. We are also explaining very little of the variance overall ($R^2 = .04$). Now, if we look at our type III output and the interaction term is not significant, we can stop here and just interpret the significant main effects and the TUKEY we requested in SAS. SAS will print out a post hoc for gender even though there are only two levels. Technically we don't need a post hoc for a two-level variable because our significant *F* test is already saying the means differ for that variable. SPSS won't even print out the post hoc for gender. If, however, the interaction is significant, we cannot use this output to interpret the main effects because the factorial ANOVA does not alter its output for the other variables correctly nor are the post hoc tests provided for the interactions.

If the interaction term is significant, before moving on to the next analysis step, one typically first seeks to interpret the term. The easiest way to do this is to plot it visually by using the cell means printed out as the second to last page of our SAS output or obtained from your descriptive statistics in SPSS. We often type the means into Excel rather than plotting them in the analysis program, due to the ease of manipulating the figure in Excel (Figure 13.43).

In this figure it is easier to see that the mean number of services is higher for females, getting treatments 2 and 3, but nearly identical and a little lower than males in treatment condition 1. This helps illustrate what we mean when we say that a significant interaction term means that you can't really understand the story behind one variable without understanding what the level of a second variable is.

Now the fun part: Our next step is actually a return to the one-way ANOVA. Because of the interaction term's

FIGURE 13.43. Excel Output.

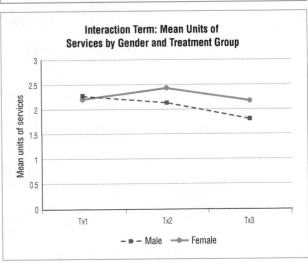

significance, we have to run a one-way ANOVA for each level of the gender (0/1) variable. This means you actually split your data into two groups. Could you do it the other way and split it into groups according to treatment levels? Well, yes, but then you would have three two-level tests, and it's just easier to do it the other way.

SAS AND ONE-WAY ANOVA FOLLOW-UP AFTER SIGNIFICANT INTERACTION

In SAS the easiest way to do this is to create two data sets using data set statements:

```
Data males;
Set temp;
If gender=0; run;

Data females;
Set temp;
If gender=1; run;
```

Now we run regular one-way ANOVAs of "logserv" by treatment groups for each data set. Refer back to one-way ANOVAs for PROC GLM code. SAS output is shown in Figure 13.44.

SPSS AND ONE-WAY ANOVA AFTER SIGNIFICANT INTERACTION

In SPSS you can split your files for analysis without creating two separate data sets:

Go to Data $\Rightarrow$ Split File $\Rightarrow$ select "Compare Groups" and then insert the gender variable in the "Groups based on" box

Now, just as in SAS, we go back and run the one-way ANOVA, but in SPSS we need to run it only once. Because we have told it to compare groups, it will simply output one result for each gender group (Figure 13.45).

Once again, we look at the F values if you want to compare SPSS and SAS output. OK, now I'm done, right? Wrong. Your F values for these one-way ANOVAs have to be corrected because after all we want to answer

FIGURE 13.44. **SAS Output.**

Male model:

The GLM Procedure
Class Level Information

Class	Levels	Values
treat	3	1 2 3

Number of observations   2140

Source	DF	Sum of Squares	Mean Square	F Value	Pr > F
Model	2	103.103639	51.551819	45.41	<.0001
Error	2137	2425.997712	1.135235		
Corrected Total	2139	2529.101350			

R-Square	Coeff Var	Root MSE	serve Mean
0.040767	51.96248	1.065474	2.050468

Source	DF	Type III SS	Mean Square	F Value	Pr > F
treat	2	103.1036388	51.5518194	45.41	<.0001

SAS OUTPUT

Female model:

Class Level Information

Class	Levels	Values
treat	3	1 2 3

Number of observations 341

Source	DF	Sum of Squares	Mean Square	F Value	Pr > F
Model	2	3.1517821	1.5758911	1.45	0.2350
Error	338	366.2177854	1.0834846		
Corrected Total	340	369.3695675			

R-Square	Coeff Var	Root MSE	serve Mean
0.008533	46.53796	1.040906	2.236681

Source	DF	Type III SS	Mean Square	F Value	Pr > F
treat	2	3.15178211	1.57589106	1.45	0.2350

FIGURE 13.45. **SPSS Output.**

Tests of Between-Subjects Effects

Dependent Variable: units

1=female; 0=male	Source	Type III Sum of Squares	df	Mean Square	F	Sig.
.00	Corrected Model	19.447(a)	2	9.723	45.411	.000
	Intercept	1472.083	1	1472.083	6875.079	.000
	treatment	19.447	2	9.723	45.411	.000
	Error	457.572	2137	.214		
	Total	2174.044	2140			
	Corrected Total	477.018	2139			
1.00	Corrected Model	.594(b)	2	.297	1.454	.235
	Intercept	278.077	1	278.077	1360.736	.000
	treatment	.594	2	.297	1.454	.235
	Error	69.073	338	.204		
	Total	391.427	341			
	Corrected Total	69.667	340			

a R Squared = .041 (Adjusted R Squared = .040)
b R Squared = .009 (Adjusted R Squared = .003)

the research question related to our two-way model. To do this, take the MS for your new table and divide it by the MS of the old summary table. Here you need the old-fashioned "look it up in the table in the book" to assess significance. So using SAS output for males, our adjusted *F* value would be:

$$\text{Corrected } F\text{value} = \frac{51.5518}{1.128} = 45.702 \quad F\text{crit} = 3.00 < .05$$

The critical value from an *F* table in the back of a statistics book or online happens to be 3. Our value is much higher, so among males there are significant differences in the means of services between treatment levels. We knew this before, right? Well, yes, normally this adjustment will make a difference only if you have a marginally significant model. Now we can look at the Tukeys for males but not for females. Why? Our model for females was not significant. If you recall from our one-way ANOVA discussion, we only look at post hoc tests if we have significant *F* values. The same rule applies to the one-way ANOVAs you run when your interaction term in a factorial ANOVA is significant. To conserve space, we will just include the SAS output (Figure 13.46).

Among males, treatment groups 1 and 2 both differ from treatment 3, but groups 1 and 2 do not differ from each other. So, we have completely answered our research question. The mean services do differ according to treatment group and gender, as we discovered in the first full model including the interaction term. On further investigation we discover that

mean units of services differ only by treatment group among males.

What if my assumptions are violated? There is a nonparametric alternative called Friedman's two-way nonparametric ANOVA. Do you want to impress your friends? Tell them that the famous Milton Friedman, a University of Chicago economist and Nobel Prize winner, invented this. Once again this is a ranking procedure. Friedman's test is similar to classical balanced two-way ANOVA, but it tests only for column effects after adjusting for possible row effects. It does not test for row effects or interaction effects. Unlike two-way analysis of variance, Friedman's test does not treat the two factors symmetrically. Instead, it is a test for whether the columns are different after adjusting for possible row differences. Friedman's test is appropriate when columns represent treatments that are under study, and

FIGURE 13.46. **SAS Output.**

```
            Tukey's Test for serve

                   Difference
   treat           Between      Simultaneous 95%
 Comparison        Means        Confidence Limits
 1   - 2           0.13349      -0.01965   0.28664
 1   - 3           0.47650       0.35739   0.59561  ***
 2   - 1          -0.13349      -0.28664   0.01965
 2   - 3           0.34301       0.18910   0.49691  ***
 3   - 1          -0.47650      -0.59561  -0.35739  ***
 3   - 2          -0.34301      -0.49691  -0.18910  ***
```

rows represent nuisance effects (blocks) that need to be taken into account but are not of any interest. Check it out at www.mathworks.com/access/helpdesk/_help/toolbox/stats/friedman.shtml.

SAS AND NONPARAMETRIC TWO-WAY ANOVA

To do this procedure in SAS, you run a PROC RANK statement that creates a ranking of the untransformed outcome variable by grouping level. The Rserve is simply the name of the new ranked variable:

```
PROC RANK data=temp;
BY treatment;
VAR serve;
RANKS Rserve;
RUN;
```

You then use the PROC ANOVA or PROC GLM statement using the rank variable as the outcome:

```
PROC ANOVA; CLASSES treat gender;
MODEL Rserve = treatment gender
treatment*gender;
Means Treatment/bon;
TITLE2 'FRIEDMAN''S TWO-WAY NON-PARAMETRIC
ANOVA';
RUN;
```

SAS output is shown in Figure 13.47. The good news is that we interpret the output like a regular ANOVA. This isn't exactly a true Friedman ANOVA, which gives you a chi-square. SAS can do this, but the procedure is not as easy to find—it's in the sample library. The bad news is that once again we lack the

same post hoc procedures we had before. One can use the LSMEANS statement with this model with a PDIFF option or MEANS with a Bonferroni option to obtain a multiple comparison analysis of the column effect only.

SPSS AND NONPARAMETRIC TWO-WAY ANOVA

To our knowledge, this is not available in SPSS at the present time.

SECTION 13.9
AN INTRODUCTION TO REGRESSION

Now we will give an introduction to regression using a simple bivariate model. The extension of the topics to a multivariate model is covered in the next chapter. Some things stay the same as when we were discussing the use of ANOVAs:

- We still have interval/ratio scale dependent or criterion variables.
- We still want normal data.
- We still want homogeneity of variance.
- We still want independence of observations.

We also bring back an old friend now, correlation. And we use familiar tools in slightly different ways: the ANOVA table and the R^2. But now we can use continuous predictor variables! Why the exclamation point? It happens to be a big deal, because many predictor variables we use are continuous. These include things such as age, scores on most instruments (tests), frequency counts, and the like.

FIGURE 13.47. **SAS Output: Friedman's Two-Way Nonparametric ANOVA.**

```
                              The ANOVA Procedure

Dependent Variable: Rserve      Rank for Variable serve

                                Sum of
Source                  DF      Squares         Mean Square    F Value    Pr > F
Model                   5       32928902.5      6585780.5      88.81      <.0001
Error                   2475    183543317.7     74158.9
Corrected Total         2480    216472220.2

              R-Square      Coeff Var     Root MSE      Rserve Mean
              0.152116      59.26271      272.3213      459.5155

Source                  DF      Anova SS        Mean Square    F Value    Pr > F
treatment               2       32099779.65     16049889.83    216.43     <.0001
gender                  1       197083.87       197083.87      2.66       0.1032
treatment*gender        2       632038.96       316019.48      4.26       0.0142
```

The research question and hypotheses for a simple bivariate correlation are:

- *Research question:* "Is variable *X* associated with dependent variable *A*?"
- *Null hypothesis:* There is no association of *X* with *A*.
- *Alternative hypothesis:* *X* is associated with *A*.

Assumptions of regression include:

1. Dependent variables must be interval or ratio, and the predictors may be either nominal/ratio or categorical.

2. For any combination of the predictor (independent) variables, the dependent variable should be normally distributed.

3. For any combination of the predictor (independent) variables, the dependent variable should have equal variance.

4. There must be independence of observations.

5. There must be a linear relationship between dependent or criterion and the independent variables.

6. The error associated with a given observation should not be correlated with the error of another observation or with the error associated with an independent variable. Also, the errors associated with prediction should be normally distributed with equal variance

7. There must be an absence of specification error, meaning that needed variables are included in the model and that the assumption of a linear relationship is correct. *What?* The first part of this is really about methods (we called this "content validity" in the methods section). Are you sticking all the independent variables in the model that need to be there, or are you leaving out a tremendously important factor? Obviously, leaving out an important factor will weaken the model and could even cause you to badly misinterpret results. Of course, in social science we don't always know what these are, so you are likely to violate this part of number 7 from time to time. The second part has to do with that linear relationship issue in item 5. You can enter variables in the model that correct for certain forms of nonlinear relationships, but you have to know that is a problem. So this whole assumption is basically about knowing about your dependent variable.

8. There must be absence of measurement error because error in how predictors are measured may lead to underestimation of the regression coefficient for those predictors.

You're probably thinking, "How does anyone ever use this technique with so many assumptions?" Well, fortunately multiple regression is generally robust for minor violations of all assumptions except items 4, 7, and 8. In addition to the assumptions, we want a big enough sample to reasonably test the number of variables in our model. In general, one wants a minimum of about 20 to 25 observations for each predictor variable and a minimum overall sample of about 100.

Now we will be predicting individual levels on a criterion (dependent) variable instead of testing the difference in means between groups. A simple regression formula is trying to make a line:

$$y' = a + bx + e$$

a = intercept (where the regression line crosses the
y-axis on the x/y plot)

b = unstandardized coefficient for the predictor variable
(or slope of the line)

e = error of prediction

y' = the predicted point based upon the line

NOTE: There is always some error, and there are specialized ways of handling errors for certain techniques. We will not, however, be going into the treatment of error in models in this text, as that is a more advanced topic.

A regression model is trying to tell you something about the relationship of the predictor and criterion variables—both overall and specific to the predictors. In our simple regression formula above we ask: How much of the value of y' is explained by x?

The regression line created by the equation is the predicted value of y that provides the best fit. This is known as the principle of the least squares. This means that a regression procedure is trying to minimize the sum of the squared errors (or the difference between the predicted and actual value of y: $\Sigma(y-y')^2$. The best model is therefore based on the "least squares."

How is regression related to ANOVA? We will again see an ANOVA table in our output. Now the *F* test is assessing whether or not the predictor variable(s) is explaining a sufficient amount of the variance in *y*. The labels will look the same and the practical interpretation is similar, but the underlying concepts are different.

In regression:

- The sum of squares error is based on how big the difference is between predicted *data points* and actual data points; $\Sigma(y-y')^2$.

- The model sum of squares is based on how much of the variance in y' is explained by x.

In ANOVA:

- The sum of squares error was based on the difference between the observed value and the *group mean* within each group; $\Sigma_{\text{group}} \Sigma_n (y - \mu_y)^2$.
- The between group sum of squares is analogous to the model sum of squares but was based on the explained difference in group means, not the explained variance for individual values of y'.

Here is another way we build on stuff we already know. We return to our old friend the correlation. In simplest terms, regression is attempted to measure the overlap between one or more predictor variables and the outcome (or the percentage of y accounted for by x). So, in a single predictor variable model or a model in which the predictor variables are not correlated at all, the R^2 for each variable is simply the square of the correlation, and the total model R^2 is the sum of the variable R^2s.

Typically, we run bivariate correlations first before the regression. Why? For one thing, if initial correlation analyses reveal no significant correlations with the criterion variable, it is a pretty safe assumption that you will not get a significant model fit in regression. Also, we have to deal with a new issue: multicollinearity.

Multicollinearity is typically not listed under assumptions of the regression model, but you might as well consider it one. It's natural that if you have, say, two independent variables associated with a dependent variable that the independent variables may also be correlated with each other. That's fine, if those correlations are not too high. If they are too high, we violated the collinearity assumption. Generally, if your bivariate correlations are greater than .80, you should be concerned about this.

Now to be truly careful about collinearity you must go beyond simple bivariate models and test for tolerance in models. This will be covered in the next chapter.

SECTION 13.9.1: PARAMETER COEFFICIENTS

A b is what is called an unstandardized coefficient. In a simple regression with only one predictor, this is fine. In a more complex model, it is more helpful to standardize the coefficient so you can compare it to other variables that may be measured on a different scale. This is called β, or "standardized coefficient." To create β, your computer uses your old friend the z score to place all the coefficients on the same scale. Then you can compare coefficients in a table to assess relative magnitude. If you want to model y' for a certain group, however, you need to use the unstandardized coefficients in the regression formula.

SECTION 13.9.2: SAS AND BEGINNING REGRESSION

There are two main options in SAS for conducting regression analyses, PROC GLM and PROC REG. In this chapter we will use PROC GLM because you are already familiar with the command in ANOVA procedures. PROC REG has more easily accessed options once we move beyond a simple bivariate illustration, so we will use PROC REG in the next chapter.

Diagnostics for a simple bivariate regression in SAS can be run by using:

```
PROC UNIVARIATE; var gincfam gpnohigh; run;
(for normality, outliers)
PROC GPLOT data= x; plot gpnohigh*gincfam;
run; (for linearity)
PROC CORR ; var gpnohigh gincfam; run; (for
establishing whether or not an association
exists)
```

SAS code for a bivariate regression using PROC GLM is shown in Figure 13.48.

SECTION 13.9.3: SPSS AND BEGINNING REGRESSION

For diagnostics in SPSS we also use three procedures:

Go to Analyze $\Rightarrow$ Descriptive Statistics $\Rightarrow$ Descriptives $\Rightarrow$ click the "Options" button and select the various output desired for skewness $\Rightarrow$ click "OK"

Go to Graphs $\Rightarrow$ Scatter/Dot $\Rightarrow$ select 'Simple Scatter' $\Rightarrow$ click the 'Define' button $\Rightarrow$ select the desired variable for the x and y axis $\Rightarrow$ click "OK" (for linearity)

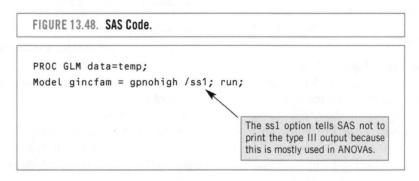

FIGURE 13.48. **SAS Code.**

```
PROC GLM data=temp;
Model gincfam = gpnohigh /ss1; run;
```

The ss1 option tells SAS not to print the type III output because this is mostly used in ANOVAs.

FIGURE 13.49. **SPSS Output.**

Variables Entered/Removed(b)

Model	Variables Entered	Variables Removed	Method
1	GPNOHIGH (a)	.	Enter

a All requested variables entered.
b Dependent Variable: GINCFAM

Model Summary

Model	R	R Square	Adjusted R Square	Std. Error of the Estimate
1	.706(a)	.498	.498	9398.493

a Predictors: (Constant), GPNOHIGH

ANOVA(b)

Model		Sum of Squares	df	Mean Square	F	Sig.
1	Regression	108171924630.344	1	108171924630.344	1224.611	.000(a)
	Residual	108912950466.342	1233	88331671.100		
	Total	217084875096.685	1234			

a Predictors: (Constant), GPNOHIGH
b Dependent Variable: GINCFAM

Coefficients(a)

Model		Unstandardized Coefficients		Standardized Coefficients	t	Sig.
		B	Std. Error	Beta		
1	(Constant)	50245.646	626.564		80.192	.000
	GPNOHIGH	−70100.254	2003.183	−.706	−34.994	.000

a Dependent Variable: GINCFAM

Go to Analyze ⇒ Correlate ⇒ Bivariate and select "gincfam" and "gpnohigh" as variables ⇒ select "OK" (to look for an association)

For bivariate regression in SPSS, the procedure is:

Go to Analyze ⇒ Regression ⇒ Linear. . . , ⇒ specify the variable "GINCFAM" under "Dependent" and "GPNOHIGH" under "Independent(s)" ⇒ click on "OK"

SPSS output is shown in Figure 13.49.

SAS output is shown in Figure 13.50 for our simple bivariate regression without standardized estimates (*b*) because we have only one predictor.

Notice that if you square the Pearson correlation coefficient from the bivariate correlation in SAS or from the *R* column in the model summary table in

SPSS, $(-.7059)^2$ is identical to our R^2 (.498) for the bivariate model. Why? A bivariate regression model is essentially identical to a correlation because correlations form the underlying foundation of the multivariate linear regression model.

CONCLUSION

Wow! You made it through the introduction to the world of statistics. You now have most of the basic tools required to do simple bivariate analyses and also the tools to begin to move to more complex multivariate techniques. Now, a cautionary note: Recall that we have purposely avoided dwelling on statistical formulae in

FIGURE 13.50. **SAS Output.**

```
Dependent Variable: GINCFAM

Source                    DF          Sum of         Mean Square      F Value      Pr > F
                                      Squares

Model                      1      108171924630       108171924630     1224.61      <.0001
Error                   1233      108912950466        88331671.1
Corrected Total         1234      217084875097


                  R-Square    Coeff Var    Root MSE    GINCFAM Mean
                  0.498293    30.89876     9398.493      30417.06


Source            DF          Type I SS        Mean Square     F Value      Pr > F
GPNOHIGH           1      108171924630        108171924630     1224.61      <.0001

                                             Standard
        Parameter              Estimate        Error        t Value    Pr > |t|
        Intercept            50245.64586     626.564472        80.19    <.0001
        GPNOHIGH            -70100.25396    2003.182586       -34.99    <.0001
```

favor of concentrating on the application. So you have an applied understanding of how to use these tools in SAS and SPSS but not the same level of mathematical understanding that someone in a biostatistics or math department would have.

Of course, our example researchers will be moving beyond univariate and bivariate analyses to answer their research questions. The next chapter provides an introduction to some of the more common advanced quantitative techniques used in social sciences. Students who are not prepared to conduct more advanced analyses may still find the introductory portions for the specific analyses useful. Why? Well, the articles you read to review literature will typically move into the multivariate level, and so having a way to refer to what the results mean will help you evaluate their findings.

Exercises

1. *SAS users:* Choose a data set provided with this text or one in your class. Use a libname statement to read in a data set. Use a data step command to change it from a permanent to a temporary data set. Select an interval/ratio and a nominal variable and examine it using PROC FREQ (or PROC UNIVARIATE with FREQ option) and PROC PRINT.

   SPSS users: Choose a data set provided with this text or one in your class. Practice using the pull-down menus under Analyze ⇒ Descriptive Statistics to obtain a frequency for an interval/ratio and a nominal variable.

2. Choose two continuous-level variables in a data set and create a frequency distribution. Use SPSS or SAS to examine the measures of central tendency, variance, kurtosis, and skewness. Print out both the numeric and graphic options available to assess the distribution of the variable. *Assignment:* Describe the distribution, variance, presence of outliers, and any issues related to normality for these variables.

3. Select two dichotomous variables that you think might be associated. Use SAS or SPSS to conduct a bivariate chi-square analysis. Write a research question that is appropriate for the variables selected. Use APA style to report the results. Interpret the results including significance and the direction of the association.

4. Identify three interval/ratio variables. In either SPSS or SAS conduct a bivariate correlation test. Don't forget to assess for linear relationship with a graphic display as well as normality. Write a research question that is appropriate for the variables selected. Enter the results in a table form as illustrated in a journal or use the APA manual. Discuss significant relationships, including the strength and the direction.

5. Select a dichotomous (independent) and a continuous (dependent) variable from one of the class data sets. Explore assumptions for the use of an independent-sample *t* test. If the dependent variable violates the assumptions too badly, choose another variable. Run the *t* test. Then use the Wilcoxon-Mann-Whitney test. Comment on the process of exploring the assumptions. Write a research question and the hypothesis for a

two-tailed test. Discuss the results of the *t* test compared to the Wilcoxon-Mann-Whitney test. Did you reject the null hypothesis?

6. Identify a categorical variable or recode an interval/ratio variable so that you have three or more groups. Then identify a dependent interval/ratio variable. Conduct an ANOVA and post hoc using the Tukey method. Students should also attempt to use the same variables to run a Kruskal-Wallis test using the NPAR1WAY procedure. Write a research question that fits the variables you have selected. Report the findings of the ANOVA in a table according to the APA style. Write a paragraph explaining the results of the ANOVA and post hoc analyses.

7. Using the same three-level group variable and dependent variable as in question 6, now add a second nominal variable to run a two-way (factorial) ANOVA. Students should run and report on appropriate descriptive statistics. Write a research question for your ANOVA. Look at the possible interaction term, then write one or two paragraphs interpreting the results of each analysis. As these data are being used to evaluate the effect of a program, what might you say to the program operators based on your analyses?

REVIEW

---

1. Which measure of central tendency is most sensitive to outliers?

2. You ask the following question on a survey:

How satisfied are you with the new playground equipment?

1	2	3	4
Not at all	Somewhat	Satisfied	Very satisfied

What type of data will this produce?

3. What does it mean when we say there are assumptions for a statistical test?

4. What is the difference between parametric and nonparametric statistics?

5. If a researcher decides to set her alpha level or *p* value to .0001 instead of .05, will she be increasing her type I or her type II error and why?

6. Why is it important to consider both practical significance and statistical significance when interpreting findings?

7. Dr. Jones has discovered the presence of some outliers in her data. Can she just delete them? Explain your answer.

8. What is the difference between a correlation and a chi-square?

9. You wanted to test the difference in knowledge of child development in a class before and after a lecture and gave everyone a pre- and posttest. What statistic might you use to see if there was a significant change?

10. Juan reports a significant *t* test in his study of gender differences in GRE scores. What other information do you need as a reader to assess the results?

11. Write a research question for an ANOVA.

12. What is a coefficient alpha used for?

13. Please draw lines to match the parametric test to its appropriate nonparametric alternative in the second column:

	George Wishman procedure
Independent samples *t* test	Spearman correlation
Paired-samples *t* test	The pet psychic
Pearson correlation	Wilcoxon rank sum test
One-way ANOVA	Kruskal-Wallis
Two-way ANOVA	Wilcoxon Signed-Rank test
	Friedman's two-way nonparametric ANOVA

14. When we say a test is robust against violations of assumptions, what do we mean?

15. Mara wants to look at the association of gender with likelihood of signing up for sports activities (yes or no). What type of data does she have, and what type of statistical test might she use?

16. Todd runs a factorial ANOVA looking at income levels by educational level and high or low unemployment. He has a significant interaction term. Look at the accompanying graph of the interaction. In simple language, what can Todd say about the association of unemployment and education with income

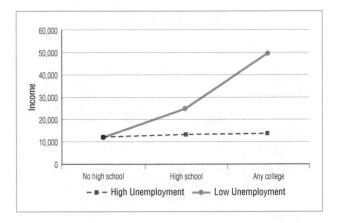

SUPPLEMENTAL READINGS

This list is not the result of a comprehensive review of all available texts on basic introductory statistics, but for the student who is interested in additional resources for this chapter here are a few commonly used in the social sciences, including two that are helpful with SAS or SPSS:

- Gonick, L., & Smith, W. (1993). *The Cartoon Guide to Statistics.* New York: Harper Collins.

- Hatcher, L., & Stepanski, E. (1994). *A Step by Step Approach to Using the SAS System for Univariate and Multivariate Statistics.* Cary, NC: SAS Institute Inc.

- Norusis, M. (2005). *SPSS 13.0 Guide to Data Analysis.* Upper Saddle River, NJ: Prentice Hall.

- Pagano, R. (2001). *Understanding Statistics in the Behavioral Sciences* (6th ed.). Belmont, CA: Wadsworth.

- Rosenthal, J. (2001). *Statistics and Data Interpretation for the Helping Professionals.* Belmont, CA: Brooks/Cole—Thompson Learning.

CHAPTER 14

MOVING ON IN QUANTITATIVE ANALYSIS

In this chapter we introduce more advanced statistical procedures. Never fear! These are extensions of ideas we have learned in Chapter 13. We begin by covering correlation and ANOVA concepts; this is followed by an introduction to logistic regression and then survival analyses. Although master's-level student may not be ready to use this level of statistics in their own work, the content of this chapter will still be helpful in understanding what researchers are talking about in articles.

Of course, this text offers only an introduction to the use of the techniques presented; in many cases, there are entire text books devoted to these approaches. Further, there are many other techniques that are gaining popularity in social science, such as generalized estimating equations and mixed models. We have chosen to concentrate only on those building directly on approaches covered in Chapter 13, with the additional beginning look at survival analyses. More advanced students are invited to check the list of other resources provided at the end of this chapter.

SECTION 14.1

ADDITIONAL IMPORTANT TERMS

Here we introduce a bit more vocabulary to help the reader digest this chapter and the more advanced research literature. If the terms seem hard to grasp at first, well, that's often because they are either difficult ideas or just not discussed in a straightforward way. It is not possible to cover all the techniques that accompany all of these terms:

■ *Clustered data:* Many of you have seen those Russian dolls that stack one within another. With clustered data, some of your subjects or cases are grouped together within some other classification, like students in a classroom. It is not possible to cover the methods used to account for this in this book, but there is a small section related to this at the end of the chapter and some references for further study. If data are clustered, you will see researchers talk about multilevel modeling or hierarchical models.

■ *Confounding factors:* Confounding factors or variables basically mess up our ability to know if a particular association of interest or predicted outcome is actually related to something else. For example, let's say you find that murder is associated with ice cream sales. Should we ban the sale of ice cream? Probably not. It's likely that there is a confounding factor, such as "heat." If we are able to measure heat, then we can "control" for that.

■ *Controlling for effects:* In statistics, "controlling for" something usually means that we have entered a variable that measures something that may not be the main variable of interest but is also associated with the outcome. In many techniques, this means that the value associated with one independent variable is interpreted as the magnitude of the relationship to the outcome of interest while holding the other variables in the model constant. So we can say that we are looking at the association of ice cream sales and murder rates while holding temperature constant (essentially removing its confounding impact).

- *Covariates:* This is just another word for the independent and control variables entered in a model. When we measure a confound, it becomes a covariate.

- *Fixed effects:* This does get confusing; at a basic level, a fixed effect is fixed either because it's a characteristic of a subject like race or because it's something that is deliberately set, such as testing one program condition against usual care for homeless males. Why do you care? In the statistics we use here, thinking of our variables as just variables in the equation is fine. However, in some techniques it is important to differentiate between variables that are fixed and those that are assumed to vary (also called "random effects"). So, an article using this term is probably doing so because it includes both kinds of variables and is trying to control for change over time or across levels of data.

- *Goodness of fit:* If we are estimating something or modeling (see the following discussion) that we cannot exactly know, then we need some measure of how well this is working overall. So various statistics are used to answer the question of how well the particular set of variables and the analysis chosen represent the sample data. If your goodness-of-fit measure says that representation is not too good, you really shouldn't go forward with interpreting the meaning of coefficients in the model.

- *Longitudinal data:* These data include measuring something over time either in discrete intervals, as in panel studies where we interview people at baseline then three years later, then three years after that; or in continuous time intervals, such as measuring recidivism by observing a sample over an entire period of time.

- *Models:* In multivariate statistics we say that we are "modeling" something. Why? This is because, as we learned in Chapter 13, statistics are about probability. So we are using numbers to try to represent a given thing in which we are interested. This becomes a model of reality.

- *Multivariate:* The term **multivariate** means involving lots of variables as compared to one or two

(Weisstein, 2006). In some cases, this is because we are interested in knowing a value for the level of association with a dependent variable for several independent variables. In other cases, we may have a primary interest in the outcome of treatment versus no treatment but are trying to control for other confounding variables through entering more covariates.

- *Parameter estimate:* When you conduct or read about analyses that include multiple variables, the analysis will print out some value that is a measure of the association between a given variable and the outcome of interest; this is the **parameter estimate.** In a linear model, this is a change in the slope; in a probability model or categorical model it is a magnitude of association.

- *Random effects:* Basically a variable is fixed, or it varies. If the levels of some variable included in the investigation are a random subset from a larger population of levels that are also of interest, then that is considered a "random effect." In multilevel models, the grouping level (e.g., a family in a study that looks at multiple children per family) might be treated as a random effect.

- *Standardized estimate:* You have probably heard some version of the expression, "That's like comparing apples to oranges." Often we are interested in comparing the relative association of independent variables in our model with the dependent variable. For example, does income or education have a greater influence on marital satisfaction? The problem is that we may measure income in dollars from say $100 to $500,000 per year but measure education from 8 to 15 years. These are not on the same scale. So if we just look at the raw parameter estimates, we do not have values that can be compared. But, if we look at **standardized estimates,** then the computer places the variables on an artificial scale that is the same. These estimates can then be compared.

- *Variance explained:* Let's say you tell me your age, gender, and high school grades, and I try to use a statistical model to predict your income after graduating from college. If these variables have a decent association with later income, my model's goodness of fit may be fine. However, there are probably a lot more factors that go into your later income, such as college major, grades, and the like. So if we think of all the things that would go into constructing a pie chart of your future income, my model may include only a small slice of that pie chart. The remaining part is the variance that I did not explain. Many, but not all, multivariate models include some type of statistic that gives you an idea of how much of the outcome has been explained by the variables you included in the model.

- *Weighting:* Let's say you are interested in the relationship of child abuse to domestic violence among individuals of Chinese American heritage. Sometimes specific groups of individuals do not have very high representations in a given population. So, you might oversample (try to get more than you normally would through a random sample process) to insure that there are enough representatives of this group to look at separately in your analyses. The problem is that this creates an artificial importance (numerically speaking) in your data set compared to the sample frame population. We can, however, adjust the parameter estimates to reflect the actual true population figures by using a "weight" or numerical value that tells the computer to make this adjustment. Weighting schemes can be as simple as adjusting a mean between two groups to reflect a different sample size or as complex as multilevel processes that require specialized software to handle.

SECTION 14.2

ADVANCED APPLICATIONS OF CORRELATION—MULTIPLE REGRESSION

We begin with multiple regression as it picks up where we left off in the last chapter with a simple bivariate regression. In the prior chapter, we introduced some of the basic concepts behind multiple regression using a simple bivariate example. Now we move forward to consider the use of two or more predictor variables in a regression model. In social science it is rare that we would have either so perfect an experimental design or so powerful a single predictor as to be able to explain the dependent or outcome variable of interest. It is more common that there are three or more variables that we wish to include in trying to understand our dependent variable. You have already started thinking this way when you learned about including two variables and an interaction term in Chapter 13 using the factorial ANOVA. So the good news is that we are building on what you already know. First, let's review and extend some ideas that are important to consider in the multivariate context:

- *Research question:* "Are variables *X, Y,* and *Z* associated with dependent variable *A?*"

- *Null hypothesis:* There is no association of *X, Y,* or *Z* with *A.*

- *Alternative hypothesis:* At least one of the variables is associated with *A.*

You'll recall that assumptions of the test include:

1. Dependent variables must be interval or ratio, and the predictors may be either nominal/ratio or categorical.

2. For any combination of the predictor (independent) variables, the dependent variable should be normally distributed.

3. For any combination of the predictor (independent) variables, the dependent variable should have equal variance.

4. There must be independence of observations.

5. A linear relationship must exist between dependent or criterion and the independent variables.

6. The error associated with a given observation should not be correlated with the error of another observation or with the error associated with an independent variable. Also the errors associated with prediction should be normally distributed with equal variance.

7. There must be an absence of specification error, meaning that needed variables are included in the model and that the assumption of a linear relationship is correct.

8. There must be no measurement error because error in how predictors are measured may lead to underestimation of the regression coefficient for those predictors.

SECTION 14.2.1: MULTICOLLINEARITY

As you will recall, we mentioned that one reason you begin with bivariate correlations prior to running a multivariate regression is to do a basic assessment of multicollinearity. To truly be sure, however, you really need to assess the variables in a multivariate context. This is done by examining what are called **variance inflation factors (VIF)** for the explanatory variables. Variance inflation factors are a scaled version of the multiple correlation coefficient between variable *j* and the rest of the independent variables:

$$VIF = \frac{1}{1 - R_j^2}$$

Sometimes you will also see "tolerance" reported. This is just the reciprocal of the VIF. VIF ranges from a low of 1 to very high numbers. Some sources indicate that a VIF greater than 10 is normally the cutoff for concern regarding multicollinearity (Cody & Smith, 2006). Other sources suggest that when the VIF is more than 4, you may have issues (Garson, n.d.). Even lower values are sometimes considered problematic if there is an extremely large value for one or more variables when compared to the other independent variables.

Fortunately this is an easy option to add to your SAS command, as we will see in the following discussion. Of course, if you have this, you must then do something about the offending variables and rerun your model. Why? Because it can create several problems in the model:

1. It can severely limit the model R^2 because the explanatory or independent variables are trying to explain the same variability in the response variable.

2. It makes determining the importance of a given variable difficult because the effects of the explanatory variables are confounded due to the intercorrelations.

3. It increases the variance of the regression coefficients, making the parameter estimates less reliable (Der & Everitt, 2001, p. 84).

There are at least two means of dealing with multicollinearity. First, one can simply choose to delete one of the variables that is collinear. While this solves one problem, it may not make theoretical or practical sense to fully omit the influence of the deleted variable. For example, if we were interested in how education and income were associated with asset building, it is easy to see how income and education might be highly collinear:

> Model: Education ⟶ Income ⟶ Assets

If we drop education and education's effect on assets is fully explained by income, then there is no problem. If, however, education also uniquely contributes to assets (perhaps as related to understanding how to use available resources), then we may be underspecifying our model, which would really be like this:

> Model: Education ⟶ Income ⟶ Assets

Another option to address multicollinearity, without losing the unique contribution of independent variables that are correlated with each, is the use of principal components analysis to reduce variables to uncorrelated constructs (this technique is covered in the next section).

SECTION 14.2.2: PARSIMONY

More is not always better, as we discussed in Chapter 3. Although adding more variables will often (but not always) increase the amount of the variance explained, you are also increasing the degrees of freedom in a model and often making it harder to interpret. We seek **parsimony,** or the simplest model that maximizes the variance we can explain with the minimum number of variables and interactions. We achieve this by keeping a close eye on both whether a variable is significant and how its inclusion or exclusion impacts the R-square. If we have a model with four variables, and leaving one out results in less than 1% change in the R-square, then we will likely choose to keep the more parsimonious (smaller) three-variable model. In other words, we aren't losing practically significant information by dropping the fourth variable. Of course, if you are testing a theory, for example, you may choose to keep that variable, so that you can show statistically how important theoretically key concepts actually turn out to be. So the ideal of parsimony must be balanced with the need to include more variables if they are needed to assess a conceptual model.

SECTION 14.2.3: RESIDUAL ANALYSIS

We won't go into much depth regarding model diagnostics in this chapter, but you should understand what is meant when authors talk about analysis of residual values. Recall that a multiple regression model is attempting to fit a line that minimizes the difference between the actual measured values of your dependent variable and the predicted values. These values or distances between the actual and predicted y have a distribution. Recall from page 305 that assumption 6 includes "the errors associated with prediction should be normally distributed with equal variance." If the data met the assumptions of the regression technique, these residual values (difference between predicted and actual) should be randomly distributed. Most people use a graphic plot to assess this. A nice illustration of typical plots and interpretation can be found in online course notes from C. Friel (www.shsu.edu/~icc_cmf/cj_742/multipleRegression.doc).

SECTION 14.2.4: SAMPLE SIZE

Before jumping to analyze your data using multiple regression, remember that multiple regression analyses prefer larger samples. Generally, a minimum of 100 is suggested, but this varies according to the number of independent or predictor variables you wish to enter. Most sources will tell you that you should have a minimum of 15 subjects for every variable entered into the model. Practically, this means the smaller the sample, the fewer the variables that can be analyzed. Be aware, however, that this does not mean that the computer program will always stop running. A given analysis program may still provide results without significant cautionary warnings when, in reality, there are too few observations per variable to include all the variables entered.

SECTION 14.2.5: SUPPRESSOR VARIABLES

In some cases, a couple of predictor variables are correlated with each other (although not sufficiently to get concerned about multicollinearity), but only one is correlated with the outcome or criterion of interest. In many cases, one might leave out the variable that is not associated with the outcome. But sometimes that unassociated variable is helping us out in another way. Let's say we have predictor variable *A* and predictor variable *B*. There is a lot of variability in *A* in our sample. Error can occur in models due to "noise" or variance within a predictor variable. This will be reflected in some instability in the coefficient in our final model. Now, in our case, variable *B* is correlated with *A* but not with the outcome. If we put *B* in the model with *A,* it may be able to "calm *A* down a bit." It's similar to having a donkey walk along with a high-powered race horse because the friendship with the donkey calms the horse. So, sometimes by entering another variable in the model that is related only to the predictor and not to the dependent variable, you can help control for the background noise and improve the model. This is what is meant by a **suppressor** effect.

Of course we always run our basic descriptive statistics first, right? So we would use a univariate procedure in SAS or SPSS (not shown) to check the distribution of the dependent variable. Then we would use bivariate correlations to obtain descriptive information to look for bivariate associations as well as glance at collinearity. Finally we would use some form of graphic plot to assess a basic linear relationship. If we meet the basic requirements, then we move on to the multivariate model.

SECTION 14.2.6: SAS AND MULTIPLE REGRESSION

We will learn a new SAS procedure. For a simple bivariate regression, the SAS code used in Chapter 13 works fine. Another SAS procedure (PROC REG), however, offers more options and is more efficient for multivariate regression models (see Figure 14.1). SPSS commands follow below.

SECTION 14.2.7: SPSS AND MULTIPLE REGRESSION

Go to Analyze ⇒ Regression ⇒ Linear . . . , ⇒ specify the variable under "Dependent" and your predictor variables under "Independent(s)" ⇒ click on "Statistics" ⇒ select "Estimates" under "Regression Coefficients" to obtain the parameter estimates ⇒ select "Model Fit," "Descriptives," and "Collinearity diagnostics" to obtain the model information ⇒ click on "Continue" ⇒ click "OK"

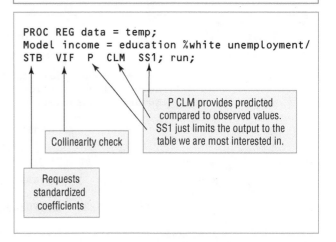

FIGURE 14.1. SAS Procedure.

Let's look at some more variables from a census data set to see how a multiple regression looks. Let's pretend we are interested in how education, unemployment, and race are associated with median family income. All of our variables are associated, but one of these associations looks problematic (too much correlation). The GINCFAM and the GPNOHIGH are highly correlated ($r = -.70$). Because the first is a measure of income and the second is high school completion, the relationship makes a lot of sense. In our case, because one is the dependent variable (income) and the other is a predictor, we are satisfied with the correlation. But if they were both predictors (independent variables), then we would be worried about multicollinearity if we entered both in the model. Let's say that again: High correlation between predictor and outcome variables is OK, but high correlation among different predictor variables may mean you have multicollinearity. Now we run our regression model, still requesting the VIF data because collinearity can show up in a multivariate context even if it seems OK in the bivariate check (see Figure 14.2).

First, we glance at the VIF or multicollinearity statistics. As can be seen in the SAS and SPSS output, none of the variables are terribly high. On the other hand the "percent White" (GPERWHT) and unemployment (GPUNEMP) are higher, and GPERWHT does not appear to be even close to significant. So, we rerun our model without the "percent White" (model not shown) and find that the variance explained remains nearly identical. This indicates that the GPERWHT was not functioning as a suppressor variable. Further, the VIF is now 1.20 for both remaining variables. We are therefore happier with the more parsimonious model.

Note the standardized estimates in SAS (labeled "BETA" in SPSS) help us understand the relative magnitude of the relationship between the independent and dependent variables. Our measure of high school completion (GPNOHIGH) has the strongest influence

FIGURE 14.2a. **SAS Output.**

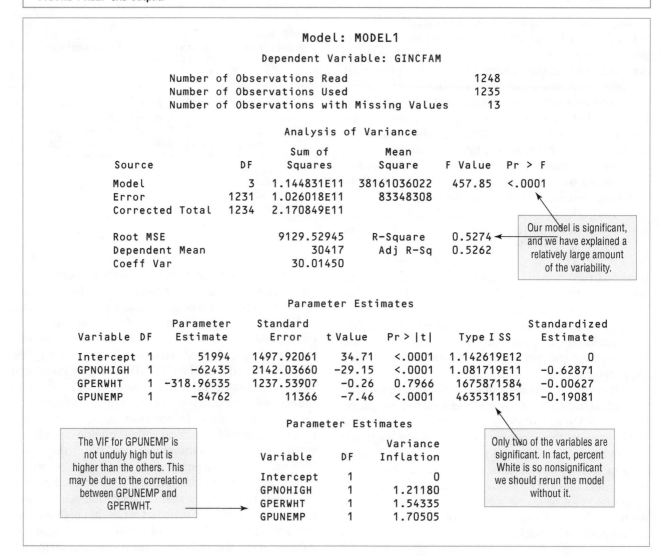

```
                         Model: MODEL1
                   Dependent Variable: GINCFAM
          Number of Observations Read              1248
          Number of Observations Used              1235
          Number of Observations with Missing Values  13

                      Analysis of Variance
                              Sum of        Mean
       Source        DF      Squares       Square    F Value   Pr > F
       Model          3   1.144831E11   38161036022    457.85   <.0001
       Error       1231   1.026018E11      83348308
       Corrected Total 1234 2.170849E11

       Root MSE            9129.52945    R-Square    0.5274
       Dependent Mean           30417    Adj R-Sq    0.5262
       Coeff Var             30.01450
```

Our model is significant, and we have explained a relatively large amount of the variability.

```
                      Parameter Estimates
                   Parameter    Standard                                Standardized
     Variable DF    Estimate       Error    t Value   Pr > |t|    Type I SS      Estimate
     Intercept  1       51994   1497.92061    34.71    <.0001   1.142619E12           0
     GPNOHIGH   1      -62435   2142.03660   -29.15    <.0001   1.081719E11    -0.62871
     GPERWHT    1  -318.96535   1237.53907    -0.26    0.7966   1675871584     -0.00627
     GPUNEMP    1      -84762        11366    -7.46    <.0001   4635311851     -0.19081

                      Parameter Estimates
                                         Variance
                     Variable    DF     Inflation
                     Intercept    1             0
                     GPNOHIGH     1       1.21180
                     GPERWHT      1       1.54335
                     GPUNEMP      1       1.70505
```

The VIF for GPUNEMP is not unduly high but is higher than the others. This may be due to the correlation between GPUNEMP and GPERWHT.

Only two of the variables are significant. In fact, percent White is so nonsignificant we should rerun the model without it.

on median income (GINCFAM). One can also compute a "uniqueness index," or variance explained by each additional variable, by running the model with one variable, then rerunning it with two variables and subtracting the *R*-square:

$$\text{uniqueness} = R^2_{full} - R^2_{reduced}$$

We'll stop here, acknowledging that there are many more options and topics related to multiple regression that simply extend beyond this introductory glimpse. There are several references useful for further study of multiple regression with SAS or SPSS listed at the close of this chapter.

SECTION 14.3

PRINCIPAL COMPONENTS ANALYSIS

Principal components analysis is a technique sometimes used in survey research to see if the subscales that are supposed to exist really still exist when used with a new population. This type of analysis is also very useful if you have a lot of highly correlated independent variables (multicollinearity; see Chapter 13) and need to decide which to keep and which to exclude from your model. In this chapter we are interested in its use as a variable reduction procedure to help us with multicollinearity.

A word of warning: While the process is similar to that of factor analysis, there are critical conceptual differences (Cody & Smith, 2006). When you conduct a factor analysis, you assume that there is a causal structure that underlies the results. In other words, there is a

FIGURE 14.2b. SPSS Output: Variables Entered/Removed(b).

Model	Variables Entered	Variables Removed	Method
1	GPUNEMP, GPNOHIGH, GPERWHT(a)	.	Enter

This indicates that all variables were entered simultaneously.

a All requested variables entered.
b Dependent Variable: GINCFAM

Model Summary

Model	R	R Square	Adjusted R Square	Std. Error of the Estimate
1	.726(a)	.527	.526	9129.529

Note the *R*-square and betas are rounded to one less digit than in SAS.

a Predictors: (Constant), GPUNEMP, GPNOHIGH, GPERWHT

ANOVA(b)

Model		Sum of Squares	df	Mean Square	F	Sig.
1	Regression	114483108065.073	3	38161036021.691	457.850	.000(a)
	Residual	102601767031.613	123	83348307.905		
	Total	217084875096.685	123			

a Predictors: (Constant), GPUNEMP, GPNOHIGH, GPERWHT

b Dependent Variable: GINCFAM

Coefficients(a)

Model		Unstandardized Coefficients		Standardized Coefficients	t	Sig.	Collinearity Statistics	
		B	Std. Error	Beta			Tolerance	VIF
1	(Constant)	51994.463	1497.921		34.711	.000		
	GPNOHIGH	−62434.571	2142.037	−.629	−29.147	.000	.825	1.212
	GPERWHT	−318.965	1237.539	−.006	−.258	.797	.648	1.543
	GPUNEMP	−84761.940	11366.056	−.191	−7.457	.000	.586	1.705

a Dependent Variable: GINCFAM

belief that a latent variable (underlying unmeasured construct) is explaining the relationship you find among a set of variables (see Hatcher & Stepanski, 1994). The concept of principal components involves only manifest (i.e., actually measured) variables. There is no assumption of a causal structure, only the construction of a grouping based on intercorrelations. Factor analysis and principal components are therefore used for different things. Here is another way of explaining the difference:

... components are not latent variables; they are linear combinations of the input variables,

and thus determinate. Factors, on the other hand, are latent variables, which are indeterminate. If your goal is to fit the variances of input variables for the purpose of data reduction, you should carry out principal components analysis. If you want to build a testable model to explain the intercorrelations among input variables, you should carry out a factor analysis. (Wikipedia, 2005b)

In simple terms, we can define a component as a way to represent all the unique variance in separate variables in one big variable. In our last section, we learned that sometimes our predictor or independent variables are correlated too much to enter as separate variables in a regression equation (that's the multi-collinearity issue). You want to maximize the separate information available and think that there is value in combining some items in your data. This is our interest in the principal components analysis.

As with regression, your computer will be looking for linear models that optimize the variance explained—but now it's the variance of interrelationships in the data. We are now modeling a new variable rather than a subject's predicted value on a scale. It's a bit difficult to visualize, but this is similar to mixing colors. We know red and blue make purple. Purple is created by the unique aspects of red and blue joined together. Any shared characteristics of red and blue would be done away with.

We have some new language to learn. We now have an EIGENEQUATION rather than a regression equation:

$$c_1 = b_{11}X_1 + b_{12}X_2 + \dots$$

The c in the equation is the subject's score for the component extracted through the analysis process. Similar to regression, b = coefficient (or weight) that uniquely contributes to the observed variable. X = subject's actual score on the observed variable.

■ *Research question:* "Can I explain the variance in the data by a simplified set of components that are uncorrelated?"

Assumptions of principal components analysis are based on correlations, so we need:

1. Interval or ratio-level data (Likert or similar are OK here)
2. Independence of observations (one subject contributes to only one score on each variable)
3. Linearity (relationships between variables are not curvilinear)
4. Normality for each observed variable (you can transform variables if they aren't normal, as we discussed earlier with other parametric procedures)

There are different kinds of solutions that you can ask SAS to produce. A solution is the best combination of the variables. They are called "rotations." If you ask for an oblique rotation, this will result in components that are mostly their own units but are still allowed to correlate to other components. This type of solution is more likely to be used in survey design. In this introductory text we will cover only orthogonal rotations. What does this mean? It means that final resulting components will not be correlated with each other. This is good because it solves our multicollinearity problem.

How many components will I get? Well, the reality is that the procedure itself creates as many components as there are variables. So how is that useful? The answer is that the first few components will typically explain most of the variance in the data. These components can then be used as summary variables in later analyses. So at some point, you make a judgment that you will use only components that have a sufficiently large eigenvalue. An **eigenvalue** is a measure of how much variance is accounted for by a component. A low eigenvalue means that the component does not explain much of the dependent variable and therefore isn't very important. The most common rule used is to include components that have an eigenvalue greater than 1 (Hatcher & Stepanski, 1994). As we will see in the following discussion, components with eigenvalues less than 1 actually are less explanatory of the dependent variable than are existing single independent variables, and so there isn't much reason to bother with them.

How big a sample do I need? Well, this is an issue, as principal components is designed to be used with larger samples. Hatcher and Stepanski (1994) recommend a minimum of 100 subjects or a minimum of 5 times the number of variables being analyzed, whichever is bigger.

Finally, we will want to understand which variables go with which components and how strongly related they are (also known as the loading) to that component. This is where that orthogonal solution comes in. It rotates the items to develop uncorrelated components and then shows you the variables that are the major contributors.

SECTION 14.3.1: FIVE "EASY" STEPS TO PRINCIPAL COMPONENTS

STEP 1.

■ Make sure you reverse code items if necessary before you run this procedure.

■ Run univariates and plots to check assumptions of normality.

■ Look at a correlation matrix of your variables. With a small number of variables you may actually be able to see some underlying groupings.

SAS Diagnostics.

```
PROC UNIVARIATE data=X;
var m1-m22; run;
PROC CORR data=X;
var m1-m22; run;
```

SPSS Diagnostics.

> Go to Analyze ⟹ Descriptive Statistics ⟹ Explore ⟹ select variables m1–m22
>
> Go to Analyze ⟹ Correlate ⟹ Bivariate ⟹ select variables m1–m22

Each variable should be correlated relatively strongly with two or three other variables, or you are unlikely to get components with high eigenvalues. Principal components says, "Aha!" Let's reduce this mess by dividing up these variables into underlying groups according to how much overlap there is. Principal components analysis then magically gets rid of the overlap by creating a new variable based on the nonoverlap. So, if there are no relatively strong correlations among your variables, this procedure is unlikely to produce much. Then again, if we didn't have these correlations we wouldn't have to do this right?

STEP 2. Set your evaluation standards for the computer. We will use MINEIGEN=1 (minimum eigenvalue = 1). Each variable you enter theoretically contributes one unit of variance overall. So, any factor or component that is over 1 accounts for the variance contributed by more than 1 variable (which is why we are doing this, anyway).

STEP 3. Enter the long list of commands. The meaning of these commands is given immediately following. To see how they look when in use on the SAS screen, see the display immediately following that.

SAS and Principal Components. SAS can be asked to perform a principal components analysis using PROC PRINCOMP or PROC FACTOR. Obviously, PROC FACTOR is the procedure of choice in factor analysis, but it is also our preferred method here. It produces a few things more easily, such as the "scree plot" that provides you with a visual way of assessing the components rather than just the eigenvalues in a list. The commands include:

PROC FACTOR This is the procedure command for either principal components or factor analysis.

SIMPLE This requests some basic descriptive statistics, such as the mean and standard deviations for the variables used and the number of usable cases.

Method=PRIN Here is where you tell the computer you want to do principal components, not factor, analysis.

PRIORS=one This also has to do with telling the computer to do the right procedure.

MINEIGEN=1 This says we are really interested only in components that include variance from more than one variable.

SCREE This is a visual plot. If you are lucky you will see a nice break between important and unimportant factors.

ROTATE=VARIMAX We have to transform the output into something understandable. This has to do with the mathematics of the EIGENEQUATION. This is also requesting the orthogonal solution.

ROUND This keeps you from using up too much space with endless decimal places.

FLAG = .40 This is another means of assessing the LOAD of a variable on a component. We will use .40 (which is a moderate relationship in correlation language).

Var This is where you tell the computer which variables to use.

All together, this will look like:

```
PROC FACTOR data=X simple method=prin
priors=one mineigen=1 scree rotate=varimax
round flag=.40; var m1-m22;
run;
```

SPSS and Principal Components. We will also use the factor procedure in SPSS and, unfortunately, the list of SPSS steps is equally imposing:

> Go to Analyze ⟹ Data Reduction ⟹ Factor . . . , ⟹ specify the variables to be analyzed ⟹
>
> click on the "Descriptives" button ⟹ select "Coefficients" under "Correlation Matrix" ⟹
>
> click on "Extraction . . ." ⟹ select "Principal components" under "Method" ⟹ select "Correlation matrix" under "Analyze" ⟹ under "Display" check "Unrotated factor solution" and "Scree plot" ⟹ under "Extract" select "Eigenvalues over" and specify "1" ⟹ click on "Continue" ⟹ click on "Rotation . . ." ⟹ under "Method," select "Varimax" ⟹ under "Display" check "Rotated solution" ⟹ click on "Continue" ⟹ click on "Options . . ." ⟹ under "Coefficient Display Format," check "Suppress absolute values less than:" and specify the desired value (0.4 in our example) ⟹ click on "Continue" ⟹
>
> click "OK"

STEP 4. Look at the output and see whether you will be keeping all the variables you entered. Perhaps you have heard the old saying "You can't make a silk purse out of a sow's ear"? Sometimes the computer is unable to fully separate a variable onto a single component. We can't have correlated components, so that means you have to get rid of the variable. If you have to throw out an item, you must rerun the whole process again. To do this you leave the undesirable variable out of your variable list the second time. This can be a tedious process sometimes.

STEP 5. After examining your output to see how many components seem to have significant and unique variance, you must look back at the original items and see if they make conceptual sense. This is rather intuitive when you think about it. You want to enter the component(s) into a regression model. When you do this, the coefficient for your variable will be for the component, not the individual variables in it. If it makes no sense, then it will be next to impossible to interpret. If you find groupings that make no sense, you should reconsider the variables in the principal components model. If you can't conceptually rid yourself of the problem, you will need to seek consultation on another procedure. And your computer can't test whether or not the component makes sense; only you can.

So I bet you're just dying to try one of these, right? Let's say we have a set of 22 variables. Some are highly correlated. A principal components analysis was done to see if we can reduce these variables into some bigger uncorrelated items.

We will skip the univariate output but display a few bivariate correlations to illustrate what we meant by obvious groupings. We'll use just the SAS output to save space (Figure 14.3). Looking at the correlation in Figure 14.3, you can see that there may be a component that includes items 1, 2, 3, and 8, as they all seem to have relatively strong correlations with each other.

Now let's look at our SAS and SPSS output for the procedure (Figures 14.4 and 14.5). In both SPSS and

---

FIGURE 14.3. SAS Output.

Pearson Correlation Coefficients

	m1	m2	m3	m4	m5	m6	m7	m8
m1	1.00000	0.76463	0.64786	0.07893	0.13065	0.43276	−0.16654	0.60481
	<.0001	<.0001	0.2950	0.0822	<.0001	0.0259	<.0001	<.0001
	179	179	179	178	178	179	179	179

FIGURE 14.4. SAS Output.

The FACTOR Procedure
Initial Factor Method: Principal Components
Prior Communality Estimates: ONE

Eigenvalues of the Correlation Matrix: Total = 22 Average = 1

	Eigenvalue	Difference	Proportion	Cumulative
1	6.65505971	3.94734752	0.3025	0.3025
2	2.70771218	0.81687031	0.1231	0.4256
3	1.89084187	0.68044008	0.0859	0.5115
4	1.21040179	0.14381085	0.0550	0.5665
5	1.06659093	0.02820385	0.0485	0.6150
6	1.03838709	0.15807210	0.0472	0.6622
7	0.88031499	0.05601752	0.0400	0.7022
8	0.82429747	0.05492222	0.0375	0.7397
9	0.76937525	0.03907928	0.0350	0.7747
10	0.73029598	0.10362136	0.0332	0.8079
11	0.62667462	0.08834193	0.0285	0.8364
12	0.53833269	0.02945214	0.0245	0.8608
13	0.50888055	0.08265717	0.0231	0.8840
14	0.42622338	0.01966681	0.0194	0.9033
15	0.40655657	0.07726945	0.0185	0.9218
16	0.32928712	0.03808308	0.0150	0.9368
17	0.29120404	0.00991643	0.0132	0.9500
18	0.28128761	0.04454945	0.0128	0.9628
19	0.23673816	0.00949178	0.0108	0.9736
20	0.22724638	0.03394984	0.0103	0.9839
21	0.19329654	0.03230146	0.0088	0.9927
22	0.16099508		0.0073	1.0000

Note: 6 factors will be retained by the MINEIGEN criterion.

FIGURE 14.5. **SPSS Output.**

Total Variance Explained

Component	Initial Eigenvalues			Extraction Sums of Squared Loadings			Rotation Sums of Squared Loadings		
	Total	% of Variance	Cumulative %	Total	% of Variance	Cumulative %	Total	% of Variance	Cumulative %
1	6.655	30.250	30.250	6.655	30.250	30.250	4.778	21.717	21.717
2	2.708	12.308	42.558	2.708	12.308	42.558	2.787	12.668	34.386
3	1.891	8.595	51.153	1.891	8.595	51.153	2.635	11.976	46.362
4	1.210	5.502	56.655	1.210	5.502	56.655	1.629	7.407	53.769
5	1.067	4.848	61.503	1.067	4.848	61.503	1.480	6.729	60.498
6	1.038	4.720	66.223	1.038	4.720	66.223	1.259	5.725	66.223
7	.880	4.001	70.224						
8	.824	3.747	73.971						
9	.769	3.497	77.468						
10	.730	3.320	80.788						
11	.627	2.849	83.636						
12	.538	2.447	86.083						
13	.509	2.313	88.396						
14	.426	1.937	90.334						
15	.407	1.848	92.182						
16	.329	1.497	93.678						
17	.291	1.324	95.002						
18	.281	1.279	96.281						
19	.237	1.076	97.357						
20	.227	1.033	98.390						
21	.193	.879	99.268						
22	.161	.732	100.000						

Note: Extraction Method: Principal Component Analysis.

SAS, following the correlations you will find a list of eigenvalues for up to 22 components (because we have 22 items). You'll recall that we told the computer that we were interested only in components that had eigenvalues greater than 1. So although the computer will not continue to consider the components that go beyond our cutoff, it will still list them initially. As you can see, the first parts of each output are similar, although SPSS prints out more information about the six components that have an eigenvalue of more than 1.

On the next portion of the output we find a **scree plot.** To save space we have provided only the SAS scree plot (Figure 14.6). The SPSS simply uses circles rather than the numbers of the components on the plot. This gives us a visual reference so that we can better understand the relative import of the six retained components. Does anyone know what scree is? Anyone familiar with mountaineering or geology may know that scree is the rocky rubble at the bottom of a cliff. The scree plot is designed to look as though your 22 components have been thrown off a cliff. Those with little unique importance group together at the bottom. The important ones look as though they are suspended in air. The bigger the

FIGURE 14.6. **Scree Plot of Eigenvalues.**

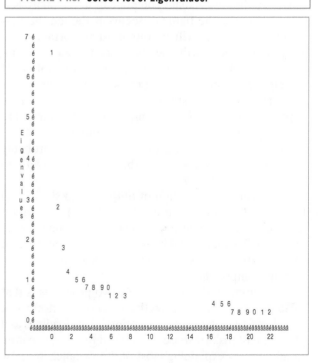

FIGURE 14.7. **SAS.**

Rotated Factor Pattern

	Factor1	Factor2	Factor3	Factor4	Factor5	Factor6
m1	84*	6	−2	5	−10	9
m2	79*	20	−9	−2	−5	8
m3	84*	16	−16	0	−11	−14
m4	24	−4	25	−13	31	−61*
m5	5	81*	4	18	−6	−10
m6	42*	24	−6	65*	−13	−5
m7	−12	8	46*	2	29	−35
m8	81*	14	−17	21	0	−10
m9	−6	−14	75*	5	−4	−22
m10	19	77*	−17	9	−12	18
m11	36	73*	−5	−3	−14	23
m12	−38	−6*	62*	16	23	19
m13	70*	5	−13	33	12	13
m14	57*	−4	2	37	23	41*
m15	9	67*	−28	29	11	−5
m16	37	30	−4	72*	−13	3
m17	−2	−17	33	0	58*	−11
m18	2	−17	67*	−30	10	−7
m19	−10	−4	79*	−4	7	−2
m20	69*	23	4	29	−4	0
m21	−8	−1	2	−12	84*	−2
m22	29	41*	−10	−18	7	58*

Printed values are multiplied by 100 and rounded to the nearest integer. Values greater than 0.4 are flagged by an '*'.

space between the numbers, the more important that component is. (By the way, your computer is calling them factors because of the name of the procedure—so keep in mind that they are actually components in this analysis.)

Looking at the figure, it seems as though the first three components will be our most important ones. Why? After the fourth one, the space between components really narrows. You can verify this by looking at the eigenvalue matrix in Figure 14.4. The values in the proportion row illustrate the amount of variance explained by each of the components. Of course, the computer will "keep" all the components with an eignevalue of 1—meaning the first six. We will probably want to rerun it later with only the first three, but let's go on with our output first.

We will skip a portion of output to go straight to the rotated pattern (Figures 14.7 and 14.8). A rotation is a linear transformation that allows us to more easily interpret the loadings. The loadings are a measure of the strength of the association between a given variable and the component.

The primary difference in the two programs is that SPSS prints only the loadings that exceed the cutoff value we select (0.4 in this case). SAS prints all the loadings and places an asterisk by those that exceed the chosen cutoff. In addition to explaining most of the variance, we now know that the first three components have more variables loading on them. Ideally we want at least three variables for each component. Also, we notice that m22 and m14 load on both the first and sixth factor. So, we decide that we are really interested only in the first three components. And, yes, that means we have to rerun it again.

SAS and Rerunning Our Model. In SAS we rerun the analysis using the NFACT statement instead of the MINEIGEN statement to say we are keeping only three components:

# of factors to keep

We also add the following line before the "RUN" statement to create a data set with the final factors:

= Dataset name;

This new data set will include the components and the original variables.

SPSS and Rerunning Our Model. In SPSS we change an option under the "Extract" section:

Go to "Extraction . . ." submenu, ⇒ select "Number of factors:" and specify the number of factors required (three in this example)

FIGURE 14.8. SPSS Output.

Rotated Component Matrix(a)

	Component					
	1	2	3	4	5	6
m1	.837					
m2	.791					
m3	.836					
m4						−.610
m5		.812				
m6	.419			.645		
m7			.462			
m8	.806					
m9			.754			
m10		.771				
m11		.729				
m12			.624			
m13	.703					
m14	.569					.407
m15		.671				
m16				.720		
m17					.582	
m18			.671			
m19			.794			
m20	.691					
m21					.842	
m22		.408				.583

Extraction Method: Principal Component Analysis.
Rotation Method: Varimax with Kaiser Normalization.
a Rotation converged in 11 iterations.

When we rerun the data, we go directly back to the rotated factor pattern portion of our output because we have already chosen the components and don't need to check eigenvalues or the scree plot. Unfortunately, we discover that items m6 and m16 are split across factors:

	Factor1	Factor2	Factor3
m6	54 *	41 *	−6
m16	50 *	50 *	−6

We would drop these items and rerun a final time before we discussed the final components we found. So when do you know you are done? According to Hatcher and Stepanski, we check for four things:

1. Are there at least three variables with significant loadings on each retained component?

2. Do they share some conceptual meaning that makes sense?

3. Do the variables that do not load on one component appear to be measuring something else?

4. Is there a simple structure, meaning that most variables have high loadings on only 1 component? (Hatcher & Stepanski, 1994)

Then it is up to you to give your components or subscales names that describe them. This is sort of an interesting and little-known thing that happens in social science. You may do the stats and find that a number of questions hang together. Interestingly, you can say that you have a series of questions that hang together and seem to be reliably measuring the same thing, but no statistic will tell you what to call that thing. You therefore make a name based on an understanding of the variables.

WHAT'S IN A NAME? (INFORMATION CHANGED TO PROTECT THE INNOCENT)

Once there was a brilliant but also very unlucky Ph D student. This person had located a new instrument from a respected researcher. The instrument included a subscale measuring what we will call "trait X." Because trait X was a key construct in the student's dissertation, and because there was no other known scale measuring trait X, this new one seemed perfect. The student called the researcher, got a copy of the test along with access to the pilot data, examined the statistical properties of the test (which looked good), and then used the test in her dissertation. The good news is that the test performed well for her, and the components hung together much as they had for the designer of the study.

The bad news came when the student later contacted the original scale inventor to share her findings. The original inventor had decided that the scale didn't really measure trait X at all but was now calling it a subscale measuring trait Y (this would be similar to deciding that your depression scale no longer measures depression but measures fatigue instead). Now these were very different concepts theoretically, and the second concept did not fit well into the doctoral student's dissertation or theoretical model. Ouch.

So what was really being studied, X or Y? Does a researcher have a right to arbitrarily decide what a scale is measuring and later change his or her mind? Who checks up on all this anyway? And what did our poor doctoral student do? Well, in answer to the first set of questions, yes, scales are typically named by their designers, just as you will name your components. Hopefully, these assertions of what the components or subscales mean are checked with regard to criterion validity (do scales have similar findings to other measures of the construct you claim the scale is measuring?) and construct validity (does the scale perform as theory says it should, based on the construct you say it measures?). This can take a while, meaning that scales can be "discovered" to mean different things over time. With regard to our student, you might say that our student got involved in the process before the scale was really finalized and was just unlucky. The data were used in the dissertation, but the student had to explain the ambiguity present regarding the meaning of the scale in the conclusion section. The lesson here is that computers just output numbers; it is the researcher and the research process that provide the meaning and report the limitations of what is known.■

SECTION 14.4
ANCOVA AND MANOVA: COMBINING IDEAS OF REGRESSION AND ANOVA

Although we will not cover these in depth, the reader may find it useful to understand two other techniques that are extensions of ideas used in regression and ANOVA. There is the **ANCOVA**, or **analysis of covariance**, and the **MANOVA**, or **multivariate analysis of variance**. An ANCOVA is useful in treatment studies where there is no randomization. You use this technique to provide a statistical control. MANOVA is useful when you are testing multiple possible outcomes from a treatment study.

- *Research question for ANCOVA:* "Are the means in score *X* according to group *A* and controlling for continuous variable *Y*?"
- *Null hypothesis for ANCOVA:* The means of the groups are equal even after controlling for other variables.
- *Research question for MANOVA:* "Are the differing means of dependent variables different according to groups being tested?"
- *Null hypothesis for MANOVA:* The mean of the groups are equal for all dependent (criterion) variables.

Because ANCOVA is somewhat more commonly used in social science, particularly in intervention research where you have treatment and comparison groups, we will limit the discussion of how to do these techniques to the ANCOVA.

The ANCOVA is a hybrid of ANOVA and regression. Assumptions for this test include:

1. Independence of observations
2. Dependent variable measured at interval/ratio level
3. Normality
4. Homogeneity of variance
5. Linear relationships between covariates and outcome
6. Homogeneity of regression slopes
7. Measurement of the covariate without error

The ANCOVA model uses covariates to adjust for initial differences in groups in pre- and posttest studies. For example, the pretest is often used in an ANCOVA as a covariate. This adjusts the resulting model means by the initial pretest levels. ANCOVA improves over ANOVA by reducing the MS_{within} or MSerror. An estimate of the improvement can be made by running a regular ANOVA and then adjusting the MS_{within} by the squared bivariate correlation between the covariate and the outcome:

$$MS_{remaining} = MS_{within} (1 - r_{xy}^2)$$

Technically, you need to adjust this for the error degrees of freedom:

$$MS_{remaining} = MS_{within} (1 - r_{xy}^2) [1 + 1/(df - 2)]$$

However, if you have an $N > = 50$, this adjustment will not make a practical difference.

Although we have discussed not having too many variables in a regression with a small sample, covariates can help with small ANOVA group sizes because of the reduction in error. How many covariates should we have at most? There is a fairly straightforward formula that can be used to provide an estimate:

$$\frac{(C + J - 1)}{N} < .10$$

where C = number of covariates
  J = number of groups
  N = total number of subjects

So with $J = 3$ and $N = 60$, $C < 4$. We would limit the number of covariates to three or less. How do we choose covariates?

1. They must not occur after or be affected by the treatment.
2. They must be linearly associated with the criterion (outcome).
3. They should make conceptual sense—we should pick them prior to analysis, not after "fishing."
4. If we have more than one covariate, they should not be heavily correlated with each other.
5. The covariates should be accurately measured.

Before you happily proceed to the use of ANCOVA be forewarned that the cautions associated with ANCOVA are many:

1. Covariates cannot completely control for factors as well as random assignment can. Sometimes controlling for one factor can make groups unequal on another unknown factor. Remember that spurious causality is completely ruled out only when there is random assignment.

2. Because the model adjusts the outcome so that groups are equal on covariates, it may not be a good model of reality.

3. Assumptions of linearity and homogeneity of regression slopes can be hard to satisfy.

4. Growth/change in groups may be differential (see Bryk & Weisberg, 1977, for more on options to deal with this).

5. Measurement error in a covariate can mask or alter the effect of the groups (see Huitema, 1980, for more on this).

This sounds like those ominous caution lists associated with new drugs advertised on television, doesn't it? So why use it? Because sometimes it's the best option available, given a particular study design. You just need to understand its limitations and interpret your results accordingly. There are alternatives such as the Johnson-Neyman procedure, but as yet these are not integrated as separate procedures in SAS or SPSS and require a special module (Alonzo, 2004).

SECTION 14.4.1: SAS, SPSS, AND ANCOVA DESCRIPTIVES

First we check for linear relationships between the dependent variable and the covariate(s) using PROC GLPOT in SAS or the "Scatterplot" pull-down option in the SPSS graphics menu. Then we sort the data by the groups so you can look at normality and homogeneity of variance assumptions (PROC UNIVARIATE in SAS or ANALYZE ⇒ DESCRIPTIVE STATISTICS ⇒ EXPLORE . . . in SPSS).

Now, we are ready to build the model using Yuan's data.

SAS AND ANCOVA

The SAS commands will look like Figure 14.9.

SPSS AND ANCOVA

Go to Analyze ⇒ General Linear Model ⇒ Univariate . . . ⇒ specify POSTA under "Dependent Variable" ⇒ specify CBT under "Fixed Factor(s)" ⇒ specify PREA under "Covariate(s)" ⇒ click on "Model . . . ," ⇒ select "Custom" under "Specify model," ⇒ build the terms "CBT PREA PREA*CBT" under "Model:" ⇒ click "Continue" ⇒ click "OK"

Let's look at an ANCOVA research question involving a pre- and a posttest design. Yuan is interested in whether or not a cognitive behavioral intervention (CBT) affects scores on a measure of avoidance of conflict. Because we have not randomly assigned participants, we want to control for some possible differences

FIGURE 14.9. Yuan's Data in SAS.

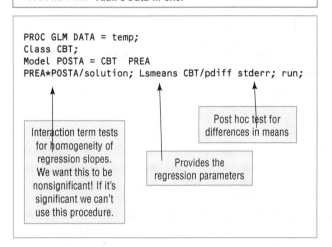

between groups. In this simplest case, we control only for the pretest avoidance scores:

- *Research question:* "Is there a difference in mean scores of avoidance scale posttests for subjects receiving CBT compared to subjects not receiving CBT controlling for pretest scores?"

- *Null hypothesis:* There is no difference in scores between groups.

- *Alternate hypothesis:* There is a difference in scores between groups.

Figure 14.10 shows an example of a plot checking for linear relationship (only the SAS plot is displayed).

FIGURE 14.10. SAS Plot Checking for a Linear Relationship.

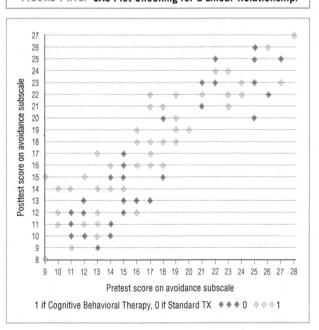

Then we print out the means procedure to look at our variance for groups (Figure 14.11).

Finally we have our SAS and the SPSS model output. Much of this has the same interpretation process as the factorial ANOVA output. We run the model this way first to make sure our interaction term is not significant. If it is, we can't use the ANCOVA. If it's not, we should rerun without so we do not inflate our degrees of freedom (Figure 14.12).

In SPSS, the ANOVA table and the type III sum of squares information for the variables are all in one table, so you may have to look back and forth a couple of times to find all the same numbers. The main thing we are interested in initially is the interaction term significance. This is at the bottom of the SAS output and about midway down the table in the SPSS output (Figure 14.13).

With a *p* value of .568, we see that it is not significant, and thus we can interpret the ANCOVA. We rerun the model without the interaction so that we have the correct degrees of freedom. The SAS output is shown in Figure 14.14 and the SPSS in Figure 14.15.

Once again, the default output from the two analysis programs differs, but the practical results of interest for us are the same. One of the differences is that SPSS prints out the full output for the intercept, while SAS includes the intercept only in the parameter estimate table. In both cases, the programs output the *F* table first, followed by estimates for the parameters. CBT=1 is held constant in the model. All have a pretest score, so this will function as a slope estimate (in regression lingo).

Recall that we said this was a hybrid of ANOVA and regression. The regression formula produced by this output is shown in Figure 14.16.

Last but not least, we have our test for the differences in means after controlling for the covariate. SAS is shown in Figure 14.17 then SPSS in Figure 14.18.

In SAS, the means and the significance test are in a single table. In SPSS, the means are printed out in one table, and the results of the significance test are in the second. So, viola—the difference is significant between treatment groups adjusting for the

FIGURE 14.11. Means Procedure.

```
1 IF COGNITIVE BEHAVIORAL THERAPY, 0 IF STANDARD TX=0 ---

                           The MEANS Procedure

        Variable          Mean          STD Dev         Variance        N
        PREA           16.7547170      4.9142871      24.1502177        53
        POSTA          16.4339623      4.9904117      24.9042090        53
- 1 IF COGNITIVE BEHAVIORAL THERAPY, 0 IF STANDARD TX=1 -
        Variable          Mean          STD Dev         Variance        N
        PREA           16.7500000      4.9621113      24.6225490        52
        POSTA          17.3076923      4.7918986      22.9622926        52
```

FIGURE 14.12. Checking for Significant Interaction with SAS.

```
                           The GLM Procedure

Dependent Variable: POSTA POSTTEST score on AVOIDANCE subscale

                               Sum of
Source              DF         Squares        Mean Square      F Value     Pr > F
Model               3        1990.375617      663.458539       135.17      <.0001
Error              101         495.757716       4.908492
Corrected Total    104        2486.133333

     R-Square     Coeff Var     Root MSE       POSTA Mean
     0.800591     13.13545      2.215512       16.86667

Source              DF       Type III SS       Mean Square      F Value     Pr > F
cbt                 1          6.142914          6.142914         1.25      0.2659
PREA                1       1968.725436       1968.725436       401.09      <.0001
PREA*cbt            1          1.609889          1.609889         0.33      0.5681
```

FIGURE 14.13. **Checking for Significant Interaction with SPSS Output.**

Tests of Between-Subjects Effects

Dependent Variable: POSTTEST score on AVOIDANCE subscale

Source	Type III Sum of Squares	df	Mean Square	F	Sig.
Corrected Model	1990.376(a)	3	663.459	135.165	.000
Intercept	34.280	1	34.280	6.984	.010
Cbt	6.143	1	6.143	1.251	.266
PREA	1968.725	1	1968.725	401.086	.000
cbt * PREA	1.610	1	1.610	.328	.568
Error	495.758	101	4.908		
Total	32357.000	105			
Corrected Total	2486.133	104			

a R Squared = .801 (Adjusted R Squared = .795)

FIGURE 14.14. **SAS Output without Interaction.**

```
Dependent Variable:      POSTA POSTTEST score on AVOIDANCE subscale

Source              DF            Sum of Squares      Mean Square      F Value      Pr > F

Model                2              1988.765728        994.382864       203.93       <.0001
Error              102               497.367605          4.876153
Corrected Total    104              2486.133333

R-Square        Coeff Var        Root MSE         POSTA Mean
0.799943        13.09210         2.208201         16.86667

Source              DF            Type III SS         Mean Square      F Value      Pr > F

cbt                  1                20.229545          20.229545        4.15       0.0443
PREA                 1              1968.728186        1968.728186      403.75       <.0001

                                                   Standard
Parameter                       Estimate             Error          t Value      Pr > |t|

Intercept                 2.477875104 B          0.79904908          3.10        0.0025
cbt        0             -0.877906280 B          0.43101636         -2.04        0.0443
cbt        1              0.000000000 B               .                .            .
PREA                      0.885362221            0.04406226         20.09        <.0001
```

pretest values ($p = .044$). The mean for the treatment group improved (which is good). Of course, it is up to your knowledge of the scale used to assess the outcome to determine whether the statistically significant result has practical significance for the individuals treated. In other words, you need to decide if the difference between groups (16.43 versus 17.31) is practically meaningful in terms of people's day-to-day lives.

There are many more advanced topics one could learn related to regression and ANOVA, but these extend beyond the scope of the present text. Instead we return our attention to dealing with categorical outcomes (dependent variables). Why? Because we often have interests in such issues as whether a person dies, or if a family moves off income maintenance, or whether someone enters a hospital. These are not scale scores or continuous variables, so we need different tools.

FIGURE 14.15. SPSS ANCOVA Output Without INTERACTION.

Tests of Between-Subjects Effects

Dependent Variable: POSTTEST score on AVOIDANCE subscale

Source	Type III Sum of Squares	df	Mean Square	F	Sig.	Partial Eta Squared	Noncent. Parameter	Observed Power(a)
Corrected Model	1988.766(b)	2	994.383	203.928	.000	.800	407.855	1.000
Intercept	34.282	1	34.282	7.031	.009	.064	7.031	.747
PREA	1968.728	1	1968.728	403.746	.000	.798	403.746	1.000
Cbt	20.230	1	20.230	4.149	.044	.039	4.149	.523
Error	497.368	102	4.876					
Total	32357.000	105						
Corrected Total	2486.133	104						

a Computed using alpha = .05
b R Squared = .800 (Adjusted R Squared = .796)

Parameter Estimates

Dependent Variable: POSTTEST score on AVOIDANCE subscale

Parameter	B	Std. Error	t	Sig.	95% Confidence Interval	
					Lower Bound	Upper Bound
Intercept	2.478	.799	3.101	.002	.893	4.063
PREA	.885	.044	20.093	.000	.798	.973
[cbt=0]	−.878	.431	−2.037	.044	−1.733	−.023
[cbt=1]	0(a)	.	.	.	.	.

a This parameter is set to zero because it is redundant.

FIGURE 14.16. Regression for ANCOVA Results.

```
    Regression slope b = .88536
    Intercept 1   = 2.47767 + ( .87790)
    Intercept 2   = 2.47767 + 0
When CBT=0:
Y= 2.47767 +( .8779) +.88536x

When CBT=1:
Y= 2.47767 +.88536x
```

FIGURE 14.17. SAS Output for ANCOVA Results.

```
        The GLM Procedure
        Least Squares Means

                                    H0:LSMean=1
          POSTA      Standard   H0:LSMEAN=0  LSMean2
    cbt   LSMEAN     Error      Pr > |t|     Pr > |t|
    0     16.4318940 0.3033198  <.0001       0.0443
    1     17.3098003 0.3062224  <.0001
```

SECTION 14.5

INTRODUCTION TO ADVANCED CATEGORICAL ANALYSES

One of the more commonly used methods in social science is a logistic regression approach to the multivariate analysis of categorical outcomes. Before we look at logistic regression, however, we will return briefly to the chi-square and introduce some more advanced techniques related to assessing magnitude (how strong an association is) and nested or confounding effects (associations of two variables, controlling for a third).

You'll recall that we learned that variations of the chi-square statistic were useful for testing associations between nominal variables, between nominal and ordinal variables, and between two ordinal variables when the ordinal categories are too limited to use a Spearman correlation. Now we will learn about two more related techniques, the request for an odds ratio to measure the magnitude of the association and the use of the Mantel-Haenszel test for the association of two variables while controlling for a third (also known as stratified analysis). These concepts are useful foundations to cover prior to moving on to logistic regression.

FIGURE 14.18. SPSS Output for ANCOVA Test of Difference in Means.

Estimates

Dependent Variable: POSTTEST score on AVOIDANCE subscale

1 IF COGNITIVE BEHAVIORAL THERAPY, 0 IF STANDARD TX	Mean	Std. Error	95% Confidence Interval	
			Lower Bound	Upper Bound
0	16.432(a)	.303	15.830	17.034
1	17.310(a)	.306	16.702	17.917

a Covariates appearing in the model are evaluated at the following values: PRETEST score on AVOIDANCE subscale = 16.75.

Dependent Variable: POSTTEST score on AVOIDANCE subscale

(I) 1 IF COGNITIVE BEHAVIORAL THERAPY, 0 IF STANDARD TX	(J) 1 IF COGNITIVE BEHAVIORAL THERAPY, 0 IF STANDARD TX	Mean Difference (I−J)	Std. Error	Sig.(a)	95% Confidence Interval for Difference(a)	
					Lower Bound	Upper Bound
0	1	−.878(*)	.431	.044	−1.733	−.023
1	0	.878(*)	.431	.044	.023	1.733

Based on estimated marginal means.
* The mean difference is significant at the .05 level.
a Adjustment for multiple comparisons: Least Significant Difference (equivalent to no adjustments).

SECTION 14.5.1: CONTROLLING FOR OTHER FACTORS IN CHI-SQUARE

So we know how to use chi-square to test the association between two variables. What happens when we want to stratify by a third variable or control for a third variable? Eventually this will lead us to a multivariate model, but first it is helpful to know that there is an intermediate ability to test sets of tables using the Mantel-Haenszel test.

Suppose you are interested in whether receiving a group intervention was associated with increasing savings, but the study was conducted in two different communities. What if the association of interest varies by community? We can represent this by two cross-tabulation tables (Table 14.1). We want to know if the relationship between the intervention and savings is the same in Community 1 as it is in Community 2.

This is similar to the idea behind adding the block group in a two-way ANOVA. The Mantel-Haenszel test is a type of chi-square also known as the average partial association statistic. This test helps answer the question:

- *Research question:* "Does the association between the intervention and savings hold controlling for the community location?"
- *Null hypothesis:* There is no association between the intervention and savings when controlling for community location.

TABLE 14.1. Cross-Tabulation Tables.

	SAVINGS	NO SAVINGS
Community 1		
Group intervention	A_1	B_1
No intervention	C_1	D_1
	SAVINGS	NO SAVINGS
Community 2		
Group intervention	A_2	B_2
No intervention	C_2	D_2

Assumptions include:

1. Independence of observations in each cell
2. Nominal or limited ordinal categories
3. When rows are totaled, an *n* size of at least 30

Let's use an example data set. Here we are interested in who is receiving counseling in a school sample. Our research question is: Is gender associated with receipt of counseling when controlling for a referral for academic problems?

SAS AND ANALYZING SETS OF TABLES

To do this in SAS, we extend our use of the PROC FREQ; Tables command to make a three-way request with the first variable being the stratification variable (Figure 14.19).

Now let's examine portions of the SAS output (Figure 14.20). First, we see that SAS gives us a 2 × 2 table for each level of the first variable in the procedure statement. (Always be sure that the first variable is the right one given your question.) This time we will look at the CMH chi-square underneath each table rather than the Pearson chi-square (not shown to con-

serve space). It is possible for both tables to have significant associations, only one to be significant, or neither to be significant.

In the SAS output in Figure 14.20, we find two sets of cross-tabulations, one for gender and counseling when there is no referral for academic reasons and one for gender and counseling when there is a referral for academic reasons. After this, one finds a set of summary statistics. We look for the value of the CMH that tells us if our association is significant while controlling for the third factor. Any of the stats in this table will tell us the same thing when we have just a 2 × 2 table. The general

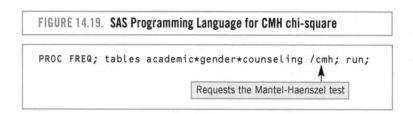

FIGURE 14.19. **SAS Programming Language for CMH chi-square**

```
PROC FREQ; tables academic*gender*counseling /cmh; run;
```
                                                    ↑
                                          Requests the Mantel-Haenszel test

---

FIGURE 14.20. **SAS Output.**

```
                        The FREQ Procedure
                     Table 1 of female by couns
                       Controlling for acad=0
female(1=female;)
couns(1=provided direct counseling to student;)
Frequency,
Percent    ,
Row Pct    ,
Col Pct    ,        0 ,        1 , Total
*********^*********^*********^
       0 ,      441 ,      418 ,      859
         ,    24.18 ,    22.92 ,    47.09
         ,    51.34 ,    48.66 ,
         ,    51.70 ,    43.05 ,
*********^*********^*********^
       1 ,      412 ,      553 ,      965
         ,    22.59 ,    30.32 ,    52.91
         ,    42.69 ,    57.31 ,
         ,    48.30 ,    56.95 ,
*********^*********^*********^
Total           853        971       1824
               46.77      53.23     100.00

         Frequency Missing = 46


                     Table 2 of female by couns
                       Controlling for acad=1
female(1=female;)
couns(1=provided direct counseling to student;)
 Frequency,
 Percent   ,
 Row Pct   ,
 Col Pct   ,       0,        1,  Total
```

```
*********^*********^********^
    0 ,    161 ,    189 ,   350
       ,  25.04 ,  29.39 , 54.43
       ,  46.00 ,  54.00 ,
       ,  62.89 ,  48.84 ,
*********^*********^********^
    1 ,     95 ,    198 ,   293
       ,  14.77 ,  30.79 , 45.57
       ,  32.42 ,  67.58 ,
       ,  37.11 ,  51.16 ,
*********^*********^********^
Total      256       387       643
           39.81     60.19    100.00


           Frequency Missing = 8
```

                      Summary Statistics for female by couns
                             Controlling for acad

              Cochran–Mantel–Haenszel Statistics (Based on Table Scores)

Statistic	Alternative Hypothesis	DF	Value	Prob
1	Nonzero Correlation	1	24.5154	<.0001
2	Row Mean Scores Differ	1	24.5154	<.0001
3	General Association	1	24.5154	<.0001

              Estimates of the Common Relative Risk (Row1/Row2)

Type of Study	Method	Value	95% Confidence	Limits
Case–Control	Mantel–Haenszel	1.4981	1.2763	1.7585
(Odds Ratio)	Logit	1.4975	1.2756	1.7580
Cohort	Mantel–Haenszel	1.2480	1.1426	1.3631
(Col1 Risk)	Logit	1.2414	1.1368	1.3555
Cohort	Mantel–Haenszel	0.8345	0.7765	0.8969
(Col2 Risk)	Logit	0.8323	0.7747	0.8943

                         Breslow–Day Test for
                    Homogeneity of the Odds Ratios
                 ****
                    Chi-Square   1.4225
                    DF   1
                    Pr > ChiSq   0.2330

                 Effective Sample Size = 2467
                 Frequency Missing = 54

association (in bold) is the CMH chi-square of interest for this type of analysis. We will discuss the remainder of the output a little further on in this section.

SPSS AND ANALYZING SETS OF TABLES

Go to Analyze ⇒ Descriptive Statistics ⇒ Crosstabs . . . , ⇒ specify the variable "gender" for the "Row(s)," the variable "counseling" for the "Column(s)," and the control variable "academic" under "Layer 1 of 1"⇒ click on "Statistics . . ." ⇒select "Risk" and "Cochran's and Mantel-Haenszel statistics"⇒click on "Continue"⇒click on "Continue"⇒click "OK"

SPSS output is shown in Figure 14.21.

Unless you request a chi-square statistic, the cross-tabulation table in SPSS will be only frequencies. As we did with our SAS output, we will skip some of the SPSS output for now. The final table in the output contains the significance tests of interest. SPSS uses a slightly different formulation that accounts for the difference in values between the "general association" value in SAS and the Mantel-Haenszel value in SPSS. The practical meaning, however, should be identical. In our case, it is significant. Gender is associated with receipt of

---

FIGURE 14.21. SPSS Output.

Case Processing Summary

	Cases					
	Valid		Missing		Total	
	N	Percent	N	Percent	N	Percent
1=female; * 1=provided direct counseling to student; * 1=referral for academic problems;	2467	97.9%	54	2.1%	2521	100.0%

1=female; * 1=provided direct counseling to student; * 1=referral for academic problems; Cross-tabulation

Count

1=referral for academic problems;			1=provided direct counseling to student;		Total
			0	1	
0	1=female;	0	441	418	859
		1	412	553	965
	Total		853	971	1824
1	1=female;	0	161	189	350
		1	95	198	293
	Total		256	387	643

Risk Estimate

1=referral for academic problems;	Value		95% Confidence Interval	
			Lower	Upper
0	Odds Ratio for 1=female; (0 / 1)	1.416	1.177	1.704
	For cohort 1=provided direct counseling to student; = 0	1.202	1.090	1.326
	For cohort 1=provided direct counseling to student; = 1	.849	.778	.927
	N of Valid Cases	1824		
1	Odds Ratio for 1=female; (0 / 1)	1.775	1.286	2.451
	For cohort 1=provided direct counseling to student; = 0	1.419	1.161	1.734
	For cohort 1=provided direct counseling to student; = 1	.799	.705	.906
	N of Valid Cases	643		

Tests of Homogeneity of the Odds Ratio

	Chi-Squared	df	Asymp. Sig. (2-sided)
Breslow-Day	1.422	1	.233
Tarone's	1.422	1	.233

Mantel-Haenszel Common Odds Ratio Estimate

Estimate			1.498
ln(Estimate)			.404
Std. Error of ln(Estimate)			.082
Asymp. Sig. (2-sided)			.000
Asymp. 95% Confidence Interval	Common Odds Ratio	Lower Bound	1.276
		Upper Bound	1.758
	ln(Common Odds Ratio)	Lower Bound	.244
		Upper Bound	.564

NOTE: The Mantel-Haenszel common odds ratio estimate is asymptotically normally distributed under the common odds ratio of 1.000 assumption. So is the natural log of the estimate.

Tests of Conditional Independence

	Chi-Squared	df	Asymp. Sig. (2-sided)
Cochran's	24.535	1	.000
Mantel-Haenszel	24.115	1	.000

Note: Under the conditional independence assumption, Cochran's statistic is asymptotically distributed as a 1 df chi-squared distribution, only if the number of strata is fixed, while the Mantel-Haenszel statistic is always asymptotically distributed as a 1 df chi-squared distribution. Note that the continuity correction is removed from the Mantel-Haenszel statistic when the sum of the differences between the observed and the expected is 0.

counseling when controlling for having been referred for academic problems.

"Aha!," you say, but what are those odds ratios and a relative risk measures in the output? Why do I care about them?

SECTION 14.5.2: THE ODDS RATIO

The **odds ratio** is one of the measures of risk frequently used in epidemiological research and is also a widely used method of reporting the results for coefficients in a logistic regression model. Pretend you are interested in understanding something about the occurrence of homelessness, which we will call H. You are interested in whether or not a risk factor such as history of substance abuse (S) is associated with a higher or lower rate of homelessness. Let's say we measure each at a nominal or "yes/no" level.

We might notate this relationship by the following probability statements:

- $Pr(H|S)$ =The probability of homelessness with a substance abuse history
- $Pr(H$ not $S)$ = The probability of homelessness without a history of substance abuse

The odds of an event are calculated as the number of events divided by the number of nonevents. If, for example, on average 100 men are homeless per 5,000 men total, the odds of any randomly chosen man becoming homeless would be expressed as:

$$\frac{\text{Number of homeless 100}}{\text{Number of not-homeless 4,900, or about .02}}$$

If the odds of an event are greater than one, the event is more likely to happen than not (the odds of an event that is certain to happen are infinite); if the odds are less than one, the chances are that the event won't happen (the odds of an impossible event are zero).

An odds ratio is the odds of homelessness for group 1 (substance abuse history) divided by the odds of homelessness for group 2 (no substance abuse history). So, if we had an odds ratio of 1.50, then we would say that there is about a 50% increase in the odds of homelessness for the group with a substance abuse history compared to the group without. In a cross-tabulation of two variables, the odds ratio is the cross-product (Table 14.2).

Odds Ratio Compared to Relative Risk. A **relative risk** is simply a relative incidence. For example, it is the

TABLE 14.2. **An Odds Ratio.**

	HOMELESS	NOT HOMELESS	PROPORTION YES
No substance abuse	A = percent	B = percent	$P_1 = a/a+b$
Substance abuse	C = percent	D = percent	$P_2 = c/c+d$

Odds ratio = $a*d/c*b = (a/b)/(c/d)$

incidence or number of new cases of homelessness in a group of individuals exposed to a factor, compared to the incidence of homelessness in a group of individuals not exposed to the factor. If the relative risk is two, it means that the condition occurs twice as often in those exposed to the factor than it does in those not exposed to the factor.

$$\text{Relative risk} = \frac{P1}{P2} \text{ or RR=odds ratio*} \left[\frac{1+(c/d)}{1+(a/b)}\right]$$

The relative risk is a more intuitive measure, but it cannot be used in case control or cross-sectional studies. In most cases, the odds ratio is essentially equivalent to a relative risk if the outcome of interest is rare (see "Relative Risk," Wikipedia for easy to read discussion). When the outcome is not rare, the odds ratio will overestimate the relative risk.

To return to our CMH output: SAS and SPSS will also print out odds ratios and relative risk, but they provide only one overall measure. This makes sense in a way because our research question is really related to the overall relationship between gender and counseling when controlling for the academic problem referral. Because of the fact that it is an overall measure, the odds ratios related to the individual sets of tables must be homogeneous to be able to use the OR or RR from this analysis. What do we mean by homogeneous? If the relationships are very different in direction or magnitude between gender and counseling for each level of academic problem the overall OR won't be a very accurate description of the relationship. How do we know? That's what the Breslow-Day or Breslow-Day-Tarone statistic tells us. By now you should be getting used to the idea that these tests of whether assumptions can be met generally assume the positive. In other words, the null hypothesis for our test is that the odds ratios for the two sets of tables are homogeneous, so a significant Breslow-Day test is "bad." This means that the overall estimates in the "common relative risk" table are not useful. In our example, our Breslow-Day was not significant, so we can interpret the overall OR of 1.49, and controlling for a referral for academic problems, females are nearly 50% more likely to be receiving counseling than males.

Of course, if our Breslow-Day is significant, all is not lost. We can go back to our individual tables and request an odds ratio to go along with a regular chi-square. Here is the language for requesting the appropriate statistic in SAS and SPSS.

SAS AND SIMPLE ODDS RATIOS

```
    PROC FREQ data=temp;
    tables gender*counseling / chisq measures; run;
```

```
    "measures" requests various measures of
    association , including the OR and RR.
```

SPSS AND SIMPLE ODDS RATIOS

Go to Analyze ⟹ Descriptive Statistics ⟹ Crosstabs . . . , ⟹ specify the variable "gender" for the "Row(s)," the variable "counseling" for the "Column(s)⟹ click on "Statistics . . ." and select "Chi-square" and "Risk"⟹ click on "Continue"⟹ click on "Cells . . . ," ⟹ under "Percentages," check "Row," "Column" and "Total" ⟹ click on "Continue"⟹ click "OK"

In both cases the programs will output a cross-tabulation with chi-square statistics just like we learned in the prior chapter. SAS will then print out a variety of forms of correlations that we will ignore here so they are not displayed (Figure 14.22). Finally it will print out the "Estimates of Relative Risk" table that contains our statistics of interest. SPSS does not include the correlation output table unless requested (Figure 14.23).

Of course, as with other statistics we have learned about (post hoc tests for ANOVA, parameter estimates in regression), if the initial overall test is not significant (in this case our Pearson chi-square), we don't go on to interpret magnitude. So, if there is no association as measured by the chi-square, then one does not go on to look at the odds ratio or relative risk. In the SAS and SPSS output in Figures 14.22 and 14.23, we see our test is significant, and the odds ratio is pretty close to the one we found in our CMH test (1.47 compared to 1.49 previously). You will note there is a confidence interval as well. Any time the confidence interval for an odds ratio spans the number 1, the odds ratio is not significant. In other words, if the confidence interval in our data were .999 to 1.723, then we would not attempt to interpret the odds ratio (although SAS and SPSS will still provide the OR). This is because the OR is not stable. We cannot be 95% certain that if we reran the statistic the OR would be different from 1.00. The outcome is not terribly rare, so the odds ratio is greater in magnitude than the relative risk.

We now know how to control for one other nominal variable while looking at a two-nominal variable association. We have also learned a new way to assess the magnitude and direction of a categorical association. Frequently, however, we want to go beyond that and ask how a number of variables are associated with a categorical outcome. The most common technique seen in the social science literature to accomplish this is logistic regression.

SECTION 14.6

LOGISTIC REGRESSION

Most multivariate statistics like linear relationships with parametric assumptions. Often, however, we just don't have those kinds of outcome variables. We may study whether a child is reported again to child welfare (yes/no) or whether an adult relapses after treatment

FIGURE 14.22. **SAS Output.**

```
Table of female by couns
                    female(1=female;)
                             couns(1=provided direct counseling to student;)
                    Frequency,
                    Percent  ,
                    Row Pct  ,
                    Col Pct  ,        0,        1, Total
                    *********^*********^*********^
                        0 ,       602 ,      607 ,     1209
                          ,     24.40 ,    24.60 ,    49.01
                          ,     49.79 ,    50.21 ,
                          ,     54.28 ,    44.70 ,
                    *********^*********^*********^
                        1 ,       507 ,      751 ,     1258
                          ,     20.55 ,    30.44 ,    50.99
                          ,     40.30 ,    59.70 ,
                          ,     45.72 ,    55.30 ,
                    *********^*********^*********^
                    Total       1109        1358        2467
                                44.95       55.05      100.00
                    Frequency Missing = 54
             Statistics for Table of female by couns

    Statistic                    DF            Value        Prob

    ****************************************************************
    Chi-Square                    1          22.4431       <.0001
    Likelihood Ratio Chi-Square   1          22.4729       <.0001
    Continuity Adj. Chi-Square    1          22.0612       <.0001
    Mantel-Haenszel Chi-Square    1          22.4340       <.0001
    Phi Coefficient                          0.0954
    Contingency Coefficient                  0.0949
    Cramer's V                               0.0954

    [NOTE: We deleted the Fisher's Exact table and the table containing the
    correlation statistics from the SAS output to save space.]


          Estimates of the Relative Risk (Row1/Row2)

    Type of Study                Value        95% Confidence Limits

    ****************************************************************
    Case-Control (Odds Ratio)   1.4691         1.2526      1.7229
    Cohort (Col1 Risk)          1.2355         1.1315      1.3490
    Cohort (Col2 Risk)          0.8410         0.7824      0.9040

             Effective Sample Size = 2467
                Frequency Missing = 54
```

(yes/no), or whether someone enters a given service system, and the like. None of these variables fit traditional parametric approaches, and running numerous chi-squares is not a satisfying alternative to multivariate models. We are ready to take the next step in thinking about controlling for multiple variables rather than just one when faced with categorical data. The most common multivariate method used for this is **logistic regression** for a dichotomous outcome.

There are many variations in the use of logistic regression. For example, you can also use this technique to explore multilevel or ordinal outcomes or even models that integrate time into the dependent variable. So, once again, we are touching on only the simplest case of this technique. You are encouraged to review other applied sources to use with SAS and SPSS listed at the end of the chapter. This section draws heavily on Paul Allison's material (see references)

FIGURE 14.23. **SPSS Output.**

1=female; * 1=provided direct counseling to student; Cross-tabulation

			1=provided direct counseling to student;		Total
			0	1	
1=female;	0	Count	602	607	1209
		% within 1=female;	49.8%	50.2%	100.0%
		% within 1=provided direct counseling to student;	54.3%	44.7%	49.0%
		% of Total	24.4%	24.6%	49.0%
	1	Count	507	751	1258
		% within 1=female;	40.3%	59.7%	100.0%
		% within 1=provided direct counseling to student;	45.7%	55.3%	51.0%
		% of Total	20.6%	30.4%	51.0%
Total		Count	1109	1358	2467
		% within 1=female;	45.0%	55.0%	100.0%
		% within 1=provided direct counseling to student;	100.0%	100.0%	100.0%
		% of Total	45.0%	55.0%	100.0%

Chi-Square Tests

	Value	df	Asymp. Sig. (2-sided)	Exact Sig. (2-sided)	Exact Sig. (1-sided)
Pearson Chi-Square	22.443(b)	1	.000		
Continuity Correction(a)	22.061	1	.000		
Likelihood Ratio	22.473	1	.000		
Fisher's Exact Test				.000	.000
Linear-by-Linear Association	22.434	1	.000		
N of Valid Cases	2467				

a Computed only for a 2 × 2 table

b 0 cells (.0%) have expected count less than 5. The minimum expected count is 543.49.

Risk Estimate

	Value	95% Confidence Interval	
		Lower	Upper
Odds Ratio for 1=female; (0 / 1)	1.469	1.253	1.723
For cohort 1=provided direct counseling to student; = 0	1.236	1.132	1.349
For cohort 1=provided direct counseling to student; = 1	.841	.782	.904
N of Valid Cases	2467		

because he does such a good job of presenting statistics in an applied context.

We have learned that nonparametric approaches create alternatives to parametric statistics by doing such things as creating ranked data or expected compared to observed outcomes. These constructed variables allow the computer to approximate parametric models (in an abstract sense). Logistic regression (also

called binary logit analysis) does this by taking the logarithm of the odds of something in your data. This removes the lower bound of zero that we have when we calculate odds. We move from discussing the odds ratio to talking about a relative of the odds ratio, the logit. The logit is the statistic used in the multivariate technique of logistic regression and is expressed on a logarithmic scale. Because some people find it helpful to see how things are related, the log of the odds ratio can be written as the difference between two logits:

$$\log(OR) = \log[p1/(1-p1)] - \log[p2/(1-p2)]$$

More advanced students and researchers will of course note that the "logit" function is not the only way of specifying a multivariate binary response model (e.g., functions like probit or loglog). Given the introductory nature of this chapter, however, we will discuss only the logit function. The references at the close of the chapter include more detail. A nice summary of similarities and differences between SPSS and SAS done by Dr. I Ibrahim can be found online (www.ats.ucla.edu/stat/mult_pkg/library/CompBinary.doc):

- *Research question:* "Are variables *X*, *Y*, and *Z* associated with a greater likelihood of event *A*?"

- *Null hypothesis:* There is no association between variables *X*, *Y*, and *Z* and event *A*.

- *Alternative hypothesis:* At least one of the variables is associated with A.

Assumptions for logistic regression include:

- There must be independence of observations.

- There must be a nominal (binary logistic regression) or ordinal (multinomial logistic regression) outcome variable.

- Approximately 25 observations per variable are entered into the model. For aggregate model fit statistics:

  - 80% of the predicted values must be at least 5.

  - All others must be greater than 2.

- Independent variables are associated with but do not perfectly predict a 0 or 1 for the outcome variable.

- There is no problematic multicollinearity.

You can use categorical or continuous predictors. We can write the formula equation for logistic regression in much the same way we did when we introduced multivariate linear regression, $y = a + bx$, except that now this formula is modeling an outcome on a different scale: log

$[p/1 - p]$. This outcome variable is called the logit or log-odds. Probably few people on this planet think easily on a logarithmic scale, but if we exponentiate the parameters produced by this model, we get our friend, the odds ratio. This is what is typically reported.

So, we know that the model for our logistic regression looks similar to the one for multivariate regression, but wait ... the intercept can't be the same because it's not a line this time. So rather than a point for starting the line, the intercept α is equal to the log-odds of the outcome of interest when all the other parameters (β = parameter estimate) are set to 0. You'll recall from multiplication that anything times 0 is 0. For example, if we want to know how gender and referral for maltreatment relate to the probability of delinquency, we could write this out like this:

$\beta1 = 1$ when a child was female and 0 when a child was male

$\beta2 = 1$ when a child is referred for maltreatment and 0 when a child is not referred for maltreatment

When the parameter estimates $\beta1$ and $\beta2$ are set to 0, then the value of α is the probability of delinquency for males not referred for maltreatment. Your values for the coefficients can be expressed as the logit model, a probability of delinquency or the odds of delinquency (see Table 14.3).

Table 14.3 illustrates how you can develop a predicted value for various types of subjects in your data (format taken from Table 8.2, Stokes, Davis, & Koch, 2000, p 186).

In the model output, any variable coded as a binary variable means that the odds ratio for that variable is the odds ratio when the variable equals 1. The value of the odds ratio provided for the variable is compared to a value of 1.00 when the variable equals 0. So in our example, if females (gender = 1) had an odds ratio of 2.00 in the model, then that is compared to a value of 1.00 for males (gender = 0). For a multilevel categorical variable such as race, the common practice is to dummy code each value of that variable, then leave the one out you wish to use as a comparison. For example, if you have African Americans, Caucasians, and Other, and you want to compare minority populations to Caucasians,

---

TABLE 14.3. Values for Coefficients Expressed as the Logit Model.

GENDER	MALTREATMENT REFERRAL	LOGIT	Pr(DELINQUENCY)	ODDS OF DELINQUENCY
Females	No	$\alpha + \beta1$	$e^{\alpha + \beta1}/(1 + e^{\alpha + \beta1})$	$e^{\alpha + \beta1}$
Females	Yes	$\alpha + \beta1 + \beta2$	$e^{\alpha + \beta1 + \beta2}/(1 + e^{\alpha + \beta1 + \beta2})$	$e^{\alpha + \beta1 + \beta2}$
Males	No	α	$e^{\alpha}/(1 + e^{\alpha})$	e^{α}
Males	Yes	$\alpha + \beta2$	$e^{\alpha + \beta2}/(1 + e^{\alpha + \beta2})$	$e^{\alpha + \beta2}$

then you would enter African American (0/1) and Other (0/1) in the model and leave the variable Caucasian out. This means that the odds ratio for African American is comparing to Caucasians and the odds ratio for Other is comparing to Caucasians.

Logistic regression can also accommodate continuous variables and interaction terms. An odds ratio of 1.02 for a continuous variable such as age is essentially a 2% increase in the odds of the outcome per year of age. To interpret an interaction term between two dichotomous variables, one must keep in mind the multiplication issue. An interaction term between gender and race would be providing an odds ratio when those two variables both are equal to 1. In order to enter an interaction term in the model, both of the main effects must also be there (even if one is not significant). Why? Because it is part of the underlying formula; it makes sense that to have 1*1 both ones must be in the model:

$$\log[p/1 - p] = \alpha + \beta1 + \beta2 + \beta1 * \beta2$$

Maximum likelihood is the typical method used to estimate the logit model for individual level data (Allison, 2001). This method attempts to develop a solution that produces parameters that are closest to what we have observed. In other words, it tries to minimize the difference between the observed and expected values. This iterative process seeks the best possible model out of several options rather than a sole solution. If the analysis program finds one it likes, we call this "convergence."

It's possible to have a model that does not converge—the iterations (attempts to build a model) do not improve over time. This often occurs when there are separation problems related to the association between the independent and dependent variables. No, this is not separation, as in attachment theory. If you have "complete separation"—every observation in your data has exactly one value (either 1 or 0)—then there is no maximum likelihood estimate because there is a perfect association. For example, let's take a simple case where our outcome is incarceration = 1 or not = 0, and gender is our predictor. Being female cannot be associated with incarceration likelihood because it never happens (see Table 14.4).

The computer program, therefore, cannot develop a model where females have a probability of incarceration or males have a probability of no incarceration.

TABLE 14.4. Incarceration Predicted by Gender.

	INCARCERATION	NO INCARCERATION
Female	0	100
Male	100	0

Quasi-complete separation is also bad and means that there are one or two observations that could be 0 or 1, but all the rest are completely identified by the independent variable value.

Problems with separation of data are good reasons to run your cross-tabulations for all the variables in the model before you run the logistic regression. If you find a cell size = 0 or 1 in your cross-tabulations, then you have found a problem. You may be able to resolve this by dropping that variable from further analysis. Or, in our preceding example, we might restrict the sample to males because no females had the event of interest. Such means of dealing with these problems, however, should be noted in your methods section and make sense according to your research question. This is another reason to get a firm grasp on available literature while planning your study. If the outcome for a subgroup of interest is particularly rare, then you may need to oversample a group or just go after a particularly large overall sample.

What about multicollinearity? Unfortunately, the similarities noted between the formulas for the logit model compared to multiple regression also hold for problems with multicollinearity. Yes, we still call it this even though the relationship of categorical variables isn't thought of as a line. Unlike procedures for multiple regression, there is no diagnostic test specific to use with logistic regression. However, because collinearity has to do with the independent variables, not the dependent variables, you can use the multiple regression procedure with the VIF TOL options (see the prior section on multiple regression) to diagnose this problem (Allison, 2001). The procedure for dealing with problematic (collinear) variables is the same as discussed in prior sections on regression.

SECTION 14.6.1: SAS AND LOGISTIC REGRESSION

You can obtain a logistic regression model in SAS through more than one procedure command, but we will talk only about PROC LOGISTIC in this text. The first statement is the procedure command. Because SAS will model the binary outcome in ascending order, we want to tell SAS to model the outcome when it equals one so that the results are easy to interpret. We do this by adding the word *descending:*

```
PROC LOGISTIC data=x descending;
```

Next we use a model statement:

```
Model outcome = variable1 variable2 variable3 /
```

The forward slash indicates that you are done entering variables, and you now specify options for the model. Some of these will depend on what type of variables you are using as independent or predictor variables:

- `scale=none aggregate:` You can use this option to obtain one type of model fit *if* your independent variables are all categorical or nominal. This restriction is because this option groups the data (or aggregates it) into profiles. This provides you with a Pearson and deviance chi-square. Nonsignificant values for these tests are what you want—particularly over .20. The word *none* can be replaced by Pearson to adjust for problems in the data—we will discuss this later on.

- `LACKFIT:` With continuous variables or very rare events, the standard approach is to request the Hosmer-Lemeshow statistic. This is also a test that you want not to be significant, but it has significant critiques (Kuss, 2005).

- `PLCL` or `clparm=CL:` This provides adjusted confidence intervals for parameter estimates when samples are not large.

- `PLRL` or `CLODDS=PL:` These request the confidence intervals for odds ratios that adjust for smaller samples.

- `PLRL Units variable name = increment:` This additional subcommand lets you create odds ratios specific to various increments (for example, years of life or dollars) of a continuous predictor variable.

- `RSQ:` This is one measure of predictive power frequently referred to as the pseudo *r*-square. It is still not entirely accepted: $R^2 = 1 - \exp[-L^2/n]$. The max rescaled R^2 is provided to fix the upper bound of the regular measure so that it goes all the way to one (see Generalized Coefficient of Determination, SAS, 2003).

- Other predictive measures. You can also request options to look at the sensitivity and specificity according to a set probability level or request the receiver operating curve. We'll look at these options after we discuss the primary aspects of a logistic regression output.

First, we will take a simple case using Yuan's data and only nominal variables:

- *Research question:* Is domestic violence recidivism associated with type of treatment and marital status?

```
PROC LOGISTIC data=Yuan descending;
Model recid=cbt married /scale=none aggregate
rsq; run;
```

SAS output (Figure 14.24) will provide information on the sample size used in the analysis, which is the "used" compared to the "read." If they differ, it is because you had missing values in one of your variables. The "probability modeled" statement lets you know if the

results are related to the 1 or 0 value of your dependent variable. Next, SAS prints out the Pearson and deviance goodness-of-fit tests that we want to be nonsignificant. Most people rely on the Pearson statistic (see Hosmer, Hosmer, Cessie, & Lemeshow, 1997, for discussion). This is followed by the requested pseudo *r*-square and model chi-square statistics that we want to be significant. The most commonly reported statistic is the −2 log likelihood chi-square. (This is the only model chi-square reported by SPSS.) The practical meaning of this statistic is much like the *F* test in regression or ANOVA. It just tells us that at least one of our independent variables was significant enough to make the model worthwhile to look at. Finally, the parameter estimates, odds ratios, and some additional model statistics (we will discuss later) are printed.

SECTION 14.6.2: SPSS AND LOGISTIC REGRESSION

In SPSS (output shown in Figure 14.25) one of the differences is that only the Hosmer-Lemeshow statistic is available for assessing model fit in the checkbox menus for binary logistic regression:

> Go to Analyze ⇒ Regression ⇒ Binary Logistic . . . ⇒specify your dependent variable "recid" under "Dependent:" and the predictor variables "cbt" and "married" under "Covariates:" ⇒click on "Options . . ." ⇒check "Hosmer-Lemeshow . . ." and "CI for exp(B): 95%" ⇒click on "Continue"⇒ click "OK"

In both the SAS and SPSS output, we find a significant −2 LogLikelihood chi-square of 8.79. We look at our goodness-of-fit tests. The Pearson chi-square (SAS) and the Hosmer-Lemeshow (SPSS) are nonsignificant—this is all good. We now can go on to look at the independent variables. Here we find that the treatment model (CBT) is significant but marital status is not. In SAS we find the odds ratio in the point estimate column underneath the parameter information. In SPSS this information is all in one table. As you can see, our confidence interval for "married" spans 1.00 because the parameter is not significant; so persons who received the CBT treatment were slightly over four times less likely to be among those with later recidivism events.

SECTION 14.6.3: SAS AND LOGISTIC REGRESSION WITH CONTINUOUS VARIABLE

Now let's look at a model with a continuous variable. We make some changes to our SAS statement (see below) but in SPSS we just add the variable:

```
PROC LOGISTIC data=Yuan descending;
Model recid=cbt married age /lackfit rsq; run;
```

FIGURE 14.24. SAS Output.

```
          Number of Observations Read        105
          Number of Observations Used        105

                    Response Profile

          Ordered                    Total
          Value        RECID       Frequency
          1              1             22
          2              0             83
```

Probability modeled is RECID=1. ← *Tells you what your model is attempting to predict.*

```
                Model Convergence Status
     Convergence criterion (GCONV=1E-8) satisfied.

     Deviance and Pearson Goodness-of-Fit Statistics

   Criterion     Value      DF    Value/DF     Pr > ChiSq
   Deviance      0.5417      1     0.5417         0.4617
   Pearson       0.6147      1     0.6147         0.4330
```

Nonsignificant values are a good sign!

```
            Number of unique profiles: 4
                Model Fit Statistics

                      InterceptIntercept and
           Criterion  OnlyCovariates
           AIC        109.798      105.004
           SC         112.452      112.966
           -2 Log L   107.798       99.004
```

```
                The LOGISTIC Procedure
   R-Square  0.0803  Max-rescaled  R-Square  0.1252
```
← *An attempt to talk about variance explained*

```
         Testing Global Null Hypothesis: BETA=0

   Test               Chi-Square    DF    Pr > ChiSq
   Likelihood Ratio     8.7940       2      0.0123
   Score                8.3816       2      0.0151
   Wald                 7.5648       2      0.0228

       Analysis of Maximum Likelihood Estimates

                          Standard      Wald
   Parameter  DF  Estimate   Error   Chi-Square  Pr > ChiSq
   Intercept   1   -0.6718   0.3165    4.5050      0.0338
   cbt         1   -1.5098   0.5568    7.3528      0.0067
   married     1   -0.4473   0.7068    0.4006      0.5268

                Odds Ratio Estimates

                  Point         95% Wald
   Effect       Estimate   Confidence Limits
   cbt           0.221     0.074      0.658
   married       0.639     0.160      2.555
```

Tests of whether there is a significant association of variable with the dependent variable

```
  Association of Predicted Probabilities and Observed Responses

   Percent Concordant     51.9     Somers' D     0.367
   Percent Discordant     15.1        Gamma      0.549
   Percent Tied           33.0        Tau-a      0.123
   Pairs                  1826           c       0.684
```

FIGURE 14.25. SPSS Output (a few nonrelevant portions are not displayed).

Case Processing Summary

Unweighted Cases(a)		N	Percent
Selected Cases	Included in Analysis	105	100.0
	Missing Cases	0	.0
	Total	105	100.0
Unselected Cases		0	.0
Total		105	100.0

a If weight is in effect, see classification table for the total number of cases.

Dependent Variable Encoding

Original Value	Internal Value
0	0
1	1

Omnibus Tests of Model Coefficients

		Chi-square	df	Sig.
Step 1	Step	8.794	2	.012
	Block	8.794	2	.012
	Model	8.794	2	.012

Model Summary

Step	22 Log likelihood	Cox & Snell R Square	Nagelkerke R Square
1	99.004(a)	.080	.125

a Estimation terminated at iteration number 5 because parameter estimates changed by less than .001.

Hosmer and Lemeshow Test

Step	Chi-square	df	Sig.
1	.615	2	.735

Variables in the Equation

		B	S.E.	Wald	df	Sig.	Exp(B)	95.0% C.I.for EXP(B)	
								Lower	Upper
Step 1(a)	Cbt	21.510	.557	7.354	1	.007	.221	.074	.658
	Married	2.447	.707	.401	1	.527	.639	.160	2.555
	Constant	2.672	.317	4.505	1	.034	.511		

a Variable(s) entered on step 1. cbt, married.

FIGURE 14.26. **SAS Output.**

```
                    Model Convergence Status
          Convergence criterion (GCONV=1E-8) satisfied.

                    Model Fit Statistics

                                         Intercept
                          Intercept         and
         Criterion          Only         Covariates
         AIC              109.798          103.175
         SC               112.452          113.791
         -2 Log L         107.798           95.175


R-Square     0.1133     Max-rescaled R-Square     0.1765

          Testing Global Null Hypothesis: BETA=0

    Test                 Chi-Square     DF     Pr > ChiSq
    Likelihood Ratio      12.6233        3       0.0055
    Score                 11.7854        3       0.0082
    Wald                  10.2864        3       0.0163

        Analysis of Maximum Likelihood Estimates
                         Standard
Parameter    DF    Estimate    Error    Chi-Square    Pr > ChiSq
Intercept     1     -3.6362    1.6110      5.0942        0.0240
cbt           1     -1.5468    0.5688      7.3949        0.0065
married       1     -1.4838    0.9239      2.5792        0.1083
age           1      0.0979    0.0515      3.6110        0.0574

              Odds Ratio Estimates
                    Point            95% Wald
    Effect        Estimate       Confidence Limits
    cbt            0.213        0.070        0.649
    married        0.227        0.037        1.387
    age            1.103        0.997        1.220

     Partition for the Hosmer and Lemeshow Test
                         RECID = 1        RECID = 0
  Group   Total   Observed   Expected   Observed   Expected
    1       11        1         0.46        10       10.54
    2       14        0         1.03        14       12.97
    3       12        2         1.17        10       10.83
    4       12        1         1.54        11       10.46
    5       12        2         2.18        10        9.82
    6       13        3         3.45        10        9.55
    7       15        6         5.06         9        9.94
    8       16        7         7.11         9        8.89

     Hosmer and Lemeshow Goodness-of-Fit Test
        Chi-Square     DF     Pr > ChiSq
         2.9904         6       0.8101
```

> This is good—
> if it doesn't converge,
> SAS can't come up
> with a workable model.

> Nonsignificant value—good fit with
> data! This is not a really powerful
> test, so we want this to be
> quite nonsignificant (bigger than .20).

In the partial display SAS output in Figure 14.26, you will notice that the Pearson and deviance chi-square tests are no longer present.

SECTION 14.6.4: SPSS AND LOGISTIC REGRESSION WITH CONTINUOUS VARIABLE

Go to Analyze ⇒ Regression ⇒ Binary Logistic . . . ⇒ specify your dependent variable "recid" under "Dependent:" and the predictor variables "age," "cbt" and "married"

under "Covariates:" ⇒ click on "Options . . ." and check "Hosmer-Lemeshow . . ." and "CI for exp(B): 95%"⇒ click on "Continue" ⇒ click "OK"

SPSS output is shown in Figure 14.27.

The Hosmer-Lemeshow test displayed next attempts to group subjects into deciles based on the model-predicted probabilities. Then it compares the numbers of expected versus observed subjects. If there is not a big difference, the test will be nonsignificant. This is what we want because it shows us our model is

---

FIGURE 14.27. Partial SPSS Output.

Omnibus Tests of Model Coefficients

		Chi-square	df	Sig.
Step 1	Step	12.623	3	.006
	Block	12.623	3	.006
	Model	12.623	3	.006

Hosmer and Lemeshow Test

Step	Chi-square	df	Sig.
1	3.377	7	.848

Contingency Table for Hosmer and Lemeshow Test

		1 IF RECIDIVISM REPORTED DURING 6 MO FOLLOWUP = 0		1 IF RECIDIVISM REPORTED DURING 6 MO FOLLOWUP = 1		Total
		Observed	Expected	Observed	Expected	
Step 1	1	10	10.535	1	.465	11
	2	14	12.974	0	1.026	14
	3	10	10.833	2	1.167	12
	4	11	10.456	1	1.544	12
	5	10	9.824	2	2.176	12
	6	10	9.553	3	3.447	13
	7	6	5.416	2	2.584	8
	8	6	7.017	5	3.983	11
	9	6	6.392	6	5.608	12

Variables in the Equation

		B	S.E.	Wald	df	Sig.	Exp(B)	95.0% C.I.for EXP(B)	
								Lower	Upper
Step 1(a)	Cbt	−1.547	.569	7.395	1	.007	.213	.070	.649
	Married	−1.484	.924	2.579	1	.108	.227	.037	1.387
	Age	.098	.052	3.611	1	.057	1.103	.997	1.220
	Constant	−3.636	1.611	5.094	1	.024	.026		

a Variable(s) entered on step 1: cbt, married, age.

fitting the data well. Although SAS and SPSS use slightly different calculations, both display a very non-significant result. We also note that although age is not quite statistically significant, the change in the model chi-square from 8.79 to 12.6 does suggest we have improved the model by adding the variable.

A word about Hosmer-Lemeshow tests: The reader should be aware that the Hosmer-Lemeshow tests used in most current statistical packages make certain assumptions about being able to group the data that don't always make sense. The argument against reliance on this test does not seem to have filtered into the social science literature heavily as yet, but you should be aware that there are alternative tests that are considered much more reliable. Unfortunately, these are yet to be easily accessed in SAS and SPSS. You can request other goodness-of-fit tests in SAS using a special program called a "macro." As of the writing of this chapter there was not a similar "fix" for SPSS. The following macro is taken directly from an article by Kuss (2005) that compares and contrasts some alternative means of assessing model fit with continuous or very rare event variables:

```
%goflogit(data=,y=,m=,xlist=,logistic=,
work=2000,syms=200)
```

In the above SAS code:

- `data=` specifies the data set you are using.
- `y=` specifies the variable that contains the number of observed events (yi) for each covariate pattern.
- `m=` specifies the variable that contains the number of observed individual observations (mi) for each covariate pattern.
- `xlist=` specifies the list of covariates in the model.
- `logistic=` controls the optional running of PROC LOGISTIC (default: logistic = on).
- `work=` specifies the worksize for SAS/IML (default: work=2000).
- `syms=` specifies the size of symbol space for SAS/IML (default: SYMS=200).

Note that **%GOFLOGIT** expects observations to be grouped by covariate patterns. If your data show extreme sparseness (*mi*≡1) and every covariate pattern consists of a single individual observation, you should specify a variable that constantly equals 1 in a previous DATA step (for example: numobs = 1;) (Kuss, 2005).

Ahh . . . all done with the basics of logistic regression, right? Not exactly. One additional word related to model fit should be given. There is a potential problem

FIGURE 14.28. Yuan's Data in SAS.

```
PROC LOGISTIC descending data=yuan;
Model recid = dbt married prior /
scale=pearson
Aggregate rsq; run;
```
Here's our adjustment for overdispersion.

called **overdispersion** with grouped or discrete data. This occurs when the discrepancy between the observed and expected values is greater than what the model would predict. Sometimes a model that uses categorical and nominal variables does not fit due to incorrect specification (more interactions or nonlinearities are need) or lack of independence due to clustering. In the following example of SAS output we see that the values in the Value/DF column, which is the value of the chi-square divided by the degrees of freedom, are over 1. This indicates we have a possible problem with overdispersion:

Criterion	DF	Value	Value/DF	Pr > ChiSq
Deviance	4	5.1002	1.2751	0.2772
Pearson	4	7.2582	1.8145	0.1229

When this occurs, we can ask SAS to adjust for the overdispersion in the logistic regression model by specifying after the forward slash one of the following:

- `Scale=deviance` (which many statisticians do not like)
- `Scale=Pearson` (the generally preferred method)

Unfortunately, the point-and-click menu of SPSS lacks this option. So now let's reanalyze Yuan's data using SAS and adjusting for overdispersion (Figure 14.28). We see that the value/DF is over 1.0, but now there is a statement saying that our data have been adjusted for any problem with overdispersion.

```
Deviance and Pearson Goodness-of-Fit
Statistics
```
Criterion	Value	DF	Value/DF	Pr > ChiSq
Deviance	6.6482	4	1.6621	0.1557
Pearson	6.6222	4	1.6556	0.1573

```
      Number of unique profiles: 8

NOTE: The covariance matrix has been multi-
plied by the heterogeneity factor (Pearson
Chi-Square/DF) 1.65555.
```

Comparing the coefficient for CBT=1 in a corrected model to the uncorrected model we can see that we sometimes have more conservative estimates—which is sometimes disappointing (see below):

```
Uncorrected
                                                 Standard
                Parameter    DF    Estimate      Error     Chi-Square    Pr > ChiSq
                Intercept     1     -0.6478      0.4562       2.0169        0.1556
                cbt           1     -1.5114      0.5573       7.3556        0.0067
   Corrected
                Intercept     1     -0.6478      0.6145       1.1115        0.2918
                cbt           1     -1.5114      0.7507       4.0537        0.0441
```

SECTION 14.6.5: REVIEW: INTERPRETING ODDS RATIOS

We'd like to go back to interpretation of the values for coefficients for a moment, because we've noticed that some people have trouble with this material. Let's look at a set of example odds ratios and see what they mean. Basically, the odds ratio shows the likelihood of change in the dependent variable per unit change in the independent variable. For dichotomous independent variables, this is easy to interpret, but for continuous independent variables, this is harder. We hope the examples in Table 14.5 will clarify things.

Notice in the last two cases, the ratio seems to be very different (1.0001 versus 1.1). In reality, the reason the first number is so small (1.0001) is that we are looking at the change in the dependent variable per dollar of monthly income, a very small increment. If we modify the independent variable to represent thousands of dollars (INCOME=INCOME/1000), then the ratio becomes much easier to interpret. We've had risk ratios associated with yearly income that were significant at the .0001 level but that were reported by SAS as 1.0000, because the effect of each dollar of income was only visible at the 1/100,000 level. This sounds small, but in

TABLE 14.4. **Examples of Odds Ratios.**

INDEPENDENT VARIABLE	DEPENDENT VARIABLE	ODDS RATIO	INTERPRETATION (MEANING) OF THE NUMBER
Gender (Female = 1, Male = 0)	**Graduated** (Yes = 1, No = 0)	2.0	Females are twice as likely as males to graduate.
Gender (Female = 0, Male = 1)	**Graduated** (Yes = 1, No = 0)	0.5	Males are half as likely to graduate as females. (*Notice this is exactly the same result as above, but gender was coded differently.*)
Age (ranges from 20 to 50)	**Criminal recidivism** (Yes = 1, No = 0)	0.98	For each year of age over 20, the chance of criminal recidivism goes down about 2%.
Number of prior convictions (ranges from 1 to 10)	**Commission of domestic violence** (1 = Yes, 0 = No)	1.23	For each prior criminal conviction, the chance of committing domestic violence goes up by about 23%.
Income per month in *dollars* (ranges from 0 to 10,000)	**Family was reported to CPS in 2004** (1 = Yes, 0 = No)	1.0001	For each dollar of monthly income, a family is 1/10,000 more likely (.001%) to have a CPS report.
Income per month in *thousands of dollars* (ranges from 0 to 10)	**Family was reported to CPS in 2004** (1 = Yes, 0 = No)	1.1	For each $1000 of monthly income, a family is 10% more likely to have a CPS report. (*Note: This is exactly the same finding as the above row.*)

terms of thousands of dollars per year of income, this could be a 1% change per thousand dollars of income per year, which means that someone earning $50,000 a year has a 40% effect compared to someone earning $10,000.

SECTION 14.6.6: PREDICTIVE UTILITY OF THE LOGISTIC REGRESSION MODEL

We have already mentioned one way of assessing predictive utility—the pseudo *r*-square. In our three-variable model, including CBT, marriage, and age, we had a maximum rescaled *r*-square of about .176. It is not actually correct to interpret this as a percentage variance explained as we do in multiple regression models, but the general notion is the same—bigger is better (see Allison, 2001, pp. 56–57 for further discussion). There are other means of assessing the predictive utility of your model as well.

CROSS-TABULATION OF PREDICTED EVENTS

One way to assess predictive utility is to construct a cross-tab table of predicted versus observed events for various probability levels that you can specify. Both SPSS and SAS can perform this function. If you don't specify a probability for the event, the programs will just use the observed proportion of events. SAS and SPSS commands are similar, except that now you are asking the programs to create a new data set that includes the predicted probabilities. In SAS there are extra lines of programming related to printing the predicted probability table as well.

SAS Analysis and Cross-Tab of Predicted Events.

```
PROC LOGISTIC descending data=yuan;
model recid = cbt married age /lackfit rsq;
output out=probs predicted=phat;
run;
data probs1;
set probs;
predicts=(phat>=.50);
run;
proc freq data=probs1;
tables outcome*predicts;run;
```

SAS output is shown in Figure 14.29.

SPSS Analysis and Cross-Tab of Predicted Events.

Go to Analyze ⇒ Regression ⇒ Binary Logistic . . . ⇒ specify your dependent variable "recid" under "Dependent:" and the predictor variables "age," "cbt," and "married" under "Covariates:"⇒ click on "Options . . ." and check "Hosmer-Lemeshow goodness-of-fit" and "CI for exp(B): 95%"⇒ click

on "Continue"⇒ click on "Save . . ." ⇒check the option "Probabilities" and "Group membership" under "Predicted Values" ⇒click on "Continue"⇒click "OK"

SPSS output is shown in Figure 14.30. As we can see, 82/105 (78.1%) of our cases were correctly classified by the model. It did very well classifying nonevents (97.6%), but it did not do well correctly classifying events (4.5%).

Now, the problem with this method of assessing predictive utility is that when you use the same data to create the prediction table as to fit the logistic model you introduce bias. One way to get around this is to randomly split your sample into two parts and use one to build the model and another to run again to create the table, but this is difficult to do if your data set is small. Another option to assess predictive utility is to create some new observations with missing data for the outcome variable. These new observations get left out of the logistic regression model but are included in the table by creating a new outcome variable that references just the missing values.

CLASSIFICATION TABLE

Another, more clear, way to get around the bias problem available in SAS is to create a classification table instead that has a bias adjustment built into it. Here is a model looking at 602 cases and trying to predict case resolution. We used the actual proportion of events for our probability of event (.40).

FIGURE 14.29. SAS Output.

```
           Table of RECID by predicts
RECID(1 IF RECIDIVISM REPORTED DURING 6 MO
FOLLOWUP) predicts

Frequency,
Percent  ,
Row Pct  ,
Col Pct  ,         0,         1,    Total
*********^*********^*********^
       0 ,       81 ,        2 ,       83
         ,    77.14 ,     1.90 ,    79.05
         ,    97.59 ,     2.41 ,
         ,    79.41 ,    66.67 ,
*********^*********^*********^
       1 ,       21 ,        1 ,       22
         ,    20.00 ,     0.95 ,    20.95
         ,    95.45 ,     4.55 ,
         ,    20.59 ,    33.33 ,
*********^*********^*********^
   Total          102          3        105
                97.14       2.86     100.00
```

FIGURE 14.30. SPSS Output.

Classification Table(a)

Observed			Predicted		
			1 IF RECIDIVISM REPORTED DURING 6 MO FOLLOWUP		Percentage Correct
			0	1	
Step 1	1 IF RECIDIVISM REPORTED DURING 6 MO FOLLOWUP	0	81	2	97.6
		1	21	1	4.5
Overall Percentage					78.1

a The cut value is .500.

SAS Classification Table Commands.

```
PROC LOGISTIC descending data=temp;
model outcome = variable list /ctable
pprob=(.20 to .80 by .10)
pevent=.40;
run;
```

We omitted the bulk of the SAS output to focus on the last part that is the classification table (Figure 14.31). These values are adjusted for the bias factor, and SAS has the advantage of printing out various results for false positives and false negatives at different probability levels.

SPSS Classification Table Commands. SPSS classification table commands are not currently available.

ROC TABLE

A third means of assessing predictive utility, available in both SAS and SPSS, is the **ROC (receiver operating characteristic) curve.** It is a plot of the true positive rate against the false-positive rate for the different possible cutpoints of a diagnostic test. The more quickly the curve rises and the larger the area under the curve, the better the predictive accuracy of the model.

SAS and ROC.

```
PROC LOGISTIC descending data=tempm;
model outcome = variable list /outroc=roc1
run;
```

FIGURE 14.31. SAS Output.

Classification Table

		Correct		Incorrect			Percentages			
Prob Event	Prob Level	Event	Non-Event	Event	Non-Event	Correct	Sensi-tivity	Speci-ficity	False POS	False NEG
0.400	0.200	16	53	30	6	67.4	72.7	63.9	42.7	22.2
0.400	0.300	11	65	18	11	67.0	50.0	78.3	39.4	29.9
0.400	0.400	4	77	6	18	62.9	18.2	92.8	37.4	37.0
0.400	0.500	0	81	2	22	58.6	0.0	97.6	100.0	40.6
0.400	0.600	0	82	1	22	59.3	0.0	98.8	100.0	40.3
0.400	0.700	0	83	0	22	60.0	0.0	100.0	.	40.0

The following commands in SAS set up the display and then ask SAS to print the curve:

```
goptions cback=white
colors=(black)
border;

axis1 length=2.5in;
axis2 order=(0 to 1 by .1) length=2.5in;

proc gplot data=roc1;
symbol1 i=join v=none;
title1;
title2 'Case Disposition ROC Curve: All
Cases';
plot _SENSIT_*_1MSPEC_ / haxis=axis1
vaxis=axis2; run;
```

SAS will output the curve in the graphics window, and then we go back to the logistic regression portion of the output to obtain the value for the *c* statistic (see explanation following). The resulting diagram is shown in Figure 14.32.

SPSS and ROC.

Go to Graph ⇒ ROC Curve . . . ⇒ specify "pred_1" as the "Test Variable:" and "recid" as the "State Variable:"⇒ provide the "Value of the State Variable:" (which is 1 in our case)⇒ click "OK"

The SPSS output is shown in Figure 14.33. SPSS prints the *c* statistic (.741) out in the same window as the curve (which is convenient). References differ in how

FIGURE 14.32. **SAS Output.**

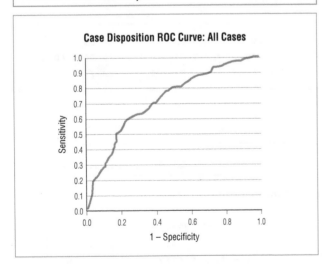

Case Disposition ROC Curve: All Cases

Area Under the Curve
Test Result Variable(s): Predicted probability

Area
.741

The test result variable(s): Predicted probability has at least one tie between the positive actual state group and the negative actual state group. Statistics may be biased.

FIGURE 14.33. **SPSS output.**

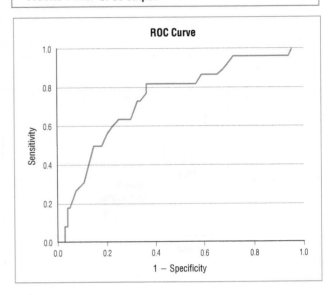

they talk about assessing the ROC, so two examples are provided here. The first is from the Cleveland Clinic Foundation (note that AUC refers to area under curve):

> . . . in a study involving rating data, an AUC of 0.84 implies that there is an 84% likelihood that a randomly selected diseased case will receive a more-suspicious (higher) rating than a randomly selected nondiseased case. Note that an AUC of 0.50 means that the diagnostic accuracy in question is equivalent to that which would be obtained by flipping a coin (i.e., random chance) (2005).

The second example is from an online text:

> . . . guide for classifying the accuracy of a diagnostic test is the traditional academic point system:

- .90–1 = excellent (A)
- .80–.90 = good (B)
- .70–.80 = fair (C)
- .60–.70 = poor (D)
- .50–.60 = fail (F) (Tape, 2005).

From the logistic regression printout in SAS, we look for a statistic called *c*. Our *c* = 0.742 and 0.741 in the SPSS output. This is the statistic that represents the area under the curve. So, basically, we do not have the level of predictive quality we would want, but we are improving the likelihood of knowing the outcome over chance.

There is much more to learn about multivariate analyses of binary or categorical outcomes that simply goes beyond the scope of the present text. Instead we now turn to the issue of analyzing outcomes that occur over time and encourage more advanced readers to check out the resources presented at the end of the chapter.

SECTION 14.7

CONTROLLING FOR TIME

There are many instances in which one wants to look for the development of events or characteristics or intervention effects over time. Indeed there has been an increasing emphasis on longitudinal studies in social science. There are entire books devoted to analyzing longitudinal data, and this text touches on only a tiny part of the options available. Again, this is just meant as an introduction to give you a feel for what's out there.

First, we will explore the longitudinal extension of our familiar friend the ANOVA. This is called a repeated measures ANOVA and is useful for looking at intervention effects over time. Now researchers (particularly those with nonexperimental designs) are much more likely to use more powerful models such as mixed model regression or generalized estimating equations. Again, however, the goal of this text is to introduce foundational concepts, so we have chosen to build on what we have already learned. Next, we will briefly introduce survival analyses, or the examination of categorical outcomes while controlling for the time at risk of that given outcome.

You should be aware that longitudinal data analysis is an area of rapid growth in social science. New techniques and better integration into software are emerging all the time. So, this text provides an introduction to some common approaches, but you will certainly find yourself in need of further training in this area to remain a good consumer and user of longitudinal analytic methods.

In addition to differences in data analyses, there are also tricks to programming with longitudinal data that, while not covered in this text, are useful to understand. Interested readers may want to check out a relatively new and straightforward SAS publication by Ron Cody, *Longitudinal Data and SAS. A Programmer's Guide* (2001).

SECTION 14.7.1: REPEATED MEASURES ANOVA

We know that in a simple pre- and posttest design that we can use the paired-samples *t* test. In a more complex situation we can use the ANCOVA to look at pre- and posttest results while controlling for other variables. What if we are interested in maintenance of effect? In other words, suppose we want to stop substance abuse in a population. We may be relatively secure in thinking

that following a residential treatment program, subjects will not be using at the time they exit. But what about later? Once subjects return to an uncontrolled environment, will they be able to continue to abstain from the problem substance? To answer this question, we must take repeated measures of the dependent variable: pretest, posttest, and at least one follow-up measure. One means of analyzing this type of data is to extend the ANOVA technique to a repeated measures ANOVA:

- *Research question:* "Does the mean value of *X* change between measurement time periods?"
- *Null hypothesis:* There is no difference in the mean value of *X* over time.

Assumptions of Repeated Measures ANOVA include:

- Like the regular ANOVA, normality is an important assumption of this technique. The same criteria hold for robustness, though. If you have equal cell sizes and/or a large sample, small to moderate departures from this assumption can be tolerated.
- Here we see a change in terms from homogeneity of variance to homogeneity of covariance. Why? Because we no longer have the pure between-groups conditions. The criterion variables covary. The idea is that the covariance between time 1 and time 2 should be similar to that between time 2 and time 3, and so on. Now, it is largely accepted that this is not as big an issue as initially thought and a check for sphericity (see following) is deemed to suffice (Baguley, 2004).
- Subject groups are not "independent" here. The same subjects are exposed to the different conditions over time.
- In repeated measures we are concerned with a special case called **sphericity.** Put simply, this means that the conditions should affect the subjects in the same way over time. If for some reason our treatment affects women in our data differently than men at different time periods, then sphericity will be violated. Of course, the reality is that this is to be somewhat naturally violated due to the measurement of the same subjects over time. We will go over the techniques used to assess and adjust for violations of this assumption.

Another way of understanding assumptions for a repeated measures model can be to state them as a general principle:

The groups in such an analysis are, after all, potentially intercorrelated. Actually, it is a cluster of assumptions that go by such names as "compound symmetry," "homogeneity of covariance," "circularity," and "sphericity," all of which are more complex than can be dealt with at the introductory level. For practical purposes you can think of it this way. Suppose we were to calculate all possible correlation coefficients (r) among the k groups of measures. The homogeneity of covariance assumption requires that all of these correlation coefficients be positive and of approximately the same magnitude. Essentially, it is a requirement that the differential effects of the k conditions are consistent among the subjects in the repeated measures design, or among the matched sets of subjects in the randomized blocks design. (Part III, Chapter 15; Lowry, 2005)

Assessing for assumptions begins much the same way as with other ANOVA techniques, and we will not repeat the computer commands (refer back to Chapter 13). First we look at our descriptive statistics (we are presenting only SAS univariate output to conserve space).

```
                              The MEANS Procedure
Variable   Label                     N      Mean       Std Dev    Minimum       Maximum
**************************************************************************************
e1         Errors made (session 1)   60   9.1333333   5.9102516    0          24.0000000
e2         Errors made (session 2)   60   8.9833333   5.6433301    0          23.0000000
e3         Errors made (session 3)   60   9.0666667   7.1943167    0          33.0000000
```

We have group sizes of 60, and they are equal. This will help our model to be robust against normality issues. We can use this output to graph our means—this allows you to take a guess about whether or not you might have findings that support your hypothesis.

To test for sphericity, we have to actually run the model. The test is called **Mauchly's criterion.** Yes, you guessed it; we want it to be nonsignificant. If it is significant, there are problems violating the assumption of sphericity (Hatcher & Stepanski, 1994). *Warning:* This test is very sensitive and not universally accepted as the best means of assessing sphericity (see Baguley, 2004, for discussion). For practical purposes, if it's just barely significant, you're probably OK (.03, .04, .05, and so on). The good news is that even when the assumption is violated, we do not have to rerun a lot of different procedures. Both SAS and SPSS print out the necessary "fixes" for problems associated with a significant Mauchly's:

STEP 1: Find the Mauchly's test on the output.

STEP 2: Is the Mauchly's test significant?

STEP 3A: If the Mauchly's is not significant, use the unadjusted *p* value associated with the *F* test.

STEP 3B: If the Mauchly's is significant, follow the process in the following discussion.

STEP 4: If the *F* test is significant, move on to the contrast statements (SAS) or pairwise comparisons (SPSS) to look at where differences are.

A SIGNIFICANT MAUCHLY'S

There are a few options for adjusting findings for sphericity based on the severity of the problem. The most common adjustments are just to make the *F* test more conservative. In SAS, there are *p* values printed out beside the *p* value for the regular *F*. In SPSS, these adjusted values are in rows below the main statistic. Generally, in statistics it is best to be conservative, so if the Mauchly's is significant and the Greenhouse-Geisser or G-G value is greater than .75, you simply use the adjusted *p* value labeled G-G on the SAS output and Greenhouse-Geisser on the SPSS output. The H-F or Huynh-Feldt *p* value is a less conservative adjustment.

If the Mauchly's test is really, really violated (very significant, as in <.001) and/or the G-G epsilon (another statistic output by SAS) is less than .75, you will want to use the significance level associated with the MANOVA approach instead. The MANOVA does not require sphericity and is included with the default output. There are different options for which test statistic to choose within the MANOVA section of the output. Depending on the software, this may not be clearly labeled as a MANOVA section. So, you can look for the name of the test statistic of choice. We will choose to use the Wilk's lambda (most commonly mentioned) in this class in cases requiring the MANOVA approach.

SAS AND REPEATED MEASURES ANOVA

One of the biggest differences you will note between other ANOVAs and the repeated measures ANOVA is that the model statement changes. In the case of a one-way repeated measures design, there are no study groups or class variable—only three time periods of the criterion variable. Thus, all you have are the three levels

FIGURE 14.34. SAS Output.

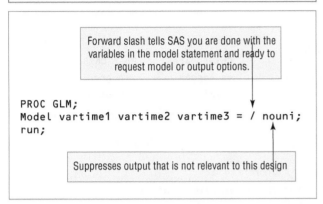

Where "vartime1..." are the names of variables for measuring the outcome variable at different times.

FIGURE 14.35. SAS Model Statement.

```
Model vartime1 vartime2 vartime3
= groupvariablename/;
```

Where "vartime1..." are the names of variables for measuring the outcome variable at different times and groupvariablename is the variable signifying group membership.

and nothing following the equals sign other than output or test options after the forward slash (see Figure 14.34).

In a two-way or factorial repeated measures ANOVA, the model statement looks more like what we are used to (Figure 14.35).

In the preceding factorial scenario, the group is typically the experiment versus the control, so group-variablename would probably be something similar to "group" and would be 1 if the treatment group and 0 if the control group.

Contrast Statements. Another change in SAS compared to the regular ANOVA is the use of contrast statements rather than multiple comparison tests like Tukey or Bonferroni. You can specify which time variable (time 1, or time 2, or time 3) will be the comparison. SAS will then compare the other values for time to that group. The use of multiple comparisons can be done with another procedure, but this text will not cover that. The SAS command for contrasts goes after the model statement and before requesting the sphericity test or other optional statistics (Figure 14.36).

SPSS AND REPEATED MEASURES ANOVA

Go to Analyze ⇒ General Linear Model ⇒ Repeated Measures . . . ⇒ specify Time as the "Within-Subject Factor Name" and three as "Number of Levels" in this factor ⇒ click on "Add" ⇒ click on "Define" and specify time 1, time 2, and time 3 as the "Within-Subject

FIGURE 14.36.

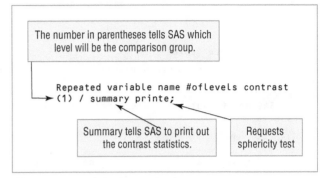

Where "variable name" is whatever you want printed on the output to reprresent the time periods and #oflevels is the number of time periods.

Variables" ⇒ to request for a graph of the data, click on "Plots . . ." and specify Time for the "Horizontal Axis" ⇒ click on "Continue" ⇒ click on "Options . . ." ⇒ specify the option to "Display Means for" Time and select "Compare main effects" ⇒ click on "Continue" ⇒ click "OK"

Results of Repeated Measures ANOVA. Similar to the other ANOVA procedures, the overall model fit just specifies that at least two of the time periods differ. The F test is the same type of test in terms of interpretation as the other ANOVA tests, although the algebra behind it varies because it partials out the within error. So, we need post hoc measures to assess which time periods differ.

The output of a repeated measures ANOVA looks a little different. (SAS output is shown in Figure 14.37, SPSS in Figure 14.38.) The correlation material in the output is part of this test but goes beyond this class in terms of explaining the mechanics, so we will skip over this part of the output. Let's use some of Professor Kathy's data:

- *Research question*: "Does the mean number of errors differ across three time measures?"

Our Mauchly's is not significant, and this is great news! We can skip the MANOVA results and move right to the model results for interpretation. For the sake of understanding the output, however, note that the Greenhouse-Geisser epsilon is over .75. If our Mauchly's test had indicated that we had sphericity problems but they were not severe, we would simply use the G-G p value instead of the $Pr > F$ to correct for the issue. If the G-G was less than .75 and Mauchly's had been very significant, then we would have looked at the Wilk's lambda (which is printed out before the GLM results) instead of the adjusted F test.

In our example, our F test is only .01 and very non-significant. We now know that the mean errors in three

---

FIGURE 14.37. **SAS Output.**

```
                                Sphericity Tests

                                        Mauchly's
        Variables              DF       Criterion    Chi-Square    Pr > ChiSq
        Transformed Variates    2       0.8103189    12.198988     0.0022
        Orthogonal Components   2       0.9849575     0.8790955    0.6443
```

SAS prints out two tests under the sphericity section. We want to read the orthogonal components results.

```
The GLM Procedure            Repeated Measures Analysis of Variance
        MANOVA Test Criteria and Exact F Statistics for the Hypothesis of no time Effect
                        H = Type III SSCP Matrix for time
                             E = Error SSCP Matrix

                        S=1      M=0      N=28

    Statistic                 Value      F Value    Num DF    Den DF    Pr > F
    Wilks' Lambda           0.99944675     0.02        2        58      0.9841
    Pillai's Trace          0.00055325     0.02        2        58      0.9841
    Hotelling-Lawley Trace  0.00055356     0.02        2        58      0.9841
    Roy's Greatest Root     0.00055356     0.02        2        58      0.9841
```

```
The GLM Procedure            Repeated Measures Analysis of Variance
              Univariate Tests of Hypotheses for Within Subject Effects

                                                                      Adj Pr>F
Source        DF    Type III SS    Mean Square    F Value    Pr > F    G - G     H - F
time           2     1.111111       0.555556       0.01      0.9854    0.9845    0.9854
Error(time)  118  4444.222222      37.662900
```

```
The GLM Procedure                    Greenhouse-Geisser Epsilon         0.9852
                                      Huynh-Feldt Epsilon               1.0190

                     Repeated Measures Analysis of Variance
                     Analysis of Variance of Contrast Variables

              time_N represents the contrast between the nth level of time
                    and the 1st Contrast Variable: time_2
    Source            DF         Type III SS      Mean Square    F Value    Pr > F
    Mean               1           1.666667         1.666667       0.03     0.8748
    Error             59        3924.333333        66.514124
```

```
Contrast Variable: time_3

    Source            DF         Type III SS      Mean Square    F Value    Pr > F
    Mean               1           1.666667         1.666667       0.02     0.8838
    Error             59        4562.333333        77.327684
```

time periods do not differ in Professor Kathy's data. If the *F* value was significant, we would move on to the contrast statement in SAS or the pairwise comparison table in SPSS. In our example, of course, both are nonsignificant.

One of the interesting aspects of the repeated measures ANOVA is that the post hoc tests really don't tell you a lot about what the differences look like. So it's nice to look back at the original means. You can do this graphically as well by putting the means in a program such as Excel. Because our researcher's data weren't terribly interesting, let's look at a fictitious set of means. In the graph in Figure 14.39, time 2

FIGURE 14.38. **SPSS Output.**

Within-Subjects Factors

Measure: MEASURE_1

time	Dependent Variable
1	e1
2	e2
3	e3

Multivariate Tests(b)

Effect			Value	F	Hypothesis df	Error df	Sig.	
Time	Pillai's Trace		.000	.010(a)	2.000	58.000	.990	
	Wilks' Lambda		1.000	.010(a)	2.000	58.000	.990	
	Hotelling's Trace		.000	.010(a)	2.000	58.000	.990	
	Roy's Largest Root		.000	.010(a)	2.000	58.000	.990	

a Exact statistic

b Design: Intercept

Within Subjects Design: time

Mauchly's Test of Sphericity(b)

Measure: MEASURE_1

Within Subjects Effect	Mauchly's W	Approx. Chi-Square	df	Sig.	Epsilon(a)		
					Greenhouse-Geisser	Huynh-Feldt	Lower-bound
Time	.979	1.237	2	.539	.979	1.000	.500

Tests the null hypothesis that the error covariance matrix of the orthonormalized transformed dependent variables is proportional to an identity matrix.

a May be used to adjust the degrees of freedom for the averaged tests of significance. Corrected tests are displayed in the Tests of Within-Subjects Effects table.

b Design: Intercept

Within Subjects Design: time

Tests of Within-Subjects Effects

Measure: MEASURE_1

Source		Type III Sum of Squares	Df	Mean Square	F	Sig.
Time	Sphericity Assumed	.678	2	.339	.009	.991
	Greenhouse-Geisser	.678	1.959	.346	.009	.990
	Huynh-Feldt	.678	2.000	.339	.009	.991
	Lower-bound	.678	1.000	.678	.009	.926
Error(time)	Sphericity Assumed	4537.989	118	38.458		
	Greenhouse-Geisser	4537.989	115.562	39.269		
	Huynh-Feldt	4537.989	118.000	38.458		
	Lower-bound	4537.989	59.000	76.915		

(continues)

FIGURE 14.38. **(Continued)**

Pairwise Comparisons

Measure: MEASURE_1

(I) time	(J) time	Mean Difference (I-J)	Std. Error	Sig.(a)	95% Confidence Interval for Difference(a)	
					Lower Bound	Upper Bound
1	2	.150	1.051	.887	−1.953	2.253
	3	.067	1.150	.954	−2.234	2.367
2	1	−.150	1.051	.887	−2.253	1.953
	3	−.083	1.191	.944	−2.467	2.301
3	1	−.067	1.150	.954	−2.367	2.234
	2	.083	1.191	.944	−2.301	2.467

Based on estimated marginal means.

a Adjustment for multiple comparisons: Least Significant Difference (equivalent to no adjustments).

is significantly different from time 1, but time 3 was not significantly different from time 1. If this were treatment data, we can see that the scores on the outcome measure increased at posttest but then rapidly decreased between the posttest and follow-up period. When we refer to the graph we made according to the means of our time groups (Figure 14.39), we can see that subjects are not doing well at follow-up. So, although our treatment may have had the initial desired effect, at follow-up subjects are at a similar level to that at pretest.

SECTION 14.7.2: ALTERNATIVE METHODS FOR REPEATED MEASURES ANALYSES

As stated, there is a trend now toward using the **generalized estimating equation** (or **GEE**) or mixed model regression instead of methods like the repeated

measures ANOVA. In SAS, these are invoked through PROC GENMOD or PROC MIXED. In SPSS, the mixed model is available under "Analyze⇒Mixed Models," but GEE is not readily available on the pull-down menus.

One advantage of these methods is that you can specify an underlying model that assumes some correlation. This means you don't have to worry about sphericity. Further, the procedures are quite robust. GEE can be used for categorical outcomes and is easily used in a multivariate context (many of these types of models will also handle missing data). Typically these procedures will require data in a "per period" format. For example, if you had a seven-year data set, the repeated variables would be recoded within each year—so it would be essentially seven data sets concatenated (stacked) together. The use of these techniques is beyond the scope of the present text (your head hurts now anyway, right?). But, you should be aware of them and may want to seek training in their use as you advance in your research career. There are a couple of references to these techniques included at the close of the chapter to get you started.

SECTION 14.8

CATEGORICAL TIME TO EVENT DATA

Now we will turn our attention to data in which we are measuring and considering the impact of the time from the start of the study to an event or behavior of interest. We will focus on categorical data outcomes for this chapter. In other words, we are interested in some type of discrete outcome rather than a change in a scale score.

There are two ways in which data may be structured for such analyses. You may have data struc-

FIGURE 14.39. **Subject Score at Pretest, Posttest, and Follow-up.**

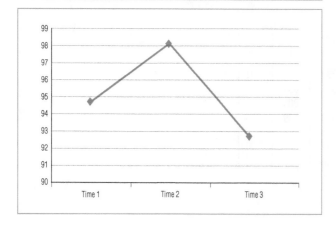

tured according to periods of time, such as monthly or yearly observations. This type of data might be analyzed with a variety of techniques including life tables with CMH tests (which we will explore) or generalized estimating equations (not covered in this text). The second structure may include exact dates. With exact dates we are typically measuring the change in risk of a given behavior or event over an exact period of time. We will explore a bivariate approach (survival curves) and provide a brief introduction to a multivariate extension called the Cox regression model.

Because this form of statistics was primarily used first in the medical and public health field, we have inherited some medically oriented words. We will introduce an old word used a new way: *survival*. A subject "survives" until the event of interest occurs or the study period ends. One would think then that the opposite term would be *dies*, but *fails* is used instead; a person who has the event "fails." So, if we want to see how long it takes until someone becomes pregnant, she "survives" until the pregnancy occurs (or until the study ends, and she is still not pregnant) and she "fails" if and when she becomes pregnant within the study period. (Don't blame us, we didn't make the labels up.)

- *Research question:* For the following techniques our question is: "Is X associated with event Y while controlling for time at risk of event Y?"

- *Null hypothesis:* There is no association of X with event Y over time.

- Assumptions:
  - There is independence of observations.
  - Data include time intervals or exact dates for each observation.
  - Event or outcome of interest is a nominal or limited ordinal variable.
  - Withdrawals for reasons other than the outcome are known.

SECTION 14.8.1: GROUPED INTERVALS

A life table is one method of considering a change in some rate of an event over time. With grouped data, it's similar to the idea of analyzing sets of tables that you learned about with the CMH chi-square. In fact, we will use the CMH commands in SAS and SPSS. This technique is particularly useful for studies with periods or intervals rather than exact dates of occurrence, studies with small samples, or studies with large samples but extremely rare events of interest.

Because certain subjects will "fail" or not survive during each period, the next period risk must be

adjusted according to the number of subjects who are still at risk for the event. The survival rate for each period is the probability of survival for that period given the remaining persons at risk. This might sound complex, but it's quite intuitive when thought of in context. Let's say you want to know if persons who install your new experimental airbag in their cars are less likely to die following a serious traffic accident than those without the new airbag. You follow a group of people for 12 months, and at the end of each month record the number of accident fatalities. Well, if John dies in January, then John cannot still be at risk of death in February, right? So we have to remove John from the possible persons who could die in February. The remaining persons for each period include:

Total for the prior period − (those who had the event + those who withdrew for other reasons)

Why use this if you have exact dates? Well, if your event of interest is rare (such as death from cancer among children or suicide), then there are so few events for each day or month at risk that it will be difficult to assess differences in rates by various variables. So, we may need to collapse our nicely dated information into discrete time intervals to have enough events per interval to examine various related factors of interest.

Let's look at an example. Imagine you have three periods of data collection and you want to figure out the survival rate for each interval for males compared to females following a substance abuse intervention program:

- *Research question:* "Is gender associated with relapse after treatment controlling for time?"

Given the small numbers of those who successfully complete the program, it's unlikely that a detailed date to date analysis will be possible. We can, however, group the data into intervals and think about whether or not a given individual "survives" or avoids recidivism within that interval. The survival rates for each period can be hand-calculated fairly easily as long as you keep your components straight (see Stokes, et al., 2000, for further discussion). The formulas for calculating the survival rates and the standard errors for three intervals follow for females. You would repeat the same formula for the other value of gender. In other words, you would have six estimated survival rates—one for each time period by gender. What is p? This is the probability that a subject will withdraw from the study. If you assume uniform probability of withdrawals, then $p = .5$. In other words, there is no particular systematic reason people drop out—it's by chance.

- First Interval for Females:

$$X1 = \frac{\text{no event1} + p * \text{withdrawals1} \; (p = \text{probability of withdrawal})}{\text{no event1} + \text{event1} + p * \text{withdrawals1}}$$

$$\text{standard error} = X1 * \left(\frac{\text{event1} / \text{no event1} + \text{event1} + p * \text{withdrawals1}}{\text{no event1} + p * \text{withdrawals1}} \right)^{1/2}$$

- Second Interval for Females:

$$X2 = X1 * \left(\frac{\text{no event2} + p * \text{withdrawals2}}{\text{no event2} + \text{event2} + p * \text{withdrawals2}} \right)$$

$$\text{standard error} = X2 * \left(\frac{\text{event1} / \text{no event1} + \text{event1} + p * \text{withdrawals1}}{\text{no event1} + p * \text{withdrawals1)}} \right)$$

$$+ \left(\frac{\text{event2} / \text{no event2} + \text{event2} + p * \text{withdrawals2}}{\text{no event2} + p * \text{withdrawals2}} \right)^{1/2}$$

- Third Interval for Females

$$X3 = X2 * \left(\frac{\text{no event3} + p * \text{withdrawals3}}{\text{no event3} + \text{event3} + p * \text{withdrawals3}} \right)$$

$$\text{standard error} = X3 * \left(\frac{\text{event1} / \text{no event1} + \text{event1} + p * \text{withdrawals1}}{\text{no event1} + p * \text{withdrawals1}} \right)$$

$$+ \left(\frac{\text{event2} / \text{no event2} + \text{event2} + p * \text{withdrawals2}}{\text{no event2} + p * \text{withdrawals2)}} \right)$$

$$+ \left(\frac{\text{event3} / \text{no event3} + \text{event3} + p * \text{withdrawals3}}{\text{no event3} + p * \text{withdrawals3}} \right)^{1/2}$$

Then we would repeat this same process for males.

We can also use statistics programs to calculate this for us. To do the test, we have to recode our data to group the withdrawals with the no events or drop the withdrawals from our data. Most drop the withdrawals as a more conservative approach. The easiest means of doing this is to create four variables: a variable that defines the interval; a status or event variable that is 1 or 0, depending on whether one has the event; a frequency of individuals for each time period and each event level; and gender.

Interval = time periods

Gender = 0/1

Status = relapse in substance use (yes/no)

Frequency count

Our data might look like Table 14.6. Notice that for every time interval, those who had the event in the prior interval are no longer included. We had 35 males to start with, and 20 had the event in the first interval, so there are only 15 males in the second interval, and so on.

TABLE 14.6 **Calculating in Statistics Program**

INTERVAL (MONTHS)	GENDER (1 = FEMALE)	RELAPSE (1 = YES)	FREQUENCY
1–3	0	0	30.00
1–3	0	1	5.00
1–3	1	0	15.00
1–3	1	1	30.00
4–6	0	0	12.00
4–6	0	1	3.00
4–6	1	0	18.00
4–6	1	1	7.00
7–9	0	0	9.00
7–9	0	1	3.00
7–9	1	0	14.00
7–9	1	1	4.00

SAS AND TIME INTERVAL DATA

```
PROC FREQ data=libname.x; weight frequency;
Tables interval*gender*relapse /cmh; run;
```

The "weight" statement tells SAS to associate the values for "frequency" with the other variables. We will read the "Nonzero correlation" result in the SAS output table.

SPSS AND TIME INTERVAL DATA

In SPSS we also have to tell the program this is grouped frequency data first:

> Go to Data⇒select "Weight cases"⇒ select "Weight Cases by" circle ⇒enter the name of the variable with the frequency counts under "Frequency variable"⇒ click "OK"

Now

> Go to Analyze⇒Descriptive Statistics⇒Crosstabs⇒ specify the variable "female" for the "Row(s)," the variable "relapse" for the "Column(s)," and the control variable "interval" under "Layer 1 of 1"⇒click on "Statistics . . ." ⇒ select "Cochran's and Mantel-Haenszel statistics"⇒ click on "Continue"⇒ click "OK"

We read the Mantel-Haenszel chi-square from the SPSS output.

We do not display output here as it looks the same as that we saw in the prior section on CMH chi-square tests. If our test is significant, this tells us that gender is associated with relapse while controlling for time period.

SECTION 14.8.2: EXACT DATES

Sometimes you have exact start, end, and event dates and larger data sets. For example, you may have data that include the date of the entry into the data set, the date of a female becoming a teen parent (if occurred), and then a date at which you stopped following the sample for several thousand females. You want to know how the risk of becoming a teen mother is associated with a prior history of trauma while controlling for time at risk. This time instead of cross-tabulations of time intervals and CMH tests, we turn to another procedure using life tables and survival curves.

There are some different forms of testing bivariate associations with exact date information. For small samples, we will want to use the Kaplan-Meier method, which calculates survival rates for a subject at each measured time. For larger samples we will group the output into time intervals to save space and analyze according to persons who "fail" or "survive" within a given interval. This will print out a table with various columns by

strata. The idea is similar to the one we discussed for intervals. The procedure adjusts the estimates for survival at each time period according to those left in the sample at the next measured time (see Allison, 1995, for a more in-depth presentation of these concepts).

First, a bit of data programming. You need a "yes/no" variable that indicates the occurrence of the event of interest just like the outcome for a logistic regression:

> teen motherhood=1 if "yes"; or 0 if "no"

Then we must calculate the time at risk. This time variable can be on any scale (minutes, days, months, years). For a person who has the event (or "fails") in our example this is:

> time at risk = (date of child birth − date of entry into study)

For a person who "survives" (does not get pregnant) this is:

> time at risk = (date of study end [or withdrawal] − date of entry into study)

Obviously, a person who has the event is removed from the subsequent time period. This removal is also called **censoring.** There can be other reasons for withdrawal, however, such as death or moving out of the study area. Assuming you know that this occurs and when, you simply adjust the end date for the time at risk to equal the date for the other reason for withdrawal. So for Jane the time at risk might be:

> time at risk = (date of child birth − date of entry into study)

but for Tina, who moved out of the area when she was 13, the time at risk might be:

> time at risk = (date moved out of study area − date of entry into study)

This type of censoring is also called "right censoring" because typically we think of time on a time line that moves from left to right (beginning to end). You can also have "left censoring." Left censoring refers to instances in which cases entered the study at different times. For example, let's say you were following survival rates for cancer patients. People get cancer at different ages, so therefore their time at risk must be adjusted for the age at which they became cancer patients. Because this is only an introduction to survival analyses, we deal only with right censoring here.

Finally, we need a nominal or limited ordinal variable if we wish to do bivariate analyses. In other words, in our example we are interested in whether or not child trauma status is associated with becoming a teen mom while controlling for time. Therefore we need a third variable called trauma that is a nominal variable:

- *Research question:* "Is childhood trauma associated with the risk of becoming a teen mother controlling for time?"

Because the SAS and SPSS output are significantly different, we will go through each one separately.

SAS AND EXACT DATE TIME DATA

If you have a relatively small sample, a version of the life table using exact dates with small samples can be produced by using the PROC LIFETEST with no method specified (Figure 14.40).

Figure 14.41 is an example of part of the SAS output for the lifetest measuring time in years of age and using the default Kaplan-Meier method. As you can see, it looks as if there is a lot of missing information, but this is because it prints an entry for each subject. This makes it unwieldy for large samples. The alternative is to use the method=life option, which can group our data into intervals (Figure 14.42). This tells SAS to examine our data by year intervals rather than individual subjects. In this case, our data cover ages 13 through 17, so we start before and end after to make sure the complete intervals are included. We have also requested some graphic plots that we will talk about in a minute.

FIGURE 14.40. SAS Code.

```
PROC LIFETEST data=X;
     time riskmom*teenmom(0);
     strata CTS; run;
```

Where "riskmom" is the time at risk (number of months that the mother was observed prior to censoring) and "teenmom" is 1 if the mother gave birth and 0 if she didn't, and "CTS" is 1 if there is a child trauma history.

FIGURE 14.42. SAS Programming Language for Bivariate Survival Curve

```
PROC LIFETEST data=temp method=lt
intervals=12.1 to 18.1 by 1 plots=(s,lls);
         time riskmom*teenmom(0);
         strata CTS; run;
```

You will see two levels of output this time. The output will be arranged according to the strata (in our case a variable called 1 if there was a child trauma history and 0 if there was not). The output in Figure 14.43 presents data on survival and failure for each level of the stratifying variable. This is followed by information on bivariate tests of association. In addition, SAS will print out any plots requested on the separate graphics screen. To conserve space, we display only one level of the strata output and then the association tests and plots. We have also chosen to discuss only the most commonly used aspects of the output.

Interpretation of Commonly Used Output for the SAS Lifetest Method.

- *Interval:* Period of time defined in your statement
- *The number failed:* Those who have the event within that interval
- *The number censored:* Those who have reached the end of the study period or withdrawn in a given interval without the event
- *Effective sample size:* Who is left for that period
- *Conditional probability of failure:* Estimate of the probability that a person will have the event within that interval, given that she did not have it prior to that interval
- *Survival column:* Probability that an event will occur at a time greater than or equal to the start of that interval (0 to 1)

FIGURE 14.41. SAS Output.

		Survival			
riskmom	Survival	Failure	Standard Error	Number Failed	Number Left
0.0000	1.0000	0	0	0	58
16.0000	.	.	.	1	57
16.0000	0.9655	0.0345	0.0240	2	56
17.0000	.	.	.	3	55
17.0000	0.9310	0.0690	0.0333	4	54
19.0000	.	.	.	5	53
19.0000	.	.	.	6	52

FIGURE 14.43. SAS Output.

The LIFETEST Procedure

Stratum 1: CTS = 1

Life Table Survival Estimates

Interval (Lower, Upper)		Number Failed	Number Censored	Effective Sample Size	Conditional Probability of Failure	Conditional Probability Standard Error	Survival	Failure
0	12.1	0	1492	1758.0	0	0	1.0000	0
12.1	13.1	2	184	920.0	0.00217	0.00154	1.0000	0
13.1	14.1	1	174	739.0	0.00135	0.00135	0.9978	0.00217
14.1	15.1	4	156	573.0	0.00698	0.00348	0.9965	0.00352
15.1	16.1	12	149	416.5	0.0288	0.00820	0.9895	0.0105
16.1	17.1	12	208	226.0	0.0531	0.0149	0.9610	0.0390
17.1	18.1	0	110	55.0	0	0	0.9100	0.0900

Evaluated at the Midpoint of the Interval

Interval (Lower, Upper)		Survival Standard Error	Median Residual Lifetime	Median Standard Error	PDF	PDF Standard Error	Hazard	Hazard Standard Error
0	12.1	0	.	.	0	.	0	.
12.1	13.1	0	.	.	0.00217	0.00154	0.002176	0.001539
13.1	14.1	0.00154	.	.	0.00135	0.00135	0.001354	0.001354
14.1	15.1	0.00204	.	.	0.00696	0.00347	0.007005	0.003503
15.1	16.1	0.00402	.	.	0.0285	0.00811	0.029233	0.008438
16.1	17.1	0.00900	.	.	0.0510	0.0143	0.054545	0.01574
17.1	18.1	0.0167	.	.	0	.	0	.

- *Failure:* 1 (representing everyone) – survival (see above)
- *Hazard:* Probability of an event at the midpoint of the interval given survival or a lack of an event to that point

Next, SAS will give you a summary of the failed and censored cases by the strata you requested (Figure 14.44). In addition to errors listed in the log file, it is a good idea to check this table to make sure the sample size is correct. For example, we wouldn't want to include males in an analysis of who becomes a teen mother. So, our sample size should be correct according to the number of females in the study.

Finally, at the end of the output of the survival table you will find the test statistics (Figure 14.45). Two test statistics are relevant to assessing the association with the stratifying variable, and they are similar to chi-square tests. Significance indicates an association between the strata and the outcome controlling for time. The Wilcoxon is more sensitive to differences in strata at the beginning of the study, and the log rank test is more sensitive to differences toward the middle and later (Allison, 1995). The log rank is the most commonly reported.

FIGURE 14.44. Summary of the Number of Censored and Uncensored Values.

Stratum	CTS	Total	Failed	Censored	Percent Censored
1	1	2504	31	2473	98.76
2	0	2534	16	2518	99.37
Total		5038	47	4991	99.07

FIGURE 14.46. SPSS Life Table.

First-order Controls	Interval Start Time	Number Entering Interval	Number Withdrawing during Interval	Number Exposed to Risk	Number of Terminal Events	Proportion Terminating	Proportion Surviving	Cumulative Proportion Surviving at End of Interval	Std. Error of Cumulative Proportion Surviving at End of Interval	Probability Density	Std. Error of Probability Density	Hazard Rate	Std. Error of Hazard Rate
CTS 1	0	2504	3	2502.500	0	.00	1.00	1.00	.00	.000	.000	.00	.00
	1	2501	0	2501.000	0	.00	1.00	1.00	.00	.000	.000	.00	.00
	2	2501	3	2499.500	0	.00	1.00	1.00	.00	.000	.000	.00	.00
	3	2498	9	2493.500	0	.00	1.00	1.00	.00	.000	.000	.00	.00
	4	2489	7	2485.500	0	.00	1.00	1.00	.00	.000	.000	.00	.00
	5	2482	16	2474.000	0	.00	1.00	1.00	.00	.000	.000	.00	.00
	6	2466	13	2459.500	0	.00	1.00	1.00	.00	.000	.000	.00	.00
	7	2453	116	2395.000	0	.00	1.00	1.00	.00	.000	.000	.00	.00
	8	2337	280	2197.000	0	.00	1.00	1.00	.00	.000	.000	.00	.00
	9	2057	288	1913.000	0	.00	1.00	1.00	.00	.000	.000	.00	.00
	10	1769	277	1630.500	0	.00	1.00	1.00	.00	.000	.000	.00	.00
	11	1492	250	1367.000	0	.00	1.00	1.00	.00	.000	.000	.00	.00
	12	1242	230	1127.000	0	.00	1.00	1.00	.00	.000	.000	.00	.00
	13	1012	184	920.000	2	.00	1.00	1.00	.00	.002	.002	.00	.00
	14	826	174	739.000	1	.00	1.00	1.00	.00	.001	.001	.00	.00
	15	651	156	573.000	4	.01	.99	.99	.00	.007	.003	.01	.00
	16	491	149	416.500	12	.03	.97	.96	.01	.029	.008	.03	.01
0	0	2534	3	2532.500	0	.00	1.00	1.00	.00	.000	.000	.00	.00
	1	2531	1	2530.500	0	.00	1.00	1.00	.00	.000	.000	.00	.00
	2	2530	3	2528.500	0	.00	1.00	1.00	.00	.000	.000	.00	.00
	3	2527	10	2522.000	0	.00	1.00	1.00	.00	.000	.000	.00	.00
	4	2517	7	2513.500	0	.00	1.00	1.00	.00	.000	.000	.00	.00
	5	2510	8	2506.000	0	.00	1.00	1.00	.00	.000	.000	.00	.00
	6	2502	15	2494.500	0	.00	1.00	1.00	.00	.000	.000	.00	.00
	7	2487	119	2427.500	0	.00	1.00	1.00	.00	.000	.000	.00	.00
	8	2368	263	2236.500	0	.00	1.00	1.00	.00	.000	.000	.00	.00
	9	2105	269	1970.500	0	.00	1.00	1.00	.00	.000	.000	.00	.00
	10	1836	294	1689.000	0	.00	1.00	1.00	.00	.000	.000	.00	.00
	11	1542	250	1417.000	0	.00	1.00	1.00	.00	.000	.000	.00	.00
	12	1292	244	1170.000	0	.00	1.00	1.00	.00	.000	.000	.00	.00
	13	1048	194	951.000	0	.00	1.00	1.00	.00	.000	.000	.00	.00
	14	854	173	767.500	2	.00	1.00	1.00	.00	.003	.002	.00	.00
	15	679	164	597.000	3	.01	.99	.99	.00	.005	.003	.01	.00
	16	512	142	441.000	4	.01	.99	.98	.01	.009	.004	.01	.00

FIGURE 14.45. Test of Equality over Strata.

Test	Chi-Square	DF	Pr > Chi-Square
Log-Rank	5.9324	1	0.0149
Wilcoxon	5.1269	1	0.0236
-2Log(LR)	5.1904	1	0.0227

Notice that both the log rank and the Wilcoxon are relatively close in value. If a person's risk changed significantly with more risk at the beginning or end, these statistics would likely be quite different.

SPSS AND EXACT DATE TIME DATA

Go to Analyze ⇒ Survival⇒ Life Tables . . . ⇒ specify the "time" variable under "Time:" and define the "Display Time Intervals" ⇒ specify the outcome variable under "Status" and define the value(s) whereby the outcome occurs with "Define Event" ⇒specify the predictors under "Factor:," and define the range of the factor values (1 = maltreatment history, etc.)⇒ click on "Options . . ." ⇒select "Life table(s)" ⇒choose the "Survival" plot⇒ select "Overall" for "Compare Levels of First Factor"⇒ click on "Continue"⇒click "OK"

There are several differences in the SPSS output (Figure 14.46). First, the information is printed in a single table, one strata of CTS after another. SPSS also prints all results in the single table, rather than wrapping it into two tables. SPSS prints out only one test for bivariate significance, the Wilcoxon.

Interpretation of Commonly Used Output for the SPSS Lifetest Method.

- *Withdrawing:* SPSS does not use the term *censored;* it uses the word *withdrawing.*
- *Terminal events:* Instead of the number "failing," SPSS calls it the number "with terminal events."
- *Cumulative proportion surviving:* This is equivalent to the survival column in SAS.
- *Hazard:* This is the same as SAS.

Overall Comparisons(a)

Wilcoxon (Gehan) Statistic	df	Sig.
5.127	1	.024

a Comparisons are exact.

Our test bivariate statistics (Log Rank and Wilcoxon for SAS and Wilcoxon only for SPSS) are clearly significant. For this example, it means that those females in the CTS = 0 (no trauma) were less likely to have the event (becoming a teen mother) than those in the CTS = 1 (trauma) group. So we answer our research question in the affirmative.

SECTION 14.8.3: SURVIVAL CURVES

A survival curve provides a visual display of when events occur over time by strata without printing out the whole survival table. It provides another means of summarizing our findings. You'll recall that we mentioned we were asking SAS and SPSS for some plots. We asked for something called a survival curve in both and the log-log survival plot in SAS. The survival curve from SPSS is displayed in Figure 14.47.

It can be hard to manipulate an SAS or SPSS graphic, so we typically cut and paste the survival rates from the tables in SAS or SPSS into Excel to make our own curve if we want to use it in an article or presentation. In Figure 14.48, we have cut off the early years of the data because no female had an event before age 12.

As you can see, our Excel version is much more readable. The lines indicate events. The area under the curve represents those who have "survived" or not had the event. The *Y*-axis is basically a percent, so we are displaying the results only down to 86% of the sample. This provides visual confirmation of what we saw in our statistics. The females who have a history of trauma are at greater risk of the event, and this difference appears to increase with age.

Now you want to know why we were interested in that other plot in SAS. If we want to extend our analysis to a multivariate model, we may want to use something called Cox regression or proportional hazards. As might be deduced from the second name, something needs to be proportional. It turns out that this multivariate model "assumes" that the risk of a given event behaves similarly over time for all values of the independent variable. This second plot in SAS helps us assess this assumption. We can also get this in SPSS, but we have to use a different procedure. We'll discuss this more in the following section.

COX REGRESSION

A Cox regression is one of a variety of event history models and is generally preferred in social science unless you are attempting to forecast the future or time itself is of interest rather than just something you want to control for. As can be gathered from its other name, this type of event history model has an assumption that the risk of a given event for one strata is constant compared to another strata. Thus, running the bivariate analysis with the "log-log survival" option is a way of

FIGURE 14.47. **SPSS Survival Curve.**

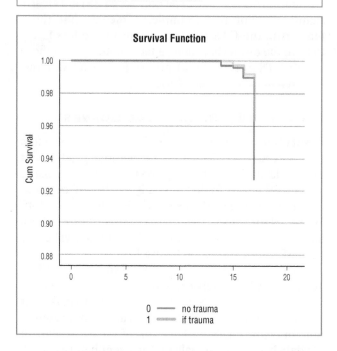

FIGURE 14.48. **Excel Version of Survival Curve.**

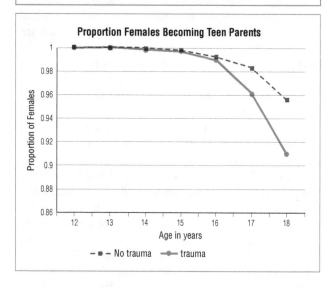

method of choice for many researchers for determining if the risk of an event is proportional over time. While both SAS and SPSS produce this plot, we find that the SAS plot is easier to use as a diagnostic tool.

SAS and Diagnostics for Proportionality. In SAS we request this plot in our life table statement. It is the "lls" in the parentheses after the word *plots*.

```
PROC LIFETEST data=temp method=lt
intervals=12.1 to 18.1
by 1 plots=(s,lls);
time riskmom*teenmom(0);
strata CMS; run;
```

SPSS and Diagnostics for Proportionality.

Go to Analyze⇒Survival⇒Cox Regression⇒ select the time variable and the event variable⇒skip the covariate section⇒ go down to the "Strata" and select "CMS"⇒ click on the "Plots" button⇒select "log minus log" ⇒click "Continue" ⇒click "OK"

We display the SAS plot output in Figure 14.49. As you can see, in the log-log plot, our lines are not perfectly parallel, but they are close. If the lines crossed or had a distinctive funnel shape, then we would assume that the risk of the event changed over time in a different way for one level of the strata compared to another in a practically significant way.

That's all very well for our example, but what if the dreaded funnel shape appeared? Good news: If we had a strong indication of lack of proportionality for a given strata, we could still proceed with a Cox regression. We do have to create a new variable that is a special form of interaction term. This variable adjusts the model for the time interaction and is an interaction term between the independent variable of interest and your time at risk variable (e.g., an interaction between CMS and riskmom).

checking for violations of this assumption before moving on to multivariate models (Allison, 1995). Given the slight departure from parallel lines in our example, the procedure would be robust against this level of violation.

Now because our Wilcoxon and log rank were relatively close in our earlier example, there is probably not a problem meeting the proportionality requirement of the multivariate technique. However, a second type of plot is useful to further check this phenomenon in our data. The other graphic produced is the negative log-log survival plot. When used with strata, this is the

FIGURE 14.49. **SAS Plot Output.**

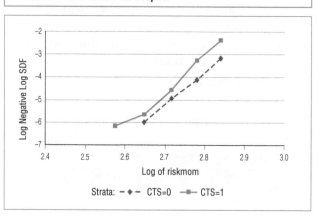

Like a regular interaction term, a significant value for this coefficient means that you cannot interpret the main effect for that variable without considering the interaction with time. Of course it is possible to have different types of nonproportionality, including a curvilinear effect. Thus, it may be necessary to create an interaction term that is tied to a recoded version of time that acknowledges the shape or location of the nonproportionality.

A thorough introduction to the use of the multivariate Cox regression model is beyond the scope of this text. However, it is helpful to know what it is and the basics of its interpretation so that you can understand results that you may read. This procedure helps a researcher answer the question about what factors are associated with an increase or decrease in the risk of an event given the time period that a subject was at risk for the event.

The time variable and censor variable (outcome) are the same as those we discussed for the bivariate model. Cox regression produces output that looks somewhat similar in format to a logistic regression model. The difference is that this is modeling the logarithm of the hazard (or risk of event) for a person at time t. The dependent variable portion of the equation includes time as well as the event. The procedure uses a form of chi-square to test the model fit and also the coefficients. Instead of producing odds ratios, however, this procedure produces what some people call "risk ratios" (technically hazard ratios). It has a similar practical interpretation to the odds ratio in that a hazard ratio below 1 indicates a decrease in the estimated hazard of the event and above 1 indicates an increased hazard of the event.

If a lack of proportionality is indicated during bivariate analyses prior to running the model, one of the nice features of this procedure is that the interaction term can be created in the model statement instead of having to do so in the data step. Sometimes bivariate problems with proportionality are not an issue in the multivariate model. To test this, a time/variable interaction for each variable that displays the problem should be included and tested separately. If either the interaction term is significant or the inclusion of the term significantly alters the model fit or coefficients for other variables, then the interaction should be retained in the model.

SAS and Cox Regression.

```
PROC PHREG data=X;
model riskmom*teenmom(0)= X Y Z X*Y X*time /
ties=efron rl;
X*time; x*Y;
run;
```

Terms and their definitions include:

- `PROC PHREG:` This is the procedure command in SAS to request a Cox regression.

- `Model:` This is the statement letting SAS know that these are the variables and options you want to use.

- `Riskmom:` This is the variable you created in the data set that is basically the end of the study period—start of the study period adjusted to the metric of interest (days, months, years, and so on). Yes, of course there are more complicated issues in creating this value—such as determining whether the subject is at risk during the whole period—but you get the basic idea. It's basically telling the computer to adjust the outcome variable by the time at risk of the outcome.

- `Teenmom(0):` This first part "Teenmom" will be the name of your outcome of interest. The (0) is telling the computer what the censoring value is.

- *Variables* (`x, y, z`): After the equals sign, you list the variables you wish to include in the model. This includes the name of any interaction terms.

- *Options:* These are listed after a forward slash following the variable list. The "ties" statement is telling the computer how to settle ties in times. In other words, let's say inchworm one reaches the apple in the same amount of time as inchworm two. SAS needs to differentiate between the inchworms. The "Ties = Efron" option is the option of choice in most cases. Please see Allison (1995) for an explanation of why. Finally, "rl" requests the confidence intervals for the risk ratios in the output.

- *Interaction Terms:* After the line concluding with OPTIONS, the PHREG procedure has the convenient feature of allowing you to create interaction terms in the model statement. Each interaction is created as a separate statement followed by a semicolon (e.g., X*time and X*Y in our example above).

SPSS and Cox Regression.

Go to Analyze⇒Survival⇒Cox Regression⇒ select the time variable "riskmom" and the event "teenmom" and define the event as "1"⇒select our covariates "CMS" and "Race"⇒because these are categorical covariates, we click on the categorical button and enter them in the box as indicators⇒click "Continue" ⇒ click on "Options" ⇒ select the "confidence interval" option⇒ click "Continue" ⇒click "OK"

We display two examples, one a simple example model of teen parenting using two variables, past trauma history and race (White versus non-White), and a second including an interaction term between race and time. To conserve space we will use the SPSS output for the first model (Figure 14.50) and the SAS output for the second (Figure 14.51).

It's tempting to skip things like the initial model information, but don't succumb to the temptation! This is a great way to check out whether the computer appears to be doing what you asked with the right amount of data.

SPSS provides us with a single-model chi-square, which is significant. This means we can go on and interpret our hazard ratios (the "Exp(B)" column). Remember, the hazard ratio reported is not the same as an odds ratio (we'll skip the math here because this is just an introduction to this technique), so although its practical interpretation is very similar you should use the right terminology. Both covariates are significant. It appears that White females in this sample had

a lower risk of pregnancy when also controlling for trauma history, and females with a trauma history had a higher (over twice as high) rate of pregnancy.

Now we use SAS to model the same outcome, but there are the two variables and an interaction term between race and time. SAS provides a few options for model fit, but we will look at the top one, which is the likelihood ratio chi-square. As before, it is significant, so we may move on to look at the covariates. The interaction term with race is not statistically significant, but it does approach significance. Remember that a nonsignificant interaction can still have a significant influence on a model. When this model was rerun without the interaction term the -2Log likelihood chi-square was reduced to 16.2543 with DF = 2. If we look at the difference in model chi-squares and use a chi-square table, the number 3.84 is the critical value for significance with 1 degree of freedom. The difference in chi-square is 3.19, not significant. We might well choose

---

FIGURE 14.50. SPSS Output.

Case Processing Summary

		N	Percent
Cases available in analysis	Event(a)	47	.9%
	Censored	2013	40.0%
	Total	2060	40.9%
Cases dropped	Cases with missing values	0	.0%
	Cases with negative time	0	.0%
	Censored cases before the earliest event in a stratum	2978	59.1%
	Total	2978	59.1%
Total		5038	100.0%

a Dependent Variable: riskmom

Omnibus Tests of Model Coefficients(a,b)

-2 Log Likelihood	Overall (score)			Change from Previous Step			Change from Previous Block		
	Chi-square	df	Sig.	Chi-square	df	Sig.	Chi-square	df	Sig.
629.672	13.862	2	.001	15.978	2	.000	15.978	2	.000

a Beginning Block Number 0, initial Log Likelihood function: -2 Log likelihood: 645.650
b Beginning Block Number 1. Method = Enter

Variables in the Equation

	B	SE	Wald	df	Sig.	Exp(B)	95.0% CI for Exp(B)	
							Lower	Upper
Caucasian	-1.741	.724	5.782	1	.016	.175	.042	.725
CTS	.837	.309	7.355	1	.007	2.309	1.261	4.227

FIGURE 14.51. **SAS Output.**

```
                        The PHREG Procedure
                        Model Information

        Data Set              WORK.TEMP
        Dependent Variable    riskmom
        Censoring Variable    TEENMOM        1 = became teen mother
        Censoring Value(s)    0
        Ties Handling         EFRON

               Number of Observations Read      5038
               Number of Observations Used      5038
        Summary of the Number of Event and Censored Values

                                          Percent
            Total    Event   Censored     Censored

            5038      47       4991         99.07

                       Convergence Status

        Convergence criterion (GCONV =1E-8) satisfied.
                      Model Fit Statistics

                        Without           With
         Criterion     Covariates       Covariates

         -2 LOG L       644.877          625.437
         AIC            644.877          631.437
         SBC            644.877          636.987

            Testing Global Null Hypothesis: BETA=0

         Test           Chi-Square    DF      Pr > ChiSq

         Likelihood Ratio  19.4401     3       0.0002
         Score             15.3133     3       0.0016
         Wald              12.0463     3       0.0072
```
← Model fit measures

```
                     The PHREG Procedure
            Analysis of Maximum Likelihood Estimates
```

Variable	DF	Parameter Estimate	Standard Error	Chi-Square	Pr > ChiSq	Hazard Ratio	95% Hazard Ratio Confidence Limits	
CTS	1	0.85046	0.30843	7.6029	0.0058	2.341	1.279	4.284
Caucasian	1	13.64158	8.59109	2.5213	0.1123	840358.2	0.041	1.727E13
whitetime	1	-1.00212	0.58293	2.9553	0.0856	0.367	0.117	1.151

to eliminate the interaction term—particularly given how rare our event is and power issues related to that and how unstable the race term has become relative to the confidence interval.

In both models, a prior report of maltreatment remained significant and nearly identical (HR = 2.34, compared to the SPSS output of 2.31). So, a rough practical interpretation is that a female without a trauma report history had about half of the risk of becoming a teen mother in this sample. White subjects were about five times less likely to become teen parents. Note the broad confidence interval for race in the SPSS output (0.42, 0.72), however, meaning that there was a lot of variability.

Be warned: This was just a small taste of analyses that consider time. There is much more to learn. Though many of the techniques for analyzing such data have existed for some time, their use in social science has become commonplace only in the last five years. Because of the rapidly evolving nature of these techniques, you are encouraged to read further and feel free to seek consultation with a statistician.

There are numerous special issues you will encounter as you move on to more advanced uses of statistics. It is beyond the scope of this chapter to introduce the use of additional statistical procedures. We do, however, briefly review three important issues that we find commonly occurring and provide some direction as to resources to address those issues.

SECTION 14.9.1: CLUSTERING OF OBSERVATIONS

Sometimes you are analyzing only individuals (e.g., what happens to John and Jane?), and sometimes you are analyzing only groups (e.g., do poor people use more services?), but sometimes your data include individuals or other units of analysis who are grouped in some way that is part of the focus of the research. For example, let's say you are studying parental participation in a child's school and want to control for income in the census tract. Unless you selected only one person from each census tract (which is unlikely), you have more than one parent who comes from each tract. If you simply attach the census tract data without controlling for the fact that some of your parents come from the same tract, you run the risk of error in the coefficient estimates for your model because aspects of persons within the census tracts are intercorrelated. In other words, there is some lack of independence in your observations if you include a grouped variable like census data without special controls in your model. You may also see the words "cluster" or "design effect" in the literature (Allison, 1996; Cochran, 1977). The effect of the clustering on the outcome is also called a "random effect" in the literature (Fitzmaurice, Laird, & Ware, 2004). Some techniques treat clusters as a nuisance and provide essentially an average adjustment for them. Others provide the capability of assessing variation within and between those clusters and outputting that specific information.

Covering all the ways of handling this issue is beyond the scope of this textbook, but the multivariate models introduced in this chapter all have options or counterparts that can be used to analyze data that are clustered in some way. Perhaps the most commonly heard term related to this issue is *hierarchical linear modeling,* which typically refers to techniques analyzing continuous dependent variables (Raudenbush & Bryk, 2001). Mixed model regression can also be used to handle clustering (Hedeker, 2005). SAS procedures like PROC MIXED and SPSS mixed model can be used to address clustering and provide estimates of the differences between clusters with continuous data (SAS Institute Inc., 2005). PROC NLMIXED can be used to address clustering and provide estimates of the differences between clusters for categorical data but is not currently available in SPSS (SAS Institute Inc., 2005). Also, PROC NLMIXED is currently limited to two levels and can have difficulty with longitudinal data that have a degree of correlation between measures over time (Fitzmaurice et al., 2004; Van Ness, O'Leary, Byers, & Dubin, 2004). In such cases one will need to use specialized software such as HLM (see the publisher Web site for more detail about HLM: www.ssicentral.com/hlm/index.html). Yes, it's both a technique and the name of a computer program.

Sometimes we really don't care about the variation of a given cluster, we just want to control for it as a nuisance. There are several options for more familiar methods that can do this. For example, Cox and logistic regression have available options that use special estimating techniques to account for clustering as a nuisance (Allison, 1991 & 2005; Lee, Wei, & Amato, D, 1991; SAS Institute, 2003). Further, generalized estimating equations (GEE) can also be used to model data that are clustered (Hardin & Hilbe, 2003). SPSS does not currently have a procedure for GEE models.

SECTION 14.9.2: CORRELATIONS OVER TIME IN LONGITUDINAL DATA

Recall that we discussed a repeated measures model for an ANOVA. Sometimes you want a multivariate regression model of how an individual changes over time and capture repeated measures of the same thing for multiple years. This seems straightforward, but unfortunately you are likely to encounter a problem that is similar in its effect to clustering but is related to time and the individual. For example, let's say you are measuring treatment impact on 500 depressed people, and you remeasure their level of depression each year. Within an individual there are unmeasured personal aspects that will influence his or her subsequent scores. In other words, there is a sort of within-subject correlation between the person's scores over time. This is also called a "random effect." You need to use a statistical model that can take this into account. For panel designs where the interest is between group change, a generalized estimating equation might be a good choice (Hardin & Hilbe, 2003). For measuring individual level variation in change, a mixed model regression might be used (Hedeker, 2005). As of the writing of this chapter, SPSS cannot be used for GEE models, but SAS and STATA (another statistical analysis package) are capable of running this technique.

SECTION 14.9.3: COMPLEX DATA SETS, GIS, AND OTHER ANALYTIC NEEDS

This text focuses on SAS and SPSS, which are two very popular and highly capable statistical packages. There are, however, complex survey designs and other specialized data analyses that are either only or better suited to other programs. For example, LISREL is a popular choice for structural equation modeling. Programs like SUDAAN or Mplus are used for some of the larger national-level data sets that have complex weighting systems that need to be used to generalize results back to the population of interest. Geospatial analyses (using geocoded data and also called GIS for short) are becoming increasingly popular in social science, particularly in public health. These data are typically prepared using software such as ArcView or MapInfo and analyzed using a variety of software packages. The more widespread software packages like SAS or SPSS do update their capabilities but tend to lag behind other programs that are sometimes specifically designed by a particular statistician to handle a given data situation.

As stated early in the text, research is a cyclical and dynamic process. The choice of statistical software is as dependent on good planning and research design as the analyses themselves. Once a research question is formed, it is important to think about the type of data as well as the kinds of analyses to be performed. The more complex the situation or cutting edge the statistics, the more likely the social science researcher will wish to consult with a statistician. This individual can assist the project leader in identifying the appropriate analyses as well as the appropriate software. Depending on the expertise available at your site, this process may involve bringing in someone from another university or traveling to attend training on a specific system. This, too, becomes a part of the research process.

CONCLUSION

Whew! You made it! This chapter has provided a whirlwind introduction to more advanced methods used in social science research to analyze data. For the beginning researcher and the more advanced student who need a refresher or are unfamiliar with how to invoke the procedures in SAS and SPSS, this chapter provides a basic working knowledge of the statistical techniques covered. There are many options, provisos, advanced topics, and the like whose omission may make the statistician cringe a bit. Now we will see how our researchers have chosen to apply this knowledge to their studies.

EBP MODULE

As may be evident by now, even if you never conduct your own research study, a basic grasp of statistics is imperative for the evidence-based practitioner. For example, the policy advocate must be able to understand that a statistically significant test of association between two things does not mean that the association is large enough to be meaningful or that it is causal. To understand what factors to target to prevent delinquency requires an adequate research design combined with appropriate statistical procedures. The EBP practitioner asks not only whether findings were statistically significant but whether they are practically significant. How much of the variance in the subject of interest is explained by the variables included in the study? In an analysis of an intervention, were the significant effects large enough to matter?

But how can you hope to master all the different statistical techniques? The answer is that you can't. But all well-written articles should include variables that are operationalized so you can understand what they mean. All good research should include some information beyond *p* values that say "yes, this was significant." There should be some kind of indicator of the relative magnitude of the relationship in the form of a coefficient (i.e., a beta, an odds ratio). If there was a significant loss of sample or a low response rate, a good article should include some basic statistics comparing the remaining subjects to those who exited. You may not understand everything that a given researcher did statistically, but you should be able now to look for those reported results that tell you whether or not there is substantial and practical meaning there.

EXERCISES

1. Using the data set provided, calculate and interpret two separate bivariate regression models using the same dependent variables for both models. Then run a multiple regression model in which both independent variables are entered simultaneously. *Assignment:* Assess for multicollinearity in the multiple regression model.

Do the regression coefficients and the independent variables change when they are both in the equation? Why or why not? Write the regression results in journal format.

2. Use the zip code census data provided and run a principal components procedure using at least seven variables. *Assignment:* Discuss your results. How many components did you keep? What type of variables seemed to hang together? Did the resulting components make intuitive sense? What did you label them and why?

3. You will select three nominal variables to use from a course data set. At least two of the three variables must have a bivariate association. Using a computer, compute the CMH statistic for a set of 2×2 tables. *Assignment:* Write up the results in a paragraph. What did you learn about the relationships among the variables you examined?

4. Use the same outcome and two independent variables from exercise 1 and construct a logistic regression model using PROC LOGISTIC. Enter the independent variables one at a time. *Assignment:* Compare the model chi-square with one as compared to the two variables and interpret the results in a paragraph. What did you learn about the relationships between the variables and the outcome you examined? Were the variable coefficients significant? Look at the odds ratios—are they practically and statistically significant?

5. Use the same data as last week, but this time add age as a continuous variable in the model and then rerun the model with an interaction term in PROC LOGISTIC. Request the output for ROC for both models. *Assignment:* Interpret both models, including the overall fit and the results for the continuous variable and interaction term. Was the interaction term significant? Did it alter the model fit or predictive value in a significant way?

6. Using a data set provided, run a one-way repeated measures ANOVA. *Assignment:* Write a research question for your ANOVA. Then write one or two paragraphs interpreting the results of the analysis.

7. You will be given a small data set with a start and end dates, a dichotomous independent variable, and a dichotomous count of an event. Create a time variable using SAS. Use PROC LIFETEST to produce a survival curve and significance test. *Assignment:* Interpret the output. Were there significant differences in the occurrence of the event over time for the two groups? Look at the survival curve; does the occurrence of the event seem proportional over time for both groups?

1. What are the primary assumptions for a multiple regression model?

2. One of the main differences between regression and ANOVA is:

   a. Regression is sensitive to normality, and ANOVA is not.

   b. ANOVA assesses linear relationships, and regression does not.

   c. Regression is predicting a point (or single value) of the dependent variable, and ANOVA tests group differences.

   d. Cool researchers use ANOVAs.

   e. none of the above

3. Why is it important to look at the standardized betas for a multiple regression model instead of the raw parameter estimates?

4. You are interested in the association between spirituality (coded as spiritual = 1 or not = 0) and recovery from depression without medication (no medication = 1; medication = 0). You think that this relationship may vary by gender. The statistical procedure most appropriate to help you assess this association is:

   a. *T* test

   b. correlation

   c. principal components analysis

   d. Cochran-Mantel-Haenszel chi-square

5. John uses a CMH chi-square to examine the association between taking psychotropic medication (yes = 1; no = 0) and gender, controlling for participation in a program (yes = 1; no = 0). Both tables have significant CMH chi-square, and his general association statistic is significant. He now looks at the Breslow-Day-Tarone test. Why? What is this test for? If it's significant, what does that mean?

6. Why might you use a principal components analysis technique?

7. How do you know how many factors to keep in a principal components analysis (circle any that apply)?

   a. educated guess

   b. minimum Eigenvalue

   c. Mauchly's test

   d. scree test

   e. *R* square

8. Sigurd has run a principal components analysis of several variables that were highly correlated. After he runs the procedure, he finds that

variables 6 and 7 are both flagged as loading at .4 or above on two of his components. What should Sigurd do next?

9. You run an analysis of the likelihood of drug use among incarcerated youth, and the results indicate that the odds ratio for violent offenders is 1.50 (compared to nonviolent offenders). Briefly explain what that means.

10. Write a research question for a logistic regression model of homelessness (yes/no) controlling for at least three other variables.

11. A public health student runs a logistic regression model to better understand risk factors associated with the onset of asthma. The odds ratio for age (measured in years) is 0.98 and statistically significant. Please interpret the practical meaning of this finding.

12. As a researcher you are interested in understanding whether a family exits poverty or not. You run a logistic regression model and want to understand something about the predictive utility of the model. You might use the following to do that (circle any that apply):

    a. phi correlation

    b. ROC curve and *c* statistic

    c. pseudo *r* square

    d. astrological reading

13. Tina is the director at a small domestic violence agency. They have just begun a new intervention program for perpetrators. Tina wants to understand if the program is associated with a decrease in the participant scores on an anger control scale. She also wants to know if this decrease lasts over time. The agency collects data on 25 perpetrators at three periods: (1) prior to start, (2) at end of program, (3) six months later. They will use _____ to analyze the result.

14. Before Tina interprets her result, what assumptions will she first check for?

15. Why might a social science researcher use survival analysis?

16. Write a research question for a bivariate survival analysis of smoking cessation controlling for treatment (yes/no).

17. The multivariate extension of the bivariate survival curves is called _____.

SUPPLEMENTAL READINGS

This list is not the result of a comprehensive review of all available texts on statistics, but the readings were chosen based on the techniques mentioned in this book, the authors' experience, ease of use for a nonstatistician, and the fact that the books include references on how to use the techniques with SAS and/or SPSS.

- Agresti, A. (2002). *Categorical Data Analysis* (2nd ed.). New York: Wiley.
- Allison, P. (1991). *Logistic Regression: Using the SAS System*. New York: Wiley & Sons.
- Allison, P. (1995). *Survival Analysis Using the SAS System: A Practical Guide*. Cary, NC: SAS Institute Inc.
- Allison, P. (2002). *Missing Data. Quantitative Applications in the Social Sciences*. Thousand Oaks, CA: Sage.
- Allison, P. (2005). *Fixed Effects Regression Methods for Longitudinal Data Using SAS*. Cary, NC: SAS Institute Inc.
- Cai, L., & Weinfort, K. (1999). A SAS/IML Module for the Johnson-Neyman procedure. *Applied Psychological Measurement, 23*, 308.
- Cody, R., & Smith, J. (2006). *Applied Statistics and the SAS Programming Language* (5th ed.). Upper Saddle River, NJ: Pearson Prentice-Hall.
- Der, G. & Everitt, B. (2001). *Handbook of Statistical Analyses Using SAS* (2nd ed.). London: Chapman & Hall.
- Field, A. (2004). *Discovering Statistics Using SPSS for Windows*. Thousand Oaks, CA: Sage.
- Fitzmaurice, G., Laird, N., & Ware, J. (2004). *Applied Longitudinal Analysis*. Hoboken, New Jersey: John Wiley & Sons, Inc.
- Freund, R.J., & Littell, R.C. (2000). *SAS System for Regression* (3rd ed.). Wiley Series in Probability and Statistics. Cary, NC: SAS Institute Inc.
- Hardin, J., & Hilbe, J. (2003). *Generalized Estimating Equations*. New York: Chapman & Hall.
- Hedeker, D. & Gibbons, R. (2006). *Longitudinal Data Analysis*. Hoboken, NJ: John Wiley & Sons, Inc.
- Lawal, B. (2003). *Categorical Data Analysis with SAS and SPSS Applications*. Hillsdale, NJ: Lawrence Erlbaum Associates.
- Norusis, M. (2005). *SPSS 13.0 Advanced Statistical Procedures Companion*. Upper Saddle River, NJ: Prentice Hall.
- O'Rourke, N., Hatcher, L., Stepanksi, E. J. (2005). *A Step-by-Step Approach to Using SAS for Univariate and Multivariate Statistics* (2nd ed.). Cary, NC: SAS Institute Inc.
- Schafer, J. (1997). *Analysis of Incomplete Missing Data*. London: Chapman & Hall.

- Stevens, J. (2002). *Applied Multivariate Statistics for the Social Sciences* (4th ed.). Hillsdale, NJ: Lawrence Elrbaum.

- Stokes, M., Davis, C., & Koch, G. (2000). *Categorical Data Analysis Using the SAS System* (2nd ed.). Cary, NC: SAS.

- Tabachnick, B. G., & Fidell, L. S. (2001). *Using Multivariate Statistics* (4th ed.). Needham Heights, MA: Allyn & Bacon.

Students should also note that support documentation, help for specific techniques, and publications produced by the SAS and SPSS software companies can be found at the software Web sites. These Web sites change and are quite complex, so we have listed two good starting places:

- For SAS go to: http://support.sas.com/documentation/index.html.

- For SPSS go to: www.spss.com/spss/data_analysis.htm

CHAPTER

ANALYSIS EXAMPLES

We have just completed reviewing various statistical procedures and the interpretation of the related computer output. Now we will return to our five researcher friends and see what procedures the five researchers chose and what they found. Our final researcher, John, used primarily qualitative methods, but he did do some quantitative summing of themes as found among his sample.

SECTION 15.1

PROFESSOR KATHY

Kathy needs to decide what statistical procedures can answer her questions. As you may recall, Kathy is doing an experimental design study looking for the effects of background music on file coding. She has a three group balanced design (equal numbers per group): classical music ($n = 20$), easy listening ($n = 20$), and no music ($n = 20$). She wants to know if group membership is associated with coding speed and coding accuracy. Because the outcomes are measured as continuous variables (total number coded and number of errors per file), she can probably use a parametric procedure

(if the assumptions are met) to look for differences between groups. You may recall from the previous chapter that this sounds just like an ANOVA.

SECTION 15.1.1: DO PROFESSOR KATHY'S DATA MEET THE ASSUMPTIONS OF ANOVA?

First, Kathy runs her descriptive statistics to check to see if her data meet the assumptions required to use the ANOVA procedure (refer back to Chapter 13). We will now turn to the program Professor Kathy has written to do the analysis ("Kathy3.SAS"—available to you electronically at www.ablongman.com/mysocialworkkit). This program looks like Figure 15.1. Kathy sorts the data by group—this is a style thing that permits her to more easily scan the files visually. Following this, she looks to see that the data are in the right format (PROC CONTENTS) and that they "look" right when printed out (PROC PRINT). She also does a PROC MEANS (by group) to get a feel for how key variables "FALL" and "EPFALL" look by group. Everything seems cool, and she is ready to check to see that her data meet requirements for normality needed for the PROC GLM she plans to run (See Chapter 13). She does this

---

FIGURE 15.1. **Professor Kathy's SAS Analysis Program.**

```
/*********************** KATHY3.SAS *****************************/
/*********************** KATHY3.SAS *****************************/
/*********************** KATHY3.SAS *****************************/
/*********************** KATHY3.SAS *****************************/
/*********************** KATHY3.SAS *****************************/
/*********************** KATHY3.SAS *****************************/
/*********************** KATHY3.SAS *****************************/
/*           does data analysis for music study               */
/***************************************************************/

libname music "u:\drake and jonson-reid\book\projects\kathy";

/**************create temporary dataset for analyses***/
data kathy;set music.kathydata;run;

/** sort by group - it will make it easier to look at***/
proc sort data=kathy; by group fall;run; /**sort by #files*/

/**check it out - are variables OK and in the right format?****/
proc contents data=kathy; run;

/**check it out pt. 2 - do variables look right & not missing***/
proc print  data=kathy; run;

/*** more checking - look at means to get a better "feel" for the data**/
proc means; var epfall fall; by group; run;

/********check it out again, see if the key variables   ***
********meet statistical requirements for normality     **/
proc univariate plot normal data=kathy; var epfall fall;run;

/***do main analysis (# of files coded ("fall") ****/
PROC GLM data =kathy;  CLASS  group;
MODEL fall=group;
MEANS group /TUKEY HOVTEST=LEVENE WELCH; /**check homog. of var.**/
MEANS group; run;

/***********do main analyses for errors per file ("epfall")*****/
PROC GLM data =kathy;  CLASS group;
MODEL epfall=group;
MEANS group /TUKEY HOVTEST=LEVENE WELCH; /**check homog. of var.**/
MEANS group; run;
```

by running a PROC UNIVARIATE with the PLOT NORMAL option. Everything looks OK there, the box-plot is adequately centered, there are not too many outliers, and the normal probability plot looks very good. Kathy knows that the observations are independent (no student is in more than one group). She also checked to see that the largest group variance is less than 1.5 times the smallest. She then decides to do the analysis proper.

She proceeds to run a one-way ANOVA for both number of files coded (FALL) and errors per file (EPFALL). She will request Levene's test for homogeneity of variance in the ANOVA procedures so that when she writes her report she can report a statistical assessment for homogeneity of variance. A significant Levene's test is a bad thing; it means that there is not sufficient homogeneity of variance. This would screw up the F statistic. She also makes the computer calculate a revised F statistic using the WELCH option. Welch's test provides a corrected F statistic if Levene's test is significant (although it turns out later this will not be needed). Let's revisit Kathy's questions to see exactly how the ANOVAs she performs answer her questions.

SECTION 15.1.2: ANSWERING THE QUESTIONS

QUESTION 1: DOES BACKGROUND MUSIC AFFECT SPEED OF CODING?

- Q1: Do CBM, ELBM, and NBM coders have different speeds of coding?
- H1: CBM, ELBM, and NBM coders will have different rates of files coded per hour.

Partial SAS output is shown in Figure 15.2.

For question 1, Kathy will say "No," or more correctly she will be "unable to reject the null hypothesis."

There appears to be no significant difference in the speed of coding according to membership in the different background music groups. Because the ANOVA model is not significant, she doesn't bother to assess the TUKEY mean group comparisons. Now she runs a second ANOVA for question 2 using the errors per file as the dependent variable.

QUESTION 2: DOES BACKGROUND MUSIC AFFECT ACCURACY OF CODING?

- Q2: Are CBM, ELBM, and NBM coders equally accurate?
- H2: CBM coders will have different accuracy rates compared to ELBM and NBM codes as determined by file review.

See the SAS output in Figure 15.3.

Professor Kathy finds that the mean errors per file did vary according to background music group. Her hypothesis is supported. The students who listen to classical music (group 1) have a lower error rate than either the easy-listening or the no background music conditions. But how much is the difference? Is it important? The mean numbers of errors are what's important here, and group 1 has an error rate of 1.26 compared to about 1.90 (roughly) in the other two groups. Because 1.26/1.90 = .663, the classical group makes only .66 times as many errors. Cutting errors by one-third seems to be a big enough difference to be worthwhile.

SECTION 15.2

ABIGAIL

Abigail's interest is in how organizational and social support factors help child welfare workers cope with

---

FIGURE 15.2. **Professor Kathy's SAS Output for Question 1.**

```
                        The ANOVA Procedure

      Dependent Variable: fall        All files coded (all sessions)

                                 Sum of
      Source              DF     Squares      Mean Square   F Value   Pr > F
      Model                2    105.633333    52.816667       1.78    0.1771
      Error               57   1686.700000    29.591228
      Corrected Total     59   1792.333333


              R-Square     Coeff Var     Root MSE     fall Mean
              0.058936     18.65068      5.439782     29.16667


                        The ANOVA Procedure

            Levene's Test for Homogeneity of fall Variance
            ANOVA of Squared Deviations from Group Means

                                 Sum of       Mean
            Source          DF   Squares      Square     F Value   Pr > F
            group            2    1325.4       662.7        0.47    0.6303
            Error           57   81177.6      1424.2
```

Her model is not significant!

FIGURE 15.3. More of Kathy's SAS Output.

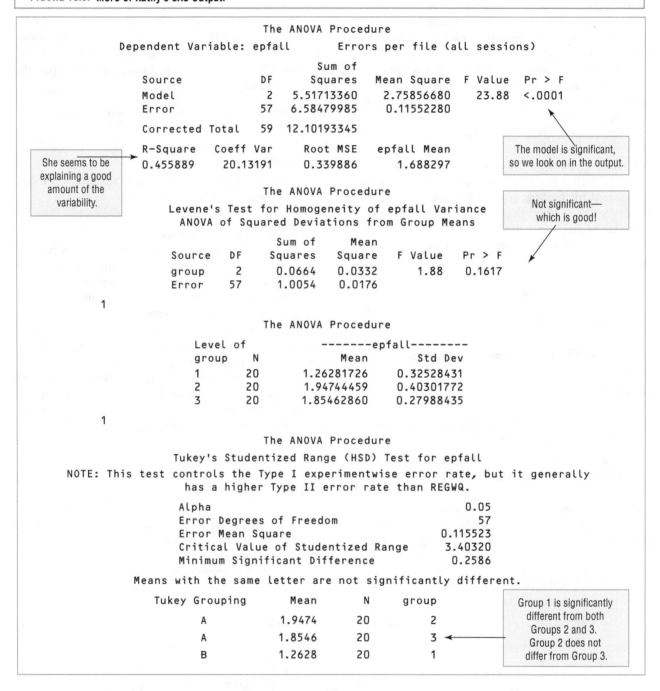

The ANOVA Procedure

Dependent Variable: epfall   Errors per file (all sessions)

Source	DF	Sum of Squares	Mean Square	F Value	Pr > F
Model	2	5.51713360	2.75856680	23.88	<.0001
Error	57	6.58479985	0.11552280		
Corrected Total	59	12.10193345			

R-Square	Coeff Var	Root MSE	epfall Mean
0.455889	20.13191	0.339886	1.688297

> *The model is significant, so we look on in the output.*

> *She seems to be explaining a good amount of the variability.*

The ANOVA Procedure

Levene's Test for Homogeneity of epfall Variance
ANOVA of Squared Deviations from Group Means

Source	DF	Sum of Squares	Mean Square	F Value	Pr > F
group	2	0.0664	0.0332	1.88	0.1617
Error	57	1.0054	0.0176		

> *Not significant—which is good!*

1

The ANOVA Procedure

Level of group	N	-------epfall-------- Mean	Std Dev
1	20	1.26281726	0.32528431
2	20	1.94744459	0.40301772
3	20	1.85462860	0.27988435

1

The ANOVA Procedure

Tukey's Studentized Range (HSD) Test for epfall

NOTE: This test controls the Type I experimentwise error rate, but it generally
has a higher Type II error rate than REGWQ.

Alpha	0.05
Error Degrees of Freedom	57
Error Mean Square	0.115523
Critical Value of Studentized Range	3.40320
Minimum Significant Difference	0.2586

Means with the same letter are not significantly different.

Tukey Grouping	Mean	N	group
A	1.9474	20	2
A	1.8546	20	3
B	1.2628	20	1

> *Group 1 is significantly different from both Groups 2 and 3. Group 2 does not differ from Group 3.*

child fatalities, so she collects data from workers who experience these events.

SECTION 15.2.1: ABIGAIL DECIDES WHAT STATISTICAL PROCEDURES CAN ANSWER HER QUESTIONS

Unlike Kathy, Abigail has a single group. Like Kathy, she has continuous outcome variables of interest. She is looking for associations between the factors of interest and the outcomes and wants to control for some demographic factors. It doesn't sound like an ANOVA. It sounds as though, to answer her main questions, she will need a multivariate model to provide control for the demographic factors. Associations, continuous (interval/ ratio) outcomes, and multiple variables: these issues indicate that Abigail will attempt to use multiple regression. She will also use some bivariate techniques, such as correlation and *t* tests, to test relationships between different variables and to review assumptions. Figure 15.4 includes Abigail's program (Abigaildataanalysis. sas). This program is available to you at www.ablongman.com/mysocialworkkit.

FIGURE 15.4. **Abigail's SAS Analysis Program.**

```
/***************** ABIGAILANALYSIS.SAS ****************/
/***************** ABIGAILANALYSIS.SAS ****************/
/***************** ABIGAILANALYSIS.SAS ****************/
/*****       Data analysis program for Abigail   ******/
/******************************************************/
libname mouse "U:\drake and jonson-reid\book\projects\abigail";
data temp;set mouse.abigail1;

/****take a look at what we got - get oriented ****/
proc contents;run;                        /**see what's there***/
proc print data=temp;run; /***look at data visually**/

/***check normality in vars. **/
proc univariate plot normal data=temp;
var iesavo iesint /*DV's*/
ocscon ocssup ssbada ssbadb ssbema ssbemb /*IV's*/
active age childage jobyears monthago timeopen; /*controls*/;run;
/*** note- gender, being dichotomous, is not included****/

/* run corr.matrix (what's related? - check multicollinearity */
proc corr; var iesint ocscon ocssup iesavo; run;

/****modify childage variable and transform CALog varaible, check**/
data temp;set temp;
childage=childage+.5;  /**done to avoid values of 0 when logging**/
CALog=.; CALog=log(childage);label CALog="Child Age Logged";
proc univariate; var CALog; run;

/*******get ready to do regressions***************************/
/**** need to look for significant bivariate relationships   */
/**** that we will want to include in the multivariate models*/
/*************************************************************/
/***look for bivariate relationships between IV's and DV's ***/
/*** check corrs between IV's(OCS...) and DV's(IES...) for Q1*/
proc corr data=temp; var
ocscon ocssup iesint iesavo;run;
/*** check corrs between IV's(SSB...) and DV's(IES...) for Q2**/
proc corr data=temp;
var  ssbema ssbemb ssbsoa ssbsob ssbada ssbadb iesint iesavo;run;
/******bivariates for control variables***/
/*********run ttests for dichotomous variables**********/
/***gender***/
proc ttest; class female; var iesint; run;
proc ttest; class female; var iesavo; run;
/***active case at time of death***/
proc ttest; class active; var iesint; run;
proc ttest; class active; var iesavo; run;
/*********run correlations for continuous variables******/
proc corr data=temp;
var iesint iesavo  /*DV's*/
active age CALog jobyears monthago timeopen;run; /*Control Vars*/

/*************run regression analyses*********/
PROC Reg data=temp;
Model iesint = jobyears SSBEMA/ STB VIF SS1; run;

PROC Reg data=temp;
Model iesavo = jobyears CALog OCSCOn/ STB VIF SS1; run;
```

SECTION 15.2.2: DO ABIGAIL'S DATA MEET THE ASSUMPTIONS OF CORRELATION, *T* TESTS, AND REGRESSION?

First, Abigail looks at her data as Kathy did, using PROC UNIVARIATE to check for normality in her continuous variables. Then she runs a bivariate correlation to look for associations and begin thinking about multicollinearity. Because she has some dummy coded demographic variables of interest, she will use *t* tests to examine bivariate relationships with the outcomes of interest. Because Abigail has only 78 observations, her data set is a bit small for multiple regression. Her preliminary analyses will be critical to her ability to focus in on a few key variables of importance so she can properly use the multivariate test. Further, her first three questions can be answered using bivariate correlations.

After examining her data using PROC UNIVARIATE Abigail discovers that "child age" is positively skewed at 1.92 (which makes sense, as child fatalities are much more common among young children). She decides to transform this variable using the logarithm method (see Chapter 13). Before she does this, she changes the child age variable by adding .5. This is done to avoid having to log a value of "0," which is generally a bad idea. It is also really more accurate when you think about it, because someone who is "1" year old is, on the average, really 1 year and six months old, since one-year-olds are, in reality, all people from age 12 months 1 day to age 23 months, 29 (or whatever) days. She creates a new variable name "youth" because she is careful not to overwrite her original data!

Abigail reruns a PROC UNIVARIATE on the new variable and discovers that the skewness is now at an acceptable level at .33.

SECTION 15.2.3: ANSWERING THE QUESTIONS

Abigail now begins to answer her research questions 1 through 3 with correlations.

QUESTION 1: ARE ORGANIZATIONAL FACTORS (SUPPORTIVE COMMUNICATION, CONFLICTUAL COMMUNICATION) ASSOCIATED WITH THE IMPACT (INTRUSIVENESS, AVOIDANCE) OF CLIENT FATALITIES?

The correlation matrix shown in Figure 15.5 was generated from the PROC CORR under the "Get ready to do regressions . . . for Q1" section in Abigaildataanalysis.sas.

■ H1A1: Organizational supportive communication will be associated with lower levels of worker-reported postfatality event intrusive experiences.

  If this statement were true, we would expect a negative correlation between OCSSUP and IESINT. The relationship is in the expected direction ($r = -.06$) but it is clearly not significant ($p = .5935$). This hypothesis is not supported.

■ H1A2: Organizational conflictual communication will be associated with higher levels of worker-reported postfatality event intrusive experiences.

  If this statement were true, we would expect a positive correlation between OCSCON and IESINT. The relationship is not in the expected direction ($r = -.08$), and it is clearly not significant ($p = .4770$). This hypothesis is not supported.

■ H1B1: Organizational supportive communication will be associated with lower levels of worker-reported postfatality event avoidance reactions.

  If this statement were true, we would expect a negative correlation between OCSSUP and IESAVO. The relationship is in the expected direction ($r = -.05$), but it is clearly not significant ($p = .6899$). This hypothesis is not supported.

■ H1B2: Organizational conflictual communication will be associated with higher levels of worker-reported postfatality event avoidance reactions.

  If this statement were true, we would expect a positive correlation between OCSCON and IESAVO. The relationship is in the expected direction ($r = .48$), and it is clearly significant ($p = .0001$). *Good news:* This hypothesis is supported. How big

---

FIGURE 15.5. **Abigail's Correlation Matrix from SAS.**

```
Pearson Correlation Coefficients, N = 78
Prob > |r| under H0: Rho=0
```

	OCSCON	OCSSUP	IESINT	IESAVO
OCSCON OCS CONFLICTUAL SUBSCALE	1.00000	20.33666 0.0026	20.08171 0.4770	0.48033 <.0001
OCSSUP OCS SUPPORTIVE SUBSCALE	20.33666 0.0026	1.00000	20.06137 0.5935	20.04590 0.6899
IESINT IES intrusion subscale total	20.08171 0.4770	20.06137 0.5935	1.00000	20.02151 0.8517
IESAVO IES avoidance subscale total	0.48033 <.0001	20.04590 0.6899	20.02151 0.8517	1.00000

a deal is $r = -.48$? Most people would call this a moderate association.

Now for question 2. Some key variables:

SSBEMA = Emotional support from family

SSBEMB = Emotional support from friends

SSBSOA = Social support from family

SSBSOB = Social support from friends

SSBADA = Advice/guidance from family

SSBADB = Advice/guidance from friends

> NOTE: We do not show the output from the correlation matrix for Question 2 here. It looks very much like the one pictured for H1, just a bit bigger. You are welcome to run it yourself if you would like to see it.

- H2A1: Emotional support by friends will be associated with lower levels of worker-reported postfatality event intrusive experiences.

  If this statement were true, we would expect a negative correlation between SSBEMB and IESINT. The relationship is in the expected direction ($r = -.11$), but it is clearly not significant ($p = .3424$). This hypothesis is not supported.

- H2A2: Emotional support by friends will be associated with lower levels of worker-reported postfatality event avoidance reactions.

  If this statement were true, we would expect a negative correlation between SSBEMB and IESAVO. The relationship is in the expected direction ($r = -.09$), but it is clearly not significant ($p = .4347$). This hypothesis is not supported.

- H2A3: Emotional support by family will be associated with lower levels of worker-reported postfatality event intrusive experiences.

  If this statement were true, we would expect a negative correlation between SSBEMA and IESINT. The relationship is in the expected direction ($r = -.51$), and it is clearly significant ($p = .0001$). This hypothesis is supported.

- H2A4: Emotional support by family will be associated with lower levels of worker-reported postfatality event avoidance reactions.

  If this statement were true, we would expect a negative correlation between SSBEMA and IESAVO. The relationship is in the expected direction ($r = -.04$), but it is clearly not significant ($p = .7383$). This hypothesis is not supported.

- H2B1: Social support by friends will be associated with lower levels of worker-reported postfatality event intrusive experiences.

  If this statement were true, we would expect a negative correlation between SSBSOB and IESINT. The relationship is in the expected direction ($r = -.07$), but it is clearly not significant ($p = .5519$). This hypothesis is not supported.

- H2B2: Social support by friends will be associated with lower levels of worker-reported postfatality event avoidance reactions.

  If this statement were true, we would expect a negative correlation between SSBSOB and IESAVO. The relationship is not in the expected direction ($r = .05$), but it also is clearly not significant ($p = .6517$). This hypothesis is not supported.

- H2B3: Social support by family will be associated with lower levels of worker-reported postfatality event intrusive experiences.

  If this statement were true, we would expect a negative correlation between SSBSOA and IESINT. The relationship is in the expected direction ($r = -.03$), but it is clearly not significant ($p = .8236$). This hypothesis is not supported.

- H2B4: Social support by family will be associated with lower levels of worker-reported postfatality event avoidance reactions.

  If this statement were true, we would expect a negative correlation between SSBSOA and IESAVO. The relationship is not in the expected direction ($r = .02$), and it is clearly not significant ($p = .8729$). This hypothesis is not supported.

- H2C1: Advice/guidance by friends will be associated with lower levels of worker-reported postfatality event intrusive experiences.

  If this statement were true, we would expect a negative correlation between SSBADB and IESINT. The relationship is in the expected direction ($r = -.02$), but it is clearly not significant ($p = .8909$). This hypothesis is not supported.

- H2C2: Advice/guidance by friends will be associated with lower levels of worker-reported postfatality event avoidance reactions.

  If this statement were true, we would expect a negative correlation between SSBADB and IESAVO. The relationship is in the expected direction ($r = -.02$), but it is clearly not significant ($p = .8225$). This hypothesis is not supported.

- H2C3: Advice/guidance by family will be associated with lower levels of worker-reported postfatality event intrusive experiences.

  If this statement were true, we would expect a negative correlation between SSBADA and

---

FIGURE 15.6. **Abigail's Multivariate Regression Analysis (IESINT).**

```
                      Analysis of Variance
                  Sum of          Mean
      Source      DF    Squares      Square    F Value   Pr > F
      Model        2   519.40812   259.70406    14.44    <.0001
      Error       75  1349.30983    17.99080
      Corrected Total  77  1868.71795

              Root MSE          4.24156    R-Square   0.2779
              Dependent Mean   13.79487    Adj R-Sq   0.2587
              Coeff Var        30.74734
```

Significant model

OK, but not a terrific amount of variability explained

```
                        Parameter Estimates

                                        Parameter   Standard
Variable   Label                   DF   Estimate    Error    t Value   Pr > |t|
Intercept  Intercept                1   20.10922   1.90026    10.58    <.0001
jobyears   years in this job        1    0.11016   0.09759     1.13    0.2626
SSBEMA     SSB TOTAL, EMOTIONAL SUBSCALE 1 -0.32164 0.07353   -4.37    <.0001
           (Family)
```

```
                        Parameter Estimates
                                              Standardized   Variance
Variable   Label                   DF   Type I SS   Estimate    Inflation
Intercept  Intercept                1      14843        0           0
jobyears   years in this job        1   175.18742    0.12066    1.18686
SSBEMA     SSB TOTAL, EMOTIONAL SUBSCALE 1 344.22069 -0.46757   1.18686
```

Collinearity check is fine.

FIGURE 15.7. **Abigail's Multivariate Regression Analysis (IESAVO).**

```
                      Analysis of Variance
                  Sum of          Mean
      Source      DF    Squares      Square    F Value   Pr > F
      Model        3   886.52062   295.50687    10.77    <.0001
      Error       74  2031.01785    27.44619
      Corrected Total  77  2917.53846

      Root MSE          5.23891    R-Square   0.3039
      Dependent Mean   17.92308    Adj R-Sq   0.2756
      Coeff Var        29.22997
```

Similar to model 1 fit and r² statistics

```
                        Parameter Estimates
                                        Parameter   Standard
Variable   Label                   DF   Estimate    Error    t Value   Pr > |t|
Intercept  Intercept                1    9.88609   1.58551     6.24    0.0250
CALog      Child Age Logged         1    0.95847   0.52791     1.82    0.0735
OCSCON     OCS Conflict Subscale    1    0.78926   0.18931     4.17    <.0001
```

```
                        Parameter Estimates
                                              Standardized   Variance
Variable   Label                   DF   Type I SS   Estimate    Inflation
Intercept  Intercept                1      25056        0           0
jobyears   years of work at fatality 1  230.84288   0.22613    1.03818
CALog      Child Age Logged         1   178.62331   0.17911    1.03446
OCSCON     OCS Conflict Subscale    1   477.05442   0.41581    1.05742
```

Collinearity check is fine.

IESINT. The relationship is in the expected direction ($r = -.10$), but it is clearly not significant ($p = .3863$). This hypothesis is not supported.

- H2C4: Advice/guidance by family will be associated with lower levels of worker-reported postfatality event avoidance reactions.

    If this statement were true, we would expect a negative correlation between SSBADA and IESAVO. The relationship is not in the expected direction ($r = .11$), and it is clearly not significant ($p = .3492$). This hypothesis is not supported.

QUESTION 3: WHAT OTHER PERSONAL CHARACTERISTICS ARE ASSOCIATED WITH INCREASES IN THE IMPACT OF CHILD FATALITIES?

Now we will look at question 3.

To answer this, Abigail must test associations of each personal characteristic with intrusive experiences and avoidance separately to determine which have statistically significant associations.

To look for associations, Abigail runs a correlation between her personal characteristics and event avoidance and event intrusiveness. Because whether the case was active at the time of the fatality and gender were *nominal dichotomous* variables, she uses a *t* test to examine the relationship between these variables and the outcome variables. Based on the *t* tests and correlations, she sees that the logged child age (CALog) was significantly associated with IESAVO, and JOBYEARS was associated with both IESAVO and IESINT. These will have to be included in the multivariate models.

QUESTION 4: DO EFFECTS FOUND IN Q1 AND Q2 PERSIST IN THE PRESENCE OF CONTROLS FOR PERSONAL CHARACTERISTICS?

To answer question 4, Abigail must retest H1 and H2 elements in multivariate equations including controls from Q3.

Fortunately for Abigail, few variables are associated with the outcomes of interest. We say "fortunately" because her sample was fairly small, so it would be impossible for her to include a large number of variables in a multivariate equation. She is looking for association and has dependent interval/ratio data and acceptably normal distribution of her dependent variables. She will use a multiple regression equation to reexamine relationships found in questions 1 and 2 while also controlling for years on the job (Figure 15.6).

The relationship between a lower level of event intrusiveness and emotional support from the worker's family remains when controlling for years on the job. "Years on the job" is not significant in the model.

Abigail then runs the model for IESAVO, includ-ing both jobyears and calog as control variables (Figure 15.7).

In the multivariate model (Figure 15.6), OCSCON remains significantly ($p < .0001$) correlated with avoidance (IESAVO) at a moderate level (standardized estimate is .41581). Years on the job shows a low correlations (standardized estimate is about .23, $p = .0250$). CALog approaches significance ($p = .0735$). The adjusted *r* square shows that the model explains 27.56% of the total variance. Not bad.

SECTION 15.3

MARIA

Maria is interested in relationships between homicide and suicide rates and community characteristics. Her variables are measured at the zip code level.

SECTION 15.3.1: MARIA DECIDES WHAT STATISTICAL PROCEDURES CAN ANSWER HER QUESTIONS

Maria's dependent variables of interest (homicide and suicide rates) are measured at ratio level. Maria is looking for associations. She will actually use the same statistical procedures as Abigail with the exception that she will not be using a *t* test because all of her variables are ratio level (Figure 15.8).

SECTION 15.3.2: DO MARIA'S DATA MEET THE ASSUMPTIONS OF CORRELATION AND REGRESSION?

First Maria runs PROC UNIVARIATE to look at her data. She notices that her outcome variables and all of the independent and control variables except age, proportion White, and density are positively skewed above 1.5. She will need to transform these variables, but unlike Abigail's results, Maria's 0 values are actual zeros and cannot be changed. So, she uses a square root transformation instead (see "Transform Variables . . ." part of program).

The transformations successfully reduce the skewness.

SECTION 15.3.3: ANSWERING THE QUESTIONS

Maria runs some correlations to produce the following output (only partly shown) in Figure 15.9.

QUESTION 1A: ASSOCIATIONS BETWEEN RESIDENTIAL DENSITY AND HOMICIDE RATES

- H1A1: More residents per square mile (2000 Census) will be correlated with a higher homicide rate (2000–2001) in San Diego zip codes.

    This hypothesis is supported. There is a moderate positive correlation between residents

FIGURE 15.8. Maria's SAS Analysis Program.

```
/******************maria2.sas***************/
/******************maria2.sas***************/
/******************maria2.sas***************/
/******************maria2.sas***************/
/******************maria2.sas***************/
/**** Maria's data analysis program ******/
libname book "U:\drake and jonson-reid\book\projects\maria";run;

/**************let's take a look at what's in the dataset*********/
proc contents data=book.maria2; run;
proc univariate data=book.maria2; run;

/***Transform variables and put in new temporary dataset "TEMP"*/
data temp;
set book.maria2;
hom=.;hom=sqrt (HRate);·              suic=.;suic=sqrt (srate);
byself=.;byself=sqrt (PCTalone);      poverty=.; poverty=sqrt (PCTpoor);
hisp=.;hisp=sqrt (PCThispa);
label hom      = "homicide rate /1K /yr (sqrt)"
      suic     = "suicide rate /1K /1yr (sqrt)"
      byself   = "% living alone (sqrt)"
      poverty  = "% in poverty (sqrt)"
      hisp     = "% Hispanic (sqrt)"; run;
/*check to see how that all went*/
proc univariate; var    hom suic byself poverty hisp; run;
proc freq;        tables hom suic byself poverty hisp; run;

/**** run correlation matrix to answer bivariate Q's****/
proc corr data=temp; var hom suic poverty byself density pct25up
PCTblack PCThispa PCTasia PCTwhite PCTother; run;

/******** perform multivariate regressions ********/
PROC Reg data=temp;
Model srate = byself poverty density/ STB VIF SS1; run;

PROC Reg data=temp;
Model Hrate = pct25up density poverty/ STB VIF SS1; run;
```

FIGURE 15.9. Maria's SAS Correlation Matrix.

The CORR Procedure

Pearson Correlation Coefficients, N 5 77
Prob > |r| under HO: Rho50

	hom	suic	poverty	byself	Density	PCT25up
hom homicide rate/1K/yr (sqrt)	1.00000 0.1046	0.18640 <.0001	0.52820 0.8846	0.01681 <.0001	0.48385 0.0017	−0.35129
suic suicide rate/1K/1yr (sqrt)	0.18640 0.1046	1.00000 0.4147	0.09428 0.0009	0.36992 0.4462	−0.08808 0.0601	0.21527
poverty % in poverty (sqrt)	0.52820 <.0001	0.09428 0.4147	1.00000 0.4327	0.09070 <.0001	0.56080 <.0001	−0.47954
byself % living alone (sqrt)	0.01681 0.8846	0.36992 0.0009	0.09070 0.4327	1.00000 0.2039	0.14639 <.0001	0.71657
Density people per acre of developed land	0.48385 <.0001	−0.08808 0.4462	0.56080 <.0001	0.14639 0.2039	1.00000 0.0156	−0.27464
PCT25up Percentage of people 25 and over	−0.35129 0.0017	0.21527 0.0601	−0.47954 <.0001	0.71657 <.0001	−0.27464 0.0156	1.00000
PCTblack percentage African–American/Black	0.52478 <.0001	−0.08143 0.4814	0.46923 <.0001	−0.16181 0.1597	0.61401 <.0001	−0.45299 <.0001

per square mile and the homicide rate ($r = .48$, $p < .0001$).

- H1A2: Higher percentages of single-person residences (2000 Census) will be correlated with a higher homicide rate (2000–2001) in San Diego zip codes.

    This hypothesis is not supported. There is no significant correlation between percentage of residents living alone and the homicide rate ($r = .016$, $p = .88$).

QUESTION 1B: IS LOWER INCOME ASSOCIATED WITH HIGHER HOMICIDE RATES?

- H1B: Lower income (2000 Census) will be correlated with a higher homicide rate (2000–2001) in San Diego zip codes.

    This hypothesis is supported. Household income has a moderate to strong negative association with the homicide rate ($r = -.55, p < .0001$). "Percent of residents in poverty" has a positive, moderate association with the homicide rate ($r = .52, p < .0001$). These two income variables are also highly correlated at $r = -.79$ (p < .0001).

QUESTION 2A: ASSOCIATIONS BETWEEN RESIDENTIAL DENSITY AND SUICIDE RATES

- H2A1: More residents per square mile (2000 Census) will be correlated with a higher suicide rate (2000–2001) in San Diego zip codes.

    This hypothesis is not supported. There is no significant correlation between population density and the suicide rate ($r = -.09, p = .44$).

- H2A2: Higher percentages of single-person residences (2000 Census) will be correlated with a higher suicide rate (2000–2001) in San Diego zip codes.

    This hypothesis is supported. There is a significant positive correlation between percent residents living alone and the suicide rate ($r = .36, p < .0001$).

QUESTION 2B: IS LOWER INCOME ASSOCIATED WITH HIGHER SUICIDE RATES?

- H2B: Lower income (2000 Census) will be correlated with a higher suicide rate (2000–2001) in San Diego zip codes.

    This hypothesis is not supported. There is no significant correlation between either measure of income and the suicide rate.

QUESTION 3: WHAT OTHER COMMUNITY FACTORS ARE ASSOCIATED WITH HOMICIDE RATES?

Proportions of Black ($r = .55, p < .0001$) and Hispanic ($r = .53, p < .0001$) residents were positively correlated with the homicide rate. Proportion of White residents was negatively correlated with homicide rates ($r = -.54$,

$p < .0001$). The racial categories aforementioned are also strongly correlated to income. The proportions of Black and Hispanic residents have a strong negative correlation with income ($r = -.56, p < .0001$ and $r = -.63$, $p < .0001$, respectively). The proportion of White residents has a strong positive correlation with income ($r = .53, p < .0001$). The percent of Black residents is also strongly correlated with population density ($r = .63$, $p < .0001$). Percentage "age 25 and up" had a negative correlation with homicide rate ($r = -.35, p < .0001$). The suicide rate approached significance at $r = .19$ ($p = .10$).

QUESTION 4: WHAT OTHER COMMUNITY FACTORS ARE ASSOCIATED WITH SUICIDE RATES?

There was a trend toward significance for percent Hispanic ($r = -.19, p = .09$) and proportion over age 25 ($r = .21, p = .06$), but no other variables correlated with suicide rate.

Maria now retests questions 1 and 2 while controlling for the other significant relationships discovered in questions 3 and 4. She begins with a linear regression model of homicide rate. Maria has a bit of a problem developing the homicide model. The proportion race categories are strongly correlated to income and, in addition, proportion Black is strongly correlated with population density. When she enters the three racial categories that were significantly correlated to the homicide rate (% Black, %Hispanic, %White), the VIF goes from above 2 to over 12 for the racial groups and density. There is probably no reason to suspect that race in and of itself is a causal factor in homicide. It seems more likely that other factors related to race, such as income, may be more directly associated with homicide. Age, on the other hand, is associated with violent crime—with violent crime becoming much less likely after age 30. The literature also supports the theoretical rationale for density and poverty being associated with homicides. Maria doesn't have enough variables in her model or really enough observations to try to use principal components to reduce the variables, so she decides to drop the race variables from the model. Her model is significant with an adjusted r square of .34, meaning she is explaining just over a third of the observed variance (see Figure 15.10).

Concerns about multicollinearity are no longer strong. Looking at the standardized estimates, poverty has the strongest association with homicide rates. Age also matters; when the proportion of adults over age 25 goes up, the homicide rate goes down. An increase in population density code was associated with a trend toward statistical significance and was related to an increase in homicide rates.

Now Maria constructs a model for suicide rate. She includes the percent living alone and also the two community variables that approached significance—

FIGURE 15.10. **Maria's SAS Regression Output (Homicides).**

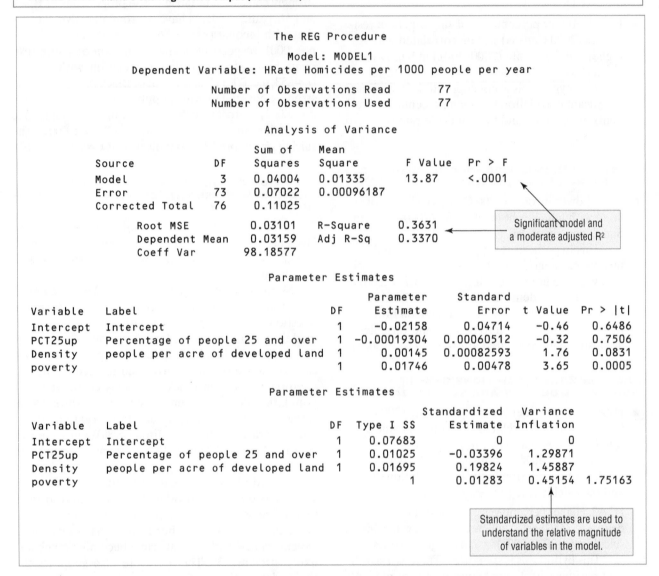

The REG Procedure

Model: MODEL1

Dependent Variable: HRate Homicides per 1000 people per year

Number of Observations Read   77
Number of Observations Used   77

Analysis of Variance

Source	DF	Sum of Squares	Mean Square	F Value	Pr > F
Model	3	0.04004	0.01335	13.87	<.0001
Error	73	0.07022	0.00096187		
Corrected Total	76	0.11025			

Root MSE	0.03101	R-Square	0.3631	
Dependent Mean	0.03159	Adj R-Sq	0.3370	
Coeff Var	98.18577			

Significant model and a moderate adjusted R²

Parameter Estimates

Variable	Label	DF	Parameter Estimate	Standard Error	t Value	Pr > |t|
Intercept	Intercept	1	-0.02158	0.04714	-0.46	0.6486
PCT25up	Percentage of people 25 and over	1	-0.00019304	0.00060512	-0.32	0.7506
Density	people per acre of developed land	1	0.00145	0.00082593	1.76	0.0831
poverty		1	0.01746	0.00478	3.65	0.0005

Parameter Estimates

Variable	Label	DF	Type I SS	Standardized Estimate	Variance Inflation
Intercept	Intercept	1	0.07683	0	0
PCT25up	Percentage of people 25 and over	1	0.01025	-0.03396	1.29871
Density	people per acre of developed land	1	0.01695	0.19824	1.45887
poverty		1	0.01283	0.45154	1.75163

Standardized estimates are used to understand the relative magnitude of variables in the model.

percent over the age of 25 and proportion of Hispanic residents. Unfortunately, she once again has multicollinearity issues. The VIF for percent 25 and up was over 3.5, and the VIF for Hispanic was over 2. The percent 25 variable was also not significant, so Maria decides to drop this variable. The proportion Hispanic variable was collinear with the percent living alone variable. She has theoretical grounds to keep the percent living alone variable and so omits the Hispanic variable. Some further exploration leads to the inclusion of population density as well (Figure 15.11).

By deleting the "percent 25 and up" and "proportion Hispanic" variables, Maria finds that the multicollinearity is no longer a problem. In contrast to the model of homicide rate, the adjusted *r* square for this model was under .24. Thus less of the variability in suicide rate was explained. Isolation (percent living alone and decreased population density) and poverty are all associated with an increase in suicide rates.

WARNING: This example uses real data and is messy in the way real analyses are. The need for the researcher to make decisions about which variables to retain and which to exclude is a common one faced by researchers. Maria chose to retain and exclude collinear variables based on theoretical grounds. This is a common practice. Is it the "right" practice? Some might say "yes" and some "no." A different researcher might have done it differently based on the theory being applied or because he or she had questions that emphasized a different set of variables. Sometimes statistics is as much art as science. For your purposes, if you are in doubt, first get advice from others who have dealt with the issue before. Next, make sure you have a logical reason for doing what you do and make sure you can explain it clearly to anyone questioning your decisions.

FIGURE 15.11. **Maria's SAS Regression Output (Suicides).**

```
                            Model: MODEL1
               Dependent Variable: SRate Suicides per 1000 people per year

                      Number of Observations Read        77
                      Number of Observations Used        77

                             Analysis of Variance

                                   Sum of        Mean
        Source            DF      Squares       Square    F Value    Pr > F

        Model              3      0.19189      0.06396       8.83    <.0001
        Error             73      0.52879      0.00724
        Corrected Total   76      0.72068


               Root MSE            0.08511    R-Square    0.2663
               Dependent Mean      0.11977    Adj R-Sq    0.2361
               Coeff Var          71.05896

                             Parameter Estimates

                                        Parameter    Standard
Variable    Label                  DF    Estimate      Error     t Value   Pr > |t|

Intercept   Intercept               1    -0.05595     0.04550     -1.23     0.2228
byself                              1     0.04838     0.01135      4.26    <.0001
poverty                             1     0.02687     0.01197      2.24     0.0279
Density     people per acre of      1    -0.00733     0.00228     -3.21     0.0020
            developed land

                             Parameter Estimates

                                                     Standardized    Variance
Variable    Label                  DF    Type I SS       Estimate    Inflation

Intercept   Intercept               1     1.10463              0            0
byself                              1     0.11494        0.43204      1.02201
poverty                             1     0.00220        0.27170      1.45894
Density     people per acre of      1     0.07474       -0.39160      1.47862
            developed land
```

SECTION 15.4

YUAN

Yuan is interested in understanding the relative effectiveness of two forms of treatment for domestic violence offenders.

SECTION 15.4.1: YUAN DECIDES WHAT STATISTICAL PROCEDURES CAN ANSWER HIS QUESTIONS

Yuan has a two-group design but has been unable to collect all data points for both groups. For both the CBT and standard treatment groups, he collects pretest scale data (avoidance, empathy, forethought, and usefulness), recidivism occurrence (yes or no) and select control variables (age in years, married [yes or no], prior incidents [1 to 7]). For the CBT group only, he collects pre-, post-, and 6-month follow-up data on the four scales. His scale scores are continuous (interval/ratio) data. A simple pre/post design for the CBT group using the avoidance, empathy, forethought, and usefulness scales would require paired *t* tests, but he is also interested in whether the posttest scores change at follow-up. This will require a repeated measures ANOVA.

To further complicate things, Yuan is measuring recidivism rates as a "yes/no" or nominal variable. This question asks if the subjects in the two treatment groups have different rates of recidivism. Both variables are measured at the nominal level, so he will use a chi-square. Then he wants to control for scale scores at pretest and the other control variables; this will require moving to a multivariate model. Because the time elapsed from posttest to follow-up is the same for all individuals, Yuan will use a logistic regression model. His program is shown in Figure 15.12.

SECTION 15.4.2: DO YUAN'S DATA MEET THE ASSUMPTIONS OF THE PAIRED *T* TEST, FACTORIAL ANOVA, CHI-SQUARE, AND LOGISTIC REGRESSION?

Like our other researchers, Yuan will be using PROC UNIVARIATE to explore the characteristics of his scale outcomes to see if they meet the assumptions for using the repeated measures ANOVA. Yuan knows that he has an interval or ratio level dependent variable. Like the regular ANOVA, normality is an important assumption of this technique. Yuan runs univariate statistics on the scales at each time period. Yuan finds that he has no significant departures from

FIGURE 15.12. Yuan's SAS Data Analysis Program.

```
/*********************** YUANDATAANALYSIS.SAS *******************/
/*********************** YUANDATAANALYSIS.SAS *******************/
/*********************** YUANDATAANALYSIS.SAS *******************/
/*********************** YUANDATAANALYSIS.SAS *******************/
/*********************** YUANDATAANALYSIS.SAS *******************/
libname Y "u:\drake and jonson-reid\book\projects\yuan";

/**********examine variables********/
proc contents data=Y.yuandata; run;
/*** yow! lots of 'em...***/

/**** sort by CBT group for analysis********/
proc sort data=Y.yuandata; by cbt; run;

/** univariates for scale outcomes -check for normality***/
proc univariate data=Y.yuandata;
var prea posta pree poste pref postf preu postu;by CBT; run;

/************look at pre/post means by for CBT group       *******/
/*** see if it "looks like" pre/post change happens        **/
data temp; set Y.yuandata;
if cbt=1; proc means;
var prea posta folla pree poste folle
pref postf follf preu postu follu; run;

/****** time to get ready to do ANOVAs****/
/*** prior to ANOVAs, check bivariate pre-post using t-test    **/
PROC TTEST alpha=.01 data=Y.yuandata;
PAIRED prea*posta pree*poste pref*postf preu*postu; run;

/*******************************************do ANOVAs***********/
/*** see if pre/post/follow up scores are significantly different*/
/***/
/*** compare pre. post, follow-up scores on avoidance scale */
PROC GLM data=Y.yuandata;
model prea posta folla = /nouni;
Repeated time 3 contrast (2) / summary printe; run;
/*** compare pre. post, follow-up scores on empathy scale */
PROC GLM data=Y.yuandata;
model pree poste folle = /nouni;
Repeated time 3 contrast (2) / summary printe; run;
/*** compare pre. post, follow-up scores on forethought scale */
PROC GLM data=Y.yuandata;
model pref postf follf = /nouni;
Repeated time 3 contrast (2) / summary printe; run;
/*** compare pre. post, follow-up scores on usefulness scale   */
PROC GLM data=Y.yuandata;
model preu postu follu = /nouni;
Repeated time 3 contrast (2) / summary printe; run;
/********done with ANOVAs*****/

/***prepare to do recidivism analyses ****/
/**/
/*** do chisquares on recid for dichotomous vars, make       */
/*** sure that we don't have complete separation (ch. 14)    */
/*** also checking to see that expected cell counts are >=5  */
/*** also seeing if bivariate relationship exists,           */
proc freq data=Y.yuandata;
tables cbt*recid /chisq; run;/*<- Looks OK and p<0.0001*/
proc freq data=Y.yuandata;
tables married*recid /chisq;run;/*<- OK, very NS, drop from model*/
/* since priors is a continuous variable, we will dichotomize it */
/* as a new variable "prior". This allows us to do a check for   */
/* association with recidivism. Dichotomizing costs power, but   */
/* allows us to get a quick feel for the general relationship    */
data temp;set Y.yuandata;
prior=0;if priors ge 3 then prior=1;
label prior = "0 if <3 priors, 1 if >=3 priors";
proc freq data=temp; tables prior*recid /chisq;run;
/** NS. Retain in model, though, for theoretical reasons*/
/**/
```

(Continued)

FIGURE 15.12. **(Continued)**

```
/**another thing to check - do check for multicollinearity *******/
PROC Reg data=Y.yuandata;
Model recid = CBT priors married
              prea pref preu pree/ STB VIF SS1; run;
/*** done now getting ready for logistic regresssion...yay!**/

/**************** run logistic regression ***/
proc logistic descending data=y.yuandata;
model recid = CBT priors prea pref preu pree
/lackfit plrl rsq ;
run;

/*** the below text will print out an ROC curve **/
goptions cback=white
colors=(black) border;
axis1 length=2.5in;
axis2 order=(0 to 1 by .1) length=2.5in;
proc gplot data=roc1;
symbol1 i=join v=none;
title2 "Recidivism ROC Curve";
plot _sensit_*_1mspec_ / haxis=axis1 vaxis=axis2; run;
```

normality and no missing data over time. Yuan will go ahead and run the ANOVA, requesting the test for sphericity.

Based on PROC means, Yuan sees only minor changes over time in his scale scores (Figure 15.13). It appears that a small (two point) improvement in empathy was found that remained stable at follow-up.

SECTION 15.4.3: ANSWERING THE QUESTIONS

After looking the means over, Yuan (being a careful guy) decides to run a set of *t* tests to check for significant pre/post relationships (see "Time to get ready to do ANOVAs . . ." in his program). This gives Yuan a much better feel for what's going on in his data. Yuan proceeds with the repeated measures ANOVA for each scale. He begins with the avoidance scale. The Mauchly's

criterion is highly significant (Figure 15.14). This tells Yuan that he must use the Wilk's lambda test rather than the *F* test reported for the model (Figure 15.15). The repeated measures ANOVA allow Yuan to answer questions 1 and 2 with the same analysis.

As shown in Figures 15.14 and 15.15, the tests provide similar results. There is a statistically significant difference between at least two of the mean scores. Yuan now examines the contrast statements. Only the contrast between the mean at posttest and the mean at pretest is significant (see output in Figure 15.16). This makes sense, as the mean at follow-up decreases compared to the posttest (pre = 17.5; post = 18.1; follow-up = 17.96). Yuan requested that the contrast statements compare to the second time period (that's the "2" in the parentheses below) because this provides output that most closely mimics his research questions. The following code is used:

FIGURE 15.13. **Yuan's PROC MEANS Output (Partial).**

Variable	Label	N	Mean	Std Dev	Minimum	Maximum
PREA	PRETEST score on AVOIDANCE subscale	100	17.47	5.00	8.0	27.0
POSTA	POSTTEST score on AVOIDANCE subscale	100	18.08	4.84	9.0	27.0
FOLLA	FOLLOWUP score on AVOIDANCE subscale	100	17.96	5.05	9.0	28.0
PREE	PRETEST score on EMPATHY subscale	100	19.10	3.66	9.0	26.0
POSTE	POSTTEST score on EMPATHY subscale	100	21.19	3.18	14.0	27.0
FOLLE	FOLLOWUP score on EMPATHY subscale	100	21.10	3.21	11.0	26.0
PREF	PRETEST score on FORETHOUGHT subscale	100	17.44	4.09	7.0	26.0
POSTF	POSTTEST score on FORETHOUGHT subscale	100	17.24	3.44	9.0	26.0
FOLLF	FOLLOW-UP score on FORETHOUGHT subscale	100	17.37	3.97	10.0	25.0
PREU	PRETEST score on USEFULNESS subscale	100	17.83	4.65	10.0	27.0
POSTU	POSTTEST score on USEFULNESS subscale	100	17.28	4.47	8.0	26.0
FOLLU	FOLLOW-UP score on USEFULNESS subscale	100	17.48	4.66	9.0	27.0

(Author's note: shortened for inclusion in book–this PROC MEANS output is from the CBT group.)

FIGURE 15.14. **ANOVA Output for Mauchly's Scale.**

```
                              Mauchly's
Variables              DF    Criterion    Chi-Square    Pr > ChiSq
Transformed Variates   2     0.7721695    25.33802        <.0001
Orthogonal Components  2     0.8553528    15.311642       0.0005
```
We examine the orthogonal value.

FIGURE 15.15. **ANOVA Output for Wilk's Lambda and *F* Test.**

```
Statistic           Value      F Value    Num DF    Den DF    Pr > F
Wilks' Lambda     0.91389155    4.62         2         98     0.0121


ANOVA

Source        DF    Type III SS    Mean Square    F Value    Pr > F    G - G     H - F
time           2    20.8866667     10.4433333      3.05      0.0494    0.0566    0.0558
Error(time)  198   677.1133333      3.4197643
```

FIGURE 15.16. **ANOVA Output for Contrast.**

```
time_N represents the contrast between the nth level of time and the 2nd
Contrast Variable: time_1

Source    DF    Type III SS    Mean Square    F Value    Pr > F
Mean       1    37.2100000     37.2100000      8.78      0.0038
Error     99   419.7900000      4.2403030
```

```
Repeated time 3 contrast (2) / summary printe;
run;
```

Full ANOVA output is not shown to save space.

QUESTIONS 1 AND 2: DO SUBJECTS RECEIVING CBT SHOW CHANGES IN AS SUBSCALE SCORES FROM PRETEST TO POSTTEST?

The repeated measures ANOVA allows Yuan to answer questions 1 and 2 using the same analysis. We will therefore present the analyses to questions/hypotheses 1 and 2 in the order they are addressed in the programming:

First (Avoidance) repeated measures ANOVA:

■ H1A: Subjects receiving CBT will show different levels of change in the AS *avoidance* subscale from pretest to posttest (change during treatment).

There is a significant difference in the mean avoidance subscale between the pre- and posttest ($F = 8.78$, $p < .0038$). This hypothesis is supported by the contrast statement, but Yuan must remember that the statistical significance does not mean that the slight increase in the average avoidance scale score is sufficient to have practical therapeutic significance.

■ H2A: Subjects receiving CBT will show different levels of change in the AS *avoidance* subscale from posttest to follow-up (change during treatment).

There was no significant difference from posttest to follow-up, which is good (the treatment gains do not seem to be fading over time).

Second (Empathy) repeated measures ANOVA:

■ H1B: Subjects receiving CBT will show different levels of change in the AS *empathy* subscale from pretest to posttest (change during treatment).

Once again the Mauchly's criterion indicates problems with sphericity, so he looks at the Wilk's Lambda F test ($F=24.65$, $DF=2$, $p<.0001$). Once again there is no practical difference in the results between the ANOVA model F-test and the Wilk's Lambda. Both indicate that there is a statistically significant difference between at least two of the mean scores. Yuan now examines the contrast statements. Once again, the first hypothesis, that there will be a significant change between pre and posttest scores is supported ($F=49.02$, $p<.0001$) (pretest mean=19.1 v. posttest mean=21.19).

■ H2B: Subjects receiving CBT will show different levels of change in the AS *empathy* subscale from posttest to follow-up (change during treatment).

There was no significant difference between posttest and follow-up scores. Again, this is good, showing that treatment gains are maintained over the six month follow up period.

Third (Forethought) repeated measures ANOVA:

■ H1C: Subjects receiving CBT will show different levels of change in the AS *forethought* subscale from pretest to posttest (change during treatment).

■ H2C: Subjects receiving CBT will show different levels of change in the AS *forethought* subscale from posttest to follow-up (change during treatment).

Yuan repeats the process for the Forethought subscale. This time the Mauchly's criterion is not significant. Yuan can proceed with the ANOVA F-test. This test is also not significant. There is no statistically significant change between pretest and posttest or posttest and follow-up or pretest and follow-up scores on the Forethought scales.

Fourth (Usefulness) repeated measures ANOVA:

- H1D: Subjects receiving CBT will show different levels of change in the AS *usefulness* subscale from pretest to posttest (change during treatment).

- H2D: Subjects receiving CBT will show different levels of change in the AS *usefulness* subscale from posttest to follow-up (change during treatment).

Mauchly's criterion is not significant. The ANOVA F-test is trending toward significance at $p=.0972$. This happens because the contrast statement testing the difference in pre and posttest Usefulness scale scores is significant, but the difference is quite small (17.83 v. 17.28). Because of the model test, Yuan will ignore the contrast statement.

Question 3: Do Subjects Receiving CBT and ST Show Different Rates of Reported Violence?

- H3: Subjects receiving CBT and ST will show different rates of recidivism during the six months following treatment.

Yuan will do a cross-tabulation with a chi-square to check for the needed cell size for his categorical data analyses of recidivism:

```
proc freq; tables cbt*recid /chisq; run;
```

It looks as if there is an association present between treatment group and recidivism (see Figure 15.17). Yuan decides to proceed with the logistic regression model to see if the original subscale scores help predict recidivism in addition to treatment group. He examines his other control variables to see if age, marital status, or prior arrests for DV should be included in the model as well. Age and marital status are highly associated with each other in this sample. See "Prepare to do Recidivism Analyses . . ." in program. Further, bivariate tests indicate that neither age nor marital status was significantly associated with recidivism. Prior arrests were also not associated with recidivism, but he decides to retain a control for prior arrests for DV because there is a theoretical reason to believe that an established behavior pattern is more difficult to affect. Yuan enters the subscale scores, treatment indicator, and "priors" variable into a linear regression model first to test for multicollinearity between variables (see "Another thing to check. . ." in program). The variance inflation factors are all close to 1.00 with no indication of problems with multicollinearity. Yuan proceeds with the logistic regression model.

The logistic regression model statement used was:

FIGURE 15.17. Yuan's FREQ Output (CBT * RECID).

```
                    Table of cbt by RECID

cbt(1 IF COGNITIVE BEHAVIORAL THERAPY, 0 IF STANDARD TX)
           RECID(1 IF RECIDIVISM REPORTED DURING 6 MO FOLLOWUP)
    Frequency ,
    Percent   ,
    Row Pct   ,
    Col Pct   ,         0,         1,     Total
    **********^********^********^
         0 ,      53 ,      47 ,      100
           ,   26.50 ,   23.50 ,    50.00
           ,   53.00 ,   47.00 ,
           ,   38.41 ,   75.81 ,
    **********^********^********^
         1 ,      85 ,      15 ,      100
           ,   42.50 ,    7.50 ,    50.00
           ,   85.00 ,   15.00 ,
           ,   61.59 ,   24.19 ,
    **********^********^********^
    Total         138        62       200
               69.00     31.00    100.00


          Statistics for Table of cbt by RECID

Statistic              DF       Value        Prob
**************************************************
Chi-Square              1     23.9364      <.0001
```

FIGURE 15.18. The LOGISTIC Procedure.

```
                          Model Information
Data Set                      Y.YUANDATA
Response Variable             RECID   1 IF RECIDIVISM REPORTED DURING 6 MO FOLLOWUP
Number of Response Levels     2
Model                         binary logit
Optimization Technique        Fisher's scoring

              Number of Observations Read        200
              Number of Observations Used        200
```

Yuan glances to make sure all his observations were included.

```
                      Response Profile
        Ordered                     Total
        Value        RECID        Frequency
          1            1             62
          2            0            138

        Probability modeled is RECID=1.

             Model Convergence Status
      Convergence criterion (GCONV=1E-8) satisfied.

               Model Fit Statistics

                                  Intercept
                      Intercept   and
        Criterion     Only        Covariates
        AIC           249.640     191.005
        SC            252.939     214.093
        -2 Log L      247.640     177.005
      R-Square 0.2975 Max-rescaled R-Square 0.4190
```

The pseudo-*r* square (Max-rescaled *R* square) indicates that a moderate portion of the variability of recidivism rate is explained by the model.

```
        Testing Global Null Hypothesis: BETA=0
        Test               Chi-Square   DF   Pr > ChiSq
        Likelihood Ratio    70.6353      6     <.0001
        Score               60.5834      6     <.0001
        Wald                43.2898      6     <.0001
```

The −2 log likelihood chi-square indicates that the model fits the data relatively well.

```
                   The LOGISTIC Procedure
         Analysis of Maximum Likelihood Estimates
                            Standard       Wald
Parameter   DF   Estimate   Error       Chi-Square   Pr > ChiSq
Intercept   1     5.8770    1.7183       11.6976      0.0006
cbt         1    -1.5859    0.3984       15.8439      <.0001
priors      1     0.1210    0.0823        2.1639      0.1413
PREA        1     0.0492    0.0387        1.6157      0.2037
PREF        1    -0.0310    0.0540        0.3288      0.5663
PREU        1    -0.0477    0.0430        1.2277      0.2679
PREE        1    -0.3365    0.0615       29.9404      <.0001

                  Odds Ratio Estimates
                  Point         95% Wald
        Effect   Estimate   Confidence Limits
        cbt       0.205      0.094      0.447
        priors    1.129      0.961      1.326
        PREA      1.050      0.974      1.133
        PREF      0.970      0.872      1.078
        PREU      0.953      0.876      1.037
        PREE      0.714      0.633      0.806

  Association of Predicted Probabilities and Observed Responses
        Percent Concordant    84.4    Somers' D   0.688
        Percent Discordant    15.5    Gamma       0.689
        Percent Tied           0.1    Tau-a       0.296
        Pairs                 8556    c           0.844
```

```
proc logistic descending data=y.yuandata;
model recid = CBT priors prea pref preu pree
/lackfit plrl rsq;
run;
```

The descending option insures that SAS models recidivism rather than lack of recidivism. This will make the output easier to talk about (Figure 15.18).

Yuan finds that his model is significant and the -2 Log likelihood chi-square and psuedo-r square suggest a good model fit. Because he has independent variables that are continuous, he requests the "lackfit" option to get the Hosmer and Lemeshow Goodness-of-Fit Test:

```
Hosmer and Lemeshow Goodness-of-Fit Test
Chi-Square          DF        Pr > ChiSq
   7.0761            8          0.5284
```

This is nonsignificant, offering another indication of model fit. Only the treatment group (CBT) and the pretest empathy score (PREE) are significant (see rows marked in bold in Figure 15.18). Those in the CBT group were less than 25% as likely to have a record of later recidivism. A one-unit increase in the score on the pretest empathy scale was associated with over a 25% decrease in the likelihood of recidivism. If Yuan wishes to publish his findings, some journals may want to see an assessment of the "predictive power" of the model. He can request an ROC curve using the following programme:

```
proc logistic data=y.yuandata;
model recid = CBT priors prea pref preu pree
/outroc=roc1;
run;

goptions cback=white
colors=(black) border;
axis1 length=2.5in;
axis2 order=(0 to 1 by .1) length=2.5in;

proc gplot data=roc1;
symbol1 i=join v=none;
title2 "Recidivism ROC Curve";
plot _sensit_*_1mspec_ / haxis=axis1
vaxis=axis2; run;
```

This results in the graph in Figure 15.19. The "c statistic" from the preceding output accompanies the graph. The higher the c value and the steeper the line without a significant dropoff, the better the predictive power.

Yuan is careful, however, to remember that his design does not allow him to establish causality with confidence. The idea of "prediction" is best understood as the computer's ability to assign cases that did and

did not have recidivism correctly according to the variables in the model.

FIGURE 15.19. Yuan's ROC Curve.

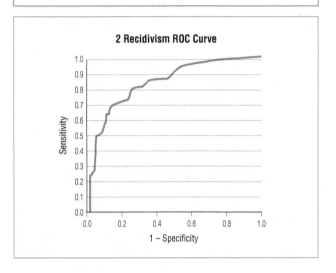

SECTION 15.5
JOHN

John sits down and looks at his pile of transcripts. He is excited about the richness of the data before him and utterly frightened. He's frightened about how to start and what to do. It all seems so wide open and unstructured. John takes several deep breaths, gets himself a cup of coffee, and calmly plans how he might move forward. He does the following:

- He remembers to focus on his research question, which involves seeing how people fit into different parts of Berry's model (assimilation, integration, separation). He wants to find out what strengths and issues seem to occur within those groups of people. Sticking to his research question will help guide everything he does and tells him *what* he must do.

- He remembers that his design is exploratory, involving a grounded theory approach. He means to let the data "speak for itself," and he means to "code up" from the data. This informs *how* he will do his work.

We might take a second to remember that John's theory, as modified from Berry, looks like the diagram in Figure 15.20.

John hopes that each of his transcripts will be easily identifiable as falling into one of the three boxes on the right, and he hopes they will have lots of nice detail about how people's strengths helped decide those outcomes. John figures he has to tackle four main tasks:

1. *Assign each transcript (person) to one of Berry's groups.* If this doesn't work, major rethinking of the project will be necessary—scary.

2. *Code the transcripts.* John will use a grounded theory approach and will run NVivo 2.0 as his qualitative analysis package.

3. *Analyze the coded transcripts.* John will do this while focusing on the following questions:

   ■ What strengths are evident?

   ■ What issues are faced?

   ■ How do persons in the four groups differ?

4. *Present his analysis in the form of a short paper.*

SECTION 15.5.1: ASSIGNING TRANSCRIPTS TO BERRY'S GROUPS

Within ten minutes of sitting down and looking at the transcripts, John realizes that they do not fall neatly into separation, assimilation, and integration groups. Four of the transcripts were obviously not fitting into any of those categories. They were all people who just were telling sad stories and not doing well. John quickly realized that Berry's model was not failing him, but that these were people who were still "marginalized." That meant that John would have to classify each person (transcript) as falling into one of these four (not three) categories. He put together the following operational definitions of each category:

■ *Integration:* Showing substantial social and economic integraton into U.S. culture while also maintaining Bosnian ties or identity

■ *Assimilation:* Showing a clear predominance of social and economic integraton into U.S. culture with low emphasis on Bosnian ties or identity

■ *Separation:* Showing little social and economic integraton into U.S. culture with strong emphasis on Bosnian ties or identity

■ *Marginalization:* Not showing successful economic or social integration with either the U.S. or Bosnian community

These categories were a compromise. John would like finer operationalization, but he wants to stay close to Berry's model. He classifies four subjects under marginalization, three under separation, two under assimilation, and three under integration. To check reliability of these classifications, John gives the written operationalizations to three friends in his program and asks them to rate the subjects. To his great relief, only one other rater disagrees with his ratings, and then only with one individual. For John's purposes, he feels this demonstrates an adequate level of reliability for his main coding variable.

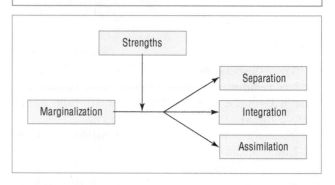

FIGURE 15.20. **John's Model.**

SECTION 15.5.2: ASSIGNING ATTRIBUTES TO THE DOCUMENTS

Assignment of attributes is done as described in Chapter 10 and is sorted by the attribute "Berry-Status," giving the results shown in Figure 15.21. These data are mainly quantitative and show John some interesting things. John is careful to remember that the numbers involved are so small that they can give him *hints* about how trends might be shaping up, but there are nowhere near enough cases (and they weren't sampled in the right way) to generalize to Bosnians in general or "prove" anything. John is trying to explore and inductively create theory. John can't help but notice that:

■ *Age seems to matter.* Both assimilated people are under 30, and all the integrated and separated people are over 30. The marginalized people are all over the place. Both assimilated people pursued U.S. education, and nobody else did. This could have to do with age because younger people are probably more likely to go to school.

■ *Language seems to matter.* Of the four people with less than good English, three were experiencing separation.

John finds it harder to form clear ideas about the remaining categories and decides to start coding.

SECTION 15.5.3: CODING THE TRANSCRIPTS

John decides to use NVivo for coding and analysis. He enters the documents into NVivo using the Launch Pad and the "Create a Document" commands (see Chapter 10 for specifics on loading documents and coding). John then starts coding (Project Pad/ Documents/Explore a Document/right-click on document icon/Browse-Edit-Code Document/Coder). He has vague ideas about a coding scheme that may look something like this:

FIGURE 15.21.   **NVivo Attribute Explorer.**

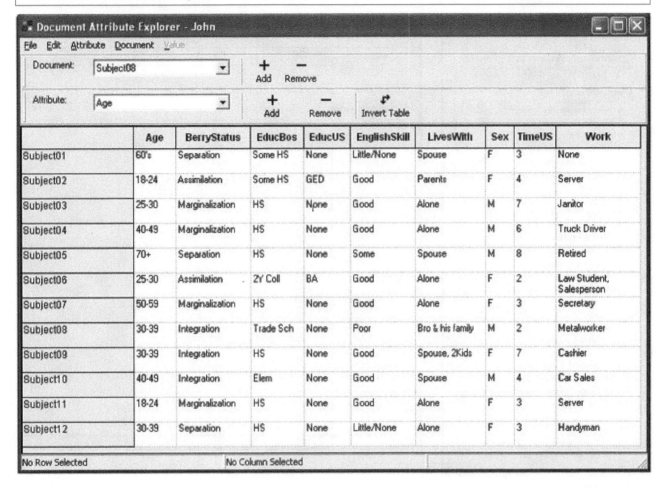

	Age	BerryStatus	EducBos	EducUS	EnglishSkill	LivesWith	Sex	TimeUS	Work
Subject01	60's	Separation	Some HS	None	Little/None	Spouse	F	3	None
Subject02	18-24	Assimilation	Some HS	GED	Good	Parents	F	4	Server
Subject03	25-30	Marginalization	HS	None	Good	Alone	M	7	Janitor
Subject04	40-49	Marginalization	HS	None	Good	Alone	M	6	Truck Driver
Subject05	70+	Separation	HS	None	Some	Spouse	M	8	Retired
Subject06	25-30	Assimilation	2Y Coll	BA	Good	Alone	F	2	Law Student, Salesperson
Subject07	50-59	Marginalization	HS	None	Good	Alone	F	3	Secretary
Subject08	30-39	Integration	Trade Sch	None	Poor	Bro & his family	M	2	Metalworker
Subject09	30-39	Integration	HS	None	Good	Spouse, 2Kids	F	7	Cashier
Subject10	40-49	Integration	Elem	None	Good	Spouse	M	4	Car Sales
Subject11	18-24	Marginalization	HS	None	Good	Alone	F	3	Server
Subject12	30-39	Separation	HS	None	Little/None	Alone	F	3	Handyman

Strengths

- Personal
- Social
- Professional

Issues

- Personal
- Social
- Professional

He starts coding that way and gets into a couple of transcripts, but it just doesn't feel right. Too many things aren't covered, and it feels as if content units (ideas) are being forced into places they don't belong. John then remembers that he's supposed to be using grounded theory and coding up, not coding down. Feeling more than a little stupid, John erases the codes he put in and starts over.

This time, John moves through the transcripts putting logical codes in that seem to come up from the content units. He comes up with things like "lure of America" and "community—Bosnian" that cover the

issues people bring up. After about five transcripts, John feels good about the codes he's using. He goes back to the first few transcripts and recodes them to make sure that they match with the more evolved coding scheme. Coding the last several transcripts goes quickly. His final coding scheme as seen through the NVivo Node Explorer looks like Figure 15.22.

There are four major categories: "Immigration Process," "Emmigration—Decision to Leave," "Issues," and "Social Contexts." Categories are up to three levels deep (e.g., Issues/Transitioning Cultures/Problems).

John decides that he doesn't have the resources to have another person or persons check his coding. In a more formal project, this would be an absolute must.

ANALYSIS: LOOKING AT CODING STATISTICS

John is curious as to how much was coded under each code label. He can easily display this from the project pad by going to the gray bar at the top and hitting "Nodes" and then "Profile Node Information." This gives him a chart like the one in Figure 15.23.

This chart can show many things, depending on what part you look at. John has moved to the part of the chart

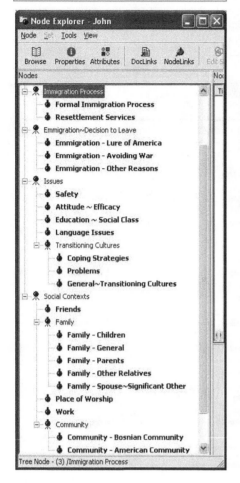

FIGURE 15.22. NVivo Node Explorer.

FIGURE 15.23. Node Information.

Nodes	Characters Coded	Paragraphs Coded	Documents Coded	Passages Coded
(3) Immigration Process	0	0	0	0
(3 2) Formal Immigration Process	1086	14	4	4
(3 3) Resettlement Services	833	13	5	6
(4) Emmigration - Decision to Leave	0	0	0	0
(4 1) Emmigration - Lure of America	1238	16	4	5
(4 2) Emmigration - Avoiding War	3128	37	9	11
(4 3) Emmigration - Other Reasons	691	9	2	2
(5) Issues	0	0	0	0
(5 1) Safety	344	6	2	3
(5 2) Attitude ~ Efficacy	1501	24	8	10
(5 3) Education ~ Social Class	821	11	2	3
(5 5) Language Issues	2299	37	11	17
(5 6) Transitioning Cultures	0	0	0	0
(5 6 1) Coping Strategies	3098	45	5	10
(5 6 3) Problems	2545	38	5	8
(5 6 6) General~Transitioning	7621	105	12	30
(6) Social Contexts	0	0	0	0
(6 1) Friends	163	3	2	2
(6 2) Family	0	0	0	0

showing the number of characters (letters, basically) coded, the number of paragraphs coded, and the thing he is most interested in, the number of documents with that code. It appears that the more popular codes include "Emmigration—Avoiding War," "Attitude—Efficacy," "Coping Strategies," "General—Transitioning" (under "Transitioning Cultures"), "Work," "Community—Bosnian" and "Community—American." This all makes sense. There is also a lot of family material, spread out over a lot of different subcategories. Overall, looking at this table has shown John that his questions did seem to evoke a range of responses that are congruent with themes in the literature and that seem to relate to his research question. So far, so good.

ANALYSIS: LOOKING AT THE CONTENT UNITS IN THE CODING SCHEME

The next thing John does is to use the "Node Explorer" screen (Figure 15.22) to review coded text in each part of the coding scheme. For example, when he right-clicks "Issues/Education—Social Class," and selects "Browse/Code Node," a list of all the text from all the documents bearing that code pops up (Figure 15.24).

Doing this gives John the ability to view the data in the structure of his coding scheme. Looking at it in an organized way helps him really get a sense for what was said.

FIGURE 15.24. **Social Class Nodes.**

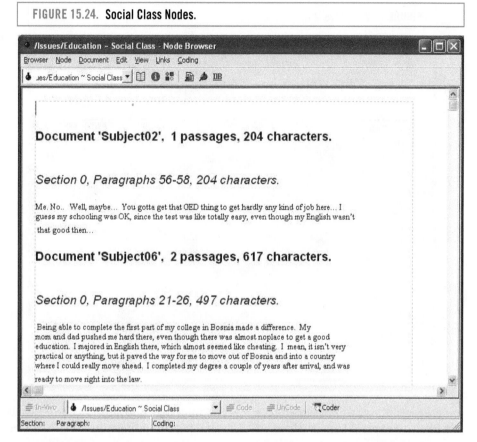

ANALYSIS: LOOKING AT THE CONTENT UNITS BY BERRY'S CATEGORIES

To do this, John needs a matrix (see the example in Chapter 10). John crosses the four labels in the document attribute "BerryStatus" with all the coding nodes. This gives him a table looking like Figure 15.25.

John can now move to each box on the table and display the coded text inside by simply right-clicking and hitting "Browse/Code Node." For example, hitting the lower right box in Figure 15.25 would bring up coding from three documents (second from bottom right side box) relating to "General—Transitioning" codes for people with BerryStatus of "Integration." This is the main place John will do most of his analysis. Why? Because it allows him to consider the subjects in each part of Berry's model separately and look for similarities and differences.

By moving through all the codes and condensing their meaning into notes, John comes up with a working document summarizing his findings (johnsnotes.doc, available at www.ablongman.com/mysocialworkkit). This simple table in MSWord shows each code item, the number of documents coded for each item, and John's summary of the meaning of the coded text. He could have used some NVivo features to do this, but he has an idea of how he wanted the table to look in Word, so he switches to that format. Maybe he'll want to actually print his notes out as part of a poster presentation, and he wants them to look a certain way.

SECTION 15.5.4: PUTTING IT ALL TOGETHER AND WRITING IT UP

John's purpose in doing the research is to better understand the local Bosnian population as a preliminary step in his dissertation process. He has hoped he can use the findings as part of an application for a dissertation support grant. It also turns out that John has a research paper due for one of his classes, so he decides to write up his work. This will both help him organize his conclusions and take care of the class assignment. The purpose of the paper will be to present his general findings and discuss how they might inform future work.

John decides he can present his main findings as follows:

1. Berry's model is a useful way to categorize Bosnian immigrants. This is very important for John's dissertation. It demonstrates that the model he has chosen is appropriate for use with this population.

2. Several constructs emerge as important in understanding Bosnian immigrants and their status in Berry's model:

■ *Leaving Bosnia and coming to America:* Marginalized individuals were more likely to describe very serious trauma and loss prior to leaving Bosnia. They were also less likely to express excitement at coming to America and taking existing opportunities.

FIGURE 15.25. NVivo Matrix.

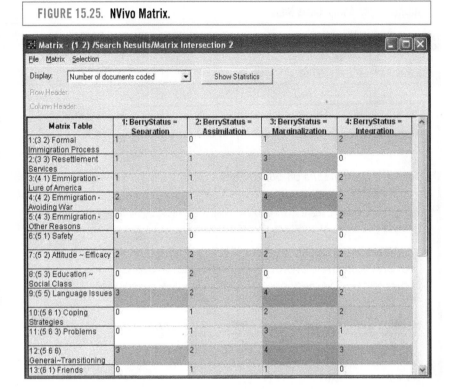

Matrix Table	1: BerryStatus = Separation	2: BerryStatus = Assimilation	3: BerryStatus = Marginalization	4: BerryStatus = Integration
1:(3 2) Formal Immigration Process	1	0	1	2
2:(3 3) Resettlement Services	1	1	3	0
3:(4 1) Emmigration - Lure of America	1	1	0	2
4:(4 2) Emmigration - Avoiding War	2	1	4	2
5:(4 3) Emmigration - Other Reasons	0	0	0	2
6:(5 1) Safety	1	0	1	0
7:(5 2) Attitude ~ Efficacy	2	2	2	2
8:(5 3) Education ~ Social Class	0	2	0	0
9:(5 5) Language Issues	3	2	4	2
10:(5 6 1) Coping Strategies	0	1	2	2
11:(5 6 3) Problems	0	1	3	1
12:(5 6 6) General~Transitioning	3	2	4	3
13:(6 1) Friends	0	1	1	0

■ *Attitude and efficacy:* Marginalized individuals were far less likely to express high levels of efficacy (belief in their own ability to succeed). The marginalized group expressed general themes of sadness and passivity.

■ *Age and language issues:* Separated individuals tended to be older and to not have learned English well.

■ *Social contexts:* Family were frequently noted as important in providing support. Places of worship were described as key supports, particularly in the Separated group. Friends were not noted as particularly important. There was no clear consensus regarding the role of work, except that the Marginalized group appeared to have a very passive view of their employment.

■ *Community context:* Separated individuals had almost all social ties confined to the Bosnian community. Their lack of language skills seemed to exacerbate this, and they appeared content to remain separated. There appeared to be little evidence of any Bosnians being aggressively supported or "drawn in" by the general American community. Involvement in American community contexts seemed to come mainly from internal motivations held by the Bosnian immigrants themselves.

John gets started on his paper, in which he overviews the literature, introduces his study, describes his methods, and presents and discusses his findings. This paper, "johnsnotes.doc," can be found at www.ablongman.com/mysocialworkkit.

Now it is time for our five friends to think about how they will make sense of and present their results. The next chapter will discuss issues of interpretation and dissemination.

REVIEW

We assume you will be doing your own analysis of some of your own data. Please answer the following questions.

1. What statistical method(s) or qualitative analysis approach(es) did you use? Justify how these sprang logically from your question and design.

2. Explain how statistical assumptions underlying the approaches you used were explored and satisfied.

3. Present your statistical results or qualitative coding scheme and some kind of summary or presentation of your coded content units.

4. Explain the limitations in the analysis approach you used.

5. Explain how the reader should interpret or understand your results. Use simple English.

16

INTERPRETATION AND DISSEMINATION

This chapter will move you through the part of the research process that comes after your data have been analyzed. This includes two main tasks, interpreting your data and writing it up in some format so that other people can see what you've done. We will discuss these two tasks together because interpretation is a culmination of all the work that goes into a project and is most easily understood in terms of what you have to tell other people about the work you've done.

In this chapter, we will also overview the main components of any scientific work (introduction and background, methods, results, and discussion). We will discuss the various audiences your work might be aimed at, and finally we will discuss each type of product you might produce (i.e., journal article, presentation, etc.). We will include finished products from our five sample cases as examples of the major types of academic product.

As far as specifics regarding style, use of fonts, headings, how to put tables together, and the like, you should spend the $30 and buy yourself a copy of the *Publication Manual of the American Psychological Association* (www.apastyle.org). This is the standard reference for writing in the social sciences and is a necessary resource for any researcher. We will not cover the specifics of style here, but you can use the included paper from Kathy as an example of the current APA format.

SECTION 16.1

FOUR COMPONENTS OF SCIENTIFIC REPORTING

Every scientific product should have four main components. These elements are most formalized in the case of journal articles but should be present in any work. They are the introduction and background, the methods, the results, and the discussion.

SECTION 16.1.1: INTRODUCTION AND BACKGROUND

The introduction and background are the first part of any product and may be partitioned into several smaller components. Journal articles generally start with an abstract, which is usually about 150 to 200 words and is meant to summarize the article. The abstract is separate from the body of the text and probably should be written after the paper is otherwise finished, allowing you to look at the final product and then write the clearest, most concise description possible in the limited space provided.

The abstract is followed by an introduction to the issue being studied and a review of the theoretical and empirical literature in the area. Many researchers will present their research question and hypotheses as the final part of this section. A typical introduction and background section will be structured as follows:

1. *Brief (one paragraph at most) description of goal of the work:* This might be, for example, a statement that the paper will focus on evaluating different means of fostering economic self-sufficiency among the rural poor in Alabama. The aim of your work should be presented here.

2. *Overview of current knowledge (literature), both theoretical and empirical:* This shows the need for the current work and the approach taken in studying it. This section should:

   ■ Describe the practical importance of the work. Most applied articles will cite statistics showing the extent and impact of the issue being studied.

   ■ Describe the literature providing a theoretical foundation for the work and describe the theoretical foundation for the current work.

   ■ Overview prior similar work, including methods and findings. It is important that key issues, such as areas of consistent methodological weaknesses or contradictory empirical findings, be highlighted.

   This section's job is to set the groundwork for the presentation of your work. The reader should come away from this section knowing about theory, empirical findings, and other key issues in your area. The next section must flow logically from this foundation.

3. *Description of the current project:* This section introduces your work in detail. It must at a minimum show the following:

   ■ How your work flows from or tests theory.

   ■ How your work builds on prior work. Most importantly, you must state explicitly how your work fills current gaps in the literature.

   ■ What your general design is (this may include an overview of sample, type of design, key variables).

   ■ What your specific research questions and hypotheses are.

SECTION 16.1.2: METHODS

The methods section is where you say exactly how you did what you did. It must be sufficiently precise to allow for replication of your work. This section builds on and operationalizes the overview of your design, which was begun in the prior section. They must be clearly linked. Here you will provide details on your sample, procedures, instruments, and data analysis plan. Planned statistical tests that are complex or unfamiliar to readers should be discussed in some detail. Methods sections can vary dramatically. A methodology section using simple statistics on Census information may be well under a page long, whereas a section detailing a complex recruitment of subjects to different types of groups with multiple tests and other instruments being administered under differing contingencies may actually be the longest part of the paper. The methods section must not include presentation of results as such, although references to some preliminary results (such as normality of data) may be necessary in describing the statistical approaches used. Methodology sections should always discuss details about sample recruitment and response rates if appropriate.

SECTION 16.1.3: RESULTS

The results are your findings. This section presents data, commonly in tables or figures, and describes them in text. The results section does not include commentary or discussion of findings, it only presents them.

A description of the sample is a common first step in any results section. Typically, a results section will begin with a table or text describing the sample used, broken down by groups if groups exist. This is important so that the reader can understand your sample and how representative it might be. Statistical tests, such as *t* tests or chi-square, will often be used to demonstrate similarities or differences between treatment and control or comparison groups.

Univariate and bivariate relationships are often presented next. Many studies will show simple univariate statistics (mean, median, standard deviation, proportions, and so on) of their main variables. In addition, simple bivariates (correlations, chi-squares) can be presented to show simple relationships between variables.

Finally, full models are presented to provide the reader with the definitive study results. In a true experimental design study, the primary analysis may be as simple as a bivariate ANOVA. Most studies, however, use multivariate statistics to allow for statistical control, and some studies will present more complex findings derived from such means as factor analysis or structural equation modeling.

The statistical models are almost always presented in tables. Sometimes figures are used instead of or in addition to the tables for examples with structural equation modeling. Many researchers will use figures to highlight particularly important findings or to graphically show results not easily understood in tabular form, such as interaction effects.

The text accompanying the tables need not list all findings individually but should describe the important findings. In addition, any confusing findings or findings that highlight possible methodological issues should be highlighted. Sometimes results not included in tables will be in the text. It is important to highlight to the reader when you are describing information in a table or figure and when you are presenting separate information. It is critically important that opinion not be present in the results section. Statements to be avoided include even minor comments like "It is interesting that . . ." to introduce results.

SECTION 16.1.4: DISCUSSION

Discussion sections are the final parts of most academic products. They commonly start with a very brief (one paragraph) summary of the purpose of the work and the principal findings. The discussion section is unique in that the writer is expected to give his or her opinion. It is the author's only real chance to say what he or she thinks, as opposed to simply describing what was done. Typical components of a discussion section include the following.

A strengths and limitations section tells the reader what you think the assets and flaws of your work are. This is your chance to both describe why you think your method was strong and to defend the weaknesses of the approach. Wise and ethical writers will highlight the weaknesses in their own work so that the reader does not conclude that the researcher was too ignorant to understand them or was trying to be deceptive. It is fine to present special circumstances or considerations that might moderate the concerns about a particular weakness. Strengths and limitations can apply to any part of the work, ranging from theory to design to sample to statistics used.

A discussion of findings comprises the major focus of this section. The writer must discuss what was found, with an emphasis on the following issues:

- How were the research questions answered? Were the hypotheses (if any) supported?
- In light of the findings, does the methodology appear appropriate?
- Are the findings consistent with or divergent from prior empirical work? If they are divergent, why is this?
- How do the findings relate to the theory underlying the work?
- What are the implications for practice, policy, and research?

Suggestions for future research comprise the final part of many papers or other academic products. Here, the authors give their views about how future studies can build on the current work.

SECTION 16.2
DIFFERENT AUDIENCES

You've got to know whom you're writing for, what they need, and what will hold their interest. Most research is written for academic audiences, but other key constituencies include agency or governmental personnel, the general public, and consumers. Even among academic audiences, different journals vary remarkably in their emphasis on different things.

Academic audiences are generally reached through professional journals, conference presentations, and books. Academics tend to want a precise description of the methodology, and they want to see descriptions of samples and multivariate statistics. Depending on the relative "newness" of an area, they may also be particularly interested in the background review and theoretical foundation. They tend to be less interested in your opinion of your findings and more interested in how they build on or diverge from prior work. They also tend to be more interested in implications for research rather than practice and policy implications. If you are writing for this audience, you must place relatively more emphasis on the methods and results sections.

Governmental and agency audiences are commonly reached through presentations and reports (particularly executive summaries) and less commonly through academic journals. Some of these people are interested in methodology, but most of them want to know what you found and what should be done about it. They will often not understand arcane statistics such as unstandardized regression coefficients but will respond well to simple statistics ("for every female who commits suicide, four males commit suicide"). They tend to understand and like *USA Today*–style graphics featuring pie and bar charts. This does not mean that you avoid conducting more complex analyses, but it does mean that you must find simple ways of communicating the results in a more understandable way. There is no point in presenting a table nobody but you can read.

Additionally, you will have to be ready to show the potential impact of your work. Why was your work important? What practical implications exist? What should your audience do about it now? The aforementioned executive summary can be a great tool here. Many people will not read beyond the first couple of pages of anything you give them, so you'd better give them the meat of the issue fast. One of the best ways to do this is to begin with half a dozen or so specific findings or implications, phrased so that they will be easily understood. This is what is meant by an executive summary. You provide this abbreviated version and then include the larger reports so that they can review

details if needed. If you do this, you stand a better chance of having an effect on people and on the world. For an example of an executive summary, see Yuan's final product.

The use of anecdotal stories to introduce the work or implications can help people understand what is going on. People understand human events far more easily than they understand statistics, so it can be useful to pick a story and relate it to the audience, so long as the story accurately reflects your main findings.

Consumers and the general public are often quite unfamiliar with the language of research, and require clear and straightforward presentation of main findings. As with agencies and governmental audiences, the emphasis must be on providing simple descriptions of findings that will have some relevance to the real world. Ideally, researchers should use short, clear sound-bite sentences and should by no means attempt to describe methodological complexities, unless some overview of the methods is absolutely necessary to understanding the findings. It is surprising how difficult it can be to approach these audiences because you need a very thorough understanding of your work to be able to break it down into a format that is both simple to understand and informative. There is a need for a kind of cultural competency here. Different consumer groups may prefer different forms of dissemination (e.g., in a community meeting rather than a newsletter).

Now that we've briefly discussed the components of a final product and spent a little time considering how the final product will vary depending on your audience, we will move to a specific description of different types of products that you might produce.

SECTION 16.3
DIFFERENT TYPES OF PRODUCTS

There are many forms that your final product can take. This section will describe each and will provide examples from the projects we've been following throughout the text. Among the most common are the following.

Peer-reviewed journal articles are the "gold standard" by which academic productivity is judged. These articles are usually between about 15 and 30 double-spaced pages long (including tables and references). Most academic articles use a blind peer review process, in which you submit an article to a journal and the editor sends it out for other experts to review, without telling them who you are. Typically, you will hear from the journal in three to six months, and the most common action is for them to either reject your article or to request revisions. It is quite rare that articles are accepted without revision. The revision process can take several more months, during which time you communicate with the editor, and the articles may be sent back to the original reviewers for rereview. After acceptance, it may still be a year or more before the article appears in print, depending on whether or not the journal has a backlog of article submissions. For a typical example of a paper that would be sent to a peer-reviewed journal, see Professor Kathy's final product.

Books and book chapters tend to give authors the chance to spend a little more time and page space discussing their ideas or their work. The peer-review process is either absent or less stringent than in article publication. Typically a publisher receives a proposal for a book from authors or an editorial team. The publisher may send the proposal out for a peer review to judge interest in the manuscript. After a publisher accepts the idea, the author completes the work, or editors guide the chapter authors in completing the work. In an edited work, most of the review process is handled between the editors and the chapter authors, but it can involve peer review as well. Book chapters often undergo fewer alterations prior to publication than journal articles. After a complete draft is compiled, some publishers will again send the book out for review to solicit comments about improvements. This process typically takes over a year. We have chosen not to provide an example of a book chapter here due to concerns about length.

Agency reports are written for agencies to describe clientele, needs, programs, and outcomes. They are typically more heavily focused on practical issues (population demographics, services provided, outcomes) and place less emphasis on methodology. The primary audience for an agency report is often administrative staff. Sometimes, however, these reports are also provided to funders. Most agency reports have an executive summary, a one- or two-page overview of the report, usually in a bulleted format. More text may then follow. For an example of a typical agency report, see Yuan's final product.

Presentations can be made to agencies, interested groups, or, most commonly, at conferences. These usually involve your standing up and telling people about what you've done. Most people use overheads, handouts, or, more commonly, a PowerPoint presentation. The typical presentation lasts about 15 to 30 minutes, so your ability to budget your time wisely is a very important part of a good presentation. Unlike most other scientific products, presentations provide you with the additional challenge of having to respond to questions from the audience, requiring you to be very well versed in what you are talking about. The ability to "think on your feet" is a real benefit here.

Most academic conferences are centered around presentations, which are usually combined by the organizers in two to four presentation groups, which usually share a similar theme. Presentation sessions are usually 90 to 120 minutes long, leaving each presenter somewhere between 20 and 45 minutes—including time for questions. Presentations are a great way to get feedback and meet people. Most conferences require that you submit an abstract between six months to a year in advance of the conference and will screen the abstracts through a type of peer review, accepting only a subset for their conference. In other words, you have to apply, and you may be rejected.

Presentations to agencies or other nonacademic audiences are similar in content but will tend to focus less on methodological issues and more on practical implications. These may be done in more informal situations in a meeting format. It is important to know how many people will be attending the presentation and be prepared to use whatever format is convenient given the purpose of the presentation, audience size, and available technology at the agency site. For an example of a presentation in PowerPoint format, see Abigail's final product.

Posters are used at many conferences. A poster presentation is sometimes a set of slides made in PowerPoint and printed out to fit in the space required, or it may just be a document file. In a poster presentation, you put your poster up, and people come by and look at it, sometimes with you present, sometimes not. Posters generally include between four to eight pages of text and graphics. They are far less impressive on an academic résumé than a journal article, and most professors won't bother with them. They can be a good way for a student or young investigator to get a start and make connections, though. Similar to the way a presentation works, it is important that you can think on your feet so that you can respond to questions from people who come by and look at the poster. You should have cards or some type of handout available with your contact information so that viewers can request further information about your work after the conference. For a typical poster, see Maria's final product.

SECTION 16.4
PRACTICAL ADVICE FOR GETTING PRESENTATIONS AND ARTICLES ACCEPTED

The peer-review process can be a particularly confusing aspect of dissemination for the beginning researcher. This section provides a brief guide or checklist for the person making an initial effort to become published by a peer-reviewed journal. The principles are similar for submitting a conference presentation abstract for competitive review, except that only steps 1 through 3 really apply.

SECTION 16.4.1: DETERMINE WHOM YOU WILL SUBMIT TO

This is probably the most important part of the process. You probably know what journals exist in your area, but you need to take another look from the point of view of a prospective author. Journals should be thought of along the following dimensions:

- *What is the subject matter of the articles they publish?* You should try to match your article to the journal that has published the most similar articles.

- *What is the emphasis on methodology and statistics in the journal?* Look through the journal. Are all the articles using very advanced statistical methods, or are there relatively few statistics reported? Are they publishing mainly true experimental designs, or are descriptive and correlational designs also welcome? Do they prefer certain types of data (e.g., administrative, primary data collection, qualitative interviews)? In other words, you are trying to assess how well the methods and statistical techniques in the journal match those in your paper.

- *Who is the target audience of the journal?* Some journals are written mostly for researchers (e.g., *Social Work Research*), while others are written more for the field in general (e.g., *Social Work*). Some journals have a cross-disciplinary reputation (e.g., *American Journal of Orthopsychiatry*), while others are specific to a field of practice (e.g., *Children & Schools*). Whom is your article meant to reach?

- *How well-respected and well-read is the journal?* A good article should be sent to a good, widely read journal. The reputation of the journal is important to your career, as colleagues will tend to more highly value a work in a more respected journal. A widely read journal (not all well-respected journals are widely read) will help insure that your article has the most impact on building knowledge in your area. It is true that these journals are also harder to get into, and this can be intimidating. Many beginning researchers make the mistake of sending their articles to journals that are less well respected or read but have higher publication rates. It is important to remember that if it is rejected, you can always scale down your ambitions later and submit to another journal.

- *What specific requirements does the journal have for the length and format of submitted papers?* Make sure that your article fits within the required page limitations. This information can be found either in the journal, usually at the front or back, or on the journal's Web site. You also need to note the required style (usually APA) and any other requirements, such as length of abstract and the like. If you are at a university, make sure you ask a faculty member in your area for advice on this issue. This whole process is something like playing a game; it takes learning the rules and practice to get good at it. They know how to play it. You probably don't.

SECTION 16.4.2: MAKE SURE YOUR ARTICLE IS READY

Your paper must be carefully checked for spelling, grammar, APA style, and the like. It also needs to convey your message as clearly and as succinctly as possible. Sometimes it is hard to make the transition from writing long research papers, a thesis, or a dissertation to writing a 15-page article. Have someone look it over and give critical feedback on the writing, logic, and presentation. If you have a tendency to write too much, ask the person to identify areas that could be cut. It may seem intimidating at first to have a peer you know review your work, but it's better to have your friends find a weakness than to have the reviewers find it.

You should also print out your article and check for two issues. First, note whether the citations in the text agree with the reference list at the end of the article. It's easy during the editing process to leave a reference out or have one remain that is no longer cited in the text. Second, carefully review the text in your results section with the tables and figures. Do the sample sizes agree? Do any columns or rows that are totaled equal the right number? Do numbers and descriptions in the text match the tables? Some reviewers may just casually note one or two errors, but others will see this as a "red flag" regarding the quality of the work. While few manuscripts make it through the review process without having to "revise and resubmit," you don't want an outright rejection because of a few editing errors. This little in-house review can save a lot of trouble later.

SECTION 16.4.3: MAIL IT AND WAIT FOR A RESPONSE

Make sure you send the right number of copies to the right location and addressed to the right person. Follow instructions regarding format. What will happen next is as follows:

- *The editor will get the paper and probably assign it for review.* He or she will either reject it outright or send it out for blind review. Outright rejections usually occur when the article is seen by the editor as simply very poor quality (relatively rare) or as not appropriate to the journal, due to length or subject matter. You will typically receive a card or letter from the editor telling you what happens.

- *Reviewers will read the article and send comments back to the editor.* Editors usually ask for three to five reviews and usually get about three back. These reviewers are asked for general comments on the paper and to make a recommendation as to whether the paper should be rejected outright, accepted outright (rare), accepted provisionally, or rejected with a request for the author to revise and resubmit (common if the article is appropriate for the journal).

The editor will make a decision and forward the reviewer's comments to you. This process should take about three months. If it takes longer, call the editor's office and politely inquire as to the state of the review process.

SECTION 16.4.4: YOU GET THE EDITOR'S RESPONSE BACK AND DECIDE WHAT TO DO

If the article is accepted outright, fine; but this almost never happens. The authors have had about 70 articles published and have had outright acceptance letters in only three or four cases.

- If the letter just says the article is rejected, then look at the reviewer's comments (most journals forward complete comments as a courtesy to the author, but a few do not). Make any needed changes and submit it somewhere else. Hemingway is alleged to have said that the most important key to getting published is "postage." So give yourself a day at most to be disappointed then "get back on the horse" (i.e., fix it and mail it out again). A quick response allows you to make changes while the study is fresh in your mind. If you let it sit, there is a good chance that you will become depressed about the paper or get distracted by a newer project and never get back to it.
- If the letter says your article is rejected, but that the editor is willing to look at a revised draft that addresses the reviewer's concerns, then this is very good. This is the most common way that published articles move through the process. If the changes make sense to you, make the changes and resubmit. If some of the suggested changes do not make sense, you can respond to the editor and defend why the changes should not be made, or you can send it somewhere else. When you return the

article, you must provide a cover sheet explaining to the editor what you have done and why. We discuss this more later.

- If the letter says your article is accepted pending revisions, then you are in pretty much the same situation as above.

SECTION 16.4.5: REVISE AND RESUBMIT

You will probably have received three or so different reviews, ranging from a short paragraph to a 10-page itemized set of concerns. You will have to convince the editor and reviewers that you understand and have addressed their issues. The best way to do this is by sending your resubmission in two parts. The first part, of course, is the revised article. The second part is your cover letter and attached list of changes and rationale for those changes. Each reviewer's comment should be specifically mentioned, and you should describe how you deal with each issue. If you do not agree with the reviewer, say so, and say why. Sometimes changes alter the length or organization of the article. If so, it is helpful to direct the editor and reviewers to the specific page numbers where the changes can be found.

Obviously, tact and a certain amount of humility are important here. Figures 16.1 and 16.2 show the text of the cover letter and enumerated changes that the authors provided to the editor of *Child Maltreatment* for their article "Substantiation and Recidivism." You might note, for example, the gentle language used regarding reviewers. Because these comments may be read by the reviewers, it is important to be nice to them.

FIGURE 16.1. **Text of Cover Letter for Resubmission.**

Dr. Mark Chaffin,
Editor, *Child Maltreatment*
University of Oklahoma Health Sciences Center CHO 3406
POB 26901
Oklahoma City, Oklahoma 73190

October 7, 2002

Dear Mark,

I have made the changes requested. I appended a list of changes along with a copy of the original reviewer's comments. Sorry if the original draft was a bit rough. Let me know if there is anything else I can do.

Thanks.

_____
Brett Drake Ph.D.
Associate Professor

FIGURE 16.2. Accompanying Responses to Reviewer's Concerns (Partial text only, full response was 3 pages long).

Responses to Reviewer's Issues:
Reviewer C raises a number of issues that need to be dealt with. We have attempted to do so to his or her satisfaction and have included both a revised document and this compilation of changes made. It is nice to see a reviewer who really takes the time to help improve both the big things and the little things on a paper.

Reviewer's concerns (page 1 of reviewer's comments).

ISSUE: The reviewer voices concerns regarding a lack of a theoretical model.

RESPONSE: We apologize for not more clearly specifying the theoretical model tested. We have done so in a new section (approx. ½ page) entitled "The Harm/Evidence Model," which is in the introduction.

ISSUE: The reviewer desired more clarity regarding the last two sentences of paragraph one.

RESPONSE: We have revised these to make them more clear.

ISSUE: Emotional Abuse excluded

RESPONSE: We stand by our reasoning for excluding this type, which is that it is simply too physically large a task to present the data in one article that is already long and burdened by large tables.

ISSUE: Means of classifying type of case (Sex, Physical, Mixed, etc...) unclear.

RESPONSE: We have substantially improved our description of how this was done and have included a reference to the citation the reviewer suggests on page 4.

Reviewer's concerns (page 2 of reviewer's comments).

ISSUE: Reviewer dislikes technical jargon re STF1 and 3 in census.

RESPONSE: Deleted.

ISSUE: Reviewer wants description of ecological fallacy.

RESPONSE: Provided on page 5.

ISSUE: Reviewer wants clarification of median tract income.

RESPONSE: We now say "median family income in census tract."

ISSUE: Reviewer dislikes our dropping names of states that have had their data analyzed in similar ways; says to delete.

RESPONSE: Done.

ISSUE: Reviewer dislikes our naming of SAS version and procedures used.

RESPONSE: We took out SAS version. We feel it does no harm for less experienced readers to be exposed to the type of procedures used, but will remove if reviewer wants.

ISSUE: Clumsy wording on our part regarding interpreting significant but small effects

RESPONSE: Language clarified on page 9.

ISSUE: Reviewer suggests increased recidivism of neglect cases may be due in part to their greater likelihood of occurrence.

RESPONSE: We agree. This has been addressed in substantial detail in another article, currently in press, which we have now cited.

ISSUE: Reviewer suggests we move summary sentence at end of pgph 1 pg 10 forward.

RESPONSE: We'd rather not do this because this sentence deals with looking at percentages of recidivism cases originally unsubstantiated (not the reverse). While this is important to note, it does not stem so directly from our basic question, and therefore we don't want to lead off with it.

ISSUE: FPS not written out

RESPONSE: Corrected.

SECTION 16.4.6: REVISE AND RESUBMIT AGAIN

No, this is not an error in the textbook. There is a very strong chance your editor will come back to you and request more changes, particularly for your first few articles. You may have to revise the paper several times. If the cycle goes on too long, you may have to use your judgment about giving up and sending to another journal. One of the authors had a paper revised five times and then rejected. This is very rare. It is a good idea to consult with a more senior colleague if you are thinking that the process is going nowhere and you should change journals. That colleague can help you assess whether being patient is wiser than retracting the article.

SECTION 16.4.7: GALLEYS

After final acceptance, you can now list the article as "in press" on your vitae and congratulate yourself and any coauthors. There will be a delay, however, while the article awaits its turn for publication. Indeed, the reputation of a journal is sometimes positively correlated with the length of time between acceptance and publication. Prior to publication, you will be sent galleys, which are final copies of your paper for your review. You are supposed to assure only that they are correct and to make only those changes related to appearance or accuracy. There will almost certainly be an appended list of queries for you about such things as misspellings and issues with your references being cited correctly. Generally, major changes should not occur at this point. The galleys are already set into a certain page length. If such a change is needed, you should include a comment in a cover letter as to why this is needed and assurance that it doesn't have an impact on the overall meaning of the paper (i.e., the change is not so great as to need a new review).

SECTION 16.5
VALUES AND ETHICS IN DISSEMINATION

Many ethical guidelines apply to dissemination. These issues apply while writing papers as well as during the publication process:

- You must be honest and fair in your introduction section. It is very common for writers to disregard or omit material that would cast doubt on the merit of their work. You must do your best to accurately show the state of the research, theory, and methods in your area and explain how your work builds on past work. Obviously, you must avoid plagiarism here, as always.

- You must be accurate in your presentation of methods. Every study has weaknesses in methodology, and you must present them clearly. Again, it is tempting simply to omit damaging information, such as high rates of sample attrition. You might think that if you can sneak it by the reviewers, it's OK to do. Avoid such sloppy or intentionally dishonest practices.

- You must accurately present your findings. You must not only avoid direct lies, but you must do your best to convey the actual meaning of the data. For example, consider the following IQ scores for males and females, before and after an experimental intervention, shown in Figure 16.3.

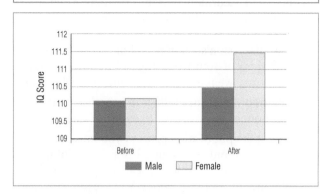

FIGURE 16.3. IQ Scores Before and After Treatment.

At first glance, this table appears to show that males might have had a slight improvement after treatment, while females made a big jump. It looks this way because the male bar goes up a reasonable amount (about 25% of its height), and the female bar goes up a lot. Of course, looking at the left column, we see that the jump for males was from about 110 to about 110.5, a totally meaningless jump of .5 IQ points (which is 1/30 of a standard deviation). The jump for females was almost equally meaningless, being about 1 IQ point. Why is this chart so utterly misleading? Because the values on the vertical axis range across only three IQ points. A less misleading bar chart would appear as in Figure 16.4 and would tell a very different visual story with exactly the same numerical data.

One interesting point is that the misleading chart in Figure 16.3 is the default table produced by Microsoft Excel. We didn't have to try to create this misleading table, it was done automatically for us! To create the chart in Figure 16.4, we had to go in and manually adjust the y-axis. As you become a more experienced researcher, you will gain the ability to do many things that misrepresent your data without technically presenting false data. For example, including or removing some variables in a multivariate design may help a different variable perform the way you want or

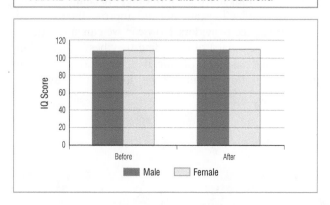

FIGURE 16.4. IQ Scores Before and After Treatment.

expect it to. Try to avoid such cheap and dishonest tactics and try to accurately present the clearest picture of what your data are telling you. More tips:

- Your discussion section must honestly portray the limitations of your work. Again, intentional omission of key weaknesses is a definite ethical no-no.

- You should present findings in a method that is both honest and sensitive to cultural issues.

- During the publication process, you must submit an article to only one journal at a time. Multiple submissions of the same article are unethical. The rules are different for books. You are allowed to shop around until a contract is signed.

- You should try very hard to avoid what our friend Dr. Martha Ozawa calls "salami publications." Also termed the "least publishable unit" or "LPU," this phenomenon is when a researcher breaks the work up into many small articles to get his or her publication count up. You should determine what to include in a given work by the scholarly merit of the material and the space available and should not simply remanufacture articles with slightly different variables or methods.

- You must give credit to people in order according to their contributions, especially with respect to the lead author. You must cite all significant contributors. You may not leave out people who contributed, but you also must not include people who did not significantly contribute, just to give them a publication.

- We believe that it is unethical not to disseminate your work simply because you have a politically or personally motivated dislike for your findings. This may not be a universally held ethical principle, but it is codified in the American Sociological Association's Code of Ethics (section 13.04a).

CONCLUSION

Dissemination is a critical aspect of the scientific process. Without sharing our findings, we cannot hope to build knowledge in academia and improve the evidence base for service providers. How can we can stay true to the ethical standard of providing the "best practice" in the applied aspects of social science (e.g. service providers, policy makers) if we don't understand the magnitude and etiology of problems and the most effective and efficient means of ameliorating them?

In our experience, students and practitioners are too hesitant about getting involved in publication. Many journals and conferences have created special venues for students and practitioners to encourage their contributions. For example, some journals have "practice highlights" sections that are designed for shorter notes from the field. When you consider the numbers of research faculty in relation to the number of bio-psycho-social needs and models of service, there is clearly a need for contributions from all levels. Talk to someone familiar with the process and see if your work strikes them as appropriate. If so, there is no reason at all why you shouldn't give it a try. After all, you've already done the work, and someone is waiting for that information to move ahead.

REVIEW

1. What goes in each of the following sections: Introduction and Background, Methods, Results, Discussion?

2. What are the three kinds of audiences discussed in this chapter, and what are two considerations you might keep in mind when writing for each?

3. Assuming you have done work that you wish to disseminate, which type of dissemination (probably either article, presentation, or poster) would you think is right for you? Why?

4. What are the main criticisms of your work that a reviewer might mention?

SUPPLEMENTAL READINGS

- American Psychological Association. (2001). *Publication Manual of the American Psychological Association* (5th ed.). Washington, DC: American Psychological Association. The gold standard for both psychology and many other social sciences, APA format is by far the most common formal writing style you will encounter.

- Mitchell, M. L., Jolley, J. M., & O'Shea, R. P. (2004). *Writing for Psychology*. Belmont, CA: Thomson-Wadsworth. For people interested in more detail about the writing process than is provided above, this is a nice reference.

Random Number Table

	1 2 3 4 5	6 7 8 9 10	11 12 13 14 15	16 17 18 19 20	21 22 23 24 25
1	96 08 82 39 60	97 69 79 56 31	39 18 02 19 61	76 50 23 76 55	78 98 52 36 58
2	60 21 12 66 22	42 52 08 52 10	64 47 78 54 58	20 10 03 81 54	55 83 47 81 36
3	71 88 06 99 93	27 17 90 85 70	49 43 84 96 83	19 17 59 21 43	81 22 00 94 32
4	66 63 21 37 97	73 10 45 91 21	04 05 93 40 57	90 85 64 17 04	77 42 43 21 21
5	85 31 54 94 33	21 43 81 72 09	44 16 07 45 25	46 46 32 00 81	96 98 39 46 99
6	72 27 43 02 26	03 96 84 32 65	24 83 93 79 05	55 97 01 19 90	24 65 34 69 28
7	66 06 56 06 75	73 75 33 90 23	69 48 82 70 66	08 26 37 36 11	32 77 29 76 27
8	19 61 40 99 93	20 55 05 65 26	75 05 99 69 35	83 09 81 85 83	10 70 96 09 57
9	38 13 96 04 13	32 81 74 36 03	24 26 81 32 31	39 19 89 00 45	03 85 99 06 58
10	09 48 86 63 52	95 64 65 70 35	46 37 71 49 57	50 83 18 47 12	02 82 93 82 94
11	38 22 00 78 07	76 76 34 28 15	63 83 75 21 80	23 51 36 00 16	08 18 65 16 79
12	74 32 13 89 79	44 42 36 28 37	35 81 89 78 68	93 00 02 47 04	91 63 33 46 79
13	09 37 31 80 56	38 80 77 73 66	30 62 14 35 57	60 84 04 19 36	20 79 44 92 27
14	99 67 72 49 63	38 45 87 19 84	81 54 82 05 31	78 01 32 98 36	32 77 22 26 74
15	86 94 31 39 44	20 53 80 03 83	45 14 73 63 49	63 90 36 98 91	84 14 49 32 36
16	25 54 36 29 90	13 40 93 06 56	70 42 15 89 95	02 39 99 65 01	78 15 04 73 05
17	62 01 69 11 87	50 56 91 23 35	43 66 68 46 73	12 95 40 47 66	66 93 65 03 71
18	28 40 67 88 95	87 88 35 55 77	93 13 92 19 89	46 30 67 48 60	10 22 15 54 87
19	00 83 41 49 98	69 44 96 00 06	02 41 54 25 16	10 40 94 48 90	78 07 74 91 35
20	97 60 04 50 18	41 69 55 66 66	70 87 52 40 19	08 51 75 06 32	24 49 97 36 26
21	00 54 58 87 22	65 50 07 95 34	33 25 23 42 93	97 12 44 28 60	09 18 93 51 79
22	18 44 88 39 77	41 80 80 95 86	44 83 56 36 31	73 51 32 76 84	98 63 02 15 57
23	07 96 60 89 30	63 85 15 10 38	51 96 54 72 27	79 70 57 63 74	43 55 37 11 10
24	70 37 68 51 27	30 52 39 78 96	03 02 87 54 02	29 11 73 79 09	64 47 09 40 37
25	64 58 52 10 98	55 48 22 82 74	17 18 24 68 36	14 47 54 31 30	10 74 29 12 58
26	61 52 43 76 59	00 91 80 35 24	42 34 43 23 01	27 69 25 58 84	18 12 30 47 85
27	09 76 00 36 61	70 22 29 66 32	07 33 51 31 81	40 43 45 71 51	49 10 06 49 19
28	78 72 66 29 71	86 26 23 68 04	54 52 90 01 59	42 80 71 51 52	52 00 81 97 53
29	44 38 24 25 47	87 52 81 17 48	73 54 62 02 68	14 20 61 88 04	61 53 96 92 03
30	81 05 82 92 57	10 55 66 17 65	39 91 95 27 76	22 37 65 92 70	41 05 12 86 34
31	13 25 13 64 21	53 68 93 83 86	47 40 62 36 86	24 20 00 95 29	97 52 46 06 10
32	57 25 76 79 01	75 08 98 38 85	08 14 82 48 63	68 83 83 63 34	41 95 69 14 69
33	53 52 49 01 98	63 64 61 23 56	56 65 85 22 58	93 63 01 21 28	32 99 61 47 00
34	28 04 82 25 89	94 28 09 89 68	70 87 65 49 65	36 66 65 13 79	96 79 23 15 27
35	09 46 09 69 26	93 42 37 74 30	84 87 26 87 47	14 71 05 62 06	83 82 11 25 65
36	18 95 92 09 10	98 18 35 60 64	80 68 26 80 94	84 80 25 13 61	95 27 33 49 59
37	20 16 61 31 26	05 32 58 23 84	36 14 15 08 53	65 70 44 47 51	83 08 84 55 37
38	82 86 58 57 07	76 40 41 30 65	72 95 12 75 10	33 27 30 67 70	49 50 46 73 67
39	70 04 06 09 51	57 32 62 71 06	92 95 11 58 14	07 87 64 70 38	55 42 60 46 85
40	34 65 11 60 76	91 03 13 98 76	82 56 92 30 14	78 88 33 43 30	49 58 55 85 80
41	24 59 19 06 09	98 31 35 76 66	97 92 96 33 57	56 19 59 89 21	81 20 15 13 45
42	73 16 06 14 30	16 49 27 59 98	45 54 86 31 58	19 18 84 93 48	31 41 56 80 85
43	74 72 00 50 82	33 02 24 04 30	77 59 88 01 90	89 90 83 76 95	29 29 20 28 25
44	08 59 22 52 47	50 01 98 43 90	05 57 75 59 77	50 76 02 96 95	69 49 36 83 82
45	47 75 28 78 50	75 43 38 10 48	29 46 50 97 26	70 41 24 94 48	38 61 60 26 98

AN APPLICATION OF BERRY'S MODEL OF ACCULTURATION TO A BOSNIAN REFUGEE POPULATION

JOHN PRESTON, MA
Washington College, Collegetown, Missouri

ABSTRACT

Twelve Bosnian refugees were interviewed in an attempt to explore the relationship between strengths and acculturation status (marginalization, separation, integration, and assimilation). Interview transcripts were analyzed qualitatively using grounded theory. The respondents were all adults and had been in the United States for between two and eight years. Results highlighted differences between those individuals experiencing marginalization and other respondents. Marginalized individuals appeared to show fewer positive attitudes, less self-efficacy, and less future orientation. They also reported higher levels of trauma prior to leaving Bosnia and less enthusiasm for opportunities in the United States. Individuals experiencing separation also appeared different from the other groups, being generally older, with less English language skills, and having social contacts restricted almost entirely to the Bosnian community. This preliminary study suffers from small sample size and failure to include individuals with children in the home but does support the utility of Berry's (Berry & Kim, 1988) model in framing qualitative inquiries into this population.

AN APPLICATION OF BERRY'S MODEL OF ACCULTURATION TO A BOSNIAN REFUGEE POPULATION

The literature on refugee acculturation suffers from several major shortcomings, including the lack of a cohesive unifying theoretical model, differences within and between immigrant populations, and an almost exclusive focus on certain issues (e.g., posttraumatic stress disorder). This paper seeks to move the literature forward by presenting findings from a qualitative exploratory study seeking to understand linkages between strengths and acculturation status. The emphasis on strengths derives partly from the almost complete lack of focus on this area in the literature and partly from the recent emphasis on strength-based work with other populations and in other areas (e.g., Perez, Peifer, & Newman, 2002; Ronch & Goldfield, 2003).

BACKGROUND

Well over 100,000 Bosnian refugees live in the United States (Coughlan & Owens-Manley, 2005). These individuals are mainly Muslims who have fled the ethnic genocide that occurred in the Balkans in the 1990s. The empirical study of immigrants, particularly Bosnian immigrants, is still at an early stage. The aspect of the Bosnian experience that has received the most attention is clearly the study of posttraumatic stress disorder, or PTSD (Mollica, Saraljic, Chernhoff, Lavelle, Sarajilic-Vukovic & Massagli, 2001; Weine, Kuc, Dzurdra, Razzano, & Pavkovic 2001; Witmer & Culver, 2001). Identifying the prevalence and correlates of trauma-related mental health diagnoses is clearly important work. A sole focus on diagnoses and disorder, however, can reduce our ability to see and use strengths present within the Bosnian community. Social service practitioners have traditionally blended deficit and strengths models in assessment and treatment (McMillen, Morris, & Sherraden, 2004). Indeed, other immigrant populations have been studied with respect to strengths such as self-efficacy (Schwarzer, Hahn, & Schroder, 1994; Yong, 2005). One researcher to look at self-efficacy among Bosnian immigrants was Ferren (1999). This work advanced the study of PTSD by looking at the association of prior trauma with current self-efficacy among refugees postemigration.

Interestingly, prior trauma, with or without PTSD symptomatology, was associated with higher levels of self-efficacy in adolescent boys but not girls.

One of the more interesting studies on strengths among refugees was done by Yau (1996). Yau looked at self-esteem and self-efficacy among Southeastern Asian immigrants and used Berry and Kim's (1988) model. This is an influential model of acculturation that splits responses to immigration into four categories. Marginalization is an initial phase in which individuals feel separated from their former country and have not learned to fit in with their new host country. Over time, some people move from marginalization to integration, in which they identify more with and function within their new country, while still maintaining customs and other connections to their old country and community. Other people move more completely into a social role within their new country, abandoning ties to their former culture. This is called *assimilation.* Another aspect of the model is *separation,* in which individuals move into a new country but never really identify with it or function in it outside of enclaves from their own place of origin.

Given the formative nature of the literature on Bosnian immigrants, this paper will use an inductive approach to attempt to identify strengths within the Bosnian immigrant community and to understand these strengths in relation to acculturation status according to Berry and Kim. Methods used will include face-to-face interviewing of Bosnian immigrants and qualitative analysis of interview transcripts. This study is preliminary and exploratory and is intended only as an initial look at the issues studied.

METHODOLOGY

This study uses grounded theory (Glaser & Strauss, 1967) to attempt to build knowledge about strengths and acculturation in a Bosnian immigrant community. Grounded theory is an inductive approach in which theory arises from data collected. This approach was chosen due to the very limited data currently available on strengths in the Bosnian immigrant population. The sample was recruited from a refugee resettlement community in a large midwestern metropolitan area with a large Bosnian community. Participants were reimbursed for their time. Interviews were based around a set of questions intended to elicit responses regarding participants' acculturation experiences (see Table 1). In keeping with a grounded theory approach, these questions were kept intentionally general to allow participants to provide the information that they felt was most salient or important. Basic demographic information was also collected. All but three respondents were fluent in English. A translator was present for those three individuals.

TABLE 1 Questions Used in Study.

Q #1: How would you describe your adaptation to life in the United States?

Q #2: What were the most important things that made a difference in how you adapted to life here?

Q #3: What can you tell me about your decision to leave Bosnia?

Q #4: What things about yourself or your past experiences were important in your adjustment to life in the United States?

Q #5: What role did your family play in how you adjusted to adaptation to life in the United States?

Q #6: What things about your neighborhood or community were important in your adjustment to the United States?

Q #7: What was most helpful in your adjustment to the United States?

Q #8: What was least helpful in your adjustment to the United States?

Q #9: What abilities or strengths were most important to you in helping you adapt to the United States?

Q #10: Is there anything else that you can tell us that would help us understand your adaptation to the United States?

The interviews were taped and transcribed. Transcripts were analyzed using NVivo, Version 2.0. Primary analytic tasks included identifying and coding content units and arranging them into a hierarchical structure. In addition, all respondents were assigned to one of Berry and Kim's four categories of acculturation. These were operationally defined as follows:

- *Integration*: Showing substantial social and economic integration into U.S. culture while also maintaining Bosnian ties or identity.

- *Assimilation*: Showing a clear predominance of social and economic integration into U.S. culture with low emphasis on Bosnian ties or identity.

- *Separation*: Showing little social and economic integration into U.S. culture with strong emphasis on Bosnian ties or identity.

- *Marginalization*: Not showing successful economic or social integration with either the U.S. or Bosnian community.

To determine reliability in applying the above classifications, classification of subjects into one of these four categories was performed independently by four raters. Raters disagreed about classification on only one subject, with one rater disagreeing with the other three. Coding of content units was performed by the author, not in conjunction with other coders. This was done according to a "coding up" strategy (Bazeley & Richards, 2000) where the coding scheme evolves from the data.

RESULTS

A description of the demographics of the sample can be found in Table 2. The sample includes seven women and five men, almost all of whom were employed. Respondents varied in age from young adults to elderly. Time in the United States ranged from two to eight years. Eight of the respondents had a high school–level education, while two had not graduated high school. One had a bachelor's degree, and one had attended trade school after high school.

Application of grounded theory produced four major coding areas: emigration—decision to leave, immigration process, social contexts, and issues. Each of these major areas includes subthemes, and these will be discussed below. Special care will be taken to explore emerging similarities and differences between subjects experiencing different acculturation statuses.

EMIGRATION—DECISION TO LEAVE

Two major themes were identified with regard to subjects' decision to leave Bosnia. The most common theme, mentioned across all acculturation statuses,

TABLE 2 Characteristics of Subjects.

Gender	Female	7
	Male	5
Age	18–30	4
	30–59	6
	60+	2
Years in US	3 or less	6
	4 to 8	6
Education Level	Not HS graduate	2
	GED or HS graduate	8
	Some college	1
	4-year college graduate	1
Current Employment	Employed	10
	Unemployed	1
	Retired	1

but especially by marginalized subjects, was the desire to avoid war. Two of the four subjects coded as marginalized reported losing close family members, while no other respondents did. The general level of war trauma appeared higher in this group. One subject reported, "After I lost my family, it was a bad time. I didn't know what to do. If I stayed there, I'd just go crazy. Couldn't . . . [PAUSE]. I just couldn't stay anymore." This sense of confusion and helplessness was echoed by other marginalized individuals. Those from other groups were often more proactive in their desire to leave. One individual in the assimilated group stated that, "I [darn] near begged my family to get me out of there every day! They were kinda slow coming to it, and maybe they wouldn't have gone at all except the kid down the street got kinda messed up by a land mine."

The second subtheme in this area consisted of comments made about the lure of coming to America. While this was not evident in the marginalized group, at least one person in each of the other categories mentioned this issue. Responses varied in intensity, with some appearing almost casual, such as, "I saw America on TV, and I decided I'd want to come here," while others were more intensive: "They say the U.S. is the land of opportunity, and it sure is!"

IMMIGRATION PROCESS

There were two main areas of comment regarding the immigration process, and responses were consistent among groups for both. With regard to the formal process of resettlement, there was general dissatisfaction with official procedures and paperwork. One representative view was as follows:

> You people have rules and paperwork and requirements for breathing. I got my citizenship, and that was unnecessarily complicated, and the university wanted all kinds of stuff about my life before I came here, like school records, and I had to convince them that a lot of that stuff was sort of destroyed. The school I went to doesn't even exist anymore. The entire getting-here process was like that too. The whole refugee resettlement thing was like run by totally clueless people. That isn't exactly fair, a couple of them were really nice . . .

The reaction to refugee support services was completely different. Four respondents noted that the resettlement agency had been a big help, while only one had not found the services useful. It was interesting to note that three of the four marginalized individuals noted that the agency had been helpful to them.

SOCIAL CONTEXTS

A variety of individuals, organizations, and contexts were noted by our participants as important in their acculturation. There was relatively little mention of friends as important, with only two individuals mentioning these. No respondents had minor children in the home. Key persons identified by respondents were very diverse. Two individuals from the marginalized group made general comments about how family can provide a safe base. Two of the assimilated individuals stressed that their desire to succeed in America was based on parental motivation. Other family members, such as an uncle, were also mentioned as important, and some respondents specifically mentioned how important and helpful spouses had been to their transition. This was particularly true for the one woman and one man who met their (American) spouses after immigration.

Religious institutions were mentioned as important by two of the four marginalized respondents and two of the three individuals in the separation category. The responses from the separation group in particular were very strong, suggesting that religious institutions have been a primary node in their new lives. One respondent noted that, "I do almost all my things at the mosque. I work there, and they help me."

Work was mentioned as an important context by members of all groups, with seven out of twelve respondents commenting. The main difference between groups was that the marginalized group had a more passive tone in describing their work (e.g., "The work gives me something to do and some money"), while some respondents from other groups seemed to see work as more central to their lives. One respondent, describing his work in selling previously owned cars, said, "Hey, you make your life, you know? Back in Bosnia I used to sell stuff on the side . . . I made three sales the first day I was on my own. They couldn't believe it. I guess I just found my place."

Descriptions of community were largely consistent with acculturation status, with individuals experiencing separation being more likely to report close ties to the Bosnian community. Ties to mainstream American communities were noted by many respondents. These ties did not seem to be particularly strong and generally seemed to be initiated by the Bosnian immigrants themselves. There seemed to be little aggressive "pull" from the mainstream community toward integration.

ISSUES

This category is something of a catch-all, including themes of safety, attitude, education, language, and transitioning cultures. Two responses noted the relief of living in a country not at war. Eight different responses were made regarding attitude and efficacy. There was a dramatic difference between the marginalized and other groups. One comment from a marginalized person was that

> I'm just so tired. Sometimes I think I should be trying to make more of myself, you know, but I just can't get up the energy. I see other people doing well, and it looks like there's room for that in this country, but I just don't seem to be doing anything about it. It makes me feel bad sometimes.

Responses from other groups tended to show more efficacy and a more aggressive attitude toward life in the United States. One person noted: "I think I feel like I can get by anywhere, and I think that helped."

A pair of issues that could pose barriers to success are education and language. Two individuals from the assimilated group noted that education was important in achievement in the United States. While many respondents noted English language skills as important to successful acculturation, this issue was most evident among the group experiencing separation. Individuals in this category noted ongoing limitations with language, and this seemed to contribute to their lack of contacts with the American mainstream culture.

Other issues identified by clients included coping strategies, problems, and a few general comments. Again, comments from marginalized groups were characterized by a passive tone (e.g., "I feel like I'm drifting") while other groups were more positive. Apart from this distinction in tone, there were few consistent findings in these areas.

DISCUSSION

This study demonstrated the feasibility of using Berry and Kim's acculturation model to classify Bosnian refugees. Main findings included the distinctness of the marginalized group from other groups, especially as regards preimmigration experiences and reports of self-efficacy. In addition, language issues and older age appear to be associated with separation. Before discussing these issues and their implications further, a review of the limitations of this study is in order.

LIMITATIONS AND STRENGTHS

This very modest study suffers from substantial limitations. Perhaps the most serious is the small sample size. This study did not achieve saturation, a condition in which data coming from respondents has become almost entirely repetitive. It is therefore likely that themes important to this population were not obtained in this study. This problem was seriously exacerbated by the fact that four separate conceptual populations (assimilated, separated, marginalized, and integrated) were being studied. Ideally, a study would have sufficient subjects to achieve saturation for each group. In addition, the sample was not adequately diverse. There were, for example, no adults interviewed who had young children in the home. The emphasis on a resettlement service for sample recruitment is another weakness, as there may be entirely distinct groups of Bosnian refugees who do not use these services.

A second major problem includes the cross-sectional nature of the work. Berry and Kim's model has a time component, with marginalization being viewed as a preliminary stage to the other three. This is at variance with other models. For example, Galan (1978) sees marginalization as frequently a terminal stage, with a preliminary "transitional" stage often preceding other stages. Without longitudinal data, it is difficult to evaluate Berry's model, because one cannot determine if all or many refugees passed through the marginalization phase. Another critical problem attending cross-sectional data is the difficulty of sequencing and determining causality. For example, the finding that lower self-efficacy and marginalization are associated might either imply that low self-efficacy contributes to marginalization, or that marginalization wears down one's self-efficacy. A longitudinal study could present a much clearer picture of this issue.

Strengths of the study include the good fit between Berry and Kim's categories and the responses. It was relatively easy to use the four acculturation categories, and these groupings did appear to have utility in analyzing responses, with specific trends developing. This was particularly true of the marginalization and separation groups. Another strength was the congruence between current study findings and prior studies (e.g., Ferren, 1999).

IMPLICATIONS FOR PRACTICE

The finding that self-efficacy appears to be associated with positive outcomes cannot be overlooked. If self-efficacy actually causes better outcomes, which is possible but cannot be definitively determined from this data, then specific early interventions to support self-efficacy may be of substantial help to this population. Early educational, vocational, and social supports may be able to provide individuals with success in their early transition, both forming a basis for continued growth and supporting efficacy.

The extremely traumatic histories reported by many respondents in the marginalized group suggest that unmet trauma needs may be limiting the ability of this group to successfully acculturate. While trauma services may not be wanted or needed by all refugees,

this study suggests that careful screening of this population may well be a necessary first step in supporting positive outcomes.

The group experiencing separation is very interesting from a practice perspective. Given the age, limited English skills, and apparent lack of internal motivation to change found in this group, the most appropriate social response may be to support these people in place. The presence of a vibrant Bosnian community, especially centered around religious institutions, may be the best means of assuring that this population is able to be supported and have their needs met. The informal social support network found in these communities must be recognized as a key support for this portion of the Bosnian refugee community, and relocation of such individuals to areas without preexisting Bosnian community infrastructure should probably be avoided.

IMPLICATIONS FOR FUTURE RESEARCH

As stated previously, future work could well benefit from using Berry and Kim's model or perhaps a similar model. Longitudinal work with much larger samples that will allow tracking of individuals as they move through various acculturation stages is also needed. Ideally, such tracking should start with individuals as they come to the United States and persist for several years. This would also avoid some of the bias involved in an agency-based sample, where people not using or needing the agency will be necessarily underrepresented.

REFERENCES

Bazely, P., & Richards, L. (2000). *The NVivo qualitative project book*. London: Sage.

Berry, J. W., & Kim, U. (1988). Acculturation and mental health. In P. R. Dasen, J. W. Berry, & N. Sartorius (Eds.). *Health and cross-cultural psychology: Toward applications*. (pp. 207–236). Newbury Park, CA: Sage.

Coughlan, R., & Owens-Manley, J. (2005). *Bosnian refugees in America: New communities, new cultures*. New York: Springer.

Ferren, P. (1999). Comparing perceived self-efficacy among adolescent Bosnian and Croatian refugees with and without posttraumatic stress disorder. *Journal of Traumatic Stress, 12*(3), 405–420.

Galan, F. (1978). *Alcohol use among Chicanos and Anglos: A cross-cultural study*. Doctoral dissertation, University of Michigan.

Glaser, B. G., & Strauss, A. L. (1967). *The discovery of grounded theory: Strategies for qualitative research*. Chicago: Aldine.

McMillen, C., Morris, L., & Sherraden, M. (2004). Ending social work's grudge match: Problems versus strengths. *Families in Society, 85*(3), 317–325.

Mollica, R., Sarajlic, N., Chernoff, M., Lavelle, J., Vukovic, I, & Massagli, M. (2001). Longitudinal study of psychiatric symptoms, disability, mortality and emigration among Bosnian Refugees. *Journal of the American Medical Association, 286* (5) 546–554.

Perez, L., Peifer, L., & Newman, M. (2002). A strength-based and early relationship approach to infant mental health assessment. *Community Mental Health Journal, 38*(5), 375–390.

Ronch, J., & Goldfield, J. (2003). *Mental wellness in aging: Strengths-based approaches.* Baltimore, MD: Health Professions Press.

Schwarzer, R., Hahn, A., & Schroder, H. (1994). Social integration and social support in a life crisis: Effects of macrosocial changes in East Germany. *American Journal of Community Psychology, 22,* 685–706.

Weine, S. M., Kuc, G., Dzudza, E., Razzano, L., & Pavkovic, I. (2001). PTSD among Bosnian refugees: A survey of providers' knowledge, attitudes and service patterns. *Community Mental Health Journal, 37,* 261–271.

Witmer, T. A. & Culver, S. M. (2001). Trauma and resilience among Bosnian refugee families: A critical review of the literature. *Journal of Social Work Research and Evaluation, 2,* 173–187.

Yau, T. (1996). *The level of acculturation, self-esteem, and self-efficacy of Southeast Asian refugee adolescents.* Doctoral Dissertation, University of Denver.

Yong, L. (2005). *Resilience in ex-refugees from Cambodia and Vietnam.* Doctoral dissertation, University of Rhode Island.

APPENDIX C

NOTE: EXAMPLES WITH FICTITIOUS RESEARCHER AND FICTITIOUS DATA.

Reaction to Child Fatality among Child Welfare Workers: The Role of Organizational and Social Support

Abigail Braintree, MSW
Washington College

Background: Child Fatalities

◆ Approximately 41,600 children ages 14 or under die in the United States each year.
(Statistical Abstract of the United States, 2000, p 92)

◆ Approximately 1,300 children are reported as victims of fatal child maltreatment each year.
(Child Maltreatment 2001, U.S. DHHS)

◆ The number of officially substantiated child abuse fatalities almost certainly understates the true number of child abuse fatalities and also understates the number of fatalities that occur in workers' caseloads.

◆ In one demographically representative medium-sized state (Missouri), approximately 50 children are reported as substantiated child abuse fatalities per year, but 10 times as many child deaths are reviewed by the state child fatality review program each year.
(www.dss.mo.gov/re/cfrar03/section1.pdf)

Background: Workers

◆ All 50 states employ Child Protective Services (CPS) workers. These workers generally have a bachelor's or master's level education.

◆ Nationwide, they receive approximately 3 million reports of child maltreatment per year.
(Child Maltreatment 2001, U.S. DHHS)

Background: Prior Research

◆ Very little literature exists that addresses worker reactions to caseload fatalities, a serious gap in the literature (Gustavson & MacEachron, 2002).

◆ Research regarding reactions to caseload fatalities among allied disciplines (mainly health care providers) stresses the importance of social support and a supportive organizational context (Bendiksen, Bodin, & Jambois, 2001; Burrell, 1996; Burns & Harm, 1993).

Research Question

◆ This study is an attempt to better understand whether organizational and social factors are associated with better outcomes for workers who have suffered fatalities in their caseloads.

◆ Child welfare workers who had experienced child fatalities within the past 12 months were surveyed and asked about their organizations, social support, and coping.

Sample

◆ Packets were mailed to 110 workers from a large child welfare agency who had had children in their caseload die in the last 12 months. 78 returned the forms for a response rate of 71%.

◆ 71% of respondents were female, the median worker age was 35, and the median time of employment at the agency was 4 years. Median victim age was one year.

Instruments and Variables: Independent (Predictor) Variables

◆ The Organizational Climate Scale (OCS; Thompson & McCubbin) provides measures of organizational conflictual communications and organizational supportive communications.

◆ The Social Support Behaviors scale (SSB; Vaux, Reidel, & Stewart) measures emotional support, social support, and advice/guidance from family and friends separately (6 subscales).

Instruments and Variables: Dependent (Outcome) Variables

◆ The Impact of Events scale (IES; Horowitz) measures two separate constructs: Intrusive experiences and avoidance behaviors.

Hypotheses

◆ It was hypothesized that each of the OCS subscale scores (conflictual and supportive communication) would separately predict both intrusive and avoidance outcome measurements from the IES.

◆ It was also hypothesized that each of the six SSB social support subscales would separately predict both intrusive and avoidance outcome scores.

Bivariate Analyses

◆ Analyses were first performed at the bivariate level using simple regression.

◆ Results for organizational climate and social support will be reported separately.

Bivariate Results (Organizational)

◆ Organizational conflictual communication scores predicted higher levels of post-event avoidance reactions ($r = .48$, $p = .001$).

◆ Organizational conflict did not predict intrusive experiences at the $p < = .05$ level.

◆ Organizational supportive communication predicted neither intrusive nor avoidance reactions at the $p < =.05$ level.

Bivariate Results
(Social Support)

◆ Family emotional support predicted lower levels of intrusive experiences ($r = -.51$, p < .0001).

◆ No other form of social or emotional support or advice/guidance from friends or family predicted either intrusive experiences or avoidant behavior.

Bivariate Results
(Other Factors)

◆ Years on the job was associated with event avoidance ($r = .28$, $p = .0126$).

◆ Event intrusiveness was predicted by years on the job ($r = .31$, $p = .0064$).

Multivariate Analyses

◆ To control for the effects of other factors on the relationships found to be significant at the bivariate level, multivariate models were run with other significant and near significant factors (e.g., years on the job) included.

Multivariate Results
(Intrusiveness)

	Standardized Estimate	Significance
Years in Job	.121	.2626
Emotional Support (Family)	−.468	< .0001
Full Model DF =2	F =14.44	p < .0001

Multivariate Results
(Avoidance)

	Standardized Estimate	Significance
Years in Job	.201	.0405
Conflictual Communication (OCS)	.446	< .0001
Full Model DF =2	F =14.07	p < .0001

Summary of Findings

Multivariate analyses found:

◆ Emotional support from family predicts lower levels of intrusive experiences. This effect is moderate ($r = -.468$).

◆ Higher conflictual communication in agencies predicts moderately ($r = .446$) higher levels of avoidance behaviors.

◆ Years on the job has a low positive association ($r = .208$) with avoidance behaviors.

◆ Other relationships that were explored failed to reach significance.

Implications for Agencies

◆ Supportive communication in agencies did not show any relationship to how workers cope with caseload fatalities. Conversely, conflictual communication styles at work made matters worse. It is therefore suggested that agencies make direct efforts to be aware of and reduce conflictual communication styles in the workplace.

Implications for Agencies

◆ Family support of workers was also important in reducing negative outcomes. It is not clear what direct role agencies can play in this regard, except possibly to make workers aware of the importance of family support and to encourage workers to take advantage of this resource.

Implications for Agencies

◆ There is some slight evidence that workers with more work experience may be at greater risk for negative outcomes. This is somewhat counterintuitive and may suggest that conventional wisdom that experienced workers are better at handling trauma may be mistaken.

Suggestions for Future Research

Future research could be undertaken to:

◆ Better understand what aspects of organizational conflict and family support relate to post-fatality worker outcomes and why.

◆ Expand the research question to other kinds of negative case outcomes, such as re-abuse, which are more commonly encountered by workers.

BACKGROUND MUSIC AND ITS IMPACT ON SPEED AND ACCURACY OF CODING

KATHY CRONIN, PhD

KATHY CRONIN, PhD
Washington College, Collegetown, Missouri

NOTE: THIS PAPER IS AN EXAMPLE.
AUTHOR AND DATA ARE FICTIONAL.

ABSTRACT

Academic researchers often employ research assistants who hand-code files. This study uses a randomized experimental design to compare speed of coding and coding accuracy among 60 students assigned to one of three conditions. The conditions were classical background music, easy-listening background music, and no background music. Speed of coding was not found to vary by condition, but the classical music condition coders had lower rates of errors per file than the other two conditions. It is suggested that researchers consider using classical background music in coding environments.

BACKGROUND MUSIC AND ITS IMPACT ON SPEED AND ACCURACY OF CODING

Social scientists often need to hand-code existing files or other documents into more useful formats, such as summative forms or checklists. Such work is tedious and time consuming and is frequently left to paid undergraduate assistants. While various techniques for checking the accuracy of such coding exist, any techniques or procedures that can enhance original accuracy will enhance the overall validity of the data. This research uses a randomized experimental design to determine if undergraduate file coders exposed to classical background music (CBM) or easy-listening background music (ELBM) differ from no-music controls (NBM) in accuracy and speed of coding. The main practical goal of this research is to assist researchers in determining if their coders will benefit from the addition of background music.

BACKGROUND

The study of the effect of background music on task accuracy and speed has a history spanning at least forty years. Smith (1961) studied people engaged in old-style computer card-punching tasks and found that background music did not seem to have any meaningful effect on performance. Despite this, the workers reported that they enjoyed the task more if background music was provided. Fox and Embrey (1972) examined factory workers engaged in repetitive tasks and concluded that there was some benefit to the presence of background music.

In more recent studies, Furnham and Bradley (1997) found little support for background music helping in the completion of complex tasks, while Furnham later found (Furnham & Strbac, 2002) that introverted individuals are more likely to be distracted by music or noise than are extroverts. This suggests an interaction between personality characteristics and the presence or absence of background music. Stephensen (2002) found that classical music may increase the speed of undergraduate subjects finishing spatial tasks. Johnson (2000), on the other hand, found that classical background music might negatively affect the academic performance of junior high school students. In a study of older people, Otto, Cochran, Johnson, and Clair (1999) were not able to detect any differences in task completion associated with the presence or absence of background music. Halam, Price, and Katsarou (2002) found that calming music increased children's memory and ability to do arithmetic. This same study found that students did not do well with music perceived as arousing or aggressive or unpleasant.

In the only overview article identified to date, Rauscher and Shaw (1998) reviewed the existing literature to determine the degree to which classical music might influence task performance. They concluded that such music might have a slight effect on task performance. This appears to be a reasonable summary of the available literature.

In relating the conclusions of past studies to the issue at hand, it appears possible that background music may have a slight positive effect on coding performance. Both speed and accuracy have been studied in the prior literature, and both seem reasonable dimensions for future analysis. Classical music seems to be consistently identified as potentially helpful, while faster-paced or otherwise distracting music could be detrimental to performance. The current study therefore compares three musical conditions, classical, easy-listening, and no music, across two outcome measures, speed and accuracy. The research question for the current study is therefore "do classical (CBM), easy-listening (ELBM), and no music (NBM) conditions affect coding speed and accuracy?" and operationalized by the following hypotheses: hypothesis 1—coders in CBM, ELBM, and NBM conditions will have different rates of files coded per hour; hypothesis 2—coders in CBM, ELBM, and NBM conditions will have different numbers of errors per file coded.

METHOD

This study uses data and coders engaged in an ongoing study of self-sufficiency among elderly nursing home residents. Resident files representing one day of care were copied at the agency and provided to the author for coding by trained undergraduate coders.

PROCEDURE

Each file represents one day of client care. Entries are made every half-hour. If a client has needed assistance with an activity of daily living, such as washing or going to the bathroom, the care provider enters a description of the service provided, prefaced with the word *assist*. The coders use a coding sheet broken down into half-hours (48 entries) for each daily file and make a check mark during each half-hour block in which an *assist* code is recorded in the file. Coding was done in nine cubicles, which had their musical conditions rotated on a daily basis to control for any possible environmental differences. Coders were assigned to the correct type of cubicle as they reported for work each day. Classical music was from the "Classical, Symphonic, Orchestral, Volume 1" collection procured from RoyaltyFreeMusic and described as "Classical, Symphonic, Orchestral Music performed by The Moscow International Symphony Orchestra. The Classical Series includes elegantly and compellingly performed selections from

Tchaikovsky, Bach, Vivaldi, Rossini, Grieg, Liszt and others" (RoyaltyFreeMusic, n.d.). The easy-listening music was from the same company's "Soft Moods, Volume 1," described as "Warm and glowy light jazz feel, on the guitar based tracks. Ethereal, water sound soft melodic pieces. Dreamy keyboard based tracks" (RoyaltyFreeMusic, n.d.).

SUBJECTS

Sixty undergraduate coders were randomly assigned to the two experimental conditions and the control condition, giving 20 coders per condition The subjects were 50% male ($n = 30$), and 83% White ($n = 50$). The remaining 10 students were Asian ($n = 7$), African American ($n = 2$), and Hispanic ($n = 1$). All were between 18 and 24 years of age (median age = 21.4). Each coder was followed for his or her first 10 coding sessions. Each coding session could run up to three hours at the student's discretion, but only files completed within the first hour of each session were treated as coded for purposes of this study.

ACCURACY OF CODING

Correctness of coding was checked by having other trained checkers blind double-code the files and having a third checker identify discrepancies between their coding and the original coder's rating, to determine if the original coding was in error. All coding and checking was blind with regard to the identity and group membership (CBM, ELBM, NBM) of the coder. All double-coding and third-tier coding was done without background music. A database was constructed reflecting the total files coded and the total numbers of errors made, and mean errors per file coded for each rater.

RESULTS

All analyses were performed using SAS 9.1. One-way ANOVAs (SAS PROC GLM) were run to determine if there were differences in means for number of files coded (hypothesis 1) and numbers of errors per file coded (hypothesis 2). Levene's test for homogeneity was nonsignificant in both models. Results can be seen in Table 1. The model associated with hypothesis 1, using numbers of files coded as the dependent measure, was nonsignificant ($F = 1.78$, $df = 2$, $p = 0.1771$). The model for the second hypothesis, using errors per file coded as the dependent measure, was significant ($F = 23.88$, $df = 2$, $p \leq .0001$). The R square for this model was 0.4559.

TABLE 1 **Mean Files Coded and Mean Errors Per File Coded.**			
GROUP	CLASSICAL	EASY LISTENING	NO MUSIC
Files coded per hour ($F = 1.78$, $df = 2$, $p = 0.1771$)	2.755 (SD = .485)	3.080 (SD = .597)	2.915 (SD = .544)
Errors per file ($F = 23.88$, $df = 2$, $p \le .0001$).	1.263(a) (SD = .325)	1.947 (SD = .403)	1.855 (SD = .280)

NOTES: (a) Tukey post hoc, alpha = .05, Error $df = 57$. Classical condition significantly different from both other groups for errors per file.

DISCUSSION

The goal of this paper was to compare classical music, easy-listening music, and no music conditions in terms of their impact on speed and accuracy of file coding. Varying the background music for coders produced no differences in speed of coding but did produce a lower number of errors per file in the classical music condition (1.26 errors per file coded) as compared to easy-listening and no music conditions (1.94 errors per file coded and 1.855 errors per file coded, respectively).

STRENGTHS AND LIMITATIONS

Strengths of this study included the randomized experimental design employed and the fact that this research was done as a part of an ongoing study using fairly typical coders, source materials and, coding procedures. The main limitations of this study included the choice of specific background music used, which cannot represent the entire domain of either classical or easy-listening music. It is possible that a choice of a different kind of classical or easy-listening music might have yielded different results. In addition, music may interact with specific types of coding tasks.

SUGGESTIONS FOR RESEARCHERS USING CODERS

In the current study, the use of classical background music reduced the number of errors per file coded. There appears to be no reason for researchers not to use classical background music for their coders. The cost of setting up coding facilities with background music should be minimal compared to the overall cost of coding.

FUTURE RESEARCH NEEDS

Future studies in this area should compare larger selections of music. Tempo, style, and volume could be varied. Ideally, different selections of music would be compared across different types of tasks. If it is possible to move outside a university setting, it would be interesting to vary subjects along age, class, and racial dimensions to determine if different populations respond differently to music.

REFERENCES

Fox, J. G., & Embrey, E. D. (1972). Music—an aid to productivity. *Applied Ergonomics, 3*(4), 202–205.

Furnham, A., & Bradley, A. (1997), Music while you work: The differential distraction of background music on the cognitive test performance of introverts and extraverts. *Applied Cognitive Psychology, 11,* 445–455.

Furnham, A., & Strbac, L. (2002). Music is as distracting as noise: The differential distraction of background music and noise on the cognitive test performance of introverts and extraverts. *Ergonomics, 45*(3), 203–217.

Halam, S., Price, J., & Katsarou, G. (2002). The effects of background music on primary school pupil's test performance. *Educational Studies, 28*(2), 111–122.

Johnson, M. (2000). *The effects of background classical music on junior high school student's academic performance.* Doctoral Dissertation. The Fielding Institute.

Otto, D., Cochran, V., Johnson, G., & Clair, A. (1999). The influence of background music on task engagement in frail, older persons in residential care. *Journal of Music Therapy, 36*(3), 182–195.

Rauscher, F., & Shaw, G. (1998). Key components of the Mozart effect. *Perceptual and Motor Skills, 86*(3), 835–841.

RoyaltyFreeMusic (n.d.). Retrieved September 20th, 2004 from www.royaltyfreemusic.com/clips.html.

Smith, W. A. S. (1961). Effects of industrial music in a work situation requiring complex mental activity. *Psychological Reports, 8,* 159–162.

Stephensen, V. (2002). *The effect of classical background music on spatial reasoning skills as measured by completion of a spatial task: A study of selected college undergraduates.* Doctoral Dissertation, Universidad de Guadalijara.

DEMOGRAPHIC PREDICTORS OF HOMICIDE AND SUICIDE
THE CASE OF SAN DIEGO COUNTY

MARIA ESTEVEZ, BA, WASHINGTON COLLEGE

NOTE: EXAMPLE PAPER WITH FICTITIOUS RESEARCHER FOR ACTUAL DATA.

THEORY AND BACKGROUND

There is a long and rich history of sociological inquiry into environmental correlates of homicide and suicide. Durkheim's *Le Suicide* (1897) used national-level data to empirically explore theoretical explanations for suicide. Modern sociologists have continued this tradition with regard both to suicide (Connoly & Lester, 2001; Wenz, 1977) and also homicide (Centerwall, 1995; Harries, 1995). Major findings have included increased rates of both homicide and suicide at lower income levels and in times of economic stress.

AIMS AND QUESTIONS

This study seeks to determine if demographic characteristics of specific zip codes are associated with increases or decreases in rates of homicide and suicide. The specific variables chosen (rate of poverty, percentage of individuals living alone, residential density per acre, age of the population) were selected due to their prior validation as relevant to homicide or suicide (e.g., poverty rate) or their theoretical relatedness to homicide or suicide. Percentage of persons living alone is used in an attempt to quantify social isolation, whereas number of persons per acre of developed land is used as a proxy for possible overcrowdedness. *Specific hypotheses were that poverty, more persons per square mile, and more people living alone would be associated with both homicide and suicide rates.* In addition, racial composition and age within the zip codes were explored to determine their effect on the models. These hypotheses were tested in multivariate analysis of variance models.

DATA SOURCES

It is becoming increasingly possible to perform studies using data available in the public domain. This study uses publicly available data from the U.S. Census (Summary File 3 DVD data) and from the San Diego County Coroner's Office (www.sdcounty.ca.gov/cnty/cntydepts/safety/medical/stat). The combined database includes 77 zip codes, their associated census-derived demograpic characteristics, and the mean number of homicides and suicides per zip code per year as reported to the San Diego Coroner's Office in 2000 and 2001.

DESCRIPTION OF DATA USED

- *The number of residents* in each zip code ranged from 3247 to 98214 (median = 35471).

- There were a total of *206 homicides* in 77 zip codes in 2000 and 2001.

- There were a total of *591 suicides* in 77 zip codes in 2000 and 2001.

- The median zip code had a population density of 5.41 individuals per acre of developed land.

- The median zip code had 11.15% of the population living below the poverty line.

- The median zip code had 7.57% of the population living alone in single-residence households.

- The median zip code had 63.89% of the population at or over age 25.

- Racial composition varied widely among the zip codes studied. Race was associated with a number of predictor variables, as well as with homicide and suicide rates. However, given the lack of theoretical and empirical justification for inclusion of the race variable (see Centerwall, 1995) and the fact that the association between race, suicide, and homicide was reduced when other factors (e.g., poverty) were included, race was excluded from the analysis.

MULTIVARIATE RESULTS

Homicides in 77 San Diego County Zip Codes

Regression Model: $F = 13.87$, $df = 3$, $p < .0001$ Adjusted R Square $= 0.3370$		
	Standardized Estimate	$Pr > t$
% of residents over 25 years old	−0.03396	0.7506
Persons per acre of developed land	0.19824	0.0831
% of residents in poverty	0.45154	0.0005

Age did not produce a significant relationship in the multivariate model but was retained due to the strong relationship between age and violent crime noted in the literature. While population density was not significant at the $p <= .05$ level, it was trending toward significance. Percentage of residents in poverty was by far the strongest predictor, with a standardized estimate of 0.45154 ($p = 0.0005$). The model explained slightly over one-third of the variance in the dependent variable. Percentage living alone was not significant at the bivariate level, nor was there strong empirical or theoretical reason for inclusion, so it was omitted from the model.

Suicides in 77 San Diego County Zip Codes

Regression Model: $F = 8.83$, $df = 3$, $p < .0001$ Adjusted R Square $= 0.2361$		
	Standardized Estimate	$Pr > t$
% of persons living alone	0.43204	<.0001
% of residents in poverty	0.27170	0.0279
Persons per acre of developed land	−0.39160	0.0020

Percentage of persons living alone, population density, and percentage of persons in poverty all predicted suicide rates at the zip code level. Percent of persons living alone was a particularly strong predictor, with a standardized estimate of 0.43204 ($p < .0001$). The R square was less strong than for homicides, however, with slightly less than a quarter of the variance explained. Interestingly, *higher* residential density was associated with *lower* suicide rates. Percentage of persons over 25 was not a significant predictor of suicide and was omitted.

SUMMARY AND DISCUSSION

SUBSTANTIVE CONCLUSIONS

- **The hypothesized associations between poverty and both homicide and suicide were supported.** This is consistent with prior work (Centerwall, 1995; Wenz, 1977).

- **The hypothesized association between higher numbers of persons living alone and suicide was supported.** Both higher numbers of people living alone (% in single-person households) and lower population density (persons per acre of developed land) were significant predictors of increased rates of suicide.

- **The significant *inverse relationship* between population density and suicide contrasts with the near-significant ($p = .0831$) *positive relationship* between population density and homicide.** This can be seen as consistent both with theories of increased stress (overpopulation) leading to violent acts (homicide) and with theories suggesting that social isolation leads to increased rates of suicide.

METHODOLOGICAL CONSIDERATIONS

- **The study was underpowered, with a small sample size ($N = 77$).** This limited power to avoid type II errors (false negatives) and the ability to include large numbers of variables and interactions in multivariate models.

- **The study was forced by the nature of the coroner's data to use zip codes, rather than census tracts.** This resulted in the inclusion of geographic units that were not homogenous with regard to the predictor variables. This introduces statistical noise.

- **Regardless of these limitations, this study was able to replicate prior empirical work, and the findings, particularly with regard to suicide, were supportive of current theory.** This can be seen as highlighting the utility of public domain administrative and census data as a means for evaluating sociological theory.

REFERENCES

Centerwall, B. (1995) Race, socioeconomic status, and domestic homicide. *JAMA: Journal of the American Medical Association, 273* (22), 1755–1758.

Connoly, J., & Lester, D. (2001). Suicide rates in Irish counties: 10 years later. *Irish Journal of Psychological Medicine, 18*(3), 87–89.

Durkheim, E. (1897). *Le Suicide.* Paris: Felix Alcan.

Harries, K. (1995). The ecology of homicide and assault: Baltimore City and County, 1989–91. *Studies on Crime & Crime Prevention, 4* (1), 44–60.

Wenz, F. (1977). Ecological variation in self-injury behavior. *Suicide and Life-Threatening Behavior, 7*(2), 92–99.

COGNITIVE BEHAVIORAL THERAPY VERSUS TREATMENT AS USUAL: WHICH WORKS BETTER FOR US?

AN EMPIRICAL COMPARISON OF TWO METHODS USED AT SAFE HAVEN

YUAN HAN
October 22, 2006

NOTE: EXAMPLE PAPER WITH FICTITIOUS RESEARCHER AND FICTITIOUS DATA.

EXECUTIVE SUMMARY

At Safe Haven, we have been treating court-ordered perpetrators of domestic violence using a treatment method that draws from many kinds of therapy and has been developed over the years. Recently, there has been some concern that this method may not be the most effective means to treat our clients. Published studies have suggested that using a cognitive behavioral therapy (CBT) approach might prove effective in working with our batterers. Safe Haven administrators decided to test these two approaches against each other to determine which was more helpful for us.

DESIGN OF STUDY

We assigned 100 clients to five treatment groups led by therapists recently trained in CBT. One hundred other clients attended five treatment groups that were run as normal here at Safe Haven. Clients in the CBT group were followed to determine if the treatment changed their attitudes toward arguing with their partners, and both groups were tracked to determine how many reoffended against their spouses, measured by number of reports to law enforcement.

QUESTIONS

- Do clients treated with CBT show improvements in their attitudes toward their partners?
- Do clients treated with CBT and treatment as usual (TAU) show similar rates of reoffense against their partners in the six months following treatment? This was done by tracking reports to law enforcement.

RESULTS

- With regard to question 1, clients did seem to experience improvements in **avoidance** of arguments and **empathy** toward partners while in treatment, and this effect did seem to persist for the six-month follow-up period. **Forethought** and **usefulness** scores showed no improvement with treatment.
- Clients receiving CBT recidivated (were rereported to law enforcement) at a much lower rate (15% versus 47%) than clients receiving TAU.

PROGRAM IMPLICATIONS

In our study, clients receiving CBT were less than one-third as likely to be rereported for domestic violence as were clients receiving treatment as usual. *It is recommended that CBT replace TAU as the means of treating batterers at Safe Haven. We anticipate this will result in dramatic reductions of reoffending by our clients.*

COGNITIVE BEHAVIORAL THERAPY VERSUS TREATMENT AS USUAL: WHICH WORKS BETTER FOR US?

INTRODUCTION

Safe Haven is a large domestic violence counseling provider serving several hundred batterers per year. Clients are court-ordered and complete a three-month (12-session) weekly treatment module. Treatment is in a group format, with 20 clients generally attending each group. The treatment model in use to date has been eclectic, blending psychodynamic, humanist, and behavioral principles and methods.

In late 2004, Safe Haven administrators wished to determine if the current means of treating our clients was effective. Review of books, scientific journal articles, and Internet sources suggested that one option was to try a Cognitive Behavioral Therapy (CBT) approach (Babcock, Green & Robie, 2004; Morrel, 2000). CBT stresses changing how the perpetrator thinks about what he does so that his behaviors will then change. For example, if perpetrators can be taught to notice when they are becoming angry, and if they can be taught to take steps to reduce that anger, then it is thought that subsequent violence can be prevented.

STUDY APPROACH AND METHODS

By July of 2005, Safe Haven administrators had decided to begin to implement CBT groups side-by-side with our normal treatment groups to see which worked better. Ten therapists were selected by Safe Haven, and five were randomly assigned to receive CBT training. Random assignment was used to make sure that differences in subsequent success or failure would not be due to self-selection on the part of the therapists. Training occurred during August and September. Groups were run using CBT and TAU starting in October (Groups 1–4), November (Groups 5–8) and December (Groups 9–10). Each group lasted 12 sessions. All clients were appraised of their rights not to participate in the study and signed consent forms.

Ten groups of clients were assigned in order of referral, with even-numbered groups receiving CBT and odd-numbered groups receiving TAU. Clients in the CBT groups had their attitudes toward arguing with their spouses evaluated at the first session, at the last session, and six months later, by mail. This was done by the administration of the argument scales, a test that measures **avoidance** of arguments, **empathy** toward their partner, **forethought** before entering arguments, and their judgment of the **usefulness** of arguing. We had also hoped to check attitudes of TAU clients, but this turned out not to be feasible in the current study. These particular kinds of attitudes were targeted because they are consistent with the attitudes we are attempting to change with CBT.

In addition, Safe Haven routinely receives law enforcement reports when any of our clients has a re-report for domestic violence. These reports were tracked for six months following treatment.

RESEARCH QUESTIONS AND RESULTS

There were two main questions in this study: "Does CBT change the attitudes of perpetrators?" and "Do CBT and TAU result in similar recidivism rates?" Results are presented below.

QUESTION 1: DOES CBT CHANGE ATTITUDES?

Attitudes were measured with a written instrument called the "argument scales." The argument scales include a series of 24 questions, each of which is rated on a scale from "never" to "always." These are assigned a value of 1 to 5 for scoring, with "always" counting as 5. There are four separate scales, measuring avoidance, forethought, empathy, and usefulness. An example from the empathy scale is presented below:

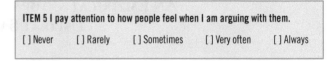

ITEM 5 I pay attention to how people feel when I am arguing with them.

[ ] Never   [ ] Rarely   [ ] Sometimes   [ ] Very often   [ ] Always

The total responses from each of the subscales can range from 6 to 30. The CBT groups filled out this measure at pretest, posttest, and six-month follow-up. Mean (average) scores are shown in Table 1.

TABLE 1 **Changes in Attitude**			
	PRETEST	POSTTEST	FOLLOWUP
Avoidance	17.47(a)	18.08(a)	17.96
Empathy	19.10(b)	21.19(b)	21.10
Forethought	17.44	17.24	17.37
Usefulness	17.83	17.28	17.48

NOTE: a: $F = 8.78$, $p = .0038$.   b: $F = 49.02$, $p < .0001$.

The blue shaded areas represent statistically significant differences, that is, differences that are unlikely to be due to just luck. The avoidance scale improved slightly during treatment (17.47 to 18.08), and the empathy scale improved somewhat more dramatically (19.10 to 21.19). In addition, these scores did not show significant decay during the posttest to follow-up time period, suggesting that the gains made were not lost. The forethought and usefulness scales showed no changes.

These figures are displayed in a graph in Figure 1. This graph shows more clearly the relatively dramatic change in the empathy scores, the smaller change in the avoidance scores, and the relatively flat results from the other two scales.

QUESTION 2: DOES CBT OR TAU RESULT IN HIGHER RECIDIVISM?

Average (mean) pretest, posttest, and six-month follow-up scores are shown in Table 2.

There was a statistically significant and large difference between CBT and TAU groups with regard to recidivism. Only 15 CBT clients had rereports for

FIGURE 1 Changes in Attitude (Graph).

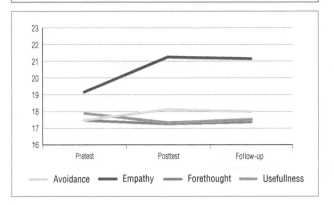

TABLE 2 Recidivism rates for CBT and TAU Groups.

	WITH RECIDIVISM	WITHOUT RECIDIVISM
CBT Clients (100)	15	85
TAU Clients (100)	47	53

NOTE: Chi-Square = 23.94, *df* = 1, *p* < .0001.

domestic violence to law enforcement during the six months following treatment. The TAU group suffered more than three times as much recidivism, with almost half (47%) being rereported. The TAU rate is similar to the Safe Haven six-month recidivism rate for the prior (2004) year, which was 45% (284 of 632 people served).

Caution: As with most studies, there are some things about this study that could possibly have resulted in misleading findings. Therapists who have been recently trained in a new method may be more involved or enthusiastic than therapists providing services as usual.

It is possible that the reduced recidivism in the CBT group may be partly due to this factor. In addition, membership in CBT versus TAU groups was not random but was done in the order clients reported to our agency. While very unlikely, it is possible that a truly random assignment of clients might have yielded weaker results. To make sure that the findings from this study will hold at Safe Haven, it is recommended that rates of recidivism of future groups be reviewed frequently, perhaps quarterly, to make sure that the gains made by the CBT group in this model are maintained.

SUMMARY OF FINDINGS AND RECOMMENDATIONS:

The CBT group showed only a third as much recidivism as the TAU group. While attitude measured did not show such consistent differences, the CBT group also did better on measures of avoiding arguments and empathizing with the other party. Based on these findings, it is recommended that CBT training be provided to all staff, and that this model become the basis for all future batterer groups run at Safe Haven. We also recommend ongoing monitoring of recidivism rates, to make certain that the low rates obtained continue. If these rates should rise in the future, management should consider retraining or refresher courses for therapists.

REFERENCES

Babcock, J., Green, C., & Robie, C. (2004). Does batterer's treatment work? A meta-analytic review of domestic violence treatment. *Clinical Psychology Review, 23*(8), 1023–1053.

Morrel, T. (2000). *Changes in self-efficacy, self-esteem and aggression in male batterers: A comparison of cognitive-behavioral and supportive group therapies.* Doctoral Dissertation, University of Maryland at Baltimore.

YUAN'S SAS PROGRAM AND CODEBOOK

YUANDATAMGMT.SAS

```
/************************ YUANDATAMGMT.SAS ********************************/
/************************ YUANDATAMGMT.SAS ********************************/
/************************ YUANDATAMGMT.SAS ********************************/
libname book "C:\book\projects\yuan";
/******** bring in .xls file ******************/
PROC IMPORT OUT= BOOK.YUANDATA
            DATAFILE= "C:\Book\projects\Yuan\yuandata.xls"
            DBMS=EXCEL2000 REPLACE;
        GETNAMES=YES;
RUN;
DATA BOOK.YUANDATA;SET BOOK.YUANDATA;
/** REVERSE THOSE ITEMS NEEDING REVERSE SCORING **/
PRE1A    = 6-PRE1A ;       PRE9A    = 6-PRE9A ;
PRE8E    = 6-PRE8E ;       PRE11E   = 6-PRE11E ;     PRE819E   = 6-PRE19E;
PRE3F    = 6-PRE3F ;       PRE13F   = 6-PRE13F ;     PRE18F    = 6-PRE18F;
PRE10U   = 6-PRE10U;       PRE17U   = 6-PRE17U ;     PRE23U    = 6-PRE23U;
POST1A   = 6-POST1A ;      POST9A   = 6-POST9A ;
POST8E   = 6-POST8E ;      POST11E  = 6-POST11E;     POST819E  = 6-POST19E;
POST3F   = 6-POST3F ;      POST13F  = 6-POST13F;     POST18F   = 6-POST18F;
POST10U  = 6-POST10U;      POST17U  = 6-POST17U;     POST23U   = 6-POST23U;
FOLL1A   = 6-FOLL1A ;      FOLL9A   = 6-FOLL9A ;
FOLL8E   = 6-FOLL8E ;      FOLL11E  = 6-FOLL11E;     FOLL819E  = 6-FOLL19E;
FOLL3F   = 6-FOLL3F ;      FOLL13F  = 6-FOLL13F;     FOLL18F   = 6-FOLL18F;
FOLL10U  = 6-FOLL10U;      FOLL17U  = 6-FOLL17U;     FOLL23U   = 6-FOLL23U;
/************************************ create subscale totals *************************/
PREF=PRE2F+PRE3F+PRE7F+PRE13F+PRE18F+PRE20F;
PREU=PRE6U+PRE10U+PRE12U+PRE16U+PRE17U+PRE23U;
PREA=PRE1A+PRE4A+PRE9A+PRE15A+PRE21A+PRE24A;
PREE=PRE5E+PRE8E+PRE11E+PRE14E+PRE19E+PRE22E;
POSTF=POST2F+POST3F+POST7F+POST13F+POST18F+POST20F;
POSTU=POST6U+POST10U+POST12U+POST16U+POST17U+POST23U;
POSTA=POST1A+POST4A+POST9A+POST15A+POST21A+POST24A;
POSTE=POST5E+POST8E+POST11E+POST14E+POST19E+POST22E;
FOLLF=FOLL2F+FOLL3F+FOLL7F+FOLL13F+FOLL18F+FOLL20F;
FOLLU=FOLL6U+FOLL10U+FOLL12U+FOLL16U+FOLL17U+FOLL23U;
FOLLA=FOLL1A+FOLL4A+FOLL9A+FOLL15A+FOLL21A+FOLL24A;
FOLLE=FOLL14E+FOLL5E+FOLL19E+FOLL8E+FOLL22E+FOLL11E;
/*************** label variables ***************************/
LABEL
PREA    = "PRETEST score on AVOIDANCE subscale"
POSTA   = "POSTTEST score on AVOIDANCE subscale"
FOLLA   = "FOLLOWUP score on AVOIDANCE subscale"
PREE    = "PRETEST score on EMPATHY subscale"
POSTE   = "POSTTEST score on EMPATHY subscale"
```

```
FOLLE    = "FOLLOWUP score on EMPATHY subscale"
RECID    = "1 IF RECIDIVISM REPORTED DURING 6 MO FOLLOWUP"
AGE      = "AGE IN YEARS"
CBT      = "1 IF COGNITIVE BEHAVIORAL THERAPY, 0 IF STANDARD TX"
GROUP    = "NUMBER OF GROUP (1-5 = CBT, 6-10 = STANDARD TX)"
ID       = "ID number (1-105)"
married  = "1 IF MARRIED"
PRIORS   = "NUMBER OF PRIOR REPORTS BEFORE TREATMENT"
PRE1A    = "PRETEST ITEM 1      (AVOIDANCE SUBSCALE) [REVERSED]"
PRE4A    = "PRETEST ITEM 4      (AVOIDANCE SUBSCALE)"
PRE9A    = "PRETEST ITEM 9      (AVOIDANCE SUBSCALE) [REVERSED]"
PRE15A   = "PRETEST ITEM 15     (AVOIDANCE SUBSCALE)"
PRE21A   = "PRETEST ITEM 21     (AVOIDANCE SUBSCALE)"
PRE24A   = "PRETEST ITEM 24     (AVOIDANCE SUBSCALE)"
PRE5E    = "PRETEST ITEM 5      (EMPATHY SUBSCALE)"
PRE8E    = "PRETEST ITEM 8      (EMPATHY SUBSCALE) [REVERSED]"
PRE11E   = "PRETEST ITEM 11     (EMPATHY SUBSCALE) [REVERSED]"
PRE14E   = "PRETEST ITEM 14     (EMPATHY SUBSCALE)"
PRE19E   = "PRETEST ITEM 19     (EMPATHY SUBSCALE) [REVERSED]"
PRE22E   = "PRETEST ITEM 22     (EMPATHY SUBSCALE)"
POST1A   = "POSTTEST ITEM 1     (AVOIDANCE SUBSCALE) [REVERSED]"

POST4A   = "POSTTEST ITEM 4     (AVOIDANCE SUBSCALE)"
POST9A   = "POSTTEST ITEM 9     (AVOIDANCE SUBSCALE) [REVERSED]"
POST15A  = "POSTTEST ITEM 15    (AVOIDANCE SUBSCALE)"
POST21A  = "POSTTEST ITEM 21    (AVOIDANCE SUBSCALE)"
POST24A  = "POSTTEST ITEM 24    (AVOIDANCE SUBSCALE)"
POST5E   = "POSTTEST ITEM 5     (EMPATHY SUBSCALE)"
POST8E   = "POSTTEST ITEM 8     (EMPATHY SUBSCALE) [REVERSED]"
POST11E  = "POSTTEST ITEM 11    (EMPATHY SUBSCALE) [REVERSED]"
POST14E  = "POSTTEST ITEM 14    (EMPATHY SUBSCALE)"
POST19E  = "POSTTEST ITEM 19    (EMPATHY SUBSCALE) [REVERSED]"
POST22E  = "POSTTEST ITEM 22    (EMPATHY SUBSCALE)"
FOLL1A   = "FOLLOW-UP TEST ITEM 1      (AVOIDANCE SUBSCALE) [REVERSED]"
FOLL4A   = "FOLLOW-UP TEST ITEM 4      (AVOIDANCE SUBSCALE)"
FOLL9A   = "FOLLOW-UP TEST ITEM 9      (AVOIDANCE SUBSCALE) [REVERSED]"
FOLL15A  = "FOLLOW-UP TEST ITEM 15     (AVOIDANCE SUBSCALE)"
FOLL21A  = "FOLLOW-UP TEST ITEM 21     (AVOIDANCE SUBSCALE)"
FOLL24A  = "FOLLOW-UP TEST ITEM 24     (AVOIDANCE SUBSCALE)"
FOLL5E   = "FOLLOW-UP TEST ITEM 5      (EMPATHY SUBSCALE)"
FOLL8E   = "FOLLOW-UP TEST ITEM 8      (EMPATHY SUBSCALE) [REVERSED]"
FOLL11E  = "FOLLOW-UP TEST ITEM 11     (EMPATHY SUBSCALE) [REVERSED]"
FOLL14E  = "FOLLOW-UP TEST ITEM 14     (EMPATHY SUBSCALE)"
FOLL19E  = "FOLLOW-UP TEST ITEM 19     (EMPATHY SUBSCALE) [REVERSED]"
FOLL22E  = "FOLLOW-UP TEST ITEM 22     (EMPATHY SUBSCALE)"
PRE2F    = "PRETEST ITEM 2      (FORETHOUGHT SUBSCALE)"
PRE3F    = "PRETEST ITEM 3      (FORETHOUGHT SUBSCALE)"
PRE7F    = "PRETEST ITEM 7      (FORETHOUGHT SUBSCALE)"
PRE13F   = "PRETEST ITEM 13     (FORETHOUGHT SUBSCALE)"


PRE18F   = "PRETEST ITEM 18     (FORETHOUGHT SUBSCALE)"
PRE20F   = "PRETEST ITEM 20     (FORETHOUGHT SUBSCALE)"
PRE6U    = "PRETEST ITEM 6      (USEFULNESS SUBSCALE)"
PRE10U   = "PRETEST ITEM 10     (USEFULNESS SUBSCALE)"
```

(Continued)

```
YUANDATAMGMT.SAS (Continued)

PRE12U      = "PRETEST ITEM 12     (USEFULNESS SUBSCALE)"
PRE16U      = "PRETEST ITEM 16     (USEFULNESS SUBSCALE)"
PRE17U      = "PRETEST ITEM 17     (USEFULNESS SUBSCALE)"
PRE23U      = "PRETEST ITEM 23     (USEFULNESS SUBSCALE)"
POST2F      = "POSTTEST ITEM 2     (FORETHOUGHT SUBSCALE)"
POST3F      = "POSTTEST ITEM 3     (FORETHOUGHT SUBSCALE)"
POST7F      = "POSTTEST ITEM 7     (FORETHOUGHT SUBSCALE)"
POST13F     = "POSTTEST ITEM 13    (FORETHOUGHT SUBSCALE)"
POST18F     = "POSTTEST ITEM 18    (FORETHOUGHT SUBSCALE)"
POST20F     = "POSTTEST ITEM 20    (FORETHOUGHT SUBSCALE)"
POST6U      = "POSTTEST ITEM 6     (USEFULNESS SUBSCALE)"
POST10U     = "POSTTEST ITEM 10    (USEFULNESS SUBSCALE)"
POST12U     = "POSTTEST ITEM 12    (USEFULNESS SUBSCALE)"
POST16U     = "POSTTEST ITEM 16    (USEFULNESS SUBSCALE)"
POST17U     = "POSTTEST ITEM 17    (USEFULNESS SUBSCALE)"
POST23U     = "POSTTEST ITEM 23    (USEFULNESS SUBSCALE)"
FOLL2F      = "FOLLTEST ITEM 2     (FORETHOUGHT SUBSCALE)"
FOLL3F      = "FOLLTEST ITEM 3     (FORETHOUGHT SUBSCALE)"
FOLL7F      = "FOLLTEST ITEM 7     (FORETHOUGHT SUBSCALE)"
FOLL13F     = "FOLLTEST ITEM 13    (FORETHOUGHT SUBSCALE)"

FOLL18F     = "FOLLTEST ITEM 18    (FORETHOUGHT SUBSCALE)"
FOLL20F     = "FOLLTEST ITEM 20    (FORETHOUGHT SUBSCALE)"
FOLL6U      = "FOLLTEST ITEM 6     (USEFULNESS SUBSCALE)"
FOLL10U     = "FOLLTEST ITEM 10    (USEFULNESS SUBSCALE)"
FOLL12U     = "FOLLTEST ITEM 12    (USEFULNESS SUBSCALE)"
FOLL16U     = "FOLLTEST ITEM 16    (USEFULNESS SUBSCALE)"
FOLL17U     = "FOLLTEST ITEM 17    (USEFULNESS SUBSCALE)"
FOLL23U     = "FOLLTEST ITEM 23    (USEFULNESS SUBSCALE)"
PREF        = "PRETEST score on FORETHOUGHT subscale"
PREU        = "PRETEST score on USEFULNESS subscale"
POSTF       = "POSTTEST score on FORETHOUGHT subscale"
POSTU       = "POSTTEST score on USEFULNESS subscale"
FOLLF       = "FOLLOW-UP score on FORETHOUGHT subscale"
FOLLU       = "FOLLOW-UP score on USEFULNESS subscale";RUN;

proc contents;run;

proc print;run;
```

YUANCODEBOOK.DOC

Variable	Description	Type	Range	Missing Data	Source
Subject General Information					
AGE	Age in years at pretest (from agency files)		18–100		Agency Files
CBT	1 if CBT group (see below)		0 or 1		From Group #
GROUP	1 if CBT (Groups 2,4,6,8,10), else 0		1–10		Researcher
ID	Id Number given by researcher	Num	1–105	.	Researcher
MARRIED	1 if married, else 0		0 or 1		Agency Files
PRIORS	Number of prior police reports for domestic violence (from agency files)		0+		Agency Files
RECID	1 if recidivism (report of domestic violence to agency) during 6 month follow-up.		0+		Agency Files

Avoidance Subscale Data (Pretest)					
PRE1A	Pretest Item 1 (Avoidance subscale) [Reversed]				
PRE4A	Pretest Item 4 (Avoidance subscale)				
PRE9A	Pretest Item 9 (Avoidance subscale)) [Reversed]	Num	1–5	.	AS Pretest
PRE15A	Pretest Item 15 (Avoidance subscale)				
PRE21A	Pretest Item 21 (Avoidance subscale)				
PRE24A	Pretest Item 24 (Avoidance subscale)				
Avoidance Subscale Data (Posttest)					
POST1A	Posttest Item 1 (Avoidance subscale) [Reversed]				
POST4A	Posttest Item 4 (Avoidance subscale)				
POST9A	Posttest Item 9 (Avoidance subscale)) [Reversed]	Num	1–5	.	AS Pretest
POST15A	Posttest Item 15 (Avoidance subscale)				
POST21A	Posttest Item 21 (Avoidance subscale)				
POST24A	Posttest Item 24 (Avoidance subscale)				
Avoidance Subscale Data (Follow-up)					
FOLL1A	Follow-up Item 1 (Avoidance subscale) [Reversed]				
FOLL4A	Follow-up Item 4 (Avoidance subscale)				
FOLL9A	Follow-up Item 9 (Avoidance subscale)) [Reversed]	Num	1–5	.	AS Pretest
FOLL15A	Follow-up Item 15 (Avoidance subscale)				
FOLL21A	Follow-up Item 21 (Avoidance subscale)				
FOLL24A	Follow-up Item 24 (Avoidance subscale)				
Empathy Subscale Data (Pretest)					
PRE5E	Pretest Item 5 (Empathy subscale)				
PRE8E	Pretest Item 8 (Empathy subscale) [Reversed]				
PRE11E	Pretest Item 11 (Empathy subscale) [Reversed]	Num	1–5	.	AS Pretest
PRE14E	Pretest Item 14 (Empathy subscale)				
PRE19E	Pretest Item 19 (Empathy subscale) [Reversed]				
PRE22E	Pretest Item 22 (Empathy subscale)				
Empathy Subscale Data (Posttest)					
POST5E	Posttest Item 5 (Empathy subscale)				
POST8E	Posttest Item 8 (Empathy subscale) [Reversed]				
POST11E	Posttest Item 11 (Empathy subscale) [Reversed]	Num	1–5	.	AS Pretest
POST14E	Posttest Item 14 (Empathy subscale)				
POST19E	Posttest Item 19 (Empathy subscale) [Reversed]				
POST22E	Posttest Item 22 (Empathy subscale)				
Empathy Subscale Data (Follow-up)					
FOLL5E	Follow-up Item 5 (Empathy subscale)				
FOLL8E	Follow-up Item 8 (Empathy subscale) [Reversed]				
FOLL11E	Follow-up Item 11 (Empathy subscale) [Reversed]	Num	1–5	.	AS Pretest
FOLL14E	Follow-up Item 14 (Empathy subscale)				
FOLL19E	Follow-up Item 19 (Empathy subscale) [Reversed]				
FOLL22E	Follow-up Item 22 (Empathy subscale)				

(Continued)

YUANCODEBOOK.DOC *(Continued)*

	Forethought Subscale Data (Pretest)				
PRE2E	Pretest Item 2 (Forethought subscale)				
PRE3E	Pretest Item 3 (Forethought subscale) [Reversed]				
PRE7E	Pretest Item 7 (Forethought subscale)	Num	1–5	.	AS Pretest
PRE13E	Pretest Item 13 (Forethought subscale) [Reversed]				
PRE18E	Pretest Item 18 (Forethought subscale) [Reversed]				
PRE20E	Pretest Item 20 (Forethought subscale)				
	Forethought Subscale Data (Posttest)				
POST2E	Posttest Item 2 (Forethought subscale)				
POST3E	Posttest Item 3 (Forethought subscale) [Reversed]				
POST7E	Posttest Item 7 (Forethought subscale)	Num	1–5	.	AS Pretest
POST13E	Posttest Item 13 (Forethought subscale) [Reversed]				
POST18E	Posttest Item 18 (Forethought subscale) [Reversed]				
POST20E	Posttest Item 20 (Forethought subscale)				
	Forethought Subscale Data (Follow-up)				
FOLL2E	Follow-up Item 2 (Forethought subscale)				
FOLL3E	Follow-up Item 3 (Forethought subscale) [Reversed]				
FOLL7E	Follow-up Item 7 (Forethought subscale)	Num	1–5	.	AS Pretest
FOLL13E	Follow-up Item 13 (Forethought subscale) [Reversed]				
FOLL18E	Follow-up Item 18 (Forethought subscale) [Reversed]				
FOLL20E	Follow-up Item 20 (Forethought ubscale)				
	Usefulness Subscale Data (Pretest)				
PRE6E	Pretest Item 6 (Usefulness subscale)				
PRE10E	Pretest Item 10 (Usefulness subscale) [Reversed]				
PRE12E	Pretest Item 12 (Usefulness subscale)	Num	1–5	.	AS Pretest
PRE16E	Pretest Item 16 (Usefulness t subscale)				
PRE17E	Pretest Item 17 (Usefulness subscale) [Reversed]				
PRE23E	Pretest Item 23 (Usefulness subscale) [Reversed]				
	Usefulness Subscale Data (Posttest)				
POST6E	Posttest Item 6 (Usefulness subscale)				
POST10E	Posttest Item 10 (Usefulness subscale) [Reversed]				
POST12E	Posttest Item 12 (Usefulness t subscale)	Num	1–5	.	AS Pretest
POST16E	Posttest Item 16 (Usefulness t subscale)				
POST17E	Posttest Item 17 (Usefulness subscale) [Reversed]				
POST23E	Posttest Item 23 (Usefulness subscale) [Reversed]				
	Usefulness Subscale Data (Follow-up)				
FOLL6E	Follow-up Item 6 (Usefulness subscale)				
FOLL10E	Follow-up Item 10 (Usefulness subscale) [Reversed]				
FOLL12E	Follow-up Item 12 (Usefulness subscale)	Num	1–5	.	AS Pretest
FOLL16E	Follow-up Item 16 (Usefulness subscale)				
FOLL17E	Follow-up Item 17 (Usefulness subscale) [Reversed]				
FOLL23E	Follow-up Item 23 (Usefulness subscale) [Reversed]				

FOUNDATION GRANT EXAMPLE

(NOTE: DATA ARE FICTIONAL.)

Grants for research can come from large research organizations (like the National Institute of Health) or foundations. The advantage of foundations is that their review process may require a shorter application and they often respond faster than research institutes. They are often looking for smaller projects that fit within the particular focus of the foundation. Some foundations retain the same focus over time while others change their interests, so it is important to get current information. The Foundation Center Web site offers a host of options (some free and some for a fee) to help identify the right funder fdncenter.org/learn/faqs/html/subject.html. If you are a student, your university, school, or even your department probably has a person devoted to helping people locate funding sources.

For purposes of this example let's say Yuan sought some funding from a foundation to conduct his evaluation of the effect of CBT versus usual care. The foundation requires an initial letter of inquiry that is actually a 4–6 page mini-proposal. The letter guidelines require the following additional components be included: an application form, an abstract of 100 words, and resumes for research team members (not shown).

Mini-proposal must include:

a. **Major questions** guiding this work;

b. **Theoretical and empirical rationale,** including basic and intervention theory on changing setting structures, processes and practices, related empirical findings, and discussion of how the project will add to theory and policy/practice;

c. **Specific hypotheses and/or questions** to be tested or addressed;

d. **Intervention,** including a rationale for its appropriateness for the setting and age group specified; details on how it will be implemented and by whom; and brief information on prior pilot or other quasi-experimental studies that indicate that the intervention is promising;

e. **Research methods**, including sample definition and selection procedures, research design, random assignment procedures, key constructs, measures/data sources, and data collection procedures, methods for assessing implementation of the intervention and parallel assessments in the control group; and

f. **Data analysis plan** for addressing hypotheses and/or questions.

Of course, this particular format is just being used as an example. While these components are typical parts of a grant, each foundation or granting organization will have its own application process and required format. It is important to carefully read through the instructions and follow them exactly. Sometimes not following instructions can lead to not getting considered. If something is confusing, grant agencies are normally happy to have potential applicants call or e-mail questions.

INVESTIGATING THE EFFECT OF COGNITIVE BEHAVIORAL THERAPY ON DOMESTIC VIOLENCE RECIDIVISM

ABSTRACT

This study asks whether Cognitive Behavioral Therapy (CBT) is more effective than treatment as usual (TAU) in reducing male domestic violence recidivism. Safe Haven is a community-based agency treating court-ordered perpetrators of domestic violence. Research on similar populations suggests that a Cognitive Behavioral Therapy (CBT) approach might improve outcomes, but too few studies of CBT use with batterers have been done to know if this is a significantly better approach than treatment as usual. Perpetrators in CBT ($n = 100$) and TAU ($n = 100$) will be compared on change in conflict strategies and police report recidivism up to two years post-treatment.

INVESTIGATING THE EFFECT OF COGNITIVE BEHAVIORAL THERAPY ON DOMESTIC VIOLENCE RECIDIVISM

Major Questions: Safe Haven's primary goal is to reduce or prevent domestic violence through work with perpetrators and victims. Typical results for domestic violence perpetrator interventions have not met with high levels of success in reducing the likelihood of re-offending behavior. Some research suggests that CBT can be an effective approach, but the literature is too underdeveloped to understand what types of batterers benefit the most from this approach. Thus, the major research question is: Does CBT produce better outcomes than typical services?

Theoretical and Empirical Rationale: Every year in the United States there are over 3 million incidents of reported domestic violence (Bureau of Justice Statistics, no date). Unfortunately recidivism rates are also very high (American Bar Association, no date). The consequences of domestic violence range from economic impacts due to lost work or medical injury, health, and mental health related issues (US Surgeon General, 2005; Wilt & Olson, 1996). It is important to understand how to improve our ability to intervene in these emotionally, socially, and economically costly situations. Yet, research comparing varying approaches to dealing with domestic violence have "generated weak or inconsistent evidence of deterrent effects" on recidivism repeat offending (Fagan, 1996).

Cognitive behavioral treatment. The cognitive-behavioral therapy (CBT) model was developed mostly by psychologists. It views violence as a learned behavior, and believes that non-violent behavior can be learned as well (Stith, Rosen, & McCollum, 2003). Further CBT approaches can vary in their particular focus. Some research suggests that violent couples can be identified separately from nonviolent couples based on conflict strategies used (Lloyd, 1990). Safe Haven has chosen a CBT model that focuses on altering the way individuals handle conflict.

In general, program evaluations report a success rate of between 50% and 80% across various program approaches (Stith, Rosen & McCollum, 2003). CBT has been found to be either equally effective as or more effective than other practices, though some studies report it only works with certain kinds of batterers (Buttell, 2001; Morrel, 2000). Studies of treatment effectiveness have suffered from numerous methodological problems that make it hard to draw conclusions about treatment methods. These include differing measures of effectiveness, differing follow-up times, reliance on partner self-report of continued violence, and treatment dropout rates.

This study improves upon the current literature in several ways. First, official reports of offenses will be measured as well as changes in conflict strategies. Staff providing the CBT treatment will all be trained at the same program, which will improve treatment fidelity. There will be six months of follow-up time and the study will test a specific theory of change. The theoretical framework for the program effect is as follows:

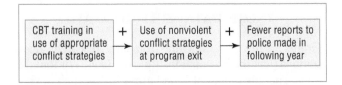

Thus far, no studies have examined this CBT model in comparison to a typical eclectic group therapy used in community-based agencies. This study will not only benefit the client population of Safe Haven but also substantially add to the literature on the use of CBT with batterers.

Specific Hypotheses and/or Questions. The specific questions and hypotheses for the proposed study include the following:

Q1: Do subjects receiving CBT and TAU show different changes in AS subscale scores?

> H1A1: Subjects receiving CBT and TAU will show different levels of change in the AS avoidance subscale from pretest to posttest (change during treatment).
>
> H1A2: Subjects receiving CBT and TAU will show different levels of change in the AS avoidance subscale from posttest to six-months post-treatment (change following treatment).
>
> H1B1 & H1B2 mirror the above except the AS Empathy subscale is the DV.
>
> H1C1 & H1C2 mirror the above except the AS Forethought subscale is the DV.
>
> H1D1 & H1D2 mirror the above except the AS Usefulness subscale is the DV.

Q2: Do subjects receiving CBT and TAU show different rates of reported violence?

This would yield the following hypothesis:

H2: Subjects receiving CBT and TAU will show different rates of recidivism during the six months following treatment.

Yuan is also considering adding a couple of new hypotheses, to see if the AS subscales predict recidivism rates. Those two new hypotheses would be under a new question and would look like this:

Q3: Do empathy and argument avoidance predict recidivism?

H3A: People with higher AS empathy scores at posttest will have lower rates of recidivism.

H3B: Same as 3A except Empathy subscale is used.

H3C: Same as 3A except Forethought subscale is used.

H3D: Same as 3A except Usefulness subscale is used.

Intervention. Safe Haven is a large domestic violence counseling provider serving several hundred batterers per year. Clients are court-ordered and complete a three-month (12 session) weekly treatment module. Treatment is in a group format, with 20 clients generally attending each group. The planned intervention is specific to these court-ordered batterers. Although this excludes batterers who may volunteer for intervention, voluntary clients make up a small proportion of Safe Haven clients. With the increased focus on criminal prosecution of batterers, it is also important to understand what works with court-ordered batterers. Although there are female batterers, Safe Haven (and most domestic violence agencies) offer gender-specific groups. There are too few females to participate in the study. Care will be taken to compare characteristics of the present sample with men in other studies to assess generalizability.

The batterer groups will be conducted by Safe Haven staff. All Safe Haven staff have been trained on the current treatment method. The treatment model in use to date has been eclectic, blending psychodynamic, humanist, and behavioral principles and methods. On average, facilitators have been with Safe Haven for three years. Treatment group staff will be selected to participate in a three-day training on CBT prior to the intervention.

Research methods. The sample will include 200 men who are court-ordered to participate in the Safe Haven program. Because of the nature of the service, clients must be assigned on a space available basis. Ten groups of clients will be assigned in order of referral, with even numbered groups receiving CBT and odd-numbered groups receiving Treatment as Usual (TAU).

Although clients are court-ordered, informed consent will be obtained for participation in the study. Clients will be informed that their participation in the study will in no way impact their services or reports back to the court. Data will be kept by id number only. Police reports are already collected on mandated clients as part of the court-ordered process. The scale to

be given does not contain sensitive questions. It is not anticipated, therefore, that participation in the study will cause any additional burden or stress or in any way harm the client. If possible, clients who do not consent will be assigned to a separate group. If this is not possible they will be excused from completing the pre- and post-test scales and be excluded from follow-up.

This study is a quasi-experimental investigation comparing outcomes of CBT with TAU. The groups will be conducted by different therapists to help prevent treatment contamination. To assess treatment fidelity, two sessions will be taped at random from each therapist. A graduate student who is well-versed in CBT will review the tapes to note each time a therapist uses a CBT intervention technique. In this way, he will compare the degree to which CBT is used in CBT and TAU groups. The rater will be kept blind to the nature (CBT vs. TAU) of each group.

Although clients are court-ordered, informed consent will be obtained for participation in the study. Two outcome measures will be assessed: (1) A pre and post and follow-up assessment of conflict strategies using the Argument Scales (subscales include: Empathy, Avoidance, Forethought and Usefulness) will be conducted. This scale has been used in several other recent investigations and has good reliability and validity ratings (citations for validity and support for use of this scale go here[1]); (2) Police records of domestic violence will be examined for six months post-treatment. The argument scales will be given at the first and last group and then again at a six-month follow-up meeting. The scales will be administered in a group context at pre-and post-test and during an individual meeting for the follow-up. The principal investigator, who is not one of the paid group facilitators, will collect the scale data while the group facilitators are outside the room.

Should clients withdraw from the program, efforts will be made to provide the post-test and continue to check for police record of recidivism. Because random assignment was not possible, models of outcomes will also control for client demographics, marital status, and prior domestic violence history. These control variable data will be collected from agency files.

The principal investigator is a graduate student at X University and an intern at Safe Haven. He has completed his research methods and foundations of statistics coursework. He will work under the supervision of Professor Y at X University to insure that the analyses are correctly implemented and interpreted.

Data Analysis Plan. Data will be entered into an Excel spreadsheet then exported to SAS for Windows. Software and computers are available to the principal

---

[1]Note: Yuan's scale is a fictitious example and therefore citations for its use do not exist.

investigator at his university. All computerized data will be anonymized, meaning only an ID number will be entered.

Pre- and post-test change in conflict strategies by subscale will be assessed using paired t-tests. Because there is also interest in whether the post-test scores change at follow-up, a repeated measures ANOVA will be conducted.

To assess recidivism (yea or no) and control for argument scale scores at pretest and the other control variables, requires moving to a multivariate model. Because the time elapsed from posttest to follow-up is the same for all individuals, a logistic regression model will be used. Odds ratios will be used to discuss the magnitude of the coefficients in the model.

SUMMARY

Increasingly, agencies such as Safe Haven are seeking ways to improve practice by drawing on evidence-based interventions. Thus far, research is inconclusive regarding the efficacy of CBT with batterers. This study will build on the literature in this area and further our understanding of the efficacy of CBT. This study will also contribute to the agency's ability to serve this important population. This study is also in keeping with the foundation's interest in violence prevention.

REFERENCES

American Bar Association (no date). *American Bar Association Commission on Domestic Violence.* Available on-line: www.abanet.org/domviol/stats.html

Bureau of Justice Statistics (no date). *Disturbing Facts about Domestic Violence.* Available on-line: www.lapdonline.org/bldg_safer_comms/gi_ domestic_violence/domestic_disturbing.html

Fagan, J. (1996). T*he Criminalization of Domestic Violence: Promises and Limits NIJ Research Report.* Available www.ncjrs.org/ txtfiles/crimdom.txt.

Lloyd, S. (1990). Conflict types and strategies in violent marriages. *Journal of Family Violence* 5(4), 269–284.

Stith, S. M., Rosen, K. H., McCollum, E. E. (2003). Effectiveness of couples treatment for spouse abuse. *Journal of Marital and Family Therapy*, Available www.findarticles.com/p/articles/mi_qa3658/is_200307/ai_n9254960

US Surgeon General (1999). *Adults and Mental Health in Mental Health.* A report of the surgeon general. www.surgeongeneral.gov/library/mentalhealth/chapter4/ sec1_1.html#stressful.

Wilt, S., & Olson, S. (1996). Prevalence of domestic violence in the United States. *Journal of the American Medical Women's Association,* 51, 77–82.

NATIONAL SCIENCE FOUNDATION
GRANT EXAMPLE

NOTE: PILOT PROJECT WORK AND
AGENCY DATA ARE FICTIONAL.

Grants for academic research often come from federal funding bodies like the National Institute for Health (NIH) or the Centers for Disease Control (CDC), among others. Federal funding sources such as these are very interested in the scientific rigor of the application. It is absolutely essential to have very clear and defensible questions, sampling protocols, and discussions of how the design maximizes internal and external validity. The work must explicitly address existing gaps in the literature. The linkages between theory questions and design must be crystal clear. Some federal funders (e.g., NIH) will want the work to have at least some field relevance, although this emphasis is generally less than with foundation grants. Other funders, like the National Science Foundation (NSF), are more interested in doing basic research that develops knowledge.

John wants money for his doctoral education. He is interested in pursuing some of the leads he developed in his study of Bosnian immigrants. His work, like most doctoral dissertations, will be rather more basic than applied. As you will see, he is interested in exploring issues of acculturation among refugees, with particular attention to the role of trauma in acculturation. His work is strongly rooted in theory. John looked around for some funding sources dealing specifically with refugees and couldn't find any. Given the very theoretical nature of his work, he felt what he was doing might interest NSF. He therefore decided to send his application there. Checking out the NSF Web site (nsf.gov), John found a very broad array of areas of investigation and funding opportunities. An hour or two of familiarization with the rather complex NSF opportunities showed him that he needed to print and read their grant proposal guide (http://nsf.gov/publications/pub_summ.jsp?ods_key=gpg). He figured out he would have to apply under the "Social, Behavioral and Economic Sciences" section and that dissertation support was available—so far so good. The proposal guide showed John that he had to do several things, including:

- A cover sheet
- A project summary (one page, stressing "intellectual merit" and "broader impacts")
- A table of contents
- The project description (15 pages maximum)
- References
- Biographical sketches of personnel
- A budget

This establishes the format of John's application. This all seems simple enough, especially because his academic department will handle most of the budgeting section. John has been warned by his professors to make sure he does two things: First, stick exactly to the required format (preceding list); and second, carefully read the review criteria and stick to them, too. The review criteria can be found at (http://nsf.gov/pubs/gpg/nsf04_23/3.jsp#IIIA) and include the material shown in Figure A.1.

FIGURE A.1 **NSF Criteria.**

What is the intellectual merit of the proposed activity? How important is the proposed activity to advancing knowledge and understanding within its own field or across different fields? How well qualified is the proposer (individual or team) to conduct the project? (If appropriate, the reviewer will comment on the quality of prior work.) To what extent does the proposed activity suggest and explore creative and original concepts? How well conceived and organized is the proposed activity? Is there sufficient access to resources?

What are the broader impacts of the proposed activity? How well does the activity advance discovery and understanding while promoting teaching, training, and learning? How well does the proposed activity broaden the participation of underrepresented groups (e.g., gender, ethnicity, disability, geographic, etc.)? To what extent will it enhance the infrastructure for research and education, such as facilities, instrumentation, networks, and partnerships? Will the results be disseminated broadly to enhance scientific and technological understanding? What may be the benefits of the proposed activity to society?

Why should John be so obsessed with review criteria? Because this is essentially the "grading sheet" that the reviewers will use. Close adherence to both the required format and the required criteria are absolutely necessary.

John's idea for his dissertation is based on a number of things he learned in his qualitative research, combined with additional literature he has found. You may remember that one of John's primary findings was that those people who did not have an aggressive approach to taking advantage of opportunities in America and who did not have high self-efficacy seemed to be more likely to become marginalized. John also found that those individuals experiencing lots of trauma before moving to the United States seemed to be more likely to be marginalized. This suggests to John that those refugees with very traumatic preimmigration experiences may be less focused on learning how to actively build their lives in the US post-immigration. Interestingly, research in Australia (Nesdale, 2002) suggests that immigrants who had lower self-esteem and less desire to live according to Australian standards and values had lower identification with their host country. John's own work supports this but also highlighted that those immigrants who were not actively integrating into American culture also tended to have worse preimmigration experiences. John's dissertation will focus on this nexus between desire to integrate into the host country and preimmigration trauma.

AUTHOR'S NOTE: FOR PURPOSES OF THIS BOOK, WE PRESENT ONLY THE COVER SHEET, PROJECT SUMMARY, TABLE OF CONTENTS, PROJECT DESCRIPTION, AND REFERENCES. BIOGRAPHICAL SKETCHES AND BUDGET SECTIONS ARE OMITTED TO SAVE SPACE AND BECAUSE THEIR STRUCTURE CAN VARY SUBSTANTIALLY ACROSS FUNDING AGENCIES. WE WOULD ALSO LIKE TO REMIND YOU THAT THE DATA FROM JOHN'S PRIOR (QUALITATIVE) WORK IS FICTIONAL.

PROJECT SUMMARY: TRAUMA, ATTITUDES, AND REFUGEE ACCULTURATION (TARA)

The proposed work is a longitudinal panel design surveying refugees resettled in the St. Louis area. The purpose of the proposed research is to better understand the linkages between preimmigration trauma, acculturation-related psychological characteristics at arrival, and acculturation, functioning, and psychological well-being two years postarrival. Specific questions include:

- What is the relationship of preimmigration trauma to refugee characteristics at arrival and 18 months after arrival?
- How do attitudes toward host country and country of origin at arrival predict various refugee characteristics 18 months after arrival?
- What interactions between attitudes toward host country and country of origin exist with regard to predicting subsequent refugee characteristics?
- How stable are acculturation constructs (attitude, identity toward host and origin countries) over time? Do trauma and arrival status factors predict changes in these constructs?

Theoretical Significance: This is the first longitudinal study linking trauma theory with an orthogonal model of acculturation. The proposed work is an evolutionary step forward, based on methodology developed with refugees being done in Australia and New Zealand (Nesdale, 2002; Nesdale & Mak, 2000; Pio, 2005). The above referenced body of work has used an orthogonal conceptualization of acculturation and has demonstrated good construct validity across a number of immigrant populations. The theoretical significance of the current work is that it expands this prior work in three ways:

- **The proposed work explores existing theory and constructs specifically with regard to one subset of the immigrant population—refugees.** Many of the key correlates of acculturation status (e.g., self-efficacy, attitude toward country of origin) are likely to manifest very differently among those immigrants who are refugees, and the current literature on immigrants may or may not apply well to this subpopulation.
- **The proposed work study explores preimmigration trauma in relation to the emerging orthogonal model of acculturation.** In this way the vast literature on PTSD among refugees can be connected to the nascent literature on refugee acculturation.
- **Study variables will be studied longitudinally, allowing predictive, not simply correlational, relationships to be established.** The dominance of cross-sectional and retrospective designs in the literature may be the single most serious roadblock to understanding the acculturation process among refugees.

Practical Significance: The American commitment to refugees is enshrined both legally and within our national character. Substantial monies are appropriated to support the transition of refugees, but the application of these funds is not adequately supported by empirical research. Our constructs and outcome variables have been chosen to both reflect theoretical interest and to provide practical relevance (psychological well-being, employment, and the like). It is hoped that by identifying predictors of positive (integration or assimilation) versus negative (separation or marginalization) acculturation outcomes our ability to target services more effectively will be greatly enhanced.

Questions and hypotheses are operationalized in the project description but can be broken down into the following categories: (1) the association of preimmigration trauma with psychological and attitudinal factors at arrival; (2) the testing of theoretically derived main effects and mediating and moderating relationships between pre-immigration trauma and psychological and attitudinal factors at arrival and subsequent outcome variables (orthogonal acculturation status, employment, depression, and the like) at two years postarrival.

TRAUMA, ATTITUDES, AND REFUGEE ACCULTURATION (TARA) PROJECT DESCRIPTION

The United States receives more refugees than any other nation, approximately one million in the last decade (UNHCR, 2003). Successful acculturation of this population is a national priority. The U.S. government earmarked $552,000,000 in federal funds for refugee services in fiscal '06 (OMB, 2005). The social sciences have not, as yet, provided a comprehensive theoretical or empirical basis in support of positive refugee acculturation. This study seeks to remedy that gap in the following ways:

- Through use of a more sophisticated theoretical (orthogonal) model of acculturation
- Through the employment of a longitudinal design
- Through inclusion of issues of trauma in modeling acculturation

In many ways, this work is based on the emerging Australasian body of work, conducted most notably by Nesdale (Nesdale, 2002; Nesdale & Mak, 2000). This work was chosen to inform the proposed study for both theoretical and methodological reasons. Nesdale's work and instrumentation were designed to conform specifically with an orthogonal theoretical model of acculturation. This model can be seen as a refinement of currently dominant (Berry & Kim, 1983) acculturation theory, in that it allows separate consideration

and operationalization of both host-country relevant attitudinal and affiliative factors. Nesdale has developed and validated instruments specifically to study refugees of various ethnic origins. His are the only existing measures of acculturation attitudes and status that have been validated across multiple dissimilar cultures (e.g., Vietnamese and Indian).

OBJECTIVES OF THE PROPOSED STUDY

The present study is a two-wave panel survey design, interviewing refugees settling in the Metroland area during the 2007 calendar year (expected $N = 294$). Refugees will be interviewed twice, once at resettlement in the Metroland area (typically six to ten weeks postarrival in the United States) and once 18 months later. A full list of study objectives and questions are specified in the "Theoretical Model, Questions, and Hypotheses" section below but can be summarized as including:

- Determining the association of preimmigration trauma with identification toward origin and host cultures at arrival
- Determining the association of trauma, cultural attitudes, and identification (host and origin, measured separately at arrival) and other selected factors (self-esteem, self-efficacy, PTSD symptomatology, educational and job preparedness) with vocational success, PTSD symptomatology, depression, and cultural attitudes and identification 18 months later

The proposed work builds on qualitative pilot work carried out by the author in the past year (Preston, 2006).

PRIOR LITERATURE AND THEORY

Due to the paucity of refugee-specific theory and empirical research, much of our literature review will center around work done regarding the broader immigrant population.

The immigrant adaptation literature is largely based on Berry's (1998) very influential model of acculturation. This model includes marginalization as a preliminary phase, followed either by continued marginalization (no cultural affiliation), separation (original cultural affiliation only), assimilation (host cultural affiliation only), or integration (dual cultural affiliation).

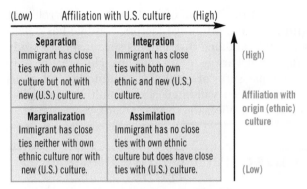

The preceding model is essentially an orthogonal presentation of the concepts of affiliation with origin and ethnic cultures. This four-part model has received almost general acceptance in the immigration and acculturation literature. However, it is not a predictive theory and thus cannot be subjected to scientific falsification. We view the above theoretical model as a conceptual framework and starting point. We use it mainly to guide our criticism and identification of gaps in the current research and to assist in selecting and operationalizing constructs of theoretical interest.

Unfortunately, the literature on refugees is strong in only one area: the understanding of trauma-related psychiatric disorders, principally posttraumatic stress disorder (PTSD). While some attention will be paid to PTSD, it is not our central interest. Trauma is included mainly as a predictor variable, and PTSD is measured not because of its innate theoretical importance in our model but mainly to provide linkage between the proposed work and the bulk of the existing literature. The next several paragraphs will familiarize the reader with key gaps in the refugee literature:

Gap in the literature: Despite the challenges, service needs, and historical importance of refugees in the United States, there has been relatively little research on refugee (as opposed to "immigrant") acculturation in America. There has been voluminous work on refugees, some quite strong (e.g., Cusak, 2002; Mollica, Saraljic, Chemoff, Lavelle, Sarajilic-Vukovic, & Massagli, 2001). This research, however, has focused almost exclusively on refugees and their relationship to trauma, most notably vis-à-vis PTSD. Specific acculturation research on refugees in the United States is virtually nonexistent.

Gap in the literature: The temporal sequencing of attitudes and acculturation outcomes remains underdeveloped. The process of adaptation to a new culture is widely acknowledged to take time (Pio, 2005). Reliance on retrospective, cross-sectional designs has left us without a clear understanding of the predictive (as opposed to associative) relationship of attitudes on acculturation. It is quite possible that attitudes toward origin and host cultures flux dramatically. If one wishes to understand the effect of immigrant attitudes on subsequent acculturation, a longitudinal design is clearly necessary.

Gap in the literature: There has been a remarkable lack of interest in studying immigrant attitude toward their host country. Attitudes of immigrants toward maintaining affiliation with their culture of origin have been the subject of much attention. One review article (Phinney, 1990) cites over 70 empirical studies prior to 1990. Interestingly, there has been an almost complete lack of attention given to immigrant attitudes toward and affiliation with their host cultures (Nesdale, 2002). While the existing theoretical and empirical work on identification and affiliation with one's origin culture is very helpful in helping understand acculturation, this work is almost completely unsupported by a corresponding focus on host-country identification and affiliation. There is some evidence that early acculturation experiences may have greater long-term impact on acculturation outcomes than pre-immigration trauma among refugees (Westermeyer & Uecker, 1997). If these preliminary findings are found to hold, they will have substantial importance with regard to how we provide early services for refugees.

HOW TARA ADDRESSES EXISTING KNOWLEDGE GAPS

TARA will broaden the existing research on refugees by addressing issues of acculturation and postimmigration status (depression and employment status). These are practically relevant constructs that will help us to expand our knowledge of refugee functioning beyond the issue of PTSD.

TARA uses an orthogonal conceptualization of acculturation, exploring both ethnic and host-country attitudes and identities. This substantially expands our existing acculturation knowledge base, which is almost uniformly unidimensional, excluding host-country attitudes and identification.

TARA is longitudinal and will allow us to determine the associations of preimmigration trauma to arrival attitudinal factors (self-efficacy, host culture identification, origin ethnicity identification). These factors will then be explored relative to their ability to predict both attitudinal factors and well-being at 18 months postimmigration. In this way, TARA affords us our first look at the development of acculturation attitudes and identities and establishment of well-being over time.

The inclusion of varied constructs (acculturation attitude and identity, well-being, trauma) allows us to move research on refugees beyond a strict mental-health model.

PRELIMINARY WORK

A small qualitative pilot study was performed by the principal investigator on a population of Bosnian refugees in the St. Louis area (Preston, 2005; see

Appendix B). This very preliminary work supported the utility of applying Berry's framework to this population. Most importantly for the current study, the pilot work found that trauma and acculturation attitudes seemed to be strongly predictive of functioning. Those subjects who remained marginalized (low host and ethnic identification and involvement) appeared to have had far more traumatic preimmigration experiences. There was some suggestion in the data that the inability of these individuals to move forward in their new country may have been due to ongoing effects of the trauma. A different mechanism also appeared to exist.

Among those who did well (vocationally, socially, and the like), there appeared to be a higher proportion of refugees who were mainly motivated by a desire to come to America and aggressively take advantage of opportunities here. It may be that refugees can be conceptualized both along a continuum of the degree to which they are "running from" traumatic experiences in their host country and the degree to which they are "running to" the United States. The resultant theoretical proposition is that trauma and host-country attitudes and identification may separately predict depression and vocational success. This study has been designed, in part, to test this proposition.

THEORETICAL MODEL, QUESTIONS, AND HYPOTHESES

We propose the following theoretical framework as a starting point for understanding early acculturation among refugees.

GENERAL CONCEPTUAL FRAMEWORK

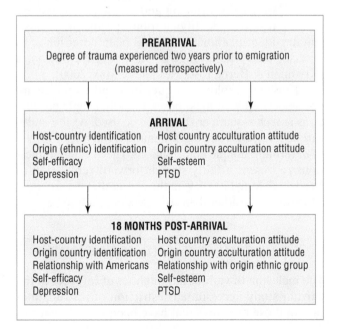

PREARRIVAL
Degree of trauma experienced two years prior to emigration (measured retrospectively)

ARRIVAL
Host-country identification   Host country acculturation attitude
Origin (ethnic) identification   Origin country acculturation attitude
Self-efficacy   Self-esteem
Depression   PTSD

18 MONTHS POST-ARRIVAL
Host-country identification   Host country acculturation attitude
Origin country identification   Origin country acculturation attitude
Relationship with Americans   Relationship with origin ethnic group
Self-efficacy   Self-esteem
Depression   PTSD

THEORETICALLY DERIVED QUESTIONS

While the general exploratory questions detailed below are important, we feel the main value of this study will be found in the degree to which theoretically derived propositions are tested. We present the following questions and hypotheses.

QUESTION SET 1: THE RELATIONSHIP OF PREIMMIGRATION TRAUMA TO REFUGEE CHARACTERISTICS AT ARRIVAL AND AT 18 MONTHS POSTARRIVAL

Our temporally precedent independent variable is trauma. There is substantial reason to believe that trauma has an impact on subsequent attitudes and functioning.

Hypothesis 1.1: Degree of preimmigration trauma will be negatively associated with self-esteem, self-efficacy, and depression at arrival and at 18 months, as well as with employment at 18 months. This hypothesis is grounded in the larger trauma literature (e.g., Cusak, 2002; Miller, Worthington, Muzurovic, Tipping, & Goldman, 2002) and attempts to replicate those efforts. These hypotheses will be analyzed using both bivariate (correlation) and multivariate (OLS) approaches for most variables, although logistic regression will be used for prediction of employment, as it will be categorized dichotomously.

Hypothesis 1.2: Degree of preimmigration trauma will be negatively associated with positive host-country attitudes and identification at arrival and at 18 months. This hypothesis is an attempt to empirically test previously discussed qualitative observations from the pilot work and will use similar analytic approaches to the hypothesis (H1.1) above.

QUESTION SET 2: EFFECTS OF HOST-COUNTRY ATTITUDES AT ARRIVAL

Many studies using immigrant samples have found that integration or assimilation outcomes are supportive of immigrant well-being (Phinney, Horenczyk, Liebkind, & Vedder, 2001). Such outcomes require high levels of host-country identification by definition (see Berry's model). Nesdale's cross-sectional work with refugees (Nesdale & Mak, 2000) has also suggested the importance of host-country attitudes and identification. We will explore the following relationships.

Hypothesis 2.1: Positive host-country attitudes at arrival will predict depression, self-efficacy, self-esteem, and employment at 18 months postimmigration.

Hypothesis 2.2: Positive host-country identification at arrival will predict depression, self-efficacy, self-esteem, and employment at 18 months postimmigration. This hypothesis is more theoretically tenuous. It may be unreasonable to expect that any degree of identification with the host country could develop quickly after arrival.

QUESTION SET 3: EFFECTS OF ORIGIN COUNTRY IDENTIFICATION AT ARRIVAL

This question set, in conjunction with question set 2, supports an orthogonal conceptualization of acculturation.

Hypothesis 3.1: Positive host-country attitudes at arrival will predict depression, self-efficacy, self-esteem, and employment at 18 months postimmigration.

Hypothesis 3.2: Positive host-country identification at arrival will predict depression, self-efficacy, self-esteem, and employment at 18 months postimmigration. This hypothesis is more theoretically tenuous. It may be unreasonable to expect that any degree of identification with the host country could develop quickly after arrival.

QUESTION SET 4: INTERACTIONS OF ATTITUDES TOWARD THE HOME AND HOST COUNTRIES WITH REGARD TO DEPRESSION, SELF-EFFICACY, SELF-ESTEEM, AND EMPLOYMENT AT 18 MONTHS POSTIMMIGRATION

Hypothesis 4.1A: Attitude toward the home country will uniquely explain variance in the dependent variables measured at 18 months.

Hypothesis 4.1B: Attitude toward the host country will uniquely explain variance in the dependent variables measured at 18 months.

Hypothesis 4.1C: Attitude toward the host country will interact with attitude toward the home country in explaining variance in the dependent variables measured at 18 months. This hypothesis will allow us to determine if the absence (or presence) of high levels of positive attitudes toward both the home and host countries have unique effects. Such an interaction, if identified, would demonstrate the predictive power of client attitudes best classified as supporting marginalization or integration outcomes separate from orthogonal main effects.

Question set 4 will repeat question set 3 but will use identification constructs in place of attitudinal constructs (see Constructs and Measures, below).

QUESTION SET 5: STABILITY OF ACCULTURATION CONSTRUCTS OVER TIME

This set of questions is less theoretically derived than it is inductive. Acculturation is generally studied cross-sectionally, even retrospectively, raising the question of its stability over time. We therefore explore the consistency of attitudinal and identification factors relating to acculturation with the following hypotheses.

Hypothesis 5.1: Attitude toward the home country will significantly change between arrival and 18 months postarrival.

Hypothesis 5.2: Attitude toward the host country will significantly change between arrival and 18 months postarrival.

Hypothesis 5.3: Home country identification will significantly change between arrival and 18 months postarrival.

Hypothesis 5.4: Host country identification will significantly change between arrival and 18 months postarrival.

Given the lack of supporting longitudinal research, these hypotheses are nondirectional. If significant changes are found, we will perform multivariate analyses to determine what factors predict these changes.

GENERAL (EXPLORATORY) QUESTIONS

Given the paucity of data available in the literature, and following the lead of Nesdale (2002), we believe it would be irresponsible to collect the proposed data without performing basic statistical analyses to chart relationships between study variables over time. We confess to being somewhat uncomfortable that these general questions might be interpreted as theoretical "fishing." We believe that, given the fact that data such as these have not been collected heretofore, some basic exploration of connections between constructs is necessary. Given the theoretical justifications for the inclusion of these general constructs, we feel that such an approach is not irresponsible. In general, we will ask:

- To what degree is prearrival trauma predictive of characteristics on arrival?
- To what degree are prearrival trauma and arrival characteristics predictive of characteristics at 18 months?

With regard to both of the above questions, we are particularly interested in identifying robust predictors of psychological well-being and employment. We are also interested in identifying robust predictors of host-country identification, as this has been determined to be associated with a range of other positive outcomes (Krishnan & Berry, 1992; Nesdale & Mak, 2000).

These are exploratory questions and therefore are not associated with hypotheses. Initially, simple correlations and chi-square analyses will be used. At the multivariate level, OLS and logistic analyses will be performed to determine unique contributions. These general questions represent a fairly straightforward replication of Nesdale & Mak (2000), with the caveat that we are using a longitudinal, rather than cross-sectional, approach.

CONSTRUCTS AND MEASURES

The inclusion of various nationalities of refugees in the current study necessitated restriction of instrumentation to those measures that have been validated across many ethnic groups. This required an almost item-by-item replication of the measures used by Nesdale and his colleagues in their work on Australian immigrants, as these are often the only cross-ethnicity validated scales available. The majority of available scales are tailored to specific immigrant or refugee populations, most notably, Mexican nationals immigrating to the United States.

MEASUREMENT OF PREARRIVAL AND ARRIVAL CONSTRUCTS

Prearrival Trauma. The level of prearrival trauma will be captured by the traumatic life events questionnaire (TLEQ), which has shown good psychometric properties and has been validated across several different refugee populations (Hubbard, Realmuto, Northwood, & Masten, 1995; Realmuto, Masten, Carole, & Hubbard, 1992). While the Harvard Trauma Questionnaire is more commonly used, it could not be used for this study because it can be applied only to ethnic groups of refugees for which it has been specifically tailored. The TLEQ is meant to capture both exposure and responses (separate questions) to 21 types of trauma that can occur both in civilian experience and in war. For our purposes, the degree of exposure to trauma will constitute our primary variable of interest.

The next five instruments have been previously used and validated in Australia on a diverse group of refugees by Nesdale and colleagues (Nesdale & Mak, 2000).

Acculturation Attitudes. Host (American) and culture of origin attitudes will be measured by separate single-item scales as used by Nesdale and colleagues. These seven-point scaled items assess the degree to which the respondent believes "It is very important to me to live according to the standards and values of American (American attitude)/my ethnic group (Ethnic Attitude)."

American identity will be measured using five items from the Universal Ethnic Identity Scale (Nesdale, Rooney, & Smith, 1997).

Ethnic identity will be measured using six other items from the same scale.

Self-efficacy will be measured using five items from the General Self-Efficacy Scale (Sherer, Maddux, Mercandandante, Prentice-Dunn, Jacobs, & Rogers, 1982).

Self-esteem will be measured using the Rosenberg Self-Esteem Scale (Rosenberg, 1965). Both of these measures were used successfully with immigrant populations (Nesdale & Mak, 2003).

PTSD symptomatology will be measured with the well-known PTSD Checklist Civilian Version (PCL-C), a standardized 17-item questionnaire that uses a five-point scale to capture reactions to traumatic events.

Depression will be measured with the familiar Beck Depression Inventory-II. This easily administered standardized test has shown remarkable flexibility across various ethnic groups (see Wang, Andrade, & Gorenstein, 2005).

MEASUREMENT OF CONSTRUCTS AT 18 MONTHS POSTARRIVAL

The above items will all be included except the TLEQ. In addition, two further items used by Nesdale (2002) will be included; relationship with Americans will be measured using a three-item scale, and relationship with own ethnic group will be measured using a separate item scale. All of these scales are seven-point scales and have been shown by Nesdale (2002) to have acceptable subscale reliability.

SAMPLING

The sample will be drawn from the Central Metro Refugee Center (CMCR), a resettlement support agency in St. Louis, Missouri. This is one of the nation's most active centers. During 2005, this agency was involved in the resettling of approximately 300 refugee households (including approximately 600 immigrants) per month. Of these, two-thirds were English speakers. For the purposes of this study, only English-speaking individuals will be considered for inclusion in the study. This is to avoid the necessity of using an interpreter during the interviews, which could adversely impact the psychometrics of the instruments being used. The eligible sample for study purposes, therefore, is approximately 400 households.

CMCR has agreed to allow sampling of their population and has also agreed to allow administration of study instruments as part of their standard refugee resettlement and 18-month follow-up process. One English-speaking adult refugee per household will be randomly selected for inclusion in the study. Households with no English speakers will not be eligible for inclusion.

Selection of one individual per household will ensure independence of observations. An honorarium of $20 per subject will be paid at both interview sessions to compensate subjects for their time. We anticipate that 80% of those approached will agree to participate in the study. In the past, CMCR has achieved a 92% success rate in performing their 18-month follow-ups. This study will attempt to sample one individual from each household during a two-month period. We anticipate that 320 (80% of selected individuals from 400 households) will agree to participate, and at previously achieved follow-up rates (92%), we anticipate that we will have a final sample of 294 individuals who have completed both the initial and the follow-up interviews.

During 2005, the refugees served by CMCR were classified as follows:

- 35% Central American (Venezuelan, Columbian, others)
- 22% Eastern European (Ukrainian, Russian, Bulgarian, Rumanian, others)
- 24% East African (chiefly Somali, Bantu, and Ethiopian)
- 19% Other (West African, South American, Pacific Islanders, others)

While it is impossible to predict the exact combination that we will obtain when the sample is recruited, we expect these four groups to remain a viable means of classification.

IMPLEMENTATION

Human subjects approval has been given by RIBs at both the host university and CMCR. Project implementation will include six main elements:

- Start-up, interviewer training (month 1)
- Sample selection and initial interviews (months 2 and 3)
- Data management of initial data, preliminary analyses (months 4 through 19)
- Follow-up interviews (months 20 and 21)
- Data management and analysis (months 22 and 23)
- Report generation (months 18 through 24)

This time frame may seem compressed toward the end. The above schedule will be practical because the PI will be working full-time on the project at that time and because many of the tasks involved in performing final analyses and preparing the final report will already be done. For example, questions pertaining to the relationship of preimmigration trauma and arrival factors can

be answered before the follow-up data are collected. Furthermore, data management tasks for the follow-up data will be radically simplified because the first wave of data uses mainly the same constructs and measures. Data management issues will therefore be minimized.

START-UP AND INTERVIEWER TRAINING

Main tasks of this period will include training of the four agency staff who will implement the interviews as part of their standard resettlement work with the refugees. CMCR currently uses four workers in their initial resettlement and follow-up program, and each has agreed to participate in this study. Each staff member will receive two hours of training on administering the packet. This training will be done by the PI. Each staff member will pilot the interview on three volunteer refugees. These volunteers will be reimbursed for the initial interview but will not be interviewed a second time, nor will their data be electronically stored or kept longer than is necessary to ensure the interviews are being executed properly.

SAMPLE SELECTION AND INITIAL INTERVIEWING

As previously stated, all incoming refugee households in project months 2 and 3 will be eligible for inclusion. CMCR typically works intensively with clients during their first three months in St. Louis. Our project will sample individuals as they reach their sixtieth day in St. Louis. This represents an effort to capture information from individuals after they have had some initial exposure to America but before the acculturation process can really have started in earnest.

One household member will be randomly selected from each household and asked by the worker if he or she would like to participate in the study. It will be stressed that participation in the study will not have any effect on services provided to refugees. Consent forms will be completed on agreement to participate. We anticipate approximately four to ten individuals per day will be interviewed (about two per interviewer

Task	Month																							
	1	2	3	4	5	6	7	8	9	10	11	12	13	14	15	16	17	18	19	20	21	22	23	24
Start-up tasks																								
Interview training																								
Sample selection																								
Initial interviews																								
Data management																								
Preliminary analyses																								
18 month interviews																								
Final analyses																								
Report generation																								

on an average day). Day care will be offered at CMCR's onsite facility during the interview.

The interviews will be held in one of three small rooms used by CMCR for meeting with their clients. These are fairly standard clinical interview rooms with a desk, a chair for the interviewer, and several comfortable chairs. Interviews are anticipated to last approximately 45 minutes.

DATA MANAGEMENT AND PRELIMINARY ANALYSES

Data will be transferred from paper to Excel format by the PI as they become available. Analyses will be performed in SAS and will include basic descriptive and associative statistics. Analyses to be run include categorical coding of each main ethnic category to determine if there are any substantial ethnicity interactions that would require refinement of the analytic approach (e.g., including control variables or interaction terms for certain groups).

FOLLOW-UP INTERVIEWING

Follow-up interviews will be done in subject's homes as part of the standard CMCR 18-month follow-up. Subjects will be reminded that interviewing for this project is voluntary, and a second consent form will be signed.

FINAL DATA MANAGEMENT AND ANALYSES

Management of data from the second interviews will be the same as from the first. Analyses will be more sophisticated and will be based on the research questions specified above. Again, ethnicity-specific categorical coding will be done and analyses performed to determine if ethnicity has to be included in final models or if some groups need to be analyzed separately.

REPORT GENERATION

The following dissemination products are planned:

- Two to four peer-reviewed journal articles focusing on the research questions presented
- Two to three presentations at professional conferences
- One agency report, which will be given to CMCR

These products will be supplemented by the PI's doctoral dissertation, which is anticipated to be finalized and approved around month 30. We do not believe that the above schedule is overly optimistic because much of the writing (introduction, literature review, methods, and the like) can be done well in advance and because there will be substantial overlap between the above three categories of products.

HUMAN SUBJECTS AND IRB APPROVAL

Human subject clearance has been granted by the IRBs of both the supporting university and the collaborating agency. Risks to subjects are most likely during recall of traumatic events. Because all interviewers are clinically trained in refugee work and have strong connections to mental health agencies to whom they can refer, these risks were considered minimal. All data from the project will be deidentified on completion of the follow-up interviews to protect confidentiality.

SUMMARY: STRENGTHS AND LIMITATIONS OF PROPOSED WORK

Several of the limitations of the proposed work involve the sample. The restriction of the study to one metro area and one agency will reduce its generalizability. It will be necessary to replicate a similar approach at other locations to gain confidence in the degree to which external validity is established. Another problem relating to the sample is the restriction of the sampling frame to English-speaking adults. While this restriction minimizes concerns regarding instrumentation, it will limit the population to which findings can be confidently applied.

Another practical constraint limiting the work is time. Longer follow-up periods allow more time for practically significant changes and acculturation processes to manifest, but longer time frames also can increase subject attrition. Given the practical importance to refugees of establishing themselves quickly in their new country, we believe that the 18-month follow-up period is a good compromise.

Yet another potential limitation is lack of control of the country of origin of refugees who will be included in the sample. As previously described, 81% of 2005 refugees seen by the agency were from three general areas (Central America, Eastern Europe, and Eastern Africa). These numbers are not very dissimilar from 2004 numbers at the same agency and are also not dissimilar from national rates. It is hoped that a similar distribution of clients will obtain during the study period.

Theoretical strengths of the study include that this study will be the first study to use the emerging orthogonal model of acculturation on a refugee population in the United States. This is important because acculturation has been studied mainly as it relates to maintenance of positive attitudes toward and identification with the immigrant's country of origin. This has persisted despite the importance of studying the immigrant's relationship to the host country, which is not only empirically important (Nesdale & Mak, 2000) but is more theoretically consistent with Berry's acculturation model. The proposed work will also link the current refugee literature, which is primarily trauma based, to the larger immigrant literature on acculturation. There exists an almost startling disconnect between the literature on refugees, with its heavy emphasis on PTSD, and the literature on immigrants, with its primary emphasis on acculturation issues. This study looks at both factors.

Practical strengths of the study stem partly from the study's collaboration with a local refugee resettlement agency. The collaborating agency's preexisiting interview and follow-up process allows interviews to be carried out with a minimum of intrusion and at a much lower cost than would otherwise be possible.

Another practical advantage of the current study is that it builds directly on the work of Nesdale and his colleagues. This provides a ready set of instruments and some preliminary empirical findings that provided invaluable support to question and hypothesis formulation in the current work.

REFERENCES

Berry, J. W. & Kim, U. (1988) Acculturation and mental health. In P.R. Dasen, J. W. Berry, & N Sartorius, (Eds.) *Health and Cross-Cultural Psychology: Toward Applications.* (207–236). Newbury Park, CA. Sage.

Cusak, K. (2002) *Refugee experiences of trauma and PTSD; Effects on psychological, physical, and financial well-being.* Dissertation Abstracts International: Section B: The Sciences & Engineering Vol. 62(10), 47–78. Western Michigan University.

Hubbard, J., Realmuto, G., Northwood, A., & Masten, A. (1995). Comorbidity of psychiatric diagnoses with posttraumatic stress disorder in survivors of childhood trauma. *Journal of the American Academy of Child & Adolescent Psychiatry, 34(9),* 1167–1173.

Krishnan, A., & Berry, J. (1992). Acculturative stress and acculturation attitudes among Indian immigrants to the United States. *Psychology and Developing Societies, 4(2),* 187–212.

Miller, K., Worthington, G., Muzurovic, J., Tipping, S., & Goldman, A. (2002). Bosnian refugees and the stressors of exile: A narrative study. *American Journal of Orthopsychiatry, 72(3),* 341–354.

Mollica, R., Saraljic, N., Chemoff, M., Lavelle, J., Sarajilic-Vukovic, I., & Massagli, M. (2001). Longitudinal study of psychiatric symptoms, disability, mortality, and emigration among Bosnian refugees. *JAMA: Journal of the American Medical Association, 286(5),* 546–554.

Nesdale, D. (2002). Acculturation attitudes and the ethnic and host-country identification of immigrants. *Journal of Applied Social Psychology, 32(7),* 1488–1507.

Nesdale, D., & Mak, A. (2000). Immigrant acculturation attitudes and host country identification. *Journal of Community and Applied Social Psychology, 10,* 483–495.

Nesdale, D., & Mak, A. (2003). Ethnic identification, self-esteem and immigrant psychological health. *International Journal of Intercultural Relations, 27(1),* 23–40.

Nesdale, D., Rooney, R., & Smith, L. (1997). Migrant ethnic identity and psychological distress. *Journal of Cross-Cultural Psychology, 28,* 569–588.

OMB, (2005). *Budget of the United States Government, Fiscal Year 2006.* Washington, DC: USGPO.

Phinney, J. (1990). Ethnic identity in adolescents and adults: Review of research. *Psychological Bulletin, 108(3),* 499–514.

Phinney, J., Horenczyk, G., Liebkind, K., & Vedder, P. (2001). Ethnic identity, immigration and well-being: An interactional perspective. *Journal of Social Issues, 57(3),* 493–510.

Pio, E. (2005). Knotted strands: Working lives of Indian women migrants in New Zealand. *Human Relations, 58(10),* 1277–1299.

Preston, J. (2006). An application of Berry's model of acculturation to a Bosnian refugee population. (under review)

Preston, J. (2006). An Application of Berry's Model of Acculturation to a Bosnian Refugee Population, Unpublished Manuscript, Washington College, Collegetown Missouri.

Realmuto, G., Masten, A., Carole, L., & Hubbard, J. (1992). Adolescent survivors of massive childhood trauma in Cambodia: Life events and current symptoms. *Journal of Traumatic Stress, 5(4),* 589–599.

Rosenberg, M. (1965). *Society and the adolescent self-image.* Princeton, NJ: Princeton University Press.

Sherer, M., Maddux, J., Mercandandante, N., Prentice-Dunn, S., Jacobs, B., & Rogers, R. (1982). The self-efficacy scale: Construction and validation. *Psychological Reports, 51,* 673–671.

Ullman, C. (2001). Psychological adjustment among Israeli adolescent immigrants: A report on life satisfaction, self-concept, and self-esteem. *Journal of Youth and Adolescence, 30(4),* 449–464.

UNHCR. (2003). *2003 UNHCR Statistical Yearbook (provisional).* www.unhcr.org

Wang, Y., Andrade, L., & Gorenstein, C. (2005). Validation of the Beck Depression Inventory for a Portugeese-speaking Chinese community in Brazil. *Brazillian Journal of Medical and Biological Research, 38(3),* 399–408.

Westermeyer, J., & Uecker, J. (1997). Predictors of hostility in a group of relocated refugees. *Cultural Diversity and Mental Health, 3(1),* 53–60.

Witmer, T., & Culver, S. (2001). Trauma and resilience among Bosnian refugee families: A critical review of the literature. *Journal of Social Work Research & Evaluation, 2(2),* 173–187.

GLOSSARY

Administrative Data Common term for agency records, hopefully computerized.

Analysis of Covariance A statistical procedure that is a hybrid of ANOVA and regression. It allows for controlling for continuous independent variables using an ANOVA group means dependent variable.

Analysis of Variance A statistical procedure that tests whether or not means of groups defined by a categorical variable are significantly different.

Anonymity This is when you can't link data to specific subjects even if you wanted to.

Applied Science Science which is aimed toward practical outcomes, not the generation of knowledge for its own sake.

Archival Data Data existing in already recorded form (newspapers, computer records, etc.).

Assent When someone not legally able to give consent gives their agreement to participate in a research project.

Assumptions The basic requirements that must be satisfied in order to run a given statistical test.

Attrition When you lose people from your sample.

Basic Science Science which is aimed toward generating new knowledge. Less focus is given to immediate practical application.

Bivariate A statistical procedure that is examining the relationship between two variables.

Blocking This is when you break up the sample into sets (20–30yo, 30–40yo . . . , Black, White, Asian . . .) and then randomly assign people from each set to experimental and control/comparison conditions. It is sort of like running several mini-experiments, one for each set. This is a good way to make sure that you have good representation of key levels of each variable in both control/comparison and experimental conditions.

Breslow Day Tarone The test of homogeneity of Odds Ratios for a Cochran-Mantel-Haenszel Chi-square analysis. A non-significant result allows you to interpret the overall odds ratio provided by the CMH procedure.

Caseload Analysis Doing research to better understand the people you serve in your agency or individual caseload.

Case Study A design in which a single individual, group, organization, event, or whatever is studied. Sometimes called "N = 1" studies. A multiple case study is similar, except more than one individual or group is studied. In either case, case studies typically involve detailed and intensive examination of the subject.

Categorical Variables Variables which are not measured numerically or in which the differences between adjacent whole numbers (1, 2, 3 . . .) are not the same. The opposite of continuous variables.

Causality The idea that one thing makes something else happen. To prove causality the cause must come before the effect, it must be associated with the effect, and you must rule out spurious causality.

Censoring The removal of cases at a given time point in a longitudinal design due to subjects' withdrawal from the study for reasons other than the event or outcome of interest.

Chi-square A bivariate statistical test that examines the association between two nominal or limited ordinal variables.

Closed-Ended Question Questions which must be answered by checking a box or similar means.

Cluster Sampling Sampling people based on their affiliation with a larger grouping. *Example:* Sampling people from randomly selected zip codes.

Clustering of Observations Grouping of cases in your data based on some shared trait like coming from the same family or same census tract.

Cochran-Armitage Trend Test A statistical test that examines whether or not there is an ordered association between a nominal and an ordinal variable.

Cochran-Mantel-Haenszel Chi-square A statistical procedure that allows you to examine the association between two categorical variables while controlling for a third categorical variable.

Coding Down Starting with a coding scheme and then applying it to qualitative data.

Coding Scheme A set of labels which are applied to content units (bits of text representing ideas) in qualitative analysis.

Coding Up Starting with (usually narrative) qualitative data and then creating a coding scheme from that data.

Coefficient Alpha A test of the level of intercorrelations between items or variables. Usually used to examine the internal reliability of a scale measure.

Cohort Design A longitudinal design in which an age group of people is sampled over time. The same people need not be sampled.

Comparison Group Comparison groups are the same as control groups, but they have not been randomly assigned.

Compensation See "Inducements."

Conceptual Analysis A content analysis in which the researcher attempts to understand and track how often a given idea is expressed.

Conceptual Framework We use this term to mean the constructs and relationships you are interested in, how they might fit together, whom you are interested in (your sample), and what theories underlie your work.

Confidentiality This is when you know identifying information about subjects but keep it secret.

Consent When someone gives his or her agreement to participate in a research project. Consent must be informed, meaning subjects must know what they are getting into, especially any risks. See "Deception."

Construct Validity If a measure performs as it should according to theory, it has construct validity.

Constructs Clearly described concepts or ideas such as "self-esteem," or "income." Usually less well operationalized than variables.

Content Analysis Identifying specific words or terms or ideas in a text or spoken narrative.

Content Units One bit of narrative which expresses an idea. Content units are the things we code in accordance with a coding scheme.

Content Validity If a measure includes all key aspects of the thing it claims to measure, it has content validity.

Continuous Variables Variables in which the differences between adjacent whole numbers $(1, 2, 3 \ldots)$ are the same. Feet and pounds are continuous. Some people treat results from measures like Likert scales or summed scores from standardized instruments as continuous variables, others don't. The opposite of categorical variables.

Control The attempt by a researcher to get rid of unwanted factors in a study. *Example:* If you are measuring violent crimes on particular days and how that might be related to televised boxing matches, you might want to control for temperature, if you think that higher temperature may cause more violence.

Control Group Control groups are the groups in an experimental (not quasi-experimental) design that do not receive the experimental treatment. Randomly assigned.

Control Variables Variables which allow the researcher to remove unwanted "contaminating" factors so that the associations of other variables with the dependent variable can be more directly observed. *Example:* If you want to see if men and women are paid the same, you may want to control for years of employment.

Convenience Sampling When you just basically grab whoever is easiest to get.

Correlational Designs Designs used when you can specify constructs and wish to see if they relate to each other as theory says they should. Deductive.

Cox Regression Also known as Proportional Hazards and a type of Event History Analysis. This is a multivariate procedure used to examine a nominal or limited ordinal outcome while controlling for time elapsed from a study start and the event of interest or other exit from study or study end.

Criterion Validity If a measure agrees with other measures or indicators, it has criteria validity.

Cross-Group Contamination When you have multiple groups and people in the groups influence each other, causing the conditions of one group to "bleed over" into another group.

Cross-Sectional Usually refers to a study which collects data at one point in time only. Not longitudinal.

Debriefing Talking to research participants after they participate. The researcher tells them what was really going on. Necessary for studies using deception.

Deception Intentionally misleading research participants. Only permissible if there is no other way to do the work, if the work is important. There must be no possibility of greater than minimal harm and subjects must be debriefed afterward.

Deduction Deduction is when you move from theories or ideas to specific observations. Predicting what will happen based on a general theory is deduction.

Degrees of Freedom Related to the number of variables tested in a given statistical procedure. They are typically constructed by subtracting Number of variables − 1. Degrees of Freedom are related to how much power one has to detect significance.

Dependent Variables Variables which are influenced by or associated with (conceptually) prior independent variables.

Descriptive Designs Designs used when you can specify constructs but wish to understand them and their relationships to other constructs better. Inductive.

Dichotomous Variables Variables which are always one of two values (1 or 2, dead or living, male or female, etc.).

Directional Hypotheses Hypotheses which predict a relationship in a specific direction. *Example:* Males will ask for directions less often than females.

Distributions These relate to the way in which observed or predicted values are arranged relative to measures of central tendency: Mean median and mode. Different statistical tests are based on different assumptions about the underlying arrangement of values. The most commonly known distribution is the normal curve.

Dosage Designs Dosage designs include several experimental groups, each getting a different exposure to the experimental condition. For example, you might test the effects of running on health by having one set of people run 10 minutes per day, another group run 20 minutes per day, and a third group doing 30 minutes per day. A final group might serve as a control and not run at all.

Double-Blind When neither the subject nor the experimenters he contacts know which condition (experimental vs. control/comparison) the subject is in.

Dual Relationships When a researcher or practitioner also has another role with a subject or client (romantic, financial, etc.). Usually unethical.

Ecological Fallacy If you know something about a group of people (say, the average height of Asians) and claim that all specific members of that group are that way, then you are inappropriately generalizing from groups to individuals and are committing this fallacy.

Eigenvalue This is the cut-off point in Principal Components Analysis for determining when a "factor" should be kept in the ongoing analysis. It is a measure of how much variance in the total data is explained by a given factor.

Ethics Ways of behaving which help us to be consistent with our own values or professional values.

Ethnography This is the anthropological term for understanding and studying culture. It has been taken to mean any qualitative approach designed to understand a culture or group from the point of view of its members.

Ethnomethodology This is the branch of Sociology which deals with how people understand their world.

Evidence-Based Practice Rooted in Evidence-Based Medicine, EBP is a process for decision making in practice. It requires that you formulate an empirically answerable question, find and critique the best available evidence, and apply it in conjunction with client factors and your professional judgment.

Expectation Effects Expectation effects are threats to internal validity. Put simply, if the subject or the researcher anticipates that something might happen, that thing may be more likely to happen just for the reason of the expectation alone, and not because of any "real" effect of the independent variable.

Experimental Designs Designs using an experimental and a control/comparison group or comparison condition. Goal is to develop evidence that one thing causes another.

Experimental Group Experimental groups are the groups in an experimental or quasi-experimental design that get the experimental (new thing you are testing) treatment.

Exploratory Designs Designs used when you cannot specify constructs in advance. Goal is to discover key constructs and the relationships between them. Inductive.

External Validity The ability of a study to generalize to a given population. If you can't apply your findings to any group, you have poor external validity. Essentially synonymous with "generalizability."

Fabrication Making up your research findings. Not ethical.

Face Validity If something appears to make sense, it has face validity.

Factorial Designs Factorial designs are when you have two or more conditions (say, high and low intensity service) which are each also subjected to multiple conditions (say, group vs. individual counseling). In this example, you would have four groups: High-Group, High-Individual, Low-Group, Low-Individual. You can have far more groups, for example a 2 condition by 5 condition by 3 condition study would have $(2 \times 5 \times 3)$ 30 groups.

Falsification Lying about your research findings. Not ethical.

Feminist Research An approach to research which has a core set of assumptions about the status and oppression of women. Research is seen as a tool to liberate women from patriarchal oppression. Research techniques are often subjectivist, stressing women's own views of their worlds. Feminist research can also be entirely objectivist.

Fidelity Fidelity usually refers to the correct implementation of an experimental treatment. If you say you're testing if something works and you don't really do it right, then your study lacks fidelity and you can't say that you did a fair test.

Fisher Exact Test A statistical procedure used to measure the association of two nominal variables when the expected count in a cell is lower than 5.

Focus Groups A very common means of qualitative research where the interviewer uses a set of questions (a 'questioning route') and asks a group of (usually) 4–12 individuals to respond.

Friedman's Non-Parametric ANOVA A non-parametric alternative for a two-way or factorial ANOVA when the assumptions for the ANOVA cannot be met.

Generalizability The idea that your study should be able to be "generalized to" (applied to) some well defined population. Sometimes you might try to generalize to everyone, and sometimes you might try to generalize only to a small group (e.g., women over fifty seeking treatment for breast cancer in a given hospital). Essentially synonymous with "External Validity."

Generalized Estimating Equation A non-parametric multivariate model that can examine dichotomous or continuous outcomes. Typically used for repeated measures designs.

Geospatial analyses A family of statistical procedures that include consideration of a "case's" or "subject's" geographic location relative to another case or item of interest.

Grand Theory Grand theories are theories which attempt to explain whole domains or areas of inquiry. Examples include Freudian theory, Behaviorism, and Natural Selection.

Greenhouse-Geisser Epsilon This is a measure used in Repeated Measures ANOVA to help diagnose and correct for mild to moderate violations of sphericity. In addition to its diagnostic value (over .75 or under), it produces a modified *p*value for the ANOVA's F-test.

Grounded Scale Grounded scales present several options to the respondent, each of which is "anchored" in rich descriptive examples.

Grounded Theory Creating theory inductively from source information such as narratives.

Hawthorne Effect When people act differently just because they know they are being observed.

Hazard Rate Probability of an event at the midpoint of a time interval given lack of an event to that point.

Hazard Ratio Ratio of probabilities of an event at a given time point in a Cox Regression model. Practical interpretation is similar to an Odds Ratio (above 1 indicates an increase, below 1 indicates a decrease, and 1 indicates no association).

History A threat to internal validity. History is the idea that something that happens outside the study (e.g., current events, things that happen to a particular subject) may cause changes in your dependent variable.

Homogeneity of Variance A term used to describe consistent (or reasonably consistent) measures of variance for each group in t-test and ANOVA procedures.

Hosmer-Lemeshow Goodness of Fit A commonly used (but also commonly critiqued) diagnostic test used for model fit in logistic regression when continuous variables are included in the model.

Incidence The number of people who get something new (a cold, a need for service, etc.) over a given point in time. *Example:* The incidence of the common cold might be 2 per person per year.

Independent Variables Variables which predict, cause or are associated with a (conceptually) subsequent, dependent variable.

In-Depth Interviewing Talking to people and asking detailed questions so that you can better understand them.

Inducement Paying or otherwise giving something to someone to get them to participate in a research study. Large inducements which would get people to do things they really don't want to do are unethical.

Induction Induction is when you move from observations to theory. Darwin's ideas about natural selection were created inductively from his observations of different kinds of animals in different environmental contexts.

Informed consent A core principle of human subjects protection. People must know what they're agreeing to do in a research study. Deception is one exception but is tightly constrained (see Chapter 2).

Institutional Review Boards Bodies put in place by universities, agencies, or other organizations to assess requests for human subjects approval.

Instruments Tools to measure variables. Commonly used to refer to paper tests such as self-esteem scales.

Internal Validity If your design studies what you say it will study, we say you have strong internal validity.

Interrater Reliability If two people agree on how to rate something, they have interrater reliability.

Interval Scale Continuous variables which have no "true" zero. A true zero is when a value of zero means "not present."

For example, Fahrenheit does not have a true zero, but the Kelvin scale does.

Kappa This is a term used to describe the level of agreement between raters in a study. Over .80 is considered excellent agreement.

Knowledge Building The idea that science is a process in which prior work forms the basis for future work.

Kruskal-Wallis The non-parametric alternative procedure for a one-way ANOVA when the assumptions of the ANOVA cannot be met.

Kurtosis A measure of the "tallness" or "flatness" of a distribution. If a normal distribution is pushed down and flattened (like a pancake), this would be negative kurtosis (platykurtic). If a normal distribution is made taller and "skinnier" (like a skyscraper), then it has positive kurtosis (leptokurtic).

Latent Content The underlying ideas in a qualitative data source.

Levene's A diagnostic test for Homogeneity of Variance that can be used for one-way ANOVAs.

Likert Scale A scale where the subject chooses from numbered responses along a continuum of labeled numeric responses, ranging from terms such as "strongly disagree" to "strongly agree."

Log Rank Chi-square A test of bivariate association used in conjunction with bivariate survival curves to determine if there is an association between a variable and an outcome of interest while controlling for time. The test is most sensitive to later variation between levels of the independent variable.

Logistic Regression A multivariate statistical procedure commonly used to assess the association of either categorical or continous independent variables with a dichotomous or limited ordinal (called a multinomial logistic regression) outcomes variable.

Longitudinal Studies which collect data at different points in time.

Manifest Content The obvious, surface content in a qualitative data source.

Matching Trying to make a comparison group as much like the experimental group as possible. Usually involves selecting comparison subjects who are like the experimental subjects on certain key variables.

Maturation A threat to internal validity. Maturation is when the subject changes over time and you misinterpret these normal changes.

Mauchly's Criterion The diagnostic test used for assessing the assumption of sphericity in Repeated Measures ANOVA. A non-significant result means the assumption is met.

McNemar's A chi-square testing the association between paired nominal variables like pretest and posttest nominal variables.

Mean The average value of a variable measured at the interval, ratio, or multilevel ordinal levels.

Measurement Error Error due to failure to correctly measure the variable you are interested in. This can happen in many ways, see Chapter 5.

Measures of central tendency These are indicators of how a variable is distributed according to the average (mean), midpoint (median), and most frequent (mode) values.

Median This is a measure of the midpoint of a variable measured at the interval, ratio, or multilevel ordinal levels.

Midlevel or Midrange Theory Midlevel theories apply to many situations and contexts, but are not meant to cover entire domains of inquiry. Examples include attachment theory and crisis theory.

Mode This is a measure of the most common value for a given variable.

Model People will use the term "model" to refer to something as broad as a conceptual framework or as specific as a particular statistical analysis. Often, people mean a set of specified relationships between variables. *Example:* Maslach's model of burnout includes three constructs (emotional exhaustion, depersonalization, and personal accomplishment) which themselves have relationships to other constructs (worker effectiveness, intention to quit, etc.).

Model Fit A term used to describe how well a set of independent or control variables are aligning with the predicted values of the dependent variable of interest.

Mortality The loss of a subject from your sample.

Multicollinearity A term used to describe a situation in which two or more variables are so highly correlated that they cannot be used individually in a multivariate model due to its destabilizing effects on the parameter estimates.

Multiple Regression A multivariate statistical procedure commonly used to assess the association of either categorical or continuous independent variables with an outcome variable measured at the interval, ratio, or multilevel ordinal level.

Multistage Cluster Sampling Sampling people based on their affiliation with a series of nested groups. *Example:* Sampling people from five randomly selected classes in each of 20 randomly selected schools.

Multivariate A term used to describe a statistical model in which at least two independent or control variables are used to attempt to predict values of the outcome of interest.

Multivariate Analysis of Variance A statistical procedure used to measure simultaneous differences in more than one outcome variable while controlling for group membership.

N The full sample size of a study. *Example:* $N = 352$

n The sample size in a subgroup in a study, *Example:* full sample $N = 67$. females: $n = 34$.

Natural Experiments Experimental conditions which occur without investigator manipulation. Almost always quasi-experimental. For example, you might compare stress levels among people who were audited by the IRS and those who were not. Sometimes this is the only way something can be studied, as in the above example.

Needs Assessment Research attempting to understand what needs clients or potential clients may have.

Nominal Scale Variables which are identified by name (or similar) only. They are never continuous variables.

Non-Directional Hypotheses Hypotheses which do not predict a relationship in a specific direction. *Example:* Males and females will ask for directions at different rates.

Non-parametric A term used to describe statistical procedures that are not based on data being normally distributed.

Nonprobability Sampling When a sample is not randomly drawn, but is drawn based on convenience or is drawn for a specific reason, such as trying to sample extreme representatives of different groups.

Normality An assumption of parametric statistics, this means that a given variable is evenly distributed on either side of the mean and that the mean, median, and mode are all at the same place.

Normed Instrument An instrument which allows you to compare any person's score to population-based averages.

Nuremburg Code Ethical guidelines for human experimentation which were necessitated by the horrific conduct of Nazi "scientists" in World War II.

Objectivism An approach emphasizing countable or otherwise measurable observation.

Odds Ratio This measure is the odds of an event or outcome for one group divided by the odds of that same outcome for another group. Higher than 1, indicates that the group of interest has a greater likelihood of the event of interest than the comparison group. Lower than 1 indicates a decreased likelihood. An Odds Ratio of 1 indicates there is no association between the values for the groups and the values of the other variable.

Open-Ended Questions Questions which do not require selection from a list of responses. *Example:* "How would you describe your childhood?"

Operationalize To express something in a way that anyone else can simply understand and copy. In reference to variables, it means you have described the variable so well that anyone else can measure it just as you did. For example, saying you are going to "measure anxiety" is not well operationalized, but saying you are going to "measure anxiety using Bob's Anxiety Scale" is far more operationalized.

Ordinal Scale Variables which are identified by their rank order (1st, 2nd, etc.). They are not continuous.

Outcome Evaluation This term is generally used for research meant to determine how successful an agency or individual is in producing intended outcomes in clients.

Outliers Observations (data points) which are very different from other observations in your data. For example, if all children in a class are between 4'3'' and 4'6'', someone who is 5'5'' would be an outlier with regard to height.

Overdispersion This term is used in relation to model fit for logistic regression. It is an indicator that there is too much "distance" between the observed and expected values in the model.

Oversampling Taking more of a certain kind of subject than you would otherwise get by chance. If you were studying MSW students, you might oversample males to make sure you get enough in your sample. If you were studying Engineering students, you might oversample females.

Panel Design A longitudinal design in which the same group of people are measured over time.

Paradigm The most general way we have of understanding or looking at things. Thomas Kuhn's Structure of Scientific Revolutions suggests that some sciences are paradigmatic, meaning people agree on how to think about, talk about, and do them, and that other sciences are pre-paradigmatic, lacking this agreement. Many people feel the social sciences are preparadigmatic.

Parameter Estimate A term used to describe the value associated with the magnitude and direction of a relationship between an independent or control variable and the dependent variable.

Parametric A term used to describe statistical procedures that are based on data being normally distributed.

Parsimony The idea that you should keep frameworks and models simple. Constructs and relationships which are only of very minor importance should be excluded to keep a model simple and elegant.

Partial Correlation A statistical procedure that provides a measure of the association between two interval/ratio/or multilevel ordinal variables while "removing" the influence of a third (or more) variables.

Participant Action Research A form of research which stresses the involvement of community members in the research process. A strong value is placed on community ownership of the research process and the ability of the community to continue the research process after the researcher/consultant leaves.

Participant Observation When the researcher joins a social group in order to better understand that group.

Pearson Correlation This is the common bivariate parametric statistic used to examine the association between two interval/ratio/or multi-level ordinal variables. The statistic is measured on a scale from 0 (no association) to 1 (complete association).

Pearson Goodness of Fit A diagnostic test of model fit used in logistic regression when only categorical independent and control variables are used. A nonsignificant result indicates "good fit."

Phi correlation A measure of the magnitude of association that is used in conjunction with bivariate 2×2 chi-square in random designs. Like the Pearson correlation it is measured on a scale of 0 to 1.

Phrase Completion A scale which first presents an incomplete sentence (e.g., "this class was. . . .") and then invites the subject to respond along a numeric scale anchored by words or phrases which complete the sentence (e.g., "not useful [1] [2] [3] [4] [5] useful").

Plagiarism Taking credit for work not your own. Often failure to cite sources can be unintentional, but still constitutes plagiarism.

Population of Interest Those people you are trying to generalize to (find out about).

Positivism A complex set of ideas with many branches. Positivism is most simply described as the idea that you can observe things, build theories (laws) about what you see, and that these theories can help you understand and control things. There is an underlying assumption that there are basic laws which can be discovered and that we can progressively build more knowledge and expand our understanding of these laws through continued empirical observation and experimentation. Positivism is seen by some as a practical means of approaching social science, but is seen as overly restrictive and dehumanizing by others.

Post hoc test A test used after an ANOVA approach is used to detect whether some difference between group means exists. These tests pinpoint which groups differ and control for bias introduced by running multiple comparison tests.

Postmodernism A reaction to "modernism" which asserts that mathematics, science, and other forms of objective knowledge are nothing more than an attempt by those in power to assert and defend their status by controlling the reality of others. Postmodernists seek to "deconstruct" such knowledge. They value understanding individual "narratives."

Power A term used to describe the ability of a given study to be able to detect significant difference based on the anticipated magnitude of the effect or association as well as the sample size.

Pretest / Posttest A method of research in which scores before and after something (usually an experimental condition) are compared.

Prevalence The number of people who have something (a cold, a need for service, etc.) at a given point in time. *Example:* The prevalence of the common cold today might be that 10 million people have it right now.

Principal Components A statistical procedure commonly used for variable reduction—for example when variables are too highly correlated (multicollinearity) to be included in a model separately but the researcher hopes to retain the uncorrelated value of those variables. It can also be used to verify the existence of subscales in a measure but should not be used if items are being explored to find underlying (unmeasured or latent) connections. Then a slightly different procedure called *factor analysis* is employed. Principal components analysis can produce a set of factors or components that contain all the unduplicated variance included in the variables that load on a component.

Probability This term is used to describe the likelihood of something occurring or the existence of some relationship in your data. If something is highly likely to happen, but there is a chance that it might not we say that it has a high probability of happening. Statistics are based on the idea of probability: how likely is this finding to occur given my sample size and variables included?

Probability Sampling When a sample is randomly drawn from a population of interest.

Program Monitoring Research intended to determine how an agency and its members are functioning.

Prospective Study A design in which a sample is followed forward through time.

Pseudo r-square A statistic that attempts to measure the predictive utility of a logistic regression model. Its purpose is analogous to the r-square provided in parametric statistics, but it is not the same type of measure of variance explained. The level of acceptance among statisticians and researchers of this statistic varies.

Pseudoscience Claiming to be scientific when you're not. Pseudoscience includes the following characteristics: Lack of attention to evidence, particularly evidence which argues against the points being "proven," arguing from pre-existing conclusions, resistance to change in conclusions, unwillingness to engage in tests which could falsify the position.

Purposive Sampling When you try to sample particular kinds of subjects, not necessarily the most representative subjects.

Qualitative Research mainly focused on determining meaning. Narrative data is most commonly used.

Quantitative Research mainly focused on numeric or categorical variables.

Quasi-Experimental Design Experimental design which do not have randomly assigned control groups. Instead, they may have comparison groups or comparison conditions. Not as powerful in assessing causality due to the inability to rule out spurious factors.

Random Assignment A procedure whereby subjects have equal chances of being placed in experimental and control groups. Supports internal validity.

Random Selection A procedure whereby subjects in the sample frame each have equal chances of being put into the study sample. Supports external validity.

Ratio Scale Ratio Scales are forms of measurement in which the distance between each "unit" (number) is the same and there is a "true zero" (meaning that a score of zero means "none"). For example, the Fahrenheit scale is not a ratio scale, because zero degrees Fahrenheit does not mean "no heat present." The Kelvin scale (that starts at absolute zero—no heat present) is a ratio scale.

Receiver Operating Curve In social science this refers to a graphic display of the predictive power of a logistic regression model. The 'c' statistic describes the area under the curve. The larger the area the better.

Regression to the Mean If you measure extreme cases, chances are that the next time you measure them they will be less extreme.

Relational Analysis A content analysis focusing on how a given word or phrase is used.

Relative Risk A measure of the relative incidence of an outcome for one group compared to another. It is not used in cross-sectional or case control studies.

Reliability When a measure can be repeated consistently and continues to get the same result. Reliability does not prove validity (accuracy). A broken bathroom scale might reliably read "450 pounds" every time, but it may also be wrong every time.

Repeated Measures ANOVA A statistical procedure that examines whether the mean of a variable of interest varies across three or more time periods.

Replication The idea that scientific tests have to be repeated by many different people before their findings can be well accepted.

Research Aim The general purpose of the project. *Example:* To determine if state spending and high school achievement are associated.

Research Hypotheses Operationalized and testable statements derived from research questions. Hypotheses must include specific variables. *Example:* At the state level, higher per-pupil spending will be associated with higher graduation rates.

Research Question More specific than an aim, a question expresses what the research is trying to answer. Example: Do states that invest more money in education have more success in graduating students?

Response Rate The percentage of people in your sampling frame that you approach from whom you are able to collect data from.

Retrospective Getting data about what happened in the past. Can involve recalling past events or referring to existing archival sources.

R-square A measure of the amount of variation "explained" by the independent and control variables in a parametric model.

Sample Those people who end up in your study.

Sampling Frame Those people who might be selected to be in your study.

Saturation In qualitative research, when sufficient subjects have been interviewed to give the researcher a clear idea of all the major themes.

Scientific Method Sometimes meant to refer to the process whereby a theory is consulted, a hypothesis is formed, and an empirical test is done to rigorously test that hypothesis. To the degree that the hypothesis is supported, we gain more support for the underlying theory. To the degree you find something disconfirming or unexpected, the theory is revised.

Scree plot A graphic plot that can be used in conjunction with the eigenvalue to determine how many components or factors to retain in a Principal Components procedure. Components that explain more individual variance are separated by greater distance from other components.

Secondary Data Data which was created for some other purpose but is used by you for your project.

Semantic Differential A question is asked (e.g., "How would you describe your congressman?") and then a numeric scale is presented, anchored by opposite characteristics (e.g., "Dishonest [1] [2] [3] [4] [5] Honest").

Semi-Structured Instrument An instrument with some structured items and some broad open-ended items which allows the interviewer latitude in his or her questioning.

Single-Blind When the subject doesn't know what condition (experimental vs. control/comparison) he is in but the experimenter does.

Skip Patterns Sometimes a subject will answer a question (e.g., "have you ever used illegal drugs?") which will make some further questions (e.g., "what types of illegal drugs have you used?") unnecessary. Skip patterns tell the interviewer to "skip over" these unnecessary questions. in the example above, after the first question, there might be a statement "If 'no', skip to item 345f". Skip patterns are very useful in computer aided interviewing.

Snowball Sampling When you get your current subjects to suggest more people you should study. Very useful in studying otherwise impossible to locate groups. For example, finding a sample for a study of users of a new drug might not be possible in any other way.

Social Constructionism The idea that the world is best understood not as a purely objective reality, but in terms of how people and societies give ("construct") meanings.

Social Desirability A threat to internal validity. When someone responds in an inaccurate way to look good.

Social Justice Variously described by different authors. Some say it is equal opportunity, some say it is equal distribution or equal outcomes. Some say it is lack of oppression. John Rawls *A Theory of Justice* is among the most commonly cited sources. His "difference principle" states that inequality is only permissible in that it helps those worst off.

Spearman Correlation A non-parametric alternative for the Pearson Correlation that can handle violations of normality and more limited ordinal variables. Its practical interpretation is identical to the Pearson Correlation.

Specification Error A term that describes a situation in multivariate models when variables that should be included are not or variables that should not be included are included.

Sphericity A term that describes the assumption in Repeated Measure ANOVA that the subjects are being effected in a similar way over time.

Spurious Causality The idea that things besides the cause one expect may be causing the effect you find.

Standardized Estimate This term is used to an adjustment that is made to parameter estimates that places all the variables used in the model on a similar scale so that the magnitude of the associations of different variables can be compared.

Standardized Instruments Instruments which have been used many times and show good evidence of validity

Statistical significance This term means that the results of the analysis were unlikely to have occurred by chance. Usually $p = .05$ is the cutoff, meaning that only 5 times out of 100 would you obtain a different result.

Stratification Sampling based on groups or "strata." For example, you might first break up a college population into racial categories, and then randomly select 30 people from each racial strata.

Structured Instrument Instruments with preset questions, usually not just open-ended ones.

Subjectivism An approach emphasizing meaning and personal points of view.

Subscale Reliability If a subscale's elements "hang together" as demonstrated by a high coefficient alpha, that subscale has subscale reliability.

Suppressor This term describes an independent or control variable in a multivariate model that is associated with another independent or control variable but is not associated with the dependent variable. These two variables are not associated so highly that multicolinearity is a problem.

Survival Curve This is a graphic display of the proportion of an event of interest at a specific time interval given not having the event at a prior interval. Can be used to display bivariate associations.

Test-Retest Reliability If a test can be repeated and gives the same result, you have test-retest reliability.

Theory Theory is various described as something as simple as an idea or something as complex as a formally operationalized set of relationships between constructs.

Time-Series Design Design which incorporates time. This term is often used to refer to panel, cohort, trend and various kinds of quasi-experimental designs.

Treatment as Usual When subjects get the treatment they would normally get. This is generally used in comparison to the experimental treatment.

Trend Design A design in which (different) people are measured with regard to something year after year. For example, a study looking at each new group of incoming college freshmen would be a trend study.

True Experimental Design Design using at least one experimental group and at least one control group to which subjects are randomly assigned. Goal is always to test causality. This design provides maximum control over spurious causality.

T Test A statstical method for determining if continuous scores vary between two groups.

Tukey HSD The name of a commonly used Post Hoc Measure for ANOVA models.

Unit of Analysis The level at which you sample, measure and score. Can be people, organizations, zip codes, countries, whatever. Usually your data set has your unit of analysis as rows and variables as columns.

Univariate A term used to describes various measures of a single variable such as central tendency, missing values, etc.

Universal Population Everyone.

Validity For instruments, if the instrument measures what it should be measuring. For designs, if the design measures what it is intended to measure. Reliability is a necessary, but not sufficient, prerequisite for validity.

Values Moral principles about what is good and which (hopefully) influence our actions. They cannot be evaluated scientifically.

Variability How much a given variable moves away from measures of central tendency. In statistics, some variability is needed but too much can be a problem.

Variables Highly operationalized and measurable constructs with categorical or continuous values attached. Must be so well operationalized that it is clear how to measure them. They must vary (not all be the same) to be useful.

VIF (Variance Inflation Factor) This is a measure of multicollinearity between variables in a multivariate model. Around 1 is very good and over 10 is very bad. Values in between should be assessed carefully by the researcher.

Wilcoxon Chi-square A measure of the bivariate relationship between a categorical variable and an outcome of interest while controlling for time. This test is more sensitive to differences between levels of the categorical variable that occur early in the study.

Wilcoxon Rank Sum This is the non-parametric alternative to the independent samples *t* test.

Wilcoxon Signed Rank This is the non-parametric alternative to the paired samples t-test.

Wilk's Lambda This is the test statistic used in Repeated Measures ANOVA when the assumption of sphericity is moderately to severely violated.

Withholding Treatment Some studies use untreated "wait lists" to provide control or comparison groups. These subjects do not get treatment initially, but do receive it later. Ethical problems may arise, see Chapter 2.

REFERENCES

Agresti, A. (2002). *Categorical data analysis.* (2nd ed.). New York: Wiley.

Allison, P. (1991). *Logistic regression: Using the SAS system.* New York: Wiley & Sons.

Allison, P. (1995). *Survival analysis using the SAS System: A practical guide.* Cary, NC: SAS Institute Inc.

Allison, P. (2002). *Missing data. Series: Quantitative applications in the social sciences.* Thousand Oaks, CA: Sage Publications.

Allison, P. (2005). *Fixed Effects Regression Methods for Longitudinal Data Using SAS.* Cary, NC: SAS Institute Inc.

Alonzo, K. (2004). The Johnson Neyman Procedure as an alternative to ANCOVA. *Western Journal of Nursing Research 26*(7), 804–812.

American Psychiatric Association. (2000). *Diagnostic and Statistical Manual of Mental Disorders, Fourth Edition, Text Revision (DSM-IV-TR).* Washington, DC: APA.

American Psychological Association. (2001). *Publication manual of the American Psychological Association* (5th ed.). Washington, DC: American Psychological Association.

American Psychological Association. (2003). *Code of Ethics.* Retrieved December 30, 2005, from www.apa.org/ethics/.

American Psychological Association. (2005). *Policy Statement on Evidence Based Practice in Psychology,* APA Council of Representatives, Approved August, 2005, available online at http://www2.apa.org/practice/ebpstatement. pdf, 3/29/07

American Sociological Association. (1999). *Code of Ethics.* Retrieved December 30, 2005, from www.asanet.org/ galleries/default-file/Code%20of%20Ethics.pdf.

Amico, K., Toro-Alfonso, J., & Fisher, J. (2004). An empirical test of the information, motivation and behavioral skills model of antiretroviral therapy adherence. *Aids Care, 17*(6), 661–673.

Asch, S. E. (1955). Opinions and social pressure. *Scientific American, 193,* 31–35.

Australian Association of Social Workers. (1999). *The development of competency standards for mental health social workers: Final report.* Kingston, Australia.

Baguley, T. (2004). *An introduction to sphericity.* Retrived February 11, 2007, from www.abdn.ac.uk/~psy317/ personal/files/teaching/spheric.htm.

Bamberger, M., Rugh, J., Mabry, L. (2006). *Real world evaluation. Working under budget, time, data and political contraints.* Thousand Oaks, CA: Sage.

Barnes, S. (2005). Black American Feminisms Bibliography. University of California, Santa Barbara [online].

Retrieved December 4, 2006, from www.library.ucsb. edu/subjects/blackfeminism/introduction.html.

Bemak, F., Chung, R., Pederson, P. (2003). *Counseling refugees: A psychosocial approach to innovative multicultural interventions.* Westport, CT: Greenwood Press.

Bendiksen, R., Bodin, G., & Jambois, K. (2001). The bereaved crisis worker: Sociological practice perspective on critical incident death, grief, and loss. Lund, D. A. (Ed.). *Men coping with grief* (pp. 253–272). Amityville, NY: Baywood Publishing.

Berger, P., & Luckman, T. (1967). *The social construction of reality, a treatise in the sociology of knowledge.* New York: Anchor/Random House.

Berger, P. L., and Luckmann, T. (1966). *The Social Construction of Reality: A Treatise in the Sociology of Knowledge.* Garden City, NY: Doubleday.

Berry, J., Poortinga, Y., Segal, M., & Dasen, P. (2002). *Cross-cultural psychology : Research and applications.* Cambridge, UK: Cambridge University Press.

Berry, J. W., & Kim, U. (1988). Acculturation and mental health. In P. R. Dasen, J. W. Berry, & N Sartorius (Eds.). *Health and cross-cultural psychology: Toward applications* (pp. 207–236). Newbury Park, CA: Sage.

Bibus, A. (1993). In pursuit of a missing link: the influence of supervision on social worker's practice with involuntary clients. *Clinical Supervisor, 11*(2), 7–22.

Bleyer, L., & Joiner, K. (2002). Conducting a needs assessment in a school setting. In R. Constable, S. McDonald, & J. Flynn (Eds.). *School social work. Practice, policy and research perspectives* (5th ed.). Chicago, IL: Lyceum.

Boggs, S. (1965). Urban crime patterns. *American Sociological Review, 30,* 899–908.

Bolker, J. (1998). *Writing your dissertation in fifteen minutes a day: A guide to starting, revising, and finishing your doctoral thesis.* New York: Henry Holt and Company.

Boynton, P, Wood, G., & Greenhalgh, T. (2004). Reaching beyond the White middle classes: Hands on guide to questionnaire design. *British Medical Journal, 328,* 1433–1436.

Brantingham, P. J., & Brantingham, P. (1981). *Environmental criminology.* Prospect Heights, IL: Waveland Press.

Brantingham, P. J., & Brantingham, P. (1984). *Patterns in Crime.* New York: Macmillan.

Bronfenbrenner, U. (1979). *The ecology of human development: Experiments by nature and design.* Cambridge, MA: Harvard University Press.

Brown, J. (1997, April). Skewness and kurtosis. *Shiken: JALT Testing & Evaluation SIG Newsletter, 1*(1), 16–18.

Brown, T., Chorpita, B., Korotitsch, W., & Barlow, D. (1997). Psychometric properties of the Depression Anxiety Stress Scales (DASS) in clinical samples. *Behaviour Research and Therapy, 35,* 79–89.

Bryk, A., & Weisberg, H. (1977). Use of non-equivalent control group design when subjects are growing. *Psychological Bulletin, 84,* 950–962.

Burns, B., & Hoagwood, K. (1999). *Community treatment for youth: Evidence-based interventions for severe emotional and behavioral disorders.* New York: Oxford University Press.

Burns C. & Harm N.J. (1993). Emergency nurses' perceptions of critical incidents and stress debriefing. *Journal of Emergency Nursing,* October, 431–436.

Burrell, L. (1996). *The impact of experience, exposure and support on emergency worker health.* Dissertation Abstracts International, Section B: The Sciences and Engineering. Vol. 57(6-B). 4067.

Buttell, F. (2001). Moral development among court-ordered batterers: Evaluating the impact of treatment. *Research on Social Work Practice, 11*(1), 93–107.

Byrne, D. (2002). *Interpreting quantitative data.* Thousand Oaks, CA: Sage.

Cai, L. & Weinfort, K. (1999). A SAS/IML Module for the Johnson-Neyman procedure. *Applied Psychological Measurement,* 23, 308.

Center for Health Evidence. (2005). *User's guide to evidence-based Practice.* Retrieved November 20, 2006, from www.cche.net.

Centerwall, B. (1995). Race, socioeconomic status, and domestic homicide. *JAMA: Journal of the American Medical Association, 273*(22), 1755–1758.

Chen, H. (2004). Practical program evaluation. Assessing and improving planning, implementation and effectiveness. Thousand Oaks, CA: Sage.

Cochran, W. (1977). *Sampling techniques* (3rd ed.). New York: John Wiley and Sons.

Cody, R., & Smith, J. (2006). *Applied Statistics and the SAS Programming Language* (5th ed). Upper Saddle River, NJ: Pearson Prentice-Hall.

Cody, R. P., and Pass, R. (1995). *SAS® programming by example.* Cary, NC: SAS Institute Inc.

Connoly, J., & Lester, D. (2001). Suicide rates in Irish counties: 10 years later. *Irish Journal of Psychological Medicine, 18*(3), 87–89.

Cooper, M. (1998). *Synthesizing research: A guide for literature reviews.* Thousand Oaks, CA: Sage.

Corcoran, K., & Fischer, J. (2000). *Measures for clinical practice, a sourcebook* (3rd ed.). London: The Free Press.

Council on Social Work Education. (2001). *Educational Policy and Accreditation Standards. Available online at http://www.cswe.org/NR/rdonlyres/111833A0-C4F5–475C-8FEB-EA740FF4D9F1/0/EPAS.pdf 3/29/07*

Cusak, K. (2002). *Refugee experiences of trauma and PTSD; Effects on psychological, physical, and financial well-being.* Western Michigan University.

Cutchin, M., & Churchill, R. (1999). Scale, context and causes of suicide in the United States. *Social Science Quarterly, 80*(1), 97–114.

Dallal, G. (2001). *Multiple comparison procedures.* Tufts University. Retrieved February 11, 2007, from www.tufts.edu/~gdallal/mc.htm.

Defey, D. (1995). Helping health care staff deal with perinatal loss. *Infant Mental Health Journal, 16*(2), 102–111.

Dehejua, R. & Whaba, S. (2002). Propensity score-matching methods for nonexperimental causal studies. *The Review of Economics and Statistics, 84*(1), 151–161.

Denzin, A., & Lincoln, Y. (2005). *The Sage handbook of qualitative research* (3rd ed.). Thousand Oaks, CA: Sage.

Department of Quantitative Health Sciences. (2005). ROC Analysis. Cleveland Clinic Foundation. Retrieved April 1, 2007, from www.bio.ri-cof.org/html/rocanalysis

Der, G., & Everitt, B. (2001). *Handbook of statistical analyses using SAS* (2nd ed.). Boca Raton: Chapman & Hall.

Devellis, R. (2003). *Scale Development: Theory and Applications.* Thousand Oaks, CA: Sage.

Dowd, L. (2002). Female perpetrators of partner aggression: Relevant issues and treatment. *Journal of Aggression, Maltreatment and Trauma, 5*(2) 73–104.

Drachman, D. (1992). A stage-of-migration framework for service to immigrant populations. *Social Work, 37*(1), 68–72.

Drake, B. (1996a). Consumer and worker perceptions of key child welfare competencies. *Children and Youth Services Review, 18*(3), 261–279.

Drake, B. (1996b). Unravelling unsubstantiated. *Child Maltreatment, 1*(3), 261–271.

Drake, B., Jonson-Reid, M., Way, I., & Chung, S. (2003). Substantiation and recidivism. *Child Maltreatment, 8*(4), 248–260.

Drake, B. & Pandey, S. (1996). Understanding the relationship between neighborhood poverty and child maltreatment. *Child Abuse and Neglect, 20*(11), 1003–1018.

Dubowitz, H., & Depanfilis, D. (2000). *Handbook for child protection practice.* Thousand Oaks, CA: Sage.

Durkheim, E. (1897). *Le suicide.* Paris: Felix Alcan.

Edmonds, T. (1997). *Eye movement desensitization and reprocessing: Evaluating its effectiveness in reducing trauma symptoms in adult female survivors of adult sexual abuse.* Unpublished doctoral dissertation, University of Texas at Austin.

Eid, M., & Diener, E. (2005). *Handbook of multimethod measurement in psychology.* Washington, D.C.: APA.

Elliott, J. (2005). *Using narrative in social research: Qualitative and quantitative approaches.* Thousand Oaks, CA: Sage Publications.

Ender, P. (2002). Linear Statistical Models Course. Retrieved August 2006 at http://gseis.ucla.edu/course/ed230bci/cnotes1/check.html

Evidence-Based Medicine Working Group. (1992). A new approach to teaching the practice of medicine.

*Journal of the American Medical Association,
268,* 2425.

Faulkner, A. & Thomas, P. (2002). *User-led research and
evidence-based medicine. British Journal of Psychiatry,
180(1),* 1–3.

Fetterman, D. (1998). *Ethnography step by step* (2nd ed.)
Applied Social Research Methods Series, Vol.17.
Thousand Oaks, CA: Sage.

Fetterman, D., Kaftarian, S., & Wandersman, A. (Eds.).
(1996). *Empowerment evaluation knowledge and tools
for self-assessment and accountability.* New York:
Guilford.

Field, A. (2005). *Discovering statistics using SPSS for
Windows* (2nd ed.). London: Sage.

Fieser, J. (2005). Ethics. In *The Internet Encyclopedia of
Philosophy.* University of Tennessee at Martin.
Retrieved February 8, 2007, from
www.utm.edu/research/iep/e/ethics.htm.

Fitzmaurice, G., Laird, N. & Ware, J. (2004). *Applied
longitudinal analysis.* NY: Wiley.

Flynn, R. (2001). External influences on workplace compe-
tence: Improving services to children and families.
In Foley, P., Roche, J., et al. (Eds.). *Children in society:
Contemporary theory, policy and practice* (pp. 177–184).
Buckingham, UK: Open University Press.

Foster, E. M. (2003). Propensity score matching. An illustrative analysis of dose response. *Medical Care, 41*(10),
1183–1192.

Fox, J. G., & Embrey, E. D. (1972). Music—an aid to productivity. *Applied Ergonomics, 3*(4), 202–205.

Freund, R., & Littell, R. (2000). *SAS system for regression*
(3rd ed.). (Wiley Series in Probability and Statistics).
Cary, NC: SAS.

Friel, C. (no date). *Multiple linear regression.* Criminal
Justice Center, Sam Houston University. Retrieved
March 10, 2007, from www.shsu.edu/˜icc_cmf/ cj_742/
multipleRegression.doc.

Furnham, A., & Bradley, A. (1997). Music while you work:
The differential distraction of background music on the
cognitive test performance of introverts and extraverts.
Applied Cognitive Psychology, 11, 445–455.

Furnham, A., & Strbac, L. (2002). Music is as distracting as
noise: The differential distraction of background music
and noise on the cognitive test performance of introverts and extraverts. *Ergonomics, 45*(3), 203–217.

Gaines, J. (2004). Evidence-based practice in school social
work: A process in perspective. *Children & Schools,*
25(2), 71–86.

Gambrill, E. (2001). Social work: An authority-based profession. *Research on Social Work Practice, 11,* 166–175.

Garfinkel, H. (1967). *Studies in ethnomethodology.*
Englewood Cliffs, NJ: Prentice-Hall.

Garson, G. (2005). Multiple comparison procedures PA 765
Statnotes: An Online Textbook. Available at
http://www2.chass.ncsu.edu/garson/pa765/ANOVA.htm.

Garson, G. (2005). Nominal association: Phi, contingency
coefficient, Tschuprow's T, Cramer's V, lambda, uncertainty coefficient. *PA 765 Statnotes: An Online
Textbook.* Retrieved March 1, 2007, from www2.chass.
ncsu.edu/garson/pa765/assocnominal.htm.

Geison, G. (1995). *The private science of Louis Pasteur.*
Princeton, NJ: Princeton University Press.

General Accounting Office. (1997, February). State's
progress in implementing family preservation and
support services, GAO/ HEHS-97-34.

Gerlock, A. (1997). New directions in the treatment of men
who batter women. *Health Care for Women
International, 18*(5), 481–493.

Gillespie, D. (1995). Ethical issues in research. In R. L.
Edwards, J. G. Hopps, & R. Steiner (Eds.), *Encyclopedia
of social work* (19th ed., pp. 884–893). Silver Spring,
MD: NASW Press.

Girden, E. (1996). *Evaluating research articles from start to
finish.* Thousand Oaks, CA: Sage.

Glaser, B., & Strauss, L. (1967). *The discovery of grounded
theory: strategies for qualitative research.* Chicago, IL:
Aldine.

Glisson, C., & Durick, M. (1988). Predictors of job satisfaction and organizational commitment in human service
organizations. *Administrative Quarterly, 33,* 61–81.

Glisson, C., & Hemmelgarn, A. (1998). The effects of
organizational climate and interorganizational
coordination on the quality and outcomes of children's
service systems. *Child Abuse & Neglect, 22*(5), 401–421.

Gonick, L., & Smith, W. (1993). *The cartoon guide to
statistics.* New York: Harper Collins.

Gubrium, J., & Holstein, J. (2001). *Handbook of interview
research: Context & method.* Thousand Oaks, CA: Sage.

Gustavson, N., & MacEachron, A. (2002). Death and the
child welfare worker. *Children and Youth Services
Review, 24*(12), 903–915.

Halam, S., Price, J., & Katsarou, G. (2002). The effects
of background music on primary school pupil's test
performance. *Educational Studies, 28*(2), 111–122.

Hammersly, M., & Atkinson, P. (1997). *Ethnography:
Principles and practice.* London: Biddles.

Hamsley, J. (2001). *The efficacy of domestic violence treat-
ment: Implications for batterer intervention programs.*
Unpublished doctoral dissertation. Memphis State
University, Memphis, Tennessee.

Haney, C., Banks, W. C., & Zimbardo, P. G. (1973). Interpersonal
dynamics in a simulated prison. *International Journal of
Criminology and Penology, 1,* 69–97.

Hanusa, D. (1994). *A comparison of two group treatment
conditions in reducing domestic violence.* Unpublished
doctoral dissertation, University of Wisconsin, Madison.

Hardin, J., & Hilbe, J. (2003). *Generalized estimating
equations.* New York: Chapman & Hall.

Harkness, J., Van de Vijver, F. & Mohler, P. (2002). *Cross-
cultural survey methods.* Hoboken, NJ: Wiley-
Interscience.

Harries, K. (1974). *Geography of Crime and Justice.* New
York: McGraw-Hill.

Harries, K. (1990). *Serious violence: Patterns of homicide and assault in America.* Springfield, IL: Charles C. Thomas.

Harries, K. (1995). The ecology of homicide and assault: Baltimore city and county, 1989–91. *Studies on Crime & Crime Prevention, 4*(1), 1995, 44–60.

Harvey, G. (2003). *Excel for dummies.* Hoboken, NJ: Wiley.

Hatcher, L., & Stepanski, E. (1994). *A step by step approach to using the SAS System for univariate and multivariate statistics.* Cary, NC: SAS Institute Inc.

Hawson, C., Yule, P., Laurent, D., & Vogel, C. (2002). *Internet research methods: A practical guide for the social and behavioural sciences.* Thousand Oaks, CA: Sage.

Hedeker, D. (2005). *Longitudinal data analysis. Programs, files, datasets and examples.* University of Illinois at Chicago. Retrieved February 8, 2007, from http://tigger.uic.edu/~hedeker/long.html.

Hedeker, D., & Gibbons, R. (2006). *Applied longitudinal data analysis.* Hoboken, NJ: Wiley.

Hedeker, D., & Gibbons, R. (2006). *Longitudinal data analysis.* Hoboken, NJ: John Wiley & Sons, Inc.

Hedeker, D., & Rose, J. (2000). The natural history of smoking: A pattern-mixture random-effects regression model. In J. Rose, L. Chassin, C. Presson, & S. Sherman (Eds.). *Multivariate applications in substance abuse research. New methods for new questions.* Mahwah, NJ: Lawrence Erlbaum.

Helberg, C. (1995). Pitfalls of Data Analysis (or How to Avoid Lies and Damned Lies) Workshop: the Third International Applied Statistics in Industry Conference in Dallas, TX, June 5–7, 1995.Retrieved February 5, 2007, from www.execpc.com/~helberg/pitfalls.

Heron, G. (2004). Evidencing anti-racism in student assignments. *Qualitative Social Work, 3*(3), 277–295.

Himle, D., Jayaratne, S., & Thyness, P. (1991). Buffering effects of four social support types on burnout among social workers. *Social Work Research and Abstracts, 29,* 22–27.

Hines, T. (2003). *Pseudoscience and the paranormal.* New York: Prometheus Books.

Hite, S. (1976). *The Hite Report: A Nationwide Study of Female Sexuality.* New York: MacMillan Publishing.

Hock, R. (2004). *Forty studies that changed psychology* (4th ed.). Englewood Cliffs, NJ: Prentice Hall.

Holloway, E., & Neufeldt, S. (1995). Supervision, its contributions to treatment efficacy. *Journal of Consulting and Clinical Psychology, 63*(2), 207–213.

Hong, L., & Duff, R. (2002). Modulated participant-observation: Managing the dilemma of distance in field research. *Field Methods, 14*(2): 190–196.

Hosmer, D., Hosmer, T., Cessie, S. & Lemeshow, S. (1997). A comparison of goodness-of-fit tests for the logistic regression model. *Statistics in Medicine, 16,* 965–980.

Howard, M., Bricout, J., Edmond, T., Elze, D., Jenson, J. (2003). Evidence-Based Practice Guidelines.

Encyclopedia of Social Work, 19th ed., 2003 Supplement, 48–59, Washington D.C.: NASW Press.

Huitema, B. (1980). The analysis of covariance and alternatives. NY: Wiley.

Hussey, J., Marshall, J., English, D., Knight, E., Lau, A., Dubowitz, H., Kotch, J. (2005) Defining maltreatment according to substantiation: A distinction without a difference? *Child Abuse and Neglect: The international Journal, 29*(5), 479–492.

Institute of Medicine. (2001). *Crossing the quality chasm: A new health system for the 21st century.* Washington, DC: National Academy Press.

Israel, B., Eng, E., Schulz, A., Parker, E., & Satcher, D. (2005). *Methods in community-based participatory research for health.* San Francisco: Jossey-Bass.

Jarvis, G., Ferrence, R., Whitehead, P., & Hohnson, F. (1982). The ecology of self-injury: A multivariate approach. *Suicide and Life-Threatening Behaviors, 12*(2), 90–102.

Johnson, M. (2000). *The effects of background classical music on junior high school student's academic performance.* Unpublished doctoral dissertation. The Fielding Institute.

Jones, J. (1993). *Bad blood: The Tuskegee syphilis experiment.* New York: The Free Press.

Jonson-Reid, M. (2000). Empowerment can mean many things: Lessons learned from a community empowerment evaluation. *Journal of Community Practice, 7*(4), 57–76.

Jonson-Reid, M. (2006). Evaluating practice and using research. In L. Bye and M. Alvarez (Eds.). *School social work: A desk reference for an evolving practice.* Belmont, CA: Thompson.

Jonson-Reid, M., Drake, B., Hovmand, P., Zayas, L. (Unpublished Manuscript) Correcting the Drift in Evidence Based Practice.

Jonson-Reid, M., Kontak, D., & Mueller, S. (2001). Creating a management information system for school social workers: A field-university partnership. *Children and Schools, 23,* 198–211.

Joyner, L., & McCaughan, E. (2003). Introduction: applied research and social justice. *Social Justice, 30,* 1–5.

Kessler, R., & Zhao, S. (1999). The prevalence of mental illness in A. Horowitz & T. Scheid (Eds) *A Handbook for the Study of Mental Health.* Cambridge, Eng: Cambridge University Press, 58–78.

Kimmel, A. (1988). *Ethics and Values in Applied Social Research.* Newbury Park, CA: Sage Publications.

Kohlberg, L. (1986). *The philosophy of moral development.* San Francisco, CA: Harper and Row.

Kordy, H., Kramer, B., Palmer, L., Papezoya, H., Pellet, J., Richard, M., & Treasure, J. (2002). *Journal of Clinical Psychology, 58*(7), 833–846.

Kruger, R., & Casey, M. (2000). *Focus groups: A practical guide for applied research.* Thousand Oaks, CA: Sage.

Kuhn, T. (1962). *The structure of scientific revolutions.* Chicago, IL: University of Chicago Press.

Kuss, O. (2004). A SAS/IML Macro for goodness of fit testing in logistic regression models with sparse data. Paper. 265–266. SAS: SUG126.

Lawal, B. (2003). *Categorical data analysis with SAS and SPSS applications.* NJ: Lawrence Earlbaum Associates.

Lee, E., Wei, L., & Amato, D. (1992). Cox-type regression analysis for large numbers of small groups of correlated failure time observations. Netherlands: Kluwer Academic Publishers.

Lester, D. (1999). Suicidality and risk-taking behaviors: An ecological study of youth behaviors in 29 states. *Perceptual and Motor Skills, 88*(3), 1299–1300.

Lewins, A., & Silver, C. (2004) Choosing a CAQDAS Package, CAQDAS Networking Project. Retrieved from http://caqdas.soc.surrey.ac.uk.

Linhorst, D. (2002). A review of the use and potential of focus groups in social work research. *Qualitative Social Work, 1*(2), 208–228.

Littell, J., & Shuerman, J. (1995). A synthesis of research on family preservation and family reunification programs. Washington DC: DHHS, Office of the Assistant Secretary for Planning and Evaluation.

Loftus, E. (1975). Leading questions and the eyewitness report. *Cognitive Psychology, 7,* 560–572.

Lomax, R. & Moosavi, S. (1998, April 17). *Using humor to teach statistics: Must they be orthogonal?* Paper presented at the annual meeting of the American Educational Research Association. San Diego.

Losh, C. (2004). *Guide 5: Bivariate Associations and Correlation Coefficient Properties.* Florida State University. Retrieved March 8, 2007 from http://edf5400–01.sp04.fsu.edu/Guide5.html.

Lowry, R. (2005). One-way analysis of variance for correlated samples. *Concepts and applications of inferential statistics.* Vassar University. Retrieved March 12, 2007 from http://faculty.vassar.edu/lowry/webtext.html.

Lum, D. (2003). *Culturally competent practice. A framework for understanding diverse groups and justice issues.* (2nd ed.). Belmont, CA: Thompson/Brooks Cole.

MacKenzie, D. (1997). Criminal justice and crime prevention in L. Sherman, D. Gottfredson, D. MacKenzie, J. Eck, P. Reuter, & S. Bushway (Eds.). Preventing Crime: What works, what doesn't, what's promising. University of Maryland. Retrieved January 2007 at www.ncjrs. gov.works.

Mahoney, M. (1977). Publication prejudices: An experimental study of confirmatory bias in the peer review system. *Cognitive Therapy and Research, 1*(2), 161–175.

Mannuzza, S., Klein, R., Klein, D., Bessler, A., & Shrout, P. (2002). Accuracy of adult recall of childhood attention deficit hyperactivity disorder. *American Journal of Psychiatry, 159*(11), 1882–1888.

Marston, G., & Watts, R. (2003). Tampering with the evidence: A critical appraisal of evidence based policy. *The Drawing Board: An Australian Review of Public Affairs, 3,* 3.

Maslach, C., Jackson, S., & Leiter, M. (1997). Maslach burnout inventory: Third edition. In C. Zalaquett, & R. Wood (Eds.). *Evaluating Stress: A Book of Resources* (pp. 191–218). Lanham, MD: Usation.

McCullough, J., Philip, A., & Carstairs, G. (1967). The ecology of suicidal behavior. *British Journal of Psychiatry, 113*(496), 313–319.

McFadden, E. (1975). Helping the inexperienced worker in the public child welfare agency: A case study. *Child Welfare, 54*(5), 319–329.

McGuire, A., McCullough, L., Weller, S., & Whitney, S. (2005). Missed Expectations? Physicians' views of patients' participation in medical decision-making. *Medical Care, 43*(5), 466–470

McNemar, Q. (1969). *Psychological statistics* (4th ed.). New York: Wiley.

Mead, M. (1928). *Coming of age in Samoa.* New York: Morrow.

Meehl, P. (1998). The power of quantitative thinking. Speech delivered May 23, American Psychological Society Meeting, Washington, DC. Retrieved {3/2/2007} from www.tc.umn.edu/~pemeehl/ PowerQuantThinking.pdf.

Mental Measurements Yearbook. (2006). Retrieved March 7, 2007 from http://buros.unl.edu/buros/jsp/search.jsp.

Milgram, S. (1963). The behavioral study of obedience, *Journal of Abnormal and Social Psychology, 67,* 471–378.

Miller, K., Worthington, G., Muzurovic, J., Tipping, S., & Goldman, A. (2002), Bosnian refugees and the stressors of exile: A narrative study. *American Journal of Orthopsychiatry, 72*(3), 341–354.

Miraglia, E., Law, R., & Collins, P. (1999). *What is culture?* Retrieved May 10, 2006 from www.wsu.edu:8001/vcwsu/ commons/topics/culture/culture-index.html.

Mitchell, M. L., Jolley, J. M., & O'Shea, R.P. (2004). *Writing on Psychology.* Belmont, CA: Thomson-Wadsworth.

Mollica, R., Saraljic, N., Chemoff, M., Lavelle, J., Sarajilic-Vukovic, I, & Massagli, M. (2001). Longitudinal study of psychiatric symptoms, disability, mortality, and emigration among Bosnian refugees. *JAMA: Journal of the American Medical Association, 286*(5), 546–554.

Moore, K., & Cooper, C. (1996). Stress in mental health professionals: A theoretical overview. *International Journal of Social Psychiatry, 42*(2), 82–89.

Morales, L. (2001). Cross-cultural adaptation of survey instruments: The CAHPS experience (Chapter 2). *Assessing Patient Experiences with Assessing Healthcare in Multi-Cultural Settings.* RAND. Retrieved January 20, 2005, from www.rand.org/publications /RGSD/ RGSD157.

Moriarty, J. B., Minton, E. B., & Spann, V. (1981). Preliminary Diagnostic Questionnaire: Module 3 and 4: Administration. feedback, and interpretation.

Dunbar, WV: WV Rehabilitation Research and Training Center.

Morin, R., & Deane, C. (2005, January 20). Report acknowledges inaccuracies in 2004 exit polls. *The Washington Post*, page A06.

Morrel, T. (2000). *Changes in self-efficacy, self-esteem and aggression in male batterers: A comparison of cognitive-behavioral and supportive group therapies.* Unpublished doctoral dissertation, University of Maryland at Baltimore.

National Association of Social Workers (1999). *Code of Ethics.* Retrieved March 11, 2006, from www.socialworkers.org/pubs/code/code.asp.

Nesdale, D., & Mak, A. (2003). Ethnic identification, self-esteem and immigrant psychological health. *International Journal of Intercultural Relations, 27*(1), 23–40.

Norusis, M. (2005). *SPSS 13.0 advanced statistical procedures companion.* Upper Saddle River, NJ: Prentice Hall.

Nussbaum, N. (2001, July 20). The enduring significance of John Rawls. *The Chronicle of Higher Education.* B7.

Oetting, E. E., and Beauvais, F. (1986). Peer cluster theory: Drugs and the adolescent. *Journal of Counseling and Development, 65,* 17–22.

Oliver, P. (2003). The Students' Guide to Research Ethics. Berkshire, UK: Open University Press.

O'Rourke, N., O'Rourke, L., Hatcher, E., & Stepanksi, E.J. (2005). *A step-by-step approach to using SAS for univariate and multivariate statistics* (2nd ed.). Cary, NC: SAS Institute Inc.

Otto, D., Cochran, V., Johnson, G., & Clair, A. (1999). The influence of background music on task engagement in frail, older persons in residential care. *Journal of Music Therapy, 36*(3), 182–195.

Pagano, R. (2001). *Understanding statistics in the behavioral sciences* (6th ed.). Belmont, CA: Wadsworth.

Pan, Y. (2003). *The role of sociolinguistics in the development and conduct of federal surveys.* U.S. Census Bureau. Retrieved January 20, 2005, from www.fcsm.gov/03papers/Panfinal.pdf.

Papadopoulos, I. & Lee, S. (2002). Developing culturally competent researchers. *Journal of Advanced Nursing, 37,* 258–264.

Patton, M. (1997). *Utilization focused evaluation* (3rd ed.). Thousand Oaks, CA: Sage.

Pawson, R. (2005). *Evidence-based policy: A realist perspective.* London: Sage.

Perry, E., Kulik, C., & Zhou, J. (1999). A closer look at the effects of subordinate–supervisor age differences. *Journal of Organizational* Behavior, 20(3), 351–57.

Pope, C. (2003). Resisting evidence: The study of evidence based medicine as a contemporary social movement. *Health, 7*(3), 267–282.

Popper, K. (1959). *The logic of scientific discovery.* Toronto, Canada: University of Toronto Press.

Preston, J. (2006) An application of Berry's Model of Acculturation to a Bosnian refugee population,

Unpublished Manuscript, Washington College, Collegetown Missouri.

Proctor, E. (2004). Leverage points for the implementation of evidence-based practice. *Brief Treatment and Crisis Intervention, 4,* 227–242.

Raudenbush, S. & Bryk, A. (2001). *Hierarchical linear models: Applications and data analysis methods.* CA: SAGE Publications.

Rauscher, F., & Shaw, G. (1998). Key components of the Mozart effect. *Perceptual and Motor Skills, 86*(3), 835–841.

Rawls, J. (1971). *A Theory of Justice.* Cambridge, MA: Harvard University Press.

Reamer, F. (1995). Ethics and values. In R. L. Edwards, J. G. Hopps, & R. Steiner (Eds.), *Encyclopedia of social work* (19th ed.), pp. 893–902. Silver Spring, MD: NASW Press.

Reamer, F. (2004). *Social work values and ethics.* New York: Columbia University Press.

Rosen, A., & Proctor, E. (2003). *Developing practice guidelines for social work intervention.* New York: Columbia University Press.

Rosenbaum, D. & Hanson, G. (1998). *Assessing the effects of school-based drug education: A six-year multi-level analysis of project DARE.* University of Illinois, Chicago: Center for Research in Law and Justice.

Rosenberg, W. & Donald, A. (1995). Evidence based medicine: An approach to clinical problem solving. *British Medical Journal, 310,* 1122–1126.

Rosenthal, J. (2001). *Statistics and data interpretation for the helping professionals.* Belmont, CA: Brooks/Cole–Thompson Learning.

Rosenthal, R., & Lawson, R. (1964). A longitudinal study of the effects of experimenter bias on the operant learning of laboratory rats. *Journal of Psychiatric Research, 2,* 61–72.

Rossi, P. F., Freeman, H. W., & Lipsey, M. (1999). *Evaluation: A systematic approach.* (6th ed.). Newbury Park, CA: Sage Publications, Inc.

Rothman, J. Smith, W., Nakashima, J. & Paterson, M. (1996). Client self-determination and professional intervention: Striking a balance. *Social Work* 41(4), 396–405.

Rowe, M. (1997). Hardiness, stress, temperament, coping, and burnout in health professionals. *American Journal of Health Behavior,* 21(3), 163–171.

Royse, D., Thyer, B., Padgett, D., & Logan, T. (2006). *Program evaluation: An introduction* (4th ed.). Belmont, CA: Thomson/Brooks Cole.

Rubin, A., & Babbie, A. (2005). *Research methods for social work* (5th Ed.). Belmont, CA: Thompson/Brooks/Cole.

Rummel, J. (1976). *Understanding correlation.* Department of Political Science, University of Hawaii at Honolulu. Retrieved March 11, 2006, from www.mega.nu:8080/ampp/rummel/uc.htm#C2.

Sackett, D., Strauss, S., Richardson, W., Rosenberg, W., & Haynes, R. (2000). *Evidence-based medicine: How to practice and teach EBM* (2nd ed.). Edinburgh, UK: Churchill Livingstone.

Safer, M., & Keuler, D. (2002). Individual differences in misremembering pre-psychotherapy distress: Personality and memory distortion. *Emotion, 2*(2), 162–178.

Sales, B., & Folkman, S. (2000). *Ethics in research with human participants.* Washington, D.C.: American Psychological Association.

SAS Institute Inc. (2004). SAS help files. Retrieved from SAS Software Package version 9.1

Schafer, J. (1997). *Analysis of incomplete missing data.* London: Chapman & Hall.

Shaddish, W., Cook. T., & Campbell, D. (2002). *Experimental and quasi-experimental designs for generalized causal inference.* Boston: Houghton-Mifflin.

Shapiro, E.S. & Kratochwill, T.R. (2000). *Conducting school-based assessments of child and adolescent behavior.* New York: The Guilford Press.

Siegel, A. (1956). Film-mediated fantasy aggression and strength of aggressive drive. *Child Development, 27,* 365–378.

Simon, S. (2005). Fisher's Exact Test STATS. *Steve's Attempt to Teach Statistics.* Children's Mercy Hospitals. Kansas City, MI. Retrieve from www.cmh.edu/stats/ask/fishers. asp.

Smith, W. A. S. (1961). Effects of industrial music in a work situation requiring complex mental activity. *Psychological Reports,* 8, 159–162.

Sokal, A. (1996). Transgressing the boundaries: An afterword. *Dissent, 43*(4), 93–99.

Sokal, A. & Bricmont, J. (1998). *Fashionable nonsense: Postmodern intellectuals' abuse of science.* London: Picador.

Spradley, J. (1997). *Participant observation.* New York: Holt Rinehart & Winston.

Stanford Encyclopedia of Philosophy. (2005). Retrieved on October 3, 2005 from http://plato.stanford.edu/.

Stephensen, V. (2002). *The Effect of Classical Background Music on Spatial Reasoning Skills as Measured by Completion of a Spatial Task: A Study of Selected College Undergraduates.* Unpublished doctoral dissertation, Universidad de Guadalijara, Mexico.

Stevens, J. (2002). *Applied multivariate statistics for the social sciences* (4th ed.). Lawrence Elrbaum.

Stof, D., Breiling, J., & Maser, J. (1997). *Handbook of Antisocial Behavior.* New York: Wiley.

Stokes, M., Davis, C., & Koch, G. (2000). *Categorical data analysis using the SAS system* (2nd ed.). Cary, NC: SAS Institute.

Straus, S. & McAlister, F. (2000). Evidence-based medicine: A commentary on common criticisms. *Canadian Medical Association Journal,* 163(7), 837–841

Straus, S. E., Richardson, W. S., Glasziou, P., & Haynes, R. B. (2005). Evidence-Based Medicine: How to Practice and Teach EBM (3rd ed.). Edinburgh, UK: Elsevier Churchill Livingstone.

Strauss, A., & Corbin, J. (1998). *Basics of qualitative research: Techniques and procedures for developing grounded theory.* Thousand Oaks, CA: Sage.

Suzuki, L., Ponterotto, J., & Meller, P. (Eds.). (2000). *The new handbook of multicultural assessment: clinical, psychological, and educational applications* (2nd ed). San Francisco, CA: Jossey-Bass.

Tabachnik, B. G., & Fidell, L. S. (1996). *Using multivariate statistics* (3rd ed.). New York: HarperCollins College Publishers.

Tabachnik, B. G., & Fidell, L. S. (2001). *Using multivariate statistics* (4th ed.). New York: HarperCollins College Publishers.

Tape, T. (2003). *Interpreting diagnostic tests.* University of Nebraska Medical Center http://gim.unmc.edu/dxtests.

The Mathworks. (2005). Friedman. *Statistics Toolbox.* Retrieved February 20, 2007 from www.mathworks.com/access/helpdesk/help/toolbox/stats/friedman.shtml.

Thompson-Robinson, M., Hopson, R., & SenGupta, S. (Eds.). (2004). In search of cultural competence in evaluation: Toward principles and practices. *New Directions for Evaluation, 102,* (entire issue).

Thyer, B. (2002). Popper, positivism and practice research: A response to Munro. *Journal of Social Work Education, 38*(3), 471–474.

Thyer, B. (2004). Science and evidence-based social work practice. In H. Briggs and T. Rzepinicki (Eds.). *Using Evidence in Social Work Practice, Behavioral Perspectives,* Lyceum. 74–89.

Todman, J., & Dugard, P. (2001). *Single-case and small-N experimental designs: A practical guide to randomization tests.* Mahwah, NJ: Lawrence Earlbaum Associates.

Trials of war criminals before the Nuremberg Military Tribunals under Control Council Law No. 10, Vol. 2, pp. 181–182. Washington, DC: U.S. Government Printing Office, 1949.

Twine, F., & Warren, J. (2000). *Racing research, researching race: Methodological dilemmas in critical race studies.* New York: New York University Press.

United Nations. (2001). At the crossroads of gender and racial discrimination. Statement posted on Web site for World Conference Against Racism, Racial Discrimination, Xenophobia, and Related Intolerance. Retrieved February 18, 2007 from www.un.org/WCAR/e-kit/gender.htm.

Van de Vijver, F. & Leung, K. (1997). *Methods and data analysis for cross-cultural research.* Thousand Oaks, CA: Sage.

Van Ness, P. H., O'Leary, J., Byers, A. L., & Dubin, J. (2004). Fitting longitudinal mixed effect logistic regression models with the NLMIXED procedure. *Proceedings of the 29th Annual SAS® Users Group International Conference* (SUGI 29).

Visual Statistics with Multimedia. (2003). *Point bi-serial correlation.* Retrieved February 14, 2007, from www.visualstatistics.net/Visual%20Statistics%20 Multimedia/point-biserial_coefficient _of_correlation. html.

Weine, S., Kuc, G., Dzudra, E., Razzano, L., & Pavkovic, I. (2001). PTSD among Bosnian refugees: A survey of providers' knowledge, attitudes and service patterns. *Community Mental Health Journal, 37*(3), 261–271.

Weisstein, E. (2006). "Multivariate." From *MathWorld*— A Wolfram Web Resource. Retrieved March 21, 2007 from http://mathworld.wolfram.com/ Multivariate.html.

Wenz, F. (1977). Ecological variation in self-injury behavior. *Suicide and Life-Threatening Behavior, 7*(2). 92–99.

WGBH Educational Foundation. (1993). *The deadly deception (Nova).*

Whyte, W. (1993). *Street corner society: The social structure of an Italian slum.* Chicago, IL: University of Chicago Press.

Wikipedia. (2005a). *Culture.* Retrieved March 8, 2007 from http://en.wikipedia.org/wiki/Culture#Culture_as_values. 2C_norms.2C_and_artifacts.

Wikipedia. (2005b). *Factor analysis.* Retrieved March 16, 2007 from http://en.wikipedia.org/wiki/Factor_analysis.

Williams, P., & Wallace, D. (1989). *Unit 731: The Japanese Army's secret of secrets.* London: Hodder & Stoughton.

Witmer, T., & Culver, S. (2001). Trauma and resilience among Bosnian refugee families: A critical review of the literature. *Journal of Social Work Research & Evaluation 2*(2), 173–187.

Yin, R., & Campbell, D. (2003). *Case study research: Design and methods* (2nd ed.). Thousand Oaks, CA: Sage,

Yu, C. (2005). Illustrating degrees of freedom in terms of sample size and dimensionality. Arizona State University. Retrieved February 8, 2007, from http://seamonkey.ed.asu.edu/~alex/computer/sas/df.html.

Yuen, P., & Terao, K. (2003). *Practical grant writing and program evaluation.* Pacific Grove, CA: Brooks Cole.

Zajonc, R., & Markus, G. (1975). Birth order and intellectual development, *Psychological Review, 82,* 74–88.

Zayas, L., Gonzales, M., & Hanson, M. (2003). What do I do now? On teaching evidence-based interventions in social work practice. *Journal of Teaching in Social Work. 23*(3/4), 59–72.

Zimmerberg, B., & Gray, M. (1992). The effects of cocaine on maternal behaviors in the rat. *Physiology and Behavior, 52*(2), 379–384.

Bold page numbers indicate figures *(f)* or tables *(t)*.